Volume X.
The Sermons of John Donne

Corporis hæc Animæ fit Syndon Syndon Jesu.
Amen.

Martin D. scup. And are to be sould by R R *and* Ben. ffisher

HEAD OF DONNE IN HIS SHROUD

From an engraving by Martin Droeshout used as the
frontispiece to *Deaths Duell*, 1632

THE
SERMONS
OF
JOHN DONNE

Edited,
with Introductions
and Critical Apparatus, by
EVELYN M. SIMPSON
and
GEORGE R. POTTER

In Ten Volumes

X.

UNIVERSITY OF CALIFORNIA PRESS
BERKELEY AND LOS ANGELES
1962

UNIVERSITY OF CALIFORNIA PRESS
BERKELEY AND LOS ANGELES, CALIFORNIA

❖

CAMBRIDGE UNIVERSITY PRESS
LONDON, ENGLAND

TO
PERCY SIMPSON

Foreword

SURELY there is in our past no English divine other than Donne who has power to call into being an edition of his sermons in many volumes put forth in the best tradition of twentieth-century literary scholarship. The appearance of this tenth and final volume of *The Sermons of John Donne* brings satisfaction to all of us who have counted on that power in Donne.

The satisfaction is the greater in that completion of the edition has been accomplished very nearly according to program, though the timetable of publication has been sadly threatened. The death of Professor Potter, on April 12, 1954, came after more than eight years of collaboration with Mrs. Simpson. Each of the editors had by then done much of his allotted work, and together they had planned what remained to be done. But through seven years Mrs. Simpson has been responsible for all that remained. The tribute in Volume II that she gave to George Potter after his death is a recognition of unfailing virtue in a collaborator that he would repay now if he could.

It was agreed at the beginning of their work that Professor Potter would be mainly responsible for the first five volumes and Mrs. Simpson for the last five. At the death of Professor Potter his commitment had been fulfilled to a point where Volume I was published, Volume II was completed and at the press, and the sermons for Volumes III, IV, and V were all in typescript but with a considerable amount of editing still to be done and with the Introductions to these volumes still to be written. Mrs. Simpson had then come to the publication of Volume VI, to the reading of proofs for Volume VII, and to the completion of Volume VIII, including its Introduction, except for some minor matters.

Thus it should be understood that in accomplishing her original undertaking and what came to be added to it Mrs. Simpson has written the Introductions for Volumes III, IV, V, VI, VII, VIII, IX, and X (including for Volume X the valuable chapters on Donne's knowledge of Hebrew, Greek, and the Latin of the Vulgate and his use of the Fathers). Since 1954 she has, of course, borne an increased burden of preparing textual notes and checking for accuracy in type-script and proof. Continuing a search for suitable illustrations which Professor Potter and she had begun together, she has provided these since 1954, often with such care as she has taken in journeying to Blunham, where Donne was rector, to obtain for Volume V photographs of the church, of the chalice and paten which he presented to it, and of the pulpit there from which he preached.

It was a happy fortune that called the editors to their work in common. They came to it as devoted students of Donne both of whom possessed in high degree the necessary experience, learning, and sympathetic understanding. Each had already published an edition of a sermon of Donne's and had become familiar with the textual problems that would have to be met in making an edition of all the sermons. As early as 1911, Mrs. Simpson (who was then Miss Spearing) had formed the idea of producing such an edition and, likewise before the First World War, had published findings having to do with a chronological arrangement of Donne's sermons. Two world wars intervened and a whole new world of twentieth-century admiration for Donne was created before Mrs. Simpson and Professor Potter joined forces for the making of the edition and found a publisher for it.

The result is the first complete edition of the sermons. (Alford omits four sermons and leaves out some passages which he thought might be objectionable to Victorian taste.) It is also the first edition which employs the methods and apparatus of modern scholarship. Furthermore, it is the first edition in which the sermons are arranged, as far as possible, in chronological order. Here one is enabled to relate the sermons to the historical circumstances of their time and, more important still, to follow the growth of the mature Donne not only in his thought but in that presentation of thought married to feeling which is the sign of his poetry always.

We know what we are in relation to Donne, but we do not know what we shall be. To Donne we now give more honor by far than he had in his own day, among his fellows in that era of the English Renaissance that may be called the post-Spenserian, and he was then by no means neglected. Many now think of his revival as concomitant to a major revolution in the practice of poetry, and all can feel the force of our turning against the Victorian valuation of him. We can all wonder how Palgrave's *Golden Treasury of the Best Songs and Lyrical Poems in the English Language* could have appeared in 1861 without Donne's name in it and been reprinted in that form for decades before it gave grudging recognition to Donne. It has been said that we in the twentieth century have taken Donne as rightfully ours because he is a poet with *angst* and his *angst* is somehow deeply like our own. Could modern man eventually lose what binds him to Donne? One is not called upon to guess, however much the Victorians may lead one to ask the question. What is certain is that so long as we are drawn to the Donne we now know we shall be drawn to his sermons by the same power that draws us to his poems. And for so long this edition of the sermons will have a laudable part to play.

WILLARD FARNHAM

Preface

I AM very happy to be able to present this last volume of Donne's *Sermons* to the world. I wish to express my deep gratitude to all who have helped me in the work, and especially to the University of California, whose generosity provided me with a part-time graduate assistant for the last five years, and who have supported and helped me in many ways. In his Preface to Volume I George Potter expressed for us both our thanks to a number of friends and institutions which had given us their assistance in the first seven years of our task. In addition to those mentioned there, I should like to send my personal thanks to Professors Willard Farnham, James Hart, and Henry Nash Smith, all of the University of California, and to F. P. Wilson, Emeritus Merton Professor of the University of Oxford. Mr. John Sparrow, Warden of All Souls College, Oxford, has kindly allowed me to collate his copy of the *XXVI Sermons,* which contains some unusual variant readings, and has generously encouraged me in many ways. Sir Geoffrey Keynes lent me his valuable Ellesmere manuscript, so that I could collate it at my leisure, and I owe much to his important *Bibliography of John Donne,* especially to its latest edition. Miss Helen Gardner has been my guide and friend in all matters pertaining to Donne's poems, and she has lent me valuable books. I must express my thanks to the Delegates of the Clarendon Press for allowing me to quote at length in the present volume from her books *The Business of Criticism* and *The Divine Poems.* The Very Rev. Dr. C. A. Simpson, Dean of Christ Church, Oxford, and the Rev. J. R. Porter, Chaplain and Dean of Oriel College, have kindly helped me on the subject of Donne's knowledge of Hebrew. The Rev. Dr. J. N. D. Kelly, Principal of St. Edmund Hall, Oxford, has helped me with Donne's knowledge of St. Augustine's works. Professor R. C. Bald of the University of Chicago has imparted to me some details of Donne's life, and has sent me a useful list of misprints and mistakes to be corrected in our earlier volumes. I must also thank Professor D. C. Allen, Mr. J. B. Leishman, and Mr. J. C. Maxwell for help in various ways.

I must thank Dr. R. W. Hunt and Miss M. C. Crum, of the Bodleian Library, for their help in enabling me to reëxamine the Dowden and Merton MSS, which the Library has recently acquired through the generosity of Dr. E. de Beer. The results of this reëxamination will be found in the Addenda and Corrigenda (pp. 425–428, 435–442, of this volume). I am grateful to the Trustees of the National Library of Scotland for permission to reprint in an appendix some portion of the unidentified sermon in the Lothian MS, and also to quote the readings of that MS in textual notes. I must also thank the Librarians of Merton, Magdalen, and St. John's Colleges, and the Sub-Librarian, Mr. G. Hiscock, of Christ Church, Oxford, for their assistance, as well as the Librarian of the Princeton Theological Seminary, U.S.A.

My thanks are due to the Trustees of the Leverhulme Research Awards for a generous grant which they made towards my expenses for a two-year period.

My warmest gratitude is due to the staff of the University of California Press, and in particular to Mr. Harold A. Small, the Editor, for his unfailing kindness and diligence in supervising the printing of this edition. He has maintained a constant interest in its progress, and has accepted last-minute changes and additions with the greatest good nature. The whole edition has benefitted from the care which he has bestowed on its smallest details. I must also thank the printers for the way in which they have handled the difficult spelling and punctuation of Donne's text.

Mrs. Mary Holtby, my devoted research assistant for four years, saved me many hours of work by her knowledge of patristic Latin and of St. Augustine's works in particular. She gave me most valuable help in compiling the long list of medieval and renaissance commentaries used by Donne. Miss Elizabeth Wade White has helped me generously in procuring illustrations for several volumes. Mrs. Isabel Roberts has compiled the Index with my assistance, and has done much useful work in the Bodleian Library for me. My warm gratitude is due also to Miss Mary Anderson, who has been my housekeeper and domestic helper for fourteen years.

It is a cause for grief that George Potter did not live to see the completion of the task which he began with so much energy and enthusiasm. The notes and papers which he left behind have been of much use, and I must thank Mrs. Potter for her generosity in passing them on to me, and for her continued interest and help in the preparation of the remainder of the edition.

After all, my greatest debt is to Donne himself. It is now nearly fifty years since, as a young graduate fresh from Cambridge, I visited Exeter and saw on an open bookstall in one of the streets the six volumes of Alford's edition of the Sermons, which I bought for a total of six shillings. To them I added a sixpenny copy of Jessopp's edition of Donne's *Essays in Divinity,* and so I began my private collection of Donne's prose works. My love of Donne has grown through the years, and it has brought me many friends. It was through my early attempts to write something on Donne that I first made the acquaintance of my husband, Percy Simpson, to whom I now dedicate this volume in love and gratitude.

E. M. S.

December, 1961

Table of Contents

Volume X

Part One

Contents

List of Illustrations

Volume X

Part One

Introduction

IN THIS volume we conclude the long series of Donne's sermons. We have traced the chequered pattern of his career in the ministry from his late ordination and rather reluctant beginning through the triumphant success of his years at St. Paul's to his final illness and the last great sermon, *Deaths Duell,* which is printed here. These ten volumes show that Donne was intensely alive as a preacher. Throughout the sixteen years of his ministry he found in the great Christian doctrines a perpetual fountain of life on which the light of his mind could play in many diverse colours. The Christmas and Easter sermons which he delivered year by year show a surprising variety in their outlook. There was room for sorrow as well as joy at Christmas, and the Easter hope could be viewed from many different angles. Sometimes he preached as a poet, sometimes as a pastor, sometimes as a theologian, sometimes as a controversialist. He preached to many different types of congregation—to the Benchers of Lincoln's Inn, to the city parishioners of St. Dunstan's, to the King and Court at Whitehall, to a great concourse of all types of Londoners at St. Paul's,—and throughout he showed his power to adapt himself to the needs of each.

The scope of our edition has made it possible for us to show the sermons as more than a mere quarry for anthologists. There will always be value in a good anthology for those who have no time to read the sermons as a whole, but those who depend entirely on an anthology get a perverted idea of Donne as a preacher. In a selection of purple passages the morbid and the rhetorical will always have too large a place.[1] It is only by reading four or five entire sermons that we can realize Donne's sense of form, the carefully thought out scheme by which he arranged his material, his common sense, his

[1] Even so acute a critic as F. L. Lucas has evidently depended entirely on anthologies of the sermons, since he has written, "Beside the Sermon on the Mount, Donne's sermons seem like Solomon in all his glory beside the lilies of the field. But whether Donne's ballets of skeletons in cloth of gold have really much in common with genuine Christianity is another question."

3

shrewdness, his psychological insight, and his real religious fervour. Moreover, it is only by reading them in the order in which he delivered them that we are able to recognize the patterns of thought which keep emerging and developing from sermon to sermon. We can trace, too, a steadily growing sense of dedication to an office which at first he had accepted so reluctantly. In the later sermons he finds joy and comfort in preaching peace and forgiveness to congregations oppressed with gloom, and in visiting sick or sorrowful individuals.[2] He feels himself to be an ambassador of God to man, unworthy though he may be of so high an office. A warmth of human sympathy flows out from him to those who are poor or unhappy or laden with guilt. There is perhaps less intellectual power in the sermons of Donne's last two years, and there is much prolixity and repetition, but the man himself appears more lovable in his desire to avoid oratorical fireworks and to preach the gospel as plainly as he can.

It has been said that all Donne's many sermons are in fact one sermon. This is true if it means that Donne's one subject is the Christian Faith;[3] but because the Faith itself is living and deep-rooted in the necessities of man's nature, it can be expressed in a thousand different

[2] See in particular Vol. VII, pp. 1–2, 68–69, 133–135, and Vol. VIII, p. 249: "So that we have much exercise of this liberality, of raising dejected spirits: And by this liberality we stand. For, when I have given that man comfort, that man hath given me a Sacrament, hee hath given me a seale and evidence of Gods favour upon me; I have received from him, in his receiving from me; I leave him comforted in Christ Jesus, and I goe away comforted in my selfe, that Christ Jesus hath made me an instrument of the dispensation of his mercy; And I argue to my selfe, and say, Lord, when I went, I was sure, that thou who hadst received me to mercy, wouldst also receive him, who could not be so great a sinner as I; And now, when I come away, I am sure, that thou who art returned to him, and hast re-manifested thy selfe to him, who, in the diffidence of his sad soule, thought thee gone for ever, wilt never depart from mee, nor hide thy selfe from me, who desire to dwell in thy presence."

[3] We may perhaps except such a sermon as that on *Judges* 5.20 (Vol. IV, No. 7), since Donne was preaching at Paul's Cross by the King's express order to explain the reasons for the injunctions which James had lately issued to preachers. Another sermon of a rather similar kind is that on *Lamentations* 4.20 (Vol. IV, No. 9), which was preached at Paul's Cross on November 5, 1622, on the commemoration of the deliverance from the Gunpowder Plot.

ways. Any reader who has worked through (not merely glanced at) any one of our volumes will be surprised at the variety which Donne managed to impart to a sequence of seventeen or eighteen sermons. It is the difference of mood and of emphasis within the fixed framework of the rigid sermon form that makes such a volume interesting to the attentive reader. Donne was an artist in prose, and he knew the value of contrast and surprise. Some sermons begin with an arresting opening, and then gradually develop a carefully wrought theme. Others begin quietly, and are kept throughout on a level of sane common-sense discussion. Others are highly imaginative, and seem to have been planned as Donne might have written a poem, with a recurring refrain. Others are magnificent oratorical performances, working up to a superb climax. Some are plain and unadorned, others are rich with imagery and with every kind of literary artifice. Sometimes Donne takes a simple text from the Sermon on the Mount, sometimes an arresting sentence from the vision of Eliphaz in the Book of *Job,* or a curious verse from a little-read prophet like *Hosea.*[*]

We can find many parallels in Christian art to this divergence in detail where the general pattern is the same. A spectator who looks at the mosaics of virgins and martyrs in the church of Sant' Apollinare Nuovo in Ravenna may think at first that the twenty-six virgins on the left and the twenty-six martyrs on the right are all exactly alike within the two groups, and that the only contrast is between group and group. The virgins all have white robes and coloured cloaks, and the right hand and forearm of each is inclined in the same direction. What could be more monotonous if it had been machine-made? But because the mosaic was made by an artist the result is deeply satisfying. Though each figure is part of the pattern, it has its own individuality. There is a difference in the faces and in the folds of the drapery. The artist has obtained his grand effect by

---

[*] As examples of arresting openings we might choose the sermons on 1 *Timothy* 3.16 (Vol. III, p. 206), the Christmas sermon on *Luke* 2.29–30 (Vol. VII, p. 279), and the Whitehall sermon on *Acts* 7.60 (Vol. VIII, p. 174), though there are at least a dozen more which are almost equally effective. As examples of quiet sermons full of good sense, see Vol. III, No. 5, Vol. IV, No. 8, Vol. VI, No. 12, Vol. IX, No. 10. For sermons with a recurring refrain see Vol. VI, No. 8, Vol. VII, No. 1 and No. 10, Vol. VIII, No. 16.

the large number of his figures and the subtle differences between them. The fifty-two figures make an impression on the beholder which could not be made by a smaller number. So the very scale of Donne's performance gives a grandeur to this edition. Some monotony and repetition there may be—it was inevitable in so large a work, —but it is offset by the abiding impression of an amazingly vital personality, rich in mental and spiritual power.

⬦　⬦　⬦

The first ten sermons of this volume are undated, though we can assign conjectural dates to a few of them. For the most part they are earlier than the dated ones in Volume IX, and two of them probably belong to the same period as Volume VI. The others must be spread over the years covered by Volumes VII to IX. The last sermon of all (No. 11) is *Deaths Duell,* dated February, 1631.

Our first sermon is described in the Folio as "Preached on All Saints' Day," but no year is given. We can, however, ascribe it with some degree of probability to November 1, 1623, on account of a reference in it by Donne to "waking dreamers" who think of "tolerations" but are likely to be disappointed. On August 30, 1623, Chamberlain (*Letters,* II, 513) had written to Carleton: "...our papists are very busie and earnest (by the Spanish ambassadors meanes) to have a publike toleration, but yt seemes the King will not allow yt, yet is pleased to graunt them pardon for what is past, with a dispensation for exercise of their religion in their owne houses under the broad seale for five and twenty shillings or fowr nobles a peece..." These hopes of a "toleration" were based on the confident expectation at that date that the marriage of Prince Charles, who was then in Spain, to the Infanta would soon be celebrated. However, in the two months that elapsed between the writing of this letter and the preaching of Donne's sermon the situation changed abruptly, as in early October the Prince and Buckingham returned from Spain, and the marriage was indefinitely delayed, and finally abandoned in spite of King James's reluctance. There seems to be a discreet reference, which Donne's hearers would appreciate, to these hopes and disappointments in Donne's words:

And howsoever waking dreamers think of alterations and tolerations, howsoever men that disguise their expectations with an outward conformity to us, may think the time of declaring themselves growes on apace; howsoever the slumbring of capitall laws, and reason of State may suffer such mistakers to flatter themselves, yet God hath made this Angel of the East, this Gospel of his to ascend so far now, and to take so deep root, as that now this one Angel is strong enough for the other foure, that is, The sincere preaching of the Gospel, in our setled and well disciplined Church, shall prevaile against those foure pestilent opposites, Atheists, and Papists, and Sectaries, and Carnall indifferent men, . . .[5]

The festival of All Saints (sometimes called All Hallows) falls on November 1, and it was one of the seven days on which the Lord Mayor of London and the representatives of the twelve livery companies attended service at St. Paul's. We have only this one sermon of Donne's for this day, as against five for Candlemas Day, and it seems likely that he may have allotted this duty on most occasions to some other member of the Cathedral Chapter. In the letters which he wrote during the course of his fatal illness in the winter of 1630–31 he expressed his regret that he had not been able to preach the "fifth of *November* Sermon to the King,"[6] but said nothing about the sermon on All Saints' Day. In a later letter he wrote: "I have intreated one of my fellowes to preach to my Lord Maior, at *Pauls* upon Christmas day, and reserved Candlemas day to my self for that service, . . ."[7] and again in another lettter, "I am under the obligation of preaching at *Pauls* upon Candlemas day, . . ."[8] All this implies that Donne felt bound to preach, if his illness allowed it, on Candlemas Day, but that he had no compunction about missing the All Saints' Day sermon.

The one sermon which is here printed is long, and a little disappointing in its handling of the subject. Donne took for his text two verses (*Revelation* 7.2, 3) from a vision which was often in his mind. It had given him the opening lines of one of his most famous *Holy Sonnets,* he had mentioned it in *Essays in Divinity,* and he had preached one of his christening sermons on a verse which comes later in the same chapter of *Revelation.* In these and other passages

---

[5] P. 60 of the present volume.

[6] That is, the annual Gunpowder Plot Sermon. *Letters* (1651), p. 282.

[7] *Ibid.*, p. 243.

[8] *Ibid.*, p. 317.

of his sermons he had shown clearly that he knew that the vision described by St. John was meant to describe the heavenly triumph of the martyrs and the faithful departed, but in this All Saints' Day sermon he insists on applying the vision to the Church Militant here on earth, and especially to his present audience. In so doing much of the poetical symbolism is lost, and he obliterates the distinction clearly made by St. John, between the one hundred and forty-four thousand who were sealed of all the tribes of Israel, and the great multitude which no man could number from all nations, and races, and tongues.[9]

Though we may feel that Donne, by his persistent allegorizing of symbols which should have retained their mystery,[10] has weakened the general effect of his sermon, there are in it a number of notable passages. One of them deals with the difficulty of concentration in prayer:

None of us hath got the victory over flesh and blood, and yet we have greater enemies then flesh and blood are. Some disciplines, some mortifications we have against flesh and blood; ... but for these powers and principalities, I know not where to watch them, how to encounter them. I passe my time sociably and merrily in cheerful conversation, in musique, in feasting, in Comedies, in wantonnesse; and I never heare all this while of any power or principality, my Conscience spies no such enemy in all this. And then alone, between God and me at midnight, some beam of his grace shines out upon me, and by that light I see this Prince of darknesse, and then I finde that I have been the subject, the slave of these powers and principalities, when I thought not of them. Well, I see them, and I try then to dispossesse my selfe of them, and I make my recourse to the powerfullest exorcisme that is, I turne to hearty and earnest prayer to God, and I fix my thoughts strongly (as I thinke) upon him, and before I have perfected one petition, one period of my prayer, a power and principality is got into me againe. *Spiritus soporis,* The spirit of slumber closes mine

---

[9] This is the more surprising because Donne is usually much interested in the symbolism of numbers. See *Essays in Divinity,* ed. Simpson, pp. 10, 52–61, 111, 129. In St. John's vision the number 144,000 is made up by 12,000 taken from each of the 12 tribes of Israel. This symbolizes the perfect completion of the Jewish contingent in the Church Triumphant, according to some commentators.

[10] It is disappointing to find that the four Angels whose office is to hurt the earth, the sea, and the trees are first interpreted as devils, and then in lines 715–717 become "those foure pestilent opposites, Atheists, and Papists, and Sectaries, and Carnall indifferent men, who all would hinder the blowing of this wind, the effect of this Gospel."

eyes, and I pray drousily; Or *spiritus vertiginis,* the spirit of deviation, and vaine repetition, and I pray giddily, and circularly, and returne againe and againe to that I have said before, and perceive not that I do so; and *nescio cujus spiritus sim,* (as our Saviour said, rebuking his Disciples, who were so vehement for the burning of the Samaritans, *you know not of what spirit you are*) I pray, and know not of what spirit I am, I consider not mine own purpose in prayer; And by this advantage, this doore of inconsideration, enters *spiritus erroris,* The seducing spirit, the spirit of error, and I pray not onely negligently, but erroniously, dangerously, for such things as disconduce to the glory of God, and my true happinesse, if they were granted. Nay, even the Prophet *Hosea's spiritus fornicationum,* enters into me, *The spirit of fornication,* that is, some remembrance of the wantonnesse of my youth, some mis-interpretation of a word in my prayer, that may beare an ill sense, some unclean spirit, some power or principality hath depraved my prayer, and slackned my zeale.[11]

In another passage we find an instance of the association in Donne's mind between Christ and light, the Light of the World, which he had emphasized in his first Christmas sermon at St. Paul's, where it had been his main theme.[12] It is also linked with another sermon, the first in Volume VI,[13] where *Oriens* is used as a name of Christ:

Take the Angel of the text to be the Angel of the Covenant, Christ Jesus, and his name is The East; he cannot be knowne, he cannot bee said to have any West. *Ecce vir, Oriens nomen ejus,* (so the vulgat reads that place) *Behold the Man, whose name is the East;* you can call him nothing else; for so, the other *Zachary,* the *Zachary* of the New Testament cals him too, . . . *Visitavit nos Oriens, The East, the day spring from on high hath visited us;* And he was derived *à Patre luminum,* He came from the East, begotten from all eternity of the Father of lights, . . .[14]

The sermon also contains a number of vigorous short comments such as "The Devill is no Recusant; he will come to Church, and he

---

[11] Pp. 56–57. This should be compared with the even more vivid description in Vol. VII, pp. 264–265, and with the nineteenth *Holy Sonnet,* "Oh, to vex me, contraryes meet in one." These passages show the keenness of Donne's self-analysis, and they are a valuable testimony to the sincerity of his religious experience. The hypocrite or the merely formal Christian feels no such difficulty, but is perfectly satisfied with the lip worship of his prayer. It is the earnest seeker after God, even the potential saint, who realizes and laments his own inadequacy.

[12] See the Introduction to Vol. III, pp. 37–38.

[13] P. 59, "The name of Christ is *Oriens, The East;* . . ."

[14] P. 50.

will lay his snares there,"[15] and "Sermons unpractised are threepiled sins."[16] He has a scathing rebuke for those who give false weights and measures all the week, and yet go to church twice on Sunday.[17] The style is lively and pungent, and the sermon was evidently preached when Donne was at the height of his powers.[18]

Sermons 2 and 3 were preached "upon Candlemas Day," says the Folio, but without any date. Candlemas Day is the popular name for February 2, the Feast of the Purification of St. Mary the Virgin, otherwise known as the Presentation of Christ in the Temple.[19] The name is evidently derived from the candles and torches which were distributed and carried about in procession. In London the most important procession was that of the Lord Mayor and the representatives of the twelve great livery companies who went to St. Paul's for a service and a sermon.[20]

It is said that this custom of bearing candles was instituted by Pope Sergius in 684, in order to displace the pagan custom of burning torches and candles in honour of the goddess Februa.[21] Donne showed his knowledge of the pagan origin of the custom in his sermon which we have assigned to February 2, 1627, but he justified its continuance by the example of Christ himself.[22]

Sermons have already been assigned to the Candlemas Days of 1622, 1623, and 1627.[23] The year 1624 may be possible, though we are

---

[15] P. 58.

[16] P. 62.

[17] *Ibid.*

[18] If our attribution of it to November 1, 1623, is correct, its proper place in our edition should have been as No. 2 in Volume VI, though it would have been preached about five or six months after No. 1.

[19] These are the two names given to it in the Prayer Book of 1559.

[20] Stow, *Survey,* ed. Kingsford, I, 190.

[21] J. Brand, *Popular Antiquities of Great Britain,* revised by Sir H. Ellis (1890), I, 44. Brand adds many notes about the special customs observed in various parts of the British Isles on Candlemas Day.

[22] Vol. VII, pp. 325–326.

[23] See the Introductions to Vol. III, pp. 41–43, Vol. IV, pp. 38–39, and Vol. VII, pp. 28–31. I wish here to withdraw one of the arguments which I adduced for the assignment to 1627, although I believe that the other arguments are valid, and that 1627 is the right date for that particular sermon. The statement which is incorrect is that "internal evidence has

not certain that Donne had recovered sufficiently from his severe illness at the end of 1623 to be able to preach on February 2, 1624. Apparently he was able in February to deliver an address to the Lower House of Convocation, of which he was appointed Prolocutor. (Gosse, *Life and Letters of John Donne*, II, 196.) The letters to Sir Robert Ker which Gosse has dated as belonging "to the months of ...February and March 1624" (*ibid.*, p. 189), in the first of which Donne says that though he has left his bed he has not left his bedside, should probably be dated a little earlier. The coronation of Charles I took place on February 2, 1626, and therefore that year is unlikely, unless we assume that the St. Paul's sermon and procession were postponed for a day or two.

As to the relative order of the two sermons, we think that the one printed as No. 2 in this volume must be the earlier. Near its close Donne says:

And therefore since all the world shakes in a palsie of wars, ... let us also, who are to do the duties of private men, to obey and not to direct, ... let us endeavour to bring him [i.e., Christ] to his *Dimittuntur peccata,* to forgive us all those sins, which are the true causes of all our palsies, and slacknesses in his service; and so, without limiting him, or his great Vicegerents, and Lieutenants, the way, or the time to beg of him, that he will imprint in them, such counsels and such resolutions, as his wisdome knows best to conduce to his glory, and the maintenance of his Gospell.[24]

It is obvious that this must have been preached before England went definitely to war with Spain in the middle of 1625. Also, the general tone of the sermon is akin to that of the earlier Candlemas sermons which we have assigned to 1622 and 1623. There is in it no

---

led us to assign the four preceding Candlemas sermons to the earlier part of Donne's ministry, that is, before his severe illness in 1623" (Vol. VII, pp. 28–29). After much consideration I have assigned only *two* sermons instead of four to a date prior to Donne's illness and I have rejected the argument (p. 29) that "We have every reason to think that in the years when Donne preached on the Conversion of St. Paul he did not preach on Candlemas Day." Since the two feasts are separated by eight days, it seems quite possible that Donne may have preached on both occasions, though perhaps we should except the year 1625, when the Folio tells us that the sermon on St. Paul was preached on "the Sunday after the Conversion of St. Paul" (January 30 that year).

[24] P. 83.

allusion to the special character of the day itself. It is a quiet and not particularly interesting sermon.[25]

Sermon 3 resembles the Candlemas sermon on *Matthew* 5.8 (Vol. VII, No. 13) in that it is definitely a sermon which emphasizes the meaning of the feast. In that sermon Donne had chosen as his text "Blessed are the pure in heart, for they shall see God," and had drawn attention to the fact that the day was the feast of the Purification. He had also defended the use of candles and torches to mark the day. Our present sermon opens with the words:

Either of the names of this day, were Text enough for a Sermon, Purification, or Candlemas. Joyne we them together, and raise we only this one note from both, that all true purification is in the light; corner purity, clandestine purity, conventicle purity is not purity. *Christ gave himself for us,* sayes the Apostle, *that he might purifie to himself a peculiar people.* How shall this purification appeare? It follows; *They shall be zealous of good works;* They shall not wrangle about faith and works, but be actually zealous of good works. For, purification was accompanied with an oblation, something was to be given; A Lamb, a Dove, a Turtle; All, emblemes of mildnesse; true purity is milde, meek, humble, and to despise and undervalue others, is an inseparable mark of false purity. The oblation of this dayes purification is light: so the day names it, Candlemas-day, so your custome celebrates it, with many lights.[26]

Donne's text had reference to this custom of light-bearing. It was, "Let your light so shine before men, that they may see your good works, and glorifie your Father which is in heaven." He continued: "These are words spoken by our Saviour to his Disciples in the Mount; a treasure deposited in those disciples, but in those disciples, as depositaries for us; ... to every one of us, in them (from him, that rides with his hundreds of Torches, to him that crawles with his rush-

---

[25] It is perhaps worth noting here that Alford at first omitted this sermon and the Candlemas sermon on *Romans* 12.20 which we printed as No. 18 of Volume III of our edition. He did this, according to his preface on pp. v and vi of Volume I of his edition, because he at first intended to confine his edition to four volumes, and therefore certain sermons had to be omitted. He evidently considered these two to be comparatively uninteresting. When it was decided to enlarge the edition to six volumes, these two sermons were inserted in his Volume III as Sermons LXIII and LXIV.

[26] P. 84.

candle) our Saviour sayes, *Let your light so shine before men, that they may see your good works, &c.*"[27]

Later on Donne turns to a specific defense of the use of candles and torches on this particular feast day. He admits that Tertullian and Lactantius had argued against the Gentile superstition, followed by the Christians, of multiplying "Lamps, and Torches in Divine Service." God, who made the great and glorious sun, has no need of men's candles. Donne continues:

> It is in this Ceremony of lights, as it is in other Ceremonies: They may be good in their Institution, and grow ill in their practise. So did many things, which the Christian Church received from the Gentiles, in a harmlesse innocency, degenerate after, into as pestilent superstition there, as amongst the Gentiles themselves. For, ceremonies, which were received, but for the instruction, and edification of the weaker sort of people, were made reall parts of the service of God, and meritorious sacrifices. . . . So lights were received in the Primitive Church, to signifie to the people, that God, the Father of lights, was otherwise present in that place, then in any other, and then, men came to offer lights by way of sacrifice to God; And so, that which was providently intended for man, who indeed needed such helps, was turned upon God, as though he were to be supplied by us. But what then? Because things good in their institution, may be depraved in their practise, *Ergonè nihil ceremoniarum rudioribus dabitur, ad juvandam eorum imperitiam?* Shall therefore the people be denyed all ceremonies, for the assistance of their weaknesse? *Id ego non dico;*[28] I say not so, sayes he [i.e., Calvin]. . . . Wee must not therefore be hasty in condemning particular ceremonies: For, in so doing, in this ceremony of lights, we may condemne the Primitive Church, that did use them, and wee condemne a great and Noble part of the reformed Church, which doth use them at this day.[29]

For the most part, however, the sermon is devoted to the exposition of Donne's text, which calls for the glorification of God by the good works of Christ's disciples. It is a good sermon, and it contains a number of telling passages such as this:

> To give old cloathes, past wearing, to the poore, is not so good a worke as to make new for them. To give a little of your superfluities, not so ac-

---

[27] P. 85.

[28] Here Donne is quoting from Calvin, whose authority had great weight with the Puritans. He supplies in the margin the reference "Calv. Instit. l. 4. c. 10. §14."

[29] Pp. 90–91.

ceptable as the widows gift, that gave all. To give a poore soule a farthing at that doore, where you give a Player a shilling, is not equall dealing; for, this is to give God *quisquilias frumenti, The refuse of the wheat.* But doe thou some such things, as are truly works in our sense, such as are against the nature, and ordinary practice of worldly men to doe; some things, by which they may see, that thou dost prefer God before honour, and wife, and children, and hadst rather build, and endow some place, for Gods service, then poure out money to multiply titles of honour upon thy selfe, or enlarge joyntures, and portions, to an unnecessary, and unmeasurable proportion, when there is enough done before.[30]

The next two sermons (Nos. 4 and 5) were both preached at St. Paul's, and they can be considered together as in some way a defense of the Church of England against the attacks of Romanists and Separatists. Of the two the second is the more eloquent and memorable, but both have good passages. The following two (Nos. 6 and 7) were preached at Whitehall instead of St. Paul's, but they also contain a defense of the Church of England, chiefly against Roman attacks. It should be noted that it was largely in Court circles that the Church of Rome made most headway,[31] while Donne's audience at St. Paul's were more likely to be influenced by the Puritan attacks.

I propose to consider all these four sermons together, though they may have been preached at widely different times. It is convenient to put them together, because from them we can see that the main lines of Donne's defense were those which had already been laid down by Hooker and Andrewes. These were carefully reasoned, and thus they differ from the random attacks which Donne often introduced into his sermons.[32]

---

[30] P. 95.

[31] The ladies of the Court were particularly vulnerable during the latter years of King James's reign, and also during King Charles's. Buckingham's mother, Lady Compton, who was created Countess of Buckingham, was a Catholic, and so was Buckingham's wife, daughter of the Earl of Rutland. Weston, Lord Treasurer, created Earl of Portland, was a secret Catholic, while his wife and daughters openly declared their Catholicism. See Chamberlain, *Letters,* II, 369, for other instances.

[32] A very large number of Donne's sermons contain controversial passages against the Church of Rome. Some of these are violently abusive, but the Roman and Puritan controversialists were equally scurrilous, in the regular tradition of seventeenth-century attack and reply. Mr. J. B. Leishman, in *Review of English Studies,* n.s., VIII, 441, has supplied a list

Though sermons 6 and 7 are undated, they may perhaps belong to the reign of King Charles, for the reference on p. 161 to "the learnedst King, that any age hath produc'd, our incomparable King *James*" would probably have been worded differently if that monarch had still been on the throne. There were generally three occasions in the year on which Donne was summoned to preach at Whitehall. One of these was the first Friday in Lent, and we have a long series of dated sermons for the years 1618, 1619, 1620, 1621, 1622, 1623, 1625, 1626, 1627,[33] 1628, 1629, 1630, and 1631. Donne's two other sermons were usually preached in April.[34] In the year 1617 Donne preached at Whitehall on November 2, which was the 20th Sunday after Trinity, but this was an exception. We may take it that the two sermons on *Ezekiel* 34.19, which we are now considering, were preached in April. We do not know whether Donne preached them on successive Sundays, or on the morning and afternoon of a single Sunday,[35] but it will

---

of Donne's polemics against the Roman Church in Volumes II and VII: "Vol. II, pp. 100, 103, 160, 300, 302, 327, 360; Vol. VII, pp. 104, 120, 122–124, 129–132, 157, 158, 161, 166–168, 183–187, 191, 294–296, 309, 332–333, 377, 382, 387, 401–403, 448. [We have omitted the line references.] . . . In many of these attacks there is a kind of Miltonic savagery, and it must be admitted that Donne sometimes chooses very low ground and employs very dubious weapons. He will often introduce some long digression simply in order to lead up to such an attack, and, for one who has learnt by experience to know what is coming, it is amusing to watch both the build-up and Donne's obvious enjoyment. . . . Here, I repeat (for it seems worth insisting upon, in view of all we have been told about the great differences between them) Donne's affinity is with the polemical Milton." This is the considered verdict of one who has shown himself to be an able and sympathetic critic of Donne.

[33] This is described in the Folio as having been preached on *"the first Sunday* [not, *the first Friday*] *in Lent."*

[34] Professor R. C. Bald informs me that, apart from the Church's festivals, the Lord Chamberlain summoned preachers for the Sunday services according to the month. Evidently Donne shared April with another royal chaplain.

[35] In 1616 Donne preached at Whitehall on April 21, in 1618 on April 12 and April 19, in 1620 on April 2 and April 30, in 1625 on April 3, in 1626 on April 18 and April 30, in 1627 on April 1, in 1628 on April 5 and April 15, in 1629 in April, two sermons, no date of month given, in 1630 on April 20 [see query in Vol. IX, pp. 26–28].

be seen from the dates given in the footnote that we have a choice of years.

In Sermon 6, Donne explains that he has chosen his text from the book of *Ezekiel,* whom he asserts to be the greatest of the four major prophets. "Amongst the four great ones, our Prophet *Ezekiel* is the *greatest.* I compare not their extraction and race; ... But the extraordinary greatnesse of *Ezekiel,* is in his extraordinary depth, and mysteriousnesse, ..." Donne gives first the literal sense of the text he has chosen, that when the Israelites languished in Babylon "their own *Priests* joyned with the *State* against them, and infused pestilent doctrines into them, that so themselves might enjoy the favour of the State, ..." He then continues, "the *figurative* and *Mysticall* sense is of the same oppressions, and the same deliverance over againe in the times of *Christ,* and of the *Christian Church.*" This relates first to the deliverance of the primitive Church from the persecutions of the heathen, but Donne then applies it to "the *Reformation of Religion*" and "the oppressions of the *Roman Church.*"[36]

In this application of the text the shepherds of whom Ezekiel complains become the dignitaries of the Roman Church. Donne's complaint is first that in pre-Reformation days these dignitaries "neglected his *people,* (for Gods people are his *portion*) And then whatsoever pious men had given to the Church, is his *portion* too, and that portion they had troden under foot; ..."[37] He attacks the corruption of the Roman clergy, and then widens his attack to include the use of Latin in all services, and the supply of legends of the Saints in place of sound Scriptural teaching. He goes on to assert that in the Roman Church the traditions of men were made of equal authority with the Scriptures, and that some of these traditions were positively harmful, while others, though harmless, were misunderstood by the people. "We deny not that there are *Traditions,* nor that there must be *ceremonies,* but that maters of *faith* should depend of these, or be made of these, that we deny; and that they should be made equall to *Scriptures;* for with that especially doth *Tertullian* reproch the Heretiques, that being pressed with Scriptures, they fled to Traditions, as things equall or superiour to the word of God."[38] He proceeds to accuse the tem-

---

[36] Pp. 140–142.

[37] P. 142.

[38] P. 151.

poral power and the oppression of the Papacy, and the cruelties of the Inquisition. "They record, nay they boast, gloriously, triumphantly, of *threescore thousand of the Waldenses, slain by them in a day,* in the beginning of the Reformation; and *Possevine* the Jesuit will not lose the glory of recording the *five hundred thousand,* slain in a very few years, onely in *France,* and the *low Countrey,* for some declarations of their desire of a Reformation. . . . Let those *Israelites,* which found no way from this *Egypt,* but by *the red sea,* no way out of Idolatry, but by *Martyrdome,* as they have testified for Christ, so testifie against Antichrist, how heavy his feet, as feet signifie Power, trod upon the necks of Princes and people."[39]

In Sermon 7 Donne proceeds to justify the action of those Reformers who had established the Church of England as a separate body, free from Papal jurisdiction. He also justifies the action of the English forefathers who, holding the Christian faith, and yet desiring certain reforms in the Church, had remained so long within the fold of Rome. Continuing Ezekiel's metaphor, he calls them God's sheep,

. . . though their grasse were troden, and their water troubled, yet they did *eat* that grasse, and they did drink that water, . . . they continued *Gods sheep;* . . . And more then that, they were *Grex Dei, Gods flock;* . . . God hath *single sheep* in many corners of the *heathen,* but these, though thus fed, were his *flock, his Church.* But then, though they staid Gods leasure, and lived long upon this ill diet, yet when God was pleased to call them out of *Babylon,* out of *Babylon* they went, when God was pleased to lead our *Fathers* out of *Rome,* they left it.[40]

Donne answers an objection often raised against the Church of England:

They therefore that aske now, *Where was your Church before Luther?* would then have asked of the *Jews* in *Babylon,* Where was your Church before *Esdras?* that was in *Babylon,* ours was in *Rome.*

Now, beloved, when our Adversaries cannot deny us this truth, that our Church was enwrapped, (though smothered) in theirs, . . . they vexe us now, with that question, Why, if the case stood so, if your Fathers . . . continued sheep, and Gods sheep, and Gods flock, his Church with us, why went they from us? They ought us their residence, because they had received their Baptisme from us. And truly, it is not an impertinent, a frivo-

---

[39] Pp. 155–156.
[40] Pp. 159–160.

lous reason, that of Baptisme, where there is nothing but conveniency, and no necessity in the case. But, if I be content to stay with my friend in an aguish aire, will he take it ill, if I go when the plague comes? Or if I stay in town till 20 die of the plague, shall it be lookd that I should stay when there die 1000? The infection grew hotter and hotter in *Rome;* and their *may,* came to a *must,* those things which were done before *de facto,* came at last to be articles of *Faith,* and *de jure,* must be beleeved and practised upon salvation. They chide us for going away, and they drove us away; If we abstained from communicating with their poysons, (being now growen to that height) they excommunicated us; They gave us no room amongst them but the fire, and they were so forward to burne Heretiques, that they called it heresie, not to stay to be burnt.[41]

Donne lays stress on the fact that the Reformation in England was part of a much wider movement. He declares that "every where principall writers, and preachers, and Princes too, (as much as could stand with their safety) crying out against them *before Luther,* howsoever they will needs doe him that honour, to have been the first mover, in this blessed revolution."[42]

If we turn back now to Sermons 4 and 5, we find that in them at St. Paul's Donne maintained the same resolute defense, though more briefly, of the Church of England against attacks from Rome. In particular he urged that, judged by the laws of the primitive and the medieval Church, Anglican Orders were as valid as Roman:

When our adversaries do so violently, so impetuously cry out, that we have no Church, no Sacrament, no Priesthood, because none are sent, that is, none have a right calling, for *Internall calling,* who are called by the Spirit of God, they can be no Judges, and for *Externall calling,* we admit them for Judges, and are content to be tried by their own *Canons,* and their own evidences, for our Mission and vocation, o[u]r sending and our calling to the Ministery. If they require a necessity of lawfull Ministers to the constitution of a Church, we require it with as much earnestnesse as they; *Ecclesia non est quæ non habet sacerdotem,* we professe with Saint *Hierome,* It is no Church that hath no Priest. If they require, that this spirituall power be received from them, who have the same power in themselves, we professe it too, *Nemo dat quod non habet,* no man can confer other power upon another, then he hath himself. If they require *Imposition of hands,* in conferring Orders, we joyn hands with them. If they will have it a Sacrament, men may be content to let us be as liberall of that

---

[41] Pp. 170–171.
[42] P. 172.

name of Sacrament, as *Calvin* is; ... Whatsoever their own authors, their own Schools, their own Canons doe require to be essentially and necessarily requisite in this Mission in this function, we, for our parts, and as much as concerns our Church of *England,* admit it too, and professe to have it. And whatsoever they can say for their Church, that from their first Conversion, they have had an orderly derivation of power from one to another, we can as justly and truly say of our Church, that ever since her first being of such a Church, to this day, she hath conserved the same order, and ever hath had, and hath now, those Ambassadours sent, with the same Commission, and by the same means, that they pretend to have in *their* Church.[48]

A little later in the same sermon there occurs a passage which shows that Donne considered the Apostolic Succession and the episcopal constitution of the Church of England as important but not absolutely essential, as pertaining to the *bene esse* but not the *esse* of a Church.

This I speak of this Church, in which God hath planted us, That God hath afforded us all that might serve, even for the stopping of the Adversaries mouth, and to confound them in their own way: which I speak, onely to excite us to a thankfulnesse to God, for his abundant grace in affording us so much, and not to disparage, or draw in question any other of our *neighbour Churches,* who, perchance, cannot derive, as we can, their power, and their *Mission,* by the ways required, and practised in the Romane Church, nor have had from the beginning a continuance of Consecration by Bishops, and such other concurrences, as those *Canons* require, and as our *Church* hath enjoyed. They, no doubt, can justly plead for themselves, that Ecclesiasticall positive Laws admit *dispensation* in cases of necessity; They may justly challenge a Dispensation, but we need none; They did what was lawfull in a case of necessity, but Almighty God preserved us from this necessity.[44]

If we turn now to Donne's defense of the English Church against those Puritans who wished to secede from it, or to despoil it of all the ceremonies derived from the primitive and the medieval Church, we shall find a brief answer to them in Sermon 7. Donne argues that the differences between such Puritans and the Church are minor as compared with those which led to the separation from the Roman

[48] Pp. 128–129. Donne is here following the line of argument used earlier by Bishop Andrewes in his *Responsio ad Apologiam Card. Bellarmini,* cap. vii.
[44] Pp. 129–130.

Church. No fundamental doctrines are involved, and as for questions of order and ceremony, these should be settled by lawful authority.[45]

Donne devotes a considerable part of Sermon 4 to the need for peace and unity within the Church of England. Private opinions should be subordinated to the welfare of the Church.

> *David,* in the person of every member of the Church, submits himself to that increpation, *Let my right hand forget her cunning, and let my tongue cling to the roof of my mouth, if I prefer not Jerusalem before my chiefest joy.* Our chiefest joy, is, for the most part, our *own opinions,* especially when they concur with other learned and good men too. But then, *Jerusalem* is our love of the peace[46] of the Church; and in such things as do not violate foundations, let us prefer *Jerusalem* before our chiefest Joy, love of peace before our own opinions, though concurrent with others. . . . And when a Church hath declared her self so, in all things necessary and sufficient, let us possess our souls in peace, and not say that that Church hath, or presse that that Church would proceed to further declarations in lesse necessary particulars. . . . And let our right hand forget her cunning, (let us never set pen to paper to write) Let our tongue cleave to the roofe of our mouth, (let us never open our mouth to speake) of those things in which *Silence* was an Act of *Discretion,* and *Charity* before, but now is also an Act of *Obedience,* and of *Allegiance* and *Loy-*

---

[45] "Many of these extemporall men have gone away from us, and vainly said, that they have as good cause to separate from us, as we from *Rome.* . . . A civill man will depart with his opinion at a *Table,* at a Councell table, rather then hold up an argument to the vexation of the Company; . . . but have our *Separatists* [as at the Reformation] any such publique, and concurrent authorising of that which they doe, since of all that part from us, scarse a dozen meet together in one confession?" (Pp. 174–176.) With more earnestness Donne deplores the undervaluing of the Sacraments. "With what sorrow, with what holy indignation did I heare the Sonne of my friend, who brought me to that place, to minister the Sacrament to him, then, upon his death-bed, and almost at his last gaspe, when my service was offered him in that kinde, answer his Father, *Father, I thanke God, I have not lived so in the sight of my God, as that I need a Sacrament.* I name a few of these, because *our times* abound with such persons as undervalue, not onely all *rituall,* and *ceremoniall* assistances of devotion, which the wisdome, and the piety of the Church hath induced, but even the *Sacraments themselves,* of Christs owne immediate institution, and are alwaies open to solicitations to passe to another Church, upon their own surmises of errours in their own." (P. 162.)

[46] Donne is here playing on the original meaning of *Jerusalem,* "vision of peace."

altie.[47] But that which *David* said to the Lord, (*Psalme* 65.1) Let us also accommodate to the Lords anointed, *Tibi laus silentium,*[48] our best sacrifice to both, is to be silent in those things.[49]

Donne continues with a defense of the retention of certain ceremonies in the Church of England:

To a *Circumcision* of the *garment,* that is, to a paring, and taking away such *Ceremonies,* as were superstitious, or superfluous, of an ill use, or of no use, our *Church* came in the beginning of the *Reformation.* To a *Circumcision* we came; but those *Churches* that came to a *Concision* of the *garment,* to an absolute taking away of *all ceremonies,* neither provided so safely for the *Church* it self in the substance thereof, nor for the exaltation of *Devotion in the Church.* . . . So great a care had God, of those things, which though they be not of the *revenue* of *Religion,* yet are of the *subsidy* of Religion, and, though they be not the *soule* of the Church, yet are they those *Spirits* that unite soule and body together. . . . And therefore as this Apostle enters this *Caveat* in another place, *If yee bite one another, cavete, take heed yee be not consumed of one another,* so *cavete,* take heed of this concision of the garment, lest if the garment be torne off, the body wither, and perish. . . . Ceremonies are *nothing;* but where there are no Ceremonies, order, and uniformity, and obedience, and at last, (and quickely) Religion it selfe will vanish.[50]

While we are considering these controversial sermons of Donne's, we must not forget that in other passages he displays a sense of underlying unity among all Christian believers, which is deeper than the cleavages which seemed so profound. He recognizes the Church of Rome as a true branch of Christ's one universal Church, and so also he recognizes the Church of Geneva, and other Protestant bodies such as the Lutheran Churches.[51]

---

[47] This seems to be a reference to King James's *Directions for Preachers* in 1622 (see Vol. IV, pp. 28, 33) and may perhaps imply that Donne preached this sermon in late 1622, or in 1623.

[48] For this interpretation of *Psa.* 65.1, which in A.V. is "Praise waiteth for thee" [margin, *Heb. is silent*], see Vol. IX, pp. 134–135.

[49] P. 114–115.

[50] P. 116. For other passages in which Donne defends the ceremonies retained by the Church of England, see Vol. V, pp. 108–109, and Vol. VII, p. 430.

[51] This attitude is clearly stated in his *Essays in Divinity,* a noncontroversial work. He calls the Roman Church "that Church from which we are by Gods Mercy escaped, because upon the foundation, which we yet

Donne's desire for the reunification of the whole Christian Church as expressed in the *Essays in Divinity* should be compared with the *Holy Sonnet,* "Show me deare Christ thy spouse so bright and cleare," which was first printed by Gosse (*Life and Letters,* II, 371) from the Westmoreland MS. This was misinterpreted by Gosse, along with two other sonnets from the same MS, as betraying "a leaning to certain Romish doctrines" (II, 109–110). Gosse remarked, "They seem to prove that even after the death of his wife, and his subsequent conversion, he hankered after some tenets of the Roman faith, or at least that he still doubted as to his attitude with regard to them. In this it is probable that he found a sympathiser in secret in Lord Doncaster . . . ," a conjecture which is remarkable for the flimsy evidence adduced (see our comment on this passage in Vol. V, pp. 20–23). Gosse's insinuations have done an immense amount of harm to Donne's reputation as a loyal churchman. No one who has studied our edition of the *Sermons* with any care could possibly believe that Donne after his ordination still "hankered after some tenets of the Roman faith," except so far as those tenets were identical with those of the Church of England. Donne's subject in the sonnet is the true Universal Church, the "Bride of Christ," who is not fully represented

---

embrace together, Redemption in Christ, they had built so many stories high, as the foundation was, though not destroyed, yet hid and obscured." It remains, however, part of the true Catholic Church of Christ. "Yet though we branch out *East* and *West,* that Church concurs with us in the root, and sucks her vegetation from one and the same ground, *Christ Jesus.*" For himself, however, he prefers the *via media* of the English Church, and says that in his "poor opinion" the form of worship established in that Church is "more convenient, and advantageous then of any other Kingdome, both to provoke and kindle devotion, and also to fix it, that it stray not into infinite expansions and Subdivisions; (into the former of which, Churches utterly despoyl'd of Ceremonies, seem to me to have fallen; and the *Roman* Church, by presenting innumerable objects, into the later)." He continues, "Thus much was to my understanding naturally occasioned and presented by this variety of Names in the Scriptures: For, if *Esau, Edom,* and *Seir* were but one man, . . . so Synagogue and Church is the same thing, and of the Church, *Roman* and *Reformed,* and all other distinctions of place, Discipline, or Person, but one Church, journying to one *Hierusalem,* and directed by one guide, Christ Jesus; . . ." (*Essays in Divinity,* ed. Simpson, pp. 49–51).

by any one of the warring churches, but is hidden from our sight by our unhappy divisions.[52]

The next three sermons in this volume make up a small group of undated sermons described in the Folio as preached at St. Dunstan's. This is a statement which we take leave to doubt later, but if it were correct they must all be later than Sermons 3 and 4 of Volume VI, which were preached on April 11 and April 25, 1624, and were described in the Folio as "The first Sermon in that Church, as Vicar thereof" and "The second Sermon Preached by the Author after he came to St. Dunstanes," respectively. As Volume VI also contains a sermon preached at St. Dunstan's on Trinity Sunday, 1624, and another preached there on New Year's Day, 1624/5, it is clear that in his first twelve months as Vicar Donne kept copies of more sermons than in any other period, for we have only nine St. Dunstan's sermons in all, though he must have preached a number which he did not trouble to preserve. Just as he kept only a fraction of the large number which he preached in his six years at Lincoln's Inn, so at St. Dunstan's he wrote out only a few, which seemed to him to have special significance.

Professor Baird Whitlock has described in two articles[53] the chief

----

[52] This particular *Holy Sonnet* has been carefully examined and interpreted by Helen Gardner in her edition of Donne's *Divine Poems* (Oxford, 1952), Appendix C, pp. 121–127. In the course of her reasoning she remarks, "The sonnet is not merely 'compatible with loyalty to the Church of England'; it could hardly have been written by anyone but an Anglican. The Anglican, at this period, differed from the Roman Catholic and the Calvinist in not holding a doctrine of the Church which compelled him to 'unchurch' other Christians. The Anglican Fathers, while defending episcopacy against the Puritans, did not, as Keble had to own in his edition of Hooker, defend it as a necessity for the valid administration of the Sacraments. . . . Similarly, they did not hold that what they regarded as Roman deviations from 'primitive purity' made the Church of Rome no Church." She supports her argument by reference to Leonard Hodgson, *The Doctrine of the Church as Held and Taught in the Church of England* (Oxford, 1948), and Norman Sykes, *The Church of England and Non-Episcopal Churches in the Sixteenth and Seventeenth Centuries* (S.P.C.K., 1948).

[53] *Times Literary Supplement*, September 16 and 23, 1955, "Donne at St. Dunstan's," I and II.

items in the *Churchwardens' Accounts* and the *Vestry Minutes* of St. Dunstan's during Donne's tenure of the living. They give us a very pleasant picture of the good relations between Donne and the church officials, and of the interest which he took in the affairs of the parish. Here, as at Lincoln's Inn, he showed his wide human sympathies and his readiness to make friends. The parishioners were proud of their Vicar's high position and of his fame as a preacher, and they found him kindly and affable, willing to dine with the vestrymen after a vestry meeting,[54] and ready in time of need to give sums of money to be distributed to the poor.[55]

Soon after his appointment in March, 1624, Donne pushed forward a strong building program for the church. Whitlock quotes the *Churchwardens' Accounts* for information about the new pulpit and nine pews with other necessary repairs in the church structure. "The work was started on August 11 and completed, at the cost of £122. 2. 8d., on January 24, 1625." On May 8, 1626, it was decided at a vestry meeting to move the pulpit and to erect "five pewes or new seates in the Chancell . . . and 2 pewes more for the use of the Deane."

Donne took part in a number of vestry meetings which regulated parish affairs. At one of these the Sexton was to have five pounds deducted from his salary unless he paid his debts, and at another the vestry agreed to help a certain Mary Parker to get her children ad-

---

[54] From the *Accounts* and *Minutes* we learn that Donne dined with the vestrymen at the Horn Tavern on June 29, 1626, after he had preached the Adams memorial sermon, and after a vestry meeting on July 12 of the same year at the St. Dunstan's Tavern. Other occasions when he dined with them after a vestry meeting were October 10, 1626, January 30, 1626/7, October 10, 1627, April 19, 1628, July 16, 1628, April 21, 1630. He also attended a number of vestry meetings after which no dinner was held.

[55] At the time of the plague epidemic of 1625 Donne gave twenty shillings for the poor on August 29, and on December 23 forty shillings more. When in August, 1626, the Curate, Mr. Gray, died leaving two daughters, "the parish undertook to clear the indentures of the two girls and paid forty shillings each to apprentice them out. . . . This occurence is of interest because only one person felt personally moved to do anything for the girls. 'Item the viij of August received of Richard Collins as the guifte of Mr Deane of Paules towarde the placing of 2 daughters of Mr Gray our late Curate . . . xxˢ" (*Churchwardens' Accounts,* fo. 313ᵛ, quoted by Baird Whitlock, *op. cit.*).

mitted into Christ's Hospital [a famous charity school] at the right time. Donne and the common council gave their permission for the son of Judge Houghton to erect a monument to his father in St. Anne's chapel. On one occasion the vestry decided to relieve and keep at the charge of the parish "one William, an Irish Child of the age of 5 yeres or thereabouts who hath long since layne in the streets of this parish . . . in regard to the greate wante the said Child is in, beinge like to Starve in the Streets," until they could find out how by law they could be discharged of their responsibility.[56]

Whitlock states that other items in the records "show the interests of the church in giving help to needy sailors of all countries and to unmarried mothers and orphans." It is clear that under Donne's leadership the church of St. Dunstan's showed itself a live and vigorous community with a strong sense of social obligation to the poor and unprotected.

Sermon 8 is described in its heading as "An Anniversary Sermon preached at St. Dunstans, upon the commemoration of a Parishioner, a Benefactor to that Parish." Whitlock shows that there is an entry in the records for June 29, 1624: "paid to Mr Deane for a sermon for Mr Adams . . . x s." The 29th of June was the day (year unknown) of the funeral of the Mr. Adams who had left a sum of money for these commemoration sermons. Other benefactors had done the same thing, but most of their commemorative sermons were preached by the curate, Mr. Gray. Donne preached the Adams sermon again on June 29, 1626, but in 1627 he preached it on September 30, and received his payment for it on October 19. In 1628 he delivered it on the usual date, June 29, and this is the last time that he is recorded as having preached an Adams sermon. It seems likely, as Whitlock suggests, that the sermon we are now discussing was the first of this series of four. It is based on a curious text, the malediction on the serpent in *Genesis* 3.14: "And dust shalt thou eat all the days of thy life." To Donne the serpent was an ambivalent symbol. It represented evil personified in the Devil, as in the passage from *Genesis,* and also in *Revelation* 12.9, "that old serpent, called the Devil, and Satan, which deceiveth the whole world," and *Revelation* 20.2. On the other hand,

[56] In 1601 a Poor Law had been established by which guardians of the poor were appointed in each parish to relieve the impotent poor, and to set the ablebodied to work in workhouses.

Moses had lifted up a brazen serpent by God's command, in order that those who were bitten by poisonous serpents might look on it and recover, and Christ had compared himself to this brazen serpent in *John* 3.14, 15, "And as Moses lifted up the serpent in the wilderness, even so must the Son of man be lifted up, That whosoever believeth in him should not perish, but have eternal life." The serpent could therefore be interpreted as a symbol of divine healing power, and here we remember that Aesculapius, the Greek and Roman god of healing, frequently appeared in the form of a serpent, and tame serpents were kept in his temple at Epidaurus in Greece.[57] Worship of a divine serpent was long practiced in Mexico. Thus the serpent has fascinated many different races by its power to symbolize both good and evil.

Passages in this sermon should be compared carefully with the Latin poem which Donne sent to George Herbert with his seal of the Anchor and Christ. Both sermon and poem (with its English translation) show Donne's love of paradox, as exemplified in the Serpent. In the poem Donne compares his old seal of a sheaf of snakes, "The Crest of our poore Family," with his new seal of Christ on an anchor. He continues:

> *Nec Natalitiis penitus serpentibus orbor,*
> *Non ita dat Deus, ut auferat ante data.*
> *Quâ sapiens, Dos est; Quâ terram lambit et ambit,*
> *Pestis; At in nostra fit Medicina Cruce,*
> *Serpens; fixa Cruci si sit Natura; Crucique*
> *A fixo, nobis, Gratia tota fluat. . . .*

> Yet may I, with this, my first Serpents hold,
> God gives new blessings, and yet leaves the old;
> The Serpent, may, as wise, my pattern be;
> My poison, as he feeds on dust, that's me.
> And as he rounds the Earth to murder sure,
> My death he is, but on the Crosse, my cure.
> Crucifie nature then, and then implore
> All Grace from him, crucified there before.[58]

---

[57] See Pausanias, iii, 23; Valerius Maximus, i, 8; and Livy, Epist. xi, quoted in Smith's *Dictionary of Classical Antiquities*.

[58] H. Gardner, *Divine Poems of Donne*, pp. 52–53; *Poems*, ed. Grierson, I, 398–400. On the date and circumstances of the poem see Gardner, *op. cit.*, pp. 138–147.

In the latter part of the sermon the paradox is expounded at much greater length:

So, if he who is *Serpens serpens humi,* the Serpent condemned to creep upon the ground, doe transforme himselfe into a flying Serpent, and attempt our nobler faculties, there is *Serpens exaltatus,* a Serpent lifted up in the wildernesse to recover all them that are stung, and feel that they are stung with this Serpent, this flying Serpent, that is, these high and continued sinnes. The creeping Serpent, the groveling Serpent, is Craft; the exalted Serpent, the crucified Serpent, is Wisdome. All your worldly cares, all your crafty bargaines, ... savour of the earth, and of the craft of that Serpent, that creeps upon the earth: But crucifie this craft of yours, bring all your worldly subtilty under the Crosse of Christ Jesus, ... market and bargaine so, as that you would give all, to buy that field, in which his treasure, and his pearle is hid, and then you have changed the Serpent, from the Serpent of perdition creeping upon the earth, to the Serpent of salvation exalted in the wildernesse. Creeping wisedome, that still looks downward, is but craft; Crucified wisedome, that looks upward, is truly wisedome. Between you and that ground Serpent God hath kindled a war; ... But in the other Serpent, the crucified Serpent, God hath reconciled to himself, all things in heaven, and earth, and hell. ... That creeping Serpent, Satan, is war, and should be so; The crucified Serpent Christ Jesus is peace, and shall be so for ever. The creeping Serpent eats our dust, the strength of our bodies, in sicknesses, and our glory in the dust of the grave: The crucified Serpent hath taken our flesh, and our blood, and given us his flesh, and his blood for it.[59]

Donne devotes the last paragraph of the sermon to a commemoration of the benefactor by whose request this annual sermon was to be preached:

In this state of dust, and so in the territory of the Serpent, the Tyrant of the dead, lies this dead brother of ours, and hath lien some years, who occasions our meeting now, and yearly upon this day, and whose soul, we doubt not, is in the hands of God, who is the God of the living. And having gathered a good *Gomer* of Manna, a good measure of temporall blessings in this life, and derived a fair measure thereof, upon them, whom nature and law directed it upon, (and in whom we beseech God to blesse it) hath also distributed something to the poor of this Parish, yearly, this day, and something to a meeting for the conserving of neighbourly love, and something for this exercise. In which, no doubt, his intention was not so much to be yearly remembered himself, as that his posterity, and his neighbours might be yearly remembered to doe as he had done. For, this

---

[59] Pp. 189–190.

is truly to glorifie God in his Saints, to sanctifie our selves in their examples; To celebrate them, is to imitate them.[60]

Baird Whitlock suggests that the two undated sermons (Sermons 9 and 10) which follow this one in the Folio may also have been preached as commemoration sermons of Mr. Adams. It does not, however, seem very likely that Donne would have preserved three sermons of this type. There is nothing about Sermons 9 and 10 to suggest that they were intended to commemorate a special anniversary, and we know that Donne was in the habit of preaching at St. Dunstan's as often as he had the time and energy to do so.[61] On the other hand, Gosse and others have identified Sermon 9 with the sermon which Walton declared to have been the first which Donne preached after his wife's funeral in August, 1617. Gosse wrote:

The first time Donne left his house after the funeral of his wife, it was to preach a sermon at the church of St. Clement Danes, where she was buried. So, at least, Walton declares, but the printed copy which has come down to us says that it was delivered at St. Dunstan's. The text is from *Lamentations* 3.1: 'I am the man that hath seen affliction by the rod of His wrath.' Walton's account of this discourse is pretty, but too sentimental to be accepted; 'indeed, his very words and looks testified him to be truly such a man' [as the prophet Jeremiah describes]; 'and they, with the addition of his sighs and tears expressed in his sermon, did so work upon the affections of his hearers, as melted and moulded them into a companionable sadness; and so they left the congregation; but then *their* houses presented them with objects of diversion, and *his* presented him with nothing but[62] fresh objects of sorrow, in beholding many helpless children, a narrow fortune, and a consideration of the many cares and

---

[60] P. 190.

[61] We may take as examples of such sermons, for which no payment would be found in the records, the sermon on Trinity Sunday, 1624 (Vol. VI, No. 6), that on New Year's Day, 1624/5 (Vol. VI, No. 9), that on January 15, 1625/6 (Vol. VI, No. 18), that on Trinity Sunday, 1627 (Vol. VIII, No. 1), and the sermon to which Donne alludes in his letter to the Earl of Middlesex (Vol. VIII, pp. 24–25). In a letter to Mrs. Cokain two months before his death he defends himself from the charge that he had not preached sufficiently often at St. Dunstan's: "... my witnesse is in heaven, that I never left out S. *Dunstans* when I was able to do them that service; nor will now; ..." (*Letters*, 1651, pp. 317–318).

[62] Gosse here misquotes Walton, who wrote in the *Life of Donne* (1670), "presented him with no diversions, but with fresh objects ..." It should be noted that in the first draft of Walton's *Life*, which was pre-

casualties that attend their education.' This picture is overcharged. Walton supposed that Mrs. Donne died two years earlier than was the case; in 1617 the poet's fortune was no longer 'narrow.' Moreover, an examination of the sermon itself reveals no such emotional or hysterical appeals to sympathy as the sentimental genius of Walton conceived. It is a very dignified and calm address on the mode in which we should endure the afflictions with which God sees it fitting to chastise us. Not one word, however, applies the text or his exhortations to the speaker himself; no one would guess, from any personal emotion or parade of grief, that the preacher was more afflicted than the rest of the race of man. In no sense is this sermon a funeral oration over Anne Donne, or a record of the preacher's loss. Rather, after shutting himself up in his house until the bitterness of his anguish was over, we see Donne here putting his bereavement behind him, and resuming, with stately impassibility, his priestly task.[63]

Gosse is correct in stating that there is nothing in the sermon itself to link it with Donne's sorrow over the death of his wife. The question arises, then, whether we should dissociate this sermon from the incident described by Walton, and should accept instead the statement of the Folio that it was preached at St. Dunstan's. In that case, we should regard it as having been preached later than April 25, 1624.

The placing of Sermon 10 at St. Dunstan's also raises some questions. In the opening paragraph Donne says: "This case is so farre ours, as that in another place we have sowed in teares, and by his promise, in whose teares we sowed then, when we handled those two words, *Jesus wept,* we shall reape in Joy:..." This is an evident allusion to the sermon which Donne preached on those words (*John* 11.35) at Whitehall on "the first Friday in Lent," 1622/3 (Vol. IV, No. 13). In that sermon Donne had remarked: "There is not a shorter verse in the Bible, nor a larger Text. There is another as short; *Semper gaudete, Rejoyce evermore,* and of that holy Joy, I may have leave to speake here hereafter, more seasonably, in a more Festivall time, by my ordinary service. This is the season of generall Compunction, of generall Mortification, and no man priviledged, for *Iesus wept.*"[64]

fixed to the *LXXX Sermons* of 1640, there is no mention at all of this sermon on *Lamentations* 3.1, nor of St. Clement's Church.

[63] Gosse, *Life and Letters of John Donne,* II, 94–95.
[64] Vol. IV, pp. 324–325.

This sermon fulfilled Donne's promise that he would preach a companion sermon on the only other text of two words in the Bible, but it seems rather odd that he should have done so at a little parish church like St. Dunstan's. We note that in the passage first quoted he says "in another place we have sowed in teares," but it would have seemed more appropriate if the second sermon had been preached at St. Paul's, where at least a few of his present auditors might have come to hear him.

There is a passage later in the present sermon which affords a stronger reason for thinking that it may have been preached at St. Paul's and not at St. Dunstan's (as the Folio asserts). Donne is rebuking the irreverence of some of his listeners, and we know that this was a fault which was particularly noticeable in the congregation at St. Paul's, where divine service was held in the chancel or choir (*Quire* in Donne's spelling):

> The service of God is one entire thing; and though we celebrate some parts with more, or with lesse reverence, some kneeling, some standing, yet if we afford it no reverence, we make that no part of Gods service. And therefore I must humbly intreat them, who make this Quire the place of their Devotion, to testifie their devotion by more outward reverence there; wee know our parts in this place, and we doe them; why any stranger should think himself more priviledged in this part of Gods House, then we, I know not. I presume no man will mis-interpret this that I say here now; nor, if this may not prevaile, mis-interpret the service of our Officers, if their continuing in that unreverent manner give our Officers occasion to warn them of that personally in the place, whensoever they see them stray into that uncomely negligence. They should not blame me now, they must not blame them then, when they call upon them for this reverence in this Quire; neither truly can there be any greater injustice, then when they who will not do their duties, blame others for doing theirs.[65]

This is the tone of the Dean of a great cathedral, who had church officers to enforce his orders. It is in line with what we have lately learnt about the case which he brought against a man who disobeyed the vergers who "thrice admonished" him to kneel in St. Paul's.[66] It

---

[65] Pp. 222–223.

[66] See Baird Whitlock, "The Dean and the Yeoman," *Notes and Queries,* Vol. CXCIX, No. 9 (September, 1954), pp. 374 f. See also the rebuke administered in St. Paul's by Donne (Vol. IX of our edition, pp. 152–153).

would hardly have been necessary in a comparatively small church like St. Dunstan's to use so stern a tone, and the congregation would not sit in the choir, but in the nave and aisles.

The sermon itself is a good one, though not in Donne's grand manner. If we believe it to have been preached in St. Paul's, and to have been in some ways a pendant to the sermon on "Jesus wept," we may perhaps assign it conjecturally to a date in 1623. If it was preached at St. Dunstan's it must be later than April, 1624.

After the many undated sermons which have occupied the second half of Volume IX and the earlier part of the present volume, we come to the last and most famous of all Donne's sermons (No. 11), which was preached on February 25, 1630/1, the first Friday in Lent, at Whitehall before the King. During the autumn and winter of 1630/1 Donne had been staying at Aldborough Hatch, the home of his eldest daughter Constance, who in June, 1630, had married as her second husband Samuel Harvey, by whom she later had three sons. Harvey seems to have proved a more congenial son-in-law to Donne than Constance's first husband, Edward Alleyn, had been.[67]

According to Walton, whose dates are seldom correct, it was in August, 1630, while Donne was staying with the Harveys, that his fatal illness developed. Walton writes "... he there fell into a fever, which with the help of his constant infirmity (vapors from the spleen) hastened him into so visible a Consumption, that his beholders might say, as St. *Paul* of himself, *He dies dayly;...*" (*Life of Donne*, 1670, p. 52). It was Donne's custom, unless hindered by the business of ecclesiastical commissions, to leave London at the end of June, and visit his country parishes in turn, but we have no evidence that he did this in 1630. He may have felt the beginning of what proved to be his fatal illness as early as July, and may therefore have decided to take a rest with his daughter and new son-in-law. During the autumn and winter he wrote to George Gerrard and also to Mrs. Cokain a number of letters in which he explained, first, that he had been too unwell to preach the Gunpowder Plot sermon on November 5 though he had received the King's command through the Lord

---

[67] Alleyn's squabbles with Donne have been recorded by Gosse, II, 217–219, and by Baird Whitlock in "Yᵉ curiost Scholler in christendome," *Review of English Studies*, n.s., VI, 365–371.

Chamberlain to do so. Next, he had to excuse himself from preaching the Christmas sermon at St. Paul's before the Lord Mayor, but he wrote that he was reserving Candlemas Day to himself for that service. Finally, he had to give up Candlemas Day, but realizing then that his illness was mortal, he determined to make a last effort to preach before the King on his "old constant day," the first Friday in Lent, in obedience to the Lord Chamberlain's command.[68]

The true nature of Donne's illness seems to have been obscured for some time by a violent attack of fever, probably the ague from which he suffered half-yearly, so he tells us. He recovered from this sufficiently to be able to walk in the garden, "and (but that the weather hath continued so spitefully foul) make no doubt, but I might safely have done more," so he tells Mrs. Cokain. But the weakness, lack of appetite and sleep, and the continual wasting continued. A rumour arose that he was dead, and he wrote to a friend a letter which has almost a prophetic relation to *Deaths Duell*:

A man would almost be content to dye (if there were no other benefit in death) to hear of so much sorrow, and so much good testimony from good men as I (God be blessed for it) did upon the report of my death; yet I perceive it went not through all, for one writ to me that some (and he said of my friends) conceived I was not so ill as I pretended, but withdrew my self to live at ease, discharged of preaching. It is an unfriendly, and God knows an ill-grounded interpretation; for I have alwayes been sorrier when I could not preach, than any could be they could not hear me. It hath been my desire, and God may be pleased to grant it, that I might dye in the Pulpit; if not that, yet, that I might take my death in the Pulpit, that is, dye the sooner by occasion of those labours.[69]

So the sick man returned to his beloved London, and gave himself into the care of his old friend and physician, Dr. Fox, who had already visited him at Aldborough Hatch, and who recommended a diet of milk and cordials. His friends, seeing that his sickness "had left him onely so much flesh as did onely cover his bones," tried to dissuade him from his design of preaching on the first Friday of Lent, assuring him that the effort would shorten his life;

[68] The letters in which Donne describes his symptoms and his hopes and fears may be found in *Letters*, 1651, pp. 281–283, 316–318; Tobie Matthew, *Letters*, pp. 349–356; Gosse, II, 265–274.

[69] Walton, *op. cit.*, pp. 69–70.

but, he passionately denied their requests; saying, *he would not doubt that that God who in so many weaknesses had assisted him with an unexpected strength, would now withdraw it in his last employment; professing an holy ambition to perform that sacred work.* And, when to the amazement of some beholders he appeared in the Pulpit, many of them thought he presented himself not to preach mortification by a living voice: but, mortality by a decayed body and dying face. And doubtless, many did secretly ask that question in *Ezekiel, Do these bones live? or, can that soul organize that tongue, to speak so long time as the sand in that glass will move towards its centre, and measure out an hour of this dying mans unspent life?* Doubtless it cannot; and yet, after some faint pauses in his zealous prayer, his strong desires enabled his weak body to discharge his memory of his preconceived meditations, which were of dying, the Text being, *To God the Lord belong the issues from death.* Many that then saw his tears, and heard his faint and hollow voice, professing they thought the Text prophetically chosen, and that *Dr.* Donne *had preach't his own funeral Sermon.*

Being full of joy that God had enabled him to perform this desired duty, he hastened to his house, out of which he never moved, till like St. *Stephen, he was carried by devout men to his Grave.*[70]

The sermon which was delivered in such dramatic circumstances became the most famous and the most often printed of all Donne's discourses,[71] and has been taken to represent the norm of Donne's preaching. We should view this splendid but macabre last sermon as the climax and completion of Donne's series preached before the King at the beginning of Lent. *Deaths Duell* has the same aim as its predecessors, to prepare its hearers for Lent, Good Friday, and Easter. In addition it was to serve as Donne's farewell to the Court and to life itself, but this was subordinated to the main purpose. Lent is a season of mortification, but the mortification is not an end in itself. Lent is intended to be a preparation for our meditations on the Passion of

---

[70] Walton, *op. cit.* pp. 71–72.

[71] It was printed in quarto in 1632, and again in 1633, and was later included in *XXVI Sermons.* It was included by Alford in his 1839 edition of Donne's *Works,* and was printed together with the *Devotions* in 1840 by Pickering. Keynes included it in his *Ten Sermons,* 1923, and Hayward printed it as the only sermon given in full in his Nonesuch *Donne... Complete Poetry and Selected Prose,* 1929, second edition, 1930, reprinted by Random House, New York, 1941, and with a new Introduction, New York, 1952. In 1958 it was printed among *Sermons of John Donne,* selected by Theodore Gill (Meridian Books, New York).

Christ in Holy Week, and on his agony on the Cross on Good Friday, while these in turn lead up to the joy of Easter and the Resurrection. Donne was never privileged to preach to the Court on Easter or Palm Sunday—those days were reserved for dignitaries higher in the Church, such as Bishops Andrewes, Williams, or Laud. So that again and again he relates his Lenten sermon to the weeks that were to follow. In one of the earliest of the series, that preached on February 20, 1617/18, he had taken as his text the words of the dying thief on the cross (*Luke* 23.40), thus anticipating Good Friday. He had said then, "Now, though these words were not spoken at this time [i.e., at the beginning of Lent], when we do but begin to celebrate by a poor and weak imitation, the fasting of our Saviour Jesus Christ, but were spoken at the day of the crucifying of the Lord of life and glory; yet as I would be loath to think, that you never fast but in Lent, so I would be loath to think that you never fulfill the sufferings of Christ Jesus in your flesh, but upon Goodfriday, never meditate upon the passion, but upon that day."[72]

Four years later, at the beginning of Lent 1621/2, Donne preached at Whitehall on the text, "The last Enemie that shall be destroyed, is Death," and began his sermon with the words: "This is a Text of the Resurrection, and it is not Easter yet; but it is Easter Eve; All Lent, is but the Vigill, the Eve of Easter: to so long a Festivall as never shall end, the Resurrection, wee may well begin the Eve betimes. Forty yeares long was God grieved for that Generation which he loved; let us be content to humble our selves forty daies, to be fitter for that glory which we expect.... Make way to an everlasting Easter by a short Lent, to an undeterminable glory, by a temporary humiliation. You must weepe these teares, teares of contrition, teares of mortification, before God will wipe all teares from your eyes; You must dye this death, this death of the righteous, the death to sin, before this *last enemy, Death,* shalbe destroyed in you, and you made partakers of everlasting life in soule and body too."[73]

Again, at the beginning of Lent 1627/8 Donne preached at White-

---

[72] Vol. I, p. 253.

[73] Vol. IV, p. 45. This is one of Donne's finest sermons upon death, and it contains the oft-quoted passage which begins, "It comes equally to us all, and it makes us all equall when it comes."

hall on the text, "And when he [Stephen] had said this, he fell asleep," and began with the words: "He that will dy with Christ upon Good-Friday, must hear his own bell toll all Lent; he that will be partaker of his passion at last, must conform himself to his discipline of prayer and fasting before.... We begin to hear Christs bell toll now, and is not our bell in the chime? We must be in his grave, before we come to his resurrection, and we must be in his death-bed before we come to his grave: we must do as he did, fast and pray, before we can say as he said, that *In manus tuas,* Into thy hands O Lord I commend my Spirit."[74]

So in *Deaths Duell* Donne was treading a path which he had often trod before, and the whole sermon, with all its emphasis upon death, and the deliverance from death which God affords us, was intended to lead up to the final section, in which Donne meditates upon the death of Christ. The text which he had chosen was from his favorite book of *Psalms,* "And unto God the Lord belong the issues of death," and in this last part it is Christ who is God the Lord to whom on the Cross belonged the issues of death. This is the fullest meditation on our Lord's death which Donne has left us, for if he preached any Good Friday sermons at St. Paul's or St. Dunstan's, he has left us no record of them. This is characteristic of him, for he has told us that to him the Passion of Christ was a subject for adoring love and ecstasy, not for an exercise of rhetorical skill.[75] But now at last, when he knew himself to be a dying man, and the plaudits of men meant nothing to him, he could speak more freely than ever before of the central fact of his religion, of the amazing, the unending paradox that God could die, and would die for the love of man.

Oportuit eum pati, more can not be sayd, then *Christ* himselfe sayes of himself, *These things Christ ought to suffer;* hee had no other way but by death. So then *this part* of our *Sermon* must needes be a *passion Sermon;* since all his *life* was a *continuall passion,* all *our Lent* may well bee a *continuall good Fryday....* That *God,* this *Lord,* the *Lord* of *life could*

[74] Vol. VIII, p. 174.
[75] Vol. II, p. 132: "But for that, I shall be short, and rather leave you ... to meditate of the sufferings of Christ, when you are gone, then pretend to expresse them here. The *passion* of Christ Jesus is rather an amazement, an astonishment, an exstasie, a consternation, then an instruction."

dye, is a strange contemplation; That the *red Sea* could bee *drie,* That the *Sun* could *stand still,* . . . is strange, *miraculously strange,* but *supermiraculous* that *God could dye;* but that *God would dye* is an *exaltation* of that. . . . *love is strong as death,* stronger, it drew in death that naturally is not welcom. . . . *Many waters quench not love, Christ* tryed many; He was *Baptized* out of his *love,* and his love determined not there; He wept over *Jerusalem* out of his love, and his love determined not there; He *mingled blood* with *water* in his *agony* and that determined not his love; hee *wept pure blood,* all his blood at all his eyes, at all his pores, in his *flagellation* and *thornes* (*to the Lord our God belong'd the issues of blood*) and these *expressed,* but these did *not quench his love.*[76]

Donne ponders on the fact that Christ's death was a voluntary act, and yet it was part of God's eternal decree, his plan for the salvation of the world.

Infinite love, eternall love, be pleased to follow this home, and to consider it seriously, that what liberty soever wee can *conceive* in *Christ,* to dye or not to dye: this *necessity of dying,* this *decree* is as *eternall* as that *liberty;* and yet how small a matter made hee of this *necessity* and this *dying?* His *Father* cals it but *a bruise,* and but a *bruising of his heele* (*the serpent shall bruise his heele*) and yet that was, that the *serpent* should *practise* and *compasse* his *death.* Himselfe calls it but a *Baptisme,* as though he were to bee the better for it. *I have a Baptisme to be Baptized with,* and he was in paine till it was accomplished, and yet this *Baptisme* was *his death.* The *holy Ghost* calls it *Ioy* (*for the Ioy which was set before him hee indured the Crosse*) which was not a *joy* of his reward after his passion, but a joy that filled him even in the middest of those torments, and arose from them. When *Christ* calls his passion *Calicem, a Cuppe,* and no worse, (*Can ye drink of my Cuppe?*) he speakes not odiously, not with detestation of it: Indeed it was a *Cup, salus mundo, a health to all the world.* And *quid retribuam,* says *David, what shall I render to the Lord?* answere you with *David, accipiam Calicem, I will take the Cup of salvation;* take it, that *Cup of salvation,* his *passion,* if not into your *present imitation,* yet into your *present contemplation.* And behold how that *Lord* that was *God,* yet *could dye, would dye, must dye,* for your *salvation.*[77]

Donne goes through the last twenty-four hours of Christ's earthly life, and asks his hearers to search their own consciences before they venture to come to the Sacrament of his Body and Blood. He moves

---

[76] Pp. 242–243.
[77] P. 244.

step by step from Christ's Institution of that Sacrament to the Agony in the Garden, thence to the trials before Caiaphas and Pilate, to the scourging and mocking, and lastly to the Crucifixion itself, and he urges their contemplation in reverence and adoration of that final scene.[78]

Donne's last words from the pulpit were of hope and resurrection. "There *bath* in his *teares,* there *suck* at his *woundes,* and *lye downe in peace* in his *grave,* till hee vouchsafe you a *resurrection,* and an *ascension* into that *Kingdome,* which hee *hath purchas'd for you,* with the *inestimable price* of his *incorruptible blood."* He returned to his house with relief and joy that his task had been accomplished, and he never left it again in the five weeks which followed, till at last he was carried from it to his grave. Walton has described for us the making of his effigy, which depicted him wrapped in his shroud, and his farewells to his friends.[79] He dealt with any necessary business that was brought him, and his mind remained clear to the end.[80]

---

[78] There is a parallel between Donne's words here and one stanza of his *Hymne to God my God, in my sicknesse.* In both he remembers that Christ is the second Adam, through whom the first Adam's fall is redeemed. In the sermon he says, "...hee *gave up the Ghost,* and as *God breathed a soule into* the *first Adam,* so this *second Adam breathed his soule into God, into the hands of God.* There wee leave you in that *blessed dependancy,* to *hang* upon *him* that *hangs* upon the *Crosse..."* In the poem he writes:

> We thinke that *Paradise* and *Calvarie,*
> *Christs* Crosse, and *Adams* tree, stood in one place;
> Looke Lord, and finde both *Adams* met in me;
> As the first *Adams* sweat surrounds my face,
> May the last *Adams* blood my soule embrace.
>
> (Grierson, *Poems,* I, 368)

So at last Calvary atones for the Fall, fulfills the promise of *Genesis,* and leads man, not back to the Earthly Paradise, but onward to the Tree of Life, which is in the Paradise of God.

[79] There are some difficulties and discrepancies in Walton's account, which must be the business of Donne's biographers, but do not concern us in this edition of the *Sermons.*

[80] Professor R. C. Bald has informed us that he has examined documents relating to ecclesiastical affairs to which Donne affixed his signature three days before his death.

He lay fifteen dayes earnestly expecting his hourly change; and, in the last hour of his last day, as his body melted away and vapoured into spirit, his soul having, I verily believe, some Revelation of the Beatifical Vision, he said, *I were miserable if I might not dye;* and after those words closed many periods of his faint breath, by saying often, *Thy Kingdome come, Thy Will be done.* His speech, which had long been his ready and faithful servant, left him not till the last minute of his life, and then forsook him; not to serve another Master, but dyed before him; for that it was become useless to him that now conversed with God on earth, as Angels are said to do in heaven, *onely by thoughts and looks.* Being speechless, he did as St. *Stephen, look stedfastly toward heaven, till he saw the Son of God standing at the right hand of his Father:* and being satisfied with this blessed sight, as his soul ascended, and his last breath departed from him, he closed his own eyes; and then, disposed his hands and body into such a posture as required not the least alteration by those that came to shroud him.[81]

Donne had entered upon his ministry at St. Paul's with his Christmas sermon of 1621 on Christ as the true Light, the Light that lighteneth every man that cometh into the world.[82] He closed his ministry, as we have just seen, with a meditation on the love of Christ as expressed in his Passion and on the Cross. During his final illness he had composed his own epitaph, of which the final lines were

HIC LICET IN OCCIDUO CINERE ASPICIT EUM
CUJUS NOMEN EST ORIENS

These were translated by Archdeacon Wrangham thus: "And here, though set in dust, he beholdeth Him, Whose name is the Rising."[83] So his last message to the world which he was leaving behind him was one of hope and trust in Christ, the East, the Sun of Righteousness who rises with healing in his wings. Donne's effigy still stands in St. Paul's with this inscription.

A great poet, William Butler Yeats, has left this tribute to his fellow poet, after rereading Donne's work: "His pedantry and his obscenity—the rock and the loam of his Eden—but make me the more certain that one who is but a man like us has seen God."[84]

---

[81] Walton, *op. cit.,* pp. 77–78.
[82] Vol. III, No. 17.
[83] Again and again in his sermons Donne had used this name *Oriens,* the East, for Christ, from the Vulgate use of it in *Zech.* 6.12 and *Luke* 1.78. See pp. 304–305 of the present volume.
[84] Yeats, *Letters* (ed. Wade), p. 570.

The Sermons

Number 1.

Preached upon All-Saints Day. [? *1623*]

Apoc. 7.2, 3. *AND I SAW ANOTHER ANGEL ASCENDING FROM THE EAST, WHICH HAD THE SEALE OF THE LIVING GOD, AND HE CRYED WITH A LOUD VOYCE TO THE FOURE ANGELS, TO WHOM POWER WAS GIVEN TO HURT THE EARTH, AND THE SEA, SAYING, HURT YEE NOT THE EARTH, NEITHER THE SEA, NEITHER THE TREES, TILL WE HAVE SEALED THE SERVANTS OF OUR GOD IN THEIR FOREHEADS.*

THE SOLEMNITY and festivall with which the sonnes of the Catholique Church of God celebrate this day, is much mistaken, even by them who thinke themselves the onely Catholiques, and celebrate this day, with a devotion, at least near to superstition in the Church of Rome. For, they take it (for the most part) to be a festivall instituted by the Church, in contemplation of the Saints in heaven onely; and so carry and employ all their devotions this day, upon consideration of those Saints, and invocation of them onely. But the institution of this day, had this occasion. The heathen Romans, who
¹⁰ could not possibly house all their gods in severall Temples, they were so over-many, according to their Law, *Deos frugi colunto,* to serve God as cheape as they could, made one Temple for them all, which they

41

called *Pantheon,* To all the Gods. This Temple *Boniface* the Pope begd of the Emperour *Phocas;* (And yet, (by the way) this was some hundreds of years after the Donation of the Emperour *Constantine,* by which the Bishops of Rome pretend all that to be theirs; surely they could not finde this Patent, this Record, this Donation of *Constantine,* then when *Boniface* begd this Temple in Rome, this *Pantheon* of the Emperour) And this Temple, formerly the Temple of all their gods, that Bishop consecrated to the honour of all the Martyrs, of all the Saints of that kinde. But after him, another Bishop of the same see, enlarged the consecration, and accompanied it with this festivall, which we celebrate to day, in honour of the Trinity, and Angels, and Apostles, and Martyrs, and Confessors, and Saints, and all the elect children of God. So that it is truly a festivall, grounded upon that Article of the Creed, *The Communion of Saints,* and unites in our devout contemplation, The Head of the Church, God himselfe, and those two noble constitutive parts thereof, The Triumphant, and the Militant. And, accordingly, hath the Church applied this part of Scripture, to be read for the Epistle of this day, to shew, that *All-Saints day* hath relation to all Saints, both living and dead; for those *servants of God,* which are here in this text, *sealed in their foreheads,* are such (without all question) as received that *Seale* here, here in the militant Church. And therefore, as these words, so this festivall, in their intendiment, that applied these words to this festivall, is also of Saints upon Earth.

This day being then the day of the Communion of Saints, and this Scripture being received for the Epistle of this universall day, that exposition will best befit it, which makes it most universall. And therefore, with very good authority, such as the expositions of this booke of the *Revelation* can receive, (of which booke, no man will undertake to the Church, that he hath found the certaine, and the literall sense as yet, nor is sure to do it, till the prophecies of this booke be accomplished) (for *prophetiæ ingenium, ut in obscuro delitescat, donec impleatur,* It is the nature of prophecy to be secret, till it be fulfilled, And therefore *Daniel* was bid *to shut up the words, and to seale the booke even to the time of the end,* that is, to the end of the prophecy) with good authority, I say, we take that number of *the servants of God,* which are said to be *sealed* in the fourth verse of

Irenæus

Dan. 12.4

⁵⁰ this Chapter, which is *one hundred forty foure thousand,* and that *multitude which none could number, of all Nations,* which are mentioned in the ninth verse, to be intended of one and the same company; both these expressions denote the same persons. In the fourth verse of the fourteenth Chapter, this number of *one hundred forty foure thousand* is applied to *Virgins,* but is intended of all Gods Saints; for every holy soule is a virgin. And then this name of *Israel,* which is mentioned in the fourth verse of this Chapter, (*That there were so many sealed of the house of Israel*) is often in Scriptures applied to spirituall Israelites, to Beleevers, (for every faithfull ⁶⁰ soule is an Israelite) so that this number of *one hundred forty foure thousand Virgins,* and *one hundred forty foure thousand Israelites,* which is not a certaine number, but a number expressing a numberlesse multitude, this number, and that numberlesse multitude spoken of after, of all Nations, which none could number, is all one; and both making up the great and glorious body of all Saints, import and present thus much in generall, That howsoever God inflict great and heavy calamities in this world, to the shaking of the best morall and Christianly constancies and consciences, yet all his Saints being eternally knowne by him, shall be sealed by him, that is, so assured of his ⁷⁰ assistance, by a good using of those helps which he shall afford them, in the Christian Church, intended in this sealing on the forehead, that those afflictions shall never separate them from him, nor frustrate his determination, nor disappoint his gracious purpose upon them, all them, this multitude, which no man could number.

To come then to the words themselves, we see the safety, and protection of the Saints of God, and his children, in the person and proceeding of our Protector, in that it is in the hands of an Angel, (*I saw another Angel*) And an Angel of that place, that came from the East; The East, that is the fountaine of all light and glory, (*I* ⁸⁰ *saw another Angel come from the East*) And as the Word doth naturally signifie, (and is so rendred in this last Translation) *Ascending from the East,* that is, growing and encreasing in strength; After that we shall consider our assurance in the commission and power of this Angel, *He had the seale of the living God;* And then in the execution of this Commission; In which we shall see first, who our enemies were; They were also Angels, (*This Angel cryed to other*

Divisio

Angels) able to do much by nature, because Angels; Then we shall
see their number, they were foure Angels, made stronger by joyning
(*This Angel cryed to those foure Angels.*) And besides their malig-
⁹⁰ nant nature, and united concord, (two shrewd disadvantages, mischievous and many) They had a power, a particular, an extraordinary
power given them, at that time, to do hurt, (*foure Angels, to whom
power was given to hurt*) And to do generall, universall hurt, (*power
to hurt the Earth, and the Sea.*) After all this we shall see this Protector, against these enemies, and their Commission, execute his, first
by declaring and publishing it, (*He cryed with a loud voyce*) And
then lastly, what his Commission was; It was, to stay those foure
Angels, for all their Commission, *from hurting the Earth, and the
Sea, and the Trees.* But yet, this is not for ever; It is but *till the serv-*
¹⁰⁰ *ants of God were sealed in the forehead;* that is, till God had afforded
them such helpes, as that by a good use of them they might subsist;
which, if they did not, for all their sealing in the forehead, this Angel
will deliver them over to the other foure destroying Angels. Of which
sealing, that is, conferring of Grace and helps against those spirituall
enemies, there is a pregnant intimation, that it is done by the benefit
of the Church, and in the power of the Church, which is no singular
person, in that, upon the sudden, the person and the number is varied
in our text; and this Angel, which when he is said to *ascend from
the East, and to cry with a loud voyce,* is still a singular Angel, one
¹¹⁰ Angel, yet when he comes to the act of *sealing in the forehead,* to
the dispensing of Sacraments, and sacramentall assistances, he does
that as a plurall person, he represents more, the whole Church, and
therefore sayes here, Stay, hurt nothing, *Till we,* we *have sealed the
servants of our,* our *God in their foreheads.* And by all these steps
must we passe through this garden of flowers, this orchard of fruits,
this abundant Text.

Angelus

Psal. 19.2

First then, Man being compassed with a cloud of witnesses of his
own infirmities, and the manifold afflictions of this life, (for, *Dies
diei eructat verbum, Day unto day uttereth the same, and night unto
¹²⁰ night teacheth knowledge,* The bells tell him in the night, and fame
tels him in the day, that he himselfe melts and drops away piece-meal
in the departing of parents, and wife, and children out of this world,
yea he heares daily of a worse departing, he hears of the defection,

and back-sliding of some of his particular acquaintance in matter of
religion, or of their stifnesse and obduration in some course of sin
(which is the worse consumption) *Dies diei eructat,* every day makes
him learneder then other in this sad knowledge, And he knowes
withall, *Quod cuiquam accidere potest, cuivis potest,* that any of their
cases may be his case too) Man that is compassed with such a cloud of   [Heb. 12.1]
¹³⁰ such witnesses, had need of some light to shew him the right way,
and some strength to enable him to walk safely in it. And this light
and strength is here proposed in the assistance of an Angel. Which
being first understood of Angels in generall, affords a great measure
of comfort to us, because the Angels are *seduli animæ pedissequæ,*   Bern.
faithfull and diligent attendants upon all our steps. They doe so, they
doe attend the service and good of man, because it is *illorum opti-*
mum, It is the best thing that Angels (as Angels) can doe, to doe so:
For evermore it is best for every thing to doe that for which it was
ordained and made; and they were made Angels for the service and
¹⁴⁰ assistance of man. *Vnum tui & Angeli optimum est;* Man and Angels   Bern.
have one and the same thing in them, which is better then any thing
else that they have; Nothing hath it but they, and both they have it.
Deus nihil sui optimum habet; unum optimum totus; It is not so   Idem
with God; God hath nothing in him that is Best; but he is altogether
one intire Best. But Man and Angels have one thing common to them
both, which is the best thing that naturally either of them hath, that
is, Reason, understanding, knowledge, discourse, consideration. Angels and Men have grace too, that is infinitely better then their Reason; but though Grace be the principall in the nature and dignity
¹⁵⁰ thereof, yet it is but accessory to an Angel, or to man; Grace is not
in their nature at first, but infused by God, not to make them Angels
and Men, but to make them good Angels, and good men. This very
reason then, which is *Illorum optimum,* The best thing that Angels,
as Angels, naturally have, teaches them, that the best thing that they
can doe, is the performance of that for which they were made. And
then howsoever they were made spirits for a more glorious use, to
stand in the presence of God, and to enjoy the fulnesse of that contemplation, yet he made his spirits Angels, for the love which he had
to be with the sons of men. *Sufficit illis, et pro magno habeant,* Let   Bern.
¹⁶⁰ this content the Angels, and let them magnifie God for this, *Quòd*

cum spiritus sint conditione, ex gratia facti sunt Angeli, That whereas by nature they are but spirits, (and the devill is so) by favour and by office they are made Angels, messengers from God to man.

Now as the Angels are not defective in their best part, their Reason, and therefore do their office in assisting us, so also let us exalt our best part, our Reason too, to reverence them with a care of doing such actions onely as might not be unfit for their presence. Both Angels and we have the Image of God imprinted in us; the Angels have it not *in summo,* though they have it *in tuto;* They have it not in the

Colos. 1.15 ¹⁷⁰ highest degree, (for so Christ onely is *the Image of the invisible God*) but they have it in a deep impression, so as they can neither lose it, nor deface it. We have this Image of God so as that we cannot lose it,

Bern. but we may, and doe deface it; *Vri potest, non exuri;* The Devil hath this Image in him, and it cannot be burnt out in hell; for it is imprinted in the very naturall faculties of the soule. But if we consider how many waters beat upon us in this world to wash off this Image, how many rusty and habituall sins gnaw upon us, to eat out this Image, how many files pass over our souls in calamities, and afflic-

August. tions, in which though God have a purpose, *Resculpere imaginem,* ¹⁸⁰ to re-engrave, to refresh, to polish this Image in us, by those corrections, yet the devill hath a harsh file too, that works a murmuring, a comparing of our sinnes with other mens sinnes, and our punishments with other mens punishments, and at last, either a denying of Providence, (That things so unequally carried cannot be governed by God) or a wilfull renouncing of it in Desperation, That his Providence cannot bee resisted, and therefore it is all one what wee doe, If wee consider this, wee had need looke for Assistants.

Let us therefore looke first to that which is best in us naturally, that is, Reason; For if we lose that, our Reason, our Discourse, our ¹⁹⁰ Consideration, and sinke into an incapable and barren stupidity, there is no footing, no subsistence for grace. All the vertue of Corne is in the seed; but that will not grow in water, but onely in the earth: All the good of man, considered supernaturally, is in grace; but that will not growe in a washy soule, in a liquid, in a watery, and dissolute, and scattered man. Grace growes in reason; In that man, and in that minde, that considers the great treasure, what it is to have the Image of God in him, naturally; for even that is our earnest of

supernaturall perfection. And this Image of God, even in the Angels, being Reason, and the best act of rectified Reason, The doing of that
200 for which they were made, It is that which the Angels are naturally inclined to doe, to be alwayes present for the assistance of man; for therefore they are Angels. And since they have a joy at the Conversion of a sinner, and every thing affects joy, and therefore they indeavour our Conversion, yea, since they have an increase of their knowledge by being about us, (for, S. *Paul* sayes, *That he was made*   Eph. 3.10 *a Preacher of the Gospel, to the intent that Angels might know, by the Church, the manifold wisedome of God*) And every thing affects knowledge, these Saints of God upon earth, intended in our Text, might justly promise themselves a strong and a blessed comfort, and
210 a happy issue in all tribulations, by this Scripture, if there were no more intended in it, but onely the assistance of Angels; *I saw an Angel.*

But our security of deliverance is in a safer, and a stronger hand   *Angelus,* then this; not in these Ministeriall, and Missive Angels onely; but   *Christus* in his that sends them, yea in his that made them; *By whom, and*   Col. 1.16, 17 *for whom, they, and the Thrones, and Dominions, and Principalities, and Powers, and all things were created, and in whom they consist.* For, as the name of Angel is attributed to Christ, *Angelus Testa-*   Mal. 3.1 *menti, The Angel of the Covenant;* And many of those miraculous
220 passages in the deliverances of Israel out of Egypt, which were done by the second Person of the Trinity, by Christ, in *Exodus,* are by *Moses* there, and in the abridgement of that story, by *Stephen* after,   Acts 7.[30, attributed to *Angels,* So in this Text, this *Angel,* which doth so much   35, 38] for Gods Saints, is, not inconveniently, by many Expositors, taken to be our Saviour Christ himselfe. And will any man doubt of performance of conditions in him? Will any man looke for better security then him, who puts two, and two such into the band, *Christ,* and *Jesus;* An anointed King, able, an actuall Saviour, willing to discharge, not his, but our debt? He is a double Person, God and
230 Man; He ingages a double pawn, the old, and the new Testament, the Law, and the Gospel; and you may be bold to trust him, that hath paid so well before; since you see a performance of the Prophesies of the old Testament, in the free and glorious preaching of the Gospel, trust also in a performance of the promises of the Gospel, in timely

deliverances in this life, and an infallible, and eternall reposednesse, in the life to come. Hee tooke our nature, that he might know our infirmities experimentally; He brought down a better nature, that he might recover us, restore us powerfully, effectually; and that hee might be sure to accomplish his work, he brought more to our repa-
240 ration, then to our first building; The God-head wrought as much in our Redemption, as in our Creation, and the Man-hood more; for it began but then. And to take from us all doubt of his power, or of his will in our deliverance, he hath taken the surest way of giving

Esay 53.4 satisfaction, He hath payed beforehand; *Verè tulit, He hath truly born all our infirmities,* He hath, already; *And with his stripes are we healed;* we that are here now, are healed by his stripes received

Apoc. 13.8 sixteen hundred yeares since. Nay, he was *Occisus ab origine, The Lamb slaine from the beginning of the world;* That day that the frame of the world was fully set up in the making of man, That day
250 that the fairest piece of that frame fell down again, in the fall of *Adam,* That day that God repaired this ruine again, in the promise of a Messias, (all which we take ordinarily to have fallen in one day, the sixt day) that day, in that promise, was this Lamb slain, and all the debts not only of our fore-fathers, and ours, but of the last man, that shall be found alive at the last day, were then payed, so long beforehand.

Angelus   This security then, for our deliverance and protection, we have in
Ecclesiæ this Angel in our Text, (*I saw an Angel*) as this Angel is Christ; but yet we have also another security, more immediate, and more appli-
260 able to us. As men that lend money in the course of the world, have a desire to have a servant in the band with the Master, not that they hope for the money from him, but that they know better how to call upon him, and how to take hold of him: so besides this generall assistance of Angels, and besides this all-sufficiency of the Angel of the Covenant, Christ Jesus, we have, for our security, in this Text, (*I saw an Angel*) the servants of Christ too; This Angel is the Minister of his Word, the Administrer of his Sacraments, the Mediator betweene Christ and Man, He is this Angel, as S. *Iohn,* so often in the *Revelation,* and the Holy Ghost in other places of Scripture, styles them;
270 This Angel is indeed, the whole frame, and Hierarchy of the Christian Church. For though this Angel be called in this text *The Angel,*

in the singular, yet, (to make use of one note by Anticipation now, though in our distribution of the Branches, we reserved it to the end, because it fits properly our present consideration) though this Angel be named in the singular, and so may seeme to be restrained to Christ alone, yet, we see, the Office, when it comes to execution after, is diffused, and there are more in the Commission; for those phrases, that *Wee,* Wee may seale, the servants of *Our,* Our God, have a plurality in them, a consent, a harmony, and imply a Congregation, and doe

280 better agree with the Ministery of the Church, then with the Person of Christ alone.

So then, to let go none of our assistants, our sureties, our safety is in the Angel of the Covenant, Christ Jesus, radically, fundamentally, meritoriously; It is in the ministery of the Angels of heaven invisibly; but it is in the Church of God, and in the power of his Ministers there, manifestly, sensibly, discernibly; *They should seek* Mal. 2.7 *the Law at the Priests mouth,* (They should, and therefore they are to blame that do not, but fly to private expositions.) But why should they? *Quia angelus domini exercituum,* (as it follows there) *Because*

290 *the Priest is the Angel of the Lord of Hosts.* Yea, the Gospell which they preach, is above all messages, which an Angel can bring of himselfe; *If an Angel from heaven preach otherwise unto you, then* Gal. 1.8 *we have preached, let him be accursed.* The ministery of celestiall Angels is inferiour to the ministery of the Ecclesiasticall; The Gospel (which belongs to us) is truly *Euangelium,* the good Ministery of good Angels, the best ministery of the best Angels; for though we compare not with those Angels in nature, we compare with them in office; though our offices tend to the same end (to draw you to God) yet they differ in the way; and though the service of those

300 Angels, enlighten your understanding, and assist your belief too, yet in the ministery of these Angels in the Church, there is a blessed fulfilling, and verification of those words, *Now is salvation nearer,* Rom. 13.11 *then when we beleeved.* You beleeve, because those celestiall Angels have wrought invisibly upon you, and disperst your clouds, and removed impediments. You beleeve, because the great Angel Christ Jesus, hath left his history, his action, and passion written for you; and that is a historicall faith. But yet salvation is nearer to you, in having all this applied to you, by them, who are like you, men, and

there, where you know how to fetch it, the Church; That as you
310 beleeve by reading the Gospels at home, that Christ died for the
world, So you may beleeve, by hearing here, that he dyed for you.

Bernar. This is Gods plenteous Redemption, *Quòd linguam meam assumsit
in opus suum;* That having so great a work to doe, as the salvation
of soules, he would make use of my tongue; And being to save the
world by his word, that I should speak that word. *Docendo vos,
quod per se faciliùs & suaviùs posset,* That he calls me up hither,
to teach you that which he could teach you better, and sooner, at
home, by his Spirit; *Indulgentia ejus est, non indigentia,* It is the
largenesse of his mercy towards you, not any narrownesse in his
320 power that he needs me. And so have you this Angel in our text, in
all the acceptations, in which our Expositors have delivered him;
It is Christ, It is the Angels of heaven, It is the Ministery of the
Gospel; And this Angell, whosoever, whatsoever, S. *Iohn* saw come
from the East, (*I saw an Angel come from the East*) which was
our second Branch, and fals next into consideration.

Ab oriente   This addition is intended for a particular addition to our comfort;
it is a particular endowment, or inlargement of strength and power
in this Angel, *that he comes from the East.* If we take it, (to goe
the same way that we went before) first of naturall Angels, even
330 the Westerne Angels, *Qui habuere occasum,* Those Angels which
have had their Sun-set, their fall, they came from the East too;

Esay 14.12   *Quomodo cecidisti de cœlo, Lucifer, filius orientis? How art thou
fallen from heaven, O Lucifer, the Son of the morning?* He had his
begetting, his Creation in the East, in the light, and there might
have stayed, for any necessity of falling, that God laid upon him.
Take the Angel of the text to be the Angel of the Covenant, Christ
Jesus, and his name is The East; he cannot be knowne, he cannot

Zech. 6.12   bee said to have any West. *Ecce vir, Oriens nomen ejus,* (so the
[Vulg.]   vulgat reads that place) *Behold the Man, whose name is the East;*
340 you can call him nothing else; for so, the other *Zachary,* the *Zachary*
Luke 1.78   of the New Testament cals him too, *Per viscera misericordiæ,
Through the tender bowels of his mercy, Visitavit nos Oriens, The
East, the day spring from on high hath visited us;* And he was
derived *à Patre luminum,* He came from the East, begotten from
Iohn 16.28   all eternity of the Father of lights, *I came out from the Father, and*

came into the world. Take this Angel to be the Preacher of the Gospel, literally, really, the Gospell came out of the East, where Christ lived and dyed; and Typically, figuratively, Paradise, which also figured the place, to which the Gospel is to carry us, Heaven, that also was planted in the East; and therefore S. *Basil* assignes that for the reason, why in the Church service we turne to the East when we pray, *Quia antiquam requirimus patriam,* Wee looke towards our ancient country, where the Gospel of our salvation was literally acted, and accomplished, and where Heaven, the end of the Gospel, was represented in Paradise. Every way the Gospel is an Angel of the East.

But this is that which we take to be principally intended in it, That as the East is the fountaine of light, so all our illumination is to be taken from the Gospell. Spread we this a little thinner, and we shall better see through it. If the calamities of the world, or the heavy consideration of thine own sins, have benummed and benighted thy soule in the vale of darknesse, and in the shadow of death; If thou thinke to wrastle and bustle through these strong stormes, and thick clouds, with a strong hand; If thou thinke thy money, thy bribes shall conjure thee up stronger spirits then those that oppose thee; If thou seek ease in thy calamities, that way to shake and shipwrack thine enemies; In these crosse winds, in these countermines, (to oppresse as thou art oppressed) all this is but a turning to the North, to blow away and scatter these sadnesses, with a false, an illusory, and a sinfull comfort. If thou thinke to ease thy selfe in the contemplation of thine honour, thine offices, thy favour, thy riches, thy health, this is but a turning to the South, the Sun-shine of worldly prosperity. If thou sinke under thy afflictions, and canst not finde nourishment (but poyson) in Gods corrections, nor justice (but cruelty) in his judgements, nor mercy (but slacknesse) in his forbearance till now; If thou suffer thy soule to set in a cloud, a dark cloud of ignorance of Gods providence and proceedings, or in a darker, of diffidence of his performance towards thee, this is a turning to the West, and all these are perverse and awry. But turne to the East, and to the Angel that comes from thence, The Ministery of the Gospel of Christ Jesus in his Church; It is true, thou mayst find some darke places in the Scriptures; and, *Est*

Basil

silentii species obscuritas, To speake darkly and obscurely is a kinde of silence, I were as good not be spoken to, as not be made to understand that which is spoken, yet fixe thy selfe upon this Angel of the East, the preaching of the Word, the Ordinance of God, and thine understanding shall be enlightned, and thy beliefe established, and thy conscience thus far unburthened, that though the sins which thou hast done, cannot be undone, yet neither shalt thou bee
390 undone by them; There, where thou art afraid of them, in judgement, they shall never meet thee; but as in the round frame of the World, the farthest West is East, where the West ends, the East begins, So in thee, (who art a World too) thy West and thy East shall joyne, and when thy Sun, thy soule comes to set in thy deathbed, the Son of Grace shall suck it up into glory.

Angelus　　Our Angel comes from the East, (a denotation of splendor, and
Ascendens　illustration of understanding, and conscience) and there is more, he comes Ascending, (*I saw an Angel ascend from the East*) that is, still growing more cleare, and more powerfull upon us. Take
1 Sam. 28.13　400 the Angel here of naturall Angels; and then, when the Witch of Endor (though an evill Spirit appeared to her) yet saw him appeare so, Ascending, she attributes that glory to it, *I see gods Ascending out of the earth.* Take the Angel to be Christ, and then, his Ascension was
Bernar.　　*Fœlix clausula totius itinerarii,* The glorious shutting up of all his progresse; and though his descending from Heaven to earth, and his descending from earth to hell gave us our title, his Ascending, by which he carried up our flesh to the right hand of his Father, gave us our possession; His Descent, his humiliation gave us *Ius ad rem,* but his Ascension *Ius in re.* But as this Angel is the Ministery of the Gospel, God
410 gave it a glorious ascent in the Primitive Church, when as this Sun
Psal. 19.5　*Exultavit ut gigas ad currendam viam,* ascended quickly beyond the
[18.6 Vulg.]　reach of Heretiques wits, and Persecutors swords, and as glorious an ascent in the Reformation, when in no long time, the number of them that had forsaken Rome was as great, as of them that staid with her.

　　Now to give way to this ascent of this Angel in thy selfe, make the way smooth, and make thy soule souple; finde thou a growth of the Gospel in thy faith, and let us finde it in thy life. It is not
Iosh. 10.12　in thy power to say to this Angel, as *Ioshua* said to the Sun, *Siste, stand still;* It will not stand still; If thou finde it not ascending, it

descends; If thy comforts in the Gospel of Christ Jesus grow not, they decay; If thou profit not by the Gospel, thou losest by it; If thou live not by it, (nothing can redeeme thee) thou dyest by it. Wee speake of going up and downe a staire; it is all one staire; of going to, and from the City; it is all one way; of comming in, and going out of a house; it is all one doore: So is there *a savour of life unto life,* and *a savour of death unto death* in the Gospel; but it is all one Gospel. If this Angel of the East have appeared unto thee, (the light of the Gospel have shined upon thee) and it have not ascended in thee, if it have not made thee wiser and wiser, and better and better too, thou hast stopped that light, vexed, grieved, quenched that Spirit; for the naturall progresse of this Angel of the East is to ascend; the naturall motion and working of the Gospel is, to make thee more and more confident in Gods deliverance, lesse and lesse subject to rely upon the weake helps, and miserable comforts of this world. To this purpose this Angel ascends, that is, proceeds in the manifestation of his Power, and of his readinesse to succour us. Of his Power in this, That he hath the seales of the living God; (*I saw an Angel ascending from the East, which had the seale of the living God*) which is our next Consideration.

Of the living God. The gods of the Nations are all dead gods; either such Gods as never had life, (stones, and gold and silver) or such gods at best, as were never gods till they were dead; for men that had benefited the world, in any publique and generall invention, or otherwise, were made gods after their deaths; which was a miserable deification, a miserable godhead that grew out of corruption, a miserable eternity that begun at all, but especially that begun in death; and they were not gods till they dyed. But our Angel had the Seale of the living God, that is, Power to give life to others. Now, if we seeke for this seale in the naturall Angels, they have it not; for this Seale is some visible thing whereby we are assisted to salvation, and the Angels have no such. They are made keepers of this seale sometimes, but permanently they have it not. This Seale of comfort was put into an Angels hand, when he was *to set a marke upon the foreheads of all them that mourned;* He had a visible thing, *Inke,* to marke them withall. But it was not said to him, *Vade & signa omnes Creaturas,* Go, and set this marke upon

[2 Cor. 2.16]

Sigillum Dei viventis

Ezek. 9.4

Marke 16.15 — every Creature, as it was to the Minister of the Gospel, *Go, and preach to every Creature.* If wee seeke this seale in the great Angel, ⁴⁶⁰ the Angel of the Covenant, Christ Jesus: It is true he hath it, for,

Mat. 28.18 — *Omnis potestas data, All power is given unto me, in Heaven, and*

Iohn 5.22 — *in earth;* and, *Omne judicium, The Father hath committed all judgement to the Son;* Christ, as the Son of man executes a Judgement, and hath a Power, which he hath not but by gift, by Commission, by vertue of this Seale, from his Father. But, because it is not onely so in him, That he hath the Seale of the living God, but,

Colos. 1.15 — He is this Seale himselfe, (*Hee is the Image of the invisible God; He*

Heb. 1.3 — *is the brightnesse of his glory, and the expresse Image of his Person*) It is not onely his Commission that is sealed, but his Nature, He

Iohn 6.27 — ⁴⁷⁰ himselfe is sealed, (*Him hath God the Father sealed*) since, I say, naturall Angels though they have sometimes this seale, they have it not alwaies, they have not a Commission from God, to apply his mercies to man, by any ordinary and visible meanes, since the Angel of the Covenant, Christ Jesus hath it, but hath it so, as that he is it too, the third sort of Angels, the Church-Angels, the Ministers of the Gospell, are they, who most properly can be said to have this Seale by a fixed and permanent possession, and a power to apply it to particular men, in all emergent necessities, according to the institution of that living God, whose seale it is.

⁴⁸⁰ Now the great power which is given by God, in giving this seale to these Angels, hath a lively representation (such as a shadow can

Gen. 41.40 — give) in the history of *Ioseph. Pharaoh* sayes to him, *Thou shalt be over my house, and over all the land of Egypt,* (steward of the Kings house, and steward of the Kingdome) *And at thy word shall all my people be armed,* (Constable and Marshall too) and to invest him in all these, and more, *Pharaoh* gave him his *ring,* his seale; not his seale onely to those severall patents to himselfe, but the keeping of that seale for the good of others; This temporall seale of *Pharaoh* was a representation of the seale of the living God. But there is a more expresse type

Exod. 28.36 — ⁴⁹⁰ of it in Exodus: *Thou shalt grave* (sayes God to *Moses*) *upon a plate of pure gold, as Signets are graved, Holinesse to the Lord; and it shall be on the forehead of Aaron;* What to do? *That the people may be accepted of him.* There must be a holinesse to the Lord, and that presented by *Aaron* the Priest to God, that the people may

be *acceptable to the Lord;* So that this seale of the living God, in these Angels of our text, is, The Sacraments of the New Testament, and the Absolution of sinnes, by which (when Gods people come to a Holinesse to the Lord, in a true repentance, and that that holinesse, that is, that repentance, is made knowne to *Aaron,* to the
10 Priest, and he presents it to the Lord) that Priest, his Minister seals to them, in those his Ordinances, Gods acceptation of this degree of holinesse, he seals this Reconciliation between God and his people. And a contract of future concurrence, with his subsequent grace. This is the power given by God to this ascending Angel; and we extend that no farther, but hasten to his haste, his readinesse to succour us; in which, we proposed for the first consideration, That this Angel of light manifested and discovered to us, who our enemies were: (*He cryed out* to them who were ready to do mischiefe, *with a loud voyce*) so that we might heare him, and know them.

20 Though in all Court-cases it be not good to take knowledge of enemies, (many times that is better forborne) yet in all cases, it is good to know them. Especially in our case in the Text, because our enemies intended here, are of themselves, *Princes of darknesse;* They can multiply clouds, and disguisings, their kingdome is in the darknesse, *Sagittant in obscuro, They shoot in the darke,* (I am wounded with a tentation, as with the plague, and I know not whence the arrow came) *Collocavit me in obscuris, The enemy hath made my dwelling darknesse,* I have no window that lets in light, but then this Angel of light shews me who they are.

520 But then, if we were left to our selves, it were but a little advantage to know who our enemies were, when we knew those enemies to be Angels, persons so far above our resistance. For, but that S. *Paul* mollifies and eases it with a milder word, *Est nobis colluctatio,* That we *wrestle* with enemies, (that thereby we might see our danger is but to take a fall, not a deadly wound, if we look seriously to our worke; we cannot avoyd falling into sins of infirmity, but the death of habituall sin we may: *Quare moriemini domus Israel?* He does not say, why would ye fall? but *why will ye die, ye house of Israel?*) it were a consideration inough to make us desperate of victory, to heare
530 him say, that this (though it be but a wrestling) is *not against flesh and blood, but against principalities, and powers, and spirituall*

Manifestat inimicos

Eph. 6.12

Psal. 11.2

Psal. 143.3

Inimici, Angeli

Eph. 6.12

[Ezek. 18.31]

wickednesses in high places. None of us hath got the victory over flesh and blood, and yet we have greater enemies then flesh and blood are. Some disciplines, some mortifications we have against flesh and blood; we have S. *Pauls probatum est,* his medicine, (if we will use it) *Castigo corpus, I keep under my body, and bring it into subjection;* for that we have some assistance; Even our enemies become our friends; poverty or sicknesse will fight for us against flesh and blood, against our carnall lusts; but for these powers and 540 principalities, I know not where to watch them, how to encounter them. I passe my time sociably and merrily in cheerful conversation, in musique, in feasting, in Comedies, in wantonnesse; and I never heare all this while of any power or principality, my Conscience spies no such enemy in all this. And then alone, between God and me at midnight, some beam of his grace shines out upon me, and by that light I see this Prince of darknesse, and then I finde that I have been the subject, the slave of these powers and principalities, when I thought not of them. Well, I see them, and I try then to dispossesse my selfe of them, and I make my recourse to the powerfullest 550 exorcisme that is, I turne to hearty and earnest prayer to God, and I fix my thoughts strongly (as I thinke) upon him, and before I have perfected one petition, one period of my prayer, a power and principality is got into me againe. *Spiritus soporis,* The spirit of slumber closes mine eyes, and I pray drousily; Or *spiritus vertiginis,* the spirit of deviation, and vaine repetition, and I pray giddily, and circularly, and returne againe and againe to that I have said before, and perceive not that I do so; and *nescio cujus spiritus sim,* (as our Saviour said, rebuking his Disciples, who were so vehement for the burning of the Samaritans, *you know not of what spirit you are*) I pray, and 560 know not of what spirit I am, I consider not mine own purpose in prayer; And by this advantage, this doore of inconsideration, enters *spiritus erroris,* The seducing spirit, the spirit of error, and I pray not onely negligently, but erroniously, dangerously, for such things as disconduce to the glory of God, and my true happinesse, if they were granted. Nay, even the Prophet *Hosea's spiritus fornicationum,* enters into me, *The spirit of fornication,* that is, some remembrance of the wantonnesse of my youth, some mis-interpretation of a word in my prayer, that may beare an ill sense, some unclean spirit, some

1 Cor. 9.27

Esay 29.10
Esa. 19.14

Luke 9.55

1 Tim. 4.1

Hosea 4.12
5.4

power or principality hath depraved my prayer, and slackned my
zeale. And this is my greatest misery of all, that when that which
fights for me, and fights against me too, sicknesse, hath laid me upon
my last bed, then in my weakest estate, these powers and principalities shall be in their full practise against me. And therefore it is one
great advancement of thy deliverance, to be brought by this Angel,
that is, by the Ministery of the Gospel of Christ, to know that thou
hast Angels to thine enemies; And then another is to know their
number, and so the strength of their confederacy; for, in the verse
before the Text, they are expressed to be foure, (*I saw foure
Angels, &c.*)

Foure legions of Angels, foure millions, nay, foure Creations of
Angels could do no more harme, then is intended in these foure;
for, (as it is said in the former verse) *They stood upon the foure
corners of the earth,* they bestrid, they cantoned the whole world.
Thou hast opposite Angels enow to batter thee every where, and to
cut off and defeat all succours, all supplies, that thou canst procure,
or propose to thy selfe; absolute enemies to one another will meet
and joyne to thy ruine, and even presumption will induce desperation. We need not be so literall in this, as S. *Hierome,* (who indeed
in that followed *Origen*) to thinke that there is a particular evill
Angel over every sin; That because we finde that mention of *the
spirit of error,* and *the spirit of slumber,* and *the spirit of fornication,*
we should therefore thinke that Christ meant by *Mammon,* a particular spirit of Covetousnesse, and that there be severall princes over
severall sins. This needs not; when thou art tempted, never aske that
Spirits name; his name is *legio,* for he is many. Take thy selfe at
the largest, as thou art a world, there are foure Angels at thy foure
corners; Let thy foure corners be thy worldly profession, thy calling,
and another thy bodily refection, thy eating, and drinking, and sleeping, and a third thy honest and allowable recreations, and a fourth
thy religious service of God in this place, (which two last, that is,
recreation, and religion, God hath been pleased to joyn together in
the Sabbath, in which he intended his own glory in our service of
him, and then the rest of the Creature too) let these foure, thy calling,
thy sleeping, thy recreation, thy religion be the foure corners of thy
world, and thou shalt find an Angel of tentation at every corner;

*Quatuor
Angeli*

Mat. 6.24

Mar. 5.9

even in thy sleep, even in this house of God thou hast met them. The Devill is no Recusant; he will come to Church, and he will lay his snares there; *When that day comes, that the Sonnes of God present themselves before the Lord, Satan comes also among them.* Not ⁶¹⁰ onely so, as S. *Augustin* confesses he met him at Church, to carry wanton glances between men and women, but he is here, sometimes to work a mis-interpretation in the hearer, sometimes to work an affectation in the speaker, and many times doth more harme by a good Sermon then by a weake, by possessing the hearers with an admiration of the Preachers gifts, and neglecting Gods Ordinance. And then it is not onely their naturall power, as they are Angels, nor their united power, as they are many, nor their politique power, that in the midst of that confusion which is amongst them, yet they agree together to ruine us, but (as it follows in our text) it is *potestas* ⁶²⁰ *data,* a particular power, which, besides their naturall power, God, at this time, put into their hands; (*He cryed to the foure Angels, to whom power was given to hurt*) All other Angels had it not, nor had these foure that power at all times, which, in our distribution at first we made a particular Consideration.

It was *potestas data,* a speciall Commission that laid *Iob* open to Satans malice; It was *potestas data,* a speciall Commission, that laid the herd of swine open to the Devils transportation: Much more, no doubt, have the particular Saints of God in the assistances of the Christian Church, (for *Iob* had not that assistance, being not within ⁶³⁰ the Covenant) and most of all hath the Church of God her selfe, an ability, in some measure, to defend it selfe against many machinations and practises of the Devill, if it were not for this *Potestas data,* That God, for his farther glory, in the tryall of his Saints, and his Church, doth enable the Devill to raise whole armies of persecutors, whole swarmes of heretiques, to sting and wound the Church, beyond that ordinary power, which, the Devill in nature hath. That place, *Curse not the King, no, not in thought, for that which hath wings shall tell the matter,* is ordinarily understood of Angels; that Angels shall reveale disloyall thoughts; now, naturally Angels do not ⁶⁴⁰ understand thoughts; but, in such cases, there is *Potestas data,* a particular power given them to do it; and so to evill Angels, for the accomplishment of Gods purposes, there is *Potestas data,* a new

Marginal notes:
Job 1.6

Potestas data
Mat. 8.32

Eccles.
10.20

power given, a new Commission, (that is beyond permission; for, though by Gods permission mine eye see, and mine eare heare, yet my hand could not see nor heare by Gods permission; for permission is but the leaving of a thing to the doing of that, which by nature, (if there be no hindrance interposed) it could, and would do.)

This comfort then, and this hope of deliverance hast thou here, that this Angel in our text, that is, the Ministery of the Gospel, tels
° thee, that that rage which the Devill uses against thee now, is but *Potestas data,* a temporary power given him for the present; for, if thy afflictions were altogether from the naturall malice and power of the Devill, inherent in him, that malice would never end, nor thy affliction neither, if God should leave all to him. And therefore though those our afflictions be heavier, which proceed *ex potestate data,* when God exalts that power of the Devill, which naturally he hath, with new Commissions, besides his Permission to use his naturall strength, and naturall malice, yet our deliverance is the nearer too, because all these accessory and occasionall Commissions are for par-
° ticular ends, and are limited, how far they shall extend, how long they shall endure. Here, the *potestas data,* the power which was given to these Angels was large, it was generall, for, (as it is in the former verse) it was a power *to hold the foure winds of the earth, that the winde should not blow on the earth, nor on the sea, nor on any tree.* What this withholding of the winde signifies, and the damnification of that, is our next Consideration.

By the Land, is commonly understood all the Inhabitants of the   *Venti*
Land; by the Sea Ilanders, and Sea-faring men, halfe inhabitants of the Sea; and by the Trees, all those whom Persecution had driven
° away, and planted in the wildernesse. The hinderance of the use of the wind, being taken by our Expositors to be a generall impediment of the increase of the earth, and of commerce at Sea. But this Book of the Revelation must not be so literally understood, as that the Winds here should signifie meerly naturall winds; there is more in this then so; Thus much more, That this withholding of the winds, is a withholding of the preaching and passage of the Gospel; which is the heaviest misery that can fall upon a Nation, or upon a man, because thereby, by the misery of not hearing, he loses all light, and meanes of discerning his owne misery. Now as all the parts, and the

⁶⁸⁰ style and phrase of this Book is figurative and Metaphoricall, so is it no unusuall Metaphor, even in other Bookes of the Scripture too, to call the Ministers, and Preachers of Gods Word, by the name of

Cant. 4.16

winds. *Arise O North, and come O South, and blow on my Garden, that the spices thereof may flow out,* hath alwayes been understood to be an invitation, a compellation from Christ to his Ministers, to dispense and convey salvation, by his Gospel, to all Nations. And

Psal. 135.7

upon those words, *Producit ventos, He bringeth winds out of his treasuries,* and *Educit nubes, He bringeth clouds from the ends of the*

August.

earth, Puto Prædicatores & nubes & ventos, sayes S. *Augustine,* I
⁶⁹⁰ think that the holy Ghost means both by his *clouds,* and by his *winds,* the Preachers of his Word, the Ministers of the Gospel; *Nubes propter carnem, ventos propter spiritum,* Clouds because their bodies are seen, winds because their working is felt; *Nubes cernuntur, venti sentiuntur;* as clouds they embrace the whole visible Church, and are visible to it; as winds they pierce into the invisible Church, the soules of the true Saints of God, and work, though invisibly, upon

Psal. 18.10

them. So also those words, *God rode upon a Cherub, and did fly, He did fly upon the wings of the wind,* have been well interpreted of Gods being pleased to be carried from Nation to Nation, by the
⁷⁰⁰ service of his Ministers.

John 3.8

Now this is the nature of this wind, (of the Spirit of God breathing in his Ministers) *Spirat ubi vult,* that it blowes where it lists; and this is the malice of these evill Angels, that it shall not doe so. But this *Angel, which hath the seale of the living God,* that is, the Ministery of the Gospel established by him, shall keep the winds at their liberty; And howsoever waking dreamers think of alterations and tolerations, howsoever men that disguise their expectations with an outward conformity to us, may think the time of declaring themselves growes on apace; howsoever the slumbring of capitall laws,
⁷¹⁰ and reason of State may suffer such mistakers to flatter themselves, yet God hath made this Angel of the East, this Gospel of his to ascend so far now, and to take so deep root, as that now this one Angel is strong enough for the other foure, that is, The sincere preaching of the Gospel, in our setled and well disciplined Church, shall prevaile against those foure pestilent opposites, Atheists, and Papists, and Sectaries, and Carnall indifferent men, who all would hinder the

blowing of this wind, the effect of this Gospel. And to this purpose
our Angel in the Text is said to have cryed with a loud voice, (*He
cryed with a loud voice to the foure Angels*.)

720 For our security therefore that this wind shall blow still, that this
preaching of the Gospel which we enjoy shall be transferred upon
our posterity in the same sincerity, and the same integrity, there is
required an assiduity, and an earnestnesse in us, who are in that
service now, in which this Angel was then, in our preaching. *Clamavit*, our Angel *cryed*, (it was his first act, nothing must retard our
preaching) and *voce magna, he cryed with a loud voice;* (he gave
not over with one calling) What is this crying aloud in our Angel?
Vocis modum, audientium necessitas definit; The voice must be so
loud, as they, to whom we speak, are quick or thick of hearing.
730 *Submissa, quæ ad susurrum propriè accedit, damnanda.* A whispering voice was not the voice of this Angel, nor must it be of those
Angels that are figured in him; for that is the voice of a Conventicle,
not a Church voice. That is a loud voice that is heard by them whom
it concernes. So the catechizing of children, though in a familiar
manner, is a loud voice, though it be not a Sermon: So writing in
defence of our Religion, is a loud voice, though in the meane time
a man intermit his preaching: So the speaking by another, when
sicknesse or other services withhold him that should, and would
speak, is a loud voice even from him.
740 And therefore though there be no evident, no imminent danger
of withholding these winds, of inhibiting or scanting the liberty of
the Gospel, yet because it is wished by too many, and because we can
imagine no punishment too great for our neglecting the Gospel, it
becomes us, the Ministers of God, by all these loud voices, of catechizing, of preaching, of writing, to cry, and to cry, (though not with
vociferations, or seditious jealousies and suspitions of the present
government) yet to cry so loud, so assiduously, so earnestly, as all
whom it concernes (and it concernes all) may heare it: Hurt not the
earth, withhold not the winds, be you no occasions, by your neglect-
750 ing the Gospel of Christ Jesus, that he suffer it to be removed from
you; and know withall, that you doe neglect this Gospel, (how often
soever you heare it preached) if you doe not practice it. Nor is that
a sufficient practice of hearing, to desire to heare more, except thy

Clamavit

Basil

hearing bring thee to leave thy sinnes; without that, at the last day
thou shalt meet thy Sermons amongst thy sinnes; And when Christ
Jesus shall charge thee with false weights and measures in thy shop
all the week, with prevarication in judgement, with extortion in thy
practice, and in thine office, he shall adde to that, And besides this,
thou wast at Church twice that Sunday; when he shall have told

[Mat. 760 thee, Thou didst not feed me, thou didst not clothe me, he shall
25.42, 43] aggravate all with that, Yet thou heardst two Sermons that Sunday,
besides thine interlineary week Lectures. The means to keep this
wind awake, (to continue the liberty of the Gospel) is this loud
voice, (assiduous and pertinent preaching) but Sermons unpractised

[Psa. 109.6: are threepiled sins, and God shall turne, as their prayers, so their
Prayer preaching into sin. For this injunction, this inhibition which this
Book Angel serves upon the four Angels, That they should not hurt the
version] world by withholding the winds, that is, not hinder the propagation
and passage of the Gospel, was not perpetuall; it was limited with a
770 *Donec,* Till something were done in the behalfe and favour of the
world, and that was, *Till the servants of God were sealed in their
foreheads,* which is our last Consideration.

Donec The servants of God being sealed in their foreheads in the Sacra-
signentur ment of Baptisme, when they are received into the care of the Church,
all those meanes which God hath provided for his servants, in his
Church, to resist afflictions and tentations, are intended to be conferred upon them in that seale; This sealing of them is a communicating to them all those assistances of the Christian Church: Then
they have a way of prevention of sin, by hearing; a way to Absolu-
780 tion, by Confession; a way to Reconciliation, by a worthy receiving
the body and bloud of Christ Jesus: And these helps of the Christian
Church, thus conferred in Baptisme, keep open still, (if these be

Ephes. 1.13 rightly used) that other seale, the seale of the Spirit; *After ye heard
the Gospel, and beleeved, ye were sealed with the holy spirit of*

2 Cor. 1.22 *promise:* and so also, *God hath anointed us, and sealed us, and given
us the earnest of his Spirit in our hearts.* So that besides the seal in the
forehead, which is an interest and title to all the assistances and
benefits of the Church, publique prayer, preaching, Sacraments and
sacramentall helps, there is a seale of the Spirit of God, that that

[Rom. 8.16] 790 Spirit beares witnesse with my spirit, that I performe the conditions passed between God and me, under the first seale, my Baptisme. But because this second seale, (the obsignation and testification of the inward Spirit) depends upon the good use of the first seale, (the participation of the helps of the Church, given me in Baptisme) therefore the *Donec* in our Text, (*Hurt them not till they be sealed*) reaches but to the first seale, the seale of Baptisme, and in that, of all Gods ordinary graces, ordinarily exhibited in his Ordinances.

So then, this Angel takes care of us, till he have delivered us over to the sweet and powerfull helps of that Church, which God hath purchased with his blood; when hee hath placed us there, he looks that we should doe something for our selves, which, before we were there, and made partakers of Gods graces in his Church by Baptisme, we could not doe; for in this, this Angels Commission determines, That we be sealed in the fore-heads, That we be taken from the Common, into Gods inclosures, impayled in his Park, received into his Church, where our salvation depends upon the good use of those meanes. Use therefore those meanes well; and put not God to save thee by a miracle, without meanes. Trust not to an irresistible grace, that at one time or other God will have thee, whether thou wilt or no. *Tolle voluntatem, & non est infernus;* If thou couldst quench thine owne will, thou hadst quenched hell; If thou couldst be content, willing to be in hell, hell were not hell. So, if God save a man against his will, heaven is not heaven; If he be loath to come thither, sorry that he shall be there, he hath not the joy of heaven, and then heaven is not heaven. Put not God to save thee by miracle; God can save an Image by miracle; by miracle he can make an Image a man; If man can make God of bread, certainly God can make a man of an Image, and so save him; but God hath made thee his own Image, and afforded thee meanes of salvation: Use them. God compels no man. The Master of the feast invited many; solemnly, before hand; they came not: He sent his servants to call in the poore, upon the sudden; and they came; so he receives late commers. And there is a *Compelle intrare,* He sends a servant to compell some to come in. But that was but a servants work, The Master onely invited; he compelled none. We the servants of God, have certain compulsories, to bring men hither; The denouncing of Gods Judgements, the censures of the Church, Excommunications, and the rest, are compulsories. The

[Acts 20.28]

Bernar.

Luke 14.23

State hath compulsories too, in the penall Laws. But all this is but to bring them into the house, to Church; *Compelle intrare.* We can
⁸³⁰ compell them to come to the first seale, to Baptisme; we can compell men, to bring their children to that Sacrament; But to salvation, onely the Master brings; and (in that Parable) the Master does onely invite; he compells none: Though his corrections may seeme to be compulsories, yet even his corrections are sweet invitations; His corrections are so farre from compelling men to come to heaven, as that they put many men farther out of their way, and work an obduration, rather then an obsequiousnesse.

With those therefore that neglect the meanes, that he hath brought them to, in sealing them in the fore-head, this Angel hath no more
⁸⁴⁰ to doe, but gives them over to the power of the foure destroying Angels. With those that attend those meanes, he proceeds; and, in their behalfe, his *Donec,* (Spare them till I have sealed them) be-

Mat. 1.25 comes the blessed Virgins *Donec,* she was a Virgin till she had her Child, and a Virgin after too; And it becomes our blessed Saviours
Psal. 110.1 *Donec,* He sits at his Fathers right hand, till his enemies bee made his foot-stoole, and after too; So these destroying Angels, that had no power over them till they were sealed, shall have no power over them after they are sealed, but they shall passe from seale to seale; after

Rom. 1.16 that seale on the fore-head, *Ne erubescant Euangelium,* (*We signe*
[Prayer ⁸⁵⁰ *him with the signe of the Crosse, in token, that hereafter he shall not*
Book: *be ashamed, to confesse the faith of Christ Crucified*) He shall come
Baptism] also to those seales, which our Saviour recommends to his Spouse,
Cant. 8.6 *Set me as a seale on thy heart, and as a seale on thine arme;* S. *Ambrose* collects them, and connects them together, *Signaculum Christi in corde, ut diligamus, in fronte, ut confiteamur, in brachio, ut operemur;* God seales us in the heart, that we might love him, and in the fore-head, that we might professe it, and in the hand, that we might declare and practise it; and then the whole purpose of this blessed Angel in our Text, is perfected in us, and we our selves are
⁸⁶⁰ made partakers of the solemnity of this day, which we celebrate, for we our selves enter in the Communion of Saints, by these three seales, Of Beliefe, Of Profession, Of Works and Practise.

Number 2.

Preached upon Candlemas Day.

Mᴀᴛ. 9.2. *AND IESUS SEEING THEIR FAITH, SAID UNTO THE SICK OF THE PALSIE, MY SON, BE OF GOOD CHEARE, THY SINS BE FOR-GIVEN THEE.*

Divisio

Iɴ ᴛʜᴇsᴇ ᴡᴏʀᴅs, and by occasion of them, we shall present to you these two generall considerations; first upon what occasion Christ did that which he did, and then what it was that he did. And in the first, we shall see first some occasions that were remote, but yet conduce to the Miracle it selfe; some circumstances of time, and place, and some such dispositions, and then the more immediate occasion, the disposition of those persons who presented this sick man to Christ; and there we shall see first, that Faith was the occasion of all, for *without faith it is impossible to please God,* and without pleasing
10 of God, it is impossible to have remission of sins. It was *fides,* and *fides illorum, their faith,* all their faith; for, though in the faith of others there be an assistance, yet without a personall faith in him-selfe, no man of ripe age comes so far, as to the forgivenesse of sins; And then, this faith of them all, was *fides visa,* a faith that was seen; Christ saw their faith, and he saw it as man, it was a faith expressed, and declared in actions: And yet, when all was done, it is but *cum vidit,* it is not *quia vidit,* Christ did it When he saw, not Because he saw their faith, that was not the principle and primary cause of his mercy, for the mercy of God is all, and above all; it is the effect and
20 it is the cause too, there is no cause of his mercy, but his mercy. And when we come in the second part, to consider what in his mercy he

did, we shall see first, that he establishes him, and comforts him with a gracious acceptation, with that gracious appellation, *Fili, Son:* He doth not disavow him, he doth not disinherite him; and then, he doth not wound him, whom God had striken; he doth not flea him, whom God had scourged; he doth not salt him, whom God had flead; he doth not adde affliction to affliction, he doth not shake, but settle that faith which he had with more, *Confide fili, My son be of good cheare;* and then he seales all with that assurance, *Dimittuntur* 30 *peccata, Thy sins are forgiven thee;* In which, first he catechises this patient, and gives him all these lessons, first that he gives before we ask, for he that was brought, they who brought him had asked nothing in his behalfe, when Christ unasked, enlarged himself towards them, *Dat prius,* God gives before we ask, that is first; And then *Dat meliora,* God gives better things then we ask, All that all they meant to ask, was but bodily health, and Christ gave him spirituall; and the third lesson was, that sin was the cause of bodily sicknesse, and that therefore he ought to have sought his spirituall recovery before his bodily health: and then, after he had thus rectified 40 him, by this Catechisme, implyed in those few words, *Thy sins are forgiven thee,* he takes occasion by this act, to rectifie the by-standers too, which were the Pharisees, who did not beleeve Christ to be God: For, for proofe of that, first he takes knowledge of their inward thoughts, not expressed by any act or word, which none but God could doe; And then he restores the patient to bodily health, onely by his word, without any naturall meanes applyed, which none but God could doe neither. And into fewer particulars then these, this pregnant and abundant Text is not easily contracted.

1 Part   First then to begin with the Branches of the first part, of which the 50 first was, to consider some, somewhat more remote circumstances, and occasions conducing to this miracle, we cannot avoid the making of some use of the Time, when it was done: It was done, when Christ had dispossessed those two men of furious, and raging Devils,

Mat. 8 ult.   amongst the *Gergesens;* at what time, because Christ had been an occasion of drowning their heard of swine, the whole City came out to meet him, but not with a thankfull reverence, and acclamation, but their procession was, to beseech him to depart out of their coasts: They had rather have had their Legion of Devils still, then

have lost their hogs; and since Christs presence was an occasion of
60 impairing their temporall substance, they were glad to be rid of him.
We need not put on spectacles to search Maps for this Land of the
Gergesens; God knows we dwell in it; *Non quærimus Iesum propter
Iesum,* (which was a Propheticall complaint by S. *Augustine*) we
love the profession of Christ only so far, as that profession conduces
to our temporall ends. We seek him not at the Crosse; there most of
his friends left him; but we are content to embrace him, where the
Kings of the East bring him presents of Gold, and Myrrh, and   [Mat. 2.11]
Frankincense, that we may participate of those: we seek him not
in the hundred and thirtieth Psalme, where, though there be plenty,
70 yet it is but *copiosa redemptio, plentifull redemption,* plenty of that   [Psa. 130.7]
that comes not yet; but in the twenty fourth Psalm we are glad to
meet him, where he proclaims *Domini terra, & plenitudo ejus, The*   [Psa. 24.1]
earth is the Lords, and the fulnesse thereof, that our portion therein
may be plenteous: We care not for him in S. *Peters* Hospital, where
he excuses himselfe, *Aurum & argentum non habeo, Silver and gold*   [Acts 3.6]
have I none; but in the Prophet *Haggais* Exchequer we doe, where
he makes that claime, *Aurum meum, All the gold and all the silver*   [Hag. 2.8]
is mine. Scarce any Son is Protestant enough, to stand out a rebuke
of his Father, or any Servant of his Master, or any Officer of his
80 Prince, if that Father, or Master, or Prince would be, or would have
him be a Papist; But, as though the different formes of Religion, were
but the fashions of the garment, and not the stuffe, we put on, and
we put off Religion, as we would doe a Livery, to testifie our respect
to him, whom we serve, and (miserable *Gergesens*) had rather take   [Mat.
in that Devill againe, of which we have been dispossessed three or   8.28–34]
fourscore yeares since, then lose another hogge, in departing with
any part of our pleasures or profits; *Non quærimus Iesum propter
Iesum,* we professe not Jesus, for his, but for our owne sakes.
But we passe from the circumstance of the time, to a second, that
90 though Christ thus despised by the *Gergesens,* did, in his Justice,
depart from them; yet, as the Sea gaines in one place, what it loses
in another, his abundant mercy builds up more in *Capernaum,* then
his Justice throwes downe amongst the *Gergesens:* Because they
drave him away, in Judgement he went from them, but in Mercy he
went to the others, who had not intreated him to come.

Apply this also; And, wretched *Gergesen,* if thou have intreated
Christ to goe from thee, for losse of thy hogges, that when thou hast
found the Preaching of Christ, or the sting of thy conscience whet
thereby, to hinder thee in growing rich so hastily as thou wouldst,
100 or trouble thee, in following thy pleasures so fully as thou wouldst,
thou hast made shift to devest, and put off Christ, and seare up thy
conscience, yet Christ comes into his *Capernaum* now, that sent not
for him; he comes into thy soule now, who camest not hither to meet
him, but to celebrate the day, by this ordinary, and fashionall meeting; to thee he comes, as into *Capernaum,* to preach his owne Gospell,
and to work his miracles upon thee. And it is a high mercy in Christ,
that he will thus surprize thy soule, that he will thus way-lay thy
conscience, that what collaterall respect soever brought thee hither,
yet when he hath thee here, he will make thee see that thou art in
110 his house, and he will speake to thee, and he will be heard by thee,
and he will be answered from thee; and though thou thoughtest not
of him, when thou camest hither, yet he will send thee away, full of
the love of him, full of comforts from him.

But we passe also from this, to a third circumstance, that when he
Mat. 9.1   came to *Capernaum,* he is said to have come into *his own City;* not
Nazareth, where he was borne, but *Capernaum* where he dwelt, and
preached, is called *his own City.* Thou art not a Christian, because
thou wast borne in a Christian Kingdome, and borne within the
Covenant, and borne of Christian Parents, but because thou hast
120 dwelt in the Christian Church, and performed the duties presented
to thee there.

Againe, *Capernaum* was *his owne City,* but yet Christ went forth
of *Capernaum,* to many other places. I take the application of this,
from you, to our selves; Christ fixes no man by his example so to one
Church, as that no occasion may make his absence from thence
excusable. But yet when Christ did goe from *Capernaum,* he went
[Joh. 5.30]   to doe his Fathers will, and that, which he was sent for. Nothing but
preaching the Gospell, and edifying Gods Church, is an excuse for
[1 Cor. 9.16]   such an absence; for, *Væ si non Euangelizaverit,* if he neither preach
130 at *Capernaum,* nor to the *Gergesens,* neither at home, nor abroad,
woe be unto him: If I be at home, but to take my tithes; If I be
abroad, but to take the aire, woe be unto me.

But we must not stop long upon these circumstances; we end all
of this kinde, in this one, that when Christ had undertaken that great
work of the Conversion of the world, by the Word, and Sacraments,
to shew that the word was at that time the more powerfull meanes
of those two, (for Sacraments were instituted by Christ, as subsidiary
things, in a great part, for our infirmity, who stand in need of such
visible and sensible assistances) Christ preached the Christian Doc-
40 trine, long before he instituted the Sacraments; But yet, though these
two permanent Sacraments, Baptisme, and the Supper were not so
soon instituted, Christ alwayes descended so much to mans infirmity,
as to accompany the preaching of the Word, with certain transitory,
and occasionall Sacraments; for miracles are transitory and occasionall Sacraments, as they are visible signes of invisible grace, though
not seales thereof; Christs purpose in every miracle was, that by that
work, they should see Grace to be offered unto them. Now this history, from whence this Text is taken, begins, and ends with the principall meanes, with preaching; for, as S. *Mark* relates it, he was in   Mark 2.2
50 the act of preaching, when this cure was done; And in S. *Matthew,*   Mat. 9.35
after all was done, he went about the Cities, and Villages, preaching
the Gospell of the Kingdome: And then betweene, S. *Matthew* here,
records five of his transitory and occasionall Sacraments, five miracles,
of which every one, well considered, (as the petitions of *Abraham*   [Gen.
did upon God) may justly be thought to have gained more and more,   18.23–32]
upon his Auditory.

First, this paralytique man in our Text, who is *Sarcina sibi,* overloaded with himself, he cannot stand under his own burden, he is
cadaver animatum; It is true, he hath a soule, but a soule in a sack,
60 it hath no Lims, no Organs to move, this Paralytique, this living
dead man, this dead and buryed man, buryed in himselfe, is in-
stantly cured, and recovered. But the Palsie was a sudden sicknesse;
what could he doe, upon an inveterate disease? He cured the woman
that had had the bloudy issue twelve yeares, by onely touching the   V. 20
hem of his garment. After, he extends his miraculous power to two at
once, he cures two blinde men. But all these, though not by such   V. 27
meanes meerely, yet in nature, and in art might be possible, Palsies,
and Issues, and Blindnesses have been cured: but he went farther then
ever art pretended to goe; He raised the Rulers Daughter to life, then   V. 24

¹⁷⁰ when he was laughed to scorne, for going about to doe it. And lastly to shew his Power, as over sicknesse, and over death, so over hell it selfe, he cast out the Devill out of the dumb man, in some such extraordinary manner, as that the multitude marvailed, and said,

V. 33   *It was never so seene in Israel.* This then was his way, and this must be ours, and it must be your way too. Christ preached, and he wrought great works, and he preached againe; It is not enough in us to preach, and in you to heare, except both doe and practice, that which is said, and heard; Neither may we, though we have done all this, give over, for every day produces new tentations, and therefore ¹⁸⁰ needs new assistances. And so we passe from these more remote, to that which is our second Branch of this first part, the immediate occasion of Christs doing this miracle, *When Iesus saw their faith.*

Fides   Here then, the occasion of all that ensued, was *faith;* for, *without*

Heb. 11.6   *faith, it is impossible to please God;* Where you may be pleased to admit some use of this note, (for it is not a meere Grammaticall curiosity to note it) that it is not said in those words of S. *Paul,* It is impossible to please God, or impossible to please him, ·(which is with relation to God, as our Translation hath it,) but it is meerely, simply, onely, impossible to please, and no more, impossible to please ¹⁹⁰ any worth pleasing; but if we take away our faith in God, God will take away the protection of Angels, the favour of Princes, the obedience of children, the respect of servants, the assistance of friends, the society of neighbours; God shall make us unpleasing to all; without faith it is impossible to please any, but such, as we shall repent to have made our selves pleasing companions unto. When our Saviour Christ perfected the Apostles Commission, and set his last seale to it, after his Resurrection, he never modifies, never mollifies their instructions,

Mark 16.16   with any milder phrase then this, *He that beleeveth not, shall be*

[Mat. 5.22]   *damned.* It is not, that *he shall be in danger of a Councell;* no, nor

[Mark 9.42]   ²⁰⁰ *in danger of hell fire:* It is not, that *it were better a Mill-stone were tyed about his neck, and he cast into the Sea:* It is not, that *it will goe*

[Mat. 11.22]   *hard with him at the last day:* It is not, that *it shall be easier to Tyre, and Sidon, then to him;* For he is not bound to beleeve, but that Tyre, and Sidon, and he too, may doe well enough: Here is no modification, no mollification, no reservation; roundly, and irre-

vocably, Christ Jesus himselfe, after his Resurrection, sayes, *Qui non crediderit, he that beleeveth not, shall be damned.*
If the Judge must come to a sentence of condemnation, upon any person of great quality in the Kingdome, that Judge must not say, Your Lordship must passe out of this world, nor, your Lordship must be beheaded; but he must tell them plainly, You must be carryed to the place of execution and there hanged. Christ Jesus hath given us the Commission and the sentence there; *Goe into all the world, preach the Gospell to every creature;* And then, the sentence followes upon those that will not receive it, *He that beleeveth not, shall be damned.* These men then, who prevailed so farre upon Christ, brought faith; though not an explicite faith of all those articles, which we, who from the beginning have been Catechized in all those points, are bound to have, yet a constant assurance that Christ could, and that he would relieve this distressed person, in which assurance, there was enwrapped an implicite faith even of the Messias, that could remove all occasions of sicknesse, even sin it selfe.

[Mark 16.15]

There was faith in the case; but in whom? Whose faith was it, that Christ had respect to? To whom hath that *Illorum* in the Text, *their faith,* reference? There can be no question, but that it hath reference to those foure friends, that brought this sick man in his bed, to Christ: For, else it could not have been spoken in the plurall, and called *their faith.* And certainly S. *Ambrose* does not inconveniently make that particular an argument of Gods greatnesse and goodnesse, of his magnificence, and munificence, *Magnus Dominus, qui aliorum meritis, aliis ignoscit;* This is the large and plentifull mercy of God, that for one mans sake, he forgives another. This *Ioash* acknowledged in the person of *Elisha; when Elisha was sick, the King came downe to him, and wept over his face, and said, O my Father, my Father, the Chariot of Israel, and the horse-men thereof.* Here were all the forces of Israel mustred upon one sick bed, the whole strength of Israel consisted in the goodnesse of that one man. The Angel said to *Paul,* when they were in an evident and imminent danger of shipwrack, *God hath given thee all them that sayle with thee;* He spared them, not for their owne sakes, but for *Pauls.* God gave those passengers to *Paul* so, as he had given *Paul* himselfe before to *Stephen; Si Stephanus non sic orasset, Paulum hodiè Ecclesia non*

Illorum

2 Reg. 13.14

Act. 27.24

haberet, sayes S. *Augustine:* If *Paul* had not been enwrapped in those
[Acts 7.60] prayers, which *Stephen* made for his persecutors, the Church had
[Acts 27.24] lost the benefit of all *Pauls* labours; and if God had not given *Paul*
the lives of all those passengers in that Ship, they had all perished.
Gen. 18 For the righteousnesse of a few, (if those few could have been found)
God would have spared the whole City of Sodome: And when Gods
Gen. 19.29 fury was kindled upon the Cities of that Country, *God remembred*
²⁵⁰ *Abraham,* sayes that story, and he delivered *Lot:* And when he
delivered Jerusalem from *Sennacherib,* he takes his servant *David* by
the hand, he puts his servant *David* into Commission with himselfe,
2 Reg. 19.34 and he sayes, *I will defend this City, and save it, for mine own sake,
and for my servant Davids sake. Quantus murus Patriæ vir justus,* is
a holy exclamation of S. *Ambrose,* What a Wall to any Towne, what
a Sea to any Iland, what a Navy to any Sea, what an Admirall to any
Navy, is a good man! Apply thy selfe therefore, and make thy conversation with good men, and get their love, and that shall be an
armour of proofe to thee.
²⁶⁰   When Saint *Augustines* Mother lamented the ill courses that her
sonne tooke in his youth, still that Priest, to whom she imparted her
sorrowes, said, *Filius istarum lacrymarum, non potest perire;* That
Son, for whom so good a Mother hath shed so many teares, cannot
perish: He put it not upon that issue, *filius Dei,* the elect child of
God, the son of predestination cannot perish, for at that time, that
name was either no name, or would scarce have seemed to have belonged to S. *Augustine,* but the child of these teares, of this devotion
Mat. 8.13 cannot be lost. Christ said to the Centurion, *fiat sicut credidisti, Goe
thy way, and as thou beleevest, so be it done unto thee, and his servant*
²⁷⁰ *was healed in the selfe-same houre:* The master beleeved, and the
servant was healed. Little knowest thou, what thou hast received at
Gods hands, by the prayers of the Saints in heaven, that enwrap thee
in their generall prayers for the Militant Church. Little knowest thou,
what the publique prayers of the Congregation, what the private
prayers of particular devout friends, that lament thy carelesnesse,
and negligence in praying for thy selfe, have wrung and extorted out
of Gods hands, in their charitable importunity for thee. And therfore, at last, make thy selfe fit to doe for others, that which others,
when thou wast unfit to doe thy selfe that office, have done for thee,

²⁸⁰ in assisting thee with their prayers. *If thou meet thine enemies Oxe,* Exod.
or Asse going astray, (sayes the Law) *thou shalt surely bring it back* 23.4, 5
to him again: If thou see the Asse of him that hateth thee, lying under
his burden, and wouldest forbeare to help him, thou shalt surely
help him. Estnè Deo cura de Bobus, is the Apostles question, *Hath* [1 Cor. 9.9]
God care of Oxen? of other mens Oxen? How much more of his
owne Sheep? And therefore if thou see one of his Sheep, one of thy
fellow Christians, strayed into sins of infirmity, and negligent of himselfe, joyne him with thine owne soule, in thy prayers to God. Relieve
him, (if that be that which he needs) with thy prayers for him, and
²⁹⁰ relieve him, (if his wants be of another kinde) according to his
prayers to thee. *Cur apud te homo Collega non valeat,* sayes S.
Ambrose, why should not he that is thy Colleague, thy fellow-man,
as good a man, that is as much a man as thou, made of the same
bloud, and redeemed with the same bloud as thou art, why should
not he prevaile with thee, so farre as to the obtaining of an almes,
Cum apud Deum, servus, & interveniendi meritum, & jus habeat
impetrandi, when some fellow-servant of thine, hath had that interest
in God, as by his intercession, and prayers to advance thy salvation?
wilt not thou save the life of another man that prayes to thee, when
³⁰⁰ perchance thy soule hath been saved by another man, that prayed
for thee?

    Well then; Christ had respect to their faith, that brought this sick *Ejus*
man to him. *Consuetudo est misericordis Dei,* It is Gods ordinary
way, (sayes S. *Chrysostome) hunc honorem dare servis suis, ut propter*
eos salventur & alii, to afford this honour to his servants, that for
their sakes he saves others. But neither this which we say now out
of S. *Chrysostome,* nor that which we said before out of S. *Ambrose,*
nor all that we might multiply out of the other Fathers, doth exclude the faith of that particular man, who is to be saved. It is true,
³¹⁰ that in this particular case, S. *Hierome* says, *Non vidit fidem ejus*
qui offerebatur, sed eorum qui offerebant, That Christ did not respect
his faith that was brought, but onely theirs that brought him; but
except S. *Hierome* be to be understood so, that Christ did not first
respect his faith, but theirs, we must depart from him, to S. *Chrysos-*
tome, Neque enim se portari sustinuisset, He would neither have put
himselfe, nor them, to so many difficulties, as he did, if he had not

had a faith, that is, a constant assurance in this meanes of his recovery. And therefore the Rule may be best given thus; That God gives worldly blessings, bodily health, deliverance from dangers, and the
320 like, to some men, in contemplation of others, though themselves never thought of it, all the examples which we have touched upon, convince abundantly.

That God gives spirituall blessings to Infants, presented according to his Ordinance, in Baptisme, in Contemplation of the faith of their Parents, or of the Church, or of their sureties, without any actuall faith in the Infant, is probable enough, credible enough. But take it as our case is, *de adultis,* in a man who is come to the use of his own reason, and discretion, so God never saves any man, for the faith of another, otherwise then thus, that the faithfull man may pray for the
330 conversion of an unfaithfull, who does not know, nor, if he did, would be content to be prayed for, and God, for his sake that prayes, may be pleased to work upon the other; but before that man comes to the *Dimittuntur peccata,* that his sinnes are forgiven, that man
Habak. 2.4   comes to have faith in himselfe. *Iustus in fide sua vivit;* there is no life without faith, nor *In fide aliena,* no such life as constitutes Righteousnesse, without a personall faith of our owne. So that this *fides illorum,* in our Text, this that is called their faith, hath reference to the sick man himselfe, as well as to them that brought him.

Visa   And then, in Him, and in Them, it was *fides visa,* faith, which,
340 by an ouvert act, was declared, and made evident. For, Christ, who was now to convay into that company the knowledge that he was the Messias, which Messias was to be God, and Man, as afterwards for their conviction, who would not beleeve him to be God, he shewed that he knew their inward thoughts, and did some other things, which none but God could doe; so here, for the better edification of men, he required such a faith, as might be evident to men. For, though Christ could have seene their faith, by looking into their hearts, yet to think, that here he saw it by that power of his Divinity, *nimis coactum videtur,* It is too narrow, and too forced an interpreta-
350 tion of the place, sayes *Calvin.* They then, that is, all they declared their faith, their assurance, that Christ could, and would help him. It was good evidence of a strength of faith in him, that in a disease, very little capable of cure, then when he had so farre resolved, and

slackned his sinewes, that he could endure no posture but his bed,
he suffered himselfe to be put to so many incommodities. It was good
evidence of a strength of faith in them, that they could beleeve that
Christ would not reject them for that importunity of troubling him,
and the congregation, in the midst of a Sermon; That when they
saw, that they who came onely to heare, could not get neare the
60 doore, they should thinke to get in, with that load, that offensive
spectacle; That they should ever conceive, or goe about to execute, or
be suffered to execute such a plot, as without the leave of Christ, (if
Christ preached this Sermon in his owne house, as some take it to
have been done) or without the Masters leave, in whose house soever
it was, they should first untile or open, and then break through the
floore, and so let downe, their miserable burden: That they should
have an apprehension, that it was not fit for them to stay, till the
Sermon were done, and the company parted, but that it was likeliest
to conduce to the glory of God, that Preaching, and working might
70 goe together, this was evidence, this was argument of strength of
faith in them. Take therefore their example, not to defer that assistance, which thou art able to give to another. *Ne dicas assistam cras,*
sayes S. *Gregory,* doe not say, I will help thee to morrow; *Ne quid
inter propositum, & beneficium intercedat;* Perchance that poore
soule may not need thee to morrow, perchance thou maist have nothing to give to morrow, perchance there shall be no such day, as to
morrow, and so thou hast lost that opportunity of thy charity, which
God offered thee, to day: *Vnica beneficentia est, quæ moram non
admittit,* onely that is charity, that is given presently.

380   But yet, when all was done, when there was faith, and faith in   *Cum, non*
them all, and faith declared in their outward works, yet Christ is not   *quia*
said to have done this miracle, *quia fides,* but *cum fides,* not Because
he saw, but onely When he saw their faith. Let us transferre none of
that, which belongs to God, to our selves: when we doe our duties,
(but when doe we goe about to begin to doe any part of any of
them?) we are unprofitable servants: When God does work in us,   [Luke 17.10]
are we saved by that work, as by the cause, when there is another
cause of the work it selfe? When the ground brings forth good
corne, yet that ground becomes not fit for our food: When a man
390 hath brought forth good fruits, yet that man is not thereby made

worthy of heaven. Not faith it selfe (and yet faith is of somewhat a deeper dye, and tincture, then any works) is any such cause of our salvation. A beggars beleeving that I will give him an almes, is no cause of my charity: My beleeving that Christ will have mercy upon me, is no cause of Christs mercy; for what proportion hath my temporary faith, with my everlasting salvation? But yet, though it work not as a cause, though it be not *quia vidit,* because he saw it, yet *cum videt,* when Christ findes this faith, according to that gracious Covenant, and Contract which he hath made with us, that wheresoever, and whensoever he findes faith, he will enlarge his mercy, finding that in this patient, he expressed his mercy, in that which constitutes our second part, *Fili confide, my son be of good cheare, thy sins are forgiven thee.*

2 Part   Where we see first, our Saviour Christ opening the bowels of compassion to him, and receiving him so, as if he had issued out of his bowels, and from his loynes, in that gracious appellation, *Fili, my Son.* He does not call him brother; for greater enmity can be no where, then is often expressed to have beene betweene brethren; for in that degree, and distance, enmity amongst men began in *Cain,* and *Abel,* and was pursued in many paires of brethren after, in Sacred and in secular story. Hee does not call him friend; that name, even in Christs owne mouth, is not alwaies accompanied with good

Mat. 22.12   entertainment: *Amice, quomodo intrasti,* saies he, *Friend, how came you in? and he bound him hand and foote, and cast him into outer darknesse.* He does not call him son of *Abraham,* which might give him an interest in all the promises, but he gives him a present Adoption, and so a present fruition of all, *Fili, my Son.* His Son, and not his Son in law; he loads him not with the encumbrances, and halfe-impossibilities of the Law, but he seales to him the whole Gospell, in the remission of sinnes. His Son, and not his dis-inherited son, as the Jewes were, but his Son, upon whom he setled his ancient Inheritance, his eternall election, and his new purchase, which he came now into the world to make with his blood. His Son, and not his prodigall son, to whom Christ imputes no wastfulnesse of his former graces, but gives him a generall release, and *Quietus est,* in the for-

[Prov. 23.26]   givenesse of sinnes. All that Christ asks of his Sons, is, *Fili da mihi cor, My Son give me thy heart;* and till God give us that, we cannot

give it him; and therefore in this Son he creates a new heart, he infuses a new courage, he establishes a new confidence, in the next
⁴⁰ word, *Fili confide, My Son be of good cheere.*

Christ then does not stay so long wrastling with this mans faith,   *Confide*
and shaking it, and trying whether it were fast rooted, as he did with
that Woman in the Gospell, who came after him, in her daughters   Mat. 15.22
behalfe, crying, *Have mercy upon me O Lord, thou Son of David,*
for Christ gave not that woman one word; when her importunity
made his Disciples speake to him, he said no more, but that he was
not sent to such as she; This was far, very far from a *Confide filia,*
Daughter be of good cheere: But yet, this put her not off, but (as it
followes) *She followed, and worshipped him, and said, O Lord helpe*
⁴⁰ *me:* And all this prevailed no farther with him, but to give such an
answer, as was more discomfortable, then a silence, *It is not fit to
take the childrens bread, and cast it unto dogs.* She denies not that,
she contradicts him not; she saies, *Truth Lord,* It is not fit to take the
childrens bread, and to cast it unto dogs, and *Truth Lord,* I am one of
those dogs; but yet she persevers in her holy importunity, and in her
good ill-manners, and saies, *Yet the Dogs eate of the crums which
fall from the Masters table:* And then, and not till then comes Jesus
to that, *O Woman, great is thy faith, be it unto thee, even as thou
wilt; and her Daughter was healed.* But all this, at last, was but a
⁵⁰ bodily restitution, here was no *Dimittuntur peccata* in the case, no
declaration of forgivenesse of sinnes; But with this man in our Text,
Christ goes farther, and comes sooner to an end; He exercises him
with no disputation, he leaves no roome for any diffidence, but at
first word establishes him, and then builds upon him. Now beloved,
which way soever of these two God have taken with thee, whether   [Book of
the longer, or the shorter way, *blesse thou the Lord, praise him, and*   Common
magnifie him for that. If God have setled and strengthned thy faith   Prayer:
early, early in thy youth heretofore, early at the beginning of a Ser-   *Benedicite*]
mon now, *A day is as a thousand yeares with God,* a minute is as   [2 Peter 3.8]
⁴⁶⁰ sixe thousand yeares with God, that which God hath not done upon
the Nations, upon the Gentiles, in six thousand yeares, never since
the Creation, which is, to reduce them to the knowlege, and application of the Messias, Christ Jesus, that he hath done upon thee, in
an instant. If he have carried thee about the longer way, if he have

exposed thee to scruples, and perplexities, and stormes in thine understanding, or conscience, yet in the midst of the tempest, the soft ayre,
that he is said to come in, shall breath into thee; in the midst of those
clouds, his Son shall shine upon thee; In the midst of that flood he
shall put out his Rainbow, his seale that thou shalt not drowne, his
470 Sacrament of faire weather to come, and as it was to the Thiefe, thy
Crosse shall be thine Altar, and thy Faith shall be thy Sacrifice.
Whether he accomplish his worke upon thee soone or late, he shall
never leave thee all the way, without this *Confide fili,* a holy confidence, that thou art his, which shall carry thee to the *Dimittuntur
peccata,* to the peace of conscience, in the remission of sins.

In which two words, we noted unto you, that Christ hath instituted a Catechisme, an Instruction for this new Convertite, and
adopted Son of his; in which, the first lesson that is therein implyed,

Antequam   is, *Antequam rogetur,* That God is more forward to give, then man to
rogetur   480 aske: It is not said that the sick man, or his company in his behalfe,
said any thing to Christ, but Christ speakes first to them. If God have
touched thee here, didst thou aske that at his hands? Didst thou pray
before thou camest hither, that he would touch thy heart here? perchance thou didst: But when thou wast brought to thy Baptisme,
didst thou ask any thing at Gods hands then? But those that brought
thee, that presented thee, did; They did in thy Baptisme; but at thine
election, then when God [was] writing downe the names of all the
Elect, in the book of Life, how camest thou in? who brought thee in
then? Didst thou aske any thing at Gods hands then, when thou thy
490 selfe wast not at all?

Meliora   *Dat prius,* that's the first lesson in this Catechisme, God gives before
we aske, and then *Dat meliora rogatis,* God gives better things, then
we aske; They intended to aske but bodily health, and Christ gave
spirituall, he gave Remission of sinnes. And what gain'd he by

[Psa. 32.1]   that? why, *Beati quorum remissæ iniquitates, Blessed are they, whose
sinnes are forgiven.* But what is Blessednesse? Any more then a confident expectation of a good state in the next world? Yes; Blessednesse includes all that can be asked or conceived in the next world,
and in this too. Christ in his Sermon of blessednesse, saies first,

Mat. 5.3   500 *Blessed are they, for theirs is the Kingdome of Heaven;* and after,
and 5   *Blessed are they, for they shall inherit the earth;* Againe, *Blessed, for*

they shall obtaine mercy; and, *Blessed for they shall be filled:* Remission of sins is blessednesse, and as *Godlinesse hath the promise of this world, and the next,* so blessednesse hath the performance of both: He that hath peace in the remission of sinnes, is blessed already, and shall have those blessings infinitely multiplied in the world to come. The farthest that Christ goes in the expressing of the affections of a naturall Father here, is, That *if his Son aske bread, he will not give him a stone; and if he aske a Fish, he will not give him a Scorpion;* He will not give him worse then he ask'd; But it is the peculiar bounty of this Father, who adopted this Sonne, to give more, and better, spirituall for temporall.

Another lesson, which Christ was pleased to propose to this new Convertite, in this Catechisme, was, to informe him, That sins were the true causes of all bodily diseases. Diseases and bodily afflictions are sometimes inflicted by God *Ad pœnam, non ad purgationem,* Not to purge or purifie the soule of that man, by that affliction, but to bring him by the rack to the gallowes, through temporary afflictions here, to everlasting torments hereafter; As *Iudas* his hanging, and *Herods* being eaten with wormes, was their entrance into that place, where they are yet. Sometimes diseases and afflictions are inflicted onely, or principally to manifest the glory of God, in the removing thereof; So Christ saies of that man, that was borne blinde, that neither he himselfe had sinned, nor bore the sinnes of his parents, but he was borne blinde to present an occasion of doing a miracle. Sometimes they are inflicted *Ad humiliationem,* for our future humiliation; So S. *Paul* saies of himselfe, *That least he should be exalted above measure, by the abundance of Revelations, he had that* Stimulum carnis, *That vexation of the flesh, that messenger of Satan, to humble him.* And then, sometimes they are inflicted for tryall, and farther declaration of your conformity to Gods will, as upon *Iob.* But howsoever there be divers particular causes, for the diseases and afflictions of particular men, the first cause of death, and sicknesse, and all infirmities upon mankinde in generall, was sin; and it would not be hard for every particular man, almost, to finde it in his owne case too, to assigne his fever to such a surfet, or his consumption to such an intemperance. And therefore to breake that circle, in which we compasse, and immure, and imprison our selves, That as sinne begot

[1 Tim. 4.8]

Luk. 11.[11,] 12

Causa morborum

Acts 12.[23]

John 9.3

2 Cor. 12.7

diseases, so diseases begot more sinnes, impatience and murmuring
540 at Gods corrections, Christ begins to shake this circle, in the right
way to breake it, in the right linke, that is, first to remove the sin,
which occasioned the disease; for, till that be done, a man is in no

Amos 5.19   better case, then, (as the Prophet expresses it) *If he should flie from
a Lion, and a Beare met him, or if he should leane upon a wall, and
a Serpent bit him.* What ease were it, to be delivered of a palsie, of
slack and dissolv'd sinews, and remaine under the tyranny of a lust-
full heart, of licentious eyes, of slacke and dissolute speech and conversation? What ease to be delivered of the putrefaction of a wound
in my body, and meet a murder in my conscience, done, or intended,
550 or desired upon my neighbour? To be delivered of a fever in my
spirits, and to have my spirit troubled with the guiltinesse of an
adultery? To be delivered of Cramps, and Coliques, and Convulsions
in my joynts and sinewes, and suffer in my soule all these, from my
oppressions, and extortions, by which I have ground the face of the
poore. It is but lost labour, and cost, to give a man a precious cordiall,
when he hath a thorne in his foote, or an arrow in his flesh; for, as

[John 5.14]   long as the sinne, which is the cause of the sicknesse, remaines, *Deterius sequetur,* A worse thing will follow; we may be rid of a Fever,
and the Pestilence will follow, rid of the Cramp, and a Gout will
560 follow, rid of sicknesse, and Death, eternall death will follow. That
which our Saviour prescribes is, *Noli peccare ampliùs, sinne no more;*
first, *non ampliùs,* sinne no more sins, take heed of gravid sins, of
pregnant sinnes, of sins of concomitance, and concatenation, that
chaine and induce more sins after, as *Davids* idlenesse did adultery,
and that murder, and the losse of the Lords Army, and Honor, in
the blaspheming of his name, *Noli ampliùs,* sin no more, no such sin
as induces more; And *Noli ampliùs, sinne no more,* that is, sin thy
owne sin, thy beloved sin, no more times over; And still *Noli ampliùs,*
sin not that sin which thou hast given over in thy practise, in thy
570 memory, by a sinfull delight in remembring it; And againe, *Noli
ampliùs,* sin not over thy former sins, by holding in thy possession,
such things as were corruptly gotten, by any such former practises:
for, *Deterius sequetur,* a worse thing will follow, A Tertian will be
a Quartan, and a Quartan a Hectique, and a Hectique a Consumption, and a Consumption without a consummation, that shall never

consume it selfe, nor consume thee to an unsensiblenesse of torment.
And then after these three lessons in this Catechisme, That God
gives before we aske, That he gives better then we aske, That he
informes us in the true cause of sicknesse, sinne, He involves a tacit,
nay he expresses an expresse rebuke, and increpation, and in beginning at the *Dimittuntur peccata,* at the forgivenesse of sinnes, tels him
in his eare, that his spirituall health should have beene prefer'd before
his bodily, and the cure of his soule before his Palsie; that first the
Priest should have beene, and then the Physitian might bee consulted. That which Christ does to his new adopted Sonne here, the
Wiseman saies to his Son, *My Son, in thy sicknesse be not negligent;*
But wherein is his diligence required, or to be expressed? in that,
which followes, *Pray unto the Lord, and he will make thee whole;*
But upon what conditions, or what preparations? *Leave off from sin,*
order thy hands aright, and cleanse thy heart from all wickednesse.
Is this all? needs there no declaration, no testimony of this? Yes, *Give*
a sweet savour, and a memoriall of fine floure, and make a fat offer-
ing, as not beeing; that is, as though thou wert dead: Give, and give
that which thou givest in thy life time, as not beeing. And when all
this is piously, and religiously done, thou hast repented, restor'd,
amended, and given to pious uses, Then, saies he there, *give place to*
the Physitian, for the Lord hath created him. For if we proceed otherwise, if wee begin with the Physitian, Physick is a curse; *He that*
sinneth before his Maker, let him fall into the hands of the Physitian,
saies the Wiseman there: It is not, Let him come into the hands of
the Physitian, as though that were a curse, but let him fall, let him
cast and throw himselfe into his hands, and rely upon naturall
meanes, and leave out all consideration of his other, and worse disease, and the supernaturall Physick for that. *Asa* had had a great
deliverance from God, when the Prophet *Hanani* asked him, *Were*
not the Ethiopians, and the Lubins a huge Host? but because after
this deliverance, he relied upon the King of Syria, and not upon God,
the Judgement is, *From henceforth thou shalt have wars:* That was
a sicknesse upon the State, and then he fell sick in his own person,
and in that sicknesse, saies that story, *He sought not to the Lord, but*
to the Physitian, and then he dyed. To the Lord and then to the Physitian had beene the right way; If to the Physitian and then to the Lord,

Sanitas
spiritualis

Ecclus. 38.9

V. 15

2 Chron. 16

though this had beene out of the right way, yet hee might have returned to it: But it was to the Physitian, and not to the Lord, and
then he died. *Omnipotenti medico nullus languor insanabilis,* saies
S. *Ambrose,* there is but one Almighty; and none but the Almighty
can cure all diseases, because hee onely can cure diseases in the roote,
that is, in the forgivenesse of sins.

Scribæ &   We are almost at an end; when he had thus Catechised his Con-
Pharisæi   ⁶²⁰ vertite, thus rectified his patient, hee turnes upon them, who beheld
all this, and were scandaliz'd with his words, the Scribes and Pharisees; And because they were scandaliz'd onely in this, that he being
but man, undertooke the office of God, to forgive sins, he declares
himselfe to them, to be God. Christ would not leave even malice it
selfe unsatisfied; And therefore do not thou thinke thy selfe Christian
enough, for having an innocence in thy selfe, but be content to descend to the infirmities, and to the very malice of other men, and to
give the world satisfaction; *Nec paratum habeas illud è trivio,* (sayes
S. *Hierome*) do not arm thy self with that vulgar, and triviall saying,
⁶³⁰ *Sufficit mihi conscientia mea, nec curo quid loquantur homines,* It
suffices me, that mine own conscience is cleare, and I care not what
all the world sayes; thou must care what the world sayes, and thinks;
Christ himself had that respect even towards the Scribes, and Pharisees. For, first he declared himself to be God, in that he took knowledge of their thoughts; for they had said nothing, and he sayes to
them, why reason you thus in your hearts? and they themselves did
not, could not deny, but that those words of *Solomon* appertained
2 Chron.   only to God, *Thou only knowest the hearts of the children of men,*
6.30   And those of *Ieremy, The heart is deceitfull above all things, and*
Jer. 17.9   ⁶⁴⁰ *desperately wicked, who can know it? I the Lord search the heart,*
and I try the reines. Let the Schoole dispute infinitely, (for he that
will not content himself with means of salvation, till all Schoole
points be reconciled, will come too late) let *Scotus* and his Heard
think, That Angels, and separate soules have a naturall power to understand thoughts, though God for his particular glory restraine the
exercise of that power in them, (as in the Romane Church, Priests
have a power to forgive all sins, though the Pope restraine that power
in reserved cases; And the Cardinals by their Creation, have a voice
in the Consistory, but that the Pope for a certain time inhibits them

to give voice) And let *Aquinas* present his arguments to the contrary, That those spirits have no naturall power to know thoughts; we seek no farther, but that Christ Jesus himselfe thought it argument enough to convince the Scribes and Pharisees, and prove himselfe God, by knowing their thoughts. *Eadem Majestate & potentia,* sayes S.*Hierome,* Since you see I proceed as God, in knowing your thoughts, why beleeve you not, that I may forgive his sins as God too?

And then, in the last act he joynes both together; he satisfies the patient, and he satisfies the beholders too: he gives him his first desire, bodily health; *He bids him take up his bed and walk,* and he doth it; and he shewes them that he is God, by doing that, which (as it appears in the Story) was harder in their opinion, then remission of sins, which was, to cure and recover a diseased man, only by his word, without any naturall, or second means. And therefore since all the world shakes in a palsie of wars, and rumors of wars, since we are sure, that Christs Vicar in this case will come to his *Dimittuntur peccata,* to send his Buls, and Indulgences, and Crociatars for the maintenance of his part, in that cause, let us also, who are to do the duties of private men, to obey and not to direct, by presenting our diseased and paralytique souls to Christ Jesus, now, when he in the Ministery of his unworthiest servant is preaching unto you, by untiling the house, by removing all disguises, and palliations of our former sins, by true confession, and hearty detestation, let us endeavour to bring him to his *Dimittuntur peccata,* to forgive us all those sins, which are the true causes of all our palsies, and slacknesses in his service; and so, without limiting him, or his great Vicegerents, and Lieutenants, the way, or the time to beg of him, that he will imprint in them, such counsels and such resolutions, as his wisdome knows best to conduce to his glory, and the maintenance of his Gospell. *Amen.*

Dat sanitatem

Number 3.

Preached upon Candlemas Day.

MAT. 5.16. *LET YOUR LIGHT SO SHINE BEFORE MEN, THAT THEY MAY SEE YOUR GOOD WORKS, AND GLORIFIE YOUR FATHER WHICH IS IN HEAVEN.*

EITHER of the names of this day, were Text enough for a Sermon, Purification, or Candlemas. Joyne we them together, and raise we only this one note from both, that all true purification is in the light; corner purity, clandestine purity, conventicle purity is not purity. *Christ gave himself for us,* sayes the Apostle, *that he might purifie to himself a peculiar people.* How shall this purification appeare? It follows; *They shall be zealous of good works;* They shall not wrangle about faith and works, but be actually zealous of good works. For, purification was accompanied with an oblation, something was to be given; A Lamb, a Dove, a Turtle; All, emblemes of mildnesse; true purity is milde, meek, humble, and to despise and undervalue others, is an inseparable mark of false purity. The oblation of this dayes purification is light: so the day names it, Candlemas-day, so your custome celebrates it, with many lights. Now, when God received lights into his Tabernacle, hee received none of Tallow, (the Oxe hath hornes) he received none of Waxe, (the Bee hath his sting) but he received only lampes of oyle. And, though from many fruits and berries they pressed oyle, yet God admitted no oyle into the service of the Church, but only of the Olive; the Olive, the embleme of peace. Our purification is with an oblation, our obla-

Tit. 2.14

Levit. 12.6 [10]

[20]

84

tion is light, our light is good works; our peace is rather to exhort you to them, then to institute any solemne, or other then occasionall comparison between faith and them. Every good work hath faith for the roote; but every faith hath not good works for the fruit thereof. And it is observable, that in all this great Sermon of our Saviours in the Mount, (which possesseth this, and the two next Chapters) there is no mention of faith, by way of perswasion or exhortation thereunto, but the whole Sermon is spent upon good works. For, good works presuppose faith; and therefore he concludes   Mat. 6.30
30 that they had but little faith, because they were so solicitous about the things of this world, *O ye of little faith.* And as Christ concludes an unstedfastnesse in their faith, out of their solicitude for this world, so may the world justly conclude an establishment in their faith, if they see them exercise themselves in the works of mercy, and so *let their light shine before men, that they may see their good works, and glorifie their Father which is in heaven.*

    These are words spoken by our Saviour to his Disciples in the   *Divisio* Mount; a treasure deposited in those disciples, but in those disciples, as depositaries for us; an Oracle uttered to those disciples, but
40 through those disciples to us; Paradise convayed to those disciples, but to those disciples, as feoffees in trust for us; to every one of us, in them (from him, that rides with his hundreds of Torches, to him that crawles with his rush-candle) our Saviour sayes, *Let your light so shine before men, that they may see your good works, &c.* The words have two parts; so must our explication of them; first a precept, *Sic luceat,* (*Let your light so shine before men*) and then the reason, the purpose, the end, the effect, *ut videant,* (*that men may see your good works, and &c.*) From the first bough will divers branches spring, and divers from the other; all of good taste and
50 nourishment, if wee might stay to presse the fruits thereof. We cannot; yet, in the first we shall insist a while upon each of these three; First, the light it self, what that is, *Sic luceat lux, Let your light so shine;* And then, secondly, what this propriety is, *lux vestra,* (let *your light* shine, *yours;*) And lastly what this emanation of this light upon others is, *coram hominibus,* (let your light shine *before men.*) The second part, which is the reason, or the effect of this precept, *ut videant,* (*that men may see your good works, and glorifie*

your Father which is in heaven) abounds in particular considerations; and I should weary you, if I should make you stand all the
⁶⁰ while under so heavy a load, as to charge your memories with all
those particulars, so long before I come to handle them. Reserving
them therefore to their due time, anon, proceed we now to the three
branches of our first part, first the light in it self, then the propriety
in us, lastly, the emanation upon others, *Let your light so shine
before men.*

I Part First, for the light it self, There is a light that lightneth every man
Lux that commeth into the world. And, even this universall light is
John 1.9 Christ, sayes S. *Iohn,* (*He was that light that lighteth every man
that commeth into the world.*) And this universall enunciation, (*He
⁷⁰ lightneth every man*) moved S. *Cyril* to take this light for the light
of nature, and naturall reason. For even nature and naturall reason
John 1.3 is from Christ. *All things were made by him,* sayes S. *Iohn,* even
Colos. 1.16 nature it self. And, *By him, and for him, all things visible, and invisible were created,* sayes the Apostle. And therefore our latter men
of the Reformation, are not to be blamed, who for the most part,
pursuing S. *Cyrils* interpretation, interpret this universall light, *that
lightneth every man,* to be the light of nature. Divers others of the
Fathers take this universall light (because Christ is said to be this
light) to be Baptisme. For, in the primitive Church, as the Nativity
⁸⁰ of Christ was called the Epiphany, Manifestation, so Baptisme was
called Illumination. And so, Christ lightens every man that comes
into the world, (that is, into the Christian world) by that Sacrament
of Illumination, Baptisme. S. *Augustine* brought the exposition of
that universall proposition into a narrow roome; That he enlightned
all that came into the world, that is, all that were enlightned in the
world, were enlightned by him; there was no other light; and so he
makes this light to be the light of faith, and the light of effectuall
grace, which all have not, but they that have, have it from Christ.
Now which of these lights is intended in our Text, *Let your light
⁹⁰ shine out?* is it of the light of nature, at our comming into the world,
or the light of Baptisme, and that generall grace that accompanies
all Gods Ordinances, at our comming into the Church, or the light
of faith, and particular grace, sealing our adoption, and spirituall
filiation there? Properly, our light is none of these three; and yet

it is truly, all; for our light is the light of good works; and that light
proceeds from all the other three, and so is all those, and then it goes
beyond all three, and so is none of them. It proceeds from all; for,
if we consider the first light, the light of nature, in our creation, *We*   Ephes. 2.10
are (sayes the Apostle) *his workmanship, created in Christ Iesus*
⁰⁰ *unto good works.* So that we were all made for that, for good works;
even the naturall man, by that first light. Consider it in the second
light, in baptisme; there we dye in Christ, and are buried in Christ,
and rise in Christ, and in him we are new creatures, and with him
we make a covenant in baptisme, for holinesse of life, which is the
body of good works. Consider the third, that of faith, and as every
thing in nature is, so faith is perfected by working; for, *faith is dead,*   Jam. 2.26
without breath, without spirit, if it be *without workes.* So, this light
is in all those lights; we are created, we are baptized, we are adopted
for good works; and it is beyond them all, even that of faith; for,
¹⁰ though faith have a preheminence, because works grow out of it,
and so faith (as the root) is first, yet works have the preheminence
thus, both that they include faith in them, and that they dilate, and
diffuse, and spread themselves more declaratorily, then faith doth.
Therefore, as our Saviour said to some that asked him, *What shall*   John 6.28
we do that we might work the work of God? (you see their minde
was upon works, something they were sure was to be done) *This*
is the work of God, that ye beleeve in him whom he hath sent, and
so refers them to faith, so to another that asks him, *What shall I do,*   Mat. 19.16
that I may have eternall life? (all goe upon that, that something
²⁰ there must be done, works there must be) Christ sayes, *Keepe the*
Commandements, and so refers him to works. *He hath shewed thee*   Mic. 6.8
O man, what is good, and what doth the Lord require of thee, but
to do justly, and to shew mercy, and to walk humbly with thy God?
This then is the light that lighteth every man that goes out of the
world, *good works;* for, *their works follow them.* Their works; they   Apoc. 14.13
shall be theirs, even after their death; which is our second branch
in this first part, the propriety, *lux vestra,* let *your light* shine.

I cannot alwaies call the works that I do, my works; for sometimes   *Proprietas*
God works them, and sometimes the devill: Sometimes God works   *vestra*
³⁰ his owne worke, *The Lord will do his worke, his strange worke,*   Esay 28.21
and bring to passe his act, his strange act. Sometimes he works my

Esay 26.12
1 Cor. 12.6
Ephes. 1.11
Esay 43.13

Rom. 7.15

ver. 20

August.

Hab. 2.4

Rom. 1.17
Gal. 3.11

Heb. 10.38

Mar. 5.34

works, *Thou Lord hast wrought all our workes in us.* In us, and in all things else, *Operatur omnia in omnibus,* he worketh all in all. And all this in all these, *Secundum consilium voluntatis suæ,* After the counsaile of his owne will; for, *I will worke, and who shall let it?* But for all this his generall working, his enemy works in us too. *That which I doe, I allow not,* saies the Apostle; nay, *I know it not;* for, saies he, *what I hate, that I doe. And, if I doe that I would not doe, it is no more I that doe it, but sin that dwelleth in me.* Yet, for ¹⁴⁰ all this diverse, this contrary working, as S. *Augustine* sayes of the faculty of the will, *Nihil tam nostrum, quam voluntas,* there is nothing so much our owne, as our will before we worke, so there is nothing so much our owne, as our workes, after they are done. They stick to us, they cleave to us; whether as fomentations to nourish us, or as corrasives, to gnaw upon us, that lyes in the nature of the worke; but ours they are; and upon us our works work. Our good works are more ours, then our faith is ours. Our faith is ours as we have received it, our worke is ours, as we have done it. Faith is ours, as we are possessors of it, the work ours, as we are doers, actors in ¹⁵⁰ it. Faith is ours, as our goods are ours, works, as our children are ours. And therefore when the Prophet *Habakkuk* saies, *Fide sua, The just shall live by his faith,* that particle *His,* is a word of possession, not a word of Acquisition; That God hath infused that faith into him, and so it is his, not that he hath produced that faith in himselfe. His faith must save him; his own, and not anothers, not his parents faith, though he be the son of holy parents, not the Churches faith, (if he be of yeares) though he be within the covenant, but his own personall faith; yet not his so, as that it grew in him, or was produced in him, by him, by any plantation, or semination of his own. And ¹⁶⁰ therefore S. *Paul* in citing that place of *Habakkuk* (as he doth cite it three severall times) in all those places leaves out that particle of propriety, and acquisition, *his,* and still sayes, *The just shall live by faith,* and he sayes no more. And when our blessed Saviour sayes to the woman with the bloody issue, *Fides tua, Daughter, thy faith hath made thee whole,* it was said then, when he had seen that woman come trembling and fall down at his feet; he saw outward declarations of her faith, he saw works. And so, in divers of those places, where Christ repeats that, *fides tua, thy faith,* we finde it added, *Iesus videns fidem, Iesus seeing their faith.* With what eyes? he looked upon them with his humane eyes, not his divine; he saw not (that is, considered not at that time) their hearts, but their outward declarations, and proceeding as a good man would, out of their good works concludes faith. *Velle & nolle nostrum est,* to assent or to dis-assent is our own; we may choose which we will doe; *Ipsumque quod nostrum est, sine Dei miseratione nostrum non est;* But though this faculty be ours, it is ours, but because God hath imprinted it in us. So that still to will, as well as to doe, to beleeve, as well as to work, is all from God; but yet they are from God in a diverse manner, and a diverse respect; and certainly our works are more ours then our faith is, and man concurres otherwise in the acting and perpetration of a good work, then he doth in the reception and admission of faith. *Sed quæ non fecimus ipsi,* sayes the Poet; and he was *Vates,* a Prophet in saying so, *Vix ea nostra voco;* nothing is ours, but that which we have done our selves; and all that is ours. And though Christ refer us often to beliefe, in this life, because he would be sure to plant, and fasten safely that which is the only true root of all, that is, faith, yet when he comes to Judgement, in the next life, all his proceeding is grounded upon workes, and he judges us by our fruits. So then, God gives us faith, immediatly from himselfe, and out of that faith, he produces good works, instrumentally, by us, so, as that those works are otherwise ours, then that faith is. And this [is] the propriety, *lux vestra,* let *your light* shine, which we proposed for the second branch in this first part, that God vouchsafes to afford us an interest, in the working of our salvation; And then our third branch is, the emanation of this light, from us, to others, *Coram hominibus,* let your light shine *before men.*

There was a particular Holy-day amongst the heathen, that bore the name of this day, *Accensio luminum, Candlemas day;* A superstitious multiplying of Lamps, and Torches in Divine Service. This superstition *Lactantius* reproves, elegantly, and bitterly. *Num mentis suæ compos putandus est?* can we think that man in his wits, that offers to God, the Father, and Fountaine, the Author and Giver of all light, a Candle for an Oblation, for a Sacrifice, for a New-yeares gift? *Solem contempletur,* sayes he; Let that man but consider seriously the Sun, and he will see, that that God who could spare

Hieron.

Luceat
Emanatio

Lactant.

him so glorious a light as the Sun, needs not his Candle. And there-
Tertul.   fore sayes *Tertullian,* (reprehending the same superstition) *Lucernis
diem non infringimus,* we doe not cut off, we doe not shorten our
dayes, by setting up lights at noone, nor induce, nor force, nor make
210 night before it comes.

I would not be understood to condemne all use of candles by day,
in Divine Service, nor all Churches that have or doe use them; For,
so, I might condemne even the Primitive Church, in her pure and
innocent estate. And therefore, that which *Lactantius,* almost three
hundred yeares after Christ, sayes of those Lights, and that which
Tertullian, almost a hundred yeares before *Lactantius,* sayes, in
reprehension thereof, must necessarily be understood of the abuse,
and imitation of the Gentiles therein; for, that the thing it selfe, was
in use, before eyther of their times, I thinke, admits little question.
220 About *Lactantius* time, fell the *Eliberitan* Councell; and then the
use, and the abuse was evident. For, in the thirty fourth Canon of
that Councell, it is forbidden to set up Candles in the Church-yard:
And, the reason that is added, declares the abuse, *Non sunt enim
inquietandi spiritus fidelium,* That the soules of the Saints departed
should not be troubled. Now the setting up of lights could not trouble
them; but these lights were accompanied with superstitious Invoca-
tions, with magicall Incantations, and with howlings and ejulations,
which they had learnt from the Gentiles, and with these, the soules
of the dead, were, in those times, thought to be affected, and dis-
230 quieted. It is in this Ceremony of lights, as it is in other Ceremonies:
They may be good in their Institution, and grow ill in their practise.
So did many things, which the Christian Church received from the
Gentiles, in a harmlesse innocency, degenerate after, into as pestilent
superstition there, as amongst the Gentiles themselves. For, ceremonies, which were received, but for the instruction, and edification
of the weaker sort of people, were made reall parts of the service
of God, and meritorious sacrifices. To those ceremonies, which were
received as *signa commonefacientia,* helps to excite, and awaken
devotion, was attributed an operation, and an effectuall power, even
240 to the ceremony it selfe; and they were not practised, as they should,
significativè, but *effectivè,* not as things which should signifie to the
people higher mysteries, but as things as powerfull, and effectuall

in themselves, as the greatest Mysteries of all, the Sacraments themselves. So lights were received in the Primitive Church, to signifie to the people, that God, the Father of lights, was otherwise present in that place, then in any other, and then, men came to offer lights by way of sacrifice to God; And so, that which was providently intended for man, who indeed needed such helps, was turned upon God, as though he were to be supplied by us. But what then? Because things good in their institution, may be depraved in their practise, *Ergonè nihil ceremoniarum rudioribus dabitur, ad juvandam eorum imperitiam?* Shall therefore the people be denyed all ceremonies, for the assistance of their weaknesse? *Id ego non dico;* I say not so, sayes he. *Omnino illis utile esse sentio hoc genus adminiculi;* I think these kinds of helps to be very behoovefull for them; *Tantum hîc contendo,* all that I strive for, is but Moderation; and that Moderation he places very discreetly in this, That these ceremonies may be few in number; That they may be easie for observation; That they may be clearly understood in their signification. Wee must not therefore be hasty in condemning particular ceremonies: For, in so doing, in this ceremony of lights, we may condemne the Primitive Church, that did use them, and wee condemne a great and Noble part of the reformed Church, which doth use them at this day.

These superstitious lights, are not the lights we call for here, *sic luceat,* let your light shine out; but *lux vestra,* your light, the light of good works; let that shine out. Truly, this carrying, and diffusing of light to others is so blessed a thing, as that though *Lucifer,* (whose name signifies the carrying of light) be now an odious name, an infamous name, applyed onely to the Devill, yet a great Bishop in the Primitive Church abstained not from that name, forbore not that name, *Lucifer Talaritanus;* that he might carry about him, in his name, a remembrancer, *ferre lucem,* to carry light to others, he was content with that name, *Lucifer.* God had made light the first day, and yet he made many lights after. One light of thine shines out in our eyes, thy profession of Christ; let us see more lights, works worthy of that profession. God calls the Sun, and the Moone too, Great lights, because though there be greater in the Firmament, they appeare greatest to us; those works of ours are greatest in the sight of God, that are greatest in the sight of men, that are most

Calv. Instit. l. 4. c. 10. § 14

Gen. 1.16

²⁸⁰ beneficiall, most exemplary, and conduce most to the promoving of
others to glorifie God. To such rich men, as produce no light at all,
August.   (no works) that of S. *Augustine* is appliable, *cimices sunt,* they are
as these wormes, or flies, the *cimices, qui vivi mordent, mortui fœtent,*
They bite, and suck a man, whilst they live, and they stink pestilently, and offend so, when they are dead. The actions of such rich
men are mischievous whilst they live, and their memory odious when
they are dead. But all rich men are not such, to be absolutely without
all light. But then they may have light, (a determined purpose to
doe some good works) and yet this light not shine out. No man can
²⁹⁰ more properly be said to hide his light under a bushell, (which
because Christ sayes, (in the verse before our Text) no man does,
certainly no man should doe) then he, who hath disposed some part
of his estate to pious uses, but hides it in his will, and locks up that
will in his cabinet; For, in this case, though there be light, yet it
James 5.3   does not shine out. *Your gold, and your silver is cankered,* sayes
S. *Iames, and the rust of them shall be a witnesse, and shall eate your
flesh, as it were fire.* He does not say the gold and the silver it self,
as reproving the ill getting of it, but the rust, the hiding, the conceal-
ing therof, shall be this witnesse against thee, this executioner upon
³⁰⁰ thee. That man dyes in an ill state, of whose faith we have had no
evidence, till, after his death, his executors meet, and open his Will,
and then publish some Legacies to pious uses: And we had no
James 2.18   evidence before, if he had done no good before. For, *shew me thy
faith without thy works,* sayes the Apostle; and he proposes it, as
an impossible thing, impossible to shew it, impossible to have it. And
therefore, as good works are our owne, so are they never so properly
our owne, as when they are done with our owne hands; for this is
the true shining of our light, the emanation from us, upon others.
And so have you the three peeces, which constitute our first part, the
³¹⁰ precept, *Let your light shine before men;* The light it selfe, not the
light of nature, nor of Baptisme, nor of Adoption, but the light of
good works; And then the Appropriation of this light, how these
workes are ours, though the goodnesse thereof be onely from God;
And lastly the emanation of this light upon others; which cannot
well be said to be an emanation of our light, of light from us, except
it be whilst we are we, that is, alive. And so we passe to those many

particulars, which frame our second part, the reason, and the end of this, *That men may see your good works, and glorifie your Father which is in heaven.*

In this end, our beginning is, *ut videant,* that men may see it. The apparitions in old times, were evermore accompanied with lights; but they were private lights; such an old woman, or such a child saw a light; but *non videbant homines,* it did not shine out, so that men might see this light. We have a story delivered by a very pious man, and of the truth whereof he seemes to be very well assured, that one *Conradus* a devout Priest, had such an illustration, such an irradiation, such a coruscation, such a light at the tops of those fingers, which he used in the consecration of the Sacrament, as that by that light of his fingers ends, he could have reade in the night, as well as by so many Candles; But this was but a private light, *et non viderunt homines,* It did not shine out, so that men might see it. Blessed S. *Augustine* reports, (if that Epistle be S. *Augustines*) that when himselfe was writing to S. *Hierome,* to know his opinion of the measure and quality of the Joy, and Glory of Heaven, suddenly in his Chamber there appeared *ineffabile lumen,* sayes he, an unspeakable, an unexpressible light, *nostris invisum temporibus,* such a light as our times never saw, and out of that light issued this voyce, *Hieronymi anima sum,* I am the soule of that *Hierome* to whom thou art writing, who this houre dyed at *Bethlem,* and am come from thence to thee, &c. But this was but a private light, and whatsoever S. *Augustine* saw, (who was not easily deceived, nor would deceive others) *non videbant homines,* this light did not shine so, as that men might see it. Here, in our Text, there is a light required that men may see. Those lights of their apparitions we cannot see; There is a light of ours, which our adversaries may see, and will not; which is truly the light of this Text, the light of good works. Though our zeale to good works shine out assiduously, day by day in our Sermons, and shine out powerfully in the Homilies of our Church, composed expresly to that purpose, and shine out actually in our many sumptuous buildings, and rich endowments, (in which works, we of this Kingdome, in this last Century, since the Reformation of Religion, have perhaps exceeded our Fathers, in any one hundred of yeares, whilst they lived under the Romane perswasion) yet still they cry out, we

2 Part
Vt videant

Cantiprat.
l. 1. c. 9

Epist. 18
ad Cyrill:
Jerosolym.

are enemies of this light, and abhorre good works. As I have heard
them, in some obscure places abroad, preach, that here in England,
we had not onely no true Church, no true Priesthood, no true Sacraments, but that we have no materiall Churches, no holy Convocations,
no observing of Sundayes, or Holy dayes, no places to serve God in;
so I have heard them preach, that we doe not onely not advance, but
360 that we cry downe, and discredit, and disswade, and discountenance
the doctrine of good works. It is enough to say to them, as the Angel
said to the Devill, *Increpet te Dominus, The Lord rebuke thee.* And
the Lord does rebuke them, in enabling us to proceed in these pious
works, which, with so notorious falshood they deny; And we doe
rebuke them, the best and most powerfull way, in that, (as the Apostle
sayes) *we consider one another,* (consider the necessities of others)
and provoke one another to love, and good workes.

But then, if this be Gods end in our good works, *ut videant
homines,* that men may see them, why is Christ so earnest, in this
370 very sermon as to say, *Take heed you do not your almes before men,
to be seene of them?* Is there no contradiction in these? far from it;
The intent of both precepts together make up this doctrine, That we
doe them not therefore, not to that end, that men may see them. So
far we must come, that men must see them, but we must not rest
there; for, it is but *Sic luceat, Let your light shine out so,* it is not,
let it shine out therefore; Our doing of good workes must have a
farther end, then the knowledge of men, as we shall see, towards our
end, anon.

Men must see them then, and see them to be workes, *Vt videant
380 opera, That they may see your works:* which is a word that implies
difficulty, and paine, and labour, and is accompanied with some loath-
nesse, with some colluctation. Doe such workes, for Gods sake, as are
hard for thee to doe. In such a word does God deliver his Commandement of the Sabbath; not that word, which in that language signifies
ordinary and easie works, but servile and laborious workes, toylesome
and gainefull workes, those workes thou maist not doe upon the
Sabbath. But those workes, in the vertue of the precept of this text,
thou must doe in the sight of men; those that are hard for thee to
doe. *David* would not consecrate nor offer unto God, that which cost
390 him nothing; first he would buy *Araunahs* threshing floare at a

Iude 9

Heb. 10.24

Mat. 6.1

Opera

2 Sam. 24.24

valuable price, and then he would dedicate it to God. To give old cloathes, past wearing, to the poore, is not so good a worke as to make new for them. To give a little of your superfluities, not so acceptable as the widows gift, that gave all. To give a poore soule a farthing at that doore, where you give a Player a shilling, is not equall dealing; for, this is to give God *quisquilias frumenti, The refuse of the wheat.* But doe thou some such things, as are truly works in our sense, such as are against the nature, and ordinary practice of worldly men to doe; some things, by which they may see, that thou dost prefer God before honour, and wife, and children, and hadst rather build, and endow some place, for Gods service, then poure out money to multiply titles of honour upon thy selfe, or enlarge joyntures, and portions, to an unnecessary, and unmeasurable proportion, when there is enough done before.

Let men see that that thou doest, to be a worke, qualified with some difficulty in the doing, and then those workes, to be good workes, *Videant opera bona, that they may see your good works.* They are not good works how magnificent soever, if they be not directed to good ends. A superstitious end, or a seditious end vitiates the best worke. Great contributions have beene raised, and great summes given, to build, and endow Seminaries, and schooles, and Colledges in forraine parts; but that hath a superstitious end. Great contributions have beene raised, and great summes given at home, for the maintenance of such refractary persons, as by opposing the government and discipline of the Church, have drawne upon themselves, silencings, and suspensions, and deprivations; but that hath a seditious end. But, give so, as in a rectified conscience, and not a distempered zeale, (a rectified conscience is that, that hath the testimony and approbation of most good men, in a succession of times, and not to rely occasionally upon one or a few men of the separation, for the present) give so, as thou maist sincerely say, God gave me this, to give thus, and so it is a good worke. So it must be, *A worke* (something of some importance) and a *good worke,* (not depraved with an ill end) and then *your worke, Vt videant opera vestra, That they may see your good works.*

They are not your works, if that that you give be not your owne. Nor is it your own, if it were ill gotten at first. How long soever it have beene possessed, or how often soever it have beene transformed,

Mar. 12.42

Amos 8.6

Opera Bona

Opera bona vestra

from money to ware, from ware to land, from land to office, from office to honour, the money, the ware, the land, the office, the honour
430 is none of thine, if, in thy knowledge, it were ill gotten at first.

Luke 19.8 *Zacheus,* in S. *Luke,* gives halfe his goods to the poore; but it is halfe of his, his owne; for there might be goods in his house, which were none of his. Therefore in the same instrument, he passes that scrutiny, If I have taken any thing unjustly, I restore him foure-fold. First let that that was ill gotten, be deducted, and restored, and then, of the rest, which is truly thine owne, give cheerefully. When *Moses*

Psal. 90.10 saies, that our yeares are three score and ten, if we deduct from that terme, all the houres of our unnecessary sleep, of superfluous sittings at feasts, of curiosity in dressing, of largenesse in recreations, of
440 plotting, and compassing of vanities, or sinnes, scarce any man of threescore and ten, would be ten years old, when he dyes. If we should deale so with worldly mens estates, (defalce unjust gettings) it would abridge and attenuate many a swelling Inventory. Till this defalcation, this scrutiny be made, that you know what's your owne, what's other mens, as your Tombe shall be but a monument of your rotten bones, how much gold or marble soever be bestowed upon it, so that Hospitall, that free-schoole, that Colledge that you shall build, and endow, will bee but a monument of your bribery, your extortion, your oppression; and God, who will not be in debt, (though he owe
450 you nothing that built it) may be pleased to give the reward of all that, to them, from whom that which was spent upon it, was un-

Prov. 13.22 justly taken; for, *The wealth of the sinner is laid up for the righteous,* saies *Solomon.* The sinner may doe pious works, and the righteous may be rewarded for them; the world may thinke of one founder, and God knowes another. That which is enjoyn'd in the name of *light* here, is *works,* (not trifles) and *good works,* (made good by the good ends they are directed to) and then *your workes* (done out of that which is truly your owne) and *by seeing this light,* men will be mov'd to *glorifie your Father which is in Heaven;* which is the true
460 end of all; that men may see them, but see them therefore, *To glorifie your Father which is in Heaven.*

Patrem,   He does not say, that by seeing your good works, men shall glorifie
non Filios your sonnes upon earth. And yet truly, even that part of the reward, and retribution is worth a great deale of your cost, and your almes;

that God shall establish your posterity in the world, and in the good
opinion of good men. As you have your estates, you have your
children from God too. As it is *Davids* recognition, *Dominus pars*   Psal. 16.5
hæreditatis meæ, The Lord is the portion of mine inheritance, so the
Possedi virum à Domino, was *Eves* Recognition upon the birth of   Gen. 4.1
⁷⁰ her first son, *Cain, I have gotten, I possesse a man from the Lord.*
Now that that man that thou possessest from the Lord, thy son, may
possesse that land that thou possessest from the Lord, it behooves
thee to be righteous; for so, (by that righteousnesse) thou becomest
a foundation for posterity, (*The righteous is an everlasting founda-*   Prov. 10.25
tion) his light, (his good workes) shall be a chearefull light unto
him; (for, *The light of the righteous rejoyceth him.*) They shall be   Prov. 13.9
so in this life, and, *He shall have hope in his death,* saith *Solomon;*   Prov. 14.32
that is, hope for himself in another world, and hope of his posterity in
this world; for, saies he, *He leaveth an inheritance to his childrens*   Prov. 13.22
⁸⁰ *children;* that is, an inheritance, out of which hee hath taken, and
restored all that was unjustly got from men, and taken a bountifull
part, which he hath offered to God in pious uses, that the rest may
descend free from all claimes, and encumbrances upon his childrens
children. *The righteous is mercifull, and lendeth,* saies *David.* Merci-   Psal. 37.26
full as his Father in Heaven is mercifull; that is, in perpetuall, not   [Luke 6.36]
transitory endowments, (for, God did not set up his lights, his Sun,
and his Moone for a day, but for ever, and such should our light,
or good works be too.) Hee is mercifull, and he lendeth; to whom?
for to the poore he giveth; he looks for no returne from them, for
⁹⁰ they are *the waters upon which he casts his bread.* Yet he lendeth;   Eccles. 11.1
He that hath pity on the poore, lendeth to the Lord. The righteous is   Prov. 19.17
mercifull and lendeth, and then, (as *David* addes there) *His seed is*
blessed. Blessed in this (which followes there) that he *shall inherit*   Psal. 37.29
the land, and dwell therein for ever, (which he ratifies againe, *Surely*   Psal. 112.6
he shall not be moved for ever; that is, he shall never be moved, in
his posterity) And as he is blessed that way, blessed in the establishment of his possession upon his childrens children, so is he blessed
in this, that his honour, and good name shall bee poured out as a
fragrant oyle upon his posterity, *The righteous shall be had in*   Ibid.
¹⁰⁰ *everlasting remembrance.* Their memory shall be alwaies alive, and
alwaies fresh in their posterity, when *The name of the wicked shall*   Prov. 10.7

rot. So then, *the fruit of the righteous is the tree of life,* saies *Solomon;* that is, the righteous shall produce plants, that shall grow up, and flourish; so his posterity shall be a tree of life to many generations;

and then, *The glory of children are their Fathers,* saies that wise King; As Fathers receive comfort from good children, so children receive glory from good parents; in this are children glorified, that they had righteous Fathers, that lent unto the Lord. So that, (to recollect these peeces) it is no small reward that God affords you, 510 if men, seeing your good workes, glorifie, that is, esteeme, and respect, and love, and honour your children upon earth. But it is not onely that; your good workes shall bee an occasion of carrying glory upon the right object, They shall *glorifie your Father, which is in heaven.*

It is not *the Father* which is in Heaven; that they should glorifie God, as the common Father of all, by creation. For, for that they need not your light, your good works; *The Heavens declare the*
glory of God, saies *David;* that is, glorifie him in an acknowledgement, that he is the Father of them, and of all other things by creation.
520 *Is not hee thy Father? hath he not made thee?* is an interrogatory ministred by *Moses,* to which all things must answer with the
Prophet *Malachie,* yes, *He is our Father, for he hath made us.* But that's not the paternity of this text, as God is Father of us all by creation. Nor as he is a Father of some in a more particular consideration, in giving them large portions, great patrimonies in this world; for, thus, he may be my Father and yet disinherit me; hee may give me plenty of temporall blessings, and withhold from me spirituall, and eternall blessings. Now, to see this, men need not your
light, your good workes; for, they see dayly, That *he maketh his sun* 530 *to shine on the evill, and on the good; and causeth it to raine on the just, and the unjust;* He feeds Goates as well as Sheepe, he gives the wicked temporall blessings, as well as the righteous. These then are not the paternities of our text, that men, by this occasion, glorifie God as the Father of all men by creation, nor as the Father of all rich men, by their large patrimonies, not as he is the Father, not as he is a Father, but as he is *your Father,* as he is made yours, as he is become yours, by that particular grace of using the temporall blessings which he hath given you, to his glory, in letting

your light shine before men. For, it were better God disinherited
540 us so, as to give us nothing, then that he gave us not the grace to use
that that he gave us, well: without this, all his bread were stone, and   Mat. 7.9
all his fishes serpents, all his temporall liberality malediction. How
much happier had that man beene, that hath wasted thousands in
play, in riot, in wantonnesse, in sinfull excesses, if his parents had
left him no more at first, then he hath left himselfe at last? How
much nearer to a kingdome in Heaven had hee beene, if he had
beene borne a begger here? Nay, though he have done no ill, (of
such excessive kinds) how much happier had he beene, if he had had
nothing left him, if hee have done no good? There cannot be a more
550 fearfull commination upon man, nor a more dangerous dereliction
from God, then when God saies, *I will not reprove thee for thy*   Ps. 50.8
sacrifices; Though thou offer none, I care not, Ile never tell thee of   and 12
it, nor reprove thee for it, I will not reprove thee for thy sacrifices.
And when he saies, (as he does there) *If I bee hungry I will not tell*
thee; I will not awake thy charity, I will not excite thee, not provoke
thee, with any occasion of feeding me, in feeding the poore. When
God shall say to me, I care not whether you come to Church or no,
whether you pray or no, repent or no, confesse, receive or no, this
is a fearfull dereliction; so is it, when he saies to a rich man, I care
560 not whether your light shine out, or no, whether men see your good
works or no; I can provide for my glory other waies. For, certainly
God hath not determined his purpose, and his glory so much in that,
to make some men rich that the poore might be relieved, (for, that
ends in bodily reliefe) as in this, that he hath made some men poore,
whereby the rich might have occasion to exercise their charity; for,
that reaches to spirituall happinesse; for which use, the poore doe not
so much need the rich, as the rich need the poore; the poore may
better be saved without the rich, then the rich without the poore.
But when men shall see, that that God, who is the Father of us all, by
570 creating us, and the father of all the rich, by enriching them, is also
become your father, yours by adoption, yours by infusion of that
particular grace, to doe good with your goods, then are you made
blessed instruments of that which God seeks here, his glory, They
shall *glorifie your father which is in heaven.*

Glory is so inseparable to God, as that God himself is called *Glory,*   *Gloria*

They changed their Glory into the similitude of an Oxe; Their glory,
their true God into an inglorious Idol. *That glory may dwell in our
land,* sayes he; that is, that God may dwell therein. The first end of
letting our light to shine before men, is, that they may know Gods
⁵⁸⁰ proceedings; but, the last end to which all conduces, is, that God
may have glory. Whatsoever God did first in his own bosome, in his
own decree, (what that was, contentious men will needs wrangle)
whatsoever that first act was, Gods last end in that first act of his was
his own glory. And therefore to impute any inglorious or ignoble thing
to God, comes too neare blasphemy. And be any man who hath any
sense or taste of noblenesse, or honour, judge, whether there be any
glory in the destruction of those creatures whom they have raised,
till those persons have deserved ill at their hands, and in some way
have damnified them, or dishonoured them. Nor can God propose
⁵⁹⁰ that for glory, to destroy man till he finde cause in man. Now, this
glory, to which Christ bends all in this Text, (that men by seeing
your good works, might glorifie your Father) consists especially in
these two declarations, Commemoration, and Imitation; a due celebration of former founders and benefactors, and a pious proceeding
according to such precedents, is this glorifying of God.

    When God calls himself so often, *The God of Abraham, of Isaac,
and of Iacob,* God would have the world remember, that *Abraham,
Isaac,* and *Iacob* were extraordinary men, memorable men. When
God sayes, *Though these three men, Noah, Daniel, and Iob were*
⁶⁰⁰ *here, they should not deliver this people,* God would have it knowne,
that *Noah, Daniel,* and *Iob* were memorable men, and able to doe
much with him. When the Holy Ghost is so carefull to give men
their additions, That *Iabal was the father of such as dwell in Tents, &*
*keep Cattell, & Iubal the father of Harpers, and Organists, and
Tubal-Cain of all Gravers in Brasse and Iron,* And when he presents
with so many particularities every peece of worke, that *Hiram* of
Tyre wrought in Brasse for the furnishing of *Solomons* Temple, God
certainly is not afraid that his honour will be diminished, in the
honourable mentioning of such men as have benefited the world by
⁶¹⁰ publique good works. The wise man seemes to settle himselfe upon
that meditation; *let us now praise famous men,* sayes he, *and our
fathers that begot us;* and so he institutes a solemne commemoration,

and gives a catalogue of *Enoch,* and *Abraham,* and *Moses,* and *Aaron,*
and so many more, as possesse six Chapters; nor doth he ever end
the meditation till he end his booke; so was he fixt upon the commemoration of good men; as S. *Paul* likewise feeds and delights him-   Heb. 11
selfe in the like meditation, even from *Abel.* It is therefore a wretched
impotency, not to endure the commemoration, and honourable mentioning of our Founders and Benefactors. God hath delivered us, and
20 our Church, from those straights, in which, some Churches of the
Reformation have thought themselves to be, when they have made
Canons, That there should be no Bell rung, no dole given, no mention made of the dead at any Funerall, lest that should savour of
superstition. The Holy Ghost hath taught us the difference between
praising the dead, and praying for the dead, betweene commemorating of Saints, and invocating of Saints. We understand what *David*
meanes, when he sayes, *This honour have all his Saints,* and what S.   Psal. 149.9
Paul meanes, when he sayes, *Vnto the only wise God be honour, and*   1 Tim. 1.17
glory, for ever and ever. God is honoured in due honour given to his
30 Saints, and glorified in the commemoration of those good men whose
light hath so shined out before men, that they have seen their good
workes. But then he is glorified more, in our imitation, then in our
commemoration.

    Herein is my Father glorified, (sayes Christ) *that ye beare much*   *Gloria ex*
fruit. The seed sowed in good ground, bore some an hundred fold,   *Imitatione*
the least thirty. The seed (in this case) is the example that is before   John 15.8
you, of those good men, whose light hath shined out so, that you have
seene their good workes. Let this seed, these good examples bring   Mar. 4.20
forth hundreds, and sixties, and thirties in you, much fruit; for herein
40 is your Father glorified, that you beare much fruit. Of which plentifull encrease, I am afraid there is one great hinderance that passes
through many of you, that is, that when your Will lyes by you, in
which some little lamp of this light is set up, something given to
God in pious uses, if a Ship miscarry, if a Debtor break, if your
state be any way empaired, the first that suffers, the first that is
blotted out of the Will, is God and his Legacy; and if your estates
encrease, portions encrease, and perchance other legacies, but Gods
portion and legacy stands at a stay. Christ left two uses of his passion;
application and imitation. *He suffered for us,* sayes the Apostle; for   1 Pet. 2.21

650 us, that is, that we might make his death ours, apply his death, and then (as it follows there) *he left us an example.* So Christ gives us two uses of the Reformation of Religion; first, the doctrine, how to doe good works without relying upon them, as meritorious; and then example, many, very many men (and more by much, in some kindes of charity since the Reformation of Religion, then before) even in this City, whose light hath shined out before you, and you have seen their good works. That as this noble City hath justly acquired the reputation and the testimony of all who have had occasion to consider their dealings in that kinde, that they deale most 660 faithfully, most justly, most providently, in all things which are committed to their trust for pious uses, from others, not only in a full employment of that which was given, but in an improvement thereof, and then an employment of that emprovement to the same pious use, so every man in his particular may propose to himselfe, some of those blessed examples which have risen amongst your selves, and follow that, and exceed that; That as your lights are Torches, and not petty Candles, and your Torches better then others Torches, so he also may be a larger example to others, then others have been to him, for, *Herein is your Father glorified, if you beare* 670 *much fruit,* and that is the end of all, that we all doe, *That men seeing it, may glorifie our Father which is in heaven.*

Number 4.

Preached at Saint Pauls.

PHILIPPIANS 3.2 *BEWARE OF THE CONCISION.*

THIS IS ONE of those places of Scripture, which afford an argument for *that*, which I finde often occasion to say, That there are not so *eloquent* books in the world, as the *Scriptures*. For there is not onely that *non refugit*, which *Calvin* speaketh of in this place, (*Non refugit in Organis suis Spiritus Sanctus leporem & facetias*, The *Holy Ghost* in his Instruments, (in those whose tongues or pens he makes use of) doth not forbid, nor decline elegant and cheerfull, and delightfull expression; but as God gave his Children a bread of *Manna*, that tasted to every man like that that he liked 10 best, so hath God given us *Scriptures*, in which the plain and simple man may heare God speaking to him in his own plain and familiar language, and men of larger capacity, and more curiosity, may heare God in that Musique that they love best, in a curious, in an harmonious style, unparalleled by any. For, that also *Calvin* adds in that place, that there is no secular Authour, *Qui jucundis vocum allusionibus, & figuris magis abundat*, which doth more abound with perswasive *figures* of Rhetorique, nor with musicall *cadences* and *allusions*, and assimilations, and conformity, and correspondency of words to one another, then some of the *Secretaries of the Holy Ghost*, 20 some of the authours of some books of the Bible doe. Of this Rule, this Text is an example. These *Philippians*, amongst whom Saint *Paul* had planted the Gospell in all sincerity, and impermixt, had admitted certain new men, that preached *Traditionall*, and *Additionall* Doctrines, the *Law* with the *Gospell*, *Moses* with *Christ*,

[Wisd.
16.20, 21]

103

Circumcision with *Baptisme.* To these new Convertites, these new
Doctors inculcated often that charm, *You are the Circumcision,* you
are *they* whom God hath sealed to himself by the Seale of *Circum-*
cision; They whom God hath distinguished from all Nations, by
the marke of Circumcision; *They* in whom God hath imprinted,
³⁰ (and that in so high a way, as by a *Sacrament*) an internall Circumcision, in an externall; and will you breake this *Seale* of Circumcision? will you deface this *marke* of Circumcision? will you depart
from this *Sacrament* of Circumcision? you are the Circumcision.
Now Saint *Paul* meets with these men upon their haunt; and even
in the sound of that word which they so often pressed; he sayes they
presse upon you Circumcision, but *beware of Concision,* of tearing
the Church of God, of *Schismes,* and separations from the Church
of God, of aspersions and imputations *upon* the Church of God,
either by imaginary superfluities, or imaginary defectivenesse, in

Verse 3   ⁴⁰ that Church: for, saith the Apostle, *We are the Circumcision,* we who
worship God in the *Spirit,* and rejoyce in *Christ Jesus,* and have no
confidence in the flesh. If therefore they will set up another Circumcision beyond this Circumcision, if they will continue a significative,
a relative, a preparative figure, after the substance, the body, Christ
Jesus is manifested to us, a legall Circumcision in the flesh, after the
spirituall Circumcision in the heart is established by the Gospell,
their end is not *Circumcision,* but *Concision:* they pretend *Reforma-*
tion, but they intend *Destruction,* a tearing, a renting, a wounding
the body, and frame, and peace of the Church, and by all means,
⁵⁰ and in all cases *Videte Concisionem, Beware of Concision.*

Divisio   First then, we shall from these words consider, the lothnesse of God
to lose us. For, first, he leaves us not without a Law, he *bids* and he
forbids, and then he does not surprise us with *obsolete laws,* he leaves
not his laws without *Proclamations,* he refreshes to our memories,
and represents to us our duties, with such commonefactions as these
in our Text, *Videte, Cavete,* this and this I have commanded you,
Videte, see that ye do it, this and this will hinder you, *Cavete,* beware
ye do it not, *Beware of Concision.*

         And this, thus derived, and digested into these three branches:
⁶⁰ first, Gods lothnesse to lose us; and then his way of *drawing* us to
him, by manifestation of his will in a law; and lastly his way of

holding us with him, by making that law effectual upon us, by these his frequent commonefactions, *Videte, Cavete,* looke to it, beware of it, this will be our first part. And then our second will be the thing it self that falls under this inhibition, and caution, which is *Concision,* that is, a tearing, a renting, a shredding in peeces that which should be intire. In which second part, we shall also have, (as we had in the former) three branches; for, we shall consider, first, *Concisionem corporis,* the shredding of the *body* of Christ into fragments,
70 by unnecessary wrangling in *Doctrinall points;* and then, *Concisionem vestis,* the shredding of the *garment* of Christ into rags, by unnecessary wrangling in matter of *Discipline,* and *ceremoniall* points; and lastly, *Concisionem spiritus,* (which will follow upon the former two) the concision of thine owne spirit, and heart, and minde, and *soule,* and *conscience,* into perplexities, and into sandy, and incoherent doubts, and scruples, and jealousies, and suspitions of *Gods purpose* upon thee, so as that thou shalt not be able to recollect thy self, nor reconsolidate thy self, upon any assurance, and peace with God, which is onely to be had in Christ, and by his Church. *Videte*
80 *Concisionem,* beware of tearing the *body,* the *Doctrine;* beware of tearing the *Garment,* the *Discipline;* beware of tearing thine owne spirit, and *conscience,* from her adhæsion, her agglutination, her cleaving to God, in a holy *tranquillity,* and acquiescence in his *promise,* and *mercy,* in the *merits* of his Sonne, applyed by the holy Ghost, in the Ministery of the Church.

For our first consideration, of Gods lothnesse to lose us, this is argument enough, That we are here now, *now* at the participation of that grace, which God alwayes offers to al such Congregations as these, gathered in his name. For, I pray God there stand any one
90 amongst us here now, that hath not done something since *yesterday,* that made him unworthy of being here to day; and who, if he had been left under the damp, and mist of *yesterdayes sinne,* without the light of *new grace,* would never have found way hither of himself. If God be weary of me, and would faine be rid of me, he needs not repent that he wrapped me up in the *Covenant,* and derived me of *Christian parents,* (though he gave me a great help in *that*) nor repent that he bred me in a *true Church,* (though he afforded me a great assistance in *that*) nor repent that he hath brought me *hither*

1 Part
Vult omnes

now, to the participation of his *Ordinances,* (though thereby also
¹⁰⁰ I have a great advantage) for, if God be weary of me, and would
be rid of me, he may finde enough in me now, and here, to let me
perish. A present *levity* in me that speake, a present *formality* in you
that heare, a present *Hypocrisie* spread over us all, would justifie
God, if now, and here, he should forsake us. When our blessed

Luke 18.8   Saviour sayes, *When the Son of man comes, shall he finde faith upon
earth?* we need not limit that question so, if he come to a *West-
minster,* to an *Exchange,* to an *Army,* to a *Court,* shall he finde *faith*
there? but if he come to a *Church,* if he come hither, shall he finde

[1 Pet. 4.17]   *faith* here? If (as Christ speaks in another sense, That *Judgement*
¹¹⁰ *should begin at his owne house,*) the great and generall judgement

[1 Thes.   should begin now at this *his house,* and that the first that should be
4.17]   taken up in the clouds, to meet the Lord Jesus, should be we, that
                are met now in this his house, would we be glad of that acceleration,

[Mat. 16.8]   or would we thank him for that haste? Men *of little faith,* I feare
Iob 1.6   we would not. *There was a day, when the Sonnes of God presented
themselves before the Lord, and Satan came also amongst them;* one
Satan amongst many Sonnes of God. Blessed Lord, is not our case
far otherwise? do not we, (we, who, as we are but *we,* are all the
Sonnes of Satan) present our selves before thee, and yet, thou Lord
¹²⁰ art amongst us? Is not the spirit of slumber and *wearinesse* upon one,
and the spirit of *detraction,* and mis-interpretation upon another;
upon one the spirit of *impenitence* for former sinnes, and the spirit
of *recidivation* into old, or of *facility* and opennesse to admit tentations into new upon another? We, as we are but *we,* are all the Sonnes
of Satan, and thou Lord, the onely Sonne of God, onely amongst us.
If thou Lord wert weary of me, and wouldest be rid of me, (may
many a soule here say) Lord thou knowest, and I know many a
midnight, when thou mightest have been rid of me, if thou hadst

Ier. 31.28   left me to my selfe then. But *vigilavit Dominus,* the Lord vouchsafed
Prov. 8.31 ¹³⁰ to *watch* over me, and *deliciæ ejus,* the delight of the Lord was to be
with me; And what is there in me, but his *mercy?* but then, what is
there in his mercy, that that may not reach *to all,* as well as to *me?*
The Lord is loth to lose any, the Lord would not the death of *any;*
not of *any sinner;* much lesse if he do not see him, nor consider him
so; the Lord would not lose him, *though a sinner,* much lesse *make*

him a sinner, that he might be lost: *Vult omnes,* the Lord would have   [1 Tim. 2.4]
all men come unto him, and be saved, which was our first consideration, and we have done with that, and our second is, The way
by which he leads us to him, that he declares and manifests his will
unto us, in a *Law,* he *bids,* and he *forbids.*

   The laborers in the Vine-yard took it ill at the Stewards hand, and   *Lex*
at his Masters too, that those which came late to the labour, were   Mat. 20.12
made equall with them, who had borne the heate, and the burden of
the day. But if the Steward, or the Master had never meant, or
actually never had given any thing at all, to them that had borne
the heate and the burden of the day, there had been much more
cause of complaint, because there had passed a *contract* between them.
So hath there passed a *contract* between God, and us, *Beleeve,* and   [Luke 10.28]
thou shalt live, Do this, and thou shalt live. And in this especially
hath God expressed his love to us, and his lothenesse to lose us, that
he hath passed such a *contract* with us, and manifested to us a way,
to come to him. We say, every day, in his owne prayer, *Fiat voluntas
tua, thy will be done;* that is, done *by us,* as well as done *upon us.* But
this petition presumes another; the *Fiat* supposes a *Patefiat voluntas,*
if it must be done, it must be known. If man were put into this
world, and under an obligation of doing the will of God, upon
damnation, and had no meanes to *know* that will which he was
bound to doe, of all creatures he were the most miserable. That which
we read, *Lord what is man that thou takest knowledge of him?* the   Psal. 144.3
Vulgat edition, and the *Fathers* following the *Septuagint,* read thus,
Quia innotuisti ei, Lord what is man that he should have any knowledge of *thee,* that thou shouldest make thy selfe known to *him?*
This is the heighth of the mercy of God, this innotescence, this
manifestation of himselfe to *us.* Now what is this innotescence, this
manifestation of God to us? It is, say our old Expositors, the *law.*
That's that, which is so often called *the face of God,* and the *light of
his Countenance;* for, *facies Dei est, qua nobis innotescit,* that's Gods   August.
face, by which God is known to us, and that's his *law,* the declaration
of his will to me, and my way to him. When Christ reproaches those
hard-hearted men, that had not *fed him,* when he *was hungry,* nor
clothed him, when he was naked, and that they say, *Lord when did*   Mat. 25.44
we see thee naked, or see thee hungry? (inconsiderate men, or men

loth to give, the penurious and narrow soule, shall not see an occasion of charity, when it is presented, which is a heavy blindnesse, and
obcæcation, not to see occasions of doing good) yet those men doe
not say, when did we see thee *at all,* as though they had never seen
him? The blindest man that is, hath the face of God so turned
towards him, as that he may be seen by him; even the *naturall man*
hath so; for, therefore does the Apostle make him inexcusable, if in

Rom. 1.20

¹⁸⁰ the visible worke, he doe not see the *invisible* God. But all sight of
God, is by the benefit of a *law;* the naturall man sees him by a law
written in his *heart, the Jew,* by a law given by *Moses,* the Christian,
in a clearer glasse, for, his law is the *Gospell.* But there is more mercy,
that is, more manifestation in this text, then all this. For, besides
the naturall mans seeing God, in a law, in the faculties of his owne
nature, (which we consider to be the work of the whole *Trinity,* in

[Gen. 1.26]

that *Faciamus hominem, Let us make man in our own Image,* let
us shine out in him, so as that he may be a glasse, in which he may
see us, in himselfe) and besides the *Jews* seeing of God in the law
¹⁹⁰ written in the stone *tables,* (which we consider to be the worke of
the *Father*) And besides the Christians seeing of God, in the law
written in *bloud,* (in which we consider especially *the Sonne*) there
is in this text an operation, a manifestation of God, proper to the
Holy Ghost, and wrought by his holy suggestions and inspirations,
That God does not onely speake to us, but call upon us; not onely
give us a Law, but *Proclamations* upon that law, that he refreshes to
our memories, generall duties, by such particular warnings, and
excitations, and commonefactions, as in this text, *Videte, Beware,*
which is the last branch of this part, though it be the first word of
²⁰⁰ our text, *Videte, Beware.*

Videte

Nothing exalts Gods goodnesse towards us, more then this, that
he multiplies the meanes of his mercy to us, so, as that no man can
say, *once* I remember I might have been saved, *once* God called unto
mee, *once* hee opened mee a doore, a passage into heaven, but I
neglected *that,* went not in then, and God never came more. No
doubt, God hath come often to that doore since, and knocked, and
staid at that doore; And if I knew who it were that said this, I
should not doubt to make that suspitious soule see, that God is at

Psal. 62.11

that doore *now. God hath spoken once, and twice have I heard him;*

for the foundation of all, God hath spoken but *once,* in his Scriptures. Therefore doth Saint *Jude* call that *fidem semel traditam,* the faith *once* delivered to the Saints; once, that is, *at once;* not at once so, all at one time, or in one mans age; the Scriptures were not delivered *so;* for, God *spoke by the mouth of the Prophets, that have been, since the world beganne;* But, at once, that is, *by one way,* by *writing,* by Scriptures; so, as that after that was done, after God had declared his whole will, in the *Law,* and the *Prophets,* and the *Gospell,* there was no more to bee added. *God hath spoken once,* in his Scriptures, *and wee have heard him twice,* at *home,* in our owne readings, and againe and againe *here,* in his *Ordinances.* This is the heighth of Gods goodnesse, that he gives us his *Law,* and a *Comment* upon that Law, *Proclamations,* declarations upon that Law. For, without these subsequent helpes, even the law it selfe might be mistaken; as you see it was, when Christ was put to rectifie them, with his *Audiistis,* and *Audiistis,* this you have heard, and this hath been told you, *Ego autem dico,* but this *I say, ab initio,* from the beginning it was not so, the foundations were not thus laid, and upon the foundations laid by God in the Scriptures, and not upon the super-edifications of men, in traditionall additions, must wee build. In stormes and tempests at sea men come sometimes to cut down Galleries, and teare up Cabins, and cast them overboard to ease the ship, and sometimes to hew downe the Mast it selfe, though without that Mast the ship can make no way; but no foule weather can make them tear out the keele of the ship, upon which the ship is built. In cases of necessity, the Church may forbeare her *Galleries,* and *Cabinets,* meanes of ease and conveniency; yea, and her *Mast* too, meanes of her growth, and propagation, and enlarging of her selfe, and be content to *hull* it out, and consist in her present, or a worse state, during the storme. But to the *keele* of the *ship,* to the *fundamentall articles* of Religion, may no violence, in any case, be offered.

God multiplies his mercies to us, in his divers ways of speaking to us. *Cæli enarrant,* says *David, The heavens declare the glory of God;* and not onely by showing, but by *saying;* there is a *language* in the heavens; for it is *enarrant,* a verball declaration; and, as it followes literally, *Day unto day uttereth speech.* This is the true harmony of the Spheares, which every man may heare. Though he understand

Margin notes:

verse 3

[Luke 1.70]

Mat. 5.[21, 27, 38]
[Mat. 19.8, 9]

Psal. 19.1;
Vulg., 18.2]

no tongue but his owne, he may heare God in the motions of the same, in the seasons of the yeare, in the vicissitudes and revolutions of Church, and State, in the voice of Thunder, and lightnings, and
250 other declarations of his power. This is Gods *English* to thee, and his *French,* and his *Latine,* and *Greek,* and *Hebrew* to others. God

[Gen. 11.7]

once confounded languages, that conspiring men might not understand one another; but never so, as that all men might not under-

[Acts 2.4-8]

stand *him.* When the holy Ghost fell upon the Apostles, they spoke so, as that all men understood them, *in their owne tongues.* When the holy Ghost fell upon the waters, in the Creation, God spoke so, in his language of *Workes,* as that all men may understand them. For, in this language, the language of *workes,* the *Eye* is the *eare, seeing* is *hearing.* How often does the holy Ghost call upon us, in
260 the Scriptures, *Ecce, quia os Domini locutum, Behold, the mouth of the Lord hath spoken it?* he calls us to *behold,* (which is the office of the *eye*) and that that we are to behold, is the *voice* of God, belonging to the eare; seeing is hearing, in Gods first language, the language of *works.* But then God translates himself, in particular *works; nationally,* he speaks in particular judgments, or deliverances to one *nation;* and, *domestically,* he speaks that language to a particular family; and so *personally* too, he speaks to every particular soul. God will speak unto me, in that voice, and in that way, which I am most delighted with, and hearken most to. If I be *covetous,* God wil tel me
270 that heaven is a pearle, a treasure. If cheerfull and affected with mirth, that heaven is all *Joy.* If ambitious, and hungry of preferment, that it is all *Glory.* If sociable, and conversable, that it is a *communion of Saints.* God will make a *Fever* speake to me, and tell me his minde, that there is no health but in *him;* God will make the *disfavour,* and frowns of *him* I depend upon, speake to me, and tell me his minde, that there is no safe dependence, no assurance but in *him;* God will make a *storme* at Sea, or a *fire* by land, speake to me, and tell mee his minde, that there is no perpetuity, no possession but in *him;* nay, God will make my *sinne* speake to me, and tell me his minde; even
280 my sinne shall bee a Sermon, and a Catechisme to me; God shall suffer mee to fall into some such sinne, as that by some circumstances in the sinne, or consequences from the sinne, I shall be drawn to hearken unto him; and whether I heare *Hosannaes,* acclamations,

and commendations, or *Crucifiges,* exclamations and condemnations from the world, I shall stil finde the voice and tongue of God, though in the mouth of the Devill, and his instruments. God is a declaratory God. The whole yeare, is, to his Saints, a continuall *Epiphany,* one day of manifestation. In every minute that strikes upon the *Bell,* is a syllable, nay a syllogisme from God. And, and in my *last Bell,* God 290 shall speake too; that Bell, when it tolls, shall tell me I am going, and when it rings out, shall tell you I am gone into the hands of that God, who is the God of the living and not of the dead, for, they dye not that depart in him. *Dives* pressed *Abraham* to send a preacher from the dead, to his brethren. This was to put God to a new language, when he had spoken sufficiently by *Moses,* and the *Prophets.* And yet, even in this language, the tongue of the dead, hath God spoken too. Saint *Hierome* says, that that Prophet *Jonas,* who was sent to *Niniveh,* was the same *man,* whom, beeing then a *child,* and dead in his mothers house, the widow of *Zarepta's* house, *Elias* the Prophet 300 raised to life againe; and so, God spoke to *Niniveh* in that language, in the tongue of the *dead.* But be that but *Problematicall,* wrapped up in a Traditionall, and Historicall faith, this is *Dogmaticall,* and irrefragable, that God hath spoken to the whole world in the tongue of the dead, in his Sonne *Christ Jesus,* the Lord of life, and yet the *first borne of the dead.* God is lothe to lose us, at worst, and therefore, did not, surely, reject us, before we were ill, (And that was our first) God hath drawn us to him, by manifesting his will, and our way in a law, and therefore, will not judge us at last, by any thing never revealed to us, (And that was our second) God holds us to him by 310 these remembrances, these common manifestations in our text, *Videte, Cavete,* and therefore let no man that does not heare God speaking to him, in this present voice, despaire that hee shall never heare him, but hearken still, and in one language or other, perchance a *sicknesse,* perchance a *sinne,* hee shall heare him, for these are severall Dialects in Gods language, severall instruments in Gods Consort; And this is our third consideration, and the end of this first part, the Prohibition, the Commonefaction, *Videte, Cavete;* And wee passe to our second generall part, and the three branches of *that,* that that falls under this Prohibition, *Videte Concisionem, Beware* 320 *the Concision.*

[Mat. 22.32]
Luke 16.27

Procemium
in Jonam
1 Reg. 17

[Col. 1.18]

Saint *Paul* embraces here, that elegancy of language familiar to the holy Ghost, They pretend *Circumcision,* they intend *Concision;* there is a certaine elegant and holy delicacy, a certaine holy *juvenility* in Saint *Pauls* choosing these words of this musicall cadence and ag- nomination, *Circumcision,* and *Concision;* But then this delicacy, and juvenility presents matter of gravity and soundnesse. Language must waite upon matter, and *words* upon *things.* In this case, ,(which indeed makes it a strange case) the matter is the forme; The matter, that is, the doctrine that we preach, is the forme, that is, the Soule,
³³⁰ the *Essence;* the language and words wee preach in, is but the Body, but the *existence.* Therefore, Saint *Paul,* who would not allow *Legall figures,* not Typicall figures, not Sacramentall figures, not Circum- cision it selfe, after the *body,* Christ Jesus, was once exhibited, does not certainely allow *Rhetoricall* figures, nor *Poeticall* figures, in the preaching, or hearing of Christ preached, so, as that that should bee the principall leader of hearer, or speaker. But this Saint *Paul* au- thoriseth in his owne practise, and the holy Ghost in *him,* That in elegant language, he incorporates, and invests sound and important Doctrine; for, though he choose *words* of musicall sound, *Circum-*
³⁴⁰ *cision* and *Concision,* yet it is a matter of weighty consideration that he intends in this Concision. Saint *Chrysostome,* and Saint *Hierome* both agree in this interpretation, That whereas *Circumcision* is an orderly, a usefull, a medicinall, a beneficiall pruning and paring off, that which is superfluous, *Conciditur quod temere, & inutiliter de- cerpitur,* Concision is a hasty and a rash plucking up, or cutting downe, and an unprofitable tearing, and renting into shreds and

Ier. 19.11

fragments, such, as the Prophet speaks of, *The breaking of a Potters vessell, that cannot be made up again.* Concision is, at best, *Solutio Continui,* The severing of that, which should be kept intire. In the
³⁵⁰ State, the aliening of the *head* from the body, or of the body from the head, is Concision; and *videte,* it is a fearefull thing to be guilty of *that.* In the *Church,* (which Church is not a *Monarchy,* otherwise then as she is united in her head, Christ Jesus) to constitute a Mon- archy, an universall *head* of the Church, to the dis-inherison, and to the tearing of the Crownes of Princes, who are heads of the Churches in their Dominions, this is Concision; and *videte,* it is a fearefull thing to be guilty of *that,* to advance a forein *Prelate.* In the family, where

God hath made man and wife, *one,* to divide with others, is *Concision;* and *videte,* it is a fearefull thing to be guilty of *that.* Generally, the tearing of that in peeces, which God intended should be kept intire, is this *Concision,* and falls under this Commonefaction, which implies an increpation, *videte, beware.* But because thus, *Concision* would receive a concision into infinite branches, we determined this consideration, at first, into these three; first, *Concisio Corporis,* the concision of the *body,* dis-union in *Doctrinall* things; and *Concisio vestis,* the Concision of the *garment,* dis-union in *Ceremoniall* things; and then *Concisio Spiritus,* the Concision of the Spirit, dis-union, *irresolution,* unsetlednesse, diffidence, and distrust in thine owne minde and conscience.

First, for this Concision of *the body,* of the body of Divinity, in *Doctrinall* things, since still Concision is *Solutio continui,* the breaking of that which should be intire, consider we first, what this *Continuum,* this that should be kept intire, is; and it is, sayes the Apostle, *Jesus himself. Omnis spiritus qui solvit Jesum,* (so the Antients reade that place) *Every spirit which dissolveth Jesus,* that breakes Jesus in peeces, that makes *Religion* serve turnes, that admits so much Gospell as may promove and advance present businesses, every such spirit is *not of God.* Not to professe the whole Gospell, *Totum Jesum,* not to beleeve all the Articles of faith, this is *Solutio continui,* a breaking of that which should be intire; and this is truly *concision.* Now with concision in this kinde, our greatest adversaries, they of the *Romane* heresie, and mis-perswasion, do not charge us. They do not charge us that we deny any article of any antient Creed: nor may they deny, that there is not enough for salvation in those antient Creeds. This is *Continuitas universalis,* a continuity, an intirenesse that goes through the whole Church; a skin that covers the whole body; the whole Church is bound to beleeve all the articles of faith. But then, there is *Continuitas particularis, Continuitas modi,* a continuity, a harmony, an intirenesse, that does not go thorough the whole Church; the whole Church does not alwaies agree in the manner of explication of all the articles of faith; but this may be a skin that covers some particular limbe of the body, and not another; one Church may expound an article thus, and some other some other way, as, in particular, the *Lutheran* Church expounds the article of *Christs descent*

Concisio Corporis

1 John 4.3

into hell, one way, and the *Calvinist* another. Now, in cases, where
neither exposition destroyes the article, in the substance thereof, it is
Concision, that is, *Solutio continui,* a breaking of that which should
be kept intire, for any man to breake the peace of that Church, in
which he hath received his *baptisme,* and hath his *station,* by advanc-
400 ing the exposition of any other Church, in that. And as this is *Concision, Solutio continui,* a breaking of that which is intire, to break
the peace of the Church, where we were baptized, by teaching otherwise then that Church teaches, in these things *De modo,* of the manner of expounding such or such articles of faith, so is there another
dangerous *Concision* too. For, to inoculate a forein bud, or to engraffe a forein bough, is *concision,* as well as the cutting off an arme
from the tree; to inoculate, cleaves the rinde, the bark; and to *engraffe,* cleaves the tree: it severs that which should be entire. So when
a particular Church, in a holy, and discreet modesty, hath abstained
410 from declaring her self in the exposition of some particular Articles,
or of some Doctrines, by faire consequence deducible from those
Articles, and contented her self with those generall things which are
necessary to salvation, (As the Church of *England* hath, in the Article
of *Christs descent into Hell*) it is *Concision,* it is *solutio Continui,*
a breaking of that which should be intire, to inoculate a new sense, or
engraffe a new exposition, which howsoever it may be true in it selfe,
it cannot be truly said, to be the sense of that Church; not perchance
because that Church was not of that mind, but because that Church
finding the thing it self to be no *fundamentall* thing, thought it un-
420 necessary to descend to particular declarations, when as in such declarations she must have departed from some other Church of the
Reformation, that thought otherwise, and in keeping her self within
those generall termes that were *necessary,* and sufficient, with a good
conscience she conserved peace and unity with all. *David,* in the person of every member of the Church, submits himself to that increpa-

Psal. 137.
[5,]6
tion, *Let my right hand forget her cunning, and let my tongue cleave
to the roof of my mouth, if I prefer not Jerusalem before my chiefest
joy.* Our chiefest joy, is, for the most part, our *own opinions,* especially
when they concur with other learned and good men too. But then,
430 *Jerusalem* is our love of the peace of the Church; and in such things
as do not violate foundations, let us prefer *Jerusalem* before our chief-

est Joy, love of peace before our own opinions, though concurrent with others. For, this is that, that hath misled many men, that the common opinion in the Church is necessarily the opinion of the Church. It is not so; not so in the *Romane* Church: There the common opinion is, That the blessed *Virgin Mary* was conceived without originall sin: But [it] cannot be said to be the opinion of that Church; nor may it be safely concluded in any Church: Most Writers in the Church have declared themselves this way, therefore the Church hath declared her self, for the declarations of the Church are done publiquely, and orderly, and at once. And when a Church hath declared her self so, in all things necessary and sufficient, let us possess our souls in peace, and not say that that Church hath, or presse that that Church would proceed to further declarations in lesse necessary particulars. When we are sure we have beleeved and practised, all that the Church hath recommended to us, in these generals, then, and not till then, let us call for more declarations; but in the mean time prefer *Jerusalem* before our chiefest joy, love of peace by a generall forbearance on all sides, rather then victory by wrangling, and uncharitablenesse. And let our right hand forget her cunning, (let us never set pen to paper to write) Let our tongue cleave to the roofe of our mouth, (let us never open our mouth to speake) of those things in which *Silence* was an Act of *Discretion,* and *Charity* before, but now is also an Act of *Obedience,* and of *Allegiance* and *Loyaltie.* But that which *David* said to the Lord, (*Psalme* 65.1) Let us also accommodate to the Lords anointed, *Tibi laus silentium,* our best sacrifice to both, is to be silent in those things. So then, this is *Concisio corporis,* that Concision of the *body,* which you are to beware in *Doctrinall things,* first, *non solvere Jesum,* not to dissolve, not to break Jesus in pieces, not to depart, in any respect, with any fundamentall Article of faith, for that is a skin that covers the whole body, an obligation that lies upon the whole *Church;* and then for that particular *Church,* in which you have your station, first, to conform your self to all that, in which she had evidently declared her self, and then not to impute to her, not to call such articles *hers, as she never avowd.* And our next *consideration* is *Concisio vestis, the tearing of the garment,* matter of *discipline,* and *government.*

Concisio
vestis

To a *Circumcision* of the *garment,* that is, to a paring, and taking away such *Ceremonies,* as were superstitious, or superfluous, of an ⁴⁷⁰ ill use, or of no use, our *Church* came in the beginning of the *Reformation.* To a *Circumcision* we came; but those *Churches* that came to a *Concision* of the *garment,* to an absolute taking away of *all ceremonies,* neither provided so safely for the *Church* it self in the substance thereof, nor for the exaltation of *Devotion in the Church.* Divide the law of the *Jews* into 2 halfs, and the *Ceremoniall* will be the greater; we cannot cal the *Morall* law, the *Jews* law; that was *ours* as wel as *theirs,* peculiar to none; but of that law which is peculiar to the *Jews, judicial* and *Ceremonial,* the *Ceremonial* is far the greater part. So great a care had God, of those things, which though they be ⁴⁸⁰ not of the *revenue* of *Religion,* yet are of the *subsidy* of Religion, and, though they be not the *soule* of the Church, yet are they those *Spirits*

2 Sam. 10

that unite soule and body together. *Hanun* did but *shave the beards* of *Davids* servants, he did not cut off their heads; He did not cut their clothes so, as that he stripped them naked. Yet, for that that he did, (says that story) *he stanke in Davids sight,* (which is a phrase of high indignation in that language) and so much, as that it cost him forty thousand of his horsemen in one battell. And therefore as

Gal. 5.15

this Apostle enters this *Caveat* in another place, *If yee bite one another, cavete, take heed yee be not consumed of one another,* so *cavete,* ⁴⁹⁰ take heed of this concision of the garment, lest if the garment be torne off, the body wither, and perish. A shadow is nothing, yet, if the rising or falling Sunne shine out, and there be no shadow, I will pronounce there is no body in that place neither. Ceremonies are *nothing;* but where there are no Ceremonies, order, and uniformity, and obedience, and at last, (and quickely) Religion it selfe will vanish. And therefore *videte concisionem,* beware of tearing the body, or of tearing the garment, which will induce the other, and both will induce the third, *concisionem spiritus,* the tearing of thine owne spirit, from that rest which it should receive in God; for, when thou hast ⁵⁰⁰ lost thy hold of all those handles which God reaches out to thee, in the Ministery of his Church, and that thou hast no meanes to apply the promises of God in Christ to thy soule, which are onely applied by Gods *Ordinances* in his Church, when any thing falls upon thee, that overcomes thy *morall constancy* (which *morall constancy,* God knowes, is soon spent, if we have lost our recourse to God) thou wilt soon sinke into an irrecoverable *desperation*, which is the fearfullest concision of all; and *videte*, beware of this concision.

When God hath made himselfe one body with me, by his assuming this *nature*, and made me *one spirit* with himselfe, and that by so high a way, as making me *partaker of the divine nature*, so that now, *in Christ Jesus*, he and I are one, this were *solutio Jesus*, a tearing in peeces, a dissolving of Jesus, in the worst kinde that could be imagined, if I should teare my selfe from Jesus, or by any jealousie or suspicion of his mercy, or any horror in my own sinnes, come to thinke my selfe to be none of *his*, none of *him*. Who ever comes into a Church to denounce an *excommunication* against himselfe? And shall any sad soule come hither, to gather arguments, from our preaching, to *excommunicate* it selfe, or to pronounce an impossibility upon her owne salvation? *God did a new thing*, says *Moses*, a strange thing, a thing never done before, when the earth opened her mouth, and *Dathan*, and *Abiram* went downe quicke into the pit. Wilt thou doe a stranger thing then that? To teare open the jawes of Earth, and Hell, and cast thy self actually and really into it, out of a mis-imagination, that God hath cast thee into it before? Wilt thou force God to second thy irreligious *melancholy*, and to condemne thee at last, because thou hadst precondemned thy selfe, and renounced his mercy? Wilt thou say with *Cain, My sinne is greater then can be pardoned?* This is *Concisio potestatis*, a cutting off the *Power* of God, and Treason against the *Father*, whose Attribute is *Power*. Wilt thou say, God never meant to save me? this is *Concisio sapientiæ*, a cutting off the *wisdome* of God, to thinke, that God intended himselfe glory in a kingdome, and would not have that kingdome peopled, and this is Treason against the *Son* whose Attribute is *wisdome?* Wilt thou say, I shall never finde comfort in *Praying*, in *Preaching*, in *Receiving?* This is *Concisio consolationis*, the cutting off consolation, and treason against the *holy Ghost*, whose office is *comfort*. No man violates the *Power* of the *Father*, the *Wisedome* of the *Sonne*, the *Goodnesse* of the *holy Ghost*, so much as he, who thinkes himselfe out of their reach, or the latitude of their working. *Rachel* wept for her children, and would not be comforted; but why? *Because they were not*. If her children had been but gone for

Concisio
Spiritus
1 Cor. 6.17
2 Pet. 1.4

Numb.
16.30

[Gen. 4.13]

Mat. 2.18

a time from her, or but sicke with her, *Rachel* would have been comforted; but, *they were not.* Is that thy case? Is not thy soule, a soule
still? It may have gone from thee, in sins of *inconsideration,* it may
be sicke within thee, in sins of *habit and custome;* but is not thy soul,
a soul still? And hath God made any *species* larger then himself? is
there more soul, then there is God, more *sin* then *mercy?* Truly
Origen was more excusable, more pardonable, if he did beleeve, that
the *Devill* might possibly be saved, then that man, that beleeves that
550 *himself* must necessarily be damned. And therefore, *videte concisionem,* beware of cutting off thy spirit from this spirit of comfort;
take heed of shreading Gods *generall promises,* into so narrow propositions, as that they wil not reach home to *thee,* cover thee, invest
thee; beware of such *distinctions,* and such subdivisions, as may make
the way to heaven too narrow for thee, or the gate of heaven too strait
for thee. 'Tis true, one drop of my Saviours bloud would save me, if
I had but *that;* one teare from my Saviours eye, if I had but *that;*
but he hath none that hath not *all;* A drop, a teare, would wash away
an *Adultery,* a *murder,* but lesse then the whole sea of both, will not
560 wash away a wanton looke, an angry word. God would have *all,* and
gives all to all. And for Gods sake, let God be as good as he will; as
mercifull, and as large, as liberall, and as generall as he will. Christ
came to save sinners; thou art sure thou art one of them; At what
time soever a sinner repents, he shall be heard; be sure to be one of
them too. Beleeve that God in Christ proposes conditions to thee;
endevor the performing, repent the not performing of those conditions, and be that the issue between God and thy soule; And lest
thou end in this concision, the concision of the Spirit, beware of the
other two concisions, of the body, and of the garment, by which onely,
570 all heavenly succors are appliable to thee.

Number 5.

Preached at Saint Pauls.

---

2 Cor. 5.20. *WE PRAY YEE IN CHRISTS STEAD,*
BE YE RECONCILED TO GOD.

IN BESTOWING of *Benefits,* there are some *Circumstances,* that vitiate and deprave the nature of the benefit (as when a man gives onely in contemplation of *Retribution,* for then he is not *Dator,* but *Mercator,* this is not a giving, but a Merchandising, a permutation, or when he is *Cyminibilis Dator,* (as our *Canons* speake) one that gives Mint and Cumin, so small things, and in so small proportions, as onely keeps him alive that receives, and so *Ipsum quod dat, perit, & vitam producit ad miseriam,* that that is given is lost, and he that receives it, is but continued in misery, and so the *benefit,* hath almost the nature of an *injury,* because but for that poore benefit, hee might have got out of this life. And then there are circumstances, that doe absolutely *annihilate* a benefit, amongst which, one is, if the giver take so expresse, so direct, so publique knowledge of the wants of the receiver, as that he shall be more ashamed by it, then refreshed with it; for in many courses of life, it does more deject a man, in his own heart, and in the opinion of others too, and more retard him in any preferment, to be *known* to be *poore,* then to *be* so indeed; And he that gives so, does not onely make him that receives, his *Debtor,* but his *Prisoner,* for he takes away his liberty of applying himselfe to others, who might be more beneficiall to him, then *he* that captivated, and ensnared him, with that small benefit. And therefore many times in the Scripture, the phrase is such in doing a curtesie, as though the receiver had done it, in accepting it; so when *Jacob* made a present to his brother *Esau, I beseech thee,* says he, *to take my blessing* that *I may finde favour in thy sight;* so he compelled him to take it. So when Christ recommends here to his people, the great, and inesti- mable benefit in our text, *Reconciliation* to *God,* he delivers that bene- fit of all those accidents, or circumstances, that might vitiate it; and amongst those, of this, that we should not be confounded with the 30 notice taken of our poverty, and indigence; for he proceeds with man, as though man might be of some use to him, and with whom it were fit for him to hold good correspondence, he sends to him by *Ambas- sadors,* (as it is in the words immediately before the text) and by those Ambassadors he *prays him,* that he would accept the benefit of Reconciliation. To us, who are his *Creatures,* and therefore might be turned and wound by his *generall Providence,* without employ- ment of any particular messengers, he sends particular messengers; to us that are his *enemies,* and fitter to receive denunciations of a war, by a *Herald,* then a *Message* by *Ambassadors,* he sends Ambassadors; 40 to us, who are indeed *Rebells,* and not enemies, and therefore rather to be reduced and reclaimed by *Executioners,* then by *Commissioners,* he sends Commissioners, not to article, not to capitulate, but to pray, and to intreat, and not to intreat us to accept Gods reconciliation to us, but, as though God needed us, to intreat us to be reconciled to him; *We pray you in Christs stead, be ye reconciled to God.*

Divisio   In these words, our parts will be three: *Our* Office towards *you; yours* towards *us;* and the Negotiation it self, *Reconciliation* to God. In each of these three, there is a re-derivation into three branches: for, in the two first (besides the matter) there are two kinds of *per-* 50 *sons, we* and *you,* The *Priest* and the *People* (we *pray you.*) And in the last there are two kinds of persons too, *you* and *God; Be ye recon- ciled to God.* But because all these kinds of persons, *God,* and *we,* and *you,* fall frequently into our consideration, there is the lesse necessity laid upon us to handle them, as distinct branches, otherwise then as they fall into the Negotiation it self. Therefore we shall determine our selves in these three: First, our office towards you, and our stipu- ation and contract with you, *We pray you;* we come not as Lords or Commanders over you, but in humble, in submissive manner, *We pray you.* And then your respect to us, because in what manner so- 60 ever we come, we come *in Christs stead,* and though dimly, yet represent *him.* And lastly, the blessed effect of this our humility to you, and this your respect to us, Reconciliation to God. Humility in us, because we are sent to the poorest soul; respect in you, because we are sent to represent the highest King, work in you this reconciliation to God, and it is a Text well handled; practice makes any Sermon a good Sermon.

First, then, for *our office* towards you, because you may be apt to say, *You take too much upon you, you sonnes of Levi; We* the sonnes of *Levi,* open unto you our Commission, and we pursue but that we professe, that we are sent but to pray, but to intreat you; and we accompany it with an outward declaration, we stand bare, and you sit covered. When greater power seems to be given us, of treading upon *Dragons* and *Scorpions,* of *binding* and *loosing,* of *casting out Devills,* and the like, we confesse these are powers over *sinnes,* over *Devills* that doe, or endevour to possesse you, *not over you,* for *to you* we are sent to pray and intreat you. Though God sent *Jeremy* with that large Commission, *Behold this day, I have set thee over the Nations, and over the Kingdomes, to pluck up, and to rout out, to destroy and to throw down;* and though many of the Prophets had their Commissions drawn by that precedent, we claime not *that,* we distinguish between the extraordinary Commission of the *Prophet,* and the ordinary Commission of the *Priest,* we admit a great difference between them, and are farre from taking upon us, all that the Prophet might have done; which is an errour, of which the *Church of Rome,* and some other over-zealous Congregations have been equally guilty, and equally opposed Monarchy and Soveraignty, by assuming to themselves, in an ordinary power, whatsoever God, upon extraordinary occasions, was pleased to give for the present, to his extraordinary Instruments the Prophets; our Commission is *to pray, and to intreat you.* Though upon those words, *Ascendunt salvatores in Montem Sion,* there shall arise Saviours in Mount Sion, in the Church of God, Saint *Hierom* saith, That as Christ being the light of the world, called his Apostles the light of the world too; so, *Ipse Salvator Apostolos voluit esse Salvatores,* The Saviour of the world communicates to us the name of Saviours of the world too, yet howsoever instrumentally and ministerially that glorious name of *Saviour* may be afforded to *us,* though to a high hill, though to that Mount

1 Part
[Num. 16.7]

[Luk. 10.19]
[Mat. 18.18]
[Mar. 16.17]

Ier. 1.10

Obad. 1.21

[Luk. 24.26]

Sion, we are led by a low way, by the example of our blessed Saviour
himself; and since there was an *Oportuit pati,* laid upon him, there
¹⁰⁰ may well be an *Oportet obsecrare* laid upon us; since his way was to
be dumb, ours may well be to utter no other voyce but *Prayers;* since
he bled, we may well sweat in his service, for the salvation of your
souls. If therefore our selves, who are sent, be under contempt, or
under persecution, if the sword of the *Tongue,* or the sword of the
Tyrant be drawn against us, against all these, *Arma nostra, preces &
fletus,* we defend with no other shield, we return with no other
sword, but Tears and Prayers, and blessing of them that curse us.
Yea, if he that sent us suffer in us, if we see you denounce a warre
against *him,* nay, triumph over him, and provoke him to anger, and
¹¹⁰ because he showes no anger, conclude out of his patience, an impotency, that because he doth not, he cannot, when you scourge him,
and scoffe him, and spit in his face, and crucifie him, and practise
every day all the Jews did to him once, as though that were your pattern, and your businesse were to exceed your pattern, and crucifie your
Saviour worse then they did, by tearing and mangling his body, now
glorified, by your blasphemous oaths, and execrable imprecations,
when we see all this, *Arma nostra preces & fletus,* we can defend our
selves, nor him, no other way, we present to you our tears, and our
prayers, his tears, and his prayers that sent us, and if you will not be
¹²⁰ reduced with these, our Commission is at an end. I bring not a *Star-
chamber* with me up into the Pulpit, to punish a *forgery,* if you
counterfeit a zeale in coming hither now; nor an *Exchequer,* to punish usurious contracts, though made in the Church; nor a high *Commission,* to punish incontinencies, if they be promoted by wanton
interchange of looks, in this place. Onely by my prayers, which he
hath promised to accompany and prosper in his service, I can diffuse
his overshadowing Spirit over all the corners of this Congregation,

[Luk. 18.13]

and pray that *Publican,* that stands below afar off, and dares not lift
up his eyes to heaven, to receive a chearfull confidence, that his sinnes
¹³⁰ are forgiven him; and pray that *Pharisee,* that stands above, and
onely thanks God, that he is not like other men, to believe himself to
be, if not a rebellious, yet an unprofitable servant. I can onely tell
them, that neither of them is in the right way of reconciliation to

Aug.   God, *Nec qui impugnant gratiam, nec qui superbè gratias agunt,*

Ambros.

neither he who by a diffidence hinders the working of Gods grace, nor he that thanks God in such a fashion, as though all that he had received, were not of meer mercy, but between a *debt* and a *benefit*, and that he had either merited before, or paid God after, in pious works, for all, and for more then he hath received at Gods hand.

Scarce any where hath the Holy Ghost taken a word of larger signification, then here; for, as though it were hard, even to him, to expresse the humility which we are to use, rather then lose any soul for which Christ hath dyed, he hath taught us this obsecration, this praying, this intreating in our Text, in a word, by which the *Septuagint,* the first Translators into *Greek,* expresse divers affections, and all within the compasse of this *Obsecramus,* We pray you. Some of them we shall present to you.

Those Translators use that word for *Napal. Napal* is *Ruere, Postrare,* to throw down, to deject our selves, to admit any undervalue, any exinanition, any evacuation of our selves, so we may advance this great work. *I fell down before the Lord,* says *Moses* of himself; and *Abraham* fell upon his face, says *Moses* of *him,* and in no sense is this word oftner used, by them, then in this humiliation. But yet, as it signifies to need the favour of another, so does it also to be favourable, and mercifull to another; for so also, the same Translators use this word for *Chanan,* which is to oblige and binde a man by benefits, or to have *compassion upon him; Have pity upon me, have pity upon me, O ye my friends, for the hand of God hath touched me;* there is our word repeated. So that, whether we professe to you, that as Physicians must consider excrements, so we must consider sin, the leprosie, the pestilence, the ordure of the soule, there is our dejection of our selves, or make you see your poverty and indigence, and that that can be no way supplied, but by those means, which God conveys by us, both ways we are within our word, *Obsecramus,* we pray you, we intreat you.

They use this word also for *Calah,* and *Calah* is *Dolere,* to grieve within our selves, for the affliction of another; But it signifies also *vulnerare,* to wound, and afflict another; for so it is said in this word, *Saul was sore wounded.* So that, whether we expresse our grief, in the behalf of Christ, that you will not be reconciled to God, or whether we wound your consciences, with a sense of your sins, and

[Deut. 9.18]
[Gen. 17.3]

Job 19.21

1 Sam. 31.3

his judgements, we are still within the word of our Commission, *Obsecramus,* we pray, we intreat.

To contract this consideration, they use this word for *Cruciare,* to vex, and for *Placare* too, to appease, to restore to rest and quiet. Mic. 6.13 *Therefore will I make thee sick in smiting thee;* there it is vexation; Zech. 7.2 And then, *They sent unto the House of the Lord, Placare Dominum,* to appease the Lord, as we translate it, and well, *To pray.* And therefore, if from our words proceed any vexation to your consciences, you [Mat. 26.39] ¹⁸⁰ must not say, *Transeat calix, let that Cup passe,* no more of that matter, for it is the *physick* that must first *stirre* the humour, before it can *purge* it; And if our words apply to your consciences, the soverain balm of the merits of your Saviour, and that thereupon your troubled consciences finde some rest, be not too soon secure, but proceed in your good beginnings, and continue in hearing, as we shall continue in all these manners of praying and intreating, which fall into the word of our Text, *Obsecramus,* by being beholden to *you* for your application, or making *you* beholden to us, for our ministration, which was the first use of the word, of *grieving* for you, ¹⁹⁰ or *grieving you* for your sins, which was the second, of *troubling* your *consciences,* and then of setling them again, in a calm reposednesse, which was the third signification of the word in their Translation.

Yet does the Holy Ghost carry our *office,* (I speak of the manner of the execution of our office, for, for the office it self, nothing can be [2 Cor. 3.8] more glorious, then the *ministration* of the Gospel) into lower terms Acts 2.15 then these. He suffered his Apostles to be thought to be drunk; They were full of the Holy Ghost, and they were thought full of new wine. A dramme of zeal more then ordinary, against a *Patron,* or against a great *Parishioner,* makes us presently scandalous Ministers. Truly, ²⁰⁰ beloved, we confesse, one sign of drunkennesse is, not to remember what we said. If we doe not in our practise, remember what we preached, and *live* as we *teach,* we are dead all the week, and we 1 Sam. 1.15 are drunk upon the Sunday. But *Hannah* praid, and was thought drunk, and this grieved her heart; so must it us, when you ascribe our zeale to the glory of God, and the good of your souls, to any inordinate passion, or sinister purpose in us.

And yet hath the Holy Ghost laid us lower then this. To be drunk is an alienation of the minde, but it is but a short one; but S. *Paul*

was under the imputation of *madnesse*. Nay, our blessed Saviour
himself did some such act of vehement zeal, as that his very friends
thought him *mad*. S. *Paul,* because his madnesse was imputed to a
false cause, to a pride in his much *learning,* disavowed his madnesse,
I am not mad, O noble Festus. But when the *cause* was justifiable, he
thought his *madnesse* justifiable too; *If we be besides our selves, it is
for God;* and so long well enough. *Insaniebat amatoriam insaniam
Paulus, S. Paul* was mad for love; S. *Paul* did, and we doe take into
our contemplation, the beauty of a Christian soul; Through the
ragged apparell of the afflictions of this life; through the scarres, and
wounds, and palenesse, and morphews of sin, and corruption, we
can look upon the soul it self, and there see that incorruptible beauty,
that *white* and *red,* which the *innocency* and the *blood* of Christ
hath given it, and we are mad for love of this soul, and ready to doe
any act of danger, in the ways of persecution, any act of diminution
of our selves in the ways of humiliation, to *stand at her doore,* and
pray, and begge, that *she would be reconciled to God.*

And yet does the Holy Ghost lay us lower then this too. Mad men
have some flashes, some twilights, some returns of sense and reason,
but the *foole* hath none; And, *we are fools for Christ,* says the
Apostle; And not onely we, the persons, but the ministration it self,
the function it self is *foolishnesse; It pleased God by the foolishnesse
of preaching to save them that beleeve.* Anger will bear an action, and
Racah will bear an action, but to say *Foole,* was the heaviest imputation; and we are *fooles* for Christ, and pretend nothing to work by,
but the foolishnesse of preaching. Lower then this, we cannot be
cast, and higher then this we offer not to climbe; *Obsecramus,* we
have no other Commission but to pray, and to intreat, and that we
doe, in his words, in his tears, in his blood, and in his bowels who
sent us, *we pray you in Christs stead,* which is that that constitutes
our second Part, with what respect you should receive us.

In mittendariis servanda dignitas mittentis. To diminish the honour
of his Master, is not an humility, but a prevarication in any Ambassadour; and that is our quality, expressed in this verse. God is the
Lord of Hosts, and he is the *Prince of peace;* He needs neither the
Armies of Princes, nor the wisdome of Councell Tables, to come to
his ends. He is the Proprietary and owner of all the treasures in the

Mar. 3.21

[Acts 26.25]
2 Cor. 5.13
Theophil.

1 Cor. 4.10

[1 Cor. 1.21]

Mat. 5.[22]

2 Part

[Isa. 9.6, 7]

world; *Ye have taken my silver and my gold;* and, *The silver is mine, and the gold is mine.* All that you call *yours,* all that you can call *yours,* is *his;* your selves are but the furniture of his house, and your great hearts are but little boxes in his cabinet, and he can fill
250 them with dejection, and sadnesse, when he will. And does any Prince govern at home, by an Ambassadour? he sends Pursuivants, and Serjeants; he sends not Ambassadours; God does, and we are they; and we look to be received by you, but as we perform those two laws which binde Ambassadours, First, *Rei suæ ne quis legatus esto,* Let no man be received as an Ambassadour, that hath that title, onely to negotiate for himself, and doe his own businesse in that Country; And then, *Nemini credatur sine principali mandato,* Let no man be received for an Ambassadour, without his Letters of Credence, and his Masters Commission. To these two we submit our
260 selves.

Rei nostræ

First, we are not *Rei nostræ legati,* we come not to doe our own businesse; what businesse of ours is it, what is it to us, that you be
1 Cor. 9.16   reconciled to God? *Væ mihi si non, Necessity is laid upon me, and woe unto me, if I preach not the Gospel;* but if I doe, I have nothing to glory in; nay, I may be a *reprobate* my self. I can claim no more at Gods hand, for this service, then the Sun can, for shining upon the earth, or the earth for producing flowers, and fruits; and therefore we are not *Rei nostræ legati,* Ambassadours in our own behalfs, and to doe our own businesse.

270 Indeed where men are sent out, to vent and utter the ware and merchandises of the Church and Court of *Rome,* to proclaime, and advance the value, and efficacy of uncertain *reliques,* and superstitious charms, and incantations, when they are sent to sell particular sinnes at a certain price, and to take so much for an *incest,* so much for a *murder,* when they are sent with many summs of Indulgencies at once, as they are now to the *Indies,* and were heretofore to us, when these Indulgencies are accompanied with this Doctrine, that if the Indulgence require a certain peece of money to be given for it, (as for the most part they doe) if all the spirituall parts of the Indulgence
280 be performed by the poore sinner, yet if he give not that money, though he be not worth that money, though that Merchant of those Indulgencies, doe out of his charity give him one of those Indul-

gencies, yet all this doth that man no good, in these cases, they are indeed *Rei suæ Legati,* Ambassadours to serve their own turns, and do their owne businesse. When that Bishop sends out his *Legatos à latere,* Ambassadours from his own chair and bosome into forain Nations, to exhaust their treasures, to alien their Subjects, to infect their Religion; these are *Rei suæ Legati,* Ambassadours that have businesses depending in those places, and therefore come upon their own errand. Nor can that Church excuse it self, (though it use to do so) upon the mis-behaviour of those officers, when they are imployed; for, they are imployed to that purpose: And, *Tibi imputa quicquid pateris ab eo, qui sine te, nihil potest facere:* Since he might mend the fault, it is his fault, that it is done; he cannot excuse himself, if they be guilty, and with his privity: for, as the same devout man saith, to *Eugenius,* then Pope, *Ne te dixeris sanum dolentem latera;* If thy sides ake, (if thy Legats *à latere,* be corrupt) call not thy self well, *nec bonum malis innitentem,* nor call thy self good, if thou rely upon the counsell of those that are ill; They, those Legats *à latere,* are, (as they use to expresse it) incorporated in the Pope, and therefore they are *Rei suæ Legati,* Ambassadours that ly to doe their own businesse. But when we seek to raise no other warre in you, but to arme the spirit against the flesh, when we present to you no other holy water, but the teares of Christ Jesus, no other *reliques,* but the commemoration of his Passion in the *Sacrament,* no other Indulgencies, and acquittances, but the application of his Merits to your souls, when we offer all this without silver, and without gold, when we offer you that Seal which he hath committed to us, in *Absolution,* without extortion or fees, wherein are we *Rei nostræ Legati,* Ambassadours in our own behalfs, or advancers of our owne ends?

And as we are not so, so neither are we in the second danger, to come *sine Principali Mandato,* without Commission from our Master. Christ himselfe would not come of *himselfe,* but acknowledged and testified his Mission, *The Father which sent me, he gave me commandment, what I should say, and what I should speake.* Those whom he imployed produced their Commissions, *Neither received I it of man, neither was I taught it, but by the revelation of Jesus Christ. How should they preach except they be sent?* is a question which Saint *Paul* intended for a *conclusive* question, that none could

Bern.

Sine
Mandato

Iohn 12.49

Gal. 1.12

[Rom.
10.15]

³²⁰ answer, till in the Romane Church they excepted *Cardinals, Quibus*
sine literis creditur, propter personarum solennitatem, who for the
dignity inherent in their persons, must be received, though they have
no Commission.

When our adversaries do so violently, so impetuously cry out, that
we have no Church, no Sacrament, no Priesthood, because none are
sent, that is, none have a right calling, for *Internall calling,* who are
called by the Spirit of God, they can be no Judges, and for *Externall*
calling, we admit them for Judges, and are content to be tried by
their own *Canons,* and their own evidences, for our Mission and
³³⁰ vocation, o[u]r sending and our calling to the Ministery. If they
require a necessity of lawfull Ministers to the constitution of a
Church, we require it with as much earnestnesse as they; *Ecclesia*
non est quæ non habet sacerdotem, we professe with Saint *Hierome,*
It is no Church that hath no Priest. If they require, that this spirituall
power be received from them, who have the same power in themselves, we professe it too, *Nemo dat quod non habet,* no man can
confer other power upon another, then he hath himself. If they
require *Imposition of hands,* in conferring Orders, we joyn hands
with them. If they will have it a Sacrament, men may be content to
³⁴⁰ let us be as liberall of that name of Sacrament, as *Calvin* is; and he
says of it, *Institut. l. 4. c. 14. §20. Non invitus patior vocari Sacra-*
mentum, ita inter ordinaria Sacramenta non numero, I am not loth,
it should be called a Sacrament, so it be not made an ordinary, that
is, a generall Sacrament; and how ill hath this been taken at some of
our mens hands, to speak of more such Sacraments, when indeed
they have learnt this manner of speech, and difference of Sacraments,
not onely from the ancient Fathers, but from *Calvin* himself, who
always spoke with a holy warinesse, and discretion. Whatsoever
their own authors, their own Schools, their own Canons doe require
³⁵⁰ to be essentially and necessarily requisite in this Mission in this function, we, for our parts, and as much as concerns our Church of
England, admit it too, and professe to have it. And whatsoever they
can say for their Church, that from their first Conversion, they have
had an orderly derivation of power from one to another, we can as
justly and truly say of our Church, that ever since her first being of
such a Church, to this day, she hath conserved the same order, and

ever hath had, and hath now, those Ambassadours sent, with the
same Commission, and by the same means, that they pretend to have
in *their* Church. And being herein convinced, by the evidence of
¹⁰ undeniable Record, which have been therefore shewed to some of
their Priests, not being able to deny that such a Succession and
Ordination, we have had, from the hands of such as were made
Bishops according to their Canons, now they pursue their common
beaten way, That as in our Doctrine, they confesse we affirm no
Heresie, but that we deny some Truths, so in our Ordination, and
sending, and Calling, when they cannot deny, but that from such a
person, who is, by their own Canons, able to confer Orders, we, in
taking our Orders, (after their own manner) receive the Holy Ghost,
and the power of binding and loosing, yet, say they, we receive not
⁷⁰ the full power of Priests, for, we receive onely a power *in Corpus
mysticum,* upon the mysticall body of Christ, that is, the persons
that constitute the visible Church, but we should receive it *in Corpus
verum,* a power upon the very naturall body, a power of Consecration, by way of *Transubstantiation.* They may be pleased to pardon,
this, rather *Modesty,* then *Defect,* in us, who, so we may work fruit-
fully, and effectually upon the *mysticall* body of Christ, can be content that his reall, and true body work upon us. Not that we have no
interest to work upon the reall body of Christ, since he hath made us
Dispensers even of that, to the faithfull, in the Sacrament; but for
⁸⁰ such a power, as exceeds the *Holy Ghost,* who in the *incarnation* of
Christ, when he overshadowed the blessed Virgin, did but make man
of the woman, who was one part disposed by nature thereunto,
whereas these men make man, and God too of bread, naturally
wholly indisposed to any such change, for this power we confesse
it is not in our Commission; and their Commission, and ours was
all one; and the Commission is manifest in the Gospel; and, since
they can charge us with no rasures, no expunctions, we must charge
them with interlinings, and additions, to the first Commission. But
for that power, which is to work upon you, to whom we are sent, we
⁹⁰ are defective in nothing, which they call necessary thereunto.

This I speak of this Church, in which God hath planted us, That
God hath afforded us all that might serve, even for the stopping of
the Adversaries mouth, and to confound them in their own way:

[Joh.
20.22, 23]

which I speak, onely to excite us to a thankfulnesse to God, for his abundant grace in affording us so much, and not to disparage, or draw in question any other of our *neighbour Churches,* who, perchance, cannot derive, as we can, their power, and their *Mission,* by the ways required, and practised in the Romane Church, nor have had from the beginning a continuance of Consecration by Bishops, ⁴⁰⁰ and such other concurrences, as those *Canons* require, and as our *Church* hath enjoyed. They, no doubt, can justly plead for themselves, that Ecclesiasticall positive Laws admit *dispensation* in cases of necessity; They may justly challenge a Dispensation, but we need none; They did what was lawfull in a case of necessity, but Almighty God preserved us from this necessity. As men therefore, *Qui nec jussi*

Bern.

renuunt, nec non jussi affectant, which neither neglect Gods calling, when we have it, nor counterfeit it, when wee have it not, *Qui quod verecundè excusant, obstinatiùs non recusant,* who though wee confesse our selves altogether unworthy, have yet the seales of God, and ⁴¹⁰ his Church upon us, *Nec rei nostræ legati,* not to promove our own ends, but your reconciliation to God, *Nec sine principali mandato,* not without a direct and published Commission, in the Gospell, we come to you in Christs stead, and so should be received by you. As for our *Mission,* that being in the quality of *Ambassadours,* we submitted our selves to those two obligations, which we noted to lie

Receptio

upon Ambassadours, so here in our *Reception,* we shall propose to you two things, that are, for the most part, practised by Princes, in the reception of Ambassadours. One is, that before they give audience, they endevour, by some confident servant of theirs, to discern ⁴²⁰ and understand the inclination of the Ambassadour, and the generall scope, and purpose of his negotiation, and of the behavior that he purposeth to use in delivering his Message; lest for want of thus much light, the Prince might either be unprepared in what manner to expresse himselfe, or be surprised with some such message, as might not well comport with his honour to heare. But in these Ambassages from God to man, no man is made so equall to God, as that he may refuse to give *Audience,* except he know before hand that the message be agreeable to his minde. Onely he that will be

[2 Thes. 2.3]

more then man, that *Man of sinne,* who esteemeth himselfe to be ⁴³⁰ joyned in Commission with God, onely he hath a particular Officer to know before hand, what message Gods Ambassadour bringeth, and to peruse all Sermons to be preached before him, and to expunge, correct, alter, all such things as may be disagreeable to him. It cannot therefore become you to come to these Audiences upon conditions; to informe your selves from others first, what kinde of messages, such or such an Ambassadour useth to deliver; whether he preach *Mercy* or *Judgement;* that if he preach against *Vsury,* you will heare *Court-sermons,* where there is less occasion to mention it; If hee preach against *Incontinency,* you will goe; whither? Is there any place that ⁴⁰ doth not extort from us, reprehensions, exclamations against that sinne? But if you beleeve us to come in Christs stead, what ever our message be, you must heare us.

Doe that, and for the second thing that Princes practise in the Reception of Ambassadours, which is, to referre Ambassadours to their Councell, we are well content to admit from you. Whosoever is of your nearest Councell, and whose opinion you best trust in, we are content to submit it to. Let naturall reason, let affections, let the profits or the pleasures of the world be the *Councell Table,* and can they tell you, that you are able to maintaine a warre against God, ⁵⁰ and subsist so, without being reconciled to him? Deceive not your selves, no man hath so much pleasure in this life, as he that is at peace with God.

What an Organe hath that man tuned, how hath he brought all things in the world to a Consort, and what a blessed Anthem doth he sing to that Organe, that is at peace with God? His Rye-bread is *Manna,* and his Beefe is *Quailes,* his day-labours are thrustings at the narrow gate into Heaven, and his night-watchings are extasies and evocations of his soule into the presence and communion of Saints, his sweat is *Pearls,* and his bloud is *Rubies,* it is at peace with God. ⁶⁰ No man that is at suite in himselfe, no man that carrieth a *West-minster* in his bosome, and is *Plaintiffe* and *Defendant* too, no man that serveth himselfe with Process out of his owne Conscience, for every nights pleasure that he taketh, in the morning, and for every dayes pound that he getteth, in the evening, hath any of the pleasure, or profit, that may be had in this life; nor any that is not at peace with God. That peace we bring you; how will you receive us?

That vehemence of *zeale* which the Apostle found, we hope not

Gal. 4.14   for; *you received me as an Angell of God, even as Christ Jesus.* And,
if it had been possible, you would have plucked out your owne eyes,
470 *and have given them to me.* Consider the zeale of any Church to their
Pastor, it will come short of the Pastor to the Church. All that Saint
Paul saith of the *Galatians* towards him, is farre short of that which
[Rom. 9.3]   he said to the *Romanes,* That he *could wish himselfe separated from*
Christ, for his brethren; or that of *Moses,* that he would be *blotted*
[Exod.
32.32]   *out of the Booke of Life,* rather then his charge should. When we
consider the manner of hearing Sermons, in the Primitive Church,
though we doe not wish that manner to be renewed, yet we cannot
deny, but that though it were accompanied with many inconveni-
ences, it testified a vehement devotion, and sense of that that was
480 said, by the preacher, in the hearer; for, all that had been formerly
used in Theaters, *Acclamations* and *Plaudites,* was brought into the
Church, and not onely the vulgar people, but learned hearers were as
loud, and as profuse in those declarations, those vocall acclamations,
and those plaudites in the passages, and transitions, in Sermons, as
ever they had been at the Stage, or other recitations *of their Poets, or*
Orators. S. *Hierom* charges *Vigilantius,* that howsoever he differed
from him in opinion after, yet when he had heard him preach of the
Resurrection before, he had received that Doctrine with Acclamation
and *Plaudites.* And as Saint *Hierome* saith of himselfe, that he was
490 thus applauded in his Preaching; he saith it also of him whom he
called his Master, *Gregory Nazianzen,* a grave and yet a facetious man,
of him he telleth us this Story; That he having intreated *Nazianzen,*
Luc. 6.1   to tell him the meaning of that place, *What that second Sabbath after*
the first was? he played with me, he jested at me, saith he, *Eleganter*
lusit, and he bad me be at Church next time he preached, and he
would preach upon that Text, *Et toto acclamante populo, cogeris*
invitus scire quod nescis, and when you see all the Congregation
applaud me, and cry out that they are satisfied, you will make your
self beleeve you understand the place, as they doe, though you doe
500 not; *Et si solus tacueris, solus ab omnibus stultitiæ condemnaberis,*
And if you doe not joyne with the Congregation in those *Plaudites,*
the whole Congregation will thinke you the onely ignorant person
in the Congregation; for, as we may see in Saint *Augustin,* the manner was, that when the people were satisfied in any point which the

Preacher handled, they would almost tell him so, by an acclamation, and give him leave to passe to another point; for, so saith that Father, *Vidi in voce intelligentes, plures video in silentio requirentes,* I heare many, to whom, by this acclamation, I see, enough hath been said, but I see more that are silent, and therefore, for their sakes, I ¹⁰ will say more of it. Saint *Augustine* accepted these acclamations more willingly, at least more patiently, then some of the Fathers before had done; *Audistis, laudastis; Deo gratias;* you have heard that that hath been said, and you have approved it with your praise; God be thanked for both; *Et laudes vestræ folia sunt arborum, sed fructus quæro;* Though I looke for fruit from you, yet even these acclamations are Leafes, and Leafes are Evidences that the tree is alive. Saint *Chrysostome* was more impatient of them, yet could never overcome them. To him, they came a little closer; for it was ordinary, that when he began to speake, the people would cry out, *Audiamus* ²⁰ *tertiumdecimum Apostolum;* Let us hearken to the thirteenth Apostle. And he saith, *Si placet, hanc nunc legem firmabimus,* I pray let us now establish this for a Law, between you and mee, *Ne quis auditor plaudat, quamdiu nos loquimur;* That whilest I am speaking, I may heare no *Plaudite;* yet he saith in a Sermon preached after this, *Animo cogitavi Legem ponere,* I have often purposed to establish such a Law, *Vt decore, & cum silentio audiatis,* that you would be pleased to heare with silence, but he could never prevail.

Sidonius Apollinaris, (a Bishop himselfe, but whether *then* or no, I know not) saith of another Bishop, that hearing even *prædicationes* ³⁰ *repentinas,* his extemporall Sermons, *raucus plausor audivi,* I poured my selfe out in loud acclamations, till I was hoarse: And, to contract this consideration, wee see evidently, that this fashion continued in the Church, even to Saint *Bernards* time. Neither is it left yet in some places, beyond the Seas, where the people doe yet answer the Preacher, if his questions be applyable to them, and may induce an answer, with these vocall acclamations, *Sir, we will, Sir, we will not.* And truely wee come too neare re-inducing this vain glorious fashion, in those often periodicall murmurings, and noises, which you make, when the Preacher concludeth any point; for those impertinent In- ⁵⁴⁰ terjections swallow up one quarter of his houre, and many that were not within distance of hearing the Sermon, will give a censure upon

Hom. 30
in Act.

Hom. 31

it, according to the frequencie, or paucitie of these acclamations. These fashions then, howsoever, in those times they might be testimonies of Zeale, yet because they occasioned *vain glory,* and many times, *faction,* (as those Fathers have noted) we desire not, willingly we admit not. We *come in Christs stead;* Christ at his comming met *Hosanna's* and *Crucifige's;* A Preacher may be applauded in his Pulpit, and crucified in his *Barne:* but there is a worse crucifying then that, a piercing of our hearts, *Because we are* Ezech. 33.32 ⁵⁵⁰ *as a very lovely song, of one that hath a pleasant voyce, and can play well on an Instrument, and you heare our words, and doe them not.* Having therefore said thus much to you, first of our manner of proceeding with you, *Obsecramus,* of all those waies of humiliation, which we insisted upon, and ingaged our selves in, we pray, and intreat you, and the respect which should come from you, because we come in Christs stead, if, as the Eunuch said to *Philip, Here is* Act. 8.[36] *water, what doth hinder me to be baptized?* so you say to us, we acknowledge that you do your duties, and we do receive you in Christs stead; what is it that you would have us doe? it is but this, ⁵⁶⁰ *We pray you in Christs stead be ye reconciled to God;* which is our third, and last part, and that to which all that we have said of a good Pastor and a good people, (which is the blessedest union of this world) bendeth, and driveth, what, and how blessed a thing it is to be reconciled to God.

3 Part   Reconciliation is a redintegration, a renewing of a former friendship, that hath been interrupted and broken. So that this implyeth a present enmity, and hostility with God; and then a former friendship with God, and also a possibility of returning to that former friendship; stop a little upon each of these, and we have done.

⁵⁷⁰   Amongst *naturall Creatures,* because howsoever they differ in bignesse, yet they have some proportion to one another, we consider that some very little creatures, contemptible in themselves, are yet called *Inimicus* enemies to great creatures, as the Mouse is to the Elephant. (For the greatest Creature is not *Infinite,* nor the least is not *Nothing.*) But [Gen. 1.26] shall man, betweene whom and nothing, there went but a word, *Let us make Man,* That Nothing, which is infinitely lesse then a Mathematicall point, then an imaginary Atome, shall this Man, this yesterdayes Nothing, this to morrow worse then Nothing, be capable

of that honour, that *dishonourable honour,* that confounding honour, to be the enemy of God, of God who is not onely a multiplied Elephant, millions of Elephants multiplied into one, but a multiplied World, a multiplied All, All that can be conceived by us, infinite many times over; Nay, (if we may dare to say so,) a multiplyed God, a God that hath the Millions of the Heathens gods in himselfe alone, shall this man be an enemy to this God? Man cannot be allowed so high a sinne, as enmity with God. The Devill himselfe is but a *slave* to God, and shall Man be called his enemy? It is true, if we consider the infinite disproportion between them, he cannot; but to many sad purposes, and in many heavy applications Man is an enemy to God. *Job* could goe no higher in expressing his misery, *Why hidest thou thy face, and holdest me for thine enemy?* and againe, *Behold, he findeth occasions against me, and counteth me for his enemy.* So Man is an enemy to God; And then to adhere to an enemy, is to become an enemy; for Man to adhere to Man, to ascribe any thing to the power of his *naturall faculties,* to thinke of any beame of clearnesse in his own understanding, or any line of rectitude in his owne will, this is to accumulate and multiply enmities against God, and to assemble and muster up more, and more man, to fight against God.

A *Reconciliation* is required, therefore there is an *enmitie;* but it is but a reconciliation, therefore there was a friendship; There was a time when God and Man were friends, God did not hate man from all Eternitie, God forbid. And this friendship God meant not to breake; God had no purpose to fall out with man, for then hee could never have admitted him to a friendship. *Nec hominem amicum quisquam potest fideliter amare, cui se noverit futurum inimicum:* No man can love another as a friend this yeare, and meane to bee his enemy next. Gods foreknowledge that man and he should fall out, was not a foreknowledge of any thing that he meant to doe to that purpose, but onely that Man himselfe would become incapable of the continuation of this friendship. Man might have persisted in that blessed amitie; and, since if he had done so, the cause of his persisting had beene his owne will, I speake of the next and *immediate Cause,* (As the cause why the Angels that did persist, did persist, was *Bona ipsorum Angelorum voluntas,* the good use of their own *free-will,*

(marginal notes)

13.24
33.10

Amici

August.

Polanus
syntag.
To. 1.
fol. 784

much more was the cause of their defection and breaking this friendship in their owne will;) God therefore having made man, that is
Mankinde, in a state of love, and friendship, God having not by any
purpose of his done any thing toward the violation of this friend-
620 ship, in man, in any man, God continueth his everlasting goodnesse
towards man, towards mankinde still, in inviting him to accept the
means of Reconciliation, and a returne to the same state of friendship, which hee had at first, by our Ministery. *Be ye reconciled unto
God.*

Reconci-   You see what you had, and how you lost it. If it might not bee
liamini   recovered, God would not call you to it. It was piously declared in
a *late Synod, That in the offer of this Reconciliation, God meanes, as
the Minister meanes;* and I am sure I meane it, and desire it to you
Chrysost.   all; so does God. *Nec Deus est qui inimicitias gerit, sed vos,* it is not
Mic. 6.3   630 God, but you, that oppose this Reconciliation; *O my people what
have I done unto thee,* or *wherein have I grieved thee, testifie against
me;* testifie if I did any thing towards inducing an enmity, or doe any
thing towards hindring this Reconciliation; which reconciliation is,
to be restored to as good an estate in the love of God, as you had in
Adam, and our estate is not as good, if it be not as generall, if the
merit of Christ be not as large, as the sinne of *Adam;* and if it be not
as possible for you to be saved by him, as it is impossible for you to
be saved without him.

It is therefore but praying you in Christs stead, that you be recon-
640 ciled to God. And, if you consider what God is, The Lord of hosts,
[Num.   and therefore hath meanes to destroy you, or what he is not, He is
23.19]   not man that he can repent, and therefore it belongs to you, to repent
[Psa. 2.4,   first, If you consider what the Lord doth, *He that dwells in the
P.B.   heavens doth laugh them to scorne, and hath them in derision,* or
version]   what he doth not, He doth not justifie *the wicked balance, nor the
Mic. 6.11   bag of deceitfull waights,* If you consider what the Lord would doe,
[Mat. 23.37]   *Jerusalem, Jerusalem, how often would I have gathered thy children
together, as the Hen gathereth her Chickens, and yee would not,* or
Ezek. 33.11   what he would not doe, *As I live, sayeth the Lord, I desire not the
650 death of the wicked,* if yee consider all this, any of this, dare you, or
can you if you durst, or would you if you could, stand out in an
irreconciliable war against God? Especially if you consider, that that

is more to you, then what God is, and does, and would doe, and can doe, for you or against you, that is, what he hath done already; that he who was the party offended, hath not onely descended so low, as to be reconciled first, and to pay so deare for that, as the bloud of his owne, and onely Sonne, but knowing thy necessity better then thy selfe, he hath reconciled thee to him, though thou knewest it not; *God was in Christ, reconciling the world unto himselfe,* as it is in the former verse; there the worke is done, thy reconciliation is wrought; God is no longer angry so, as to withhold from thee the meanes; for, there it followes, *Hee hath committed to us the word of Reconciliation;* That wee might tell you the instrument of Reconciliation is drawn between God and you, and, as it is written in the history of the Councell of *Nice,* that two Bishops who died before the establishing of the Canons, did yet subscribe and set their names to those Canons, which, to that purpose were left upon their graves all night, so though you were dead in your sinne and enemies to God, and Children of wrath, (as all by nature are) when this Reconciliation was wrought, yet the Spirit of God may give you this strength, to dip your pennes in the bloud of the Lambe, and so subscribe your names, by acceptation of this offer of Reconciliation. Doe but that, subscribe, accept, and then, *Cætera omnia,* all the rest that concernes your holy history, your *Justification* and *Sanctification, nonne scripta sunt?* are they not written in the bookes of the Chronicles of the Kings of *Israel,* says the Holy Ghost, in another case; Are they not written in the books of the Chronicles of the God of *Israel?* Shalt thou not finde an eternall Decree, and a *Book of life* in thy behalfe, if thou looke for it by this light, and reach to it with this Hand, the acceptation of this Reconciliation? They are written in those reverend and sacred Records, and Rolls, and Parchments, even the skinne and flesh of our Blessed Saviour; written in those his stripes, and those his wounds, with that bloud, that can admit no *Index expurgatorius,* no expunction, no satisfaction; But the life of his death lies in thy acceptation, and though he be come to his, thou art not come to thy *Consummatum est,* till that be done.

Doe that, and then thou hast put on thy wedding garment. A man might get into that feast, without his wedding garment; so a man may get into the Church, to bee a visible part of a Christian Congre-

Binius.
To. 1.
fo. 320

[Eph. 2.1, 3]

[1 Kings
15.31, etc.]

[Rev. 20.12]

[John 19.30]

Mat.
22.[11, 12]

⁶⁹⁰ gation, without this acceptation of reconciliation, that is the *particular apprehension,* and application of Christ; but hee is still subject to a remove, and to that question of confusion, *Quomodo intrasti,* How came you in? That man in the Gospell could have answered to that question, directly, I came in by the invitation, and conduct of thy servants, I was called in, I was led in; So they that come hither without this wedding garment, they may answer to Christs *Quomodo intrasti,* How camest thou in? I came in by faithfull *parents,* to whom, and their seed thou hast sealed a Covenant; I was admitted by thy *Servants* and Ministers in *Baptisme,* and have been led along ⁷⁰⁰ by them, by comming to hear them preach thy word, and doing the other externall offices of a Christian. But there is more in this question; *Quomodo intrasti,* is not onely how *didst* thou come in, but how *durst* thou come in? If thou camest to my feast, without any purpose to eate, and so to discredit, to accuse either my meat, or the dressing of it, to quarrell at the *Doctrine,* or at the *Discipline* of my Church, *Quomodo intrasti,* How didst thou, How durst thou come in? If thou camest with a purpose to poison my meat, that it might infect others, with a determination to goe forward in thy sinne, whatsoever the Preacher say, and so encourage others by thy example, *Quomodo* ⁷¹⁰ *intrasti,* How durst thou come in? If thou camest in with thine own provision in thy pocket, and didst not relie upon mine, and think that thou canst be saved without *Sermons,* or *Sacraments, Quomodo intrasti,* How durst thou come in? Him that came in there, without this Wedding garment, the Master of the Feast cals *Friend;* but scornfully, *Friend how camest thou in?* But he cast him out. God may call us *Friends,* that is, admit, and allow us the estimation and credit of being of his *Church,* but at one time or other, hee shall minister that Interrogatory, *Friend, how came you in?* and for want of that Wedding garment, and for want of wearing it in the sight of ⁷²⁰ men, (for it is not said that that man had no such Wedding garment at home, in his Wardrobe, but that hee had none *on*) for want of *Sanctification* in a holy life, God shall deliver us over to the execution of our own consciences, and eternall condemnation.

But be ye reconciled to God, embrace this reconciliation in making your use of those means, and this reconciliation shall work thus, it shall restore you to that state, that *Adam* had in Paradise. What

would a soule oppressed with the sense of sin give, that she were in
that state of Innocency, that she had in *Baptisme?* Be reconciled to
God, and you have that, and an elder Innocency then that, the Innocency of *Paradise.* Go home, and if you finde an over-burden of
children, negligence in servants, crosses in your tradings, narrownesse, penury in your estate, yet this penurious, and this encumbred
house shall be your Paradise. Go forth, into the Country, and if you
finde unseasonablenesse in the weather, rots in your sheep, murrains
in your cattell, worms in your corn, backwardnesse in your rents,
oppression in your Landlord, yet this field of thorns and brambles
shall be your Paradise. Lock thy selfe up in thy selfe, in thine own
bosome, and though thou finde every roome covered with the soot of
former sins, and shaked with that Devill whose name is *Legion,*   [Mar. 5.9]
some such sin as many sins depend upon, and are induced by, yet
this prison, this rack, this hell in thine own conscience shall be thy
Paradise. And as in Paradise *Adam* at first needed no Saviour, so
when by this reconciliation, in apprehending thy Saviour, thou art
restored to this Paradise, thou shalt need no *sub-Saviour,* no *joint-
Saviour,* but *Cætera adjicientur,* no other Angel, but the *Angel of the*
great Councell, no other Saint, but the Holy One of *Israel,* he who   [Isa. 9.6,
hath wrought this reconciliation for thee, and brought it to thee, shall   Sept.]
establish it in thee; *For, if when we were enemies, we were recon-*   Rom. 5.10
ciled to God, by the death of his Son, much more being reconciled,
shall we be saved by his life. This is the summe and the end of all,
That when God sends humble and laborious Pastors, to souple and
appliable Congregations; That we pray, and you receive us in Christs
stead, we shall not onely finde rest in God, but, (as it is said of *Noahs*
sacrifice) God *shall finde the savour of rest* in us; God shall finde a   [Gen. 8.21,
Sabbath to himself in us, and rest from his jealousies, and anger   A.V. mg.]
towards us, and we shall have a *Sabbatary life* here in the rest and
peace of conscience, and a life of one everlasting Sabbath hereafter,
where to our Rest there shall be added *Joy,* and to our *Joy Glory,*
and this *Rest,* and *Joy,* and *Glory* superinvested with that which
crownes them all, Eternity.

Number 6.

Preached at White-Hall.

EZEK. 34.19. *AND AS FOR MY FLOCK, THEY EATE THAT, WHICH YEE HAVE TRODEN WITH YOUR FEET, AND THEY DRINK THAT WHICH YEE HAVE FOULED WITH YOUR FEET.*

THOSE FOUR Prophets, whom the Church hath called *the great Prophets, Esay,* and *Ieremy, Ezekiel* and *Daniel,* are not onely therefore called *great,* because they *writ more,* then the lesser Prophets did, (for *Zechary,* who is amongst the lesser, writ more then *Daniel* who is amongst the greater) but because their Prophecies are of a larger comprehension, and extent, and, for the most part, speake more *of the comming of Christ,* and the establishing of the *Christian Church,* then the lesser Prophets doe, who were more conversant about the temporall deliverance *of Israel from Babylon,* though there be aspersions of Christ, and his future government in those Prophets too, though more thinly shed. Amongst the four great ones, our Prophet *Ezekiel* is the *greatest.* I compare not their extraction and race; for, though *Ezekiel* were *de genere sacerdotali,* of the Leviticall and Priestly race; (And, as *Philo Judæus* notes, all nations having some markes of Gentry, some calling that ennobled the professors thereof, (in some *Armes,* and *Merchandize* in some, and the *Arts* in others) amongst the *Jews,* that was *Priesthood,* Priesthood was Gentry) though *Ezekiel* were of this race, *Esay* was of a higher, for he was of the extraction of their Kings, of the bloud royall. But the

20 extraordinary greatnesse of *Ezekiel*, is in his extraordinary depth, and mysteriousnesse, for this is one of those parts of Scripture, (as the beginning of *Genesis*, and the Canticles of *Solomon*, also are) which are forbid to be read amongst the *Jews*, till they come to be *thirty* years old, which was the *Canonicall* age to be made Priests; In so much, that Saint *Gregory* says, when he comes to expound any part of this Prophet, *Nocturnum iter ago*, that he travelled by night, and did but ghesse at his way. But, besides that many of the obscure places of the Prophets are more open to *us*, then they were to the *ancients*, because many of those prophecies are now fulfilled, and so that which 30 was *Prophecy* to them, is *History* to us, in this place, which we have now undertaken, there never was darknesse, nor difficulty, neither in the first emanation of the light thereof, nor in the reflection; neither in the *Literall*, nor in the *Figurative* sense thereof; for the literall sense is plainly that, that amongst the manifold oppressions, under which the Children of *Israel* languished in *Babylon*, this was the heaviest, that their own *Priests* joyned with the *State* against them, and infused pestilent doctrines into them, that so themselves might enjoy the favour of the State, and the people committed to their charge, might slacken their obedience to *God*, and surrender them-40 selves to *all* commandements of *all men;* This was their oppression, the *Church* joyned with the *Court*, to oppresse them; Their own *Priests gave these sheep grasse which they had troden with their feet,* (*doctrines*, not as *God* gave them to them, but as *they* had tampered, and tempered them, and accommodated them to serve *turnes*, and fit their *ends*, whose servants they had made themselves, more then *Gods*) And they gave them *water* to *drink which they had troubled with their feet*, that is, doctrines mudded with other *ends* then the glory of *God;* And that therefore *God* would take his sheep into his own care, and reduce them from that double oppression of that *Court*, 50 and that *Church*, those Tyrannous *officers*, and those over-obsequious *Priests*. This is the *literall* sense of our text, and context, evident enough in the letter thereof. And then the *figurative* and *Mysticall* sense is of the same oppressions, and the same deliverance over againe in the times of *Christ*, and of the *Christian Church;* for that's more then figurative, fully literall, soon after the Text, *I will set up one shepheard, my servant David,* And *I will raise up for them a plant of*

ver. 23
29

[Isa.] 11.1
[Jer.] 23.5

renoune; which is the same that *Esay* had called *A rod out of the stem of Jesse,* and *Ieremy* had called *A righteous branch, a King that should raigne, and prosper.* This prophecy then comprehending the
⁶⁰ kingdome of Christ, it comprehends the *whole* kingdome of Christ, not onely the oppressions, and deliverances of *our forefathers,* from the *Heathen,* and the *Heretiques* in the *Primitive Church,* but that also which touches *us* more nearly, the oppressions and deliverance of *our Fathers,* in the *Reformation of Religion,* and the shaking *off* of the yoak of *Rome,* that *Italian Babylon,* as heavy as the *Chaldæan.* We shall therefore at this time fix our meditations upon that accommodation of the Text, the oppression that *the Israel of God* was under, *then,* when he delivered them by *that* way, the *Reformation* of *Religion,* and consider how these metaphors of the holy Ghost,
⁷⁰ *The treading with their feet the grasse that the sheep were to eate, and the troubling with their feet the water that the sheep were to drink,* doe answer and set out the oppressions of the *Roman Church then,* as lively as they did in the other *Babylon.* And so, having said enough of the *primary* sense of these words, as they concern Gods *Israel,* in the first *Babylon,* and something by way of commemoration, and thankfulnesse, for Gods deliverance of his *Israel,* from the persecutions in the *Primitive Church,* insist we now, upon the severall metaphors of the Text, as the holy Ghost continues them to the *whole* reigne of Christ, and so to the *Reformation.*

Pastores
concur-
rebant

⁸⁰   First, the greatest calamity of those sheep in *Babylon,* was that their own shepherds concurred to their oppression. In *Babylon* they were a *part,* but in *Rome* they were *all;* In *Babylon* they *joyned* with the State, but in *Rome* they *were* the State. Saint *Hierome* notes out

Mal. 1.7

of a Tradition of the *Iews,* that those *loafes* which their *Priests* were to offer to the *Lord,* were to be of such corne as those Priests had sowed, and reaped and threshed, and ground, and baked all with their own *hands.* But they were so farre from that at *Babylon,* and at

Iob 4.8

Ier. 12.10

Rome, as that they *ploughed iniquity, and sowed wickednesse, and reaped the same;* and (as *God* himselfe complaines) *trod his portion*
⁹⁰ *under foot;* That is, first, neglected his *people,* (for Gods people are his *portion*) And then whatsoever pious men had given to the Church, is his *portion* too, and that portion they had troden under foot; not neglected it, not despised it, for they collected it, and audited

it providently enough, but they trod it under foot, when that which
was given for the sustentation of the Priest, they turned upon their
own splendour, and glory, and surfet. Christ will be fed in the poor   [Mat.
that are hungry, and hee will be cloathed in the poore that are naked,   25.35-36]
so he would be enriched in those poor Ministers that serve at his
Altar; when Christ would be so fed, he desires not feasts and ban-
quets; when he would be so cloathed, hee desires not soft rayment
fit for *Kings houses,* nor embroyderies, nor perfumes; when he would   [Mat. 11.8]
be enriched in the poor *Church-man,* he desires not that he should be
a spunge, to drinke up the sweat of others, and live idly; but yet, as
he would not be starved in the hungry, nor submitted to cold and
unwholesome ayre in the naked, so neither would he be made contemptible, nor beggerly in the Minister of his Church. Nor, was there
in the world, (take in Turky, and all the heathen) (for they also have
their *Clergy*) a more contemptible and more beggerly *Clergy* then
that of Rome; I speak of the *Clergy* in the most proper sense, that is,
they that minister, they that officiate, they that execute, they that
personally and laboriously do the service of the Church. The *Prela-
cies,* and *Dignities* of the Church, were multiplyed in the hands of
them, who under pretext of *Government,* took their ease, and they
that labored, were attenuated and macerated, with lean, and penurious *pensions.* In the best governed Churches there are such *Dignities,* and supplies without *Cure of soules,* or personall service; but
they are intended *for recompence of former labours,* and sustentation
of their age, of whose youth, and stronger days, the Church had received benefit. But in the *Roman* Church these preferments are given
almost in the wombe; and children have them not onely before they
can merit them, but before they can *speake* for them; and they have
some Church-names, Dean, or Bishop, or Abbat, as soon almost as
they have any *Christian names.* Yea, we know many Church dignities, entailed to noble families, and, if it fall void, whilest the child is
so incapable, it must be held *for* him, by some that must resigne it,
when it may, by any extent of dispensation, be asked for him. So then
the *Church* joyned with the *State,* to defraud the people; The Priest
was poorly maintained, and so the people poorely instructed. And
this is the first conformity between the *two Babylons,* the *Chaldæan*
and the *Italian.*

Gramen

Super
terram

Pursue we then the *holy Ghosts* purpose and manner of implying, and expressing it, the food ordained for sheep, *Grasse*. In which make we onely these two stops, that the sheep are to eate their grasse *super terram*, upon the ground; And they are to eate it *sine rore*, when the dew is off. First, upon *the ground;* that is, where the hand of *God* hath set it; which for spirituall food is the *Church*. In hard winters we give sheep hay, but in open times open grasse. In *persecutions* of Tyrans, in *Interdicts* of Antichristian Bishops, who sometimes out of passion, or some secular respect shut up Church dores and forbid
140 service, and Sacraments, to whole Cities, to whole nations, sheep must live by *hay*, Gods Children must relieve themselves at home, *by books* of pious and devout meditation; But when *God* affords abundant pastures, and free entrance thereunto, Gods sheep are to take their grasse upon the *ground*, Gods grace at the Church. *Impossibile est eum corrigere, qui omnia scit, Chrysostome,* It is an impossible thing to correct him, that thinks he knows all things already. As long as he will admit counsaile from another, he acknowledges the other, to know more then he; but if he thinks, he knows all before, he hath no room for farther instruction, nor love to the place where it is to be
150 had. We read in the *Eastern Histories,* of a navigable River, that afforded all the inhabitants exportation, and importation, and all commerce. But when every particular man, to serve his own curiosity, for the offices of his house, for the pleasures of his gardens, and for the sumptuousnesse of Grots and aqueducts, and such waterworks, drew severall channells, infinite channells out of this great River, this exhausted the maine channell, and brought it to such a shallow-nesse, as would beare no boats, and so, took from them the great and common commodities that it had afforded them. So if every man think to provide himselfe *Divinity* enough *at home,* for himselfe and
160 his family, and out of laziness and singularity, or state, or disaffection to the preacher leave the *Church* unfrequented, he frustrates the Or-dinance of God, which is, that his sheep should come to his pastures, and take his grasse upon his ground, his instructions at his house at *Church*. And this we could not doe in the *Roman* Church, where all our prayers, and all Gods service of that kinde, were in a language, not onely not understood by him that *heard* it, but for the most part, not by him that *spoake* it. It is not of their manifold, and scornfull,

and ridiculous and histrionicall *Ceremonies* in their service, nor of
the dangerous poysons, the direct *Idolatries* (in the practise of the
people) in their service, that we complain of now, but of this, that
though it had been never so wholesome grasse, it was not so to those
sheep, they could not know it to be their proper aliment; for certainly they aske without *faith,* that aske without *understanding;* nor
can I beleeve or hope that God will give me that I aske, if I know
not *what* I asked. And what a miserable supply had they for this in
their *Legends;* for many of those Legends were in vulgar tongues
and understood by them. In which Legends, the *Virgin Mary* was
every good mans wife, and every good womans mid-wife, by a neigh-
borly, and familiar, and ordinary assistance in all houshold offices, as
we see in those Legends, and revelations. In which Legends, they
did not onely *faine actions,* which those persons never did, but they
fained persons which never were; and they did not onely *mis-canon-
ize* men, made Devills Saints, but they *mis-christened* men, put names
to persons, and persons to names that never were. And these *legends*
being transferred into the Church, the sheep lacke their grasse upon
the ground, that is, the knowledge of Gods will, in his house, at
Church. And this is another conformity between the *two Babylons,*
the *Chaldean,* and the *Italian Babylon,* that the sheep lacked *due food*
in the *due place.*

So is it also, that the sheep eat their grasse, whilest the *Dew* was
upon *it,* which is found by experience to be unwholesome. The word
of God is our grasse, which should be delivered purely, simply, sincerely, and in the naturall verdure thereof. The *Dews* which we intend, are *Revelations, Apparitions, Inspirations, Motions,* and *Interpretations* of the *private spirit.* Now, though we may see the naturall
dew to descend from heaven, yet it did first ascend from the earth, and
retains still some such earthly *parts,* as sheep cannot digest. So howsoever these Revelations and Inspirations seem to fall upon us from
heaven, they arise from the earth, from our selves, from our own
melancholy, and *pride,* or our too much *homelinesse* and familiarity
in our accesses, and conversation with God, or a *facility* in beleeving,
or an often *dreaming* the same thing. And with these Dews of Apparitions and Revelations, did the *Romane Church* make our fathers
drunk and giddy; And against these does S. *Augustine* devoutly

B. Virgo
femoralia.
B. Tho.
Cantuar.
reparavit
Cantiprat.
l. 2. c. 29

*Ros super
gramen*

pray, and praise God, that he had delivered him from the curiosity of sipping these dews, of hearkening after these apparitions and revelations. But so ordinary were these apparitions *then,* as that any son, or nephew, or friend, could discern his fathers, or uncles, or companions soul, ascending out of *Purgatory* into heaven, and know them
²¹⁰ as distinctly, as if they kept the same haire, and beard, and bodily lineaments, as they had upon earth. And as a ship which hath struck Sail, will yet goe on with the winde it had before, for a while, so now, when themselves are come to acknowledge, That it was the

Maldon.   unanime opinion of the *Fathers,* that the souls of the dead did not appeare after death, but that it was stil the *Devil,* howsoever sometimes that that he proposed were holy and religious, yet we see a

Coccius   great Author of theirs attribute so much to these apparitions, and revelations, that when he pretends to prove all controversies by the *Fathers* of the Church, he every where intermingles that reverend
²²⁰ *Book,* of *Brigids Revelations,* that they might also have some *Mothers* of the *Church* too; which is not disproportionall in *that* Church; if they have had a *woman Pope,* to have Mothers of the Church too. I speak not this, as though God might not, or did not manifest his will by *women;* The great mystery of the Resurrection of Christ was revealed to women before men; and to the sinfullest woman of the company, first. But I speak of that bold injury done to the mysteries of the Christian Religion, by pouring out that dew upon the grasse, the *Revelations* of S. *Brigid,* upon the controversies of Religion. A book of so much blasphemy, and impertinency, and incredibility, that
²³⁰ if a Heathen were to be converted, he would sooner be brought to beleeve *Ovids Metamorphoses,* then *Brigids Revelations,* to conduce to Religion. And this is also another conformity between the two *Babylons,* the *Chaldean,* and the *Italian Babylon,* that we could not receive our grasse pure, but infected, and *dewed* with these frivolous, nay pernicious *apparitions,* and *Revelations.*

Gramen   But press we a little closer to the very steps, and metaphor of the
concul-   holy Ghost, who here lays the corrupting of the sheeps grasse in this,
catum   *That the shepheards had troden it down.* And this *treading* down will be pertinently considered two ways. *Tertullian* in his Book *De*
²⁴⁰ *habitu muliebri,* notes two excesses in womens dressing; One he cals *Ornatum,* the other *cultum;* One *mundum muliebrem,* the other, (ac-

cording to the liberty that he takes in making words) *Immundum muliebrem;* the first is a *superfluous diligence* in their dressing, but the other an *unnaturall addition* to their complexion; the first he pronounces to be always *ad ambitionem,* for *pride,* but the other, *ad prostitutionem,* for a worse, for the worst purpose. These two sorts of Excesses doe note these two kindes of treading down the grasse, which we intend; of which one is, the mingling of too much *humane ornament,* and secular *learning* in *preaching,* in presenting the word of God, which word is our grasse; The other is of mingling *humane Traditions,* as of things of equall value, and obligation, with the Commandements of God. For the first, *humane ornament,* if in those pastures, which are ordain'd for sheep, you either plant rare and curious flowers, delightfull onely to the eye, or fragrant and odoriferous hearbs delightfull onely to the smell, nay, be they medicinall hearbs, usefull, and behovefull for the preservation, and restitution of the health of man, yet if these specious and glorious flowers, and fragrant, and medicinall hearbs, be not proper nourishment for sheep, this is a *treading down* of the grasse, a pestering and a suppressing of that which appertained to them. So if in your spirituall food, our preaching of the Word, you exact of us more secular ornament, then may serve, a*s Saint Augustine* says, *Ad ancillationem,* to convey, and usher the true word of life into your *understandings,* and *affections,* (for both those must necessarily be wrought upon) more then may serve *ad vehiculum,* for a chariot for the word of God to enter, and triumph in you, this is *a treading down of the grasse,* a filling of that ground which was ordained for sheep, with things improper, and impertinent to them. If you furnish a *Gallery* with stuffe proper for a Gallery, with *Hangings* and *Chairs,* and *Couches,* and *Pictures,* it gives you all the conveniencies of a Gallery, walks and prospect, and ease; but if you pester it with improper and impertinent furniture, with *Beds,* and *Tables,* you lose the use, and the name of a *Gallery,* and you have made it a *Wardrobe;* so if your curiosity extort more then convenient ornament, in delivery of the word of God, you may have a good *Oration,* a good *Panegyrique,* a good *Encomiastique,* but not so good a *Sermon.* It is true that Saint *Paul* applies sentences of secular Authors, even in matters of greatest importance; but then it is to persons that were accustomed to those authors, and affected with

them, and not conversant, not acquainted at all, with the phrase and
280 language of Scripture: amongst us now, almost every man (God be
blessed for it) is so accustomed to the text of Scripture, as that he is
more affected with the name of *David,* or Saint *Paul,* then with any
Seneca or *Plutarch.* I am far from forbidding secular ornament in
divine *exercises,* especially in some *Auditories,* acquainted with such
learnings. I have heard men preach against witty preaching; and doe
it with as much wit, as they have; and against learned preaching,
with as much learning, as they could compasse. If you should place
that *beast,* which makes the *Bezoar stone,* in a pasture of pure, but
onely grasse, it is likely, that out of his naturall faculty, he would
290 petrifie the juyce of that grasse, and make it a stone, but not such a
medicinall stone, as he makes out of those herbes which he feeds
upon. Let all things concur in the name of God, to the advancing
of his purpose, in his ordinance, which is, to make his will *acceptable*
to you, by his word; onely avoid excesse in the manner of doing it.
Saint *Augustines* is an excellent rule, when after in his book *De Doctrina Christiana,* he had taught a use of all Arts in Divinity, he allows
them onely thus far, *ut cum ingenia his reddantur exercitatiora,
cavendum ne reddantur maligniora,* that when a man by these helps
is the more ful, and the more ready and the more able for Church-
300 service, he be not also thereby made the more bold and the more
confident; *Nec ament decipere verisimili sermone,* lest because he
is able to make any thing seem probable and likely to the people, by
his eloquence, he come to infuse paradoxicall opinions, or schismaticall, or (which may be beleeved either way) problematicall opinions,
for certain and constant truths, and so be the lesse conversant, and
the lesse diligent in advancing plaine, and simple, and fundamentall
doctrines and catechisticall, which are truely necessary to salvation,
as though such plaine, and ordinary, and catechisticall doctrines were
not worthy of his gifts and his great parts. In a word, in *sheep-
310 pastures* you may plant fruit trees in the *hedge-rowes;* but if you
plant them all over, it is an *Orchard;* we may transfer flowers of
secular learning, into these exercises; but if they consist of those, they
are but *Themes,* and *Essays.* But why insist we upon this? Was there
any such conformity between the two *Babylons* as that the *Italian
Babylon* can be said to have troden down the grasse in that kinde,

with overcharging their Sermons with *too much learning*. Truly it was far, very very far from it; for when they had prevailed in that Axiome, and Aphorisme of theirs, that it was best to keep the *people* in *ignorance,* they might justly keep *the Priest* in ignorance too; for when the people needed *no learned instruction,* what needed the Church a *learned instructer?* And therefore I laid hold of this consideration, the treading down of grass, by oppressing it with secular learning, there by to bring to your remembrance, the extreme ignorance that damp'd the *Roman* Church, at that time; where *Aristotles Metaphysicks* were condemned for Heresie, and ignorance in generall made not onely pardonable, but meritorious. Of which times, if at any time, you read the Sermons, which were then preached, and after published, you will excuse them of this treading down the grass, by oppressing their auditories with *over-much learning,* for they are such Sermons as will not suffer us to pity them, but we must necessarily scorne, and contemne, and deride them; Sermons, at which the gravest, and saddest man could not choose but laugh; not at the Sermon, God forbid; nor at the plainness, and homeliness of it; God forbid; but at the Solœcismes, the barbarismes, the servilities, the stupid ignorance of those things which fall within the knowledge of boys of the first forme in every School. This was their treading down of grass, not with over-much learning, but with a cloud, a dampe, an earth of ignorance. After an *Oxe* that oppresseth the grass, after a *Horse* that devours the grass, sheep will feed; but after a *Goose* that stanches the grass, they will not; no more can Gods sheep receive nourishment from him that puts a scorne upon his function, by his ignorance.

Hosius

But in the other way of treading down grasse, (that is, the word of God) by the Additions and Traditions of men, the *Italian Babylon Rome* abounded, superabounded, overflowed, surrounded all. And this is much more dangerous then the other; for this mingling of humane additions, and traditions, upon equall necessity, and equall obligation as the word of God it selfe, is a kneading, an incorporating of *grasse and earth* together, so, as that it is impossible for the weake sheep, to avoid eating the meat of the *Serpent, Dust shalt thou eate all the days of thy life*. Now man upon his transgression, was not accursed, nor woman; The sheep were not accursed; But the earth

Concul-catum per tra-ditiones

Gen. 3.[14]

was, and the Serpent was; and now this kneading, this incorporating of earth with grasse, traditions with the word, makes the sheep to eate the cursed meat of the cursed Serpent, *Dust shalt thou eat all the days of thy life.*

Now, in this treading down this grasse, this way, this suppressing it by traditions, be pleased to consider these *two applications;* some traditions doe destroy the word of God, extirpate it, annihilate it, as when a *Hog* doth root up the grass; In which case, not onely that turfe withers, and is presently useless, and unprofitable to the sheep, but if you dig never so low after, down to the Center of the earth, it is impossible ever to finde any more grass under it: so some traditions doe utterly oppose the word of God, without having under them, any mysterious signification, or any occasion or provocation of our devotion, which is the ordinary pretext of traditions, and *Ceremoniall additions* in their Church. And of this sort was that amongst the *Jews,* of which our *blessed Saviour* reproches them, that whereas by the law, children were to relieve decayed parents, they had brought in a tradition, of *Commutation,* of *Compensation,* that if those children gave a *gift* to the *Priest,* or compounded with the Priest, they were discharged of the former obligation. And of this sort are many traditions in the *Roman Church;* where, not onely the doctrines of *men* but the doctrine of *Devills,* (as the Apostle calls the forbidding of *Mariage,* and of *meats*) did not onely tread down, but root up the true grass.

The other sort of Traditions, and Ceremonies, doe not as the Hog, root up the grass, but as a *Mole,* cast a slack, and thin earth upon the face of the grass. Now, if the shepheard, or husbandman be present to scatter this earth againe, the sheep receive no great harme, but may safely feed upon the wholesome grass, that is under; but if the sheep, who are not able to scatter this earth, nor to finde the grass that lies under, be left to their own weakness, they may as easily starve in this case, as in the other; the *Mole* may damnifie them as much as the *Hog.* And of this sort, are those traditions, which induce *Ceremonies* into the Church, in *vestures,* in *postures* of the body, in *particular* things, and words, and actions, in Baptisme or Mariage, or any other thing to be transacted in the Church. These ceremonies are not the institutions of *God* immediately, but they are a kind of light earth,

Sicut Porcus

360

Mat. 15.[5]

370

1 Tim. 4.[1, 3]

Sicut Talpa

380

that hath *under it* good and usefull significations, which when they
be understood conduce much to the encrease and advancement of our
devotion, and of the glory of God. And this is the iniquity that we
complaine of in the *Roman Church,* that when we accuse them of
multiplying impertinent, and insupportable ceremonies, they tell us,
of some mysterious and pious signification, in the institution thereof
at first; They tell us this, and it is sometimes true; But neither in
Preaching nor practise, doe they scatter this earth to their own sheep,
or shew them the grass that lies under, but suffer the people, to in-
here, and arrest their thoughts, upon the ceremony it selfe, or that to
which that ceremony mis-leads them; as in particular, (for the time
will not admit many examples) when they *kneel at the Sacrament,*
they are not told, that they kneel because they are then in the act of
receiving an inestimable benefit at the hands of God, (which was the
first reason of kneeling then) And because the *Priest* is then in the
act of *prayer* in their behalfe, that that may preserve them, in body
and soule, unto eternall life. But they are suffered to go on, in kneeling in adoration of that *bread,* which they take to be God. We deny
not that there are *Traditions,* nor that there must be *ceremonies,* but
that maters of *faith* should depend of these, or be made of these, that
we deny; and that they should be made equall to *Scriptures;* for
with that especially doth *Tertullian* reproch the Heretiques, that
being pressed with Scriptures, they fled to Traditions, as things equall
or superiour to the word of God. I am loth to depart from *Tertullian,*
both because he is every where a Patheticall expresser of himselfe, and
in this point above himselfe. *Nobis curiositate opus non est, post
Jesum Christum, nec Inquisitione, post Evangelium.* Have we seen
that face of Christ Jesus here upon earth, which Angels desired to
see, and would we see a better face? Traditions perfecter then the
word? Have we read the four *Evangelists,* and would we have a
better Library? Traditions fuller then the word? *Cum credimus, nihil
desideramus ultra credere;* when I beleeve God in Christ, dead, and
risen againe according to the Scriptures, I have nothing else to beleeve; *Hoc enim prius credimus, non esse quod ultra credere de-
beamus;* This is the first Article of my Faith, that I am bound to beleeve nothing but articles of faith in an equall necessity to them. Will
we be content to be well, and thank God, when we are well? *Hilary*

tells us, when we are well; *Bene habet quod iis, quæ scripta sunt, contentus sis;* then thou art well, when thou satisfiest thy self with those things, which God hath vouchsafed to manifest in the *Scriptures.*
430 *Si aliquis aliis verbis, quàm quibus à Deo dictum est, demonstrare velit,* if any man will speake a new language, otherwise then God hath spoken, and present new Scriptures, (as he does that makes traditions equall to them) *Aut ipse non intelligit, aut legentibus non intelligendum relinquit,* either he understands not himself, or I may very well be content not to understand him, if I understand God without him. The *Fathers* abound in this opposing of Traditions, when out of those traditions, our adversaries argue an insufficiency in the Scriptures. *Solus Christus audiendus,* says Saint *Cyprian,* we hearken to none but Christ; *nec debemus attendere quid aliquis ante nos faci-*
440 *endum putarit,* neither are we to consider what any man *before us* thought fit to be done, *sed quid qui ante omnes est, fecerit;* but what he, who is *before all* them, did; *Christ Jesus* and his *Apostles,* who were not onely the primitive but the *pre-primitive Church,* did and appointed to be done. In this treading down of our grasse then in the *Roman* Church, first by their supine *Ignorance,* and barbarisme, and then by *traditions,* of which, some are pestilently infectious and *destroy* good words, some *cover* it so, as that not being declared to the people in their signification, they are uselesse to them, no *Babylon* could exceed the *Italian Babylon, Rome,* in treading down their
450 grasse.

Aqua

Psal. 23.2

Their oppression was as great in the other, *In troubling their water, My sheep drink that which you have troubled.* When the Lord is our shepherd, he leadeth us *ad aquas quietudinum,* to the waters of rest, of quietnesse; of these, in the *plurall, quietudinum,* quietness of *body,* and quietness of *Conscience* too. The endowments of heaven are *Joy,* and *Glory;* joy, and glory are the two Elements, the two Hemispheres of Heaven; And of this Joy, and this Glory of heaven, we have the best *earnest* that this world can give, if we have *rest;* satisfaction and acquiescence in our religion, for our beleefe, and for our life and
460 actions, peace of Conscience. And where the Lord is our shepherd he leads us, and *ad aquas quietudinum,* to the waters of rest, multiplyed rest; all kind of rest. But the shepherds, in our text, *troubled* the waters; and more then so; for we have just cause to note the *double*

signification of this word, which we translate *Trouble,* and to transfer
the two significations to the two Sacraments, as they are exhibited in
the *Roman Babylon;* The word is *Mirpas;* and it denotes not onely
Conturbationem, a troubling, a mudding, but *Obturationem* too, an
interception, a stopping, as the *Septuagint* translates it, *Prov.* 25.26, and
in these two significations of the word, a *troubling,* and a *stopping* of
the waters, hath the *Roman* Church exercised her tyranny, and her
malignity, in the *two Sacraments.* For, in the Sacrament of *Baptisme,*
they had *troubled* the water, with *additions* of Oile, and salt, and
spittle, and exorcismes; But in the *other* Sacrament they came *Ad
obturationem,* to a stopping, to an intercision, to an interruption of
the water, the water of life, *Aquæ quietudinum,* the water of rest to
our souls, and peace to our consciences, in *withholding the Cup* of
salvation, the bloud of Christ Jesus from us. So that if thou come to
Davids holy expostulation, *Quid retribuam, what shall I render unto
the Lord for all his benefits towards me?* And pursue it to *Davids*
holy resolution, *Accipiam Calicem,* I will take the *Cup* of salvation,
you shall be told, Sir you must take *Orders* first, or you cannot take
that Cup. But water is as common as Aire; And as that Element
Aire, in our spirituall food, that is preaching, (which is *Spiritus
Domini,* the breath of God) is common to all, *Ite, prædicate omni
Creaturæ, goe preach the Gospell to every Creature,* so is this water
of life in the Sacrament, common to all, *Bibite ex eo omnes, Drink
yee all of this;* and thereby doe the names of *Communion,* and participation accrew to it, because all have an interest in it. This is that
bloud, of which Saint *Chrysostome* says, *Hic sanguis facit, ut Imago
Dei in nobis floreat;* That we have the Image of God in our souls,
we have by the benefit of the same nature, by which we have our
souls; There cannot be a humane soule without the Image of God
in it. But, *ut floreat,* that this Image *appear to us,* and be continually
refreshed in us, *ut non languescat animæ nobilitas,* that this holy
noblenesse of the soule doe not languish nor degenerate in us, we
have by the benefit of this bloud of *Christ Jesus* the seale of our absolution in that blessed and glorious Sacrament; And that bloud
they deny us. This is that bloud of which they can make as much as
they will, with a thought, with an intention; so, as they pretend a
power, of changing a whole vintage at once, all the wine of all the

Psal. 116.12

Mar. 16.15

Mat. 26.27

nations in the world, into the bloud of Christ, if the Priest have an *intention* to doe so, in the time of his Consecration; And yet, as easily as they come by it, they will give us none. They have told us, that we had it *per Concomitantiam,* by a necessary concomitancy; That because we had the body in the bread, and that body could not be without the bloud, that therefore we had the bloud also. But if the bread alone be enough, if the Cup be impertinent, why did Christ give it? If we have no losse in their detaining it from us, what gain have they in retaining it to themselves, let all have it, or none? It is
510 true that they can performe all the *ill,* that they would doe, by the *bread* alone. They can worke the spirituall ill, of inducing *adoration* to a Creature, by the bread alone; And they could work the temporall ill, of *poysoning an Emperour* in the Sacrament, by the bread alone. They can come to all their purposes, to all *their ill,* by the bread alone; but we have not all *our good,* because we have not Christs intire Institution. And so in this troubling, and in this stopping of these waters, in these confusions, we challenge any *Babylon,* in the behalfe of this *Italian Babylon, Rome.*

Pedes
    All these oppressions are aggravated by the last, and (as weightiest
520 things sink to the bottome) so is this in the bottome the heaviest pressure, that they did this with *their feet,* they corrupted the grasse with their *feet,* and troubled the waters with their *feet.* Now, in the Scriptures, when this word, *feet,* doth not signifie that part of mans body which is ordinarily so called, but is transferred to a *Metaphori-call* signification, (as in our text it is) it does most commonly

1 Sam. 2.9   signifie *Affections,* or *Power.* So the *Lord will keep the feet* of his Saints; that is, direct their *desires,* and *affections* in the ways of holinesse. And then for *Power,* (which is the more frequent accepta-

Psal. 121.3   tion of the word) he will not suffer *thy foot* to be moved, that is, thy
530 *Power* to be shaked; And all such places, *qui festinus,* he that hasteth

Prov. 19.2   with *his feet* sinneth, our interpreters expound of a hasty abuse of

Ier. 14.10   *Power;* And those, they have not refrained *their feet,* and then, *thy*
38.22   *feet* are sunk in the mire, are still interpreted of *Power,* of a wanton abuse of Power, or of a withdrawing this Power from man, *by God; feet* signifies Affections, and them corrupted and depraved, and power, and that abused. *David* seems to have joyned them, (as when they are joyned, they must necessarily be the most heavy) in that

prayer, Let not *the foot of pride* come against me. The *hand* of pride,   Psal. 36.11
nay the *sword* of pride, affects not a tender soule so much, as the *foot*
of pride; to be oppressed, and that with *scorne;* not so much in an
anger, as in a *wantonnesse.* *Rehoboams* 'people' were more confounded, with that scornfull answer of his to them, when they were
come, (*My little finger shall be thicker then my Fathers loynes; my*   1 King.
father chastised you with whips, but I will chastise you with   12.10
Scorpions) then they were with the grievances themselves, for which
they came; when the King would not onely be *cruelly* sharp, but
wittily sharp upon them, this cut on every side, and pierced deep.
And so doe the *Rabbins,* the Jewish expositors expound this text,
literally, that in the captivity of *Babylon,* the great men of their
Synagogues, compounded with the State, and for certain tributes, had
commissions, by which they governed their people at their pleasure,
and so milked them to the last drop, the last drop of bloud, and
sheared them to the naked skin, and then flead off that, and al this
while *laughed* at them, contemned them, because they had no where,
to appeal, nor relieve themselves: And this we complain to have been
the proceeding in the *Italian Babylon, Rome,* with our Fathers, *They*
oppressed them, with their *feet,* that is, with *Power,* and with *scorne.*

   First, for their illimited and enormous *Power,* they had so slum-   *Pes potes-*
bred, so intoxicated the Princes of the Earth, the weaker by intimida-   *tatis*
tions, the stronger by communicating the spoile, and suffering those
Princes to take some fleeces, from some of the sheep in their
dominions, as there was no reliefe any way. They record, nay they
boast, gloriously, triumphantly, of *threescore thousand of the*
Waldenses, slain by them in a day, in the beginning of the Reformation; and *Possevine* the Jesuit will not lose the glory of recording
the *five hundred thousand,* slain in a very few years, onely in *France,*
and the *low Countrey,* for some declarations of their desire of a
Reformation. Let all those innumerable numbers of wretches, (but
now victorious Saints in the Triumphant Church) who have breathed
out their souls in the *Inquisition* (where even the solicitations of
Kings, and that for their own sons, have not prevailed) confess the
power, the immensness of that power, then, when as under some of
the *Roman Emperours,* it was treason to weep, treason to sigh, treason
to look pale, treason to fall sicke, and all these were made arguments

of discontent, and ill affection, to the present government: so in *Rome,* there were Hereticall sighes, Hereticall teares, Hereticall palenesse, and Hereticall sicknesse; every thing was interpreted to be an accusation of the present times, and an anhelation after a Reformation, and that was formall heresie, three pil'd, deep-died heresie: so 580 that a man durst scarce have prayed for the enlarging of Gods blessings to the Church, because to wish it better, seemed a kind of accusing of it, that it was not well already; and it was heresie to thinke so. Let those *Israelites,* which found no way from this *Egypt,* but by *the red sea,* no way out of Idolatry, but by *Martyrdome,* as they have testified for Christ, so testifie against Antichrist, how heavy his feet, as feet signifie Power, trod upon the necks of Princes and people.

Pes su-
perbiæ

But that that affected and afflicted most, was the *scorne* and the *contempt,* that accompanied their oppressions. To bring Kings to 590 *kisse his feet,* was a scorne; but that scorne determined in man; but it was a scorne to *God* himselfe, to say that he had said, it should be so, to apply Scripture to the justification thereof, *Kings and Queens shall bow down to thee, their faces towards the Earth, and lick up the dust of thy feet.* But limit we all considerations of their scorne in one; In this, that they did these wrongs professedly, and without any disguise. Great men will oppresse and ruine others, a great while before they will be content to be seen and known to doe it. There is such a kinde of reverence, not onely to *Law,* but even to *honour,* and *opinion,* as that men are lothe to *publish* their evill actions; To sinne 600 as *Sodome* did, and not to *hide* it, is an evidence, of neglecting, and scorning of all the world. And therefore the *Roman Historiographers* would not forbeare to note the insolency of that young gallant, who knowing what any man whom he strook could recover by action against him, would strike every poor soul or inferiour person, whom he met in the street, and then bid his man give him so much money, as the Law would for damages. And this oppressing with scorne, this proceeding without any respect of fame, we note (for hast) but in two things, in the *Italian Babylon Rome;* first, in that *Book,* their *Taxa Cameræ,* and then in that doctrine, their *Reservatio Casuum,* 610 that they durst compose, and divulge such a book, as their *Taxa Cameræ,* which is an *Index,* a Repertory for all sinnes, and in which

Esay 49.23

Taxa
cameræ

every man may see beforehand, how much money, an Adultery, an Incest, a Murder, a Parricide, or any other sinne, whose name he would never have thought of, but by that Remembrancer, that book will cost him, that so, he may sinne, and not undoe himself, sinne according to his means, and within his compasse; that they durst let the world see such a book, was argument enough that they were sear'd up, and scorned all that all men could think, or say, or doe in opposition.

So also is their Reservation of Cases; that though all Priests have an equall power of remitting all sins, yet are some sinnes reserved onely to *Prelates,* some onely to the Popes *Legats,* some onely to the Pope *himselfe.* Is not this a scornfull spurning and kicking of the world, a plain telling them that all is done for money, and shall be so, say all the world what it can? They have a nationall custome in civill curtesies in that place in *Italy,* to offer entertainments and lendings of money, and the like, but it must not be accepted. It is a discurtesie, to take their courteous offers in earnest. Will they play so with the great Seale of heaven, the remission and absolution of sins, and send out their Priests with that commission, *whose sinnes yee forgive, are forgiven,* but see you forgive none upon which we have set a higher price, and reserved to our selves. They had such a fashion in old *Rome,* whilest the Republique stood; He that was admitted to Triumph must *invite* the Consuls to the feast, and the Consuls must *promise* to come, but they must forbeare, lest their presence should diminish the glory of the Triumpher. So the Priest must professe that he hath (as he hath indeed) power to remit all sinnes, but there are a great many, that he must not meddle withall. They practise this reservation upon higher persons then their ordinary Priests, upon *Cardinals.* A Cardinall is created, and by that creation he hath a voice in all the great affairs of the world, but at his creation *Os clauditur à Papa,* he that made him, makes him dumbe, and he that out of the nature of his place is duly to be heard over all the world, must not be heard in the Consistory, the Pope gives him an universall voice, and then shuts his mouth; He makes him first a *Giant,* and then a *dwarfe* in an houre; He makes him thunder, and speechlesse, all at once; fearfull to the Kings of the earth, if he might speak, but he must not. They were not content to

Reser-
vatio
casuum

[Joh. 20.23]

make *Merchandize* of our souls, but they make *plays, jests, scornes,*
650 of matter of salvation, and play fast and loose with that soveraign
Balsamum of our souls, the absolution and remission of sins. Though,
no doubt, many of them confess in their own bosomes, that which
one of them professes ingenuously, and publiquely, *Diffiteri non*
possumus abusum Reservationum, & stragem animarum in iis; we
cannot deny the abuse of reservations, even to the butchery of those
poor souls, who, by reason of these reservations, want their absolution,
Dolendum, deflendum, pecuniâ numeratâ, omnia dispensare; This
deserves all our teares, all our sighs, that for money, and not without
it, all sinnes are dispensed withall; but there are *fixed seasons for*
660 *salvation,* (some remissions and pardons are reserved to certain times
of the year) and there are *fixt shops of salvation,* (some remissions
and pardons are appropriated to certain Fairs and Markets, and cannot be given (that is sold) at any other time, or place. And farther
we cannot (we need not) extend this accommodation of the words
of our text, literally intended of the conditions of Gods Children in
Babylon, but pregnantly appliable to the condition of our Fathers in
the *Italian Babylon, Rome.* But having at this time seen the oppressions that those shepheards inflicted there, for the rest which are many
and important considerations, as first that they staid, that they eate
670 that grasse, that yet they remained Gods sheep, and remained his
flock, his Church, though a Church under a greater Church; And
then the behaviour of the sheep, whilst they staid there, their obedience to Gods call in comming from them when he called them, and
made them way; And lastly the little ground that our Separatists
can have, for their departing from us, either by *Israels* departing from
Babylon, or our Fathers departing from *Rome,* must be the exercise
of your devotion another day.

Tapperus

Number 7.

Preached at White-Hall.

THE SECOND SERMON ON EZEK. 34.19. *AND AS FOR MY FLOCK, THEY EATE THAT, WHICH YEE HAVE TRODEN WITH YOUR FEET, AND THEY DRINK THAT WHICH YEE HAVE FOULED WITH YOUR FEET.*

A S BY WAY of accommodation, we have considered these words, as they concern the *iniquity* and *oppression* of the *shepheards*, (that is, the chief rulers amongst the *Jews*) in the *Chaldean Babylon*, and as they are appliable to the condition of our *Fathers* in the *Italian Babylon, Rome*, so now in this exercise are we to consider, the *behaviour of the sheep*, their nature, and their demeanour under all these pressures; in which we have many steps to goe; All these; first, *Manebant*, that for all this ill usage there they did stay, they did not breake out, nor scatter themselves, *manebant;*
10 And then *Edebant*, though their grasse were troden, and their water troubled, yet they did *eat* that grasse, and they did drink that water, *Edebant;* And doing so, *Manebant Oves*, they continued sheep, they lost not the nature, nor property of sheep, *Manebant Oves*, and *Oves Dei*, they continued *Gods sheep;* (for the Devill hath his sheep too) *my sheep*, says God; not those which *had* been mine, when they eat fresh grasse, and drunke pure water, but then, when they eat troden grasse, and drunke troubled water, they were Gods sheep; And more then that, they were *Grex Dei, Gods flock;* for those [1 Pet. 5.2] whom our former translation calls my *sheep*, the latter calls my *flock;*

159

²⁰ God hath *single sheep* in many corners of the *heathen,* but these, though thus fed, were his *flock,* his *Church.* But then, though they staid Gods leasure, and lived long upon this ill diet, yet when God was pleased to call them out of *Babylon,* out of *Babylon* they went, when God was pleased to lead our *Fathers* out of *Rome,* they left it. And justly, howsoever our Adversaries load us with contumelious names for that departure; in which branch, we shall see the vanity of their criminations, and imputations to us for that secession from them. And then lastly, by way of condoling and of instructing, we shall make it appear to our weak brethren, that our departing from
³⁰ Rome, can be no example, no justification of their departing from us. Our branches then, from whence we are to gather our fruit, being thus many, it is time to lay hold upon the first, which is *Manebant,* Though these sheep were thus ill fed, yet they did stay.

Optimis ovibus pedes breves; The best sheep have shortest leggs; Their commendation is, not to make hast in straying away. He that *hasteth with his feet sinneth;* that is, from the station in which God hath placed him. *Si innumera bona fecerimus,* If we have abounded in good works, and done God never so good service, *Non minores pœnas dabimus, quàm qui Christi corpus proscindebant, si inte-*
⁴⁰ *gritatem Ecclesiarum discerpserimus,* we are as guilty in the eies of God, as they that crucifyed the Lord of life himselfe, if we violate his spouse, or rent the intirenesse of his Church. *Vir quidam sanctus dixit,* (says the same father of another, *Chrysostome* of *Cyprian*) A certaine holy man hath ventured to say, *Quod audaciùs sapere videtur, attamen dixit,* That which perchance may seem boldly sayd, but yet he sayd it; what was it? This, *peccatum istud nec martyrio deleri;* That this sin of *schisme,* of renting the unity of the Church, cannot be expiated no not by Martyrdome it self. When God had made but a *hedge* about *Job,* yet that hedge was such a fence as the
⁵⁰ Devill could not break in: when God hath carryed *Murum æneum* a wall of brasse, nay *Murum igneum,* a wall of fire about his Church, wilt thou break out through that wall, that brasse, that fire? *Paradise* was not walled, nor hedged; and there were serpents in Paradise too; yet *Adam* offered not to goe out of Paradise, till God drove him out; and God saw that he would have come in againe, if the Cherubims and the flaming sword had not been placed by God to hinder him.

Charme the Charmer never so wisely, (as *David* speaks) he cannot   Psal. 58.5
utter a sweeter, nor a more powerfull charme, then that, *Ego te*
baptizo, I baptize thee in the name of the Father, and of the Sonne,
and of the Holy Ghost; And, *Nos admittimus, we receive this child,*
into the congregation of Christs flock; There is a sweet and a powerfull charm, in the *Ego te absolvo,* I absolve thee from all thy sins;
But this blessed charm I may heare from another, if I stray into
another Church. But the *Ego te baptizo* I can heare but once; and to
depart from that Church, in which I have received my baptism,
and in which I have made my Contracts and my stipulations with
God, and pledged and engaged my sureties there, deserves a mature
consideration; for I may mistake the reasons upon which I goe, and
I may finde after, that there are more true errours in the Church I
goe to, then there were imaginary in that that I left. Truly I have
been sorry to see some persons converted from the Roman Church,
to ours; because I have known, that onely *temporall respects* have
moved them, and they have lived after rather in a *nullity,* or *indif-*
ferency to either religion, then in a true, and established zeale. Of
which kinde, I cannot forbeare to report to you so much of the
story of a French gentleman, who though he were of good parts, and   Peletier
learned, yet were not worthy to be mentioned in this place, but that
he soar'd so high, as to write against the learnedst King, that any age
hath produc'd, our incomparable King *James.* This man, who was
turned from the Reformed to the Roman religion, being asked, halfe
in jest; Sir, which is the best religion, you must needs know, that
have been of both? answered, Certainely, the religion I left, the
reformed religion, must needs be the best religion, for when I
changed, I had this religion, the *Roman religion,* for it, and three
hundred Crowns a year to boot; which was a *pension* given him,
upon his conversion. Neither truely doth any thing more loosen a
mans footing, nor slacken his hold upon that Church in which he
was baptized, nor open him more to an undervaluation of all
Churches, then when he gives himselfe leave, to thinke irreverently,
slightly, negligently of the *Sacraments,* as of things, at best, *indif-*
ferent, and, many times, *impertinent.* I should thinke I had no bowels,
if they had not earn'd and melted, when I heard a *Lady,* whose child
of five or sixe daies, being ready to die every minute, she being mov'd

often that the *child might be christened,* answered, That, if it were
Gods will, that the child should live to the Sabbath, that it might be
baptized in the Congregation, she should be content, otherwise, Gods
will be done upon it, for *God needs no Sacrament.* With what sorrow,
with what holy indignation did I heare the Sonne of my friend, who
brought me to that place, to minister the Sacrament to him, then,
100 upon his death-bed, and almost at his last gaspe, when my service was
offered him in that kinde, answer his Father, *Father, I thanke God,
I have not lived so in the sight of my God, as that I need a Sacrament.*
I name a few of these, because *our times* abound with such persons as
undervalue, not onely all *rituall,* and *ceremoniall* assistances of devotion, which the wisdome, and the piety of the Church hath induced,
but even the *Sacraments themselves,* of Christs owne immediate
institution, and are alwaies open to solicitations to passe to another
Church, upon their own surmises of errours in their own. Whereas
there belongs much consideration, and a well grounded assurance,
110 of fundamentall errours in one Church, and that those errours are
repayred, and no other, as great as those, admitted, in the other
Church, before, upon any collaterall pretences, we abandon that
Church, in which God hath sealed us to himselfe in Baptisme. Our
Fathers stayd in Rome; *Manebant,* They stayd, and *Edebant,* they
eat that grasse, and they drunke that water, which was troden and
troubled.

Edebant   Alasse, what should they have eaten, what should they have
drunke? should a man *strangle* himselfe rather then take in an ill
ayre? Or forebear a *good table,* because his stomach cannot digest
120 *every dish?* We doe not call *money,* base *money,* till the Allay exceed
the pure metall; and if it doe so, yet it may be currant, and serve to
many offices; Those that are skilfull in that art, know how to sever
the base from the pure, the good parts of the religion from the bad;
and those that are not, will not cast it away, for all the corrupt
mixture. It is true, they had been better to have stayd at home and
served God in private, then to have communicated in a superstitious
Aug. Iu-   service. *Domum vestram Christi Ecclesiam deputamus,* I shall never
lianæ   doubt to call your House the Church of Christ. But this was not
viduæ   permitted to our Fathers; to serve God at home; to Church they
ep. 143   130 must come, and there, all their grasse was troden, and all their water

troubled. What should they doe? God never brings us to a perplexity, so as that we must necessarily do one sinne to avoyd another. Never. It seemes that the *Apostles* had been traduced, and insimulated of teaching this Doctrine, That in some cases evill might be done that good might follow; and therefore doth S. *Paul* with so much diligence discharge himself of it. And yet, long after this, when those men, who attempted the *Reformation,* whom they called *Pauperes de Lugduno,* taught that Doctrine, *That no lesse sinne might be done, to escape a greater,* this was imputed to them, then, by the Roman

140 Church, for an Heresie; That that was Orthodox in *Saint Paul,* was Heresie in them that studyed a Reformation. But the Doctrine stands like a rocke against all waves, That nothing that is *naturally* ill, *intrinsecally* sinne, may upon any pretence be done, not though our lifes, nor the lifes of all the Princes in the world, though the frame, and beeing of the whole world, though the salvation of our souls lay upon it; no sinne, naturally, intrinsecally sinne might be done, for any respect. *Christus peccatum factus est, sed non fecit peccatum,* Though Christ pursued our redemption with hunger, and thirst, yet he would have left us unredeemed, rather than have committed any

150 sinne. Of this kinde therefore, naturally, intrinsecally sinne, *and so known to be to them that did it,* certainly our Fathers coming to the superstitious service in the Church of Rome, was not: for had it been naturally sinne, and so known *to them,* when they did it, they could not have been saved, otherwise then by repentance after, which we cannot presume in their behalfe, for there are no testimonies of it. If any of them had invested at any time a scruple, a doubt whether they did well or no, alasse how should they devest and overcome that scruple? To whom durst they communicate that doubt? They were under an invincible ignorance, and sometimes under an indevestible

160 scruple. They had heard that Christ commanded *to beware of the leaven of the Pharisees,* and *Sadduces,* and so of the *Herodians;* that is, of the doctrines of those particular sects; of affirming *Fate,* and *Destiny,* and *Stoicall necessity,* with the *Pharisees;* of denying *Spirits,* and *Resurrection* with the *Sadduces;* of mis-applying the prophesies concerning the *Messias,* to the person of *Herod,* or any earthly King; But yet, after all this, he commands them to observe, and performe the doctrine of the *Pharisees, because they sate in Moses chaire;*

Rom. 3.8

Prateolus
Art. 23

August.

Mat. 16.6
Mar. 8.15

Mat. 23.2

Through with much vehemence and bitternesse, he call them *Hypo-crites,* though with many ingeminations upon every occasion, he
170 reiterate that name, though he aggravate that name with other names of equall reproach, *Fools, blinde guides, painted tombes,* and the like, yet he commands to obey them; and, which is most remark-able, this is sayd, not onely to the common sort, but even to *his own disciples* too; Christ had begunne his work of establishing a Church, which should empty their Synagogues; but because that worke was not yet perfected, he would not withdraw the people from their Synagogues; for there *wrought Gods Ordinance,* (though corrupted by the workmen) which Ordinance was, that the law should be publiquely expounded to the people; and so it was there; There God
180 was present; And though the Devill (by their corruption) were there too, yet, the Devill came in at the *window,* God at the dore; the Devill by stealth, God by his declared Ordinance, and *Covenant.* And this was the case of our Fathers in the *Roman Church;* They must know that all that hath passed between God and man hath passed *Ex pacto,* by way of contract and covenant.

The best   The *best* works of the *best* man have no proportion with the king-dome of heaven, for I give God but his own: But I have it *Ex pacto,*
[Luk. 10.28]   God hath covenanted so, *Fac hoc & vives, Doe this and thou shalt live;* and at the last judgement, Christ shall ground his *Venite bene-*
[Mat. 25.34] 190 *dicti,* Come ye blessed, and his *Ite maledicti,* Goe ye accursed, upon the *Quia,* and upon the *Quia non,* Because you have, and Because you have not done this and this. *Faith,* that is of infinite value above works, hath yet no proportion to the kingdome of heaven; *Faith* saves mee, as my *hand* feeds mee; It reaches the food, but it is not the food; but faith saves *Ex pacto,* by vertue of that Covenant, which
Mar. 5.36   Christ hath made, *Tantummodo crede,* Onely beleeve. To carry it to the highest, the *merit of Christ Jesus* himselfe, though it bee infinite so, as that it might have redeemed infinite worlds, yet the working thereof is safeliest considered in the School to be *Ex pacto,* by vertue
200 of that contract which had passed between the Father and him, that all things should thus and thus be transacted by Christ, and so man should be saved; for, if we shall place it meerely, onely in the in-finitenesse of the merit, Christs death would not have needed; for his first drops of bloud in his *Circumcision,* nay his very *Incarnation*

(that God was made man) and every act of his humiliation after, being taken singly, yet, *in that person,* God and man, were of infinite merit; and also, if it wrought meerly by the infinitnesse of the merit, it must have wrought, not onely upon all men, but to *the salvation of the Devill;* for, certainely there is more merit in Christ, then there
10 is sinne in the Devill. But the proceeding was *Ex pacto,* according to the contract made, and to the conditions given; *Ipse conteret caput*   [Gen. 3.15] *tuum,* That the Messias should bruise the Serpents head for us, included our redemption, That the Serpents head should be bruised, excluded the Serpent himselfe. This contract, then between God and man, as it was able to put the nature of a great fault, in a small offence, if we consider onely the eating of an apple, and so to make even a Trespass High-Treason, (because it was so contracted) so does this contract, the Ordinance of God, infuse a great vertue and efficacie, in the instruments of our reconciliation, how mean in gifts,
20 or how corrupt in manners soever they be. *Circumcision* in it self a low thing, yea obscene, and subject to mis-interpretation, yet by reason of the covenant, *He that is not circumcised, that person shall be cut off from my people.* So also *Baptism,* considered in it selfe, a   Gen. 17.14 vulgar, and a familiar thing; yet, *except a man be born of water, and of the Spirit, he cannot enter into the Kingdome of heaven.* The   Iohn 3.5 *Sacrament of the body and blood of Christ,* a domestique, a dayly thing, if we consider onely the breaking of the bread and participation of the Cup, but if we ascend up to the contract in the institution, it is to every worthy receiver, the seale, and the Conduit of all the merits
30 of Christ, to his soule. God threw down the walls of Jericho, with the   Ios. 6.4 sound of *Horns,* not of *Trumpets.* A homely sound, yet it did the worke; so neither is the weaknesse, no, nor the corruptnesse of the instruments always to be considered in the Church of God. Our Fathers knew there had passed a contract between God and man, A Church there should be *Ad consummationem,* to the end of the world, therefore they might safely make their recourse thither; and *Portæ Inferi,* the gates of hell should not prevaile against it, therefore   Mat. 16.18 they might confidently dwell there; They knew there was a *Dic Ecclesiæ,* a bill to be exhibited to the Church, upon any disorder, and   Mat. 18.17
40 a *Si noluerit,* an excommunication upon disobedience, *If he neglect to heare the Church, let him be unto thee as a heathen man, and as a*

Publican. This Church they saw, and Gods contract upon them sealed in *Baptism,* they knew, God had *revealed* no *other* Church, nor contract to them. And therefore, though they did not eat their troden grasse, with that ridiculous tentation, as the Fryar is boasted to have eaten a Toad which was set upon the Table, because he had read,

1 Cor. 10.27 *whatsoever is set before you eat;* Nor, as their *Dorotheus,* who when his man had reachd him *rats-bane,* in stead of *honey,* which he called for, refused it not, because sayd he, *If Gods will had been, that I* 250 *should have had honey, he would have directed thy hand to the honey,* but being under an invincible ignorance, and indevestible scruples, and having this contract, and this Church, to give them some satisfaction and acquiescence, they were partakers of that blessing, That though *Serpents* and *Scorpions* lurked in their grasse, they

Luke 10.19 had power to tread *on scorpions and on serpents,* and nothing could
Mar. 16.18 hurt them, and *That if they drinke any deadly thing, it shall doe them no harme.* And so our Fathers with a good conscience, *Manebant,* stayd there, and *Edebant,* they eat troden grasse, and drunke troubled water, and yet *Manebant oves,* they continued sheep 260 still.

Oves   *Sheep,* that is, without *Barking,* or *biting.* Some faint and humble *bleatings* there were alwaies in the daies of our Fathers; In every age there arose some men, who did modestly, and devoutly, but yet couragiously and confidently appear, and complaine against those treadings, and those troublings. Every age, every nation had some such *bleatings,* some men who by *writing* or *preaching* against those abuses, interrupted the tyrannicall prescriptions of that Church, and made their *continuall claime,* to their Christian liberty; But still they continued sheep, without denying either their *fleece* or their *throats* 270 to those Pastors. We read in *Naturall story* of divers pastures, and divers waters, which will change the colour of cattell, or sheep, but none that changes the *forme,* and makes them no such cattell, or no sheep. Some waters change sheep of any colour to *white.* And these troubled waters, *temporall or spirituall afflictions,* may bring Gods children to a faint and leane, and languishing palenesse. If it doe, as

1.15   *Daniel* and his fellows appeared fairer, and fatter in flesh, with their pults and water, which they desired rather then the Kings polluted delicates, then others that fed voluptuously: so the hearts of Gods

children shall be filled, as *with marrow and with fatnesse,* when
²⁸⁰ others shall have all their hearts desire, but leannesse in their soules.
There are waters that change all coloured sheep to *black.* So may
these troubled waters, *afflictions,* effect that upon Gods children, The
enemy shall come, and before him all faces shall gather *blacknesse;*
as Jerusalem complains, That their faces were *blacker* then *coals.* If
it doe, yet as long as they stay, and continue sheep, members of the
body, as long as they partake of the body, they shall partake of the
complexion of the Church, who saies of her selfe, *I am black, O*
daughters of Jerusalem, but comely, (acceptable in the sight of my
Christ) and that shall be verifyed in them, which *Salomon* says, *By*
²⁹⁰ *the sadnesse of the countenance, the heart is made better;* that is, by
the occasion of the sadnesse, Gods correction. But the strangest change
is, that some waters change sheep into red, the most unlikely, most
extraordinary, most unproper colour for sheep, of any other. Yet
there is one *rednesse* naturall to our sheep in the Text, the rednesse
of *blushing,* and modesty, and selfe-accusing; And there is another
rednesse, which is not improper, the rednesse of zeale and godly
anger. The worst rednesse that can befall them, is the rednesse of
sinne, and yet, lest that should deject them, God proceeds familiarly
with them, *Come now, and let us reason together, Though your*
³⁰⁰ *sinnes be as scarlet, they shall be as white as snow,* though they be
red like *Crimson,* they shall be as *wooll.* Yea, to shew, that where
sinne abounds, grace also may abound, to shew that that whitenesse
of Gods mercy doth pursue and overtake this rednesse of sinne, it
pleases the Holy Ghost to use such a phrase as expresses a rednesse in
whitenesse it self; He says, that the religious men of the Jewes before
that time, were whiter then milke, and redder then pearle: *Mip-*
peninim is the originall word, which the *Rabbins* translate pearle;
And the Vulgate Edition hath it, *Rubicundiores ebore antiquo,*
redder then the oldest yvory, which is the whitest thing, that can
³¹⁰ be presented. Perchance to intimate thus much, that there is neither
in the *holiest actions,* of the holiest man, any such degree of whitenesse, but that it is always accompanied with some rednes, some
tincture, some aspersion of sin, nor any such deep rednesse in sin,
any sin so often, and deeply died in grain, but that it is capable of
whitenesse, in the application of the candor, and purenesse, and

Psalm 63.5

Joel 2.6
Lam. 4.8

[Cant. 1.5]

Eccles. 7.3

Esai. 1.18

Rom. 5.20

Lam. 4.7

innocency of Christ Jesus: Therefore may the Holy Ghost have wrapped up this whitenesse in rednesse, redder then Pearl. Our Fathers were not discouraged, when they were discolored; what palenesse, what blacknesse, what rednesse soever, these troubled waters
320 induced upon them, still they were sheep; They became not *Foxes,* to delude the State with *equivocations;* nor *Wolves,* to join with the State to the oppression of the rest; nor *Horses,* to suffer themselves to be ridden by others, and so made instruments of their passions; no nor *Vnicorns,* to think to purge and purifie the waters for all the forest, to think to reforme all abuses in State, and Church at once; but they continued sheep; opened not their mouthes in biting, nor barking, in murmuring, or reproaching the present government. So our Fathers staied, *Manebant,* so they eat that grasse, so they continued sheep, and, as it followes next, *Oves Dei,* Gods sheep, *my*
330 *sheep* have eaten, *my sheep* have drunken.

Oves Dei   Gods sheep; for *nature* hath her sheep; some men by naturall constitution, are lazy, drowsie, frivolous, unactive, sheepish men. And *States* have their sheep; timorous men, following men, speechlesse men, men, who because they abound in a plentifull State, are loth to stirre. Nay the *Devill* hath his sheep too; Men whom he possesses so entirely, that, as the Law says, *Dominium est potestas, tum utendi, tum abutendi,* Onely he is truly Lord of any thing, who may doe what he will with it, he does what he will with those men, even to their own ruine. And from these folds and flocks did the
340 *Devill* always serve his shambles, in his *false Martyrdomes* in the Primitive Church; when (as *Eusebius* notes) envying the honour which the Orthodox Christians had in their thousands of Martyrs, the Heretiques studied ways of equalling them in that. And though within *four hundred* years after Christ, the Church, (who could not possibly take knowledge of all) was come to celebrate, by name, *five thousand* Martyrs (as some books have the account) for every day in the year, yet the Heretiques went so far towards equalling them, as that they had some whole sects, (particularly the *Euphemitæ*) which called themselves *Martyrians,* men exposed to the slaughter. One
350 limbe of the *Donatists,* the *Circumcelliones,* might have furnished their shambles; They would provoke others to kill them; and if they fail'd in that, they would kill themselves. And this was, as Saint

Augustine says, *Ludus quotidianus,* their daily sport, they plaid at no other game. And lest all these meanes should not have provided Martyrs enow, *Petilian,* against whom Saint *Augustine* writes, invented a new way of Martydome, when he taught, that if a man were guilty in his Conscience of any great offence to God, and onely to punish that fault, did kill himselfe, he was by that act of Justice a Martyr. The Devill had his sheep then; He hath so still; Those
60 *Emissarii papæ,* those whom the Bishop of *Rome* sends hither into this kingdome; whom *Baronius* calls *Candidatos Martyrii,* pretenders to Martyrdome, suters for Martyrdome; Men, who (as he adds there) do *sacramento spondere sanguinem,* take an oath at *Rome* that they will be hanged in *England;* and, in whose behalfe he complaines *de sterilitate Martyrii,* that there is such a dearth of Martyrdome, that they finde it hard to be hanged; and therefore, (perchance) they finde it necessary to enter into *Powder plots,* and actuall *Treasons,* because they see that for *Religion* meerly, this State would never draw drop of bloud, *et sacramento sanguinem,* they have taken an
70 oath to be hanged, and are loth to be forsworne. But the sheep of our text, were not *Natures sheep,* men naturally lazy, and unactive, nor *State sheep,* men loth to adventure, by stirring, nor the *Devills sheep,* men headlong to their own ruine, even by way of provocation; But they were *Gods sheep,* men, who, out of a rectified conscience, would not prevaricate, not betray nor forsake *God,* if his glory required the expense of their lives, and yet would not exasperate nor provoke their superiours, how corrupt soever, by unseasonable, and unprofitable complaints: so our Fathers staid in *Rome,* so they eat troden grasse, and drunke troubled waters, so they continued harm-
80 lesse *sheep* towards others, and the sheep *of God,* such as though they staid there and fed upon an ill diet, God had distinguished from Goats, and reserved for his right hand, at the day of separation. And they were more then so; they were not onely *his sheep,* but *his flock;* for so, this translation reads it, *my flock* hath eaten, *my flock* hath drunk.

God had single sheep in many nations; *Jobs,* and *Naamans,* and such; servants, and yet not in the Covenants, sheep, and yet not brought into his flock. For though God have revealed no other way of salvation *to us,* but by breeding us in his Church, yet we must be

Grex

³⁹⁰ so far, from straitning salvation, to any *particular Christian Church,*
of any subdivided name, *Papist* or *Protestant,* as that we may not
straiten it to the *whole Christian Church,* as though God *could* not,
in the largenesse of his power, or *did* not, in the largenesse of his
mercy, afford salvation to some, whom he never gathered into the
Christian Church. But these sheep in our text, were his flock, that is,
his Church. Though they durst not communicate their sense of their
miseries, and their desires to one another, yet they were a flock.

1 King.   When *Elias* complained, *I, even I onely am left,* and God told him,
19.14   that he had *seven thousand* besides him, perchance *Elias* knew none
⁴⁰⁰ of this *seven thousand,* perchance none of this *seven thousand* knew
one another, and yet, they were his flock, though they never met.
That timber that is in the forest, that stone that is in the quarry, that
Iron, that Lead that is in the mine, though distant miles, Counties,
Nations, from one another, meet in the building of a materiall
Church; So doth God bring together, living stones, men that had
no relation, no correspondence, no intelligence together, to the making of his Mysticall body, his visible Church. Who ever would have
thought, that we of *Europe,* and they of the *Eastern,* or *Western
Indies,* should have met to the making of Christ a Church? And yet,
⁴¹⁰ before we knew, on either side, that there was such a *people, God*
knew there was such a Church. He that lies buried, in the consecrated
dust under your feet, knowes not who lies next him; but one
Trumpet at last shall raise them both together, and show them to
one another, and joyn them, (by Gods grace) in the Triumphant
Church. These that knew not one another, that knew not *of* one
another, were yet Gods flock, the Church in his eye; for there, (and
onely there) the Church is always visible. So were our Fathers in
Rome, though they durst not meet, and communicate their sorrows,
nor fold themselves so in the fold of Christ Jesus, that is in open,
⁴²⁰ and free *Confessions.* They therefore that aske now, *Where was your
Church before Luther?* would then have asked of the *Jews* in
Babylon, Where was your Church before *Esdras?* that was in
Babylon, ours was in *Rome.*

Secessio   Now, beloved, when our Adversaries cannot deny us this truth,
that our Church was enwrapped, (though smothered) in theirs, that
as that *Balsamum naturale,* which *Paracelsus* speaks of, that naturall

Balme which is in every body, and would cure any wound, if that wound were kept clean, and recover any body, if that body were purged, as that naturall balme is in that body, how diseased soever that body be, so was our Church in theirs, they vexe us now, with that question, Why, if the case stood so, if your Fathers, when they eat our troden grasse, and drunk our troubled waters, were sound and in health, and continued sheep, and Gods sheep, and Gods flock, his Church with us, why went they from us? They ought us their residence, because they had received their Baptisme from us. And truly, it is not an impertinent, a frivolous reason, that of Baptisme, where there is nothing but conveniency, and no necessity in the case. But, if I be content to stay with my friend in an aguish aire, will he take it ill, if I go when the plague comes? Or if I stay in town till 20 die of the plague, shall it be lookd that I should stay when there die 1000? The infection grew hotter and hotter in *Rome;* and their *may,* came to a *must,* those things which were done before *de facto,* came at last to be articles of *Faith,* and *de jure,* must be beleeved and practised upon salvation. They chide us for going away, and they drove us away; If we abstained from communicating with their poysons, (being now growen to that height) they excommunicated us; They gave us no room amongst them but the fire, and they were so forward to burne Heretiques, that they called it heresie, not to stay to be burnt.

Yet we went not upon their driving, but upon *Gods calling.* As the whole prophecy of the deliverance of *Israel,* from *Babylon,* belongs to the Christian Church, both to the *Primitive* Church, at first, and to the *Reformed* since, so doth that voice, spoken to them, reach unto us, *Egredimini de Babylone, Goe ye out of Babylon with a voice of singing,* declare, show to the ends of the earth, that the Lord hath redeemed his servant *Jacob.* For, that *Rome* is not *Babylon,* they have but that one half-comfort, that one of their own authors hath ministred, that *Romæ regulariter malè agitur;* that *Babylon* is Confusion, disorder, but at *Rome* all sinnes are committed in order, by the book, and they know the price, and therefore *Rome* is not *Babylon.* And since that many of their authors confesse, that *Rome* was *Babylon,* in the time of the persecuting Emperours, and that *Rome shall* be *Babylon* againe, in the time of *Antichrist,* how they will hedge in a

Vox Dei

Esay 48.20

Lud. Vives.

1 Pet. 5.13

Jerusalem, a holy City, between these two *Babylons,* is a cunning peece of Architecture. From this *Babylon* then were our Fathers called by God; not onely by that *whispering* sibilation of the holy

Zech. 10.8 Ghost, *sibilabo populum, I will hisse for my people,* and so gather them, for I have redeemed them, and they shall increase, not onely *by private inspirations,* but by generall acclamations; every where ⁴⁷⁰ principall writers, and preachers, and Princes too, (as much as could stand with their safety) crying out against them *before Luther,* howsoever they will needs doe him that honour, to have been the first mover, in this blessed revolution.

Curia They reproach to us our going from them, when they drove us, and God drew us, and they discharge themselves for all, by this one evasion; That all that we complain of, is the fault of the *Court* of *Rome,* and not of the *Church;* of the extortion in the practise of their *Officers,* not of error in the doctrine of their *Teachers.* Let that be true, (as in a great part it is, for, almost all their errors proceed from ⁴⁸⁰ their covetousness and love of money) this is that that we complain most of, and in this especially lies the conformity of the *Jewish Priests* in the *Chaldean Babylon,* and these Prelates in the Roman *Babylon,* that the Court, and the Church, joined in the oppression. But since the Court of *Rome,* and the Church of *Rome* are united in one head, I see no use of this distinction, *Court* and *Church.* If the Church of *Rome* be above the Court, the Church is able to amend these corruptions in the Court. If the Court be got above the Church, the Church hath lost, or sold away, her supremacy.

Miracula To oppresse us, and ease themselves, now, when we are gone from ⁴⁹⁰ them, they require *Miracles* at our hands; when indeed it was miracle enough, how we got from them. But, *magnum charitatis argumen-*

Chrysost. *tum, credere absque pignoribus miraculorum,* He loves God but a little that will not beleeve him without a miracle. Miracles are for the establishing of new religions; All the miracles of, and from Christ and his Apostles, are *ours,* because their Religion is ours. Indeed it behooves our adversaries to provide new miracles every day, because they make new articles of Faith every day. As *Æsop* therefore answered in the Market, when he that sold him was asked what he could do, *that he could do nothing,* because his fellow had said, *that* ⁵⁰⁰ *he could do all,* so we say, we can do no miracles, because they do all;

all ordinary cures of Agues, and toothach being done by miracle amongst them. We confesse that we have no such tye upon the Trimphant Church, to make the *Saints* there do those anniversary miracles, which they do by their reliques here, upon their own *holy days,* ten days sooner every year, then they did before the *new computation.* We pretend not to raise the dead, but to cure the sick; and that but by the ordinary Physique, the Word, and Sacraments, and therefore need no miracles. And we remember them of their own authors, who do not onely say, that themselves do no miracles, in ⁰ these latter times, but assigne diligently strong reasons, why it is that they doe none. If all this will not serve, we must tell them, that we have a greater miracle, then any that they produce; that is, that in so few years, they that forsook *Rome,* were become equall, *even in number,* to them that adhered to her. We say, with Saint *Augustine,* That if we had no other miracle, *hoc unum stupendum & potentissimum miraculum esse,* that this alone were the most powerfull, and most amazing miracle, *ad hanc religionem, totius orbis amplitudinem, sine miraculis subjugatam,* that so great a part of the Christian world, should become *Protestants* of Papists, without any miracles.

⁰ They pursue us still, being departed from them, and they aske us, How can ye pretend to have left *Babylon,* confusion, *Dissention,* when you have such dissentions, and confusions amongst your selves? But neither are our differences in so fundamental points, as theirs are, (for a principall author of their own, who was employed by *Clement the eight,* to reconcile the differences between the *Jesuits* and the *Dominicans,* about the concurrence of the grace of God, and the free will of man, confesses that the principall articles, and foundations of faith were shaken between them, between the *Jesuits,* and *Dominicans*) neither shall we finde such heat, and animosity, and ³⁰ passion between any persons amongst us, as between the greatest amongst them; The succeeding *Pope* mangling the body of his predecessor, casting them into the river for buriall, disannulling all their decrees, and ordinations; their *Ordinations;* so that no man could be sure who was a Priest, nor whether he had truely received any Sacrament, or no. Howsoever, as in the narrowest way there is most justling, the *Roman Church* going that broad way, to beleeve as the Church beleeves, may scape some particular differences, which we

Ios. Acosta

Dissensiones

Benius

that goe the narrower way, to try every thing by the exact word of
God, may fall into. *Saint Augustine* tells us of a City in *Mauritania*
⁵⁴⁰ *Cæsarea,* in which they had a custome, that in one day in the year,
not onely Citizens of other parishes, but even neighbors, yea brethren,
yea Fathers, did fling stones dangerously, and furiously at one another in the streets; and this they so solemnized, as a custome received from their ancestors; which was a licentious kind of *Carnavall.*
If any amongst us have fallen into that disease, to cast stones, or dirt
at his friends, it is an infection from his own distemper, not from our
doctrine; for, *if any man list to be contentious, we have no such custome, neither the Church of God.* We departed not from them then,
till it was come to a hot plague, in a necessity of professing old opin-
⁵⁵⁰ ions to be new articles of Faith; not till we were driven by them, and
drawn by the voice of God, in the learnedest men of all nations;
when they could not discharge themselves by the distinction of the
Court of *Rome,* and the *Church* of *Rome,* because, if the abuses had
been but in the Court, it was the greatest abuse of all, for that Church,
which is so much above that Court, not to mend it. Nor can they
require *Miracles* at our hands, who doe none themselves, and yet
need them, because they induce new articles of Religion; neither can
they reproach to us our *Dissentions* amongst our selves; because they
are neither in so fundamentall points, nor pursued with so much un-
⁵⁶⁰ charitablenesse, as theirs. So we justifie our secession *from them;* but
all this justifies in no part, the secession of those distempered men,
who have separated themselves *from us,* which is our next, and our
last consideration.

When the *Apostle* says, *study* to be *quiet,* (1 *Thes.* 4.11.) me thinks
he intimates something towards this, that the lesse we *study* for our
Sermons, the more danger is there to disquiet the auditory; extemporall, unpremeditated Sermons, that serve the popular eare, vent,
for the most part, doctrines that disquiet the Church. *Study* for them,
and they *will be quiet;* consider ancient and fundamentall doctrines,
⁵⁷⁰ and this will quiet and settle the understanding, and the Conscience.
Many of these extemporall men have gone away from us, and vainly
said, that they have as good cause to separate from us, as we from
Rome. But can they call our Church, a *Babylon;* Confusion, disorder?
All that offends them, is, that we have *too much order,* too much

regularity, too much binding to the orderly, and uniforme service of
God in his Church. It affects all the body, when any member is cut
off; *Cum dolore amputatur, etiam quæ putruit, pars corporis;* and
they cut off themselves, and feel it not; when we lose but a mysticall
limbe, and they lose a spirituall life, we feel it and they doe not. When
that is pronounced *sit tibi sicut ethnicus,* if he hear not the Church,
let him be to thee as a Heathen, *gravius est quàm si gladio feriretur,*
flammis absumeretur, feris subigeretur, it is a heavier sentence, then
to be beheaded, to be burnt, or devoured with wild beasts; and yet
these men, before any such sentence pronounced by us, excommunicate themselves. Of all distempers, *Calvin* falls oftenest upon the
reproof of that which he calls *Morositatem,* a certain peevish frowardnesse, which, as he calls in one place, *deterrimam pestem,* the most
infectious pestilence, that can fall upon a man, so, in another, he gives
the reason, why it is so, *semper nimia morositas est ambitiosa,* that
this peevish frowardnesse, is always accompanied with a *pride,* and a
singularity, and an ambition to have his opinions preferred before all
other men, and to condemn all that differ from him. A civill man
will depart from his opinion at a *Table,* at a Councell table, rather
then hold up an argument to the vexation of the Company; so will
a peaceable man doe, in the Church, in questions that are not fundamentall. That reverend man whom we mentioned before, who did
so much in the establishing of *Geneva,* professes, that it was his own
opinion, that the Sacrament might be adminstred in prisons, and in
private houses; but because he found the Church of *Geneva,* of another opinion, and another practise before he came, he applied himselfe to them and departed, (in *practise*) from his own opinion, even
in so important a point, as the ministration of the Sacrament. Which
I present to consideration the rather, both because thereby it appears,
that greater matters then are now thought *fundamentall,* were then
thought but indifferent, and *arbitrary,* (for, surely, if *Calvin* had
thought this a fundamentall thing, he would never have suffered any
custome to have prevailed against his conscience) and also, because
divers of those men, who trouble the Church now, about things of
lesse importance, and this of private Sacraments in particular, will
needs make themselves beleeve, that they are *his Disciples,* and always conclude that whatsoever is practised at *Geneva* was *Calvins*

Ambros.

August.

Ep. 209.
*Feliciæ
virgini*

opinion. Saint *Augustine* saith excellently, and appliably, to a holy Virgin, who was ready to leave the Church, for the ill life of Churchmen, *Christus nobis imperavit Congregationem, sibi servavit separationem;* Christ Jesus hath commanded *us* to gather together, and recommended to us the Congregation; as for the separation, he hath reserved it to *himself,* to declare at the last day, who are Sheep and who are Goats. And hee wrought that separation which our Fathers made from Rome, by his expresse written Word, and by that which ⁶²⁰ is one word of God too, *Vox populi,* The invitation and acclamation of Doctors, and People, and Princes; but have our *Separatists* any such publique, and concurrent authorising of that which they doe, since of all that part from us, scarse a dozen meet together in one con-

Amos [3.3]

fession? When you have heard the Prophet say, *Can two walke together, except they be agreed?* when you have heard the Apostle say,

1 Cor. 1.10

I beseech you brethren by the name of our Lord Jesus Christ, that ye all speake the same things, and that there be no divisions among you, (for, if *preachers* speake one one way, another another, there will be divisions among the people) And then, it is not onely, that in obedience ⁶³⁰ to authority, they speake the same things; But, *Be perfectly joyned in the same mind,* and in the same judgement, you had need make haste to this union, this pacification; for when we are come thither, to agree among our selves, we are not come to our journeys end.

Conclusio

Our life is a warfare; other wars, in a great part, end in mariages: Ours in a divorce, in a divorce of body and soule in death. Till then, though God have brought us, from the *first Babylon,* the darknesse of the Gentiles, and from the *second Babylon,* the superstitions of Rome, and from the *third Babylon,* the confusion of tongues, in bitter speaking against one another, after all this, every man shall finde ⁶⁴⁰ a *fourth Babylon,* enough to exercise all his forces, The civill warre, the rebellious disorder, the intestine confusion of his own Concupiscencies. This is a transmigration, a transportation layd upon us all, by *Adams* rebellion, from Jerusalem to Babylon, from our innocent state in our Creation, to this confusion of our corrupt nature. God would have his children first brought to Babylon, before he would be

Mich. 4.10

glorifyed in their deliverance, *Venies usque ad Babylonem; Ibi liberaberis;* To Babylon thou shalt come; there I will deliver thee; but not till then; that is, till you come to a holy sense of the miseries you are in, and what hath brought you to them.

Though then you have suffred the calamities of all these Babylons in some proportions, though you be not *Incolæ* but *Indigenæ*, not naturalized but borne Babylonians, (Originall sinne makes you so) yet since you are within the Covenant, heare him, that sayd to you in *Abrahams* ears, *Egredere de terrâ tuâ*, Get thee out of thy Coun-   Gen. 12.1
try, and from thy kindred, unto the land I will shew thee; Come out of Babylon to Jerusalem; since ye are within his Adoption, and may cry *Abba* father, hear that voice, *Egredimini filiæ Sion*, Come forth   Cant. 3.11
ye daughters of Sion, come to Jerusalem. Though ye be *dead*, and buryed, and putrefyed in this corrupted, and corrupting flesh, yet since he cries with a loud voice, (as it is said in that Text) *Lazare veni foras*, *Lazarus* come forth, come forth of your Tombs in Baby-   Ioh. 11.43
lon, to this Jerusalem, come from your troubled waters, your waters of contention, of anxiety, of envy, of solicitude, and vexation for worldly encumbrances, and come *Ad aquas quietudinum*, to the   Psal. 23.[2]
waters of rest, the application of the merits of Christ, in a true Church: *Vinum non habetis?* have ye no wine to refresh your hearts; no merits of your own to take comfort in? *Implete Hydrias aquâ*,   Ioh. 2.7
fill all your vessels with water, that water of life, remorsefull teares, perchance he will change your water into wine, as he did in that place; perchance he will give you abundance of temporall blessings; perchance he will change that water into blood, as in Egypt; that is, into persecutions, into afflictions, into Martyrdome, for his sake, for hee will accept our water for blood, our tears of repentance and con- trition for Martyrdome, *ut cum desit Martyrium sanguinis, habeamus Martyrium aquæ*, that we may be Martyrs in his sight, and shed no blood; Martyrs of a new die, white Martyrs. That our waters of sor- row for sinne may answer our Saviours tears over *Lazarus* and over *Ierusalem;* and the sweat of our brows in a lawfull calling may an- swer our Saviours sweat of water and blood in his agony; and that our reverent and profitable receiving of the Sacrament, may answer the water and blood that issued from his side, which represented *omnia Sacramenta*, all the Sacraments; That, as we do, we may still feed upon grasse that is not troden, and drink water, that is not troubled, with the feet of others, or our own; that we be never shaked in the sinceritie nor in the integritie of Religion with their power, nor our own distempers of fears or hopes. But that our meat may be, to do the will of him that sent us, and to finish his work.   Joh. 4.34

Number 8.

An Anniversary Sermon
preached at St. Dunstans, upon the
commemoration of a Parishioner,
a Benefactor to that Parish.

Gen. 3.14. *AND DUST SHALT THOU EAT ALL
THE DAYES OF THY LIFE.*

THIS IS Gods malediction upon the Serpent in Paradise, There
in the Region, in the Store-house of all plenty, he must starve;
This is the Serpents perpetuall fast, his everlasting Lent,
(*Dust shalt thou eat all the dayes of thy life.*) There is a generation
derived from this Serpent, *Progenies viperarum,* a generation of Vipers, that will needs in a great, and unnecessary measure, keep this
Serpents Lent, and binde themselves to performe his fact; for, the
Carthusian will eat no flesh, (and yet, I never saw better bodied
men, men of better habitudes and constitution, howsoever they recom-
10 pense their abstinence from flesh) and the Feuillans will eat neither
flesh nor fish, but roots, and sallets, (and yet amongst them, amongst
men so enfeebled by roots, was bred up that man, who had both
malicious courage, and bodily strength, to kill the last King, who
was killed amongst them) They will be above others in their fasts,
Fish, and Roots will they eat, all the dayes of their life, but their
Master will be above them in his fast, (*Dust must he eat all the dayes
of his life.*)
　　It is *Luthers* observation upon this place, That in all *Moses* his
Books, God never spoke so long, so much together, as here, upon this

ɔccasion. Indeed the occasion was great; It was the arraignment of ɑll the world, and more; of mankinde, and of Angels too; of *Adam,* ɑnd *Eve,* (and there were no more of them) and then of the Serpent, ɑnd of Satan in that, and of all the fallen Angels in him. For the ꜱentence which God, as Judge gave upon them, upon all these Male-factors, of that part which fell upon the woman, all our mothers are experimentall witnesses, they brought forth us in sorrow and in travaile. Of that part of the sentence which fell upon man, every one of us is an experimentall witnesse, for in every calling, in the sweat of our face, we eat our bread. And of that part of the Judgement, which was inflicted upon the Serpent, and Satan in him, this dead brother of ours who lyes in this consecrated earth, is an experimentall witnesse, who being by death reduced to the state of dust, for so much of him, as is dust, that is, for his dead body, and then, for so long time, as he is to remaine in that state of dust, is in the portion, and jurisdiction, and possession of the Serpent, that is, in the state which the Serpent hath induced upon man, and dust must he eat all the dayes of his life.

In passing thorough these words, we shall make but these two steps; first, What the Serpent lost, by this judgement inflicted upon him; and secondly, What man gained by it; for these two considerations imbrace much, involve much; first, That Gods anger is so intensive, and so extensive, so spreading, and so vehement, as that in his Justice, he would not spare the Serpent, who had no voluntary, no innate, no naturall ill disposition towards man, but was onely made the instrument of Satan, in the overthrow of man. And then, that Gods mercy is so large, so overflowing, so super-abundant, as that even in his Judgement upon the Serpent, he would provide mercy for man. For, as it is a great waight of judgement upon the Serpent, that the Serpent must eat dust, so is it a great degree of mercy to man, that the Serpent must eate but dust, because mans best part is not subject to be served in at his table, the soule cannot become dust, (and dust must he eate all the dayes of his life). O, in what little sinne, though but a sinne of omission, though but a sinne of ignorance, in what circumstance of sinne, may I hope to scape Judgement, if God punished the Serpent who was violently, and involuntarily transported in this action? And in what depth, in what

Divisio

height, in what hainousnesse, in what multiplicity of sin can I doubt of the mercy of my God, who makes Judgment it self the instrument, the engin, the Chariot of his mercy? What room is there left for pre-
60 sumption, if the Serpent, the passive Serpent were punished? What room for desperation, if in the punishment, there be a manifestation of mercy? The Serpent must eate dust, that is his condemnation, but he shall eate no better meat, he shall eate but dust, there is mans consolation.

1 Part
Heb. 10.31

    First then, as it is a fearefull thing to fall into the hands of the living God, so is it an impossible thing to scape it. God is not ashamed of being jealous; he does not onely pronounce that he is a jealous God, but he desires to be known by none other name, (*The Lord whose name is jealous is a jealous God*) so jealous, as that he will not have
70 his name uttered in vaine; not onely not blasphemed, not sworne by, but not used indifferently, transitorily, not Proverbially, occasionally, not in vaine. And if it be, what then? Even for this, he will visite to the third, and fourth generation; and three and foure are seven, and seven is infinite. So jealous, as that in the case of the Angels, not for looking upon any other Creatures, or trusting in them, (for, when they fell, (as it is ordinarily received) there were no other creatures made) but for not looking immediately, directly upon God, but reflecting upon themselves, and trusting in their own naturall parts, God threw those Angels into so irrecoverable, and bottomelesse a
80 depth, as that the merits of Christ Jesus, though of infinite, superinfinite value, doe not boye them up; so jealous a God, is God, so jealous, as that in *Adams* case, for over-loving his own wife, for his over-tender compassion of her, for eating the forbidden fruit, *ne contristaretur delicias suas,* (as Saint *Hierome* layes his fault) lest he should deject her into an inordinate and desperate melancholy, and so make her incapable of Gods mercy, God threw the first man, and in him, all, out of Paradise, out of both Paradises, out of that of rest, and plenty here, and that of Joy, and Glory hereafter. Consider

Numb. 22.6
20.11

Balaams sin about cursing Gods people, or *Moses* sinne about strik-
90 ing the rock, and wouldst not thou be glad to change sinnes, with either of them? Are not thy sinnes greater, heavier sinnes; And yet, wouldest thou not be sorry, to undergoe their punishments? are not

Prov. 25.16

thy punishments lesse? *Hast thou found hony?* says the holy Ghost

Exod. 34.14

in *Solomon;* and, he says it promiscuously, and universally, to every body; *eate, as much as is sufficient.* Every man may. And then, *Jonathan* found that hony, and knew not that it was forbidden by *Sauls* proclamation, and did but taste it, and that in a case of extreme necessity, and *Jonathan* must die. Any man might eate enough, He did but taste, and he must die. If the Angels, if *Adam,* if *Balaam,* if *Moses,* if *Jonathan* did, if the Serpent in the text, could consider this, how much cheaper God hath made sinne to thee, then to them, might they not have colour in the eye of a naturall man, to expostulate with God? Might not *Ananias,* and *Saphira,* who onely withheld a little of that, which, but a little before, was all their own, and now must die for that, have been excusable if they had said at the last gaspe, How many direct Sacrileges hath God forborne, in such and such, and we must die? Might not *Er,* and *Onan,* after their uncleane act upon themselves onely, for which they died, have been excusable, if they had said at the last gaspe, How many direct adulteries, how many unnaturall incests hath God forborne in such and such, and we must die? How many loads of miserable wretches maist thou have seen suffer at ordinary executions, when thou mightest have said with *David, Lord I have done wickedly, but these sheep what have they done?* What had this Serpent done?

The Serpent was more subtile then any other beast. It is a dangerous thing to have a capacity to doe evill; to be fit to be wrought upon, is a dangerous thing. How many men have been drawn into danger, because they were too rich? How many women into solicitation, and tentation, because they were too beautifull? Content thy selfe with such a mediocrity in these things, as may make thee fit to serve God, and to assist thy neighbour, in a calling, and be not ambitious of extraordinary excellency in any kinde; It is a dangerous thing, to have a capacity to do evill. God would do a great work; and he used the simplicity of the Asse; he made *Balaams* Asse speake; But the Devill makes use of the subtilty, of the craft of the Serpent; The Serpent is his Instrument; no more but so, but so much he is, his instrument. And then, says S. *Chrysostome, Pater noster execratur gladium,* as a naturall father would, so our heavenly father does hate, that which was the instrument of the ruine of his children. Wherein hath he expressed that hate? not to binde our selves to *Josephus* his opin-

1 Sam. 14.27

Act. 5.8

Gen. 38.9

[2 Sam. 24.17]
Quia instrumentum
Gen. 3.1

Num. 22.28

ion, (though some of the ancients in the Christian Church have seconded that opinion too) that at that time the Serpent could goe upright, and speak, and understand, and knew what he did, and so concurred actually and willingly to the temptation and destruction of man, though he were but anothers instrument, he became odious to God. Our bodies, of themselves, if they had no souls, have no disposition to any evill; yet, these bodies which are but instruments, must burn in hell. The earth was accursed for mans sin, though the earth had not been so much as an instrument of his sin; Onely be-
140 cause it was, after, to conduce to the punishment of his children, it

Lev. 20.15

was accursed, God withdrew his love from it. And in the law, those beasts with which men committed bestiality, were to be stoned, as well as the men. How poor a plea will it be, to say, at the last day, I got nothing by such an extortion, to mine own purse, it was for my master; I made no use of that woman whom I had corrupted, it was for a friend. Miserable instrument of sin, that hadst not the profit, nor the pleasure, and must have the damnation! As the Prophet cals

Obad. v. 21

them, that help us towards heaven, Saviours, (*Saviours shall come up on Mount Sion*) so are all that concurre instrumentally to the damna-
150 tion of others, Devils. And, at the last day, we shall see many sinners saved, and their instruments perish. *Adam* and *Eve* both, God interrogated, and gave them time, to meditate and to deprecate; To *Adam,* he says, *Where art thou,* and, *who told thee that thou wast naked? And to Eve, What is this that thou hast done?* But to the Serpent no such breathing; The first word is, *Quia fecisti;* no calling for evidence whether he had done it or no, but, *Because thou hast done it, thou art accursed.* Sin is Treason against God; and in Treason there is no Accessory; The instrument is the Principall.

2 Part

We passe from that first Part, the consideration of heavy Judge-
160 ments upon faults, in appearance but small, derived from the punishment of the Serpent, though but an Instrument. Let no man set a low value upon any sin; let no man think it a little matter to sin some one sin, and no more; or that one sin but once, and no oftner; or that once but a little way in that sin, and no farther; or all this, to do another a pleasure, though he take none in it himself (as though there were charity in the society of sin, and that it were an Alms to help a man to the means of sinning.) The least sin cost the blood of

the Son of God, and the least sinner may lose the benefit of it, if he presume of it. No man may cast himself from a Pinnacle, because an Angel may support him; no man may kill himself, because there is a Resurrection of the body; nor wound his soul to death by sin, because there may be a resurrection of that, by grace. Here is no roome for presumption upon God; but, as little for desperation in God; for, in the punishment of the Serpent, we shall see, that his Mercy, and Justice are inseparable; that, as all the Attributes of God, make up but one God (Goodnesse, and Wisdome, and Power are but one God) so Mercy and Justice make up but one act; they doe not onely duly succeed, and second one another, they doe not onely accompany one another, they are not onely together, but they are all one. As Manna, though it tasted to one man like one thing, to another like another, (for it tasted to every man like that, that that man liked best) yet still was the same Manna; so, for Gods corrections, they have a different taste in different persons; and howsoever the Serpent found nothing but Judgement, yet we find mercy even in that Judgement. *The evening and the morning make up the day,* says *Moses;* as soon as he had named evening comes in morning, no interposing of the mention of a dark, and sad night between. As soon as I hear of a Judgement, I apprehend Mercy, no interposing of any dark or sad suspition, or diffidence, or distrust in God, and his mercy; and to that purpose we consider the Serpents punishment, and especially as it is heightned, and aggravated in this Text, *Dust shalt thou eate all the days of thy life.*

[Wisd. 16.20]

Gen. 1.5

There are three degrees in the Serpents punishment; First, *Super pectus, He must creep upon his belly;* And secondly, *Inimicitias ponam, I will put enmity,* God will raise him an enemy; And thirdly, *Pulverem comedes, Dust shalt thou eate all the days of thy life.* And, in all these three, though they aggravate the judgement upon the Serpent, there is mercy to us; For, for the first, that the Serpent now does but creep upon his belly, S. *Augustine,* and S. *Gregory* understand this belly to be the seat of our affections, and our concupiscencies; That the Serpent hath no power upon our heart, nor upon our brain, for, if we bring a tentation to consideration, to deliberation, that we stop at it, think of it, study it, and foresee the consequences, this frustrates the tentation. Our nobler faculties are always assisted

Super pectus

with the grace of God to resist him, though the belly, the bowels of sin, in sudden surprisals, and ebullitions, and foamings of our concupiscencies, be subject to him: for, though it may seem, that if that be the meaning, (which, from S. *Augustine* and S. *Gregory* we have given you) That the Serpent hath this power over our affections, and
²¹⁰ that is intended by that, The belly, it should rather have been said, *super pectus vestrum,* Hee shall creep upon your belly, then upon his owne, yet, indeed, all that is his own, which we have submitted and surrendred to him, and hee is upon his own, because we make our selves his; (for, *to whom ye yeeld your selves servants to obey,*

Rom. 6.16

his servants you are.) So that if he be *super pectus nostrum,* if he be upon our belly, he is upon his own. But he does but creep; He does not fly; He is not presently upon you, in a present possession of you; you may discern the beginning of sin, and the ways of sin, in the approaches of the Serpent, if you will. The Serpent leaves a slime that
²²⁰ discovers him, where he creeps; At least behinde him, after a sin, you may easily see occasion of remorse, and detestation of that sinne, and thereby prevent relapses, if you have not watched him well enough in his creeping upon you. When hee is a Lion, he does not devoure

1 Pet. 5.8

all whom he findes; *He seeks whom he may devoure;* He may not devoure all, nor any but those, who cast themselves into his jaws, by exposing themselves to tentations to sin.

An forma
mutata

He does but creep; why, did he any more before? was his forme changed in this punishment? Many of the Ancients think literally that it was; and that before the Serpent did goe upon feet; we are
²³⁰ not sure of that; nor is it much probable. That may well be true, which *Luther* says, *fuit suavissima bestiola,* till then it was a creature more lovely, more sociable, more conversable with man, and, (as *Calvin* expresses the same) *Minus odiosus,* man did lesse abhor the Serpent before, then after. Beloved, it is a degree of mercy, if God bring that, which was formerly a tentation to mee, to a lesse power over me, then formerly it had; If deformity, if sicknesse, if age, if opinion, if satiety, if inconstancy, if any thing have worn out a tentation in that face, that transported me heretofore, it is a degree of mercy. Though the Serpent be the same Serpent, yet if he be not so
²⁴⁰ acceptable, so welcome to me, as heretofore, it is a happy, a blessed change. And so, in that respect, there was mercy.

It was a punishment to the Serpent, that, though he were the same still as before, yet he was not able to insinuate himself as before, because hee was not so welcome to us. So, the having of the same form, which he had, might be a punishment, as nakednesse was to man after his fall; He was naked before, but he saw it not, he felt it not, he needed no cloathes before; Now, nakednesse brings shame, and infirmities with it. So, God was so sparing towards the Serpent, as that he made him not worse in nature, then before, and so mercifull to us, as that hee made us more jealous of him, and thereby more safe against him, then before. Which is also intimated pregnantly, in the next step of his punishment, *Inimicitias ponam,* That God hath kindled a war between him and us. Peace is a blessed state, but it must be the peace of God; for, *Simeon* and *Levi* are brethren, they agree well enough together; but they are instruments of evill; and, in that case, the better agreement, the worse. So, war is a fearfull state; but not so, if it be the war of God, undertaken for his cause, or by his Word. Many times, a State suffers by the security of a Peace, and gains by the watchfulness of a War. Wo be to that man that is so at peace, as that the spirit fights not against the flesh in him; and wo to them too, who would make them friends, or reconcile them, betweene whom, God hath perpetuated an everlasting war, The seed of the woman, and the seed of the Serpent, Christ and *Beliall,* Truth and Superstition. Till God proclaimed a warre between them, the Serpent did easily overthrow them, but therefore God brought it to a war, that man might stand upon his guard. And so it was a Mercy.

But the greatest mercy is in the last, and that which belongs most directly, (though all conduce pertinently and usefully) to our present occasion; *Dust shalt thou eat all the days of thy life.* He must eat dust, that is, our bodies, and carnall affections; Hee was at a richer diet, he was in better pasture before; before, he fed upon souls too; But for that his head was bruised, in the promise of a Messias, who delivers our souls from his tyranny; But the dust, the body, that body, which for all the precious ransome, and the rich, and large mercy of the Messias, must die, that dust is left to the Serpent, to Satan, that is, to that dissolution, and that putrefaction, which he hath induced upon man, in death. He eats but our dust, in our death, when he hath brought us to that; that is a mercy; nay he eats up our dust

Inimi-
citias
ponam

Gen. 49.5

Pulverem
comedes

before our death, which is a greater mercy; our carnal affections, our
280 concupiscencies are eaten up, and devoured by him; and so, even
his eating is a sweeping, a cleansing, a purging of us. Many times we
are better for his tentations. My discerning a storm, makes me put on
a cloak. My discerning a tentation, makes me see my weaknesse, and
fly to my strength. Nay, I am somtimes the safer, and the readier for
a victory, by having been overcome by him. The sense, and the remorse of a sin, after I have fallen into it, puts me into a better state,
and establishes better conditions between God and me then were
before, when I felt no tentations to sin. He shall eat up my dust, so, as
that it shall fly into mine eys; that is, so work upon my carnall affec-
290 tions, as that they shall not make me blinde, nor unable to discern that
it is he that works. It is said of one kinde of Serpent, that because they

Stellio   know, by an instinct they have, that their skin is good for the use of
man, (for the falling sickness) out of Envy, they hide their skin, when
they cast it. The Serpent is loth we should have any benefit by him; but
we have; even his tentations arm us, and the very falling exalts us,
when after a sin of infirmity, we come to a true, and serious repentance,
and scrutiny of our conscience. So he hath nothing to eat but our dust,
and he eats up our dust so, as that he contributes to our glory, by his

Jon. 1.17   malice. The Whale was *Jonas* Pilot; The Crows were *Elias* caters; The
1 Reg. 17.6 300 Lions were *Daniels* sentinels; The Viper was *Pauls* advocate; it
Dan. 6.22   pleaded for him, and brought the beholders in an instant, from extreme
Act.   to extreme, from crying out that *Paul* was *a murderer,* to cry that he
28.[3–6]   was *a god.* Though at any time, the Serpent having brought me to a
sin, cry out, *Thou art a murderer,* that is, bring me to a desperate
sense of having murdred mine own soul, yet in that darkness I shal
see light, and by a present repentance, and effectual application of the
merits of my Savior, I shall make the Serpent see, I am a God; thus
far a God, that by my adhering to Christ, I am made partaker of

2 Pet. 1.4   the Divine Nature. For, that which S. *Chrysostome* sayes of Baptism,
310 is true too in the second Baptism, Repentance, *Deposui terram, &
cœlum indui;* then I may say to the Serpent, Your meat is dust; and
I was dust; but *Deposui terram,* I have shak'd off my dust, by true

2 Cor. 5.17 repentance, for I have shak'd off my self, and am a new creature, and
am not now meat for your Table. *Jam terra non sum, sed sal,* says
the same Father, I am not now unsavoury dust, but I am salt; And,

Sal ex aqua & vento, says he; Salt is made of water and winde; I am made up of the water of Baptism, of the water of Repentance, of the water that accompanies the blood of Christ Jesus, and of that winde that *blows where it list,* and hath been pleased to blow upon me, the Spirit of God, the Holy Ghost, and I am no longer meat for the Serpent, for *Dust must he eat all the days of his life.* I am a branch of that Vine, (Christ *is the Vine, and we are the branches*) I am a leafe of that *Rose of Sharon,* and of that *Lilly of the valleys;* I am a plant in the *Orchard of Pomegranats,* and that Orchard of Pomegranats is the Church; I am a drop of that *dew,* that *dew* that lay upon the *head* of Christ. And this Vine, and this Rose, and Lilly, and Pomegranats, of Paradise, and this Dew of heaven, are not Dust, *And dust must thou eate all the dayes of thy life.*

So then, the Prophecy of *Esay* fulfils it self, That when Christ shall reign powerfully over us, *The wolf and the lamb shall feed together,* (*Saul* and *Ananias* shall meet in a house, (as S. *Hierome* expounds that) and *Ananias* not be afraid of a Persecutor.) *The Lion shall eate straw like the Bullock,* says that Prophet in that place, *Tradent se rusticitati Scripturarum,* says the same Father, The strongest understandings shall content themselves with the homelinesse of the Scriptures, and feed upon plain places, and not study new dishes, by subtilties, and perplexities, and then, *Dust shall be the Serpents meat,* says the Prophet there, The power of Satan shall reach but to the body, and not touch a soul wrapt up in Christ. But then, it is *Totâ vitâ, all his life.* His diet is impaired, but it is not taken away; He eats but dust, but he shall not lack that, as long as hee lives. And how long lives the Serpent, this Serpent? The life of this Serpent is to seduce man, to practise upon man, to prevaile upon man, as farre, and as long as man is dust. And therefore wee are not onely his dust, whilst wee live (all which time we serve in our carnall affections, for him to feed upon) but when we are dead, we are his dust still. Man was made in that state, as that he should not resolve to dust, but should have passed from this world to the next, without corruption, or resolution of the body. That which God said to *Adam, Dust thou art,* belonged to all, from the beginning, he, and all we were to be of dust, in his best integrity; but that which God adds there, *et in terram revertêris, (dust thou art, and to it thou shalt returne)* that

Joh. 3.8

Joh. 15.5
Cant. 2.1
4.13
5.2

Totâ vitâ
Esay 65.25

Gen. 3.19

the Serpent brought in, that was induced upon man by him, and his tentation. So that when we are living dust here he eats us, and when we are dead dust too, in the grave, he feeds upon us, because it proceeds from him both that we die, and that we are detained in the state of exinanition, and ingloriousnesse, in the dust of the earth, and not translated immediately to the joyes of heaven, as but for him, we should have been. But as, though he do feed upon our living dust,
360 that is, induce sicknesses, and hunger, and labour, and cold, and paine upon our bodies here, God raises even that dust out of his hands, and redeemes it from his jaws, in affording us a deliverance, or a restitution from those bodily calamities here, as he did abundantly to his servant, and our example *Job,* so, though he feed upon our dead dust and detain our bodies in the disconsolate state of the grave, yet, as the Godhead, the divine nature did not depart from the body of Christ when it lay dead in the grave, so neither doth the love and power of God, depart from the body of a Christian, though resolved to dust in the grave, but, in his due time, shall recollect that
370 dust, and recompact that body, and reunite that soul, in everlasting joy and glory. And till then, the Serpent lives; till the Judgement, Satan hath power upon that part of man; and that's the Serpents life, first to practise our death, and then to hold us in the state of the dead. Till then we attend with hope, and with prayers Gods holy pleasure upon us, and then begins the unchangeable state in our life, in body and soul together, then we beginne to live, and then ends the Serpents life, that is, his earnest practise upon us in our life, and his faint triumph in continuing over our dust. That time, (the time of the generall Resurrection) being not yet come, the devills thought them-
Mat. 8.28
[29]   380 selves wronged, and complained that Christ came before the time to torment them; and therefore Christ yeelded so much to their importunity, as to give them leave to enter into the swine. And therefore, let not us murmur nor over-mourne for that, which as we have induced it upon our selves, so God shall deliver us from, at last, that is, both death, and corruption after death, and captivity in that comfortlesse state, but for the resurection. For, so long we are to be dust, and so long lasts the Serpents life, Satans power over man; *dust must he eate all the days of his life.*

Conclusio   In the meane time, (for our comfort in the way) when this Serpent becomes a Lyon, yet there is a Lyon of the Tribe of *Judah,* that is too strong for him. So, if he who is *Serpens serpens humi,* the Serpent condemned to creep upon the ground, doe transforme himselfe into a flying Serpent, and attempt our nobler faculties, there is *Serpens exaltatus,* a Serpent lifted up in the wildernesse to recover all them that are stung, and feel that they are stung with this Serpent, this flying Serpent, that is, these high and continued sinnes. The creeping Serpent, the groveling Serpent, is Craft; the exalted Serpent, the crucified Serpent, is Wisdome. All your worldly cares, all your crafty bargaines, all your subtill matches, all your diggings into other mens estates, all your hedgings in of debts, all your planting of children in great allyances; all these diggings, and hedgings and plantings savour of the earth, and of the craft of that Serpent, that creeps upon the earth: But crucifie this craft of yours, bring all your worldly subtilty under the Crosse of Christ Jesus, husband your farmes so, as you may give a good account to him, presse your debts so, as you would be pressed by him, market and bargaine so, as that you would give all, to buy that field, in which his treasure, and his pearle is hid, and then you have changed the Serpent, from the Serpent of perdition creeping upon the earth, to the Serpent of salvation exalted in the wildernesse. Creeping wisedome, that still looks downward, is but craft; Crucified wisedome, that looks upward, is truly wisedome. Between you and that ground Serpent God hath kindled a war; and the nearer you come to a peace with him, the farther ye go from God, and the more ye exasperate the Lord of Hosts, and you whet his sword against your own souls. A truce with that Serpent, is too near a peace; to condition with your conscience for a time, that you may continue in such a sin, till you have paid for such a purchase, married such a daughter, bought such an annuity, undermined and eaten out such an unthrift, this truce, (though you mean to end it before you die) is too near a peace with that Serpent, between whom and you, God hath kindled an everlasting war. A cessation of Arms, that is, not to watch all his attempts and tentations, not to examine all your particular actions, A Treaty of Peace, that is, to dispute and debate in the behalf and favour of a sin, to palliate, to disguise, to extenuate that sin, this is too near a peace with this Serpent, this creeping Serpent. But in the other Serpent, the crucified Serpent, God hath

Apoc. 5.5

Numb. 21.9

[Mat.
13.44–46]

reconciled to himself, all things in heaven, and earth, and hell. You
have peace in the assistance of the Angels of heaven, Peace in the
contribution of the powerfull prayers, and of the holy examples of the
430 Saints upon earth, peace in the victory and triumph over the power
of hell, peace from sins towards men, peace of affections in your
selves, peace of conscience towards God. From your childhood you
have been called upon to hold your peace; To be content is to hold
your peace; murmure not at God, in any corrections of his, and you
doe hold this peace. That creeping Serpent, Satan, is war, and should
be so; The crucified Serpent Christ Jesus is peace, and shall be so for
ever. The creeping Serpent eats our dust, the strength of our bodies,
in sicknesses, and our glory in the dust of the grave: The crucified
Serpent hath taken our flesh, and our blood, and given us his flesh,
440 and his blood for it; And therefore, as *David,* when he was thought
base, for his holy freedome in dancing before the Ark, said he would
be more base; so, since we are all made of *red earth,* let him that is
red, be more red; Let him that is red with the blood of his own soul,
be red again in blushing for that rednesse, and more red in the
Communion of the blood of Christ Jesus; whom we shall eat all the
days of our life, and be mystically, and mysteriously, and spiritually,
and Sacramentally united to him in this life, and gloriously in the
next.

    In this state of dust, and so in the territory of the Serpent, the
450 Tyrant of the dead, lies this dead brother of ours, and hath lien some
years, who occasions our meeting now, and yearly upon this day, and
whose soul, we doubt not, is in the hands of God, who is the God
of the living. And having gathered a good *Gomer* of Manna, a good
measure of temporall blessings in this life, and derived a fair measure
thereof, upon them, whom nature and law directed it upon, (and
in whom we beseech God to blesse it) hath also distributed something to the poor of this Parish, yearly, this day, and something to a
meeting for the conserving of neighbourly love, and something for
this exercise. In which, no doubt, his intention was not so much to
460 be yearly remembred himself, as that his posterity, and his neighbours
might be yearly remembred to doe as he had done. For, this is truly
to glorifie God in his Saints, to sanctifie our selves in their examples;
To celebrate them, is to imitate them. For, as it is probably conceived,

2 Sam. 6.14

[Mat. 22.32]

and agreeably to Gods Justice, that they that write wanton books, or make wanton pictures, have additions of torment, as often as other men are corrupted with their books, or their pictures: so may they, who have left permanent examples of good works, well be beleeved, to receive additions of glory and joy, when others are led by that to do the like: And so, they who are extracted, and derived from him, and they who dwelt about him, may assist their own happiness, and enlarge his, by following his good example in good proportions. AMEN.

Number 9.

Preached at St. Dunstans.

LAMENT. 3.1. *I AM THE MAN, THAT HATH SEEN AFFLICTION, BY THE ROD OF HIS WRATH.*

YOU REMEMBER in the history of the *Passion* of our Lord and Saviour Christ Jesus, there was an *Ecce homo,* a shewing, an exhibiting of that *man,* in whom we are all blessed. *Pilat* presented him to the Jews so, with that *Ecce homo, Behold the man.* That man upon whom the wormwood and the gall of all the ancient Prophecies, and the venome and malignity of all the cruell instruments thereof, was now poured out; That man who was left *as a tender plant, and as a roote out of a dry ground, without forme, or beauty, or comelinesse, that wee should desire to see him,* as the ¹⁰ Prophet *Esay* exhibits him; That man who upon the brightnesse of his eternall generation in the bosome of his Father, had now cast a cloud of a temporary and earthly generation in the wombe of his mother, that man, who, as he entred into the wombe of his first mother, the blessed Virgin, by a supernaturall way, by the *overshadowing of the holy Ghost,* so he vouchsafed to enter into the wombe of her, whom he had accepted for his second mother, the *earth,* by an unnaturall way, not by a naturall, but by a violent, and bitter death, that man so torne and mangled, wounded with thornes, oppressed with scornes and contumelies, *Pilate* presents and exhibits ²⁰ so, *Ecce homo, Behold the man.* But in all this depression of his, in all his exinanition, and evacuation, yet he had a *Crown* on, yet he had a *purple garment* on, the emblems, the Characters of majesty

Ioh. 19.5

Esay 53.2

[Luk. 1.35]

were always upon him. And these two considerations, the *miseries* that exhaust, and evacuate, and annihilate man in this life, and yet, those sparkes, and seeds of *morality,* that lie in the bosome, that still he is a man, the afflictions that depresse and smother, that suffocate and strangle their spirits in their bosomes, and yet that unsmotherable, that unquenchable *Spirit of Adoption, by which we cry Abba Father,* that still he is a Christian, these *Thornes,* and yet these *Crownes,* these *contumelies,* and yet this *Purple,* are the two parts of this text, *I am the man, that hath seen affliction by the rod of his wrath.* For, here is an *Ecce, behold; Jeremy* presents a map, a manifestation of as great affliction, as the rod of Gods wrath could inflict; But yet it is *Ecce homo, Behold the man, I am the man,* he is not demolished, he is not incinerated so, not so annihilated, but that he is still a man; God preserves his children from departing from the dignity of *men,* and from the soveraigne dignity of *Christian men,* in the deluge, and inundation of all afflictions.

And these two things, so considerable in that *Ecce homo,* in the exhibiting of Christ, that *then* when he was under those scornes, and Crosses, he had his *Crownes,* his *purples,* ensignes of majesty upon him, may well be parts of this text; for, when we come to consider *who* is the person of whom *Jeremy* says, *I am the man,* we finde many of the ancient Expositors take these words *prophetically* of *Christ* himselfe; and that Christ himselfe who says, *Behold and see if there be any sorrow, like unto my sorrow,* says here also, *I am the man, that hath seen affliction, by the rod of his wrath.* But because there are some other passages in this Chapter, that are not so conveniently appliable to Christ, (it is not likely that Christ would say of himselfe, *That his Father shut out his prayer, even then when he cryed and shouted;* not likely that Christ would say of himselfe, *That his Father was to him, as a Beare in the way, and as a Lion in secret places;* not likely that Christ would say of himselfe, *That his Father had removed his soul far from peace*) therefore this chapter, and this person cannot be so well understood of Christ. Others therefore have understood it of *Jerusalem* it selfe; but then it would not be expressed in that *Sex,* it would not be said of *Jerusalem, I am the man.* Others understand it of any *particular man,* that had his part, in that calamity, in that captivity; that the affliction was so universall upon

[Rom. 8.15]

1.12

verse 8

10

17

⁶⁰ all of that nation of what condition soever, that *every man* might justly say, *Ego vir, I am the man that have seen affliction.* But then all this chapter must be *figurative,* and still, where we can, it becomes, it behooves us, to maintain a *literall sense* and interpretation of all Scriptures. And *that* we shall best do in this place, if we understand these words literally of *Jeremy himself,* that the *Minister* of God, the Preacher of God, the Prophet of God, *Jeremy* himself, was *the man;* the Preacher is the text, *Ego vir, I am the man:* As the *Ministers* of God are most exposed to *private contumelies,* so should they be most affected with publique calamities, and soonest come to say with

2 Cor. 11.29
⁷⁰ the Apostle, *Quis infirmatur, Who is weake, and I am not weake too, who is offended, and I am not affected with it?* when the people of God are distressed with sicknesse, with dearth, with any publique calamity, the Minister is the first man, that should be compassionate, and sensible of it.

Divisio   In these words then, (*I am the man &c.*) these are our two parts; first the *Burden,* and then the *Ease,* first the *waight,* and then the *Alleviation,* first the *Discomfort,* and then the *Refreshing,* the sea of afflictions that overflow, and surround us all, and then our emergency and lifting up our head above that sea. In the first we shall ⁸⁰ consider, first, the *Generality* of afflictions, and that first in their own nature; And then secondly in that *name* of man upon whom they fall here, *Gheber, Ego vir, I am the man,* which is that name of man, by which the strongest, the powerfullest of men are denoted in the Scriptures; They, the strongest, the mightiest, they that thought themselves safest, and sorrow-proofe, are afflicted. And lastly, in the person, upon whom these afflictions are fastned here, *Jeremy* the Prophet, of whom literally we understand this place: The dearliest beloved of God, and those of whose service God may have use in his Church, they are subject to be retarded in their service, by these af- ⁹⁰ flictions. Nothing makes a man so great amongst men, nothing makes a man so necessary to God, as that he can escape afflictions. And when we shall have thus considered the *generality* thereof, these three wayes, In the nature of affliction it selfe, In the signification of that name of exaltation *Gheber,* and in the person of *Jeremy,* we shall passe to the consideration of the vehemency and intensness thereof, in those circumstances that are laid down in our Text, First, that these afflictions are *Ejus, His, The Lords,* And then they are *in virga, in his rod,* And again, *In virga iræ, in the rod of his wrath.* And in these two branches, the extent and the weight of afflictions, and in these few circumstances, that illustrate both, we shall determine our first part, the burden, the discomfort. When we shall come at last, to our last part, of comfort, we shall finde that also to grow out into 2 branches; for, first, *Vidit, he saw* his affliction, (*I am the Man that hath seen affliction*) Affliction did not blinde him, not stupefie him, affliction did not make him unsensible of affliction, (which is a frequent, but a desperate condition) *vidit,* he saw it; that is first; And then, *Ego vir, I am the man that saw it,* he maintained the dignity of his station, still he played the man, still he survived to glorifie God, and to be an example to other men, of patience under Gods correc-tions, and of thankfulnesse in Gods deliverance. In which last part, we shall also see, that all those particulars that did aggravate the affliction, in the former part, (That they were *from the Lord, from his Rod,* from the *Rod of his wrath*) doe all exalt our comfort in this, That it is a particular comfort that our afflictions are *from the Lord,* Another that they are *from his Rod,* and another also, that they are *from the Rod of his wrath.*

First then in our first part, and the first branch thereof, *The Generality* of affliction, considered in the *nature thereof:* We met *all* generally, in the first *Treason* against our selves; without exception *all;* In *Adams* rebellion, who was not in his loins? And in a *second Treason,* we met all too; in the Treason *against Christ Jesus,* we met *all;* All our sins were upon his shoulders. In those two Treasons we have had no exception, no exemption. The penalty for our first Treason, in *Adam,* in a great part, we doe all undergoe; we doe *all die,* though not without a lothnesse and colluctation at the time, yet without a deliberate desire to live in this world for ever. How loth soever any man be to die, when death comes, yet I thinke, there is no man that ever formed a deliberate Prayer, or wish, that he might never die. That penalty for our first Treason in *Adam,* we do bear. And would any be excepted from bearing any thing deduced from his *second Treason,* his conspiracy against Christ, from *imitation of his Passion,* and *fulfilling his sufferings in his body,* in bearing cheerfully the afflictions and tribulations of this life? *Omnis*

1 Part

Genera-litas

[Col. 1.24]

caro corruperat; and thou art within that generall Indictment, *all*
flesh had corrupted his way upon Earth. Statutum est omnibus mori;
and thou art within that generall Statute, *It is appointed unto all men*
once to die. Anima quæ peccaverit, ipsa morietur: and thou art within
that generall Sentence and Judgement, *Every soul that sinneth shall*
die, The death of the soul. Out of these generall Propositions thou
140 canst not get; and when in the same universality there commeth a
generall pardon, *Deus vult omnes salvos, God will have all men to*
be saved, Because that Pardon hath in it that *Ita quod,* that condition,
Omnem filium, Hee scourgeth every sonne whom he receiveth,
wouldst thou lose the benefit of that *Adoption,* that *Filiation,* that
Patrimony and Inheritance, rather then admit patiently his Fatherly
chastisements in the afflictions and tribulations in this life? Beloved,
the death of Christ is given to us, as a *Hand-writing;* for, when Christ
naild that *Chirographum,* that first hand-writing, that had passed
between the Devill and us, to his Crosse, he did not leave us out of
150 debt, nor absolutely discharged, but he laid another *Chirographum*
upon us, another Obligation arising out of his death. His death is
delivered to us, as a *writing,* but not a writing onely in the nature of
a peece of *Evidence,* to plead our inheritance by, but a writing in
the nature of a Copy, to learne by; It is not onely given us to reade,
but to write over, and practise; Not onely to tell us *what he* did, but
how we should do so too.

All the evills and mischiefes that light upon us in this world, come
(for the most part) from this, *Quia fruimur utendis,* because we
thinke to injoy those things which God hath given us onely to *use.*
160 God hath given us a *use* of things, and we set our hearts upon them.
And this hath a proportion, an assimilation, an accommodation in the
death of Christ. God hath proposed *that* for our *use,* in this world, and
we think to enjoy it; God would have us doe it over again, and we
think it enough to know that Christ hath done it already; God
would have us *write* it, and we doe onely *read* it; God would have
us *practise* the death of Christ, and we do but *understand* it. The
fruition, the enjoying of the death of Christ, is reserved for the next
life; To this life belongs the *use* of it; that use of it, to *fulfill his*
sufferings in our bodies, by bearing the afflictions and tribulations of
170 this life. For, *Priùs Trophæum Crucis erexit, deinde Martyribus*

Gen. 6.12
Heb. 9.27

Ezek. 18.4

1 Tim. 2.4

Heb. 12.6

Col. 2.14

August.

Ambros.

tradidit erigendum; first Christ set up the victorious Trophee of his Crosse himself, and then he delivered it over to his Martyrs to do as he had done. Nor are they onely his *Martyrs* that have *actually* died for him, but into the signification of that name, which signifies a *Witnesse,* fall all those, who have glorified him, in a patient and constant bearing the afflictions and tribulations of this life. All being guilty of Christs death, there lies an obligation upon us all, to fulfill his sufferings. And this is the *generality* of afflictions, as we consider them in their own nature.

180 Now, this generality is next expressed, in this word of exaltation, *Gheber, Ego vir, I am the man;* It was that man, that is denoted and signified in that man, that hath lien under affliction, and therefore no kinde of man was likely to scape. There are in the Originall Scriptures, *four words,* by which man is called; four names of man; and any of the others, (if we consider the origination of the words) might better admit afflictions to insult upon him, then this, *Gheber, vir, I am the man.* At first, man is called *Ishe;* a word, which their Grammarians derive *à sonitu,* from a sound, from a voice. Whether mans excellency be in *that,* that he can *speak,* which no other creature 190 can doe; or whether mans impotency be in *that,* that he comes into the world *Crying,* in this denomination, in this word, man is but a *sound,* but a *voyce,* and that is no great matter. Another name of man is *Adam,* and *Adam* is no more but *earth,* and *red earth,* and the word is often used for *blushing.* When the name of man imports no more but so, no more but the frailty of the earth, and the bashfull acknowledgement and confession of that frailty, in infinite infirmities, there is no great hope of scaping afflictions in this name, *Adam.* Lesse in his third name, *Enosh:* for *Enosh* signifies *ægrum, calamitosum,* a person naturally subject to, and actually possest with all kindes of 200 infirmities. So that this name of man, *Enosh,* is so farre from exempting him, as that it involves him, it overflows him in afflictions: He hath a miserable name, as well as a miserable nature, *Put them in fear, O Lord,* (says *David*) *that they may know that they are but men;* but such men, as are denoted in that name of man, *Enosh,* (for there that name is expressed) weak and miserable men. Now, (to collect these) as man is nothing but a frivolous, an empty, a transitory sound, or but a sad and lamentable voice, (he is no more

Gheber
Vir

Ps. 9.20

in his first name *Ishe*) As man is nothing but *red earth,* a moldring
clod of infirmities, and then, *blushing,* that is, guilty, sensible, and
²¹⁰ ashamed of his own miserable condition, (and man is no more, as
hee is but *Adam*) As man is nothing but a receptacle of diseases in
his body, of crosses in his estate, of immoderate griefes for those
crosses in his minde, (and man is no more as hee is but *Enosh*) so
there is no wonder, why man in generall should be under affliction,
for these names import, these names inforce it: As *Adam* gave names
to the creatures according to their natures, so God hath given names
to man, according to his nature, miserable names, to miserable
wretches. But when man is presented in this Text, in this fourth and
great name, *Gheber,* which denotes excellency, Excellency in *virtue,*
²²⁰ (his minde rectified) Excellency in *wealth,* (his estate enlarged)
Excellency in *power,* (his authority extended) Excellency in *favour,*
(all seas calm on the top, and foordable at the bottome to him) when
man is expressed in that word, which *Isaac* used to *Jacob,* in his
abundant blessing, *Be Lord over thy brethren, and let thy mothers
sonnes bow down to thee:* And then, in this heighth, this heighth of
vertue and merit, of wealth and treasure, of command and power,
of favour and acclamation, is thrown down into the pit of misery, and
submitted to all afflictions, what man can hope to be exempted? Man
carries the spawn and seed and egges of affliction in his own flesh,
²³⁰ and his own thoughts make haste to hatch them, and to bring them
up. We make all our worms snakes, all our snakes vipers, all our vipers
dragons, by our murmuring. And so have you this generality of affliction, considered in this name of Exaltation *Gheber.*

Now, in our third consideration of this extent of affliction, in that
this person, this *Prophet Jeremy,* (for, of *him* literally we understand
these words, *Ego vir, I am the man*) is thus submitted to these
extraordinary afflictions, we see first, that no man is so necessary to
God, as that God cannot come to his ends without that man; God can
lack, and leave out any man in his service. If Christ had revealed to
²⁴⁰ his Apostles, before he called them to be Apostles, or qualified them for
that service, that he had a purpose to subdue and convert the whole
world, by the labour and the meanes of *twelve men,* would it ever
have faln or entred into their imaginations, that any of *them,* should
have been any of those twelve? Men of low rank, and estimation,

Gen. 27.29

Ieremy

Nemo
neces-
sarius
Deo

men disfurnished, not onely of all helps of learning, but of all experience in *Civill* or in *Ecclesiasticall* affairs? And as Christ infused new abilities into these men that had none, so can he effect his purposes without *them,* who think they have all. And therefore, when he had chosen his twelve Apostles, and had endowed and qualified
50 them for that service, when in their sight some of his Disciples forsook him, because he preached *Duros sermones,* Doctrines hard to flesh and bloud, Christ was not afraid to say to the twelve, *Numquid & vos vultis abire, Will ye also goe away?* Hee says it to the twelve; and hee does not say, *Will any of you,* but *will you, you twelve, all, goe away?* I can doe my work without you. And therefore let no man goe about to promove or advance his own fancies, his own singularities, his own *Schismaticall* opinions, because he hath done God service before, because he hath possessed himself of the love of that *Congregation,* because no mans preaching is so acceptable there, as
260 *his,* and that the Church cannot be without him; for, no man hath made God beholden to him, so far, as that he should be afraid to offend him. So also let no man be disheartned nor discouraged, if hee have brought a good conscience, and faithfull labour to the service of God. Let him not thinke his wages the worse paid, if God doe mingle bodily *sicknesse,* temporall *losses,* personal *disgraces,* with his labours; Let him not think that God should not doe thus to *them* that wear out themselves in his service; for the best part of our wages is *adversity,* because that gives us a true fast, and a right value of our prosperity. *Jeremy* had it; the best of his rank must.
270   In his example, we have thus much more, that no man is excused of subsequent afflictions, by precedent, nor of falling into more, by having born some already. *Elias* reckoned too hastily, when he told God, *Satis est, now it is enough, Lord take away my life;* God had more to lay upon him. A *last years fever* prevents not this, nor a sicknesse in the *fall,* another in the *spring.* Men are not as such *Copises,* as being felled now, stand safe from the Axe for a dozen year after; But our *Afflictions* are as beggers, they tell others, and send more after them; *Sicknesse* does but usher in *poverty,* and poverty *contempt,* and contempt *dejection of spirit,* And *a broken*
280 *spirit who can bear?* No man may refuse *a Privy Seal,* because he hath lent before. And, though Afflictions be not of *Gods revenue,*

Ioh. 6.67

Non excusamur à futuris per præterita
1 Reg. 19.4

[Prov. 18.14]

(for, Afflictions are not reall services to God) yet they are of his *Subsidies,* and he hath additionall glory out of our Afflictions; and, the

Cap. 20.2
32.2
38.9

more, the more. *Ieremy* had been scornfully and despitefully put in the stocks by *Pashur,* before; He had been imprisoned in the Kings house, before; He had been put in the dungeon, and almost starved in the mire, before; And yet he was reserved to this farther calamity. Affliction is truly a part of our patrimony, of our portion. If, as the

[Luk. 15.13]

prodigall did, we wast our portion, (that is, make no use of our ²⁹⁰ former affliction) it is not the least part of Gods bounty and liberality towards us, if he give us a new stock, a new feeling of new calamities, that we may be better emproved by them, then by the former; *Ieremies* former afflictions were but preparatives for more; no more are ours.

Publi-
cavit

And, in his example wee have this one note more, That when the hand of God had been upon him, he declared, he published Gods hand-writing: not onely to his owne conscience, by acknowledging that all these afflictions were for his sins, but by acknowledging to the world, that God had laid such and such afflictions upon him. There ³⁰⁰ is not a neerer step to obduration, nor a worse defrauding of God of his glory, then to be loth to let the world know, what God hath laid upon us. Say to your selves, *These afflictions are for my sins,* and say to one another, *Ego vir,* I am the man whom God hath thus, and thus afflicted. For, as *Executions* in *criminall justice,* are done as much for *example* of others, as for *punishment* of delinquents, so would God faine proceed that cheap way, to make those afflictions which he lays upon *thee,* serve *another* too; as they will, if thou be content to glorifie God, in letting others know, how he hath afflicted *thee.* Shut we up this first branch of this first part (The extent and *universality* ³¹⁰ of afflictions) which we have considered first in the *nature* of the case, (we have all contributed to the afflictions of Christ, and therefore must all *fulfill his sufferings in our flesh*) And then secondly, in this *name of Exaltation, Gheber,* (man, in the highest consideration of man, is the subject of affliction) And lastly, in the person of *Ieremy,* in whom we have made our use of those three observations; First, That no man is so necessary to God, as that God cannot be without him, Then, That no man is excused of future calamities, by former, And lastly, That he whom God hath exercised with afflictions, is

bound to glorifie God in the declaration thereof; shut wee up this
branch, with that story of S. *Ambrose,* who, in a journey from *Milan*
to *Rome,* passing some time in the evening with his *Host,* and hearing
him brag that he had never had any crosse in his life, S. *Ambrose*
presently removed from thence to another house, with that protestation, That either *that* man was very unthankfull to God, that would
not take knowledge of his corrections, or that Gods measure was by
this time full, and hee would surely, and soundly, and suddenly poure
down all together. And so we passe to our other branch of this first
part, from the extent and generality of afflictions, to the *weight* and
vehemence of them, expressed in three heavy circumstances, That
they *are His,* the Lords, That they are *from his Rod,* That they are
from *the Rod of his wrath: I am the man, that hath seen afflictions,
by the rod of his wrath.*

First, they are aggravated in that they are *Ejus, His,* The Lords. It
is ordinary in the Scriptures, that when the Holy Ghost would expresse a superlative, or the highest degree of any thing, to expresse
it, by adding to it, the name of God. So, in many places, *fortitudo
Domini,* and *timor Domini,* The power of the Lord, and the fear of
the Lord, doe not import that power which is in the Lord, nor that
fear which is to be conceived by us of the Lord, but the power of the
Lord, and the fear of the Lord denote the greatest power, and the
greatest fear that can be conceived. As in particular, when *Saul* and
his company were in such a dead sleep, as that *David* could enter
in upon them, and take his speare, and his pot of water from under
his head, this is there called *sopor Domini, the sleep of the Lord was
upon him,* the heaviest, the deadliest sleep that could be imagined.
So may these Afflictions in our Text be conceived to bee exalted to a
superlative heighth, by this addition, that *They,* and *the Rod,* and
the wrath, are said to be *His, The Lords.* But this cannot well be the
sense, nor the direct proceeding, and purpose of the Holy Ghost, in
this place, because where the addition of the name of God constitutes
a superlative, that name is evidently and literally expressed in that
place, as *fortitudo Dei, sopor Dei,* and the rest; But here, the name
of God is onely by implication, by illation, by consequence; All
necessary, but yet but *illation,* but *implication,* but *consequence.* For,
there is no name of God in this verse; but, because in the last verse

Ejus

1 Sam. 26.12

of the former chapter, *the Lord* is expresly named, and the *Lords Anger,* and then, this which is the first verse of this chapter, and connected to that, refers these afflictions, and rods, and wrath to *Him,* (*The rod of his wrath*) it must necessarily bee to *him* who was last 360 spoken of, The *Lord,* They are *Ejus, His,* and therefore heavy.

Then is an Affliction properly *Gods Affliction,* when thou in thy *Conscience* canst impute it to none but God. When thou disorderest thy body with a *surfeit,* nature will submit to sicknesse; When thou wearest out thy selfe with *licentiousnesse,* the sin it self will induce infirmities; When thou transgressest any law of the State, the *Justice of the State* will lay hold upon thee. And for the Afflictions that fall upon thee in these cases, thou art able to say to thy selfe, that they would have falne upon thee, though there had been *no God,* or though God had had *no rod* about him, no anger in him; Thou 370 knowest in particular, *why,* and *by whose,* or *by what means,* these Afflictions light upon thee. But when thou shalt have thy Conscience clear towards such and such *men,* and yet those men shall goe about to oppresse thee, when thou labourest uprightly in thy calling, and yet doest not prosper, when thou studiest the Scriptures, hearkenest to Sermons, observest Sabbaths, desirest conferences, and yet receivest not satisfaction, but still remainest under the torture of scruples and 1 Cor. 4.4 anxieties, when thou art in S. *Pauls* case, *Nihili conscius,* That thou knowest nothing by thy selfe, and yet canst not give thy selfe peace, Though all Afflictions upon Gods children, be from *him,* yet, take 380 knowledge that *this* is from *him,* more intirely, and more immediately, and that God remembers something in thee, that thou hast forgot; And, as that fit of an Ague, or that pang of the Gout, which may take thee to day, is not necessarily occasioned by that which thou hast eaten to day, but may be the effect of some former disorder, so the affliction which lights upon thee in thine age, may be inflicted for the sinnes of thy youth. Thy affliction is *his,* The Lords; And the Lord is infinite, and comprehends all at once, and ever finds something in thee to correct, something that thou hast done, or something that thou wouldest have done, if the blessing of that correction had 390 not restrained thee. And therefore, when thou canst not pitch thy affliction upon any *particular sinne,* yet make not thy selfe so just,

as that thou make God unjust, whose Judgements may be unsearchable, but they cannot be unjust.

 This then is the first weight laid upon our afflictions, that they *are
His, The Lords;* and this weight consists in this, That because they
are his, they are *inevitable,* they cannot be avoyded, And because they
are *His,* they are certainly *just,* and cannot be *pleaded* against, nor can
we ease our selves with any imagination of an innocency, as though
they were *undeserved.* And the next weight that is laid upon them,
is that they are, *In virga ejus, in his rod.* For, though this Metaphore,
the Rod, may seeme to present but an easie correction, such as that,
If thou beat thy childe with a rod, he shall not dye, (It will not kill
him) yet there is more weight then so in this Rod; for the word here
is *Shebet,* and *Shebet* is such a Rod as may kill; *If a man smite his
servant with a Rod, so that he dye under his hand, he shall be surely
punished.* Beloved, whether Gods Rod, and his correction, shall have
the *savour of life unto life,* or *of death unto death,* consists much in
the *hand,* that is to receive it, and in the stomach that is to digest it.
As in Gods *Temporall blessings* that he raines downe upon us, it is
much in our gathering, and inning, and spending them, whether it
shall be *frumenti,* or *laqueorum,* whether this shall prove such a
shoure, as shall nourish our soule spiritually, in thankfulnesse to God,
and in charitable workes towards his needy Servants, or whether it
shall prove *a shoure of snares,* to minister occasions of *tentations;* so
when he raines afflictions upon us, it is much in our gathering,
whether it shall be *Roris,* or *Grandinis,* whether it shall be a *shoure
of fatning dew* upon us, or a shoure of *Egyptian haile-stones,* to batter us in peeces, *as a Potters Vessell, that cannot be renewed.* Our
murmuring makes a *rod* a *staffe,* and a *staffe* a *sword,* and that which
God presented for *physick, poyson.* The double effect and operation
of Gods Rod, and Corrections, is usefully and appliably expressed in
the Prophet *Zachary:* where God complaines, *That he had fed the
sheep of slaughter,* that he had been carefull for them, who would
needs dye, say what he could. Therefore he was forced to come to the
Rod, to correction. So he does; *And I tooke unto me,* sayes he there,
two Staves, the one I called Beauty, the other Bands; Two wayes of
correction, a milder, and a more vehement. When his milder way

August.

In Virga

Prov. 23.13

Exod. 21.20

[2 Cor. 2.16]

Psal. 11.6

[Exod. 9.25]
Ierem. 19.11

11.7

prevailed not, Then said I, *I will not feed you;* I will take no more care of you; *That which dyeth let it dye,* (sayes he) *and that which* 430 *is to be cut off, let it be cut off; And I tooke my staffe of Beauty, and cut it asunder, that I might breake my Covenant, which I had made with them.* Beloved, God hath made no such Covenant with any State, any Church, any soule, but that, being provoked, he is at liberty to break it. But then, upon this, when the stubborne, and the refractory, the stiff-necked and the rebellious were cut off, *The poore of the sheep* (sayes God) *that waited upon me, knew that it was the word of the Lord.* It is not every mans case, to mend by Gods corrections; onely *the poore of the sheep,* the broken-hearted, the contrite spirit, the discerner of his owne poverty and infirmity, could make 440 that good use of affliction, as to finde *Gods hand,* and then *Gods purpose* in it. For, this Rod of God, this *Shebet,* can kill; Affliction can harden, as well as mollifie, and entender the heart. And there is so much the more danger, that it should worke that effect, that obduration, because it is *Virga Iræ, The rod of his wrath,* which is the other weight that aggravates our afflictions.

Virga	In all afflictions that fall upon us from other instruments, there is
Iræ	*Digitus Dei,* The finger of God leads their hand that afflicts us; Though it be *sicknesse,* by our intemperance, though it be *poverty,* by our wastfulnesse, though it be *oppression,* by the malice, or by 450 our exasperation of potent persons, yet still *the finger of God* is in all these. But in the afflictions which we speake of *here,* such as fall upon us, when we thinke our selves at peace with God, and in state of grace, it is not *Digitus,* but *Manus Dei,* the whole worke is his, and man hath no part in it. Whensoever he takes the Rod in hand, there is a correction towards; but yet, it may be but his *Rod of Beauty,* of his *Correction,* not *Destruction.* But, if he take his *Rod in anger,* the case is more dangerous; for, though there be properly no anger in God, yet then is God said to do a thing in anger, when he does it so, as an angry man would do it. Upon those words of *David, O Lord, rebuke*

Psal. 6.1	460 *me not in thine anger,* Saint *Augustine* observes, that *David* knew Gods rebukes and corrections were but for his amendment; but yet, *In Ira corrigi noluit, in Ira emendari noluit, David* was loth, that God should go about to mend him in anger; afraid to have any thing to do with God, till his anger were over-passed. Beloved, to a true anger, and wrath, and indignation towards his children, God never comes; but he comes so neare it, as that they cannot discerne, whether it be anger, or no. A Father takes a Rod, and looks as angerly, as though he would kill his childe, but means nothing but good to him. So God brings a soule to a sad sense of an angry countenance in God, to a sad apprehension of an angry absence, to a sad jealousie and suspition that God will never returne to it againe; And this is a heavy affliction, whilst it lasts. Our Saviour Christ, in that case, came to expostulate it, to dispute it with his Father, *Vt quid dereliquisti, My God, my God, why hast thou forsaken me?* Do but tell me *why*. For, [Mat. 27.46] if God be pleased to tell us, *why* he is angry, his anger is well allayd, and we have a faire overture towards our restitution. But, in our infirmity, wee get not easily so farre; we apprehend God to be angry; we cannot finde *the cause,* and we sinke under the burden; we leave the disease to *concoct* it self, and we take no Physick. And this is truly the highest extent, and exaltation of affliction, That in our afflictions we take God to be angryer then he is. For, then is God said to take his Rod in anger, when he suffers us to thinke that he does so, and when he suffers us to decline, and sinke so low towards diffidence, and desperation, that we dare not looke towards him, because we beleeve him to be so angry. And so have you all those peeces which constitute both the branches of this first part, The generality and extent of afflictions, considered in the nature of the *thing,* in the nature of the *word,* this name of *man, Gheber,* and in the *person of Jeremy,* the Prophet of God, And then the intensenesse, and weight and *vehemency* of afflictions, considered in these three particulars, That they *are His,* The Lords, That they are *from His Rod,* And from *the Rod of his anger.* But to weigh down all these, we have comforts ministred unto us, in our Text, which constitute our other part.

Of these the first is *Vidi, I have seen these afflictions,* for *this* is an act of particular grace and mercy, when God enables us to *see* them: for, naturally this is the infirmity of our spirituall senses, that when the eyes of our understanding should be enlightened, our understanding is so darkened, as that we can neither see prosperity, nor adversity, for, in prosperity our light is too great, and we are *dazeled,* in adversity too little, none at all, and we are *benighted,* we do not see our afflictions. There is no doubt, but that the literall sense of this phrase,

2 Part

Vidi

Eph. 1.18
4.18

To see afflictions, is to feele, to suffer afflictions. As, when *David* sayes,

Psal. 89.48 *What man is he that liveth, and shall not see death,* and when Christ

16.10 sayes, *Thou shalt not suffer thine holy One to see corruption,* to see death, and to see corruption, is to *suffer* them. But then, the literall sense being thus duly preserved, That the children of God shall certainly *see,* that is, certainly *suffer* afflictions, receive we also that sweet odour and fragrancy which the word breaths out, That they shall *see it,* that is, *understand* it, *consider* it: For, as when the wicked come

Psal. 94.7 ⁵¹⁰ to say, *The Lord does not see it,* it is presently added, *Neither doth the God of Jacob regard it,* ⸲(It is a *seeing* that induces a *regarding*) so when the godly come to see their afflictions, they come to *regard*

35.22 them, to regard Gods *purpose* in them. *Vidisti Domine, ne sileas,* sayes David, *All this thou hast seen, O Lord, Lord do not hold thy peace. David* presumed, that if God *saw* his afflictions, he would stirre in them; when we come to *see* them, we *stir,* we wake, we rise, we looke about us, from *whence,* and *why* these afflictions come; and therein lyes this comfort, *Vidi, I have seen* afflictions, I have been content to look upon them, to consider them.

⁵²⁰ The Prophets in the Old Testament, doe often call those sights, and those prenotions which they had of the misery and destruction of others, *Onus visionis, Onus verbi Domini, O the burden of this sight, O the burden of this message of God.* It was a burden to them, to see Gods judgements directed upon others; how much more is it a burden to a man, to see his own affliction, and that in the cause thereof? But this must be done, we must see our affliction in the *Cause thereof.* No man is so blinde, so stupid, as that he doth not *see* his affliction, that is, *feele* it; but we must see it so, as to *see through* it, see it to be *such* as it is, so qualified, so conditioned, so circumstanced, as he that

⁵³⁰ sends it, intends it. We must leave out the *malice* of others in our oppressions, and forgive *that;* leave out the *severity* of the Law in our punishments, and submit to *that;* and looke intirely upon the certainty of Gods judgement, who hath the whole body of our sins written together before him, and picks out what sin it pleaseth him, and punisheth now an old, now a yesterdayes sin, as he findeth it most to conduce to his glory, and our amendment, and the edification of

Dan. 5.5 others. We must *see the hand of God upon the wall* as *Belshazzar* did, (for even *that was the hand of God*) though wee cannot read

that writing, no more then *Belshazzar* could. Wee must see the affliction, so as we must see it to be the *hand of God,* though wee cannot
presently see, *for what sinne it is, nor what will be the issue of it.*
And then when we have seen that, then we must turn to the study of
those other particulars, for, till we see the affliction to come from God,
we see nothing; There is no other light in that darknesse, but *he.*
If thou see thy affliction, thy sicknesse, in that glasse, in the consideration of thine own former *licentiousnesse,* thou shalt have no other
answer, but that soure remorse, and increpation, *you might have lived
honestly.* If thou see thy affliction, thy poverty, in that glasse, in the
malice and oppression of potent adversaries, thou wilt get no farther,
then to that froward and churlish answer, *The Law is open, mend
your selfe as you can.* But *Jactate super Dominum,* saith *David, Lay
all thy burden upon the Lord, and hee will apply to thee that Col-
lyrium, that soveraigne eye-salve, whereby thou shalt see thy affliction,* (it shall not blinde thee) And see from *whence it commeth,
(from him, who, as hee liveth, would not the death of a sinner)* And
see why it commeth, *(that thou mightest see and taste the goodnesse
of God thy selfe, and declare his loving kindnesse to the Children of
Men.)* And this is the comfort deduced from this word *Vidi, I have
seen affliction.*

And this leadeth us to our other Comfort, That though these Afflictions have wrought deepe upon thee, yet thou canst say to thy soule,
Ego vir, I am that man; Thy Morality, thy Christianity is not shaked
in thee. *It is the Mercy of God, that wee are not consumed,* saith
Jeremy here; And it is a great degree of his mercy, to let us *feele* that
wee are not consumed, to give us this sense, that our case is not desperate, but that *Ego vir, I am the man,* that there remaineth still
strength enough to gather more; That still thou remainest *a man, a
reasonable man,* and so art able to apply to thy selfe, all those medi-
cines and reliefs, which Philosophy and naturall reason can afford.
For, even these helps, deduced from *Philosophy* and *naturall reason,*
are strong enough against afflictions of this world, as long as we can
use them, as long as these helps of reason and learning are alive, and
awake, and actuated in us, they are able to sustain us from sinking
under the afflictions of this world, for, they have sustained many a
Plato, and *Socrates,* and *Seneca* in such cases. But when part of the

Psal. 55.22
Apoc. 3.18

[Ezek.
33.11]
[Psa. 34.8]
[Psa. 107.8]

Ego vir

vers. 22

affliction shall be, that God worketh upon *the Spirit* it selfe, and
damps that, enfeebles that, that he casts a sooty Cloud upon the
understanding, and darkens that, that he doth *Exuere hominem,* devest, strip the man of the man, *Eximere hominem,* take the man out
580 of the man, and withdraw and frustrate his naturall understanding so, as that, to this purpose, he is no man, yet even in this case,
God may mend thee, in marring thee, hee may build thee up in de-
jecting thee, hee may infuse another, *Ego vir,* another Manhood into
thee, and though thou canst not say *Ego vir, I am that Morall man,*
safe in my *Natural Reason* and *Philosophy,* that is spent, yet *Ego vir,*
I am that *Christian man,* who have seen this affliction in the *Cause*
thereof, so farre off, as in my *sinne in Adam,* and the *remedy* of this
affliction, so farre off, as in the death of *Christ Jesus. I am the Man,*
that cannot repine, nor murmure, since I am the *Cause;* I am the
590 man that cannot *despair,* since *Christ* is the remedy. I am that man,
which is intended in this Text, *Gheber.* Not onely an *Adam,* a man
amongst men, able to convince me, though they speak eloquently

Iob 16.20   against me, and able to prove that *God* hath forsaken me, because *he
hath afflicted me,* but able to prevail with *God* himself, as *Jacob* did,

Gen.   and to wrastle out a blessing out of him, and, though I doe halt, be-
32.24[–29]   come infirm with manifold afflictions, yet they shall be so many seals
of my infallibility in him. Now this comfort hath three gradations in
our text, three circumstances, which, as they aggravated the discomfort in the former, so they exalt the comfort in this part, That they
600 are *His, The Lords,* That they are *from his rod,* That they are *from
the rod of his wrath.*

Ejus   We may compare our afflictions that come immediately from *God,*
with those that come instrumentally from *others,* by considering the
choice and election which *David* made, and the choice which *Su-*

2 Sam.   *sanna* made in her case. The Prophet *Gad* offers *David* his choice of
24.[13]   three afflictions, *War, Famine,* or *Pestilence.* It does not appeare, it is
not expressed, that *David* determined himself, or declared his choice
of any of the three. Hee might conceive a hope, that God would for-

2 Sam. 12.14   bear all three. As, when another Prophet *Nathan* had told him, *The*
610 *childe shall surely die,* yet *David* said, for all that determined assurance, *Who can tell whether the Lord will be gracious to me, that the
child may live,* and he fasted a fast, and mourned and prayed for the

childes life. Beloved, no commination of God, is unconditioned, or irrevocable. But in this case *David* intimates some kinde of election, *Let me fall into the hands of the Lord, for his mercies are exceeding great, and not into the hands of men.* *Susanna,* when shee was surprised, (and in a straight too, though of another kind) she resolves that it is better for her to fall into the hands of *men,* (let men defame her, let men accuse her, condemn her, execute her) rather then sin in the sight of God, and so fall into his hands. So that, if wee compare offences, wee were better offend all the Princes of the earth, then offend God, because he is able to cast body and soul into hell fire. But when the offence is done, for the *punishment* which follows, God forgives a *treason,* sooner then thy neighbour will a *trespasse;* God seales thee a *Quietus est,* in the bloud of his Son, sooner then a *Creditor* will renue a bond, or withdraw an Action; and a *Scandalum magnatum,* will lie longer upon thee here, then a blasphemy against God in *that* Court. And therefore, as it is one degree of *good husbandry,* in ill husbands, to bring all their debts into one hand, so doest thou husband thy afflictions well, if thou put them all upon thy debts to God, and leave out the consideration of *Instruments;* And he shall deale with thee, as hee did with *David* there, that plague, which was threatned for three days, he will end in *one;* In that trouble, which, if men had their will upon thee, would have consumed thee, thou shalt stand unconsumed. For, if a man wound thee, it is not in his power, though hee be never so sorry for it, whether that wound shall kill thee, or no; but if the Lord wound thee to death, he is the life, he can redeem thee from death, and if hee doe not, he is thy resurrection, and recompenses thee with another, and a better life. And so lies our first comfort, that it is *Ejus, His,* The Lords, And a second is, that it is *In virga ejus, In his rod.*

Job would fain have come to a cessation of arms, before hee came to a treaty with God: *Let the Lord take away his rod from me,* sayes he, *and let not his fear terrifie me; Then would I speak.* As long as his rod was upon him, and his fears terrified him, it was otherwise; he durst not. But truly his feares should not terrifie us, though his rod be upon us; for herein lies our comfort, That all Gods rods are bound up with that mercy, which accompanied that rod that God threatned *David,* to exercise upon his son *Solomon, If he commit*

[Sus. 23]

2 Sam. 24.16

In Virga
9.34

2 Sam. 7.14

⁶⁵⁰ *iniquity, I will chasten him with the rod of men;* (I will let him
fall into the hands of *men*) This was heavy; Therefore it is eased
with that Cordiall, *But my mercy shall not depart away from him,
as I took it from Saul.* But for this mercy, the oppressions of men
were mercilesse; But all Gods rods are bound up with this mercy;
and therein lies our comfort. And for the rods of other men, *O my
people be not afraid of the Assyrian,* says God. Why, blessed Lord,
shall the Assyrian doe thy people no harm? yes, says God there, *He
shall smite them with a rod, and he shall lift up his staffe against
them;* Some harm he shall doe; (*He shall smite them with a rod*)
⁶⁶⁰ And he shall threaten more, offer at more (*he shall lift up his staffe*)
where then is the peoples reliefe, and comfort? In this; *The Lord
of Hosts shall stir up a scourge for him.* God shall appear in that notion of power, The Lord of Hosts, and he shall encounter his enemies, and the enemies of his friends, with a scourge upon them,
against their rod upon us. Gods own rods are bound up in mercy,
(they end in mercy) And, for the rods of other men, God cuts them
in pieces, and their owners, with his sword. Gods owne rods, even
towards his owne Children, are sometimes, as that rod which he put
into *Moses* hand was, chang'd into *Serpents.* Gods own rods have
⁶⁷⁰ sometimes a sting, and a bitternesse in them; but then, they are
chang'd from their owne nature; Naturally Gods roddes towards us,
are gentle, and harmlesse: When Gods rod in *Moses* hand, was
changed to a Serpent, it did no harme, that did but devoure the
other Serpents: when Gods rods are heaviest upon us, if they devoure
other rods, that is, enable us to put off the consideration of the malice
and oppression of other Men, and all displeasure towards them, and
lay all upon God, for our sinnes, these *serpentine* rods have wrought
a good effect: When *Moses* his Rod was a Serpent, yet it return'd
quickly to a Rod againe; how bitter so ever Gods corrections be, they
⁶⁸⁰ returne soone to their naturall sweetnesse, and though the correction
continue, the bitternesse does not: with this Rod *Moses* tam'd the
Sea, and divided that; but he drowned none in that Sea, but the
Ægyptians. Gods rod will cut, and divide between thy soule, and
spirit, but he will destroy nothing in thee, not thy *Morality,* not thy
Christianity, but onely thine owne *Ægyptians,* thy Persecutors, thy
concupiscencies.

Esa. 10.24

V. 26

Exod. 7.12

[Exod.
14.16]

But all this while, we have but deduced a comfort out of thy Word, *Quia Virga*, though that be a rod; but this is a comfort *Quia Virga*, therefore, because that is a Rod: for, this word which is here a Rod, is also, in other places of Scriptures, an Instrument, not of *correction*, but *direction: Feed thy sheep with thy Rod*, saies God; and there it is a *Pastorall Rod*, the direction of the Church; *Virga rectitudinis virga regni tui*, saies *David; The Scepter of thy kingdome is a right Scepter;* and there it is a *royall rod*, the protection of the state: so that all comforts that are deriv'd upon us, by the *direction* of the Church, and by the *protection* of the State, are recommended to us, and conferr'd upon us in this *His Rod*. Nor is it onely a Rod of *comfort*, by implication, and consequence; but expresly and literally it is so: *Though I should walke thorough the valley of the shadow of death, I will feare no evill; Thy rod, and thy staffe, they comfort me.* He had not onely a comfort, though he had the rod, but he had not had so much comfort, except he had had it; we have not so good evidence of the joyes of the next life, except we have the sorrowes of this.

The discomfort then lies not in this, That the affliction is *ejus, his*, the Lords, (for we have an ease in that) nor, that it is *In Virga ejus*, in his rod, (for we have a benefit by that) but it is *In Virga iræ*, in that it is the rod of his wrath, of his anger. But truely, beloved, there is a blessed comfort ministred unto us, even in that word; for that word **Gnabar*, which we translate *Anger, wrath*, hath another ordinary signification in Scripture, which, though that may seem to be an easier, would prove a heavier sense for us to beare, than this of *wrath* and *anger;* this is, *preteritio, conniventia*, Gods forbearing to take knowledge of our transgressions; when God shall say of us, as he does of *Israel, Why should ye be smitten any more?* when God leaves us to our selves, and studies our recovery no farther, by any more corrections; for, in this case, there is the lesse comfort, because there is the lesse *anger* show'd. And therefore S. *Bernard*, who was heartily afraid of this sense of our word, heartily afraid of this preterition, that God should forget him, leave him out, affectionately, passionately embraces this sense of the word in our Text, *Anger;* and he sayes, *Irascaris mihi Domine, Domine mihi irascaris, Be angry with me ô Lord, O Lord be angry with me, lest I perish!* for, till we have a sense of such an anger in God, towards us, as Children have from

Quia Virga

Mich. 7.14

Psal. 45.6

Psal. 23.4

Virga Iræ

עֶבְרָה

Esa. 1.5

their Parents, that not onely they correct them, but deny them some things that they aske, and keep them some time from their sight and presence, till we be made Partakers of this blessed anger of God, (for we doe not pray, that God would not be angry, but that *he would not be angry with us for ever*) till *then* we come not to see an affliction, that is, to discerne *what,* and *whence,* and *why* that comes: Nor ⁷³⁰ we see that not like Men, like such Men, like Christian Men, not with a faithfull and constant assurance, that all will have an end in him who suffered infinitely more for us, than he hath layd upon us.

[Book of Common Prayer, Litany]

Number 10.

A Sermon Preached in Saint Dunstans.

I THESSALONIANS 5.16. *REJOYCE EVERMORE.*

W E READE in the Naturall Story, of some floating Islands, that swim and move from place to place; and in them a Man may sowe in one place, and reape in another: This case is so farre ours, as that in another place we have sowed in teares, and by his promise, in whose teares we sowed then, when we handled those two words, *Jesus wept,* we shall reape in Joy: That harvest is not yet; it is reserved to the last Resurrection: But the Corne is above ground, in the Resurrection of our head, the first fruits of the Dead, Christ Jesus, and that being the first visible steppe of his exaltation, begins our exultation, who in him are to rejoyce evermore. *The heart knoweth his own bitternesse;* he and none but he; others feele it not, retaine it not, pity it not; and therefore saies the Text, *A Stranger doth not intermeddle with his joy:* He shall have a Joy which no stranger, not he himselfe whilest he was a stranger to God, and to himselfe, could conceive. If we aske, as Christs Disciples asked of him, *Quod signum?* what shall be the signe of thy comming, of this Joy in the midst of thy bitternesse? *Ipsæ lachrymæ lætitiæ testes, & nuncii:* The tears themselves shall be the sign, the tears shall be Ambassadours of Joy; a present gladnesse shall consecrate your sorrow, and teares shall baptize, and give a new name to your passion, for your Wormwood shall be Manna; even then when it is Wormwood, it shall be Manna, for, *Gaudebitis semper,* you shall Rejoyce evermore.

But our Text does more then imply a promise to us, for it laies a precept upon us: It is not, *Gaudebitis,* you shall Rejoyce, by way of Comfort, but it is, *Gaudete,* Rejoyce, see that you doe Rejoyce, by way

213

[1 Cor. 15.20]

Prov. 14.10

Mat. 24.3
Aug.

Divisio

of Commandement, and that shall be our first part. *Cadit sub præ-cepto;* It hath the nature of a Commandement. Angels passe not from extreame to extreame, but by the way betweene; Man passes not from the miseries of this life, to the joyes of Heaven, but by joy in this life
³⁰ too; for he that feeles no joy here, shall finde none hereafter. And when we passe from the substance of the precept, to the extent thereof (which will be our second part) from the first word, *Rejoyce,* to the other, *Rejoyce alwaies;* we shall cleave that into two periods, *Gaudete in bonis,* Rejoyce in your prosperitie, and *Gaudete in malis,* Rejoyce in your adversitie too. But because it is *in sempiternum,* that

[Heb. 13.8]   must be *in sempiterno,* because it is alway, it must be in him who is alwaies, yesterday and to day, and the same for ever, Joy in God, Joy in the Holy Ghost, which will be another branch in that second part; of which Joy, though there be a preparatory, and inchoative partici-
⁴⁰ pation and possession in this life, yet the consummation being re-served to our entrance into our Masters Joy, not onely the Joy which he gives, that's here, but the Joy which he is, that's onely there, we shall end in that, beyond which none can goe, no not in his thoughts, in some dimme contemplation, and in some faint representation of the Joyes of Heaven, and in that Contemplation we shall dismisse you.

[1] Part   First then it is presented in the nature of a Commandement, and laies an Obligation upon all, at all times to procure to our selves, and

Aquin: 1   to cherish in our selves, this Joy, this Rejoycing. What is Joy? *Com-*
2æ. 28.3   *paratur ad desiderium sic ut quies admotum;* As Rest is the end of
⁵⁰ motion, every thing moves therefore that it may rest, so Joy is the end of our desires, whatsoever we place our desires, our affections

Bannez   upon, it is therefore, that we may enjoy it; and therefore, *Quod est in brutis in parte sensitiva Delectatio, in hominibus in parte intel-lectiva est gaudium:* Beasts and carnall men, who determine all their desires in the sensuall parts, come no farther then to a delight: but men, who are truly men, and carry them to the intellectuall part, they,

[Prov. 21.15]   and onely they, come to Joy. And therefore saies *Solomon, It is the joy of the just to doe judgment;* to have lyen still, and done no wrong occasions, is not this Joy; Joy is not such a Rest, as the Rest of the

[Psa. 19.5–6]   ⁶⁰ Earth, that never mov'd; but as the *Sunne rejoyceth to runne his race, and his circuit is unto the end of heaven;* so this Joy is the rest and testimony of a good conscience, that we have done those things which belong to our calling, that we have mov'd in our Sphere. For, if men of our profession, whose Function it is, to attend the service of God, delight our selves in having gathered much in this world; if a Souldier shall have delighted himselfe, in giving rules of Agriculture, or of Architecture; if a Counsellour of State, who should assist with his counsell upon present emergencies, delight himself in writing Books of good counsel for posterity, all this occasions not this joy; because though there have been motion, and though there be Rest, yet that is not Rest after the Motion proper to them. A Man that hath been out of his way all the day, may be glad to find a good Inne at night; but yet 'tis not properly Joy, because he is never the neerer home. Joy is peace for having done that which we ought to have done: And therefore it is well expressed, *Optima conjectura an homo sit in gratia est gaudere;* The best evidence that a Man is at peace, and in favour with God, is, that he can rejoyce. To trie whether I be able by Argument and disputation to prove all, that I believe, or to convince the Adversary, this is *Academia animæ,* the soules University, where some are Graduats, and all are not: To trie whether I be able to endure Martyrdome for my beliefe, this is *Gehenna animæ,* the rack, the torture of the Soule, and some are able to hold it out, and all are not: But to trie whether I can rejoyce in the peace, which I have with God, this is but *Catechismus animæ,* the Catechisme of the Soule, and every Man may examine himselfe, and every Man must; for it is a Commandement, *Gaudete semper,* Rejoyce evermore.

Bannez
ibid.

It is, we cannot say the Office, but the Essence of God to doe good; and when he does that, he is said to rejoyce; *The Lord thy God will make thee plenteous;* (there is his goodnesse) and he will *Rejoyce again over thee for good, as he rejoyced over thy Fathers.* The Lord will love thee, there is his goodnesse; and rejoyce in thee, and *he will rest in his love.* Such a joy as is a rest, a complacency in that good which he hath done, we see is placed in God himselfe. It is in Angels too: Their office is to minister to Men, (for by nature they are Spirits, but by office they are Angels) and when they see so good effect of their service, as that a Sinner is converted, *There is joy in the presence of the Angels of God.* Christ himselfe had a spirituall office and employment, *To give light to the blind, and to inflict blindnesse upon*

Deut. 30.9

Zeph. 3.17

Luke 15.10

[Joh. 9.39]

[100] *those who thought they saw all.* And when that was done, *Exultavit*

in spiritu, in that houre Christ rejoyced in the Spirit, and said, *I thank thee ô Father, Lord of Heaven and Earth, &c.* To have something to doe, to doe it, and then to Rejoyce in having done it, to embrace a calling, to performe the Duties of that calling, to joy and rest in the peacefull testimony of having done so; this is Christianly done, Christ did it; Angelically done, Angels doe it; Godly done, God does it. *As*

the Bridegroome rejoyceth in his Bride, so doth thy God rejoyce in thee. Example, as well as the Rule, repeats it to you, *Gaudete semper.*

But how farre may we carry this joy? To what outward declara-

[110] tions? To laughing? Saint *Basil* makes a round answer to a short question. *An in Universum ridere non licet?* May a Man laugh in no case? *Admodum perspicuum est,* It is very evident, that a Man may

not, because Christ saies, *Væ vobis,* Wo be unto you that laugh; and yet Saint *Basil* himselfe in another place sayes (which we are rather to take in explanation, than in contradiction of himselfe) that that woe of Christ is cast *in obstreperum Sonum, non in sinceram hilaritatem:* upon a dissolute and undecent, and immoderate laughing, not upon true inward joy, howsoever outwardly expressed. At the prom-

ise of a Son, *Abraham fell on his face and laughed;* a religious Man,

[120] and a grave Man, 100 yeares old, expressed this joy of his heart, by this outward declaration. *Hierome's* Translation reads it, *Risit in Corde,* he laughed within himselfe, because Saint *Hierome* thought that was a weaknesse, a declination towards unbeliefe, to laugh at Gods promise, as he thinks *Abraham* did. But Saint *Paul* is a better

Witnesse in his behalf; *Against hope he believed in hope; he was not weake in faith; he staggered not at the promise of God, through unbelief. Quòd risit, non incredulitatis, sed exultationis indicium fuit,* his laughing was no ebbe of faith, but a flood of joy. It is not as S.

Hierome takes it, *Risit in Corde putans celare deum, apertè ridere*

[130] *non ausus;* he kept-in his laughing, and durst not laugh out; But as St. *Ambrose* says well, *Risus non irrisio diffidentis, sed exultatio gratulantis;* he laughed not in a doubtfull scorne of Gods promise, but in an overflowing of his own joy: It is well expressed, and, well con-

cluded, *O virum æterno risu vere dignum, & sempiternæ jucunditati bene præparatum,* This was good evidence, that he was a man well disposed for the joyes of heaven; that he could conceive joy in the

temporall blessings of God, and that he thought nothing mis-becomming him, that was an outward declaration of this joy. It is a dangerous weaknesse, to forbeare outward declarations of our sense of Gods goodnesse, for feare of mis-interpretations; to smother our present thankfulnesse, for fear that some should say it was a levity to thank God so soon, till God had done the whole work. For God does sometimes leave half his work undone, because he was not thanked for it. When *David danced and leaped, and shouted before the Arke,* if he   2 Sam. 6.14
laughed too, it mis-became him not. Not to feele joy is an argument against religious tendernesse, not to show that joy, is an argument against thankfulnesse of the heart: that is a stupidity, this is a contempt. *A merry heart maketh a cheerfull countenance.* If it be within,   Prov. 15.13
it will be without too. Except I heare thee say in thine actions, *Gaudeo,* I do rejoyce, I cannot know that thou hast heard the Apostle say, *Gaudete.*

Joy for Gods blessings to us, joy for Gods glory to himself, may come *ad Risum,* and farther: Not onely *ad Ridendum,* but *ad Irridendum,* not onely to laugh in our own prosperity, but to laugh them to scorne that would have impeached it. They are put both together in God himself, *Ridebo,* and *Irridebo, I will laugh at your calamities,*   Prov. 1.26
and I will mock when your feare cometh. And this being in that place intended of God, is spoken in the person of Wisdome; It mis-becomes not wisdome and gravity to laugh in Gods deliverances, nor to laugh to scorne those that would have blown up Gods Servants; when it is carried so high as to *the Kings of the Earth, and the Rulers that take*   Psal. 2.2
counsell against the Lord, and against his Anoynted, we may come *Ad Gaudium,* to joy in Gods goodnesse, but because their place, and persons are sacred, we leave the *Ridere* and the *Irridere* to God: who says, verse 4. *That he will laugh at them, and hold them in derision.*   Verse 4
But at lower instruments, lower persons may laugh, when they fill the world with the Doctrine of killing of Kings, and meane that that should animate men against such Kings as they call Heretiques, and then finde in experience that this hath wrought onely to the killing of Kings of their own Religion, we lament justly the event, but yet we forbeare our *Ridere* and our *Irridere,* at the crossing and the frustrat-   [Exod. 15.1]
ing of their plots and practises. *Pharaohs* Army was drowned, *Et*   [Judg. 5.1]
Cecinit Moses, Moses sung, *Sisera* was slaine, *Et Cecinit Deborah,*

Deborah sung. Thus in the disappointing of Gods enemies, Gods servants come to outward manifest signes of joy. Not by a libellous and scurrill prophanation of persons that are sacred, but in fitting Psalmes and Sermons, and Prayers, and publique Writings to the occasion, to proceed to a *Ridere* and *Irridere,* and as Saint *Augustine* reades that place of the *Proverbs, Superridere,* to laugh Gods Enemies
[180] into a confusion to see their Plots so often, so often, so often frustrated. For so farre extends *Gaudete, Rejoyce evermore.*

Joy then, and cheerefulnesse, is *Sub præcepto,* it hath the nature of a commandment, and so he departs from a commandment, that departs and abandons himself into an inordinate sadnesse. And there-

Psal. 42.5   fore *David* chides his soule, *Why art thou cast down, O my soul, why art thou disquieted within me?* And though he come after to dispute against this sadnesse of the soul, which he had let in, *Hope yet in God, and yet the Lord will command his loving kindnesse, and my prayer shall be unto the God of my life,* yet he could not put it off,
[190] but he imagines that he heares his enemies say, *Where is thy God?* and when he hath wrestled himself weary, he falls back again in the last verse, to his first faintnesse, *Why art thou cast down, O my soule,*

Prov. 25.20   *why art thou disquieted within me?* For, *As he that taketh away a garment in cold weather, so is he that singeth Songs to a heavy heart:*

[Psa. 58.5]   That heavinesse makes him uncapable of Naturall, of Morall, of Civill, of Spirituall comforts, charme the Charmer never so wisely. *Heli* heard that the Battell was lost, and that his Sonnes were slaine, and admitted so much sorrow for those, that when the last was added,

1 Sam. 4.17   *The Arke was taken by the Enemy,* he was too weake for that, and
[200] fell down and brake his neck. It was his daughter in Lawes case too; shee overcharged her soul with sadnesse for her husbands death, and her fathers death, and when the report of the Arke came, she

[verse 20]   fell into labour and died; and though the women told her, *Feare not, thou hast born a Sonne, yet shee answered not.* Though the Arke of God, the worship of his Name, bee at any time transferred from where it was, despaire not thou of Gods reducing it; for this despairing of others, may bring thee to despaire in some accident to thy self: Accustome thy selfe to keepe up the consideration of Gods mercy at the highest, lodge not a sad suspition in any publique, in any private
[210] businesse, that Gods powerfull mercy can goe but thus farre: hee that

determineth Gods Power and his Mercy, and saith here it must end, is as much an Atheist, as hee that denieth it altogether. The Key of *David* openeth and no man shutteth; the Spirit of Comfort shineth upon us, and would not be blown out. Monasterie, and Ermitage, and Anchorate, and such words of singularitie are not *Synonyma* with those plurall words *Concio, Cœtus, Ecclesia, Synagoga & Congregatio,* in which words God delivereth himselfe to us. A Church is a Company, Religion is Religation, a binding of men together in one manner of Worship; and Worship is an exteriour service; and that exteriour service is the *Venite exultemus,* to come and rejoyce in the presence of God. [Rev. 3.7]

[Psa. 95.1; 94.1 Vulg.]

If in any of these wayes God cast a Cloud upon our former joyes, yet to receive good at Gods hand, and not to receive evill; to rejoice in the calme, and not in the storme; this is to breake at least half of the Commandement, which is, *Gaudete semper.* And so from the first part, which is the substance which we have passed by these steps, That this rejoycing hath the nature of a Commandement, it must bee maintained, And that inward joy must be outwardly expressed, even to the disgrace and confusion of Gods enemies, and to the upholding of a joyfull constancy in our selves: We passe now to the extent of the Commandement, *Gaudete semper,* Evermore. [Job. 2.10]

Did God mean that we should rejoyce alwayes; when he made six dayes for labour, and but one for rest? Certainly he did. *Six dayes we are to labour, and to doe all that we have to doe:* And part of that which we have to doe, is to rejoyce in our labour. *Adam* in the state of Innocency had abundant occasion of continuall rejoycing; but yet even in that joyfull state he was *to labour, to dresse and to keep the Garden.* After the fall, when God made the labour of man more heavie *in sudore vultus, that he should not eat, but in the sweat of his browe,* yet God gave him not that penalty, that occasion of sadnesse, till he had first imprinted the roote of true Joy, the promise of a *Messias;* that promise he made before he came to denounce the penalty, first came the *Ipse conteret,* and then *in sudore vultus:* upon those words, *Thou shalt eat the labour of thy hand, Debuit dicere fructum, non laborem,* saith *Augustine, David* should have said, he shall eate the fruit, not the labour of his hands. *Sed ipsi labores non sunt sine gaudio,* but the very labours, the very afflictions of good

2 Part
Semper
[Exod. 20.9]

Gen. 2.15

3.19

Psal. 128.2
August.

men, have joy in them. *Si labor potest manducari & jucundari, manducatus fructus laboris qualis erit?* And if labour it self, affliction
²⁵⁰ it self, minister Joy, what a manner, what a measure of joy is in the full possession thereof in Heaven? And as the consideration of the words immediately after the Text, hath made more then one of the Fathers say, *Etiam Somnia justorum preces sunt,* Even the sleep of the righteous is a service to God, and their very Dreams are Prayers and Meditations, so much more properly, may wee call the sleep, and the bodily rest, nay, the bodily torments of the righteous, joye, re-joycing. So that neither weeke day, nor Sabbath day nor night, labour nor rest interrupteth this continuall Joy: Wee may, we must rejoyce evermore.

In bonis ²⁶⁰   *Gaudete in bonis,* Rejoyce when God giveth you the good things
Tempora-   of this world; First, *in Temporalibus* when God giveth you the good
libus   Temporall things of this world. *Gaudete in Terra,* Rejoyce that God hath placed you in so fertill, in so fruitfull a Land. *Gaudete in pace,* Rejoyce that God hath afforded you peace to till the Land; *Gaudete de Temporibus,* Rejoyce that God giveth good seasons, that the Earth may give her increase, and that Man may joy in the increase of the Earth: And *Gaudete de amicitiis,* Rejoyce that God giveth you friend-ship with such Nations, as may take of your superfluities, and return things necessary to you. There is a joy required for Temporall things;
²⁷⁰ for hee that is not joyfull in a benefit, is not thankefull. Next to that detestable assertion (as Saint *Augustine* calleth it) That God made any man to damn him, it is the perversest assertion, That God gives man temporall things to ensnare him. Was that Gods primary inten-
Gen. 9.20   tion in prospering *Noahs* Vineyard, That *Noah* should be drunken? God forbid.

              Doth God give any man honour or place, *Vt glorietur in malo, qui potens est,* that his power might be an occasion of mischief and op-
[Gen. 1.3, 16]   pression? God forbid. God made light at first; but wee know not what that light was: but God gathered all light into the Sun, and all
²⁸⁰ the world sees it. God infuses grace and spirituall blessings into a mans heart, and no man sees that, but the Spirit that is in that man; but the Evidence, the great Seale, that he pleads in the Eye of the world, is Gods temporall blessings. When *Assuerus* put the Royall Vesture and Ring, and Crown upon *Mordecai,* it was to shew that

hee was in his favour; in the same intention proceeds God too, when he gives riches, or honour, or favour, or command; hee would have that soul rejoyce in these, as in testimonies of his favour. God loves *hilarem datorem,* a cheerfull giver, but he that is not a cheerfull receiver, is a worse natur'd man, and more dishonours, nay, reproaches his benefactor. They then disobey this Commandment, of rejoycing in temporall things, that employ not their industry, that use not all good means to attaine them. Every man is therefore planted in the world, that hee may grow in the world; and as venomous hearbs delight in the shade, so a sullen retiring argues a murmuring and venomous disposition; To contemn Gods temporall blessings, or to neglect or undervalue those instruments, those persons, by whom God sheds such blessings upon us, is to break that branch of this Commandement *Gaudete semper,* Rejoyce evermore; for he does not rejoyce *in bonis temporalibus.* So is it also, as not to seek them before, so not to use them when we have them. When a feare of growing poore, makes us think God to be poor too, that if we spend this, God can give us no more, when for feare of lacking at our end, we lack all the way, when we abound and yet will pay no debts, not to our own bellies, our own backs, our own respect, and the decency that belongs to our rank, these men so sordid, so penurious, and suspitious of Gods Providence, breake this branch of this Commandement too, because they doe not rejoyce *in bonis temporalibus.* And as the not-seeker, and the not-user, so the abuser of these temporall blessings is in the same transgression. Hee that thinkes all the world as one Jewell, and himselfe the Cabinet, that all was made for him, and hee for none, forgets his owne office, his Stewardship, by which he is enabled and bound to the necessities of others: to collect, hee that seeks not, hee that denies all to himself, hee that denies all but himself, break this branch, for they doe not rejoyce *in bonis temporalibus.*

This we must doe; but *in bonis spiritualibus,* in the spiritual good things of this world, much more we call those the spirituall good things of this world, which advance our devotion here, and consequently our salvation hereafter. The rituall and ceremoniall, the outward worship of God, the places, the times, the manner of meetings, are in the disposition of Christian Princes, and by their favours of those Churches, which are in their government: and not

[2 Cor. 9.7]

In spiritualibus

to rejoyce in the peacefull exercise of those spirituall helps, not to be glad of them, is a transgression. Now the Prophet expresses this rejoycing thus, *Venite exultemus,* let us come and rejoyce. We must doe both. And therefore they who out of a thraldome to another Church abstaine from these places of these exercises, that doe not come, or if they doe come, doe not rejoyce, but though they be here brought by necessity of law, or of observation, yet had rather they were in another Chappell, or that another kinde of service then in this: and they also who abstain out of imaginary defects in this Church, and think they cannot perform *Davids De profundis,* they cannot call upon God out of the depth, except it be in a Conventicle in a cellar, nor acknowledge *Solomons Excelsis Excelsior,* that God is higher then the highest, except it be in a Conventicle in a garret, and when they are here wink at the ornaments, and stop their ears at the musique of the Church, in which manner she hath always expressed her rejoycing in those helps of devotion; or if there bee a third sort who abstain, because they may not be here at so much ease, and so much liberty, as at their own houses, all these are under this transgression. Are they in the Kings house at so much liberty as in their own? and is not this the King of Kings house? Or have they seene the King in his owne house, use that liberty to cover himselfe in his ordinary manner of covering, at any part of Divine Service? Every Preacher will look, and justly, to have the Congregation uncovered at the reading of his Text: and is not the reading of the Lesson, at time of Prayer, the same Word of the same God, to be received with the same reverence? The service of God is one entire thing; and though we celebrate some parts with more, or with lesse reverence, some kneeling, some standing, yet if we afford it no reverence, we make that no part of Gods service. And therefore I must humbly intreat them, who make this Quire the place of their Devotion, to testifie their devotion by more outward reverence there; wee know our parts in this place, and we doe them; why any stranger should think himself more privileged in this part of Gods House, then we, I know not. I presume no man will mis-interpret this that I say here now; nor, if this may not prevaile, mis-interpret the service of our Officers, if their continuing in that unreverent manner give our Officers occasion to warn them of that personally in the place,

[Psa. 130.1]

Eccles. 5.8

330

340

350

whensoever they see them stray into that uncomely negligence. They should not blame me now, they must not blame them then, when they call upon them for this reverence in this Quire; neither truly can there be any greater injustice, then when they who will not do their duties, blame others for doing theirs.

But that we are bound to a thankfull rejoycing in all that falls well to us, *In bonis,* admits lesse doubt, and therefore requires lesse proof: But the *semper* of our Text extends farther, *Gaudete in malis,* we doe not rejoyce always, except we rejoyce in evill days, in all our crosses and calamities. Now, if we be not affected with Gods judgements, if we conceive not a sorrow for them, or the cause of them, our sins, God is angry; will he be angry too, if we be not glad of them, if we doe not rejoyce in them? Can this sorrow and this joy consist together? very well. The School in the mouth of *Aquinas* gives instances; If an Innocent man be condemned, *Simul placet ejus justitia, & displicet afflictio,* I congratulate his innocency, and I condole his death both at once. So *Displicet mihi quod peccavi, & placet quod displicet;* I am very sorry that I have sinned, but yet I am glad that I am sorry. So that, *Ipsa tristitia materia gaudii;* Some sorrow is so far from excluding joy, as that naturally it produces it. S. *Augustine* hath sealed it with this advice, *Semper doleat pœnitens,* Let him who hath sinned always lament; But then where is the *Gaudete semper?* he tels us too, *Semper gaudeat de dolore,* Let him always rejoyce, that God hath opened him a way to mercy, by sorrow. *Lacrymæ Seminium quoddam sunt & fœnus, quibus increscit gaudium;* Sorrow is our Seminary, from whence we are transplanted into a larger Orchard, into the dilatation of the heart, Joy; sorrow, says he, *Seminium est, & fœnus est;* It is our interest, our use; And if we have sorrow upon sorrow, it is use upon use, it doubles the principall, which is joy, the sooner. *Cordæ cum distenduntur,* it is S. *Augustines* musicall comparison, when the strings of an instrument are set up, the musicall sound is the clearer; if a mans sinew be stretcht upon the rack, his joy is not the lesse perfect. Not that a man must seek out occasion of sorrow; provoke the Magistrate by seditious intemperance, and call it zeal; or macerate the body with fastings, or mangle it with whippings, and call that merit; *Non ut quærant materiam quam non habent, sed ut inveniant eam quam nescientes habent;* This is the

In malis

Aquin. 3.84
9.2

Aug.

Basil

Aug.

way of joy, not to seek occasions of sorrow, which they have not, but to finde out those which they have, and know not; that is, their secret sins, the causes of Gods judgements in themselves. To discern that that correction that is upon me, is from God, and not a naturall
[400] accident, this is a beam of joy, for I see that he would cure me, though by corosives. To discern that God is not unjust, nor cruell, and therefore it is something in me, and not in him, that brings it to this sharpnesse, this is a beam of joy too; for I see how to discharge God, and to glorifie him, and how to accuse my self; and that is a good degree of repentance.

A sensis

But to perfect my repentance, *Non sufficit dolere de peccatis, sed requiritur gaudium de dolore,* It is not enough to come to a sorrow in my sin, that may flow out into despair; but I must come to a joy in my sorrow, for that fixes me upon the application of Christ, and such
[410] a joy a man must suscitate and awaken in himselfe by these steps, *In malis temporalibus,* in all worldly crosses; Else he does not *Gaudere semper.*

In spiritu-
alibus

No nor except he finde this joy, *In malis Spiritualibus,* in Spirituall afflictions too. When I fall into new sorrow, after my former joy, relapse into those sins which I have repented (and beloved, the dangerous falling in any man, is to fall backward, he that fals forward, hath his eys to help him, and his hands to help him, but he that fals backward lacks much) yet even out of these relapses we must finde

James 1.2

joy too. For when Saint *James* says, *Count it all joy when you fall into*
[420] *divers tentations,* as he speaks of all joy, so he intends, or may justly be extended to all tentations, not onely tentations, that is, trialls, when God proves a man by affliction, where morall constancy is exercised, but even in triall of religious constancy, in tentations to sin, still there is fresh occasion of joy in discerning Gods deliverance from the falling into the sinne, or from lying in the sinne. *Ipsa*

Ambros.

tentatio sal animæ, as salt preserves flesh, so tentations preserve the Soule: not the sinning, but the discerning that it is, nay that that was a tentation to sinne, preserves the soule. And therefore he calls *tentationes custodes;* he makes even the evill Angells, our Guardians,
[430] our Tutelar Angells, because by their tentations they bring us up in the feare of God, and in the ways of joy. And therefore though it be a joyfull thing to have overcome a tentation, yet determine not your Joy in that; that if that tentation had overcome you, you might have

no more Joy, but (as Christ says) *In this rejoyce not,* that is, not onely in this, *that the Spirits are subject to you, but rather rejoyce that your names are written in heaven.* Rejoyce not in this, that is, determine not, conclude not your joy in this, that you have overcome that tentation, but rather in this; that God does not forsake you after a sinne, nor after a relapse into sinne; but manifests your election by continuall returning to you: But that this may bee the joy of the text, true Joy, not a joy that induces presumption, for that will faile, that it may bee *Semper,* it must bee *in Sempiterno,* a Joy rightly conceived, and rightly placed. *Gaudium in Domino:* and that is our next step.

Rejoyce in the Lord always, says the Apostle; and lest it should admit any interruption, he repeats it, *Iterum dico gaudete, Againe I say rejoyce,* But still in the Lord. For, *Quasi locus quidam, justorum capax est Dominus:* though God be in no place, God is the place, in whom all good men are. God is the Court of every just King: God is the Church of every holy Priest: God is the field of every valiant man; and the bed of every sickly man: whatsoever is done *in Domino,* in the Lord, is done at home in the right place; He that is settled in God, centred in God, *Lætitiæ fontem, voluptatis radicem lucratus est.* They are all considerable words; *Lucratus est,* he hath purchased something which he did not inherit, he hath acquired something which was not his before, and what? *Fontem lætitiæ;* 'tis joy, else it were nothing: for what is wealth if sicknesse take away the joy of that? Or what is health, if imprisonment take away the joy of that? Or what is liberty, if poverty take away the joy of that? but he hath joy, and not a Cistern but a fountain, the fountaine of joy, that rejoyces in God: He carries it higher in the other Metaphore; he hath *radicem voluptatis;* a man may have *Flores,* flowers of joy, and have no fruit, a man may have some fruit, and not enough, but if he have joy in God, he hath *radicem voluptatis,* if we may dare to translate it so, (and in a spirituall sense we may) it is a voluptuous thing to rejoyce in God. In rejoycing in another thing Saint *Bernards* harmonious charme will strike upon us, *Rara hora, brevis mora,* they are joyes that come seldome, and stay but a little while when they come. Call it joy, to have had that thou lovest, in thine eye, or in thine armes, remember what oathes, what false oathes, it did cost thee before it came to that? And where is that joy now, is there a *Semper*

Luke 10.20

In sempiterno
Basil

Chrysost.

Bern.

in that? Call it joy to have had him whom thou hatest, in thine hands or under thy feet, what ignoble disguises to that man, what servile observations of some greater, then either you, or he, did that cost you before you brought him into your power? and where is that joy, if a Funerall or a bloudy conscience benight it? *Currus Domini,* says *David, the Chariots of the Lord are twenty thousand, thousands of Angels,* says our translation; *Millia lætantium,* says the vulgat; thousands of them that rejoyce. How comes it to bee all thing Angells and

480 Rejoycers? *Ne miremur illos lætari continuò subiecit, Dominus in illis,* Saint *Augustine* saith, to take away all wonder, it is added, the Lord is in the midst of them, and then, be what they will, they must rejoyce; For if he be with them they are with him, and hee is Joy. The name of *Isaac* signifies joy; and the triall of *Abraham* was to sacrifice *Isaac: Immola Isaac tuum,* sacrifice all thy Joy in this world, to God, *Et non mactatus sed sanctificatus Isaac tuus,* thy Joy shall not bee destroyed, but sanctified, so farre from being made none, that it shall bee made better, better here, but not better then that hereafter; which is our last steppe, beyond which there is nothing, that even

490 true Joy, rightly placed, is but an inchoative, a preparatory Joy in this world. The consummation is for the next; *Gaudebimus semper.*

Sicut lætantium omnium habitatio est in te, as Saint *Hierome* reads those words, speaking of the Christian Church here, It is the house of all them, who do as it were rejoyce; who come nearest to true joy. And so, when the Lord turned againe the Captivity of *Sion, Facti sumus sicut consolati,* We were as it were comforted. *Quare sicut,* sayes that Father, Why is it so modified with that diminution, as it were? *Quia hic etiam in Sanctis non perfecta consolatio;* Because, sayes he, in this world, even the Saints themselves have no perfect joy.

500 Where the Apostle compares the sorrow and the joy of this world, then the *Quasi* lyes upon the sorrows side; it is but a halfe sorrow; *Quasi tristes, We are as it were sorrowfull, but indeed rejoycing;* but compare the best joy of this world, with the next, and the *Quasi* will fall upon the joy of the world. For though we be sealed with the holy Spirit of promise, which is the earnest of our inheritance, (and this is the Tropique of Joy, the farthest that Spirituall Joy goes in this Zodique, in this world) yet this carries us no farther, but *Vt ex arrabone æstimetur hæreditas;* That by the proportion of the earnest, we might value the whole bargaine: For what a bargaine would we

Psal. 68.17

August.

Bern.

Psal. 87.7
[86.7 Vulg.]

Psal. 126.[1]
[125.1 Vulg.]

2 Cor. 6.10

Eph.
1.[13,]14

Hierom.

presume that man to have, that would give 20000 *l.* for earnest? what is the Joy of heaven hereafter, if the earnest of it here, be the Seale of the holy Ghost? God proceeds with us, as we do with other men. *Operariis in Sæculo, cibus in opere, merces in fine datur:* In this world, we give labourers meat and drink by the way, but wages at the end of their work. God affords us refreshing here, but joy hereafter. The best Seale is the holy Ghost, and the best matter that the holy Ghost seales in, is in blood; in the dignity of Martyrdome; and even for that, for Martyrdome, we have a rule in the Apostle, *Rejoyce in as much as ye are partakers of Christs sufferings;* That as he suffered for you, so you suffer for him: but in what contemplation? That when his glory shall be revealed, ye may be made glad with exceeding Joy; not with exceeding Joy, till then; For till then, the Joyes of Heaven may be exceeded in the addition of the body. There is the rule, and the example is Christ himself, *Who for the joy that was set before him, endured the Crosse;* in contemplation of the *Propterea exaltatus,* that therefore he should be exalted above all in heaven. *Rejoyce and be glad;* why? *for great is your reward:* but where? *in heaven.* And therefore *Ask and you shall receive; Pray and you shall have answer:* but what answer? *That your joy shall be full.* It shall be; in heaven. For *Quis sic delectat quam ille, qui fecit omnia quæ delectant?* In whom can we fully rejoyce, but him, who made all things in which we rejoyce by the way? *In thy Name shall we rejoyce all the day,* says *David. Si in nomine suo, non tota die,* St. *Augustine* says not that to any particular person, nor any particular calling, but to any man, to every man; Any Prince, any Counsellor, any Prelate, any Generall, any Discoverer, any that goes in any way of joy, and glory, *Si nomine suo, non tota die,* If they rejoyce in their own names, their own wisdome, their own strength, they shall not rejoyce all the day, but they shall be benighted with darke sadnesse, before their dayes end; *And their sunne shall set at noon too,* as the Prophet *Amos* speaks. And therefore that shall be Christs expressing of that joy, at the last day, *Enter into thy Masters Joy,* and leave the joy of Servants (though of good Servants) behind thee; for thou shalt have a better Joy then that, *Thy Masters Joy.*

It is time to end; but as long as the glasse hath a gaspe, as long as I have one, I would breathe in this ayre, in this perfume, in this breath of heaven, the contemplation of this Joy. *Blessed is that man,*

Bernard

1 Pet. 4.13

[Heb. 12.2]

Mat. 5.12

John 16.24

August.

Psal. 89.16
August.

[Amos 8.9]

[Mat. 25.21]

Psal. 89.15

qui scit jubilationem, says *David, that knowes the joyfull sound:* For, *Nullo modo beatus, nisi scias unde gaudeas;* For though we be
550 bound to rejoyce alwayes, it is not a blessed joy, if we do not know upon what it be grounded: or if it be not upon everlasting blessed-

Cant. 5.1

nesse. *Comedite amici,* says Christ, *bibite & inebriamini. Eat and drink, and be filled.* Joy in this life, *Vbi in sudore vescimur,* where

Bernard

grief is mingled with joy, is called meat, says Saint *Bernard,* and Christ cals his friends to eat in the first word. *Potus in futuro,* says he, Joy in the next life, where it passes down without any difficulty, without any opposition, is called drink; and Christ calls his friends to drink: but the overflowing, the *Ebrietas animæ,* that is reserved to the last time, when our bodies as well as our souls, shall enter into the
560 participation of it: Where, when wee shall love every one, as well as our selves, and so have that Joy of our owne salvation multiplied by that number, wee shall have that Joy so many times over, as there shall bee soules saved, because wee love them as our selves, how infinitely shall this Joy be enlarged in loving God, so far above our selves, and all them. Wee have but this to add. *Heaven* is called by many pretious

Matt. 19.17

names; *Life,* Simply and absolutely there is no life but that. And

Luc. 12.32

Kingdome; Simply, absolutely there is no Kingdom, that is not

Esay 66.23

subordinate to that. And *Sabbatum ex Sabbato,* A Sabbath flowing into a Sabbath, a perpetuall Sabbath: but the Name that should

Psal. 16.11

570 enamour us most, is that, that it is *Satietas gaudiorum;* fulnesse of Joy. Fulnesse that needeth no addition; Fulnesse, that admitteth no leake. And then though in the Schoole we place Blessednesse, *In visione,* in the sight of God, yet the first thing that this sight of God shall produce in us (for that shall produce the Reformation of the Image of God, in us, and it shall produce our glorifying of God) but the first thing that the seeing of God shall produce in us, is Joy. The measure of our seeing of God is the measure of Joy. See him here in his Blessings, and you shall joy in those blessings here; and when you come to see him *Sicuti est,* in his Essence, then you shall have this
580 Joy in Essence, and in fulnesse; of which, God of his goodnesse give us such an earnest here, as may binde to us that inheritance hereafter, which his Sonne our Saviour Christ Jesus hath purchased for us, with the inestimable price of his incorruptible blood. *Amen.*

Number 11.

Deaths Duell,

or,

A Consolation to the Soule, against the dying Life, and living Death of the Body.

*Delivered in a Sermon at White Hall, before the Kings Majesty,
in the beginning of Lent, 1630.*

To the Reader.

THIS *Sermon was, by Sacred Authoritie, stiled the Authors owne funeral
Sermon. Most fitly: whether wee respect the time, or the matter. It was
preached not many dayes before his death; as if, having done this, there
remained nothing for him to doe, but to die: And the matter is, of Death;
the occasion and subject of all funerall Sermons. It hath beene observed of
this Reverend Man, That his Faculty in Preaching continually encreased:
and, That as hee exceeded others at first; so, at last hee exceeded himselfe.
This is his last Sermon; I will not say, it is therefore his best; because, all
his were excellent. Yet thus much: A dying Mans words, if they concerne
our selves; doe usually make the deepest impression, as being spoken most
feelingly, and with least affection. Now, whom doth it not concerne to
learn, both the danger, and benefit of death? Death is every mans enemy,
and intends hurt to all; though to many, hee be occasion of greatest goods.
This enemy wee must all combate dying; whom hee living did almost
conquer; having discovered the utmost of his power, the utmost of his
crueltie. May wee make such use of this and other the like preparatives,
That neither death, whensoever it shall come, may seeme terrible; nor life
tedious; how long soever it shall last.*

                                                                  R.

PSA. 68. VERS. 20. IN FINE. *AND UNTO GOD THE
LORD BELONG THE ISSUES OF DEATH.* i.e.
FROM DEATH.

B
UILDINGS stand by the benefit of their *foundations* that susteine
and *support* them, and of their *butteresses* that comprehend
and *embrace* them, and of their *contignations* that knit and
unite them: The *foundations* suffer them not to *sinke,* the *butteresses*
suffer them not to *swerve,* and the *contignation* and knitting suffers
them not to *cleave.* The body of our building is in the former part
of this verse: It is this, hee that *is our God* is the *God of salvation; ad
salutes,* of salvations in the plurall, so it is in the originall; the *God*
that gives us spirituall and temporall salvation too. But of this *build-*
¹⁰ *ing,* the *foundation,* the *butteresses,* the *contignations* are in this part
of the *verse,* which constitutes *our text,* and in the three divers *acceptations* of the words amongst our expositors, *Vnto God the Lord be-*
Of   *long the issues of death.* For *first* the *foundation* of this *building,*
(that our *God* is the *God of all salvations*) is laid in this; That *unto*
this *God the Lord belong the issues of death,* that is, it is in his power
to give us an *issue* and deliverance, even then when wee are brought
to the jawes and teeth of death, and to the lippes of that whirlepoole,
the grave. And so in this acceptation, this *exitus mortis,* this *issue of
death* is *liberatio à morte, a deliverance from death,* and this is the
²⁰ most obvious and most ordinary acceptation of these words, and that
upon which our *translation* laies hold, the *issues from death.* And
then *secondly,* the butteresses that comprehend and settle this building, That hee that is *our God,* is the *God of* all *salvation,* are thus
raised; unto *God the Lord belong the issues of death,* that is, the
disposition and *manner of our death:* what kinde of *issue,* and *transmigration* wee shall have out of this world, whether prepared or sudden, whether violent or naturall, whether in our perfect senses or
shaken and disordered by sicknes, there is no condemnation to bee
argued out of that, no Judgement to bee made upon that, for how-
[Psal. 116.15]   ³⁰ soever they dye, *precious in his sight is the death of his saints,* and

with him are *the issues of death*, the *wayes* of our *departing* out of this *life* are in his *hands*. And so in this *sense* of the *words*, this *exitus mortis*, the *issue of death*, is *liberatio in morte*, *A deliverance in death;* Not that *God* will *deliver* us *from dying*, but that hee will *have a care* of us in the *houre of death*, of what kinde soever our passage be. And this *sense* and acceptation of the *words*, the naturall frame and contexture doth well and pregnantly administer unto us. And then *lastly* the *contignation* and knitting of this building, that hee that is *our God* is the *God of all salvations*, consists in this, *Unto this God the Lord belong the issues of death*, that is, that this *God* the *Lord* having *united* and knit *both natures in one*, and being *God*, having also *come* into this *world*, in our *flesh*, he could have no other meanes to save us, he could have no other *issue* out of this world, nor *returne* to his former *glory*, but by *death;* And so in this sense, this *exitus mortis*, this *issue of death*, is *liberatio per mortem*, a *deliverance by death*, by the death of this *God* our *Lord Christ Jesus*. And this is Saint *Augustines* acceptation of the words, and those many and great persons that have adhered to him. In all these three lines then, we shall looke upon these words; *First*, as the *God* of *power*, the *Almighty Father* rescues his servants from the jawes of death: *And then*, as the *God* of *mercy*, the glorious *Sonne* rescued us, by taking upon himselfe this *issue of death: And then* betweene these two, as the *God* of *comfort*, the *holy Ghost* rescues us from all discomfort by his blessed impressions before hand, that what manner of death soever be ordeined for us, yet this *exitus mortis* shall bee *introitus in vitam*, our *issue in death*, shall be an *entrance into everlasting life.* And these three considerations, our deliverance *à morte, in morte, per mortem, from death, in death*, and *by death*, will abundantly doe all the offices of the *foundations*, of the *butteresses*, of the *contignation* of this our *building;* That he that is our *God*, is the *God of all salvation*, because *unto* this *God the Lord belong the issues of death*.

 First, then, we consider this *exitus mortis*, to bee *liberatio à morte*, that with *God*, the *Lord* are the *issues of death*, and therefore in all our deaths, and deadly calamities of this life, wee may justly *hope* of a good *issue* from him; and all our *periods* and *transitions* in this life, are so many passages *from death* to *death*. Our very *birth* and

A morte,
in morte,
per mortem
Foundation,
butteresses
and con-
tignation
1 Part
A morte

Exitus à
morte uteri

entrance into this life, is *exitus à morte,* an *issue from death,* for in
our mothers *wombe* wee are *dead so,* as that wee doe *not know* wee
⁷⁰ *live,* not so much as wee doe in our *sleepe,* neither is there any *grave*
so close, or so *putrid* a *prison,* as the *wombe* would be unto us, if we
stayed in it *beyond* our time, or dyed there *before* our time. In the
grave the *wormes* doe not kill us, wee *breed* and *feed,* and then *kill*
those wormes which wee our selves produc'd. In the wombe the dead
child kills the *Mother* that conceived it, and is a *murtherer,* nay a
parricide, even after it is dead. And if wee bee not dead so in the
wombe, so as that being dead, wee kill her that gave us our first life,

Psal. 115
vers. [5,] 6

our life of *vegetation,* yet wee are dead so, as *Davids Idols* are dead. In
the *wombe* wee have *eyes and see not, eares and heare not;* There in
⁸⁰ the wombe wee are fitted for *workes of darkenes,* all the while de-
prived of light: And there in the *wombe* wee are taught *cruelty,* by
being *fed with blood,* and may be *damned,* though we be *never borne.*

Psal. 139.14
[ver. 6]
Ps. 118.23
100.3 [2 in
Vulg.]
10.8

Of our very making in the *wombe,* David sayes, *I am wonderfully*
and fearefully made, and, *Such knowledge is too excellent for me,*
for even that *is the Lords doing, and it is wonderfull in our eyes. Ipse*
fecit nos, it is hee that hath made us, and not wee our selves, no, nor
our parents neither; *Thy hands have made me and fashioned me*
round about, saith *Iob,* and, (as the *originall word* is) *thou hast taken*
paines about me, and, yet, sayes he, *thou doest destroy me.* Though I
⁹⁰ bee the *Master peece* of the greatest *Master* (*man* is so,) yet if thou
doe no more for me, if thou leave me where thou madest mee, destruction will follow. The *wombe* which should be the *house of life,*
becomes *death* it selfe, if *God* leave us there. That which God
threatens so often, the *shutting of the womb,* is not so *heavy,* nor
so discomfortable a *curse* in the *first,* as in the *latter* shutting,
nor in the shutting of *barrennes,* as in the shutting of *weakenes,*

Esa. 37.3

when *children are come to the birth,* and there is not *strength to bring*
forth.

It is the *exaltation* of *misery,* to *fall* from a *neare hope* of *happines.*

Ose. 9.14

¹⁰⁰ And in that vehement imprecation, the *Prophet* expresses the highth
of *Gods* anger, *Give them ô Lord, what will thou give them? give*
them a mis-carying wombe. Therefore as soone as wee are men, (that
is, inanimated, quickned in the womb) thogh we cannot our selves,

Ro. 7.24

our parents have reason to say in our behalf, *wretched man that he is, who shall deliver* him *from this body of death?* for even the *wombe* is a *body of death,* if there bee no deliverer. It must be he that said to *Ieremy, Before I formed thee I knew thee, and before thou camest out* of *the wombe I sanctified thee.* Wee are not sure that there was no kinde of shippe nor boate to fish in, nor to passe by, till *God* pre-scribed *Noah* that absolute *form* of *the Arke.* That word which the *holy Ghost* by *Moses* useth for the *Arke,* is common to all kinde of *boates, Thebah,* and is the same word that *Moses* useth for the *boate* that he was *exposed* in, that *his mother layed him in an arke* of *bul-rushes.* But we are sure that *Eve* had no *Midwife* when she was *de-livered* of *Cain,* therefore shee might well say, *possedi virum à Do-mino, I have gotten a man from the Lord,* wholly, entirely from the Lord; It is the *Lord* that *enabled* me to *conceive,* The *Lord* that *in-fus'd* a *quickning soule* into that conception, the *Lord* that *brought into the world* that which himselfe *had quickened;* without all this might *Eve* say, My *body had bene* but *the house of death,* and *Do-mini Domini sunt exitus mortis,* to *God the Lord belong the issues of death.*

But then this *exitus a morte,* is but *introitus in mortem,* this *issue,* this deliverance *from* that *death,* the death of the *wombe,* is an *en-trance,* a delivering over to *another death,* the manifold deathes of this *world.* Wee have a winding sheete in our Mothers wombe, which growes with us from our conception, and wee come into the world, wound up in that *winding sheet,* for wee come to *seeke a grave;* And as prisoners discharg'd of actions may lye for fees; so when the *wombe* hath discharg'd us, yet we are bound to it by *cordes* of flesh, by such a *string,* as that wee cannot goe thence, nor stay there. We celebrate our owne funeralls with cryes, even at our birth; as though our *three-score and ten years of life* were spent in our mothers labour, and our circle made up in the first point thereof. We begge one Baptism with another, a sacrament of tears; And we come into a world that lasts many ages, but wee last not. *In domo Patris,* says our blessed *Saviour,* speaking of *heaven, multæ mansiones,* there *are many mansions,* divers and durable, so that if a man cannot possesse a *martyrs* house, (he hath shed no blood for *Christ*) yet hee may have a *Confessors,* he hath bene ready to glorifie *God* in the *shedding of his blood.* And if a woman cannot possesse a *virgins* house (she hath embrac'd the

1.5

Exo. 2.3

Gen. 4.1

Exitus a
mortibus
mundi

Joh. 14.2

holy state of *mariage*) yet she may have a *matrons* house, she hath brought forth and brought up *children in the feare of God. In domo patris, in my fathers house,* in heaven there *are many mansions;* but

Mat. 8.20 here upon earth *The Son of man hath not where to lay his head,* sayes he himselfe. *Nonne terram dedit filijs hominum?* how then

[Ps. 115.16] hath *God given this earth* to the *sonnes of men?* hee hath *given* them *earth* for their *materialls* to bee made of earth, and he hath given them *earth* for their *grave* and sepulture, to *returne* and resolve to

Heb. 13.14 ¹⁵⁰ *earth,* but not for their *possession: Here wee have no continuing citty,* nay no *cottage* that continues, nay no persons, no bodies that continue.

Exo. 17.1 Whatsoever moved Saint *Ierome* to call the journies of the *Israelites,* in the *wildernes,* Mansions, the *word* (the word is *Nasang*) signifies but a *journey,* but a peregrination. Even the *Israel of God* hath no

Gen. 47.9 mansions; but journies, pilgrimages in this life. By that measure did *Iacob* measure his life to *Pharaoh, The daies of the years of my pilgrimage.* And though the *Apostle* would not say *morimur,* that,

2 Cor. 5.6 whilest wee *are in the body* wee *are dead,* yet hee sayes, *Peregrinamur,* whilest wee are *in the body,* wee are but in *a pilgrimage,* and ¹⁶⁰ wee are *absent from the Lord;* hee might have sayd *dead,* for this whole *world* is but an *universall church-yard,* but our *common grave;* and the life and motion that the greatest persons have in it, is but as the shaking of buried bodies in their graves by an *earth-quake.* That which we call life, is but *Hebdomada mortium, a week of deaths,* seaven dayes, seaven periods of our life spent in dying, *a dying seaven times over;* and there is an end. *Our birth dyes in infancy,* and our *infancy* dyes in *youth,* and *youth* and the rest dye in *age,* and *age* also dyes, and *determines all.* Nor doe all these, youth out of infancy, or age out of youth arise so, as a *Phœnix* out of the ¹⁷⁰ ashes of another *Phœnix* formerly *dead,* but as a *waspe* or a *serpent* out of a *caryon,* or as a *Snake* out of *dung.* Our *youth* is *worse* then our *infancy,* and our *age worse* then our *youth.* Our *youth* is *hungry and thirsty,* after those *sinnes,* which our *infancy knew not;* And our *age* is *sory* and *angry,* that it *cannot pursue* those *sinnes* which our *youth* did. And besides, al the way, so many deaths, that is, so many deadly calamities accompany every condition, and every period of this life, as that death it selfe would bee an ease to them that suffer

10.18 them. Upon this sense doth *Iob* wish that *God had not given him* an

issue from the *first death*, from the *wombe, Wherefore hast thou*
brought me forth out of the wombe? O that I had given up the Ghost,
and no eye had seen me; I should have been, as though I had not been.
And not only the impatient *Israelites* in their murmuring (*would
to God wee had dyed by the hand of the Lord in the land of Egypt*)
but *Eliah* himselfe, when he *fled* from *Iesabell*, and went for his life,
as that text sayes, under the juniper tree, requested that *hee might
dye*, and sayd, *It is enough, now O Lord, take away my life*. So *Ionah*
justifies his impatience, nay his anger towards *God* himselfe. *Now
ô Lord take, I beseech thee, my life from mee, for it is better for me
to dye then to live*. And when *God* asked him, *doest thou well to be
angry for this*, and after, (about the Gourd) *dost thou well to be
angry for that*, he replies, *I doe well to be angry, even unto death.*
How much worse a death then death, is this life, which so good men
would so often change for death? But if my case bee as Saint *Paules*
case, *quotidiè morior*, that *I dye dayly*, that something heavier then
death fall upon me every day; If my case be *Davids* case, *tota die mortificamur, all the day long wee are killed*, that not onely every day,
but every houre of the day some thing heavier then death fall upon
me, though that bee true of me, *Conceptus in peccatis, I was shapen
in iniquity, and in sinne did my mother conceive me*, (there I dyed
one death,) though that be true of me (*Natus filius iræ*) *I was borne*
not onely the child of sinne, but *the child of wrath*, of the wrath of
God for sinne, which is a heavier death; Yet *Domini Domini sunt
exitus mortis*, with *God the Lord are the issues of death*, and after a
Iob, and a *Ioseph*, and a *Ieremie*, and a *Daniel*, I cannot doubt of a
deliverance. And if no other deliverance conduce more to his glory
and my good, yet he hath the *keys of death*, and hee can let me out
at that dore, that is, deliver me from the manifold deaths of this
world, the *omni die* and the *tota die*, the *every dayes death* and *every
houres death*, by that *one death*, the *final dissolution* of body and
soule, the end of all.
But then is that the end of all? Is that dissolution of body and soule,
the last death that the body shall suffer? (for of spirituall death wee
speake not now) It is not. Though this be *exitus à morte*, it is *introitus
in mortem*: though it bee an *issue from* the manifold *deaths* of this
world, yet it is an *entrance* into the *death of corruption* and *putrefac-*

Exo. 16.3

1 Reg. 19.4

4.3

[v. 9]

1 Cor. 15.31
Psa. 44.22

[Psa.] 51.5

[Eph. 2.3]

Apoc. 1.18

*Exitus à
morte inci-
nirationis*

tion and *vermiculation* and *incineration,* and dispersion in and from the *grave,* in which every dead man dyes over againe. It was a *prerogative* peculiar to *Christ,* not to dy this death, *not to see corruption.* What gave him this priviledge? Not *Iosephs* great proportion of
220 *gummes* and *spices,* that might have preserved his body from corruption and *incineration* longer then he needed it, longer then *three dayes,* but it would not have done it for ever. What preserved him then? did his exemption and *freedome from originall sinne* preserve him from this corruption and *incineration?* 'Tis true that original sinne hath induced this corruption and *incineration* upon us; If wee had not sinned in *Adam, mortality had not put on immortality,* (as the *Apostle* speakes) nor *corruption had not put on incorruption,* but we had had our *transmigration* from this to the other world, without any *mortality,* any *corruption at all.* But yet since *Christ* tooke *sinne*
230 upon him, so farre as made him *mortall,* he had it so farre too, as might have made him see this corruption and *incineration,* though he had no *originall sinne* in himself. What preserv'd him then? Did the *hypostaticall union* of both natures, *God* and *Man,* preserve him from this corruption and *incineration?* 'tis true that this was a most powerfull *embalming,* to be embalmd with the *divine nature* it selfe, to bee embalmd with *eternity,* was able to preserve him from corruption and *incineration* for ever. And he was embalm'd so, embalmd with the *divine nature* it selfe, even in his *body* as well as in his *soule;* for the *Godhead,* the *divine nature* did not depart, but remained still
240 *united* to his *dead body* in the *grave;* But yet for al this powerful *embalming,* this *hypostaticall union* of both natures, we see *Christ* did *dye;* and for all this *union* which made him *God* and *Man,* hee became no man (for the *union* of the *body* and *soule* makes the man, and hee whose soule and body are separated by death, (as long as that state lasts) is properly no man.) And therefore as in him the dissolution of *body* and *soule* was no *dissolution* of the *hypostaticall union;* so is there nothing that constraines us to say, that though the *flesh* of *Christ* had *seene corruption* and *incineration* in the grave, this had bene any *dissolution* of the *hypostaticall union,* for the *divine nature,*
250 the Godhead might have remained with all the *Elements* and *principles* of *Christs* body, aswell as it did with the two *constitutive* parts of his *person,* his *body* and his *soul.* This *incorruption* then was not

1 Cor. 15.33

in *Iosephs gummes* and *spices,* nor was it in *Christs* innocency, and *exemption* from *originall sin,* nor was it (that is, it is not necessary to say it was) in the *hypostaticall union.* But this *incorruptiblenes* of his *flesh* is most conveniently plac'd in that, *Non dabis, thou wilt not suffer thy holy one to see corruption.* We looke no further for *causes* or *reasons* in the *mysteries of religion,* but to the *will* and pleasure of *God: Christ* himselfe limited his *inquisition* in that *ita est, even so Father, for so it seemed good in thy sight. Christs* body did *not see corruption,* therefore, because *God* had *decreed* it shold not. The humble soule (and onely the humble soule is the religious soule) rests himselfe upon *Gods* purposes, and his decrees; but then, it is upon those purposes, and decrees of *God,* which he hath declared and manifested; not such as are *conceived* and imagined in our selves, though upon some probability, some *verisimilitude.* So, in our present case, *Peter* proceeded in his *Sermon* at *Ierusalem,* and so *Paul* in his at *Antioch.* They preached *Christ* to have *bene risen* without seeing *corruption,* not onely because *God* had *decreed* it, but because he had *manifested* that *decree* in his *Prophet.* Therefore doth Saint *Paul* cite by special number the *second Psalme* for that *decree;* And therefore both Saint *Peter* and S. *Paul* cite for it that place in the 16. *Psalme,* for when *God* declares his *decree* and purpose in the expresse words of his *Prophet,* or when he declares it in the reall execution of the decree, then he makes it ours, then he manifests it to us. And therfore as the *Mysteries* of our *Religion,* are *not* the *objects* of *our reason,* but *by faith we rest* on *Gods decree* and purpose, (It is so, ô *God,* because it is *thy will,* it should be so) so *Gods decrees* are ever to be considered in the *manifestation* thereof. All *manifestation* is either in the *word* of *God,* or in the *execution* of the *decree;* And when these two concur and meete, it is the strongest *demonstration* that can be: when therefore I finde those *markes* of *adoption* and *spirituall filiation,* which are delivered in the *word* of *God,* to be upon me, when I finde that reall *execution* of his *good purpose* upon me, as that *actually* I doe *live* under the *obedience,* and under the *conditions* which are *evidences* of *adoption* and *spirituall filiation;* then, and so long as I see these *markes* and live so, I may safely comfort my selfe in a *holy certitude* and a *modest infallibility* of my *adoption. Christ* determines himself in that, the purpose of *God;* because the purpose of *God* was

Psal. 16.10

Mat. 11.26

Acts 2.31
13.35

Vers. 10

²⁹⁰ manifest to him: S. *Peter* and S. *Paul* determine themselves in those two wayes of knowing the *purpose* of *God*, the *word* of *God* before, the *execution* of the *decree* in the *fulnes of time*. It was *prophecyed before,* say they, and it *is performed now, Christ is risen* without seeing corruption.

Now this which is so singularly peculiar to him, that *his flesh should not see corruption,* at his *second coming,* his coming to *Iudgement,* shall extend to all that are then alive, their *flesh* shall not *see corruption,* because (as the Apostle saies, and saies as a secret, as a mystery, *behold I shew you a mystery) wee shall not all sleepe,* (that is, not continue ³⁰⁰ in the state of the dead in the grave,) *but wee shall all be changed.* In an instant we shall have a *dissolution,* and in the *same instant* a *redintegration,* a *recompacting* of *body* and *soule,* and that shall be truely a death and truely a resurrection, but no sleeping, no corruption. But for us that dye now and sleepe in the state of the dead, we must al passe this *posthume* death, this *death* after *death,* nay this death after buriall, this *dissolution* after *dissolution,* this *death* of *corruption* and *putrifaction,* of *vermiculation* and *incineration,* of *dissolution* and *dispersion* in and *from* the grave. When those bodies that have beene the *children* of *royall parents,* and the *parents* of *royall* ³¹⁰ *children,* must say with *Iob, to corruption thou art my father,* and *to the Worme thou art my mother and my sister. Miserable riddle,* when the *same worme* must bee *my mother,* and *my sister,* and *my selfe. Miserable incest,* when I must bee *maried* to my *mother* and my *sister,* and bee both *father* and *mother* to my *owne mother* and *sister, beget,* and *beare* that *worme* which is all that *miserable penury;* when my *mouth* shall be *filled* with *dust,* and the *worme* shall *feed,* and *feed sweetely* upon me, when the *ambitious* man shall have *no satisfaction,* if the *poorest alive* tread upon him, nor the *poorest* receive any *contentment* in being made *equall* to *Princes,* for they *shall bee equall* ³²⁰ but *in dust.* One dyeth at his full strength, being wholly at ease and in quiet, and another dyes in the *bitternes of his soul,* and never *eates* with *pleasure,* but they lye downe *alike* in *the dust,* and the *worme covers them;* The worm covers them in *Iob,* and in *Esay, it covers them and is spred under them,* the worme is spred *under thee,* and the worme *covers thee;* There's the *Mats* and the *Carpets* that *lye under,* and there's the *State* and the *Canapye,* that *hangs over the*

1 Cor. 15.51

17.14

24.20

Iob 21.23

[Isa.] 14.11

greatest of the sons of men. Even those bodies that were *the temples of the holy Ghost,* come to this *dilapidation,* to ruine, to rubbidge, to dust: even the *Israel of the Lord,* and *Iacob* himselfe hath no other specification, no other denomination, but that *vermis Iacob,* thou *worme of Iacob.* Truely the consideration of this *posthume death,* this death after buriall, that after *God,* (with whom are the *issues of death*) hath delivered me from the *death* of the *wombe,* by bringing mee into the *world,* and from the manifold *deaths* of the *world,* by laying me in the *grave,* I must dye againe in an *Incineration* of this *flesh,* and in a dispersion of that dust: That that *Monarch,* who spred over many nations alive, must in his dust lye in a corner of that *sheete of lead,* and there, but so long as that lead will laste, and that privat and *retir'd man,* that thought himselfe his owne for ever, and never came forth, must in his dust of the grave bee published, and (such are the *revolutions* of the *graves*) bee mingled in his dust, with the dust of every high way, and of every dunghill, and swallowed in every puddle and pond: This is the most inglorious and contemptible *vilification,* the most deadly and peremptory *nullification* of man, that wee can consider. *God* seemes to have caried the declaration of his *power* to a great height, when hee sets the *Prophet Ezechiel* in the *valley of drye bones,* and sayes, *Sonne of man can these bones live?* as though it had bene impossible, and yet they did; The *Lord* layed *Sinewes upon them, and flesh,* and breathed into them, and *they did live:* But in that case there were *bones* to bee *seene,* something visible, of which it might be sayd, can this thing live? But in this death of *incineration,* and dispersion of dust, wee see *nothing* that wee can call *that mans;* If we say, can this dust live? perchance it *cannot,* it may bee the meere *dust* of the *earth,* which never did live, nor never shall. It may be the dust of that mans worms which did live, but shall no more. It may bee the dust of *another* man, that concernes not him of whom it is askt. This death of *incineration* and dispersion, is, to naturall *reason,* the most *irrecoverable death* of all, and yet *Domini Domini sunt exitus mortis, unto God the Lord belong the issues of death,* and by *recompacting* this *dust* into the *same body,* and *reanimating* the *same body* with the *same soule,* hee shall in a blessed and glorious *resurrection* give mee such an *issue from* this *death,* as shal never passe into any other death, but establish me into a life that shall

Esa. 41.14

[37.1]

last as long as the *Lord of life* himselfe. And so have you that that belongs to the *first acceptation* of these words, (*unto God the Lord belong the issues of death*) That though from the *wombe* to the *grave* and in the grave it selfe wee passe from *death* to *death*, yet, as *Daniel* speakes, *The Lord our God is able to deliver us, and hee will deliver us.*

370 And so wee passe unto our *second accommodation* of *these words* (*unto God the Lord belong the issues of death*) That it *belongs* to *God*, and *not* to *man* to *passe a judgement* upon us at our death, or to conclude a dereliction on *Gods* part upon the manner thereof.

2 Part
Liberatio in morte

Those *indications* which the *Physitians* receive, and those *presagitions* which they give for *death* or *recovery* in the *patient*, they receive and they give out of the grounds and the *rules of their art:* But we have no such rule or art to give a *presagition* of *spirituall death* and damnation upon any such *indication* as wee see in any *dying man;* wee see often enough to be sory, but not to despaire; for the 380 *mercies* of *God* worke *momentarily* in minutes, and many times *insensibly* to *bystanders* or any other then the party departing, and wee may bee deceived both wayes: wee use to comfort our selves in the death of *a friend,* if it be testified that he went away like a *Lambe,* that is, without any *reluctation.* But, *God* knowes, that may bee accompanied with a *dangerous damp* and *stupefaction,* and *insensibility* of his *present state.* Our blessed *Saviour* suffered *colluctations* with *death,* and a *sadnes even in his soule to death,* and an *agony* even to a *bloody sweate* in his *body,* and *expostulations* with *God,* and *exclamations* upon the crosse. He was a *devout man,* who said upon

Hilarion

390 his death bed, or death-turfe (for hee was an *Heremit*) *septuaginta annos Domino servivisti, & mori times?* hast thou served a good *Master threescore and ten yeares, and now art thou loath to goe into his presence?* yet *Hilarion* was loath. He was a *devout* man (an

Barlaam

Heremit too) that sayd that day hee died, *Cogita te hodie cœpisse servire Domino, & hodie finiturum. Consider this to be the first days service that ever thou didst thy Master,* to glorifie him in a Christianly and a constant death, *and if thy first day be thy last day too, how soone dost thou come to receive thy wages?* yet *Barlaam* could have beene content to have stayd longer for it: Make no *ill conclusions* 400 upon any mans *loathnes* to *dye.* And then, upon *violent deaths* in-

flicted, as upon malefactors, *Christ* himselfe hath forbidden us by his owne death to make any *ill conclusion;* for his owne *death* had those impressions in it; He was *reputed,* he was *executed* as a *malefactor,* and no doubt many of them who concurred to his death, did beleeve him to bee so. Of *sudden death* there are scarce examples to be found in the *scriptures* upon *good men,* for *death* in *battaile* cannot be called *sud[d]en death;* But *God* governes not by *examples,* but by *rules,* and therefore make no *ill conclusion* upon *sudden death* nor upon distempers neyther, though perchance accompanied with some *words*
10 of *diffidence* and distrust in the *mercies of God.* The *tree lyes as it falles;* 'Tis true, but yet it is *not* the *last stroake* that *fells* the *tree,* nor the *last word* nor *gaspe* that *qualifies* the *soule.* Stil *pray* wee for a *peaceable life* against *violent death,* and for *time* of *repentance* against *sudden death,* and for *sober* and *modest assurance* against *distemperd* and *diffident death,* but never make *ill conclusions* upon persons overtaken with such deaths; *Domini Domini sunt exitus mortis,* to God the Lord belong the issues of death.* And *he* received *Sampson,* who went out of this world in *such* a *manner* (consider it *actively,* consider it *passively,* in his *owne death,* and in those whom he
20 *slew* with himselfe) as was subject to interpretation hard enough. Yet the *holy Ghost* hath moved S. *Paul* to celebrate *Sampson* in his *great Catalogue,* and so doth all the *Church.* Our *criticall* day is *not* the *very day* of our *death:* but the whole course of our life. I thanke him that *prayes* for me when my bell tolles, but I thank him much more that *Catechises* mee, or *preaches* to mee, or *instructs mee how to live. Fac hoc & vives, there's* my securitie, the mouth of the *Lord hath sayd it, doe this and thou shalt live:* But *though I doe it,* yet I *shall dye too,* dye a bodily, a naturall death. But *God* never mentions, never seems to consider that death, the bodily, the naturall death. *God* doth not
30 say, Live well and thou shalt dye well, that is, an easie, a quiet death; But *live well here,* and thou shalt *live well for ever.* As the first part of a sentence peeces wel with the last, and never respects, never hearkens after the *parenthesis* that comes betweene, so doth a *good life* here flowe into an *eternall life,* without any consideration, what *manner* of *death* wee dye: But whether the *gate* of *my prison* be *opened* with an *oyld key* (by a gentle and *preparing sicknes*) or the gate bee *hewen downe* by a *violent death,* or the gate bee *burnt downe*

[Eccles. 11.3]

Heb. 11.[32]

[Luk. 10.28]

by a *raging* and *frantique feaver, a gate into heaven* I *shall have,* for
from the *Lord* is the *cause* of *my life,* and *with God the Lord are the*
440 *issues of death.* And further wee cary not this *second acceptation* of
the *words,* as this *issue of death* is *liberatio in morte, Gods care* that
the *soule* be *safe,* what *agonies* soever the *body suffers* in the *houre*
of death; but passe to our *third part* and last part; as this *issue of death*
is *liberatio per mortem,* a *deliverance by the death* of another, by the
death of *Christ.*

Part 3   *Sufferentiam Iob audijstis, & vidistis finem Domini,* sayes Saint
Liberatio   *Iames* 5.11. *You have heard of the patience of Iob,* says he, All this
per mortem   while you have done that, for in every man, calamitous, miserable
                man, a *Iob* speakes; Now *see the end of the Lord,* sayth that *Apostle,*
            450 which is not that end that the *Lord* propos'd to himselfe (*salvation
                to us*) nor the end which he proposes to us (*conformitie to him*) but
                see the end of the Lord, says he, The end, *that the Lord* himselfe
                came to, *death,* and a painefull and a shamefull death. But why did
De civitate   he dye? and why dye so? *Quia Domini Domini sunt exitus mortis*
Dei lib. 17.   (as Saint *Augustine* interpreting this *text* answeres that question) be-
c. 18   cause *to this God our Lord belong'd the issues of death. Quid apertius
                diceretur?* sayes hee there, what can bee more obvious, more manifest
                then this sense of these words? In the former part of this verse, it is
                sayd, *He that is our God, is the God of salvation, Deus salvos faciendi,*
            460 so hee reads it, the *God* that must save us: Who can that be, sayes he,
Mat. 1.21   but *Iesus?* for *therefore* that *name* was *given him,* because he was to
                save us. And to this *Iesus,* sayes he, this *Saviour, belongs the issues of
                death; Nec oportuit eum de hac vita alios exitus habere quam mortis.*
                Being come into this life in our mortal nature, he could not goe out
                of it any other way then by Death. *Ideo dictum,* sayes he, *therefore
                it is sayd, To God the Lord belong the issues of death; ut ostenderetur
                moriendo nos salvos facturum, to shew that his way to save us was to
                dye.* And from this *text* doth Saint *Isiodore* prove, that *Christ* was
                truely Man, (which as many *sects* of *heretiques denyed,* as that he
            470 was *truely God*) because to him, though he were *Dominus Dominus*
                (as the *text* doubles it) *God* the *Lord,* yet to *him,* to *God the Lord
                belong'd the issues of death. Oportuit eum pati,* more can not be sayd,
Lu. 24.26   then *Christ* himselfe sayes of himself, *These things Christ ought to
                suffer;* hee had no other way but by death. So then *this part* of our

Sermon must needes be a *passion Sermon;* since all his *life* was a *continuall passion,* all *our Lent* may well bee a *continuall good Fryday.* *Christs* painefull life tooke off none of the paines of his death, hee felt not the lesse then for having felt so much before. Nor will any thing that shall be sayd before, lessen, but rather inlarge your devotion, to that which shall be sayd of his passion at the time of the due *solemnization* thereof. *Christ* bled not a droppe the lesse at the last, for having bled at his *Circumcision* before, nor wil you shed a teare the lesse then, if you shed some now. And therefore bee now content to consider with mee how to *this God the Lord belong'd the issues of death.*

That *God,* this *Lord,* the *Lord* of *life could dye,* is a strange contemplation; That the *red Sea* could bee *drie,* That the *Sun* could *stand still,* That an *Oven* could be *seaven times heat* and *not burne,* That *Lions* could be *hungry* and *not bite,* is strange, *miraculously strange,* but *supermiraculous* that *God could dye;* but that *God would dye* is an *exaltation* of that. But even of that also it is a *superexaltation,* that *God shold dye, must dye,* and *non exitus* (said *S. Augustin*) *God* the *Lord had no issue but by death,* and *oportuit pati* (says *Christ* himself) all this *Christ ought to suffer,* was bound to suffer. *Deus ultionum Deus* says *David, God* is the *God of revenges,* he wold *not passe* over the sin of man unrevenged, unpunished. But then *Deus ultionum liberè egit* (sayes *that place*) The *God of revenges workes freely,* he *punishes,* he *spares whome he will.* And wold he *not spare himselfe?* he would not: *Dilectio fortis ut mors, love is strong as death,* stronger, it drew in death that naturally is not welcom. *Si possibile,* says *Christ, If it be possible, let this Cup passe,* when his *love expressed in a former decree* with his *Father,* had *made it impossible.* Many *waters quench not love, Christ* tryed many; He was *Baptized* out of his *love,* and his love determined not there; He wept over *Jerusalem* out of his love, and his love determined not there; He *mingled blood* with *water* in his *agony* and that determined not his love; hee *wept pure blood,* all his blood at all his eyes, at all his pores, in his *flagellation* and *thornes* (*to the Lord our God belong'd the issues of blood*) and these *expressed,* but these did *not quench his love.*

Potuisse Mori
Exod. 14.21
Jos. 10.12
[Dan. 3.19]
[Dan. 6.22]

Psal. 94.1
Voluisse Mori

Cant. 8.6

[Mat. 26.39]

Vers. 7

Oportuisse
Mori

Hee *would not* spare, nay he *could not spare himselfe.* There was nothing more free, more voluntary, more spontaneous then the death of *Christ.* 'Tis true, *liberè egit,* he *dyed voluntarily,* but yet when we consider the *contract* that had passed betweene his *Father* and *him,* there was an *oportuit,* a kind of *necessity* upon him. All this *Christ ought to suffer.* And when shall we *date* this *obligation,* this *oportuit,* this *necessity?* when shall wee say *that* begun? Certainly this *decree* by which *Christ was to suffer* all this, was an *eternall decree,* and was there any thing before that, that was eternall? *Infinite love, eternall* 520 *love,* he pleased to follow this home, and to consider it seriously, that what liberty soever wee can *conceive* in *Christ,* to dye or not to dye; this *necessity of dying,* this *decree* is as *eternall* as that *liberty;* and yet how small a matter made hee of this *necessity* and this *dying?* His

Gen. 3.15

Father cals it but *a bruise,* and but a *bruising of his heele (the serpent shall bruise his heele)* and yet that was, that the *serpent* should *practise* and *compasse* his *death.* Himselfe calls it but a *Baptisme,* as though he were to bee the better for it. *I have a Baptisme to be*

Luk. 12.50

Baptized with, and he was in paine till it was accomplished, and yet

Heb. 12.2

this *Baptisme* was *his death.* The *holy Ghost* calls it *Ioy (for the Ioy* 530 *which was set before him hee indured the Crosse)* which was not a *joy* of his reward after his passion, but a joy that filled him even in the middest of those torments, and arose from them. When *Christ* calls his passion *Calicem, a Cuppe,* and no worse, *(Can ye drink of*

Mat. 20.22

my Cuppe?) he speakes not odiously, not with detestation of it: Indeed it was a *Cup, salus mundo, a health to all the world.* And *quid*

Psal. 116.12

retribuam, says *David, what shall I render to the Lord?* answere you with *David, accipiam Calicem, I will take the Cup of salvation;* take it, that *Cup of salvation,* his *passion,* if not into your *present imitation,* yet into your *present contemplation.* And behold how that *Lord* that 540 was *God,* yet *could dye, would dye, must dye,* for your *salvation.*

Mat. 17.3
Mar. 9.4
Luc. 9.31

That *Moses* and *Elias talkt with Christ* in the *transfiguration,* both Saint *Mathew* and Saint *Marke* tel us, but what they talkt of, onely S. *Luke, Dicebant excessum eius,* says he, *they talkt of his decease, of his death* which *was to be accomplished* at *Ierusalem.* The *word* is of his *Exodus,* the very word of our Text, *exitus,* his *issue by death. Moses* who in his *Exodus* had *prefigured* this *issue of our Lord,* and in passing *Israel* out of *Egypt* through the *red Sea,* had foretold in that actual *prophesie, Christs passing* of *mankind through* the *sea* of his *blood,* and *Elias,* whose *Exodus* and *issue out of* this *world* was a *figure* of *Christs ascension,* had no doubt a great satisfaction in *talking* with our *blessed Lord de excessu eius,* of the *full consummation* of *all this* in *his death,* which was to bee *accomplished* at *Ierusalem.* Our *meditation* of his *death* should be more *viscerall* and affect us more because it is of a thing already done. The ancient *Romanes* had a certain tenderness, and detestation of the name of death, they cold not name death, no, not in their wills. There they could not say *Si mori contigerit,* but *si quid humanitus contingat,* not if, or when I dye, but when the course of nature is accomplished upon me. To us that speake dayly of the *death* of *Christ,* (he was *crucified, dead and buried*) can the memory or the mention of our owne *death* bee yrkesome or bitter? There are in these latter times amongst us, that name death freely enogh, and the death of *God,* but in *blasphemous oathes* and *execrations.* Miserable men, who shall therefore bee sayd never to have named *Iesus,* because they have named him *too often;* and therfore heare *Iesus* say, *Nescivi vos, I never knew you,* because they made themselves *too familiar* with him. *Moses* and *Elias* talkt with *Christ* of his *death,* only in *a holy* and *joyfull sense* of the *benefit* which *they* and *all* the world were to *receive by that. Discourses* of *Religion* should not be *out of curiosity,* but to *edification.* And then they talkt with *Christ* of his *death* at that time, when he was in the greatest *height* of *glory* that ever he admitted in this world, that is, his *transfiguration.* And wee are afraid to speake to the *great men* of this world of their *death,* but nourish in them a *vaine imagination* of *immortality,* and *immutability.* But *bonum est nobis esse hic* (as Saint *Peter* said there) *It is good to dwell here,* in this *consideration* of his *death,* and therefore *transferre* wee our *tabernacle* (our *devotions*) through some of those *steps* which *God* the *Lord* made to his *issue of death* that *day.*

[Mat. 7.23]

Take in the *whole day* from the *houre* that *Christ received* the *passeover* upon *Thursday, unto* the *houre* in which hee *dyed* the *next day.* Make *this* present *day* that *day* in thy *devotion,* and consider what *hee did,* and remember what *you have done.* Before hee *instituted* and *celebrated* the *Sacrament,* (which was *after* the *eating of the passeover*) hee proceeded to that *act* of *humility,* to *wash his*

Conformitas

disciples feete, even *Peters, who* for a while *resisted* him; In thy *preparation* to the holy and blessed *Sacrament,* hast thou with a sincere *humility* sought a *reconciliation* with all the *world,* even with those that have beene *averse* from it, and *refused* that *reconciliation* from thee? If so (and not else) thou hast spent that *first part* of this
590 his *last day,* in a *conformity* with him. After the *Sacrament* hee spent the time till night in *prayer,* in *preaching,* in *Psalmes;* Hast thou considered that a *worthy receaving* of the *Sacrament* consists in a *continuation* of *holinesse after,* aswell as in a *preparation* before? If so, thou hast therein also *conformed* thy selfe to him, so *Christ* spent his time till night. *At night* hee *went into the garden* to *pray,* and he prayed *prolixius;* he spent *much time* in prayer. How much? Because it is literally expressed, that he *prayed there three severall times,* and that *returning to his Disciples* after his *first prayer,* and *finding them a sleepe* sayd, *could ye not watch with me one houre,* it is collected
600 that he *spent three houres* in *prayer.* I dare scarce aske thee *whither* thou *wentest,* or *how* thou *disposedst* of *thy self,* when it *grew darke* and after *last night:* If that time were spent in a *holy recommendation* of thy selfe to *God,* and a *submission* of *thy will* to *his,* it was spent in a *conformity* to him. In that *time* and in those *prayers* was *his agony* and *bloody sweat.* I will *hope* that thou didst *pray;* but not *every ordinary* and *customary prayer,* but *prayer actually* accompanied with *shedding of teares,* and *dispositively* in a readines to *shed blood* for *his glory* in *necessary cases,* puts thee into a *conformity* with him. About midnight he was *taken* and *bound with a kisse,* art thou not
610 *too conformable* to him in that? Is not that *too literally,* too exactly *thy case?* at *midnight* to have *bene taken* and *bound with a kisse?* From thence he was *caried back* to *Ierusalem,* first to *Annas,* then to *Caiphas,* and (as late as it was) then hee was *examined* and *buffeted,* and *delivered over* to the custody of those *officers,* from whome he received all those *irrisions,* and *violences,* the *covering of his face,* the *spitting upon his face,* the *blasphemies of words,* and the *smartnes of blowes* which that *Gospell* mentions. In which compasse fell that *Gallicinium,* that *crowing of the Cock* which *called up* Peter to his *repentance.* How thou passedst all that time last night, thou knowest.
620 If thou didst any thing then that needed *Peters teares,* and hast *not shed them,* let me be thy *Cock,* doe it now, Now thy *Master* (in

Luk. 22.44

Mat. 26.40

the unworthiest of his servants) *lookes back upon thee,* doe it now.
Betimes, in the morning, so soone as it was day, the *Iewes held a
counsell* in the *high Priests hall,* and *agreed upon their evidence*
against him, and then caried him to *Pilate,* who was to be his *Iudge.*
Diddest thou *accuse* thy selfe when thou *wakedst this morning,* and
wast thou content to admit even *false accusations* (that is) rather to
suspect actions to have beene sin, which were not, then to *smother*
and *justify* such as were *truly sins?* then thou spentst that *houre* in
conformity to him. *Pilate* found *no evidence against him,* and therefore to ease himselfe, and to passe a *complement* upon *Herod,
Tetrarch* of *Galilee,* who was at that time at *Ierusalem* (because *Christ*
being a *Galilean* was of *Herods jurisdiction*) *Pilat sent him* to *Herod,*
and rather as a *madman* then a *malefactor, Herod* remaunded him
(*with scornes*) to *Pilat* to proceed against him; And this was about
eight of the *clock.* Hast thou been content to come to this *Inquisition,*
this examination, this agitation, this cribration, this pursuit of thy
conscience, to *sift* it, to follow it from the *sinnes* of thy *youth* to thy
present sinnes, from the *sinnes* of thy *bed,* to the *sinnes* of thy *boorde,*
and from the *substance* to the *circumstance* of thy *sinnes?* That's *time
spent* like thy *Saviours. Pilat* wold have *saved Christ,* by using the
priviledge of the *day* in his behalfe, because that *day* one *prisoner was
to be delivered,* but they chose *Barrabas;* hee would have *saved* him
from death, by *satisfying their fury,* with *inflicting* other *torments*
upon him, *scourging* and *crowning with thornes,* and *loading* him
with many *scornefull* and *ignominious contumelies;* But this redeem'd
him not, they pressed a *crucifying.* Hast thou gone about to *redeeme
thy sinne,* by *fasting,* by *Almes,* by *disciplines* and *mortifications,* in
the way of *satisfaction* to the *Iustice* of *God?* that will not serve, that's
not the right way, *wee presse* an utter *Crucifying* of that *sinne* that
governes thee; and that *conformes* thee to *Christ.* Towards *noone
Pilat* gave *judgement,* and they made such *hast* to execution, as that
by noone hee was *upon the Crosse.* There now hangs that *sacred Body*
upon the *Crosse, rebaptized* in his owne *teares* and *sweat,* and *em-
balmed* in his *owne blood alive.* There are those *bowells of compassion,* which are so conspicuous, so manifested, as that you may *see
them through his wounds.* There those *glorious eyes* grew faint in
their light: so as the *Sun ashamed* to survive them, *departed with his*

light too. And then that *Sonne of God*, who was *never from us*, and
[660] yet had now come a *new way unto* us in *assuming our nature*, delivers
that *soule* (which was *never out* of his *Fathers hands*) by a *new way*,
a *voluntary emission* of it into his Fathers hands; For though to this
God our Lord, belong'd these issues of death, so that considered in
his owne contract, he *must* necessarily *dye*, yet at *no breach* or *battery*,
which they had made upon his *sacred Body*, issued his soule, but
emisit, hee *gave up the Ghost,* and as *God breathed a soule into* the
first Adam, so this *second Adam breathed his soule into God, into
the hands of God.* There wee leave you in that *blessed dependancy,*
to *hang* upon *him* that *hangs* upon the *Crosse,* there *bath* in his
[670] *teares,* there *suck* at his *woundes,* and *lye downe in peace* in his *grave,*
till hee vouchsafe you a *resurrection,* and an *ascension* into that *Kingdome,* which hee *hath purchas'd for you,* with the *inestimable price*
of his *incorruptible blood.* Amen.

APPENDIX

The Unidentified Sermon on Psalms 24.7 in the Lothian MS (First Section)

[The Lothian MS is now in the possession of the Trustees of the National Library of Scotland, Edinburgh. It was given in 1898 by the late Dr. Augustus Jessopp to the ninth Marquess of Lothian.]

In Volume I of our edition, p. 39, we mentioned a sermon on *Psa.* 24.7, which is found in the Lothian MS alone. It occupies the first place in the first section of that manuscript, and it is followed by eight sermons which are undoubtedly Donne's, and which have been printed in our edition. Dr. Jessopp stated that this manuscript, which was formerly in his possession, contained "18 sermons hitherto unknown, the others have been already printed." It is strange that Jessopp, who was a warm admirer of Donne's work, could have believed that all the very poor stuff found after Donne's known sermons could possibly have been by him. On pp. 39–41 we gave a brief account of the other sermons and jottings, dismissing them as obviously not Donne's. We made an exception, however, of the sermon on *Psa.* 24.7, as Mr. John Sparrow had in 1930 expressed an opinion that this might be by Donne,[1] and we stated that we intended to publish it as an appendix in Vol. X, though we held the opinion that it was not by Donne. Mr. Sparrow has now, however, retracted his opinion in a letter to us, and we feel that in view of the fact that the Lothian MS itself makes no ascription to Donne, we need not do more than print two extracts of a few pages which will show that this sermon, though better than some of the later unidentified sermons in the MS, is not in Donne's style and manner. When Mr. Sparrow's admirable article, most of which still holds good, was published in 1930, the Dobell, Dowden, and Merton MSS were not available for comparison, the St. Paul's Cathedral MS had not been examined, and the Ellesmere MS was still unknown. When all these had been collated, and were found not to contain this sermon, though there was a general consensus of most of the Donne material, the probability that the Lothian MS contained a single unprinted sermon not found in any other MS was seriously diminished.

We quote the opening of the sermon, which is the part that most resembles Donne's style, and also a longer passage from the middle where the author quotes Macarius, an author never mentioned in Donne's

---

[1] See "John Donne and Contemporary Preachers," *Essays and Studies by Members of the English Association,* XVI (1930), 174–175.

printed sermons, and quotes him in Greek, whereas Donne always quotes the Greek Fathers in a Latin translation.[2] The only Greek words found in Donne's printed sermons are taken from the Greek Testament, and they are very few in number.[3]

We have noted a number of expressions which seem alien to Donne's style, e.g. "Christs intention for the reason why he was humbled," "for sure since he humbled himself," "he will take us tardie," and so on. More important, however, than these, seems the general flatness of the sermon. In all Donne's genuine sermons we can detect occasional flashes of inspiration. There may be flat prosaic passages which last for two or three pages, but sooner or later there is a quickening and an uplift. The writer of this present sermon was learned and earnest, but he was also exceptionally boring. The monotony of his style contrasts strongly with Donne's uneven brilliance, when the sermon as a whole is compared with one of Donne's.[4]

SERMON

PSAL.: 24.7. *Lift up your heads yee gates and be ye lift up ye everlasting doores, and the King of Glory shall come in.*

HUMILIATION and exaltation, the humiliation of Christ the Son of God towards us men, and the exaltation of us men towards Christ the Son of God doe soe as it were strive whether of them should have greater interest in this great time in this day of the Lord which now approacheth, as at the first my meditations made a question, whether of them they should give the day to; whether they should venture on a text from whence we might see Christs humiliation, or on a text from whence we might learne the duty of exaltation and lifting up ourselves towards him who is the King of glory. Christs owne intention and his Churches continuall practise as they would have us at this time ever to remember and celebrate the one, soe they would have us to practise and performe the other. Christs intention for the reason why he was humbled, was that we might be exalted, he (as the Apostle speaketh) made himselfe of noe reputation, and tooke upon him the shape of a servant, that we who were base and slaves might become of great esteeme and be made sons, he was cast downe that we might be lifted up; he came down from heaven which is the throne of the King of glory as low as the earth, that we who lay groveling upon the earth, nay plunged by nature as low as the lowest helle might be exalted as high as the heavens, which is the throne of the King of glory; and according to Christs intention, soe hath his Churches practise beene, for the Church of Christ as she hath apponted us at this time to celebrate the holy Eucharist,

[2] See p. 346 of our present volume.

[3] See p. 317.

[4] Miss Helen Gardner allows us to say that in her opinion the sermon is not by Donne.

the Sacrament of our Saviours blessed body and blood, whereby we are exalted and lifted up towards him; soe you see the time requireth both; but because the declaration of the nativity and humiliation of our Lord, is the proper worke of the morrow which is the feast-day itself and belongeth to those great masters of Israel, who are appointed for the ordering and proclaiming of the feast; as likewise because Christs humiliation is already past, he hath done his part sure enough but our part of exalting and lifting up ourselves towards him remaineth yet to be performed by us in this holy sacrament: and besides since the chiefe end why Christ was humbled was both to teach us the duty and assure us of the dignity of our exaltation; teach us the duty of it, for sure since he humbled himselfe soe low as to come downe from heaven to us upon the earth we can doe noe lesse then according to the common Law of curtesie raise and lift up ourselves towards him, who is come much more then halfe way to meet us; and to assure us likewise of this dignity of our exaltation as Jerome teacheth us, cum ergo audieris etc. when therefore (saith he) thou shalt heare that the son of God for thy sake was made the son of Adam and the sonne of Abraham, doubt not but that thou likewise who art the Son of Adam and the son of Abram shalt one day be exalted and made the Son of God.[5] For these and diverse such reasons have I therefore made choise of a text which will teach us how to behave ourselves in receiving this King of glory, how to raise and lift up ourselves towards him in his holy sacrament; neither is it unfit that we should be taught this duty the day before the feast and entertainment for we know that great feasts have their Eeves and nights of preparation, the reason saith the text, why Christs body that night was taken down from the cross was because it was the preparation of the Jewes sabboth which was a great feast, and the Paschall Lambe to which the sacrament of the Supper is answerable in the new testament had 4 daies appointed for preparation, for they were commanded to take the lambe on the tenth day of the moneth and not to kill it before the 14th day,[6] we cannot then well allow less then one day and nights preparation for the receiving of this holy Sacrament for certainly the reason why soe many men doe depart from the table of the Lord without the fruit and comfort which God's ministers doe promise them to finde at it, is because men commonly doe come to the table without thinking of it before that very instant and soe they mys of the fruit and comfort of it which onely is promised upon a condition of precedent preparation: give me leave therefore I beseech you before the day of entertainment from the words of the text to teach you how to prepare yourselves for the receiving of the King of glory in this holy Sacrament.

---

[5] For : for MS.
[6] day, : day MS.

[Interval of several pages.]

But now let us see wherein this preparation consisteth; there are in the text 2 things set downe concerning it. 1, the organ or member which must especially be prepared, that is, our harts and soules, here in the text called everlasting gates and doores. Secondly the manner how this organ or member must be prepared, they must be raised and lifted up, Lift up your heads yee gates etc. First[7] then the organs or members principally to be prepared are our harts and soules here called in the text everlasting gates and doores; why they are called everlasting I will now say nothing, for it is noe fitt time to dispute of the immortality of the soule, but they are called here gates and doores; because when God entereth into any man, he first entreth into his hart and soule as by a doore; the first place you see we come into any house is the gate or doore of the house; and even soe when God would enter into any man, the first place he would come into is the hart or soule of the man;[8] in citties besieged the chiefe part of the cittie assaulted and defended was wont to be the gate of the citty, soe it is with the hart of man, when the Divell would have possession of any man, he would first be master of the hart; and when God would subdue any Christian to his obedience, he would first take in his hart. And[9] therefore is the hart of man fitly called by Macarius Θρόνος τοῦ Σατανου[10] Gods throne and the divells throne, for if either of them doe but once get possession of the hart they doe not doubt to inthrone themselves as absolute Kings and Commanders of the whole body; the reason of it is given by the same father ἡ γαρ καρδία etc. for saith he, the hart as an absolute king and captaine commandeth all the parts of the body. If[11] the hart be corrupt, the mouth will talk profanely, the hand doe wickedly, the foote run after vanity etc. we read that the divell when he hath entered into league with any man, all that he hath required of him hath beene, that after soe many yeares service he might have that mans soule; and soe when God entereth into covenant with any one all that he requireth on that mans part is his hart, my Son give me thy hart. Since therefore at this time we are to

---

[7] First : first MS.
[8] man; : man MS.
[9] And : and MS.
[10] Should we here emend to "τοῦ Θεοῦ κάι τοῦ Σατανοῦ"? It will be noted that the MS omits most of the Greek accents.
[11] If : if MS.

receive the King of glory in the Sacrament let us be sure that the doores and gates, that is, our harts and souls be first prepared and made cleane, by which he will enter into us if he enter at all. We[12] ought indeed to prepare our bodies too, and therefore as we heare David sometime protesting that he will lift up his hart to God soe else where we heare him promising, that he lift up his hands towards Gods holy Oracle, there is the preparation of the body. But[13] first I say and principally our harts must be prepared, for if they be once rightly prepared, then we need to make no question, but that the words of our mouthes, the actions of our hands and the gestures of our bodies shalbe acceptable in his sight, I believed (saith the prophet) and therefore I spake. And saith the Apostle with our harts we believe unto righteousnes and with our mouthes we confess unto salvation; soe that if we have once faith and beliefe which hath place in the hart, then our mouthes of their owne accord will speake and confess unto salvation; In this sacrament it is our soules that are fed, it is our soules that receive the King of glory and therefore they must principally be prepared; and if Joseph of Arimathea would not wrap the dead body of Jesus, but into pure and fine linnen shall we offer to receive the living body of Jesus into impure and unprepared harts? Let our preparation then first begin from thence, for this is certaine that in all religious performances which we doe unto God,[14] soe long as they doe not begin from the hart, God doth not account them as actions, but as meere actings and ceremonies; for this is the difference betweene the judgment of God and men, when we passe our judgment upon any religious action, from the externall performance we judge of the internall perfection and sincerity of it, and it is a good rule we know none better, for it is the judgment of charity: But now when God who is καρδιογνοστης,[15] the searcher of the harts commeth to make inquisition for this action, he beginneth his search at the hart and from the straightnes and sincerity of it, judgeth of the perfection of the externall performance, and this is the judgment of certainty.

---

[12] We : we MS.
[13] But : but MS.
[14] God, : G. MS.
[15] Read καρδιογνωστης (see *Acts* 1.24 and 15.8).

Textual Notes to the Sermons
in Volume X

Notes to Sermon No. 1

22   see : sea *F*

NOTE: The spelling "sea" for a bishop's see is sometimes found in the 16th and 17th centuries, but it is so misleading in this connection that we have altered it here to the usual spelling.

35   intendiment]

NOTE: This obsolete word from medieval Latin *intendimentum,* 'understanding,' is a different word from "intendment" (also "entendment"), which comes from French *entendement* (*N.E.D.*)

240   building; : building, *F*

267   Administrer]

NOTE: *N.E.D.* admits this as a rare and obsolete word, which may be compared with Old French *amenistrere, -eur,* afterward supplanted by the learned form *administrateur.* Donne uses it in *Biathanatos,* p. 41: "Poysons, which the nature of the disease, and the art of the Administrer made wholesome."

332   *Quomodo cecidisti de cœlo, Lucifer, filius orientis?*]

NOTE: In his Easter sermon, 1624, Donne showed that he was aware that in *Isa.* 14.12, from which these words are taken, they were originally applied to a man and not to the Devil or devils: "Though those words, *Quomodo cecidisti de Cœlo, Lucifer, How art thou fallen from heaven O Lucifer, the Son of the morning?* be ordinarily applied to the fall of the Angels, yet it is evident, that they are literally spoken of the fall of a man:..." (Vol. VI, p. 69). There is in the present sermon a juxaposition of several ideas and phrases which are found in the first sermon printed in Volume VI (see our Introd. to that volume, pp. 1–2) and also in the letter to Sir Robert Ker or Carr (Tobie Matthew, *Letters,* p. 305). See the following notes on lines 338–339 and 391–394.

336   Covenant, *F* in catchword : Covenant *F* on page 450

338–339   *Ecce vir, Oriens nomen ejus,...Behold the Man, whose name is the East*]

NOTE: This is the Vulgate rendering of *Zech.* 6.12, which the A.V. translates as "Behold the man whose name is the Branch." Donne was particularly fond of this Vulgate rendering, and quotes it again and again. Cp. Vol. V, p. 97; Vol. VI, p. 59;

LINE

Vol. IX, p. 49; also *Letters* (Tobie Matthew collection), 1660, p. 305. It is also used in the epitaph which Donne composed for himself.

He may have remembered the use of *Oriens* for Christ in the *O Sapientia* series of introits which begin on December 16 at the close of Advent (recorded in the black-letter calendar of the Book of Common Prayer): "O Oriens, splendor lucis et sol justitiæ, veni et illumina sedentes in tenebris et umbra mortis," for this also makes use of the passage from *Luke* 1.78–79 to which Donne refers below in lines 341 ff. The Vulgate has "... visitavit nos oriens ex alto" where the A.V. reads "the dayspring from on high hath visited us," though it supplies in the margin, against "dayspring," "or sun-rising, or branch."

391–394   but as in the round frame of the World, the farthest West is East, ... So in thee, (who art a World too) thy West and thy East shall joyne]

NOTE: Here again there is a parallel with Vol. VI, p. 59: "In a flat Map, there goes no more, to make West East, ... but to paste that flat Map upon a round body, and then West and East are all one. In a flat soule, ... there goes no more to the making of that trouble, peace, then to apply that trouble to the body of the Merits, to the body of the Gospel of Christ Jesus, and conforme thee to him, and thy West is East, ..." Cp. also the *Hymne to God my God, in my sicknesse,* 13–15:

> ... As West and East
> In all flatt Maps (and I am one) are one,
> So death doth touch the Resurrection.

411 *mg.*   Psal. 19.5   :   Psal. 19.6 *F*
488   *Pharaoh*   :   *Pharoh F*
550–570   I turne to hearty and earnest prayer to God, and I fix my thoughts strongly (as I thinke) upon him ... slackned my zeale]

NOTE: This long and careful analysis of the difficulty of concentration in prayer should be compared with the passage quoted in Vol. VII, pp. 20–21.

566   5.4   :   5.41 *in some copies of F*
627   transportation   :   tranportation *F*
639–640   naturally Angels do not understand thoughts]

NOTE: Cp. *The Dreame,* line 16: "And knew'st my thoughts,

LINE

beyond an Angels art." Donne agreed with Aquinas (Quæst.
lvii. art. 4) that though angels may be able to detect thoughts
by subtle indications, the power of reading thoughts as they are
in the intellect and will belongs to God alone. See Sermon 2 of
the present volume, lines 643–654: "... let *Scotus* and his Heard
think, That Angels, and separate soules have a naturall power to
understand thoughts, though God for his particular glory restraine the exercise of that power in them, ... And let *Aquinas*
present his arguments to the contrary, That those spirits have
no naturall power to know thoughts; we seek no farther, but
that Christ Jesus himselfe thought it argument enough to convince the Scribes and Pharisees, and prove himselfe God, by
knowing their thoughts."

685 compellation]
NOTE: 'An addressing or calling upon any one.' Now archaic or
obsolete. (*N.E.D.*)

688–689 *He bringeth clouds from the ends of the earth*]
NOTE: This is a good example of the way in which Donne, like
many other Anglicans, confuses the A.V. and Prayer Book
versions of the Psalms. In *Psal.* 135.7 the Prayer Book has "He
bringeth forth the clouds from the ends of the world," and A.V.
"He causeth the vapours to ascend from the ends of the earth."

796 to : to to *F*
841 meanes : meanns *F*

Notes to Sermon No. 2

54 Mat. 8 ult. : Mar. 8 ult. *F*
70 *redemptio* : *redemtio F*
102 Christ : Chirst *F*
303 *misericordis* : *miserecordis F*
304 *Chrysostome* : *Chysost. F*
307 *Chrysostome* : *Crhysostome F*

NOTE: The usually good printing of *LXXX Sermons* fails us
badly in these five lines which contain three mistakes. It would
be interesting to know whether there is any copy in which they
were corrected while passing through the press, as happens often
in *XXVI Sermons*. All copies which we have collated contain
the misprints.

LINE

456–457   *blesse ... magnifie him* : blesse ... magnifie him *F*

NOTE: Donne's wording is taken from the refrain of the canticle known as *Benedicite* in the office of Matins in the Prayer Book. It is derived from the short book "The Song of the Three Holy Children" in the Apocrypha, but there the refrain in A.V. is "praise and exalt him above all for ever."

459   *A day ... God* : A day ... God *F*

523 *mg.*   John 9.3 : John 5 *F*

563   concatenation : concatentation *F*

573–575   A Tertian will be a Quartan, and a Quartan a Hectique, and a Hectique a Consumption]

NOTE: "Hectic" is used, both as an adjective and a substantive, for 'that kind of fever which accompanies consumption or other wasting diseases, and is attended with flushed cheeks and hot dry skin' (*N.E.D.*). Cp. *Hamlet*, IV, iii, 68: "For like the Hecticke in my blood he rages."

586   *My Son ... negligent* : My Son ... negligent *F*

588   *Pray ... whole* : Pray ... whole *F*

589–590   *Leave ... wickednesse* : Leave ... wickednesse *F*

591–593   *Give ... beeing* : Give ... beeing *F*

596–597   *give ... him* : give ... him *F*

598–599   *He ... Physitian* : He ... Physitian *F*

619   he *F corr. in Errata* : we *F originally*

624   leave : leave, *F*

665   *Dimittuntur* : Dimit-/mittuntur *F*

Notes to Sermon No. 3

9   good : goods *F*

55   *coram* : cor am *F*

89   *your* : you *F*

135–136   *I will ... it?* : I will ... it? *F*

162 *mg.*   Heb. 10.38 : Heb. 10.36 *F*

182–183   *Sed quæ non fecimus ipsi*, sayes the Poet; ... *Vix ea nostra voco*]

NOTE: Ovid, *Metamorphoses*, XIII, 140–141. *Sed* should be *Et*.

192   this is *Al* : this *F*

220   *Eliberitan* Councell]

NOTE: The Council of Elvira (306 A.D.) was held at Eliberis in Spain.

LINE

227 ejulations]
NOTE: 'Wailings, lamentations,' from Latin *ejulatio.*

259 signification. Wee : signification; wee *F*

332 *mg.* Epist. 18 : Epist. 205 *F*

355, 359 preach : Preach *F*

437 Psal. 90.10 : Psal. 90.20 *F*

442 defalce *Al* : defalse *F*
NOTE: "Defalce" is a rare and obsolete word from medieval
Latin *defalcare,* from which also the more usual "defalk" (now
obsolete or archaic). Both words mean 'to diminish'; 'to deduct.'

477 *mg.* Prov. 14.32 : Prov. 14.23 *F*

494 *mg.* Psal. 112.6 : Psal. 112.4 *F*

515 *the Father* : the Father *F* : *the* Father *Al*
NOTE: Donne is emphasizing the difference, as we see below,
between God as *the Father* of all by creation and God as *your
Father* by grace.

577 *mg.* Psal. 85.9 : Psal. 85.10 *F*

605 *Iron,* : *Iron. F*

611 *let ... men* : let ... men *F*

611–612 *and ... us* : and ...us *F*

649 *mg.* 1 Pet. 2.21 : 1 Pet. 2.22 *F*

Notes to Sermon No. 4

22 impermixt]
NOTE: An obsolete word from Latin *impermixtus,* meaning
'unmixed.' Cp. Vol. V, No. 15, line 650, "zeale impermixt as the
Sun," and Vol. IX, No. 2, line 804.

55, 63 commonefactions]
NOTE: This obsolete word means 'the action of admonishing or
reminding; an admonition, reminder' (*N.E.D.*).

115–116 *There ... them* : There ... them *F*

129 *mg.* Ier. 31 : Ier. 21 *F*

129 *Dominus* : *Doninus F*

142 *mg.* Mat. 20.12 : Mat. 20.22 *F*

154 supposes : suposes *F*

163, 164 innotescence]
NOTE: This obsolete word, from medieval Latin *innotescentia,*
means 'a becoming known.' *N.E.D.* quotes as the only known

example of it another passage from Donne (Vol. IX, No. 4, line 757) "... who is all face, all manifestation, all Innotescence to me." In both these examples Donne adds a quotation from Augustine (*Enarratio in Psalm X. 11*): "Facies enim Dei est, qua Deus nobis innotescit."

175 obcæcation]
NOTE: Another rare and obsolete word. It means 'blindness' and is formed from the verb (also obsolete) "obcæcate" from the past participle of Latin *obcæcare* or *occæcare,* 'to blind.' See *N.E.D.*

179–180⎫
    mg.⎭ Rom. 1.20 : Rom. 1.12 F

242 mg. Psal. 19.1 : Psal. 19.2 F

252–253 languages, ... another; : languages; ... another, F

267 too, : too; F

281 mee : mee me F

324–325 agnomination]
NOTE: "A kind of word-play, or paronomasia" (*N.E.D.*).

354 dis-inherison]
NOTE: "The action of disinheriting" (*N.E.D.*).

365 things : *things* F

452–453 speake) ... things : speake ... things) F

455–456 (*Psalme* 65.1) ... *Tibi laus silentium*]
NOTE: Cp. Vol. IX, pp. 134–135: "*Te decet Hymnus,* (so the vulgar reads that place) To thee, O Lord, belong our Hymnes, our Psalmes, ... and conformably to that, we translate it, *Praise waiteth for thee, O God in Sion:* But if we will take it according to the Originall, it must be, *Tibi silentium laus est,* Thy praise, O Lord, consists in silence: ..."

474 of : *of* F

481–482 though they be not the *soule* of the Church, yet are they those *Spirits* that unite soule and body together]
NOTE: Cp. *The Extasie,* 61–64:
> As our blood labours to beget
> Spirits, as like soules as it can,
> Because such fingers need to knit
> That subtile knot, which makes us man.

Also *Sermons,* Vol. II, pp. 261–262: "... the spirits in a man which are the thin and active part of the blood, and so are of

a kind of middle nature, between soul and body, those spirits
are able to doe, and they doe the office, to unite and apply the
faculties of the soul to the organs of the body, and so there is
a man: ..."

518   to pronounce : *to* pronounce *F*
521   mouth, : mouth(*F*
527–528 *My sinne is greater then can be pardoned*]
       NOTE: A.V. reads "My punishment is greater than I can bear,"
       but supplies in the margin "Or, my iniquity is greater than that
       it may be forgiven." The Vulgate reads "Major est iniquitas
       mea, quam ut veniam merear," and Donne's text agrees with
       this. Cp. Vol. IX, p. 262: "...this word, which we translate here
       Iniquity, Gnavah, is oftentimes in the Scripture used for punish-
       ment, as well as for sinne: and so indifferently for both, as that if
       we will compare Translation with Translation, and Exposition
       with Exposition, it will be hard for us to say, whether *Cain* said,
       Mine iniquity is greater then can be pardoned, or, *My punish-
       ment is greater then I can beare;* and our last Translation, which
       seems to have been most carefull of the Originall, takes it
       rather so, *My punishment,* in the Text, and lays the other, *My
       sinne,* aside in the Margin."
561   sake, : sake; *in some copies of F*

Notes to Sermon No. 5

5–6   *Cyminibilis Dator,* (as our *Canons* speake) one that gives Mint
       and Cumin]
       NOTE: Cp. Vol. III, p. 384: "...how inexcusable are those
       Datores cyminibiles (as the Canonists call them) that give Mint,
       and Cummin for almes, a root that their Hogs will not, a broth
       that their Dogs will not eate."
176 *mg.* Mic. 6.13 : Mic. 6.3 *F*
177 *mg.* Zech. 7.2 : Zech. 7.12 *F*
180   *let that* : let that *F*
195   Gospel) : Gospel, *F*
230   *It* : It *F*
246 *mg.* Joel 3 : Amos 3 *F*
291   officers, *Al* : officers) *F*
301   *Rei suæ* : *Rei sui F*

LINE

318 *How should* : How should *F*

339 Sacrament, : Sacrament; *F*

359–360 evidence of undeniable Record, which have been therefore shewed]

Note: This is the reading of *F*, which has been retained by Alford. Should we read "Records" for "Record"? Or does the the phrase "evidence of ... Record" contain a sufficient suggestion of plurality to justify the plural "have been"?

419 some confident servant]

Note: "Confident" is here used in the sense common in the seventeenth century of 'confidential.' See *N.E.D.*

431 Ambassadour bringeth : Ambassadours bringeth *F*

454 Consort]

Note: "Consort" was used in the sixteenth and seventeenth centuries to mean 'a singing or playing in harmony'; cp. *Two Gentlemen of Verona*, III, ii, 84–85: "Visit by night your Ladies chamber-window / With some sweet consort." (*N.E.D.*)

459 it is at peace]

Note: We have retained the reading of *F*, but it is quite possible that "it is'" which may have been written "yt is" is a mistake for "that is" written as "yᵗ is" in Donne's MS.

468 *as an Angell* : as an Angell *F*

537 vain glorious]

Note: From the sixteenth to the eighteenth century the adjective "vainglorious" was often written as two separate words.

547 *Hosanna's* : Hosann'as *F*

562 people, : people; *F*

615–617 *voluntas, . . . free-will, . . .* will; : *voluntas; . . . free-will)* ... will; *F*

617 in : (in *F*

632 or : ot *F*

643–644 *He ... derision* : He ... derision *F*

645–646 *the wicked ... waights* : the wicked ... waights *F*

674–675 *nonne ... sunt?* : *nonne ... sunt, F*

Notes to Sermon No. 6

10 aspersions]

Note: Here used in the obsolete sense of 'the sprinkling in of an ingredient' (*N.E.D.*).

89–90⎱
mg.⎰ Ier. 12.10 : Ier. 12.20 *F*

96 surfet. : surfet: *F*

108 contemptible : contemtible *F*

114 macerated]
Note: This participle is used in the obsolete sense of 'wasted away.' Cp. Vol. VII, p. 298, "starving, or macerating this body," and our note on "macerable," Vol. IX, p. 423.

132 it, : it *F*

167 it. : it, *F*

177 ff.⎱
mg.⎰ B. Virgo femoralia, etc.]

Note: This is a reference to *Miraculorum et exemplorum memorabilium sui temporis libri duo,* by Thomas Cantipratani, 1605.

179 assistance : assistant *F*

280 Scripture: : Scripture *F*

304 be beleeved : bebeleeved *F*

360 *mg. Sicut* : *Scicut F*

374 *mg.* 1 Tim. 4 : 1 Tim. 1 *F*

386 in *particular* : *in particular F*

406 on *Al* : one *F*

409 maters of *faith*]
Note: The spelling "mater" or "matier" from Old French *matere, matier,* is older than the form "matter," and it continued to be used in the sixteenth and seventeenth centuries. Nevertheless Donne generally uses "matter," and the spelling here may be the compositor's.

467 *Obturationem*]
Note: Though there is a verb *obturare,* 'to stop up,' in classical Latin, the noun *obturatio* does not seem to appear till medieval times, when it is found in records.

468 *Prov.* 25.26 : *Prov.* 35 *F*

471 For : *For F*

479 *me?* : *me; F*

530 that hasteth : hath hasteth *F*

533 wanton : wonton *F*

588–589⎱
mg.⎰ *Pes superbiæ* : *Pessuperbiæ F*

616   compasse; : compasse, *F*
625   can? : can. *F*
675   us, : us *F*

Notes to Sermon No. 7

45   boldly : bodily *F*
67   deserves : deserve *F*
84   *Roman* : *Romans F*
127 ff.⎫
  mg.⎬ 143 : 242 *F*

NOTE: According to the numbering of Augustine's *Epistles* which Donne generally uses (see line 612 of this sermon, and elsewhere), the Epistle quoted here should be 143. In the modern numbering it is 188.

152   been : been, *F*
167 *mg.*   Mat. 23.2 : Mat. 23.1 *F*
185   contract *Al* : contact *F*
224–225⎫
  mg.⎬ Iohn 3.5 : Iohn 3.3 *F*
239   *Ecclesiæ,* : *Ecclesiæ F*
247–248   Nor, as their *Dorotheus, . . . honey*]

NOTE: Donne had used this story in *Biathanatos* (written *ca.* 1608 but not published till 1647), p. 139. See also *Pseudo-Martyr* (1610), pp. 177–178.

249   *that* : that *F*
276 *mg.*   1.15 : 1.13 *F*
276   fellows : fellows, *F*
289–290⎫
  mg.⎬ Eccles. 7.3 : Eccles. 7.5 *F*
320   became : become *F*
347–359   yet the Heretiques went so far . . . a Martyr]

NOTE: The examples given here of the *Euphemitæ,* the *Circumcelliones,* and of Petilian, with the quotation from Augustine about the Donatists, are all repeated from *Biathanatos,* pp. 69–70, where marginal references are supplied.

421–422   *Luther? . . . Esdras?* : *Luther, . . . Esdras; F*
479   is, : is) *F*

LINE

497 *Æsop* : *Esop F*

509 *mg.* Acosta]
NOTE: This mention of José Acosta is repeated from *Essays in Divinity* (1952 edition, p. 84), where a reference is given to Acosta's book, *De procuranda Indorum salute*, l. 2, c. 9.

517 amazing : a mazing *F*

609 particular, : particular) *F*

625 *agreed?* : *agreed, F*

667 *mg.* Ioh. 2.7 : Ioh. 2.4 *F*

683 grasse : grass *Al* : grace *F*

687 work. : work, *F*

687 *mg.* Joh. 4.34 : Joh. 4.2 *F* (where it follows "work," in the body of the sermon)

Notes to Sermon No. 8

Text Gen. 3.14 : Gen. 3.24 *F*

7 fact]
NOTE: Here used in the now obsolete sense of 'action,' which was the original meaning in the sixteenth century. See *N.E.D.*

10 Feuillans : Fueillans *F*
NOTE: The Feuillants, of Les Feuillans near Toulouse, were a community of reformed Cistercians founded by Abbot J. de la Barrière in 1577. The murderer of Henri IV, François Ravaillac, was at one time a novice of the community.

52 life). : life. *F*

66 scape] escape *Al*

68–69 *The Lord ... God* : The Lord ... God *F*

76 ordinarily : ordinarinly *F*

81 is God *F corr.* : is Gon *F originally*

83 over-tender : over tender *F*

83 for eating : foreating *F*

85 melancholy : malancholy *F*

89 *mg.* Numb. 22.6 : Numb. 22.5 *F*

93 *Hast ... hony?* : Hast ... hony, *F*

95 *eate, ... sufficient* : eate, ... sufficient *F*

95–96 *mg.* 1 Sam. 14.27 : 1 Sam. 14.17 *F*

LINE

108–109 | mg. } Gen. 38.9 : Gen. 38.2 *F*

124 *mg.* Num. 22.28 : Num. 28.22 *F*

151 *Adam* and *Eve* both, : *Adam,* and *Eve* both *F*

199–200 understand *Al* : understands *F*

214–215 | mg. } Rom. 6.16 : Rom. 6.18 *F*

214 *your selves* : *your F*
NOTE: *"selves"* must be supplied from *Rom.* 6.16.

269 occasion; : occasion;) *F*

325 *mg.* 4.13 : 4.14 *F*

346 his dust : hisdust *F*

349 *mg.* Gen. 3.19 : Gen. 3.18 *F*

393–394 | mg. } Numb. 21.9 : Numb. 12.18 *F*

399–400 bargaines,... hedgings : bargaines ... hedgings, *F*

440–441 | mg. } 2 Sam. 6 : 2 Sam. 5 *F*

453 a good *Gomer* of Manna]
NOTE: Donne always uses the form *gomer* for the Hebrew measure equal to the tenth part of an ephah, used in *Exod.* 16.33, 36, where the A.V. transliterates עֹמֶר as *Omer,* the form now used. *N.E.D.* explains that from 1000 to 1631 the English form was *gomer* or *gomor,* from the Vulgate *gomor,* Septuagint γομόρ, which is used in Aelfric's *Exodus,* and also by Wyclif. Cp. *Sermons,* Vol. IX, p. 102, "nor satisfied with his Gomer of Manna." Here, again, we see Donne's preference for the Vulgate over the more correct form in A.V.

Notes to Sermon No. 9

20 *man.* : *man, F*

21 evacuation *F corr.* : evacation *F originally*
NOTE: It has recently been discovered that the Carlisle Cathedral copy of *Fifty Sermons* has the uncorrected state of p. 446 (Pp 2ᵛ).

27–28 unsmotherable, *F. corr.* : unsmotherable *F originally*

34 inflict : inflict *F*

49 (it *F corr.* : (if *F. originally*

62   *figurative, F corr.* :   *figurative F originally*

67   *man*: As *F corr.* :   *man,* as *F originally*

70   *infirmatur, Who* :   *infirmatur who F*

80–81   afflictions, . . . nature; :   afflictions; . . . nature, *F*

117   part *Al* :   art *F*

125   colluctation]
      NOTE: 'A wrestling or struggling together; strife, conflict' (*N.E.D.*).

134–135   *all . . . Earth* :   all . . . Earth *F*

183–233   There are . . . *four words,* by which man is called . . . *Gheber.*]
      NOTE: This passage resembles one in Vol. IX, pp. 61–62: "I remember foure names, by which man is often called in the Scriptures: and of those foure, three doe absolutely carry misery in their significations: . . . One name of man is *Ish;* and that they derive *à Sonitu;* Man is but a voice, but a sound, but a noise, . . . Another name is *Enosh. Enosh* is meer Calamity, misery, depression. . . . One name man hath, that hath some taste of greatnesse, and power in it, *Gheber.* And yet, I that am that man, says the Prophet, (for there that name of man *Gheber* is used) *I am the man, that hath seen affliction, by the rod of Gods wrath.*"

254   but :   *but F*

280   *Seal* :   seal *F*

280–281   No man may refuse *a Privy Seal,* because he hath lent before]
      NOTE: *Privy Seal* is here used in the sense, now merely historical, of a warrant under the privy seal demanding a loan, hence a forced loan, or benevolence. See Vol. IV, pp. 26–27, for the use of these forced loans by James I.

284 *mg.*   Cap. 20.2 :   Cap. 20.1 *F*

321   some time *Al* :   sometime *F*

332   *the rod of his wrath* :   *the rod of his mouth F, Al*
      NOTE: Since Donne is here quoting his text (*Lam.* 3.1), and elsewhere throughout the sermon it is always printed as *the rod of his wrath,* it seems clear that *mouth* here is merely a slip, perhaps due to confusion with *Isa.* 11.4: "he shall smite the earth with the rod of his mouth."

344 *mg.*   1 Sam. 26.12 :   1 Sam. 26.22 *F*

348   be *His* :   *be His F*

386   is *his F corr.* :   *is his F originally*

LINE

400   they are : they *are F*

410   inning]

NOTE: This verbal substantive was used in the sixteenth and seventeenth centuries to denote the action of getting in, especially of crops (*N.E.D.*)

429–430 *and that . . . And* : and *that . . .* And *F*

438   broken-hearted : broken hearted *F*

537   others. We : others, We *F*

551   Psal. 55.22 : Psal. 55.23 *F*

553–554 *affliction* : *afffliction F*

563   *consumed*]

NOTE: In all copies of *F* which we have seen the "s" has failed to print.

588   *Jesus.*]

NOTE: Here the period has failed to print.

592–593 mg. Iob 16.20]

NOTE: This is the reference given in *F*, but it does not correspond with the words opposite in the text. We cannot find these exact words anywhere in *Job*, but they give the general sense of Job's complaint against his friends. Possibly the passage which Donne had in mind was *Job* 30.9–11.

609–610 mg. 2 Sam. 12.14 : 2 Sam. 12.13 *F*

613   life. : life; *F*

629   ill husbands]

NOTE: "Husband" is here used in the archaic sense of one who manages his affairs well or ill. See *N.E.D.*

632 *mg.* 2 Sam. 24.16 : 2 Sam. 24.18 *F*

653   *as I took* : as I took *F*

659   *(He . . . rod)* : (He . . . rod) *F*

660   *(he . . . staffe)* : (he . . . staffe) *F*

692–693 mg. Psal. 45.6 : Psal. 45.7 *F*

694   there it is : there its *F* : there is *Al*

711 and 732 than . . . than]

NOTE: After *Fifty Sermons* has consistently printed "then" for "than" throughout its course (as *LXXX Sermons* also does), in its last few pages it prints occasionally, as here, "than." See the notes on the variation between "than" and "then" in *A Sermon of Commemoration* (Vol. VIII, pp. 375, 376 n. 1).

Notes to Sermon No. 10

75 *mg.*   Bannez : Banner *F* (see line 52 *mg.*)
NOTE: The correct form of the name is Bañez.

92–93   *he will...love* : he will...love *F*
NOTE: *F* wrongly places "Zeph. 3.17" against line 90.

106–107 \
mg.   } Esay 62.5 : Esay 62.1 *F*

125–127   *he was...unbelief* : he was...unbelief *F*

127 *mg.*   Amb. : *Amo. F*

144   *Arke,* : *Arke; F*

158   mis-becomes]
NOTE: The hyphen is very faint, and has failed to print in some copies.

160   Servants; : Servants, *F*

173   slaine, : slaine *F*

183–184   from a commandment, ... departs : from a commandment ... departs, *F*

206   reducing]
NOTE: Here used in the sense of 'leading or bringing back,' now obsolete, but common in the sixteenth and seventeenth centuries. Cp. Vol. II, p. 159, line 559.

218   Religation]
NOTE: This rare word means 'the action of tying or binding up' (*N.E.D.*).

243   *in sudore* : in *sudore F*

261   *in Temporalibus* : in *Temporalibus F*

264–266   Rejoyce ... joy]
NOTE: *F* here prints "Reioyce ... ioy," a strange return to the earlier practice of printing "i" for "j" which had been abandoned in England soon after 1630. See also two later passages in lines 432–441 and 479–484, where there are nine examples of "i" for "j." It is possible that the compositor found a shortage of lower-case "j," but he always uses capital "J."

LINE

272   to damn : to / to damn *F*

299, 307
and   } *in bonis* : in *bonis F*
314, 315

NOTE: In lines 260 *mg.* and 365 we have correctly *In bonis,* and in line 364 *mg. In malis.*

300   When a *Edd.* : When in a *F, Al*

319–321 meetings, are ... which are : meetings, which are ... which are *F*

NOTE: The sentence as it stands in *F* lacks a principal verb. The eye of the scribe or the printer probably caught up "which" from the succeeding line.

350   part : patr *F*

410   suscitate]

NOTE: This verb meaning 'to stir up, to excite' is now rare, though *N.E.D.* quotes several nineteenth-century examples.

445   *Rejoyce ... always* : Rejoyce ... always *F*

479   all thing]

NOTE: "All thing" was used adverbially in the sixteenth and seventeenth centuries to mean 'wholly, altogether.' Cp. Shakespeare, *Macbeth,* III, i, 12–13:

> "It had been as a gap in our great feast,
> And all-thing unbecoming."

530   *delectant?* : *delectant: F*

532   way? : way, *F*

533   *David. ... die,* : *David; ... die. F*

566 *mg.* Matt. 19.17 : Mat. 9.15 *F*

566   *Life,* : *Life. F*

Notes to Sermon No. 11

[This sermon presents special difficulties to the editor. It appeared in the seventeenth century in three forms: the Quarto of 1632 (*Q1*), the Quarto of 1633 (*Q2*), and the Folio of 1660/1 (*F*). John Hayward, editor of the Nonesuch Press collection, *John Donne: Complete Poetry and Selected Prose* (1929), who has printed this sermon in full, has chosen *Q1* for his basic text, but has included a few obvious corrections from *F,* and the American publishers of the Random House editions (1941, 1952) have followed him in this. On the other hand, Alford in his *Works of Donne* (1839) based his text on *F,* and Sir Geoffrey Keynes in the Nonesuch *X Sermons* (1923) did the same. There are plausible reasons for preferring *F,* which has the authority of Donne's son and is considerably easier to read than the text of *Q1,* which uses an excessive number of italics and also the older spelling and punctuation. We have nevertheless decided to base our text on *Q1* (with occasional help from *Q2*), admitting, however, a number of corrections from *F,* which certainly in some places had the better text and often the better punctuation. In a few places we have had to emend the punctuation of both *Q* and *F* in order to make Donne's meaning clear (see lines 303, 336, 567).

We have preferred to use *Q* as our basic text because it is possible that *Q* has Donne's own authority, and it almost certainly has the authority of Henry King (later Bishop of Chichester), who was one of Donne's two executors. On the question whether Donne himself authorized the preparation of this sermon for the press, see Helen Gardner, *Divine Poems of Donne* (Oxford, 1952), pp. 112–113. Writing on the line of hexameter Latin verse, "Corporis hæc Animæ sit Syndon, Syndon Jesu," which is printed beneath the portrait of Donne in his shroud prefixed to both *Q1* and *Q2,* she states: "I cannot believe that anyone but Donne wrote this line of verse, and it was plainly written for one purpose only: to stand beneath this picture of himself in his shroud. It has no point without the picture. I wish to suggest that Donne's last sermon, with its splendid title: *Deaths Duell, or a Consolation to the Soule, against the dying Life, and living Death of the Body,* and with this striking frontispiece prefixed, was published in accordance with instructions which he himself gave; and that we should add to his activities in his last illness, the arrangements for the publication of his last sermon and the composition of this epigraph."

To this Sir Geoffrey Keynes objects that the book was not entered at Stationers' Hall until September 30, 1631, six months after Donne's death, and not published until sometime in 1632. He thinks this suggests that the plans for publication were not made till after Donne's death.[1] The

---

[1] *Bibliography of Dr. John Donne,* 3d edition, 1958, p. 43. Keynes goes on to mention that the title *Deaths Duell* was claimed as his own by Walter Colman, a friar educated at Douay, who complained in doggerel at the end of his book, *La Danse Machabre or Deaths Duel,* 1633, that the title had been stolen from him by Roger Muchill, i.e., Mitchell, a bookseller at the Bull's Head, St. Paul's Churchyard, from 1627 to 1631. "Colman's lines are headed: *The Authors Apologie for the title of his Booke iniuriously conferd by Roger Muchill, upon a Sermon of Doctor*

delay, however, was not very long, and whether or no Donne himself was responsible for the title, it seems likely that he had authorized the publication of this his last sermon.

We are on surer ground with Henry King's authority. He was the author of the first poem printed at the end of the sermon, *An elegie, On Dr. Donne, Deane of Pauls,* and though it is unsigned here, it was printed in the *Poems* of 1633 with his name. As Donne's executor he had the right to dispose of Donne's manuscripts, and in a letter printed long afterward by Walton he wrote that it was at his "restless importunity" that Donne had prepared his sermons for the press, and that "three days before his death" he had delivered the sermons into King's hands together with "all his Sermon-Notes and his other Papers, containing an Extract of near Fifteen hundred Authours."[2] When *Deaths Duell* appeared in 1632 with its portrait of Donne, its address "To the Reader," and its two elegies to Donne's memory, it was clearly intended to be the authoritative version of his last sermon.

Next, this quarto is much nearer in general appearance, in spelling, and in its use of italics to the sermons published in Donne's lifetime with his own authority.[3] Thus, throughout *Deaths Duell* "God" and "Christ" are italicized as they are in our Vol. IV, No. 7, lines 1, 6, 10, 14, 15, 18, 26, *et passim,* while in the Folio they are consistently printed in roman. Again, in the Quarto of *Deaths Duell* we frequently find italics used for any words on which Donne desired to lay a slight stress, as similarly in the sermons published in Donne's lifetime.[4] In spelling we find in the Quarto "wee," "hee," "bee" used much more frequently than "we," "he," "be," and there are many more words with an unnecessary final "e" than can be found in the Folio. Similarly, in the sermons published in Donne's lifetime, we find, e.g., "sweete" (Vol. IV, No. 7, line 1), "weake" (18),

---

Donnes, and he followed them with an abusive epitaph on 'Muchill,' who died, it seems, before the publication of either book, the rights in Donne's sermon passing to Richard Redmer." Keynes refers to his previous article on this subject in the *Times Literary Supplement* of September 24, 1938.

[2] Walton, *Lives* (1670), Life of Donne, p. 2.

[3] These are printed in our edition as Nos. 7, 10, and 15 of Vol. IV, No. 12 of Vol. VI, No. 2 of Vol. VII, and No. 2 of Vol. VIII.

[4] Many examples might be given, e.g., "There have beene *Verball Heresies,* and *Heresies* that were but *Syllabicall;* little *Præpositions* made *Heresies;* not onely *State-præpositions,* Precedencies, and Prerogatives of *Church* above *Church,* occasioned great *Schismes,* but *Literall Præpositions, Præpositions* in *Grammar,* occasioned great *Heresies.*" (Vol. VI, No. 12, lines 213–217.) *Deaths Duell* is full of similar examples.

"wee" (24), *"againe"* (43), "bargaine" (45), "zeale" (50), "weake" (51),
etc. Also, such words as "mortal," "natural," "sin," "son," and the like,
which usually appear in the Folio in their modern spelling, are almost
invariably spelt in the Quarto as "mortall" (line 230), "naturall" (27),
"sinne" (201), "sonne" (347), while in the sermons published in Donne's
lifetime we find the same doubled consonants, e.g., "wonderfull" (Vol.
IV, No. 7, line 17), "sinne" (21), "Literall" (76), "collaterall" (77),
"occasionall" (78). Since Donne himself superintended the publication
of these sermons, he must have liked their general appearance, crowded
with italics some of which seem to us unnecessary, and preserving spellings
which were beginning to be obsolete when the Folios, in particular the
Folio of 1660/1, were published. Therefore, by keeping the Quarto text
of *Deaths Duell* in these minor matters this sermon printed in 1632 is
linked with those which Donne had seen through the press in 1622, 1625,
1626, and 1628.

However, we must admit that the text of the Quarto is frequently
unsatisfactory, and its punctuation (or lack of it) often obscures Donne's
meaning. Donne may have written out the sermon himself at the time of
his fatal illness, and his punctuation, if we may judge from his autograph
letters,[5] was light and scanty. Certain words must have been very badly
written, e.g. "flesh" in lines 130 and 297 of Q appears in the extraordinary
form *"hestae,"* whereas it is correctly printed in F. However, F has a
number of bad misprints of its own, such as "havh" for "have" in line 150,
"morimer" for *"morimur"* in line 157, "peromptory" for "peremptory"
in line 344, "viseral" for "visceral" in line 553, and "humilty" for
"humility" in line 587. These have not been recorded in our textual
apparatus, as they are clearly due to scribal or printer's errors, and Q
supplies us the correct text.

Finally, as Q was published almost thirty years before F, it has a strong
prior claim on an editor's attention. In the process of time such antique
forms as "rubbidge" (line 328) or *"Canapye"* (line 326) were altered to
"rubbish" and "canopy" in F.

The text of F, however, must be carefully considered by editors of the
Sermons. It was certainly not printed from Q, as is proved by the fact
that it contains passages which had been omitted by Q through homœoteleuton, such as "...purpose of God; because the purpose of God was
manifest to him" in lines 289–290, where Q has omitted "because the
purpose of God," or in lines 504–506, where Q omits "He wept over

---

[5] We have, unfortunately, no poems or sermons in his autograph, and
are obliged to rely entirely on his autograph letters, which are few.

Jerusalem out of his love, and his love determined not there," because the clause was preceded by another "not there." Another point in which *F* differs from *Q* is in the position of the sentence "for the *mercies* of God worke *momentarily*... departing" (lines 379–381), which is more suitably placed in *F* after "but not to despaire" than in *Q*. Also there are a large number of minor variants such as "saies" or "sayes" for "saith," "which" for "that," "shall be extended" for "shall extend," and the like, which show conclusively that *F* was not derived from *Q*, but that John Donne must have been in possession of a better copy of the sermon than that used by the printer of *Q*. We have therefore made an exhaustive study of the differences between the two texts, and have recorded all the readings of *F* which are substantially different from those of *Q*.

The Second Quarto, of 1633, is much rarer than the First, and is of less importance. There are many changes in spelling, and a few in punctuation, but any substantive change of words is a change for the worse, and is clearly due to the printer's error. Thus in line 11 of the address to the reader the word "not" has been omitted, to the detriment of the sense. In the sermon itself, in lines 105–106, *Q2* omits the words "for even the *wombe* is a *body of death*," through homœoteleuton, because "*body of death*" had preceded this clause. Here *F* follows *Q1* in retaining the clause, though it reads "*the* body" for "*a* body." Again, in line 137 *Q2* omits the words "there *are many mansions*," which are found in *Q1*, while *F* reads "there are many, and mansions." In lines 278–279 the words of *Q1* (supported by *F*), "should be so) so *Gods decrees* are ever to be considered" appear incorrectly in *Q2* as "should be so) so we rest on *Gods decrees* are ever to be considered." In matters of punctuation *Q2* is sometimes better than *Q1* in providing a comma where one is needed, or a semicolon where *Q1* has only a comma. Such instances are recorded in our apparatus, where it will be found that in these particulars *Q2* and *F* generally agree. This does not imply that *F* made use of *Q2*; it is merely an indication that the printers of both *Q2* and *F* felt that the punctuation of *Q1* was inadequate.

In the following textual notes *Q* denotes the agreement of both quartos but the spelling given is that of *Q1*. Where the Quartos differ otherwise than in spelling or unimportant punctuation they are distinguished as *Q1* and *Q2*, but sheer blunders in *Q2* are not recorded except as mentioned above.

For our text of *Q1* we have collated three copies in Oxford: that in the Bodleian Library, that in the Magdalen College Library, and that in the possession of the surviving editor, and microfilms of three American copies: one in the Folger Shakespeare Library, one in the Harvard University Library, and one in the Huntington Library.]

Title DEATHS / DVELL, / OR, / A Consolation to the Soule, against / the dying Life, and liuing / Death of the Body. / *Deliuered in a Sermon at White Hall, before the* / KINGS MAIESTY, *in the beginning* / *of Lent*, 1630. / By that late learned and Reuerend Diuine, / IOHN DONNE, Dʳ in Diunity, / & Deane of S. *Pauls*, London. / *Being his last Sermon, and called by his Maiesties houshold* / THE DOC-TORS OWNE FVNERALL SERMON. / [ornament] / LONDON, / Printed by THOMAS HARPER, for *Richard Redmer* / and *Beniamin Fisher*, and are to be sold at the signe / of the Talbot in Alders-gate street. / M.DC.XXXII.

Q1 : *om.* F (which also omits the portrait of Donne)

DEATHS / DVELL, / OR, / A Consolation to the Soule, against / the dying Life, and living Death / of the Body. / *De-liuered in a Sermon at White-Hall,* / *before the* KINGS MAIESTIE, *in the* / *beginning of Lent,* 1630. / By that late Learned and Reverend Divine, / IOHN DONNE, Dr. in Divinity, / and Deane of S. Pauls, London. / *Being his last Sermon, and called by his Maiesties houshold* / THE DOC-TERS OWNE FVNERAL SERMON. /[a different ornament from that in *Q1*] / LONDON / Printed by *B. Alsop,* and *T. Fawcet,* for *Ben-*/*iamin Fisher,* and are to be sold at the Signe of / the *Talbot* in *Aldersgate-street.* / M.DC.XXXIII.

Q2

NOTE: The title page of *Q2* shows a number of inconsistencies in the printing of consonantal "i" and "u." The change to printing these as "j" and "v" was taking place in London in the years 1632–1633, and this is reflected in the fact that the "liuing," "Reuerend," "Diuine," and "Diuinity" of *Q1* have become "living," "Reverend," "Divine," and "Divinity" here, although "Deliuered" retains its medial "u," and the "i" of *"Maiesties"* and *"Beniamin"* is also retained. The *Six Sermons* of 1634 show that by then the change had become complete.

Keynes, *op. cit.,* pp. 43–44, reports that certain copies are found with the title page of *Q2* and the sheets of *Q1*. He also notes that he possesses a copy of *Q2* with a different setting of the first sheet. From the list of the variants which he has kindly sent us it seems clear that this is really an earlier state than the corrected one found in all other known copies. The variants include *"Aldersgat-streete"* for *"Aldersgate-street"* on the title page, and in the address to the reader *"the last"* for *"his last,"* and *"freely, and with least affection"* for *"feelingly, and with least affectation,"* in addition to some variants in spelling. Keynes also records (p. 42) that "A copy in the Folger Shakespeare Memorial Library at Washington (formerly the Harmsworth copy) contains an extra leaf inserted between A3 and A4 with a dedicatory letter, *To his dearest sister Mrs Elizabeth Francis of Brumstead in Norff.*, signed *Rich. Redmer."*

LINE

To the ⎱
Reader ⎰ ... *shall last.* R.] *om. F*

Text   vers. 20. In fine.] 20 *F*
      LORD : (LORD) *Q* : *Lord F*
      i.e.]*om. F*

1–2   susteine and] sustain them, *F*
2–3   comprehend and] comprehend them, *F*
4   *foundations* suffer] foundation suffers *F*
5   and the] the *F*
5   suffers] suffer *F*
6   *cleave.* : *cleave; Q* : cleave. *F*
7   our God] our God, *Q2, F*
7–8   *salvation; ad salutes F* : *salvation* and *salutes Q*
8   salvations *F* : salvation *Q*
10   *contignations*] contignation *F*
12   expositors, *F* : expositors. *Q*
13 *mg.*   *Of*] *om. F*
      NOTE: The existence of this marginal *Of* in *Q* shows that *Q* should have read *of death* also in the text.
13   *of death.* For *F* : *from death,* for *Q*
15   *belong*] *belongs F*
15   in his] his *F*
22   *secondly, Q2* : *secondly Q1* : Secondly, *F*
28   shaken] shak'd *F*
31   *wayes*] way *F*
33   *issue*] issue *F* : *issues Q*

LINE

36 this *F* : in this *Q*

NOTE: Here "this *sense*" is the object of the verb "doth . . . administer" and "the naturall frame" is the subject, so that no "in" is required.

37 us. *F* : us; *Q*

39 *salvations*] salvation *F*

39–40 *Unto this God F* : unto this *God Q*

45, 52 this *issue*] the issue *F*

50–51 *And then, Q2* : *And then Q1* : and then, *F*

56 *death,* shall . . . *life.* : *death* (shall . . . *life.*) *Q*

56–58 }
mg. } *A morte, in morte, per mortem*] *om. F*

57 considerations, *F* : considerations? *Q*

59–62 }
mg. } Foundation, butteresses and contignation] *om. F*

63 *mg.* 1 Part] First Part *F*

64 *mg.* *A morte F* : *om. Q*

65 deaths *F* : death *Q*

66 him; and all *F* : him. In all *Q*

67 *death.* Our : *death;* our *Q* : death. Our *F*

68–69 }
mg. } *Exitus à morte uteri* : *Exitus a morte uteri Q, F*

71 unto] to *F*

77 being dead, *Q2, F* : being dead *Q1*

82 and may be *damned,* though we be *never borne*]

NOTE: It would be contrary to the whole tenor of Donne's teaching to suppose he meant that the soul of an unborn infant could be damned, seeing that he held that unbaptized infants could be saved (see p. 355, n. 20, of the present volume). The whole passage is highly rhetorical, and we believe that there is here a word-play on *damned* and *dammed,* as elsewhere (Vol. VII, p. 59) "though it damne not the man, yet it dammes up that mans way." Donne has already described (lines 75–76) a dead child in the womb as "a murderer, nay a *parricide*" if it cannot be extracted, and in the same strain he says that the child may be thought of as damned, that is, *dammed* in the womb. The only difficulty is that we might have expected him to make this macabre pun more explicit by supplying "up," as in the quotation above.

LINE

83 *mg.*   Psal. 139.14 *F*   :   Psal. 139.6 *Q* (which refers, however, to the quotation "Such knowledge . . ." one line later)

84   and, *Such F*   :   and such *Q*

85   *and it F*   :   and it *Q*

85   *eyes. F*   :   *eyes; Q*

86 *mg.*   100.3] 200.3 *F*

86   *it is*   :   it is *Q*

86   no, nor *F*   :   nor *Q*

88 *mg.*   10.8 *F*   :   *om. Q*

88   saith] saies *F*

96   nor] not *F*

97 *mg.*   Esa. 37.3 *F*   :   Esay 37. *Q* (which wrongly places the reference against line 99)

97   and there is not *F*   :   and *no Q*

99   It is]
        NOTE: *F* continues without starting a new paragraph.

100 *mg.*   Ose. 9.14*F*   :   *om. Q*

100   highth *F*   :   highest *Q*

101   *Give F*   :   *give Q*

101–102   *give them a F*   :   give them a *Q*

102–103   (that is, inanimated, . . . womb) *F*   :   (that is, *inanimated*) . . . *womb) Q*

104   reason *F*   :   *om. Q*

104   behalf] behalves *F*

105–106   for even . . . *of death*] *om. Q*2

106   a *body*] the body *F*

107   *Before F*   :   Before *Q*

107   *and F*   :   and *Q*

107 *mg.*   1.5 *F*   :   *om. Q*

110   *Arke.* That] Ark; that *F*

111   useth] uses *F*

112   *Thebah F*   :   *Theball Q*

113   in, that *F*   :   *in,* That *Q*

113 *mg.*   Exo. 2.3 *F*   :   Exo. 23 *Q*

117   *enabled*] hath enabled *F*

117–118   that *infus'd* . . . that *brought*] hath infus'd . . . hath brought *F*

119   *quickened;*   :   *quickened, Q*

123–125 *mg.*   NOTE: *Q* incorrectly places *Exitus a mortibus mundi* opposite line 120.

LINE

123 But then]
NOTE: We have followed *F* in beginning a new paragraph here. The paragraphs of *Q* are inordinately long.

123 *a morte*] (*a mortibus* in margin)
NOTE: This is the reading of *Q* and *F*, so we have retained it, though *Q* has previously read "*à morte*" in line 68.

126 *world.* Wee : *world,* wee *Q*

126 which] that *F*

130 flesh, *F* : *hestæ Q*

131 there. We *F* : there; wee *Q*

132 funeralls] funeral *F*

133 *of* : *om. Q* : of *F*

134 thereof. We *F* : thereof; we *Q*

34–135 one Baptism with another, a sacrament of tears *F* : our *Baptisme,* with another *Sacrament,* with *teares Q*

136 not. *In F* : not; *in Q*

136 our blessed *F* : our *Q*

137 there *are many mansions*] *om. Q2* : there are many, and mansions *F*

145 *The Son F* : the *sonne Q*

146 *Nonne ... hominum?*] No? ... *hominum. F*

151 no persons, *Q2* : no persons *Q1* : no we, no persons *F*

153 Mansions, the *F* : mansions; The *Q*

155 that measure *F* : what measure *Q*

156 *Pharaoh, The daies of the years of F* : *Pharaoh; the dayes* of the years *of Q*

161 our] one *F*

163 their graves *F* : their grave, *Q*

164–165 *a week of deaths* : a *weeke of death Q* : a week of deaths *F*
NOTE: The genitive plural *mortium* just before indicates that the reading of *F* is to be preferred.

166 there is] ther's *F*

171 a *caryon,*] carrion, *F*
NOTE: The Harvard copy of *Q1* has a semicolon instead of a comma.

175 did. And *F* : *did; & Q*

178 them. *F* : them: *Q*

178 doth] does *F* (so also in line 270)

LINE

180   *forth ... O F* : forth ... O *Q*

181   *and no eye had seen me; I should have been, ... been F* : and no eye seene me? I should have beene ... beene *Q*

182   And not] (*Q* continues without beginning a new paragraph here)

183   *hand*] *hands F*

185   juniper tree *F* : *Iunipertree Q*

186 *mg.* 1 Reg. 19.4 *F* : Rev. 19.4 *Q*

186   *It is enough, now F* : *it is enough now, Q*

188–189 *better for me to F* : *better to Q*

190–191 *for this,* and after, (about the Gourd) *dost thou well to be angry for that,* he replies *F* : *for this,* he replyes *Q*

       NOTE: In the whole of this passage from line 185 to line 191 *F* follows A.V. more closely and accurately than *Q* does.

191–192 *death.* How *F* : *death,* how *Q*

193   as] *om. F*

194 *mg.* 1 Cor. 15.31 *F* : *om. Q*

195 *mg.* Psa. 44.22 : psa. 44.22 *F* : *om. Q*

195–196 *mortificamur, F* : *mortificamur; Q*

197   fall] fals *F*

198 *mg.* 51.5 *F* : *om. Q*

198–199 *I was shapen in* : *I was shapen* in *Q*

201   *child of wrath,* of the wrath] child of the wrath *F*

211   But then] (*Q* does not begin a new paragraph here)

212   spirituall death] spirituall deaths *F*

213   not. Though ... *morte,* it *F* : not, though ... *morte;* It *Q*

213 ff.⎫
  mg.⎬ *Exitus ... Incinerationis*]

       NOTE: This is placed by *F* against line 211.

214   the manifold *F* : manifold *Q*

218–219 *corruption.* What : *corruption:* what *Q*

222   but it] but yet *F*

222   ever. What *F* : ever: what *Q*

224   'Tis *F* : 'tis *Q*

224–225⎫
 mg.⎬ 1 Cor. 15.53 : 1. Cor. 15. vers. 33 *Q* : 1 C. 15.33 *F*

227   nor *F* : no, *Q*

232   himself. What *F* : himself; what *Q*

233   natures, *F* : *natures? Q*

LINE

233 him] his flesh *F*

234 and *incineration*] this incineration *F*

237 embalm'd so, *F* : embalmd, so *Q*

238 it selfe] *om. F*

239 remained] remain *F*

240–241 this ... this *F* : this ... his *Q*

242 all this *F* : all his *Q*

243 of the] of *F*

244–245 death, (as ... lasts) *F* : *death* as ... lasts *Q*

245 is properly] is, (properly) *F*

249 *dissolution*] dissolving *F*

252 his *soul*] soul *F*

256 that, *F* : that; *Q*

257 *corruption.* We *F* : *corruption,* wee *Q*

257 further] farther *F*

258 *religion*] our religion *F*

260 *seemed* : seemed *F* : *seemeth Q*

263–264 and his decrees; but then, it is upon those purposes, and decrees
     F : and the decrees *Q*
     NOTE: *Q* seems to have omitted the words found in *F* by
     homœoteleuton.

264–265 manifested; not *F* : manifested not *Q*

266 *verisimilitude.* So, ... case, : *veresimilitude,* so ... case *Q* :
     verisimilitude. So, ... case, *F*

267 proceeded *F* : proceeds *Q*

268 have *bene risen* without seeing] be risen without having seen *F*

270 *Prophet.* Therefore : *Prophet,* therefore *Q* : Prophet.
     Therefore *F*

273 words] word *F*

277 *rest* on] rest in *F*

277 purpose, *F* : purpose. *Q*

277 so, *F* : so *Q*

278–279 so *Gods decrees* ... considered] so we rest on *Gods decrees* are
     ever to be considered *Q*2

283 *God,* : *God Q* : God, *F*

286 then, and so *F* : Then so *Q*

287 so, *F* : so; *Q*

289 the purpose of *God;* because the purpose : the purpose *Q* :
     The purpose of God; because the purpose *F*

LINE

291 before, *F* : before *Q*
Note: The punctuation of *F* is correct, as "before" is here the adverb, not the preposition.

295 Now this]
Note: We have followed *F* in starting a new paragraph with these words.

297 extend] be extended *F*

297 *flesh* : *Hestæ Q* : flesh *F*

298–299 mg. 1 Cor. 15.51 *F* : *om. Q*

298–299 (as the Apostle ... *mystery*) *F* : as th' *Apostle* ... *mistery, Q*

300–301 *changed.* In an instant *F* : *changed in an instant, Q*

302 *redintegration* : *redintgeration Q*

303 sleeping, no *Edd.* : sleeping no *F* : sleeping in *Q*

303–304 corruption. But *F* : corruption; But *Q*

308 grave. When *F* : *grave,* when *Q*

308 those *F* : these *Q*

310 *mg.* 17.14 *F* : *om. Q*

310 *to corruption F* : *Corruption Q*

316 *mg.* 24.20 *F* : Vers. 24.20 *Q*

318 if *F* : *if Q*

320 *mg.* Iob 21.23 : Iob 23.24 *Q* : 23.24 *F*

323–324 mg. [Isa.] 14.11 : Vers. 14.11 *Q* : 24.11 *F*

323 The worm covers them in *F* : In *Q*

325–326 There's ... there's] There is ... there is *F*

327 men. *F* : men; *Q*

328 rubbidge] rubbish *F*
Note: *N.E.D.* records numerous instances of "rubbidge" as a seventeenth-century form of "rubbish," but later it became obsolete except in dialect.

329 dust: *F* : dust, *Q*

329 hath] had *F*

330–331 mg. Esa. 41.14 *F* : *om. Q*

336 dust: That *Edd.* : dust. That *Q* : dust, that *F*
Note: The period in *Q* is too heavy, and it obscures the fact that the cause beginning with "That" is part of the preceding

sentence. On the other hand, the comma of *F* is too light. The extravagant length of the whole sentence, which begins with "Truely the consideration of this *posthume death*" in line 331, may inhibit our noticing that it possesses no principal verb; but all its subordinate clauses lead up to "This is" in line 343.

336 That that *Monarch*] that all that monarch *F*

341 mingled in his dust, with *F* : mingled with *Q*

345 consider. *F* : consider; *Q*

346–347⎫
 mg.⎭ 37.1 *F* : *om. Q*

347 *these*] *these dry F*

349 and breathed into them *F* : and *breath into them Q*

351 this thing] this, this *F*

352 can call *F* : call *Q*

354 nor never *F* : never *Q*

355 worms *F* : *worme, Q*

357 askt] (The "s" has failed to print in some copies of *Q*)

360–361 *reanimating*] re-inanimating *F*

364 And so have you]

NOTE: *Q* begins a new paragraph here consisting of only a few lines. It seems better to allow this sentence to close the paragraph, and then to follow *Q* rather than *F* in starting a new paragraph with the words "And so wee passe" in line 370.

368 *The Lord* : the *Lord Q*

374–376 the *Physitians* ... and the *rules*] Physitians ... and rules *F*

374–375 *presagitions*] præsagitions *F*

NOTE: *N.E.D.* records other examples of "presagition," but it does not record "præsagition." It states, however, that the prefix "præ-" in words derived from Latin is often found in sixteenth- and seventeenth-century texts. *F* prints the word as "presagition" in line 377.

377 give] ground *F*

378 *indication* : *iudication Q* : Indication *F*

NOTE: The context shows that the word required is "indication." In the first part of the sentence Donne had spoken of "indications" and "presagitions," and he now inverts the order and gives us "presagition" and "indication." "Judication" means 'the action of judging' (*N.E.D.*).

LINE

379–382   for the *mercies* . . . wee may]
Note: We use the language but not the order of *Q*. In *Q* the
words from "for the *mercies*" to "departing" appear later, after
"*loathnes* to *dye*" in line 400, but they are more suitably placed
here. It may be that Donne wrote them in the margin of the
page, and that the scribe of *Q* inserted them in the wrong place.

380   *momentarily*] momentanely *F*
Note: The reading of *F* is tempting, for Donne uses
"momentany" instead of "momentary" in Vol. I, No. 4, line
76: "the momentany pleasures of the body," but we have retained the reading of *Q*, for *N.E.D.* offers no instance of
"momentanely" but this passage from *F*.

381   departing, and *F* : departing. *Q*
382   wayes: *F* : wayes, *Q*
382   our selves *F* : our selfe *Q*
384   without] but with *F*
384   may bee] may have been *F*
386   suffered] admitted *F*
386   *colluctations* : *coluctations Q* : colluctations *F*
389–390   who said . . . *Heremit*)] who . . . Hermit) said *F*
390   death-turfe *F* : dead turfe *Q*

390–391 }
    } Hilarion *F* : *om. Q*
mg. }

391   *annos*] *annis F*
393   loath. *F* : loath; *Q*

393–394 }
    } Barlaam *F* : *om. Q*
mg. }

393   He *F* : *Bartaam Q*
394   too] *om. F*
394   that day] that day that *F*
394   died, *F* : dyed. *Q*
394   *Cogita te . . . cœpisse*] *Cogitate cœpisse F*
397   *if . . . be* : if . . . be *Q*
398   *to receive* : to *receive Q*
398   *Barlaam F* : *Bartaam Q*
399   for it *F* : forth *Q*
399   *conclusions*] conclusion *F*
400   *dye.* : *dye, Q*

LINE

401   malefactors, *F*   :   malefactors. *Q*

405   so. *F*   :   so; *Q*

407   *death*] deaths *F*

408–409   distempers neyther, *F*   :   *distempers,* neither *Q*

410   *God.* The   :   *God:* The *Q*   :   God. The *F*

411   *falles;*   :   *falles Q*   :   falls; *F*

411   'Tis *F*   :   its *Q*

411   yet *F*   :   om. *Q*

412   *last word* nor *gaspe*] last word, nor last gaspe *F*

414–415   *death . . . death*] Deaths . . . Deaths *F*

415   *conclusions*] conclusion *F*

419   *passively,*   :   *passively Q*   :   passively; *F*

422   *Church.*   :   *Church: Q*   :   Church. *F*

424   my bell *F*   :   the *Bell Q*

     NOTE: It was the custom to toll the church bell for a dying parishioner, and "my bell" means the bell that will be tolled for me when I am dying. In his *Devotions upon Emergent Occasions* (1623) Donne wrote, "Perchance hee for whom this *Bell* tolls, may bee so ill, as that he knowes not it *tolls* for him; . . ." (Meditation 17).

426   *vives F*   :   *vive Q*

     NOTE: The Vulgate of *Luke* 10.28 reads "Hoc fac, et vives."

426   *sayd*] spoken *F*

430   Live *F*   :   live *Q*

430   well, that is] well; well, that is *F*

436–437   or . . . or *F*   :   *or . . . or Q*

437   *hewen*] hew'd *F*

439   *cause*] course *F*

439   *are the*   :   are the *Q*

440   further] farther *F*

441   is *F*   :   *is, Q*

442   *agonies . . . body suffers*] agonie . . . body suffer *F*

443   death; but *F*   :   *death.* / But *Q* (beginning new paragraph)

443   *third part*] third *F*

444–445   another, by the *death* of *Christ.*   :   another. *Q*   :   another, by the death of Christ. *F*

446 *mg.*   Part. 3. . . . *per mortem F*   :   3. Part. . . . *per morte Q*

     NOTE: *Q* places this heading against line 443, where it begins the new paragraph with "But passe to our *third part* . . ."

LINE

446 *Sufferentiam Iob*]
     NOTE: We follow *F* in beginning a new paragraph here.

446 *audijstis, & vidistis Edd.* : *audijsti, & vidisti Q* : *audiistis & judistis F*
     NOTE: The Vulgate has "audistis et vidistis," and Donne writes in line 447 *"You have heard of the patience of Iob,"* thus confirming the use of the second person plural, as in *F*. On the other hand, *F* is wrong in printing *"judistis"* for *"vidistis."* A.V. translates, "Ye have heard of the patience of Job, and have seen the end of the Lord, ..."

449 speakes; *F* : speakes. *Q*
449 Now *see*] Now *see F*
450 that the *Lord*] which the Lord *F*
453 came to, *F* : *came to Q*
453 death. But *F* : death, but *Q*
456 *the issues*] these issues *F*
458 words? *F* : words. *Q*
458 this verse] the verse *F*
459 sayd, : sayd; *Q*
459 *He that F* : He that *Q*
461 *mg.* Mat. 1.21] (Wrongly placed in *Q* against line 462)
464–465 nature, he ... of it *F* : nature; *He* ... *of it Q*
465 then by Death. *F* : *but by death? Q*
465 sayes] saith *F*
466 *sayd, To* : *sayd.* To *Q* : said, *To F*
467 *to shew* : to *shew Q*
468 *Isiodore F* : *Isodore Q*
468 prove, *F* : prove; *Q*
472 *death. Oportuit* : *death, oportuit Q* : Death. *Oportuit F*
472 *pati, F* : *pati Q*
473 sayes] saith *F*
473–474 himself, ... *suffer; F* : himselfe; ... *suffer, Q*
474 death. *F* : death: *Q*
475 needes] necessarily *F*
479–480 your devotion *F* : the devotion *Q*
480–481 of the due *F* : of due *Q*
481–482 at the last] at last *F*
482 shed *F* : *om. Q*
486 *mg.* *Potuisse Mori F* : *om. Q*

LINE

486   That *God,* this *Lord*] *That God the Lord F*
      NOTE: We follow *F* in beginning a new paragraph here.

488   That *F* : that *Q*

488 *mg.* Exod. 14.21 *F* : *om. Q*

489 *mg.* Jos. 10.12 *F* : *om. Q*

492   said] saith *F*

493   *Augustin*)]
      NOTE: In some copies of *Q* the upper part of the round bracket
      has failed to print, so that the lower part might be mistaken for
      a comma.

494   says] saith *F*

495   suffer. *F* : suffer; *Q*

495 *mg.* Psal. 94.1 *F* : Psal. 9.1 *Q*

496–497
mg. } *Voluisse Mori F* : *om. Q*

495, 501 says] saith *F*

496   sin of man *F* : *sonne of man Q*

500   *strong*] as strong *F*

500   is] was *F*

503   *Many waters* : Many *waters Q* : Many waters *F*

504–506 there; He wept over *Jerusalem* out of his love, and his love
      determined not there; He *F* : there. He *Q*
      NOTE: The clause in *F* is certainly genuine, and has been
      omitted in *Q* by homœoteleuton.

508   *flagellation*] flagellations *F*

508   *God*] God) *F*

511–512
mg. } *Oportuisse Mori F* : *om. Q*

511   Hee *would not* spare]
      NOTE: We follow *F* in beginning a new paragraph here.

511   *would ... could*] would ... would *F*

513   *liberè* : *libere Q*

517   *that*] it *F*

517   begun? *F* : *begun. Q*

525   was, that *F* : was that, *Q*

527–528
mg. } Luk. 12.50 *F* : Luk. 12.40 *Q*

529   *for the* : for *the Q*

532   from them. When *F* : from him; when *Q*

LINE

533   passion *F* : *om. Q*

533   no worse, *F* : wee worse *Q*]
      NOTE: Hayward in his 1930 Nonesuch edition, p. 794, records
      Q1 as reading "not worse." We have not found any copies with
      this reading.

533   *Can F* : *can Q*

533–534 ⎱
mg. ⎰ Mat. 20.22 *F* : Mat. 22.22 *Q*

534   *Cuppe?* : *Cuppe Q* : *cup; F*

536   *to the*] *unto the F*

537–538 *salvation; take it, that Cup of salvation* : *salvation, take it,
      that Cup is salvation Q* : salvation. Take that, that cup of
      salvation *F*

539–540 that was] who was *F*

541   That *Moses*]
      NOTE: This is a new paragraph in *F*. *Q* continues its inor-
      dinately long paragraph which lasts to the end of the sermon.

542   tel *F* : tells *Q*

542   of, *F* : of *Q*

544   *Ierusalem.* : *Ierusalem, Q*

545   Text, *F* : *text Q*

548   *Christs* : *Christ Q* : Christs *F*

549   *blood,* and : *blood.* And *Q* : blood, and *F*

555   tenderness, *F* : terdernesse *Q*

556–557 cold . . . could] would . . . would *F*

557   *contigerit*] *contingat F*

557   *humanitus*] *humanitas F*

557   not *F* : nor *Q*

560   *and* : and *Q*

561   owne] *om. F*

562   freely *F* : frely *Q*

565   *often;* and : *often.* And *Q* : often; and *F*

565   *Nescivi* : *Ne scivi Q* : *Nescive F*

565–566 *I never knew* : I *never knew Q*

567   *death,* only *Edd.* : *death,* only, *Q* : death only *F*

569   *that.*] it. *F*

570   to *edification*] edification *F*

571   was in] was at *F*

575   *It is* : It *is Q* : It is *F*

577   *devotions*] devotion *F*

577   those] these *F*

579   Take in]

    NOTE: We follow *F* in beginning a new paragraph here.

579   the *whole*] his whole *F*

579   *received*] eat *F*

580   *unto*] to *F*

584   that *act*] the act *F*

588   those that] those who *F*

589   (and not else) *F* : and not els *Q*

589–590 this his *F* : his *Q*

593   before? : before. *Q*

595   night. *F* : night; *Q*

596 *mg.* Luk. 22.44 : Luk. 22.24 *Q* : Luc. 22.24 *F*

596   *prolixius; F* : *prolixious Q*

    NOTE: The Vulgate reads "prolixius orabat" in the passage from *Luke* which Donne quotes here.

596   prayer. How *F* : *prayer,* how *Q*

603   *his,* it : *his,* It *Q* : his; that it *F*

608   him. *F* : him; *Q*

612   From : from *Q, F*

613   *Caiphas Q, F*]

    NOTE: Donne is here using the form employed by the Vulgate in *Mat.* 26.3 and 57. A.V. has "Caiaphas," which is nearer to the Greek.

613   then] there *F*

619   *repentance.* How : *repentance,* how *Q* : repentance. How *F*

619   last night, *F* : *om. Q*

620   then *F* : *om. Q*

622   now. *F* : now; *Q*

623   so] as *F*

624   *hall*] house *F*

625–626 *Iudge.* Diddest : *Iudge;* diddest *Q* : Judg. Didst *F*

627   to admit even *F* : even with *Q*

630   him. *F* : him: *Q*

638   it, to *F* : it to *Q*

643   chose *F* : *choose Q*

643   *Barrabas;* : *Barrabas, Q*

LINE

644 *death,* : *death; Q* : death, *F*

646 *ignominious* : *ignominous Q* : ignominious *F*

646 *contumelies Q2, F* : *contumlies Q1*

646 this redeem'd *F* : they regarded *Q*

NOTE: Both readings are possible, but we have preferred "re-deem'd" because in the next line Donne writes, "Hast thou gone about to *redeeme thy sinne, by fasting, . . . ?*"

648 *mortifications,* : *mortifications? Q*

648–649 in the way *F* : in way *Q*

649 that's *F* : thats *Q*

658 light *F* : sight *Q*

NOTE: Here again, though both readings are possible, we have preferred that of *F*, because Donne seems to be referring to it in the next clause, "the *Sun . . . departed with his light too.*"

659 then] there *F*

661–662 *hands*) by a *new way,* a *voluntary emission* of it into his Fathers hands] hands, into his Fathers hands, by a new way, a voluntary emission thereof *F*

663 *belong'd*] belong *F*

664 or] nor *F*

665 issued] issues *F*

NOTE: Here the reading of *Q* is clearly the better in view of the past tenses which follow, "*emisit,* hee *gave up . . . breathed his soule.*"

672 *purchas'd* : *prepared Q* : purchas'd *F*

Part Two

Chapter I
Donne's Sources

GENERAL INDEBTEDNESS TO THE SCRIPTURES

OF ALL the sources used by Donne in his *Sermons* the Bible is by far the most important. This may seem self-evident, but many preachers, while taking their text from Scripture, have filled their discourses with theological discussion, or abusive controversy, or with moral counsels, or stories from the lives of the saints. Donne is first and foremost an evangelical preacher, and he enforces his argument at every turn by direct quotation or oblique reference to the Bible. The Folios give an immense number of Scriptural marginal references, probably supplied by Donne himself, and we have nearly doubled the number by the additional references which we have supplied in brackets. Though the number of Donne's quotations from St. Augustine is large (we estimate that it exceeds 700), the number taken from Scripture must run into well over 7,000.

If we consider which books of the Bible Donne used most often, we shall first examine the texts which he chose for his 160 extant sermons. The Gospels provided texts for the largest number, 37, of which 16 were taken from *Matthew,* 16 from *John,* 3 from *Luke,* and 2 from *Mark.* The *Psalms* provided texts for 34, the Epistles of St. *Paul* for 26, *Genesis* for 9, *Acts* for 8, *Isaiah* for 6, *Job* and *Revelation* for 5 each, *Proverbs* for 4, *Ecclesiastes* and *Ezekiel* for 3 each, and *Exodus, Deuteronomy, Canticles, Lamentations, Hosea, Micah* for 2 each. Donne preached single sermons on texts from *Judges, Esther, Amos, Hebrews, James,* 1 *Peter,* 2 *Peter,* and 1 *John.* Though he often referred in his sermons to such books of the Apocrypha as *Wisdom* and *Ecclesiasticus,* he never preached on a text from any of them.

Mrs. Holtby, my research assistant, has made a detailed analysis of the marginal references in Volumes III and VIII. Of these, III (containing 18 sermons) gives a fair sample of Donne's earlier work, while VIII (containing 16 sermons) represents his later work. Vol. III contains 863 marginal references to Scripture, and Vol. VIII has 665, a total of 1,528 for the two volumes with their 34 sermons, an average of 45 such references per sermon. Since our ten volumes contain 160 sermons, this would give a total of 7,200 references in all, and even if we allow that some sermons may have fallen below this average, others certainly exceeded it, notably the very long sermon which we printed as No. 3 in Volume IV.

Mrs. Holtby has made an interesting analysis of the selection of books of the Bible from which these references are taken. They cover all the canonical books and several of the 14 books of the Apocrypha, which in the King James version of 1611 were printed between the Old and New Testaments. Since the Old Testament contains 39 books (or 38, if *Lamentations* is reckoned as an appendix to *Jeremiah*, as it is in the Vulgate) and the New Testament has 27 books, it would be tedious and futile to give figures for each of these. But it is illuminating to see which were the books which Donne quoted most often. If we group the four Gospels[1] together, we find that in Volumes III and VIII there are 113 references to them as compared with 186 references to the book of *Psalms* (the longest single book of the Bible), 80 to *Genesis*, 71 to *Isaiah*, 43 to *Job*, and 34 to *Revelation*. There are 271 references to the Epistles of St. Paul (omitting the Epistle to the *Hebrews,* which is not now ascribed to St. Paul).

This analysis shows that, as we should expect, Donne drew very heavily on the Gospels and St. Paul's Epistles, which together form the longer part of the New Testament. In the Gospels he found the grounds of his Christian belief, and in the Epistles he realized the implications of what Christ's life and death and resurrection had meant to the world. The rest of his favourite books—*Psalms, Genesis, Isaiah, Job,* and *Revelation*—are notable for their poetical or their symbolical character.

The fact that the Gospels head both lists should cause no surprise, but it may perhaps supply an answer to those critics who, like F. L. Lucas,[2] question whether Donne's sermons "have really much in

---

[1] Donne knew nothing of the modern distinction between the three Synoptic Gospels and the Fourth Gospel.

[2] See p. 3 of the present volume.

common with genuine Christianity," by which they apparently mean the Sermon on the Mount. Donne preached three sermons on texts taken from that Sermon, and in one of them he expressed his deep admiration for that wonderful example of Christ's teaching.[3] Indeed, we find that among the texts which Donne quoted most frequently there are the two petitions from the Lord's Prayer, which itself lies at the very heart and centre of the Sermon, namely, "Thy Kingdom come, Thy will be done." These recur again and again, and it is worth remembering that they are the words which Donne repeated in his dying moments. He loved the whole of the Lord's Prayer, and gave us a fine appreciation of it in one of his sermons,[4] but on his deathbed he uttered no petition for himself, not even the prayer for forgiveness, but simply prayed for the coming of God's kingdom.

Yet even the Sermon on the Mount is only a part of "genuine Christianity." Donne's sermons cover the whole range of the Gospel narratives, and they lay particular stress on St. John's interpretation of the meaning of those narratives. Christ's teaching cannot be separated from his life and death, for it is only in the power of the Spirit that men can reach the ideals which he set before them. Donne's long series of Whitsunday sermons bear witness to this truth.

As Donne grew older, his affection for the Gospels increased. In Volume I (9 sermons only), which covers the period from January, 1615, when he was ordained, to April, 1618, there is only one sermon on a text from the Gospels. In Volume IV, March, 1622, to May, 1623, four sermons are on texts from the Gospels. In Volume VII (18 sermons), January, 1626, to May, 1627, there are eight sermons on the Gospels. It might be thought that Volume IX, which has only five sermons on the Gospels, supplies evidence to the contrary, but this is not so, for IX is a composite volume, containing in its second half eight undated sermons on the Penitential Psalms which almost certainly belong to the earlier period, perhaps to the winter of 1624–25.[5] Therefore the percentage of five sermons on the Gospels out of the ten in the first part, covering the period April, 1629, to May, 1630, is even higher than that in Volume VII. From the Gospels came the

---

[3] Vol. IX, pp. 173–174.
[4] Vol. V, p. 271.
[5] See Vol. IX, pp. 35–37.

texts of most of Donne's finest sermons, such as the Christmas ones of 1622, 1625, 1626, and 1629, the magnificent one at the funeral of Sir William Cokayne in 1626, or the beautiful one, full of human compassion, on the text "Jesus wept" in March, 1624.[6] It was, on the other hand, in the period 1615 to early 1621 that he preached six sermons on the worldly-wise books of *Proverbs* and *Ecclesiastes*. As for the books of *Psalms*,[7] *Genesis, Job,* and *Isaiah,* Donne seems to have kept a steady interest in them throughout his preaching career. Even before this began, he had devoted half of his *Essays in Divinity* to the first verse of *Genesis,* and Volumes I and IX of the *Sermons* alike bear witness to his interest in this book.

Donne's fondness for the Apocalypse of St. John the Divine forms a strong link between the *Divine Poems,* the *Essays in Divinity,* and the *Sermons.* He preached three sermons[8] on the great vision in the seventh chapter, which opens with the words, "And after these things I saw four Angels standing on the four corners of the earth, holding the four winds of the earth, that the wind should not blow on the earth, nor on the sea, nor on any tree." This vision inspired his fourth *Holy Sonnet,* which begins, "At the round earths imagined corners, blow Your trumpets, Angells,..."[9] The same chapter is quoted in the peroration of the sermon for Easter, 1629, and another vision, that of the nineteenth chapter, is used at some length in the last section of Donne's finest marriage sermon.[10]

First and foremost the Bible was to Donne the record of God's revelation of himself to man. This progressive revelation culminating

---

[6] In his sermon on *Mark* 16.16, Donne remarked, "... the best texts that we can take, to make Sermons upon, are as this text is, some of the words of Christs owne Sermons:..." (Vol. V, p. 263).

[7] Since 21 sermons on the *Psalms* are undated, and 15 of these have no title giving the place where they were preached, we can rely only on the marginal references for this statement.

[8] Vol. V, No. 4; Vol. VI, No. 7; Vol. X, No. 1.

[9] The rising of the dead from earth and sea in the same sonnet comes from *Rev.* 20.13–14; the dyeing of souls in Christs blood which turns them from red to white comes from *Rev.* 7.14; and the description of Christ as the Lamb "from the worlds beginning slaine" (Sonnet 12) is from *Rev.* 13.8. For references to *Revelation* in *Essays in Divinity* see p. xviii of the Introduction in the 1952 Simpson edition.

[10] Vol. III, pp. 253–255. For the Easter sermon see Vol. VIII, p. 372.

in Jesus Christ was the single thread which united all the separate books from the first verse of *Genesis* to the last verse of *Revelation*. God had shown himself in the Creation, in the call of Abraham, in the Jewish Law given to Moses, in the poetry of the *Psalms,* in the outpourings of the Prophets, but fully and finally in the coming of our Lord as described in the Gospels. Donne's faith was firmly rooted in history, the history of the Chosen People, the Jews, and of their rejection of the Messiah when at last he came in the fullness of time. In the *Acts of the Apostles* Donne read how, through this rejection by the Jews, the way was opened for the admission of the Gentiles into the New Israel, the Christian Church, and how the Gospel was carried to the Græco-Roman world by St. Paul and his followers.

The imaginative range of Donne's sermons is immensely enlarged by his wide choice of subjects. It extends from the dawn of Creation through history to the Day of Doom in the far distant future. His audience must have felt themselves ennobled and enriched as they listened to him. Life ceased to seem tawdry and futile as they contemplated eternity. From the great deep we come, to the great deep we go. In his congregations there were some simple folk who could not always follow his arguments, and who found his Latinisms obscure; but they knew their Bibles, and when he came to the peroration in which his own words blended with those of Scripture, the roll and surge of the rhythms of the English version lifted them up and carried them beyond and above themselves.

But this revelation of God, though so firmly rooted in history, is conveyed to man not only through the narrative portions of the Old and New Testaments, but also through the medium of poetry, symbol, and image. The great Creation poem of the first chapters of *Genesis,* the vision of Jacob's ladder set up on earth but reaching to heaven, the lyrical outpourings of the Psalmists, Isaiah's vision of the Most High before whom he cried, "Woe is me, for I am undone, for mine eyes have seen the King, the Lord of Hosts"—all these fed the springs of Donne's imagination, and released an emotion which he communicated to his hearers. He meditated deeply, as few modern preachers do, on the books of *Genesis, Job,* and *Revelation. Job* is in dramatic form, with long monologues by the principal characters on the age-long problem of human suffering, completed by a prose prelude and epilogue. *Revelation* is a wonderful series of visions symbolizing the trials and final triumph of the persecuted Christian Church. Both these books have been a perpetual source of inspiration to poets and artists. William Blake's great series of drawings on the book of *Job* represent his finest achievement in art,[11] though he also produced many wonderful drawings on such other Biblical subjects as Adam and Eve, Cain, the Angels of the creation and the destruction of the world, as well as a great tempera painting of the Last Supper. But a closer parallel can be found in the work of Milton, whose life overlapped Donne's by twenty-two years. *Paradise Lost* draws on the whole biblical story for its illustrative material, but the first three chapters of *Genesis* are its main source. The War in Heaven is based on the vision of *Revelation* 12.7–11,[12] supplemented by Rabbinical, early Christian, and medieval commentators. For this great poem Milton used much the same background as that of Donne's *Sermons.* He shows the same interest in the nature of angels that Donne displays on page after page. Even the discussions in Heaven, in Book III, between the Father and the Son, tedious as they often are, are foreshadowed by the deliberations and the "contract" which Donne supposed to have been made in Heaven before the world was made.[13]

By his constant use of symbolism drawn from Scripture and also from elemental natural sources, such as the sun, the rain, the earth, the trees, Donne appealed to something in his hearers which could not be reached by argument. He stirred their imagination and appealed to their subconsciousness in the way that great religious teachers have always done. Man cannot be divorced from his past without grievous damage to his personality. London was still a com-

---

[11] In 1957, the bicentenary of Blake's birth, a number of fine facsimile reproductions of his drawings were published. Among them were his *Illustrations to the Bible* (compiled by Sir Geoffrey Keynes, Trianon Trust, pub. Collins). Blake declared, "The whole Bible is vision," a statement with which Donne would have disagreed.

[12] Donne spends some part of Sermon 1 of Vol. IV of our edition on the subject of the War in Heaven.

[13] For Donne on the Creation, and on the fall of angels, see Vol. VIII of our edition, pp. 358–365; for the question whether every man has a guardian angel, see Vol. III, pp. 153–154; that angels cannot read thoughts, *ibid.* Cp. Donne's *Poems,* ed. Grierson, I, 37.

paratively small town, and many of its inhabitants came from the countryside which was then close at hand. For untold centuries the hunter, the farmer, the fisherman lived in touch with the earth and the sea. They had religious observances of some kind which coincided with the rhythm of the seasons.

The medieval Church very wisely did not abolish these festivals altogether, but consecrated them from pagan to Christian uses. The name was changed,[14] and a celebration of the mass took the place of pagan sacrifices, human or animal, but much of the day was given up to dancing and feasting. On Candlemas Day (February 2) torches and candles were lighted and carried about. March 25, shortly after the spring equinox, became Lady Day, the Feast of the Annunciation. May Day (May 1) became the Feast of St. Philip and St. James, but townspeople as well as country folk still went out into the woods before daybreak and cut great boughs of hawthorn blossom and brought them back, and gathered flowers to deck the maypole around which they danced. Midsummer Day (June 24) became the Feast of St. John the Baptist, but on the previous night bonfires continued to be lit, and men vied with one another in leaping over them—a piece of ritual from the pagan past.

The Puritans abhorred all these customs as relics of heathenism, and did their utmost to abolish them. In his enormous book *Histrio-Mastix* (1633), William Prynne, two years after Donne's death, denounced in the most unmeasured terms the burning of candles[15] on Candlemas Day, the May games and maypoles,[16] and the feasting and mummeries[17] of Christmas, as heathenish, idolatrous, popish, and devilish. Later, under the rule of the Long Parliament, it became a punishable offense to celebrate Christmas at all. Mince pies and plum puddings became "food offered to idols," and this Puritan hatred of such delicacies continued into the latter half of the nineteenth century.[18]

[14] Not for Easter, which is the name of the spring goddess worshiped by the Anglo-Saxons.

[15] Pp. 758, 760.

[16] Pp. 253 mg., 807 mg.

[17] Pp. 751–768.

[18] Edmund Gosse, in his autobiographical *Father and Son* (1907 et seq.), tells us how his father forbade any Christmas feasting. As a child he

Donne's attitude was quite different. While the Puritans wished to exclude everything which could possibly have had a pagan origin, however far back, he wished to include all ceremonies which, whatever their origin, could be given a Christian meaning. Thus in one of his sermons he defended at some length the burning of candles on Candlemas Day:

The Church ... celebrates this day, the Purification of the blessed Virgin, the Mother of God: And she celebrates this day by the name, vulgarly, of *Candlemas day*. It is *dies luminarium,* the day of lights; The Church took the occasion of doing so, from the Gentiles; At this time of the yeare, about the beginning of February, they celebrated the feast of *Februus,* which is their *Pluto;* And, because that was the God of darknesse, they solemnized it, with a multiplicity of Lights. The Church of God, in the outward and ceremoniall part of his worship, did not disdain the ceremonies of the Gentiles; Men who are so severe, as to condemne, and to remove from the Church, whatsoever was in use amongst the Gentiles before, may, before they are aware, become Surveyors, and Controllers upon Christ himself, in the institution of his greatest seales: for Baptisme, which is the Sacrament of purification by washing in water, and the very Sacrament of the Supper it self, religious eating, and drinking in the Temple, were in use amongst the Gentiles too. . . . For the solemnizing of this Day, Candlemas-day, when the Church did admit Candles into the Church, as the Gentiles did, it was not upon the reason of the Gentiles, . . . but because he who was the light of the world, was this day presented and brought into the Temple, the Church admitted lights.[19]

This is a fine passage, and should be read in its context. If Christ himself ordained sacraments which had Gentile affinities, his followers had the right to redeem ancient ceremonies and symbols from their pagan use and to give them a higher meaning.

One example of Donne's development of symbols may be traced here. This is Light, with its cognate the Sun. In the earlier part of

---

ventured one Christmas Day into the kitchen, where the servants were secretly eating the forbidden fare. They offered him some, and he ate greedily. Afterwards his conscience reproached him, and he went to his father, and said with sobs, "Father, I have eaten of food offered unto idols."

[19] Vol. VII, pp. 325–326. Donne's facts are not quite correct; the Roman feast was in honour not of Februus or Pluto, but of Februa, a fertility goddess. But his main contention is sound, and in accordance both with reason and with human nature.

his ministry he makes comparatively little use of this symbol of the Godhead. In a sermon preached at Whitehall on April 19, 1618, he reminds his hearers that God's first work in the Creation, as described in *Genesis,* was the creation of light, *"Dixit, fiat lux,* that God hath said, *let there be light"* (Vol. I, p. 290), and this is repeated in *A Sermon of Valediction,* at Lincoln's Inn, April 18, 1619 (Vol. II, p. 240). But in the latter part of Volume III and again in Volume IV Donne realizes the full richness of this symbol. He turns from *Genesis* to the New Testament, and in an undated sermon which probably belongs to the summer of 1621, he dwells on God the Father as the "Father of lights," a phrase which he takes from the Epistle of St. James. In a fine passage which in its entirety occupies a full page, he writes, "He is *Pater,* and *Pater luminum, Father,* and *Father of lights,* of all kinds of lights, *Lux lucifica,* as S. *Augustine* expresses it, The light from which all the lights which we have, whether of nature, or grace, or glory, have their emanation.... Take these *Lights* of which S. *Iames* speaks, in any apprehension, any way, ... Every way, by every light we see, that he is *Pater luminum, the Father of lights;* all these lights are from him, and by all these lights we see that he is A Father, and Our Father."[20]

From this Donne proceeds to preach his great Christmas sermon of 1621, the first sermon which he preached as Dean of St. Paul's, on the thought expressed in the prologue to the Fourth Gospel, that Christ the Incarnate Word is the true Light, the Light that lightens every man that cometh into the world. This was Donne's manifesto to London of the theme which was to be the main subject of his preaching.[21] He followed it up four months later by an open-air sermon preached on April 22, 1622, at the Spital (St. Mary's, Bishopsgate), on the text, "For, God who commanded the light to shine out of darkness, hath shined in our hearts, to give the light of the knowledge of the glory of God, in the face of Jesus Christ" (Vol. IV, pp. 89–131). After these two full-length treatments of the theme, we find frequent echoes, as in Sermon 5 of Volume IV, where the text describes St. John the Baptist, whose feast the Church was commemorating, as "not that light, but sent to beare witnesse of that light," and

[20] Vol. III, pp. 276–277.
[21] See Vol. III, pp. 36–40 and 348–375.

again in Sermon 8, where Donne calls for witnesses to this Essential Light, because *"new Clouds of Ignorance, of Incredulitie, of Infirmitie, of Relapsing,* rise every day and call this light in question."[22]

From this date (the middle of 1622) there is an interesting development. Donne has been using the symbol of Essential Light "with whom is no variableness, nor shadow that is cast by turning," as applied to the Godhead. But Christ is not only God, but also man, the historical Jesus of Nazareth, born at Bethlehem and crucified on Calvary, and for this human figure a better symbol is that of the sun, which to us seems to rise at morning, and set in darkness at even.[23] So now at the close of his Midsummer Day sermon he looks forward to the Resurrection, and says, "I shall rise from the dead, from the darke station, from the prostration, from the prosternation of death, and never misse the sunne, which shall then be put out, for I shall see the Sonne of God, the Sunne of glory, and shine my self, as that sunne shines."[24]

A fuller treatment can be found in the Christmas sermon of 1624, where Donne says, "... now God comes to thee, not as in the dawning of the day, not as in the bud of the spring, but as the Sun at noon to illustrate all shadowes, as the sheaves in harvest, to fill all penuries," and, a page later, "One of the most convenient Hieroglyphicks of God, is a Circle; and a Circle is endlesse; ... His Sun, and Moone, and Starres, (Emblemes and Instruments of his Blessings) move circularly, and communicate themselves to all. His Church is his chariot; in that, he moves more gloriously, then in the Sun; as much more, as his begotten Son exceeds his created Sun, and his Son of glory, and of his right hand, the Sun of the firmament."[25]

The symbol of the Sun for the Messiah is found already in the Old Testament. "But unto you that fear my name shall the Sun of righteousness arise with healing in his wings" (*Malachi* 4.2)—a text which was often in Donne's mind. An offshoot from this is Donne's

---

[22] Vol. IV, pp. 145, 214.

[23] Donne knew the Copernican system and the discoveries of Kepler and Galileo (see C. M. Coffin, *John Donne and the New Philosophy,* pp. 79–87, 122–154), but in the *Sermons* he hardly mentions them.

[24] Vol. IV, p. 162. Here is the inevitable pun on *Son* and *Sun,* which recurs in so many succeeding sermons.

[25] Vol. VI, pp. 172, 173.

use of the word *Oriens* for Christ, which occurs first in an undated sermon which we have assigned conjecturally to the middle of 1623: "The name of Christ is *Oriens, The East; ...*" to which the Folio appends the reference "Zach. 6.12."[26] In the Authorized Version this reads, "Behold the man whose name is the Branch," but the Vulgate has "Ecce vir oriens nomen ejus." Also in *Luke* 1.78–79 the Vulgate has "in quibus visitavit nos, oriens ex alto; Illuminare his, qui in tenebris, et in umbra mortis sedent," for which the A.V. reads "whereby the dayspring from on high hath visited us, To give light to them that sit in darkness and in the shadow of death." In the margin A.V. supplies, for "dayspring," "Or, *sunrising;* or *branch.*"

Donne had a peculiar fondness for this title of Christ, and he used it often from 1623 onwards.[27] *Oriens* is the present participle of the Latin *orior,* I rise, and as a substantive it is used for the sunrise, and hence for the east. Thus it was associated in Donne's mind with the early morning, a time which he loved, and also with God's mercy, of which the prophet writes, in *Lamentations* 3.23–24, "It is of the Lord's mercies that we are not consumed, because his compassions fail not. They are new every morning: great is thy faithfulness."[28] It is also a title which lays stress on Christ's humanity: "Behold the *man* whose name is the East," while at the same time it possesses the suggestion of divinity, which for most races is associated with the rising sun.

There was, however, a period of melancholy and bereavement in Donne's life during the autumn and winter of 1627–28, when this imagery of light disappeared for a time from his sermons. This is evident in the sermon which he preached at the marriage of Lord Herbert's son, and in the Fifth Prebend Sermon, in which we read of the "horror of great darknesse" which fell upon Abraham before the approach of God.[29] Even the Christmas sermon of 1627 failed to give any impression of joy or light, and it was not till the Easter

---

[26] Vol. VI, p. 59. We have given this date because of the close resemblance to a passage in a letter sent by Donne to Sir Robert Ker about the middle of 1623 (see Vol. VI, pp. 1–2).

[27] See Vol. V, p. 97; VI, p. 59; IX, p. 49; X, p. 50.

[28] For Donne's love of the early morning see Vol. V, pp. 25, 280–282.

[29] Vol. VIII, p. 123: "Not onely a feare of God must, but a terror of God may fall upon the Best. When God talked with *Abraham, a horror of great darknesse fell upon him,* sayes that Text."

sermon of 1628 that Donne was able to return to the full use of this association of light with glory and the Godhead.[30] In the sermon which Donne preached before the King in April, 1629, we read: "Christs name is *Oriens,* the *East;* . . . First then we looke towards our East, the fountaine of light, and of life. There this world beganne; the Creation was in the east. And there our next world beganne too. There the gates of heaven opened to us; and opened to us in the gates of death; for, our heaven is the death of our Saviour, and there he lived, and dyed there, and there he looked into our west, from the east, from his Terasse, from his Pinacle, from his exaltation (as himselfe calls it) the Crosse."[31] Finally, in the epitaph which he composed for himself, Donne wrote, "Hic licet in occiduo cinere aspicit eum cujus nomen est Oriens,"[32] so that even through the grave and gate of death he looked towards the eternal Sunrise.

✧   ✧   ✧

Two symbols which occur in the first chapters of *Genesis* and are carried on into the *Revelation* of St. John can only be mentioned here. These are the River and the Tree of Life.[33] These two are closely linked, and they are archetypal symbols which lie deep in the subconsciousness of our race. They were always in the background of Donne's mind, and a long study might be made of them.

Hebrew Old Testament

Donne knew a certain amount of Hebrew, and made use of it in approximately 140 passsages of his *Sermons*. In the sixteenth century much interest was taken in Hebrew studies throughout Western Europe, and several great polyglot Bibles appeared, of which the chief

---

[30] See p. 20 of our Introduction to Vol. VIII.

[31] Vol. IX, pp. 49–51.

[32] See above, p. 38.

[33] For the river see *Gen.* 2.10: "And a river went out of Eden to water the ground"; also *Psa.* 46.4: "There is a river, the streams whereof shall make glad the city of God"; *Ezek.* 47.7–9: "Behold, at the bank of the river were very many trees on the one side and on the other. Then said he unto me, . . . And it shall come to pass, that . . . every thing shall live whither the river cometh"; *Rev.* 22.1: "And he showed me a pure river of water of life, clear as crystal, proceeding out of the throne of God and of the Lamb." For the Tree of Life see *Gen.* 2.9 and 3.22–24, and *Rev.* 2.7 and 22.2.

were the "Complutense," as Donne called it, printed at Alcalá de
Henares in 1514-1517, and the Antwerp of 1571-1573, which was
edited by Arias Montanus. These contained texts in Hebrew, Greek,
Chaldaic, and Latin. There were also separate Hebrew Testaments,
of which the first was published by Daniel Bomberg at Venice in
1517 and reissued in 1521, 1525-1528, 1533, and 1544-1555. Sebastian
Munster's *Hebraica Biblia* was printed at Basle in 1534, and, as this
contained the Hebrew text and Munster's Latin translation in parallel
columns, Donne may well have found it useful. Since Donne sometimes mentions the Jewish commentators, he may perhaps have used
Bomberg's rabbinical Bible containing the Hebrew text, the Chaldaic
paraphrase, and the commentaries of Rashi (whom Donne calls
Rabbi Solomon), Kimhi, Moses ben Nahman, Ibn Ezra (several
times mentioned by Donne), and others.[34]

Evidently Donne took much more interest in Hebrew studies than
in Greek, and his knowledge of the language was more extensive.
There is nothing surprising about this, for when he was at Oxford
Hebrew had more students than Greek, and there was great enthusiasm for the Hebrew language among theologians. Tremellius, the
learned Jew who became a Calvinist, in whose works Donne took a
profound interest,[35] had been a professor of Hebrew at Cambridge
from 1548 to 1553, and of theology at Heidelberg from 1562 to 1567.

In the summer of 1613, when the possibility of taking Orders had
entered Donne's mind, he wrote to a friend that he was busying himself a little "in the search of Eastern tongues, where a perpetual perplexity in the words cannot choose but cast a perplexity upon the
things."[36] This would seem to mean that he was applying himself to

---

[34] For some of the information contained in this section I am indebted to
Professor D. C. Allen's valuable pioneer study, "Dean Donne sets his
Text," *ELH, X,* 208-227. He, however, confined his examination to the
LXXX Sermons, leaving out the *Fifty* and *XXVI Sermons.*

[35] Donne translated the *Lamentations* of Jeremiah into verse from
Tremellius' new translation made from Hebrew into Latin. In the
Sermons he speaks approvingly of the closeness with which Tremellius
"sticks to the Hebrew" (Vol. IX of our edition, p. 226).

[36] From a letter formerly in the collection of J. H. Anderdon, quoted by
Gosse, *Life and Letters of John Donne,* II, 16. The MS copy is now in the
possession of Miss Mary Donne (Keynes, *Bibliography,* p. 122).

Hebrew, and perhaps to Syriac and Arabic. In the *Essays in Divinity* written at some time before he took Orders, we find him showing considerable interest in Hebrew learning, in the commentaries of the Rabbis and the heretical speculations of the Cabalists. Donne was here exercising himself in preparation for his entry into the ministry, and it is significant that he took for the subject of his meditations the first verses of *Genesis* and *Exodus*. This seems to imply that he had determined to concentrate his language study chiefly on the Old Testament.

We must not expect from Donne the knowledge of Hebrew that was possessed by Bishop Andrewes, one of the most learned scholars of the day, who was mainly responsible for the translation of the Pentateuch in the Authorized Version. Andrewes had been successively scholar, Fellow, and Master of Pembroke College, Cambridge, before he was made Bishop of Ely, and he had had the friendship of the great scholar Casaubon. Donne had spent his time studying law at Lincoln's Inn, traveling, serving in the expeditions to the Azores and the Islands, acting as secretary to Egerton, and finally writing *Biathanatos, Pseudo-Martyr,* and *Ignatius his Conclave.* Above all he was a poet, and imagination rather than exact scholarship provided his driving force.

Donne's sermons on the Sixth, Thirty-second, and Thirty-eighth Psalms[37] contain the most careful and detailed of his Hebrew expositions. Professor Allen has given a detailed analysis of Donne's treatment of Hebrew words from *Psa.* 32 (*op. cit.,* pp. 214–215), and he sums up: "His [Donne's] definitions are exact according to the lexicons of his day, and he obviously knows how to find the place in the text. His knowledge of Hebrew does not seem to go much beyond this." Earlier, Allen had remarked, "It is quite evident to me that Donne read the Sixth and Thirty-second Psalms in the original."

Usually Donne gives us a phonetic transliteration of the Hebrew word of the text with its Latin or English equivalent. However, the Hebrew characters are printed in the margin of *Fifty Sermons,* p. 266,[38] for the word transliterated as *Jakal* from *Job* 13.15. Also in the

[37] These are printed in Vol. II of our edition, Nos. 1–6 (on *Psa.* 38); Vol. V, Nos. 16–19 (on *Psa.* 6); Vol. IX, Nos. 11–18 (on *Psa.* 32).

[38] Vol. III of our edition, p. 194.

margin of *Fifty Sermons,* p. 455, we have the Hebrew characters for *Gnabar,* "that word *Gnabar,* which we translate *Anger.*"[89]

Donne's system of transliteration is not quite the same as that used by modern scholars. He seems, as we should expect, to have used the symbols employed by the translators of the King James Bible in their marginal notes, with occasional variations which he may have found in the commentaries. For example, he reproduces *"Ochim"* and *"Ziim"* from the margin of *Isa.* 13.21 (Vol. IV, p. 50). On *Dan.* 11.38 he makes a slight correction, which is nearer to the Hebrew. The margin of A.V. has "Mauzzin," translated in the text as "the god of forces." Donne corrects this incorrect form and writes *"Mauzzim,* which is, *The God of forces,* is not the name of our God, but of an Idoll" (Vol. III, p. 153). But for *tzebaoth,* translated "of hosts" in *Isa.* 1.24, Donne must have gone to the Hebrew, for there is no marginal note in A.V. Also, in the only places in A.V. (*Rom.* 9.29 and *Jam.* 5.4) where the word occurs in the text, it appears as "Sabaoth" from the intermediate Greek form *"σαβαώθ,"* Vulg. "sabaoth." Donne writes, "The name of the true God is *Dominus tzebaoth,* the *Lord of Hosts"* (Vol. I, p. 261; see also Vol. VIII, p. 128).

A curious feature of Donne's transliteration is the use of "gn" to represent the Hebrew guttural ע , which nowadays is represented by the Greek "rough breathing" ('). Thus where Donne writes "For, the first word, *Gned,* is an Hebrew word" (Vol. IX, p. 227, referring to *Job* 16.19), a modern transliterator would use *'Edh* for *Gned.* Again, in a comment on *Jer.* 17.9, the word which Donne transliterates as *Gnacob* (Vol. IX, p. 180) would appear as *'Aqob* in a modern transliteration.

There are several passages which show that Donne had consulted one or other of the polyglot Bibles to help him in expounding his text. For example, he discusses the spurious verse "Go to the bee" which appears in some texts between verses 8 and 9 of *Proverbs* 6:

> In the sixt Chapter of this booke, when *Solomon* had sent us to the *Ant,* to learne wisedome, betweene the eight verse and the ninth, he sends us to another schoole, to the *Bee: Vade ad Apem & disce quomodo operationem venerabilem facit,* Goe to the Bee, and learne how reverend and mysterious a worke she works. For, though S. *Hierome* acknowledge, that in his time,

---

[89] Vol. X, p. 211.

this verse was not in the Hebrew Text, yet it hath ever been in many Copies of the Septuagint, and though it be now left out in the Complutense Bible, and that which they call the Kings, yet it is in that still, which they value above all, the Vatican. S. *Hierome* himselfe takes it into his exposition, and other Fathers into theirs.[40]

Another example comes from a very early sermon of Donne's, preached on April 21, 1616, on *Eccles.* 8.11:

The word that is here used, *Pithgam,* is not truly an Hebrew word: And though in the Book of *Job,* and in some other parts of the Hebrew Scriptures, we finde sometimes some forreign and out-landish word, deriv'd from other Nations; yet, in *Solomons* writing very rarely; neither doth *Solomon* himself, nor any other Author, of any part of the Hebrew Bible, use this word, in any other place, then this one. The word is a *Chaldee* word; and hath amongst them, the same signification and largeness, as *Dabar* in Hebrew; and that includes all *A verbo ad legem;* from a word suddenly and slightly spoken, to words digested and consolidated into a Law. So that, though the Septuagint translate this place, *Quia non est facta contradictio;* ... and though the Chaldee Paraphrast express this place thus, *Quia non est factum verbum ultionis* ...[41]

There are also a number of passages in which Donne discusses the precise meaning of a Hebrew word by comparing its use in the text with other passages of the Old Testament. Thus when preaching on *Hosea* 3.4, "For the children of Israel shall abide many days without a king, and without a prince," he says of the last word, "The word in the originall is *Sar;* and take it, as it sounds most literally in our Translation, The *Prince* is the Kings Son; so, this very word is used in *Esay; Sar Salom;* The *Son of God,* is called the *Prince of Peace.*... But the word enlarges it selfe farther; for, *Sar* signifies a *Judge;* when *Moses* rebuked a Malefactor, he replies to *Moses, Who made thee a Judge?* And in many, very many places, *Sar* signifies a *Commander* in the Warres."[42] This is a fairly correct summary, and it suggests that Donne used a Hebrew concordance.[43] This, however, does not mean that he relied on a concordance because he had no proper knowledge

---

[40] Vol. III of our edition, pp. 231–232. D. C. Allen explains that by "Kings" Donne means the Antwerp polyglot.

[41] Vol. I, pp. 172–173.

[42] Vol. VII, p. 428.

[43] Allen (*op. cit.,* p. 215), discussing Donne's treatment of a Hebrew word in *Psa.* 32.7, also suggests that Donne may have used a concordance.

of the Hebrew Bible. To manipulate a Hebrew concordance success-
fully requires a working knowledge of Hebrew in the first place, and
it is evident from a large number of other passages that Donne
possessed this.

Occasionally Donne ventures to use the Hebrew text to correct a
reading of the Authorized Version, but it is generally with the support of the Vulgate or the Septuagint, or possibly of the Latin versions
of Munster or Tremellius. It was always to the Latin text that Donne
first turned, and where the Authorized Version differed from the
Vulgate he examined the Hebrew to see whether there was justification there for the difference. In a number of places he found that the
Authorized Version gave the true sense of the Hebrew against the
Vulgate.[44] Out of the passages in which Donne argues that the Vulgate better represents the sense of the Hebrew we may instance *Jer.*
50.25, where the A.V. has "The Lord hath opened his armory" but
the Vulgate reads *Aperuit Dominus thesaurum suum.* On this
Donne's comment is "... whatsoever mov'd our Translators to render
that word, *Armory,* and not *Treasury,* in that place, yet evidently it
is *Treasury,* and in that very word, *Otzar,* which they translate *Treasury,* in all those places of *Job* [38.22], and *David* [Psa. 135.7], and
Isaiah [45.3], which we mentioned before, and in all other places."[45]
This is rather pedantic. The Hebrew word means 'a store-place,' and
if royal treasures are in the store, "treasury" is the idiomatic English
equivalent, but as the verse continues "he hath brought forth the
weapons of his indignation" the Authorized translators were justified
in using "armory" here.[46]

While the majority of Donne's explanations are correct, there are
some in which he was at fault. For example, in commenting on

---

[44] As a sample of Donne's comments we may take the following: "But
then, because in their Translation, in the vulgat Edition of the Roman
Church, they find in Exodus [25.25] that word *Aureolam, Facies
Coronam aureolam,* Thou shalt make a lesser Crowne of gold; out of this
diminutive, and mistaken word, they have established a Doctrine ...
whereas indeed the word in the Originall in that place of Exodus is *Zer
zehab,* which is a Crowne of gold ... [so in A.V.]" (Vol. VII, pp. 129–
130). See also Vol. IV, p. 343; Vol. VIII, p. 258.

[45] Vol. IX, p. 184.

[46] I am indebted to the late Rev. Professor D. C. Simpson for comments on the Hebrew text here.

Shaddai in *Job* 13.3, after starting correctly with the statement that it means 'Almighty' (*omnipotens* in the Vulgate), he goes on to confuse it with the word in *Prov.* 19.26 from an entirely different root.[47] Again, his explanation of *Coheleth* as "a Shee-preacher" is wrong. He seems to have been misled by the commentary of Johannes Lorinus.[48]

ARAMAIC (CHALDEE), SYRIAC, AND ARABIC VERSIONS

After their return from the Babylonian exile the Jews gradually acquired an Aramaic dialect from their neighbours in Palestine, and by the beginning of the Christian era Hebrew had become unintelligible to the common people. An Aramaic translation or "Targum" had to be given in the synagogues after readings of Scripture. These translations were written down and became what was known in England during the sixteenth and seventeenth centuries as the "Chaldee paraphrases." The Aramaic language was called by the Greeks "Syriac" or "Chaldee," the latter name being due to the mistaken belief that the language spoken in Chaldæa in the days of Daniel[49] was Biblical Aramaic.

This Aramaic translation was printed in the Bomberg rabbinical Bible and in the polyglot Bibles. Since there is a Latin translation given at the foot of the Antwerp polyglot of 1571–1573, Donne probably made use of this, for he gives most of his quotations in Latin. Thus, he writes in an early sermon: "And so the Chaldee Paraphrasts, the first Exposition of the Bible, have express'd it, *Quousque rursus fiam,* Till I be made up again by death."[50] Again, on *Gen.* 31.53 he writes: "As in another place, God himselfe is called *feare,...Iacob*

---

[47] Vol. III, pp. 190–191. See our note on pp. 408–409 of the same volume.

[48] Vol. IX, p. 279; note on p. 440. See other notes on erroneous explanations or transliterations by Donne in Vol. I, p. 326; Vol. IV, p. 403; Vol. V, p. 419; and Vol. IX, pp. 439–440, 443, 444. For most of these we are indebted to the Very Rev. Dr. C. A. Simpson, Dean of Christ Church, Oxford.

[49] A small part of two of the later books of the Old Testament is written in Aramaic, namely, *Daniel* 2.6 to 7.28 and *Ezra* 4.8 to 6.12. The translators of the Authorized Version called this language "Chald." or "Cald." in their marginal notes on these passages.

[50] Vol. I of our edition, p. 231, on *Job* 14.14, where A.V. has "till my change come."

swore by the Feare of his Father Isaac; that is, by him whom his Father *Isaac* feared, as the Chalde Paraphrase rightly expresses it."[51] Here the Latin version in the Antwerp polyglot reads "per illum quem timebat pater suus Isaac," of which Donne's rendering is an exact equivalent.

Sometimes Donne compares the Chaldaic with the Vulgate translation and A.V. On *Psa.* 38.2 he writes: "*... Thy hand presses me sore;* so the Vulgat read it, *Confirmasti super me manum tuam, Thy hand is settled upon mee;* and the Chalde paraphrase carries it farther then, to *Mansit super me vulnus manus tuæ;* Thy hand hath wounded mee, and that hand keeps the wound open."[52] And on *Prov.* 8.17, where A.V. reads "They that seek me early shall find me," Donne writes: "St. *Hierom* expresses this early diligence ... well in his translation, *qui mane vigilaverint;* They that wake betimes in the morning shall finde me; but the Chaldee Paraphrase better, *qui mane consurgunt,* they that rise betimes in the morning shall finde me."[53]

On one occasion he makes a wide comparison between most of the versions known to him. On *Psa.* 2.12 he writes: "The Chalde paraphrase (which is, for the most part, good evidence) and the translation of the Septuagint, (which adds much weight) and the currant of the Fathers (which is of importance too) doe all reade this place, *Apprehendite disciplinam* [the reading of the Vulgate], *Embrace knowledge,* and not *Osculamini filium, Kisse the sonne.* Of the later men in the Roman Church, divers read it as we do, *Osculamini,* and some farther, *Amplectimini, Embrace the sonne.* Amongst the Jews, *Rabbi Solomon* reads it, *Armamini disciplina, Arme your selves with knowledge;* And another moderne man, reads it, *Osculamini pactum, Kisse the Covenant;* ... Clearly, and without exception, even from *Bellarmine* himselfe, according to the Originall Hebrew, it ought to be read, as we reade it, *Kisse the Sonne."*[54]

In this passage we can feel the eagerness with which Donne turns up one translation after another. At the very start of his sermon he had decided, in choosing his text, that the King James Bible was right

---

[51] Vol. III, p. 280.
[52] Vol. II, p. 66. See our note on p. 393 of the same volume.
[53] Vol. I, p. 248.
[54] Vol. III, pp. 314–315. "Kiss the Son" is the A.V. reading.

in following the Hebrew. But the Vulgate reading was in sharp conflict, and Donne was not disposed to dismiss it out of hand as one of the Vulgate's many errors. The Vulgate, as he says later in this sermon, is "a good and useful translation," "a reverend Translation," and he turns eagerly to the Chaldee paraphrase and the Septuagint, which both support it in this instance. Then he looks up his notes on the Fathers, and the "later men," among them Bellarmine. In his rabbinical Bible he finds that Rabbi Solomon (Rashi) has a reading very similar to that of the Vulgate. Finally he consults Luther, Calvin, and Pellicanus, and quotes Luther, "That translation, if we consider the very words only, is far from the Originall, but if we regard the sense, it is most proper." To a modern textual critic this is highly unsatisfactory, for it does not explain why the Vulgate and the Septuagint before it so differed from the Hebrew text, but neither Luther nor Donne had learnt textual criticism, and if the sense could be reconciled, that was what mattered.

Other references to the "Chaldee paraphrase" can be found in Vol. I, pp. 151, 173; Vol. III, pp. 50, 189, 381; Vol. IV, p. 251; Vol. V, p. 224; Vol. VI, p. 241; Vol. VII, p. 88; Vol. VIII, pp. 76, 290; Vol. IX, p. 227.

It seems likely that Donne did not use the Syriac Old Testament. He has a few references to the Syriac New Testament.[55] The first Syriac New Testament appeared in Vienna in 1555 and was reprinted in 1562. The polyglot Bible of Elias Hutter, published at Nuremberg in 1599, contains a version of the Syriac New Testament printed in Hebrew characters. Also, a version by Raphelengius was printed in Amsterdam in 1574–1575.

Writing on 1 *John* 5.7—a verse which, though it was retained in the King James Bible, is not included in the Revised Standard Version and other modern translations—Donne observes, "The first Translation of the new testament, (which was into *Syriaque*) hath not this verse"; and a few pages later in the same sermon he says, "For, though in the first Translation of the new Testament, into

---

[55] D. C. Allen (*op. cit.,* p. 218) suggests that Donne may not have been able to read Syriac or Arabic, but that he may "have picked up his few references from the scholia of others or from conversations with someone like William Bedwell."

Syriaque, that be said in the sixth verse, that Jesus is come *per manus aquarum,* by the power of waters, many waters, and in this verse, this witnesse is delivered in the plurall, *spirit and waters,...*"[56]

On 1 *Cor.* 13.12 (A.V. "I know in part") Donne remarks, "That which we call *in part,* the Syriack translates *Modicum ex multis;...*"[57] The Syriac reads "qallîl min saggi" or 'little from much,' which is approximately the same as Donne's rendering.[58]

It should be noted that the term "Syriac" was formerly used as equivalent to "Aramaic," that is (as used of language), "the northern branch of the Semitic family of languages, including Syriac and Chaldee" (*N.E.D.,* under "Aramaic"). Under "Syriac" *N.E.D.* quotes: "1668 Wilkins *Real Char.* 5, Those passages in the Gospel, which are said to be in the Hebrew tongue, as *Talitha Kumi,...* are properly Syriac." Modern scholars would call the words "Aramaic," and similarly *"Sahad"* would be described by them as Aramaic, not Syriac, as Donne calls it.[59]

Other passages in which Syriac is mentioned are Vol. V, p. 369; Vol. VII, pp. 118–119, 380; Vol. IX, p. 406.

There seems to be no reason for thinking that Donne knew Arabic, though he mentions it together with Syriac in a comment on *Psa.* 51.7, where A.V. reads "hyssop." He writes of "...a certain plant, which because the word in Hebrew is *Ezob,* for the nearnesse of the sound, and for the indifferency of the matter,... the Interpreters have ever used in all languages to call this word Hyssop. And though we know no proper word for Hyssop in Hebrew,... yet the other languages deduced from the Hebrew, Syriaque, and Arabique, have clearly another word for Hyssop, *Zuf;* And the Hebrew Rabbins think this word of our text, *Ezob,* to signifie any of three or foure plants, rather then our Hyssop."[60] Elsewhere he writes, "For, when *Adam* sayes of *Eve, She shall be called Woman* [*Gen.* 2.23 in margin], in the Arabique Translation, there is this name, *She shall be*

---

[56] Vol. V, pp. 139, 147.

[57] Vol. VIII, p. 229.

[58] Allen, op. cit., p. 219.

[59] Vol. IX, p. 227. "For, the first word, *Gned,* is an Hebrew word, but the other, *Sahad,* is Syriaque;..." See also Vol. I, p. 280, for *Shebat.*

[60] Vol. V, p. 309.

called Mary;..."[61] There is a comment on *John* 10.3 in the Arabic translation in Vol. IX, p. 140, and another on "the Arabique Translation of the Psalmes" in Vol. IX, p. 294, but Donne probably obtained these from one of the numerous commentaries which he consulted.

SEPTUAGINT

Donne had a high regard for the Septuagint, the famous Greek translation of the Old Testament, supposed to have been made in the third century B.C. in Egypt. He quotes or refers to it at least twenty times, and on one occasion, when comparing the different readings of *Psa.* 2.12, he uses the words "the translation of the Septuagint, (which adds much weight)."[62] He does not, however, quote the actual Greek text, but paraphrases it, or quotes it in Latin.

There were several versions of the Septuagint which Donne may have used: that which was printed in the Complutensian (or "Complutense," as Donne calls it) Bible of 1514–1517, that printed by Aldus at Venice in 1518, and that printed at Rome in 1587 and authorized by Pope Sixtus the Fifth. Donne indicates that he has consulted several versions in his discussion of the spurious passage on the bee which appears in some texts of *Proverbs* 6 after that on the ant.[63]

The variant from the Hebrew which he mentions most often is that in *Isaiah* 9.6, where the Septuagint has μεγάλης βουλῆς ἄγγελος for the words which the Vulgate renders as *"Admirabilis, Consiliarius,"* and the A.V. as "Wonderful, Counsellor." Thus in a sermon preached at Lincoln's Inn in 1620 he says: "... Christ himselfe is called *The Angel of the great Councell*, according to the *Septuagint*," and in the margin he supplies "Esay 9" (Vol. III, p. 141).[64] When he deals with texts from the book of *Job*, the Hebrew of which is often difficult, Donne frequently refers to the Septuagint. Preaching before the Countess of Bedford on *Job* 13.15 he says, "And this sense of the words, both the *Chaldee paraphrase*, and all translations, (*excepting onely the Septuagint*) do unanimously establish" (Vol. III, p. 189).

---

[61] Vol. IX, p. 192.

[62] Vol. III, p. 314. The Septuagint is several centuries older than the received Hebrew text, from which it differs in many places.

[63] Vol. III, p. 232; and see pp. 309–310 above.

[64] See also Vol. IV, p. 46, "the Angel of the great Councell, ... Christ Jesus himselfe," and p. 176; Vol. VII, p. 404, "as he is the *Angel of the great counsell*"; Vol. VIII, p. 218; Vol. IX, p. 107; Vol. X, p. 139.

In the same sermon he tries without much success to throw light on the term *Shaddai* as applied to God by saying, "For, first, this word signifies *Dishonor,* as the *Septuagint* translate it in the Proverbs, *He that Dishonoreth his parents, is a shamelesse child;* There's this word; *Shaddai* is the name of *God,* and yet *Shaddai* signifies *Dishonor.*"[65]

He is more fortunate in his observations on the Septuagint text of the Psalms. On *Psa.* 66.3 he states correctly: "Those words, *In multitudine virtutis tuæ, Through the greatnesse of thy power, thine enemies shall submit,* S. *Ierome,* and the Septuagint before, and *Tremellius* after, and all that binde themselves to the Hebrew letter, reade it thus, *Mentientur tibi inimici tui,...thine enemies will lie unto thee,...*" (Vol. IX, p. 301). Again, he observes correctly on *Psa.* 32.10: "For this Word, which we Translate *Sorrowes* here, is according to the Septuagint, *Scourges,* and *Whips*" (*ibid.,* p. 394). Preaching on *Psa.* 65.5 he notes that "the Septuagint, in their Translation of the Psalms, have, in the Title of this Psalme, added this, *A Psalme of Ieremy and Ezekiel, when they were departing out of the Captivity of Babylon,...*" (Vol. VII, p. 304).[66]

GREEK NEW TESTAMENT

Donne's knowledge of Greek was very small, almost negligible. He knew just enough of the Greek New Testament to be able to quote an occasional word—once, four words,[67]—but his comments throw little or no fresh light on the subject, and are sometimes misleading.

---

[65] Vol. III, p. 191. In our note on this passage (*ibid.,* pp. 408–409) we explain that the Hebrew word in *Prov.* 19.26 is from a different root.

[66] We have no space to consider Donne's other references to the Septuagint, which are more numerous than those to the Greek New Testament. See Vol. I, p. 159 on *Gen.* 37.28, and p. 173 on *Eccles.* 8.11; Vol. III, p. 74 on *Psa.* 144.15, p. 129 on *Exod.* 34.9, p. 315 on *Psa.* 2.12; Vol. V, p. 239 on the agreement of the translators, p. 270 on *Psa.* 90.14, p. 376 on *Isa.* 58.11, p. 387 on *Psa.* 6.5; Vol. VI, p. 48 on *Psa.* 6.8, p. 110 on *Job* 4.11 (μυρμηκολέων); Vol. VII, p. 88, on *Mal.* 2.16; Vol. VIII, p. 207 on *Psa.* 6.7; Vol. IX, pp. 57, 114–145 (general statements); Vol. X, p. 123 on *Deut.* 9.18, *Gen.* 17.3, *Job* 19.21, and 1 *Sam.* 31.3, p. 124 on *Mic.* 6.13 and *Zech.* 7.2, and p. 153 on *Prov.* 25.26.

[67] Vol. II, p. 148 of our edition: "... as it is sayd there in the Originall ὁ κύριος τῆς ἐπαγγελίας, *Dominus promissionis,* it is not only the Lord is not slacke of his promise, but the Lord of his promise is not slacke; ..." (in reference to 2 *Pet.* 3.9).

For example, when he is expounding *Hebrews* 13.22, he makes the mistake of implying that the Greek παρακλήσεως in the text is the exact equivalent of the Vulgate *solatii* and the English "of comfort," whereas the Greek word has a much wider meaning than the Latin, and is better translated here by the Authorized Version "of exhortation."[68]

There are one or two mistakes in the use which he makes of his few Greek words. In a sermon preached on Trinity Sunday, 1624, there are in the Folio three mistakes in three separate Greek words. Speaking of letters used for the Trinity, the Folio reads: "The Π was Πατρὸς, and the Υ was Υἱὸs, ... A was Αγιον ..." In our edition we have corrected Πατρὸς to Πατήρ, Υἱὸs to Υἱοs, and Αγιον to Ἅγιον.[69] It is possible that the printer may have been responsible for the smaller mistakes, but he is unlikely to have altered Πατήρ to Πατρὸς. Alford agrees with us in reading Πατήρ.

On the other hand, he is correct in his statement about *John* 20.15: "For the ordinary appellation of *Lord* in the New Testament, which is Κύριος, it is but a name of Civility, ... *Mary Magdalen* speaks of Christ, and speakes to the Gardiner, (as she thought) and both in one and the same word; it is Κύριος, *Dominus, Lord,* to both: when she sayes, *They have taken away my Lord,* meaning Christ, and when she saies to the Gardiner, *Sir, if thou hast borne him hence,* it is the same word too."[70]

Other examples of Greek words in the *Sermons* are: Εὐλογία (Vol. III, p. 259); Λόγος (*ibid.* and also Vol. VIII, p. 119); παροικίας (Vol. III, p. 287); λατρέια (Vol. IX, p. 161); and Συνέδριον (Vol. IX, p. 163).

In a few places Donne transliterates a Greek word into Roman letters. This occurs in Vol. III, p. 171: "The word from which scandall is derived (*scazein*)[71] signifies *claudicare,* to halt." In Vol. IX, p. 163,

---

[68] Vol. IX, p. 353: "...*I beseech yee, brethren, suffer a word of Exhortation.* And the strangenesse of the case is exalted in this, that the word there is παρακλήσεως, *Solatii,* and so the Vulgat reads it, and justly, *Vt sufferatis verbum solatii, I beseech yee to suffer a word of Comfort.*"

[69] Vol. VI, p. 145 (*LXXX Sermons,* p. 429). See our textual note on p. 369.

[70] Vol. III, p. 296; see also *ibid.,* p. 138, on the same text.

[71] The round brackets here are used, as often elsewhere in the Folio, to denote a quotation. See our note in Vol. III, p. 407.

after Συνέδριον has once been printed in Greek letters, it appears twice on the same page as *Synedrion*. In Vol. VII, p. 450, ὁ Παράκλητος appears in the latinized form *Paracletus*, which is not used in the Vulgate of the text which Donne is discussing (1 *John* 2.1–2), though the Vulgate uses it in *John* 14.16 and 15.26. In Vol. I, p. 310, Donne writes, "Now this [Jesus] is a name, which though the Greeks have translated it into *soter*,..." where we should have expected σωτήρ. Again in Vol. V, p. 103, he writes, "For God is *Logos, speech* and *reason:* He declares his will by his *Word*, and he proves it, he confirmes it; he is *Logos*, and he proceeds *Logically*." In Vol. IV, p. 119, he says, "*Christus Ratio*, says one of them [the early Fathers], well, (for *Logos*, is *Ratio*, and not only *Verbum*, as it is ordinarily translated)." This shows that Donne was fully aware of the dual meaning of λόγος, as "word" and "reason."

In a few places Donne does not attempt to quote the Greek, but merely notes that the Authorized Version differs from the original. Thus in Vol. IV, p. 290, on *Col.* 1.19, he writes "...for this personall name of the Father (*It pleased the Father*) is but added suppletorily by our Translators, and is not in the Originall." This is correct, but it does not prove that he had consulted the Greek, for the Authorized Version prints "the Father" in italics to indicate that the words were not in the Greek.

VULGATE AND OTHER LATIN VERSIONS

The Vulgate was the Bible of Donne's upbringing, and it was evidently the version which came first to his mind. He quotes it again and again in front of the English (either Geneva or A.V.), where to us there seems no need of doing so.[72] He regarded it with affection and respect, but he was careful to point out that in numerous places it does not adequately represent the Hebrew text. For example, he writes on *Job* 10.20: "The words in *Iob* are in the Vulgat, *Dimitte me ut plangam dolorem meum: Lord spare me a while that I may*

---

[72] See Vol. I, p. 177, "...*Ingravatum est cor Pharaonis, Pharaoh's* heart was hardned"; *ibid.*, p. 191, "*Cor mundum crea, Create, O Lord, a pure heart in me*"; Vol. IX, p. 136, "*Man is*, sayes the Prophet *Esay, Quasi stilla situlæ, As a drop upon the bucket.*" These examples come from the beginning and the end of Donne's ministry, and dozens of examples could be produced from the intervening volumes.

lament my lamentable estate: and so ordinarily the Expositors that follow that Translation, make their use of them. But yet it is in the Originall, *Lord spare me a while, that I may take comfort.*"[73] He complains that the Roman expositors have twisted the Vulgate reading of *Exod.* 25.25 to support an erroneous doctrine. "But then, because in their Translation, in the vulgat Edition of the Roman Church, they find in Exodus that word *Aureolam, Facies Coronam aureolam,* Thou shalt make a lesser Crowne of gold; out of this diminutive, and mistaken word, they have established a Doctrine, that besides those *Coronæ aureæ,* Those Crownes of gold, which are communicated to all the Saints from the Crown of Christ, some Saints have made to themselves, and produced out of their owne extraordinary merits certaine *Aureolas,* certaine lesser Crownes of their own, whereas indeed the word in the Originall in that place of Exodus is *Zer zehab,* which is a Crowne of gold, without any intimation of any such lesser crownes growing out of themselves."[74]

Perhaps Donne's longest discussion of the Vulgate and its relation to the Hebrew is to be found in his sermon on *Psa.* 2.12 in a passage which we have already quoted in part under our discussion of the Chaldee Version.[75] After the end of our quotation there Donne continues:

Now very many, very learned, and very zealous men of our times, have been very vehement against that Translation of the Roman Church, though it be strengthned, by the Chalde, by the Septuagint, and by the Fathers, in this place. The reason of the vehemence in this place, is not because that sense, which that translation presents, may not be admitted; no, nor that it does not reach home, to that which is intended in ours, *Kisse the Sonne:* ... The case then being thus, that that sense may be admitted, ... why are our late men so very vehement against it? Truly, upon very just reason: for, when those former reverent men were so moderate as to admit that translation in this place; The Church of Rome, had not then put such a sanctity, such a reverence, such a singularity, and preheminence, ... upon that Translation; It had the estimation then of a very reverend Translation, and compared with any other Translations, then the best. But when in the Councell of Trent they came to make it as

[73] Vol. IV, p. 343.

[74] Vol. VII, pp. 129–130. For other passages in which Donne corrects the Vulgate by referring to the Hebrew, see Vol. VIII, pp. 110–111, and 258.

[75] See p. 313 above.

Authenticall, to prefer it before the Originals themselves, to decide all matters of Controversie by it alone, and to make the doing so, matter of faith, and heresie, in any thing to depart from that Translation, then came these later men justly to charge it with those errors, wherein, by their own confessions, it hath departed from the Originall; Not that these men meant to discredit that Translation so, as that it should not still retain the estimation of a good and usefull Translation, but to avoyd that danger, that it should be made matter of faith, to be bound to one Translation; or that any Translation should be preferred before the Originall."[76]

On the other hand, Donne sometimes prefers the Vulgate reading as being closer to the Hebrew than that of A.V. On *Isa.* 40.2 he remarks: *"Loqui ad Cor Jerusalem,* to speak to the heart of *Jerusalem,* is ever the Scripture phrase, from God to man, to speak comfortably" (Vol. IV, p. 108). Here A.V. reads "Speak ye comfortably to Jerusalem," with a marginal note *"Heb. to the heart"* against "comfortably." Another example can be found in *Psa.* 66.3, where Donne points out that the Septuagint and the Vulgate are nearer to the Hebrew than the A.V. reading "...shall thine enemies submit themselves unto thee."[77] Perhaps the most remarkable example of Donne's enduring affection for the Vulgate is to be found in his frequent citation of the Vulgate reading of *Zech.* 6.12, "Ecce vir Oriens nomen ejus," in preference to that of A.V.[78]

Donne's quotations from the Vulgate are so numerous that it would be useless to make a list of them here. He generally quotes the words accurately, but not always in the right order, and sometimes he quotes from memory and slightly modifies the words.[79] Occasion-

---

[76] Vol. III, pp. 315–316. Compare a somewhat similar passage in Vol. VIII, p. 207: "The Translation is a reverend Translation; A Translation to which the Church of God owes much; but gold will make an Idol as well as wood, and to make any Translation equall, or better then the Originall, is an Idolatrous servility."

[77] Vol. IX, p. 301. Donne uses the term "S. *Ierome*" as equivalent to the Vulgate, here and elsewhere.

[78] See our discussion of this point on pp. 257–258 and 304–305 of the present volume.

[79] See Vol. III, p. 259, *"Calici benedictionis benedicimus"* for the Vulgate's "Calix benedictionis, cui benedicimus"; Vol. IV, p. 289, *"Ne evacuretur Crux Christi"* for "ut non evacuetur Crux Christi"; Vol. VIII, p. 342, "The Vulgar hath it, *Meditatur,"* for "meditabitur."

ally he quotes a short phrase from the Vulgate without troubling to translate it. Thus he speaks of Christ's *Consummatum est*[80] or quotes from the Lord's Prayer, *Dimitte debita,*[81] in the assurance that most of his hearers will recognize the words in their Latin form.

Our edition has made it clear that Donne must have continued throughout his ministry to use an early edition of the Vulgate (perhaps that of 1564 or 1578) before the Clementine recension of 1592, because on at least two occasions he drew attention to a Vulgate reading which was to be found only in the earlier editions. Thus he wrote in a sermon preached on March 8, 1622: "... and so much the vulgat Edition seemes to intimate, when (*Deut.* 30.19.) whereas we reade, I have set before you life and death, that reades it, *Vitam & bonum,* Life, and that which is good."[82] Another example is to be found as late as the Whitsunday sermon of 1629, where Donne wrote: "God can save from dangers, though a man went to Sea without art [*Wisd.* 14.4], *Sine rate,* saies the Vulgat, without a Ship."[83]

In addition to the Vulgate Donne consulted the Latin translation by Tremellius of the Old Testament canonical books.[84] Thus in a sermon preached at Lincoln's Inn, probably in the spring of 1620, he has three allusions to Tremellius.[85] Speaking of his text (*Job* 19.26), in which the Hebrew does not mention worms, he writes: "... both our later translations, (for indeed, our first translation hath no mention of *wormes*) and so very many others, even *Tremellius* that adheres most to the letter of the Hebrew, have filled up this place,

---

[80] Vol. V, p. 136.

[81] Vol. I, p. 189. See also Vol. V, p. 213: "Depart with an *In manus tuas,* and with a *Veni Domine Iesu* [*Luk.* 23.46 and *Rev.* 22.20]."

[82] Vol. IV, p. 54. The earlier Vulgate editions read "bonum," as Donne states, with "mortem" in the margin, but in the Clementine recension "mortem" appeared in the text. See our note in Vol. IV, p. 385.

[83] Vol. IX, p. 107. See our note, *ibid.,* p. 432.

[84] This translation, which Tremellius made with Francis Junius, was published at Frankfurt in 1575–1579. It was printed in London in 1580, along with a translation of the New Testament made from the Syriac by Tremellius alone. Donne's metrical paraphase *"The Lamentations of* Ieremy, *for the most part according to* Tremellius" (*Poems,* ed. Grierson I, 354) shows the interest which Donne took in Tremellius' version of the Old Testament.

[85] Vol. III, pp. 101, 105, 106.

with that addition, *Destroyed by worms."* In his fourth Prebend
sermon, preached in January, 1627, on *Psa.* 65.5, "By terrible things
in righteousness wilt thou answer us, O God of our salvation," he
says, "And these *Terrible things* are Reverend things; and so *Tremellius* translates it, and well; *Per res Reverendas, By Reverend things . . .
thou shalt answer us."*[86] On *Job* 16.19 he observes, "The oldest Latine
Translation received this variation, and the last Latine, even *Tremellius* himselfe, (as close as he sticks to the Hebrew) retaines this variation, *Testis,* and *Conscius."*[87] On *Psa.* 32.1 he writes concerning the
title of the psalm, "And therefore *Tremellius* hath inserted that word,
An Ode of David, we [i.e., the A.V.], *A Psalme of David, . . ."*[88] On
Psa. 66.3 he comments, "S. *Ierome,* and the Septuagint before, and
Tremellius after, and all that binde themselves to the Hebrew letter,
reade it thus, *Mentientur tibi inimici tui,* when thy power is shewed
upon them, . . . *thine enemies will lie unto thee."*[89]

Another Latin translation which Donne mentions, though he does
not seem to have made much use of it, is that which appeared at Lyons
in 1528 by Sante Pagnini, a good Oriental scholar. On *Genesis* 1.2 he
writes, "God had created Heaven and Earth, and then *The Spirit of
God, sufflabat,* saith *Pagnins* translation, (and so saith the *Chalde
Paraphrase* too) it *breathed upon the waters."*[90] Also in his sermon on
Psa. 32.9 he writes, "And that office God undertakes in the verse
before our Text, *I will instruct thee,* which is in some Latin Copies,
Faciam te intelligere, I will make thee understand, and in others,

---

[86] Vol. VII, p. 314.
[87] Vol. IX, p. 226.
[88] *Ibid.,* p. 251.
[89] *Ibid.,* p. 301. See also Vol. V, p. 340. In his quotation from *Isa.* 25.8,
"*Deus absterget omnem lacrymam . . . He will wipe all teares from thine
eyes*" (Vol. VIII, p. 201) Donne is using Tremellius, for the Vulgate reads
"auferet Dominus Deus lacrymam . . ." Also when he quotes *Micah* 2.13
as "*ascendit illa effractor*" (Vol. IV, p. 357) he must have been thinking
of Tremellius' "Ascendit effractor," for the Vulgate reads "Ascendit enim
pandens iter." On *Psa.* 90.14 he quotes the Vulgate first, and then Tremellius: ". . . with that he will satisfie us *Mane,* early, and as *Tremellius* reads
this very Text, *unoquoque mane,* betimes in the morning, and every morning" (Vol. V, p. 281).
[90] Vol. IV, p. 251.

(the vulgat) *Intellectum tibi dabo, I will give thee understanding.*[91]
We do not claim to have examined all the numerous Latin translations, but Allen (*op. cit.,* p. 225) states that the only version which
approximates to this reading is that of Pagnini, which reads "Intelligere faciam te."

ENGLISH VERSIONS

Donne has one reference to Wyclif's translation, made in the late fourteenth century, which he calls "the first Translation of all into our
Language." This occurs in his Third Prebend Sermon, and the passage is interesting, for it brings together four English translations.
Donne is discussing *Psa.* 64.10, "All the upright in heart shall glory."
He writes: "This Retribution is expressed in the Originall, in the
word *Halal;* And *Halal,* to those Translators that made up our
Booke of Common Prayer, presented the signification of *Gladnesse,*
for so it is there, *They shall be glad;* So it did to the Translators that
came after, for there it is, *They shall rejoyce;* And to our last Translators it seemed to signifie *Glory, They shall Glory,* say they. But the
first Translation of all into our Language (which was long before
any of these three) cals it *Praise,* and puts it in the Passive, *All men
of rightfull heart shall be praised.* He followed S. *Hierom* [i.e., the
Vulgate], who reads it so, and interprets it so, in the Passive, *Lauda-
buntur, They shall be praised.* And so truly *Iithhalelu,* in the Original,
beares it, nay requires it; . . ."[92]

With the exception of this single reference, Donne's quotations are
taken from one or other of the following translations: Coverdale's,
printed first at Zürich in 1535; the Great Bible of 1539, which was
largely Coverdale's work, and which was ordered for use in churches;
the Geneva Bible of 1560, which went into several editions; the
Bishops' Bible of 1568; and finally the King James's, or Authorized
Version of 1611.

Mention ought perhaps to be made of the version of the New Testament into English by Gregory Martin, printed at Rheims in 1582,
and of the Old Testament by the English College of Douai, printed
at Douai in 1609. Both of these were translated from the Vulgate

---

[91] Vol. IX, p. 382.
[92] Vol. VII, p. 248. See also p. 253.

under Roman authority, and they were intended to replace the
Protestant English versions. We have found no evidence that Donne
made use of them, though occasionally his own literal translation of
phrases from the Vulgate coincides with the Douai rendering.

There are one or two references in the *Sermons* to the Bishops'
Bible, such as that in an undated sermon on *Psa.* 6.1: "Rebuke me not
in thine anger, nor chasten me in thy hot displeasure": "For the words
themselves, all our three Translations retaine the two first words, to
Rebuke, and to *Chasten;* neither that which we call the *Bishops Bible,*
nor that which we call the *Geneva Bible,* and that which wee may
call the *Kings,* depart from those two first words. But then for the
other two, *Anger* and *Hot displeasure,* in them all three Translations
differ. The first cals them *Indignation* and *Displeasure,* the second
Anger and *Wrath,* and the last *Anger* and *Hot displeasure.*"[93]

For the most part, however, Donne's quotations are taken from
the Geneva and the Authorized Versions, with some quotations (for
the Psalms only) from the Great Bible, since the Book of Common
Prayer, in which the whole Psalter is printed, has retained the translation of the Great Bible up to the present day.[94] One or two instances
may be quoted here. In Vol. V, p. 184, Donne's *"Tush the Lord sees
it not"* is an adaptation of the Prayer Book's "Tush, the Lord shall
not see," where A.V. has "the Lord shall not see" (without "Tush"
or any equivalent word). In Vol. V, p. 207, Donne keeps the Prayer
Book's "seek peace and ensue it," where A.V. has "seek peace and
pursue it" (*Psa.* 34.14).

In his *Essays in Divinity* Donne used the Geneva Bible throughout.
In Volume I of our edition, which contains his earliest dated sermons,
we find, by detailed examination, that though Donne took his sermon
texts from the A.V., his quotations are generally nearer Geneva than
A.V. Thus in the first sermon, where Donne quotes *Gen.* 31.15 as
"He ... hath eat, and consumed the money," he is much closer to

---

[93] Vol. V, p. 332.
[94] This is a remarkable example of the power of choral music to stand-
ardize a translation. The text of the Epistles and Gospels in the Prayer
Book has been altered from the Great Bible to the Authorized Version,
but the fact that the Psalms are sung to certain chants has preserved the
inferior early translation, in spite of its many inaccuracies.

"He ... hath eaten up and consumed ..." (Geneva) than to *"He ... hath quite devoured also ..."* (A.V.) In the quotation from *Isa.* 43.3-4, the words are exactly as in Geneva, with the curious *"therfore will I give man for thee, and people for thy sake,"* which appears in A.V. as "therefore will I give men for thee, and people for thy life." In the second sermon there are twelve quotations nearer to Geneva, and three nearer to A.V., while in both sermons there are a number of quotations which are alike in the two versions.

These are the only dated sermons for the first two years of Donne's ministry, but there is an undated sermon "Preached at the Temple" for which evidence has lately been discovered indicating that it was probably preached in June, 1615.[95] In this sermon the text (*Est.* 4.16) and all the quotations are taken from Geneva, though, as we might expect, some of these are alike in both versions. There are also four undated christening sermons, which we believe to be fairly early, though we have no definite external evidence, and the texts of these four are all taken from Geneva.[96] Thus the first, which is from *Rev.* 7.17, runs thus: "For the Lamb which is in the midst of the throne, shall govern them, and shall leade them unto the lively fountains of waters, ..." where A.V. reads, "For the Lamb, which is in the midst of the throne, shall feed them, and shall lead them unto living fountains of waters ..." In the course of his sermon, Donne comments on the differences between "govern" and "feed," and between "lively" and "living," and notes that for the concluding phrase, "the originall," that is, the Greek, has "unto the fountaines of the water of life."[97] It is curious that Donne should have preferred the more archaic forms of Geneva for his text.

If we return to dated sermons we find that though the proportion of references from A.V. is higher in the sermons preached in 1617 and 1618 than in those for 1615 and 1616, Donne still made considerable use of Geneva. Thus in Sermon 3 of Volume I, preached at Paul's Cross on March 24, 1616/17, we find (lines 168–169) that *"Would to God, they were even cut off that disquiet you"* is from Geneva

---

[95] See Vol. V, pp. 15–16.

[96] These are printed in Vol. V, as Nos. 4–7, pp. 96–167.

[97] Vol. V, pp. 105, 109. The Greek has ἐπὶ ζωῆς πηγὰς ὑδάτων, and the Vulgate, "ad vitæ fontes aquarum."

·(*Gal.* 5.12), where A.V. has "I would they were even cut off which trouble you." In lines 300–301, *"Who can bring a clean thing out of filthiness? There is not one"* is from Geneva (*Job* 14.4). A.V. reads "Who can bring a clean thing out of an unclean? not one." There is a more striking instance in lines 1172–1175, quoting *Psa.* 101.5: *"Him* (says he) *that hath a proud look, and a high heart, I cannot;* and there he ends abruptly; He does not say, I cannot work upon him, ... but only, *I cannot,* and no more." Here the Geneva text runs as Donne quotes it, but adds in square brackets "[suffer]" to show that the word so added is not in the original. A.V. reads "Him that hath an high looke, and a proud heart, will not I suffer." Donne evidently expected his audience at Paul's Cross to be more familiar with Geneva than with A.V., and he was probably right; for the Geneva Bible, with its annotations and illustrations, remained the favourite book of the populace for many years.

Sometimes there was a special reason for Donne's choice of Geneva. Thus when he preached at the marriage of Margaret Washington in May, 1621, his text (from Geneva) was "And I will mary thee unto me for ever" (*Hos.* 2.19), where A.V. has "And I will betroth thee unto me for ever." Donne justified his choice by reference to the Hebrew in the first paragraph of his sermon: "The word which is the hinge upon which all this Text turns, is *Erash,* and *Erash* signifies not onely a betrothing, as our later Translation [i.e., A.V.] hath it, but a mariage; ... and so our former Translation [i.e., Geneva] had it, and so we accept it, and so shall handle it, *I will mary thee unto me for ever."*[98]

We might have thought that Donne would be careful to use the King James version when he was preaching at Whitehall, but in his sermon there on April 30, 1620, he took his text, "Blessed are the People that be so; yea blessed are the People, whose God is the Lord" (*Psa.* 144.15), from Geneva, preferring it to "Happy is that people that is in such a case; yea, happy is that people, whose God is the Lord."[99] It may be that he did this because his sermon was based on

---

[98] Vol. III, p. 241.

[99] Vol. III, p. 73. Another example can be found in Vol. II, where the text of Sermon 18, *Amos* 5.18, is not from A.V. but from either the Bishops' Bible or Geneva.

the thought of blessedness, with its suggestion of God's favour, rather than on happiness, which has a more worldly connotation.

After Donne became Dean of St. Paul's he used Geneva much less frequently. The lessons read daily in the Cathedral were taken from the Authorized Version, and gradually its splendid cadences must have impressed themselves firmly on his mind. Still there are occasional echoes of Geneva.[100] It is strange that Donne should have been so slow in realizing the superiority of the Authorized, both in accuracy and in style, over all previous versions.

Finally we note that in quoting from memory, whether from the Authorized or from earlier versions, Donne used considerable freedom. He transposed words, he altered tenses, he omitted or inserted articles or particles. In his own day he was criticized for this freedom, and he defended himself stalwartly. In preaching on *Acts* 10.44 he remarked: "S. *Peter* tooke his Text here, *ver.* 34. out of *Deuteronomy, Of a truth I perceive, that God is no respecter of persons.* Where, because the words are not precisely the same in *Deuteronomy,* as they are in this Text, we finde just occasion to note, That neither Christ in his preaching, nor the holy Ghost in penning the Scriptures of the new Testament, were so curious as our times, in citing Chapters and Verses, or such distinctions, no nor in citing the very, very words of the places.... if we consider that one place in the Prophet *Esay* ... and consider the same place, as it is cited six severall times in the new Testament, we shall see, that they stood not upon such exact quotations, and citing of the very words."[101]

In these alterations Donne never falsified the meaning of the text. His license was that of a poet. St. Paul wrote, "The letter killeth, but the spirit giveth life." As an expositor Donne sometimes failed through his lack of exact scholarship, but as an interpreter of the spirit of Scripture he stands high.

---

[100] Vol. VII, p. 284, the reference to *Prov.* 16.31 is from Geneva; Vol. VIII, p. 293, reference to *Act.* 10.34; *ibid.,* p. 198, reference to *Job* 5.7; Vol. IX, p. 106, reference to *Isa.* 44.3.

[101] Vol. V, p. 44.

APPENDIX

LIST OF HEBREW WORDS ON WHICH DONNE COMMENTS IN THE SERMONS

[The system of transliteration from the Hebrew employed by Donne was not invented by him. It seems to be roughly similar to that used by Victorinus Bythner, whose *Lingua eruditorum* was published at Oxford by G. Turner in 1638, and again at Cambridge in 1645. In our note on *Ragnah* (Vol. I of our edition, p. 326) we commented on Donne's transliteration of the ayin as "gn." The Rev. J. R. Porter has pointed out that Bythner uses the nearly similar "ghn" for the medial form and "ngh" (where Donne has "ng," as in *pashang* in *Psa.* 32.1) for the final form. In dealing with such consonants as beth, gimel, daleth, Donne ignores the presence or absence of the dagesh lene, i.e., he makes no distinction between "b" and "bh," "g" and "gh," "d" and "dh." On the other hand, he generally renders pe as "ph," though in *pashang* he correctly uses "p." He renders zayin as "z" except in *casah* (*Job* 36.25), where it is "s." Cheth is usually "ch," but at least four times "c" and four times "k." Koph is usually "k," but "ch" in *chevi* (*Lev.* 26.21). Resh is "r" except in *chevi,* which should be *cheri.* Either this is a misprint or Donne has made the easy mistake of confusing resh and vau. He usually represents sin as "s" and shin as "sh," but in *Prov.* 14.31 he has *gnoshehu* incorrectly. In several of his transliterations he follows the text or the margin of A.V., as in *teraphim* in *Hos.* 3.4 (where the Vulgate has "theraphim") and *Ziim* in *Isa.* 13.21 *mg.*]

Gen. 1.1. *Bara Elohim*
A.V. God created   Vulg. Creavit Deus

This was a well-known crux for the commentators. The word for God, *Elohim,* is a plural form, but *bara,* the verb of which *Elohim* is the subject, is in the singular. Some commentators, of whom the first appears to have been Peter Lombard, held that this lack of agreement between subject and verb was an intimation of the Trinity. After Lombard this was accepted by Burgensis, Lyra, Eugubinus, Catharinus, Luther, Chytraeus, and Ferus (Johann Wild). On the other hand Tostatus and Cajetan, followed by Calvin and most of the later sixteenth-century commentators, refused to accept this notion.[1] Some of them regarded the plural as a regal one, "used in accordance with the idiom of the Hebrew Language to denote rever-

[1] See Arnold Williams, *The Common Expositor,* Univ. of North Carolina Press, 1948, pp. 234–235. Donne certainly consulted the huge commentary of Benedictus Pererius, *In Genesin,* Rome, 1589–1598, Cologne (first complete edition), 1601, of which he had made much use in *Essays in Divinity.*

ence and honour." Paræus and Rivetus regarded the question as one of linguistic usage, and, after examining a number of scriptural passages, came to the conclusion that *Elohim* "is plural in form only, but according to the idiom of the language construed as a singular noun and correctly taking a singular verb."[2]

In Vol. VIII, sermon 1, lines 659–694, Donne recognizes that this passage affords no evidence against the Jews for an intimation of the Trinity, and states that Christians must base their belief on passages in the New Testament, but he thinks that those who already believe can find comfort in the idea that there is here some "intimation" of the Trinity. He writes: "We that have been catechized, and brought up in the knowledge of the Trinity, finde much strength, and much comfort, in that we finde, in the first line of the Bible, that *Bara Elohim, Creavit Dii, Gods created heaven and earth;* In this, that there is the name of God in the plurall, joyned to a Verb of the singular number, we apprehend an intimation of divers persons in one God; . . . The Jews, which believe not the Trinity, find no such thing." Donne continues by quoting *Gen.* 1.26, *"Faciamus hominem, . . .* God sayes, *Let us,* us in the plurall, *make man,"* and *Isa.* 6.8, *"Whom shall I send, or who shall goe for us?"* These, says Donne, are regarded by Christians as intimations of the Trinity in the Old Testament; "But what man, that had not been catechized in that Doctrine before, would have conceived an opinion, or established a faith in the Trinity, upon those phrases in *Moses,* or in *Esay,* without other evidence?" He continues: "Let us be content, to receive our light there, where God hath been pleased to give it; that is, in those places of the new Testament, which admit no contradiction, nor disputation."[3]

Elsewhere Donne quotes *Gen.* 35.7, *Exod.* 4.16, *Deut.* 6.4, *Josh.* 24.19, to show "that the name of our one God, is expressed in the plurall number" by the use of *Elohim.*[4]

Gen. 1.2. *Ruach*
A.V. Spirit   IV. 9. 517, 542, 546, 669, 685, 699.

Gen. 1.2. *Recaph*
A.V. moved   IX. 3. 268

---

[2] Williams, *op. cit.,* p. 245.

[3] Donne had written more clearly and forcibly against using this text as an argument for the Trinity, in *Essays in Divinity* (ed. Simpson, 1952), p. 26, where he mentions Peter Lombard, Galatinus, Lyra, Catharinus, and Luther as supporting the notion, but himself agrees with Calvin and Paræus that the phrase is a Hebrew idiom.

[4] III. 12. 320–326. (References in this style signify the volume of the present edition, the number of the sermon in that volume, and the line or lines of the sermon.) See also III. 13. 11–17. For the supposed derivation of *Elohim* see I. 4. 446, II. 15. 281.

Gen. 1.26, 2.7, 8, 15, etc., 3.8, 9. *Adam*
A.V. the man (mg. *Or, Adam*) in 2.15, Adam (mg. *Or, the man*) in 2.19–23.

II. 2. 240, 244–250; II. 9. 118; IX. 1. 536, 565. In all these passages Donne discussed *Adam* with the other Hebrew names for man, *Ish, Enosh, Gheber.* Following most of the commentators he explained that *Adam* denotes 'red earth.'

Gen. 1.31 and 25.25, and *Eccles.* 8.11. *Gnesau* ('Esau)
A.V. made (*Gen.* 1.31), executed (*Eccles.* 8.11), Esau (*Gen.* 25.25) as a proper name

I. 2. 214–216. "When *Esau* was born hairy, ... he was call'd by the word of this text, *Gnesau, Esau, factus, perfectus.* And so, when God had perfected all his works, ... there is the same word, *That he had perfected.*" (*Gen.* 1. ult. in mg.)

Gen. 2.4, 5, 7, etc., *Exod.* 6.3 *et passim. Jehovah*
A.V. the Lord (*Gen.* 2.4, etc.), Jehovah (*Exod.* 6.3, *Psa.* 83.18, *Isa.* 12.2 and 26.4)

I. 4. 452; II. 6. 582, 583; V. 16. 219–257. In the third of these passages, Donne discusses the form *Iehovah* found in the 1611 edition of A.V. and decides that the proper pronunciation of the *Tetragrammaton,* or sacred name of four letters, as it is in the Hebrew, is a difficult one. "How this name which we call *Iehovah,* is truly to be sounded, because in that language it is exprest in foure Consonants onely, without Vowels, is a perplext question; ... Neither doth it appeare to me, that ever the name of *Iehovah* was so pronounced, till so late, as in our Fathers time; for I think *Petrus Galatinus* was the first that ever called it so." This statement about Galatinus is confirmed by *N.E.D.* in its article on *Jehovah.* Cp. Donne's earlier discusson of the name *Jehovah* in *Essays in Divinity,* ed. Simpson, p. 25. Originally the Hebrew O.T. was only consonantal, and had no written vowels. By the time that vowel points were added, the Jews had ceased to pronounce the tetragrammaton from motives of reverence. So the scholars put under the consonants of the tetragrammaton the vowels of *Adonai,* to indicate that the latter was to be substituted in public reading. Donne is right in saying that we no longer know for certain how the tetragrammaton was pronounced.

Gen. 2.7. *Neshamah*
A.V. breath   IV. 9. 671, 685, 687, 700

Ibid. Chaiim or *Chajim*
A.V. of life   VII. 1. 668; IX. 5. 656
Donne notes correctly that *Chaiim* is a plural form, '*of lives.*'

Gen. 2.24. Ish
A.V. man   Vulg. homo
II. 2. 251. "But the first name, by which God called man in generall, *mankinde*, is *Ish*, ... And *Ish*, is but *à sonitu, à rugitu:* Man hath his name from *crying*, ..." Also II. 9. 115; IX. 1. 540.

Gen. 6.5. Jetzer
A.V. imagination   Vulg. cogitatio   II. 6. 347–348

Gen. 17.24, also *Job 18.16. Mul ... Namal*
A.V. circumcise (in *Job* cut off)   VI. 9. 438, 536–537
The first word here, *mul*, is the one used in *Gen.* 17.24, for the verb 'to circumcise,' and the second, *namal*, is really a form of it, the Niphal. It occurs in verse 26 as *nimmol*. But some older grammarians believed that there was also a root *namal* with the same meaning as *mul;* e.g., Valentinus Schindlerus gives it on p. 1124 of his *Lexicon Pentaglotton*, published at Hanover in 1612, and quotes *Gen.* 17.11 for its use. When in line 536 Donne states that "from this word *Namal*, comes *Nemâla*, which is *Formica, an Ant*, ..." he is using a fanciful etymology which was well established in his day. See Schindlerus, *op. cit.*, pp. 1124 f., where he quotes Pliny's *Natural History*, ii.1.30. In this second passage Donne is referring to *Job.* 18.16, where A.V. has "cut off." In line 535 we should read *Excidere* in place of *Excedere* (*F*). The Hebrew word in this verse is actually from another root *malal*, 'to wither or perish,' but Conradus Kircherus in his *Concordantiæ veteris Testamenti*, Frankfort, 1607, Vol. II, p. 25, puts the word under *mul*, and gives the meaning as 'incido.'

Gen. 28. 13. Nitzab
A.V. stood   Vulg. innixum
II. 10. 467–468. "... as the *Originall* hath it, *Nitzab*, that he leanes upon this ladder, as the *vulgar* hath it, *Innixus scalæ*, that he rests upon it, ..."

Gen. 31.19, also 1 *Sam.* 19.13, *Ezek.* 21.21, *Hos.* 3.4. *Teraphim*
A.V. images (teraphim in *Hos.* 3.4)   Vulg. idola (theraphim in *Hos.* 3.4)
VII. 17. 578–585. "... that which is not translated, but kept in the originall word, *Teraphim* ... though when *Rachel* stole her fathers *Teraphim*, (*Images*) though when the King of *Babylon* consulted with *Teraphim*, (*Images*) the word *Teraphim* have an ill sense, yet, when *Michal, Davids* wife, put an *Image* into his bed, to elude the fury of *Saul*, there the word hath no ill sense." The round brackets in this passage are used in the Folio as a sign of quotation.

Exod. 2.3. Thebah (Tebah)
A.V. ark   X. 11. 112

Exod. 4.25. *Damim* (plur.)
A.V. bloody   Vulg. sanguinum

IX. 1. 680–684. "That which *Zipporah* said to her husband *Moses* in anger,... *Verè sponsus sanguinum,* thou art truly a bloudy husband to me; *Damim, sanguinum,* of blouds, blouds in the plurall;..."

Exod. 22.29. *Vedingnacha* (Wedim'aka)
A.V. liquors   (mg. *Heb. tear*)

IV. 13. 653. "The word in the Originall is *Vedingnacha, lachrymarum,* and of thy teares:..." Actually the word means 'juice' (of the vine). Evidently Donne took his explanation from the margin of A.V.

Exod. 25.25. *Zer zehab* [for *zehab* read *zahab*]
A.V. a golden crown   VII. 4. 439

Exod. 34.9. *Nachal*
A.V. inheritance

III. 4. 545–547. "... the *Hebrew* word, *Nachal;* and *Nachal* is *Hæreditas cum possessione;* not an inheritance in reversion, but in possession." *Nachal* is the root, not the actual word used in this passage.

Lev. 26.21, 24. *Chevi*
A.V. contrary   Vulg. ex adverso

VII. 14. 498–502. "Nay, it is not onely in that place, *If you walk contrary to me, In occursu,* as *Calvin* hath it, *ex adverso,* as the *vulgate* hath it, which implies an *Actuall* Opposition against the wayes of God: but the word is but *Chevi,* and *Chevi* is but *In accidente, in contingente;...*" *Chevi* should be *Cheri,* according to Donne's system of transliteration.

Deut. 12.30. *Achareihem*
A.V. following them

IV. 4. 271–272. "... the Original word which we translate, *following,* is *Achareihem,* and it is only *post eos, Come not after them;...*"

1 *Sam.* 9.9. *Roeh*
A.V. seer   VIII. 13. 226

1 *Sam.* 9.9. *Nabi ... Niba*
A.V. prophet

VIII. 13. 228–232. "... for so we have it in *Samuel, He that is now called a Prophet,...* for, *Nabi,* which is a Prophet, is from *Niba;* and *Niba,* is *venire facio,* to cause, to make a thing to come to passe." This is incorrect. The verbal form is derived from the noun, and it means 'to prophesy' or 'to act like a prophet.'

1 *Sam.* 26.12. *Tardemath Jehovah*
A.V. a deep sleep from the Lord   Vulg. sopor Domini
  I. 3. 1003–05. "It is called, *Tardemath Jehovah, sopor Domini, The sleep of the Lord,* The greatest sleep that could possess a man; ..."

1 *Sam.* 31.3. *Calah*
A.V. wound
  X. 5. 166–169. "*Calah* is *Dolere,* to grieve ... But it signifies also *vulnerare,* to wound, ... *Saul was sore wounded.*"

2 *Sam.* 1.26, and *Psa.* 32.7. *Tzur*
A.V. distressed (in *Psa.* 32.7 trouble)
  IX. 15. 271–273. "But the Originall word *Tzur* hath a more peculiar sense; It signifies a straite, ... a distresse; *I am distressed for thee, my brother Ionathan,*" sayes *David,* ..." So far Donne's comment is correct, but when he goes on in the following lines to connect the word with *Isa.* 21.3, *Psa.* 78.15 and 89.43, he is confusing it with three different Hebrew roots.

1 *Kings* 3.9. *Leb shemmeany* [should be *shomea*]
A.V. an understanding heart   Vulg. cor docile   IX. 7. 202

1 *Kings* 19.15, 16. *Meshiach* [should be *Mashiach*]
A.V. anoint
  VIII. 13. 170–177. "... when God commands him [Elijah] to anoint *Hazael* King of Syria ... and to anoint *Elisha* Prophet ... But then, nothing is more evident, then that this word *Meshiach,* which signifies *Anointing,* is not restrained to that very action, a real unction, ..."

2 *Chron.* 4.9. *Gnazar* ('Azarah)
A.V. the court
  IV. 15. 432–433. "Heere the *Temple* is called *Gnazar,* that is *Auxilium:* A Helper ..." [mg. 2 *Paral.* 4.7].

2 *Chron.* 5.3. *Kag*
A.V. feast   Vulg. in die solemni   IV. 15. 460

Est. 4.16. *Gnalai* ('Alai)
A.V. for me   Vulg. pro me
  V. 11. 267. "... this *Jejunate super me,* as the word is, *Gnalai, super me,* in my behalf, is no more but *Orate pro me,* Pray for me; ..."

Est. 4.16. *Vecasher*
A.V. and if
  V. 11. 479–481. "... she may boldly say, *Si peream, peream;* It is all one though I perish; or as it is in the Original, *Vecasher, quomodocunque peream;* ..."

Job. 13.3. *Shaddai*
A.V. Almighty

III. 8. 128–130. ". . . *Iob* sets before him, that God, whom he conceives to be *Shaddai,* that is, *Omnipotens, Allmighty; I will speake to the All-mighty,* . . ." Also *ibid.,* lines 231, 234, 243. The Vulgate rendering is, as Donne says, *Omnipotens.* But in the following lines Donne goes on to confuse the issue by quoting a word used in *Prov.* 19.26 which is from an entirely different root meaning 'dishonor,' or 'do violence to.' His references to *Isa.* 33.1 and *Jer.* 4.13 are also incorrect.

Job. 13.15. *Jakal* יָחֵל
A.V. trust

III. 8. 280–282. "The word is *Jakal,* and *Jakal* signifies *Expectavit Deum,* his eye, his expectation was upon nothing but God; . . ." The Hebrew is in the margin of the Folio.

Job. 16.19, also *Gen.* 31.47. *Gned* ('Edh)
A.V. witness   IX. 9. 498

Job. 19.26. *Nakaph*
A.V. destroy   III. 3. 527

Job 27.6, also *Prov.* 14.31. *Charak*
A.V. reproach

VIII. 12. 374–378. "Our word here [i.e., *Prov.* 14.31], . . . is *Charak;* and this word *Job* uses, as it is used in our text, for reproach, *My heart shall not reproach me, so long as I live.*"

Job 36.25. *Casah . . . Casu*
A.V. may see

IV. 6. 55–57. "It is but *Casah* in the first, it is *Iabbit* in the second; in that, *every man may see,* in the other, *man may behold." Ibid.,* line 204: ". . . but in the *Originall,* in the Hebrew, it is *Casu,* and *Casu* is, *viderunt:* not, every man *may,* but every man *hath* seen God: . . ." *Casah* is the root, and *Casu* represents the actual form of the word in *Job.*

Job 36.25. *Iabbit*
A.V. may behold

IV. 6. 55, 397–413. ". . . the word in the originall, is *Iabbit,* and that is *videbit,* in the *future, he shall see;* . . . And more then see him; for *Iabbit,* is *Intuebitur,* he will *behold him,* contemplate God, . . ." In line 55, F misprints *Iabbit* as *Nibbat.*

Job 36.25. *Col-Adam*
A.V. every man

IV. 6. 231–236. "*Col-Adam, Omnis homo;* . . . *he* may see God. We have divers names for *man* in Hebrew; . . . This that makes him but earth, *Adam,* is the meanest, and yet *Col-Adam, Every man may see God.*"

Book of Psalms [title] (Book of Praises). *Sepher Tehillim*
   V. 14. 74; IX. 16. 5

Psa. 6.1. Iacach
A.V. rebuke   V. 16. 537, 606

Psa. 6.1. Iasar
A.V. chasten
   V. 16. 637. Donne's reference to 1 *Kings* 12.11 is correct, but in saying
that the word means 'to bind' he seems to be confusing it with another
word.

Psa. 6.4, also 80.3. *Shubah*
A.V. return   V. 18. 134, 136, 164, 192, 206

Psa. 6.4, and *Isa.* 58.11. *Chalatz . . . Iachalitz*
A.V. deliver (*Psa.* 6.4), make fat (*Isa.* 58.11)
   V. 18. 415, 456. Donne's comment is rather fanciful. *Chalatz* is the root
of the word used in *Psa.* 6.4. *Iachalitz* is the actual form of the verb in
Isa. 58.11.

Psa. 6.4. Iashang (Yasha')
A.V. save   V. 18. 476

Psa. 6.4. Casad
A.V. mercy   V. 19. 19

Psa. 6.6, and *Cant.* 2.12. *Anach*
A.V. groaning   VIII. 8. 179
   Anach is the root, not the actual word used.

Psa. 6.8. Shamang
A.V. heard
   VI. 1. 315–319. "*Shamang;* a word of that largenesse in the Scriptures,
that sometimes in the Translation of the Septuagint, it signifies hearing,
Shamang, is *audit,* God gives eare to our teares; . . ."

Psa. 6.10. Iashabu . . . Ieboshu
A.V. Let them return and be ashamed
   VI. 1. 597–598. ". . . those words which are here rendred, *Convertentur,*
& *Erubescent,* and which in the Originall, are *Iashabu,* and *Ieboshu, . . .*"

Psa. 8.4 and 9.20. *Enosh* (*Enos* in II. 9. 124, 130)
A.V. man (men)
   II. 2. 261; II. 9. 124–130; IX. 1. 547–561. In these three passages Donne
compares *Enosh* with *Adam, Ish,* and *Gheber.* In IX. 5. 323–325 he writes:
"But, by the name of *Enosh, Enosh* that signifies *meere misery,* Man is
never called in the Scriptures, till after the fall of *Adam.*" Donne's com-
ment about the derivation of *Enosh* is plausible, but it confuses different
Hebrew roots.

Psa. 32 [title]. *Le David Maschil*
A.V. *A Psalm* of David, Maschil (mg. *or, giving instruction*)
 IX. 11. 22

Psa. 32.1. *Pashang*
A.V. transgression   IX. 11. 271
 Donne's comment is too strong.

Psa. 32.1. *Nasa*
A.V. forgiven   IX. 11. 325

Psa. 32.1. *Catah* (Chata'ah)
A.V. sin
 IX. 11. 347–369. Donne's note on the derivation is quite wrong. *Nata* means 'to incline,' and *ḳut* (*chut*) 'a thread.'

Psa. 32.1. *Casah* (Kasah)
A.V. covered   IX. 11. 384

Psa. 32.1 (allusion to another word). *Sacac*
A.V. cover   IX. 11. 394

Psa. 32.2. See 1 *Sam.* 1.12. *Cashab* (*Chashab*)
A.V. imputeth
 IX. 11. 440–448. Donne's comment is wrong in saying that the word implies an error in thinking.

Psa. 32.2. *Gnavah* ('Awon)
A.V. iniquity   IX. 11. 449

Psa. 32.3 (and 22.1). *Shaag*
A.V. roaring   IX. 12. 519

Psa. 32.4, 5, and 7 (and *Hab.* 3.3, 9). *Selah*
A.V. Selah   IX. 12. 744–779

Psa. 32.5 (and *Gen.* 4.13). *Gnavon* ('Awon)
A.V. iniquity   IX. 13. 629
 This is the same word (more correctly printed) as *Gnavah* above.

Ps. 32.6 (and *Jer.* 8.6). *Shatach* (Shateph)
A.V. floods   IX. 14. 625

Psa. 32.7. *Sether*
A.V. hiding place   IX. 15. 62
 Sether is the root, not the form in *Psa.* 32.7.

Psa. 32.7 (and 2 *Sam.* 1.26). *Tzur*
A.V. trouble
 IX. 15. 271–280. In his comment with additional references Donne has confused several different Hebrew roots.

Psa. 32.7 (and *Psa.* 17.1, *Lam.* 2.19). *Ranan*
A.V. songs
    IX. 15. 536–539. "The word is *Ranan,* which signifies Joy, exultation, singing; But it hath another sense too. [mg. Lament. 2.19] *Arise, Cry out in the night.* And, *Attend unto my cry* [mg. Psal. 17.1], which are voyces far from singing."

Psa. 32.10. *Rabbim*
A.V. sorrows
    IX. 18. 31–33. "And as the word *Rabbim* doth as properly import, and might be as well so translated, here are *Dolores magni, Great sorrows; . . ."*

Psa. 32.11. *Tzadok* (Tsaddikim)
A.V. righteous
    IX. 18. 548–553. The word in the psalm is "righteous" (in the plural), and the second vowel of the Hebrew should be "i," not "o." Donne, however, is discussing the root, for which his form is correct.

Psa. 34.11. *Banim*
A.V. children   VI. 4. 35–36

Psa. 37.30. *Hagah*
A.V. speaketh
    VIII. 15. 260–261. "But the Original, *Hagah,* is noted to signifie, *fructificavit,* He brings forth fruits thereof; . . ."

Psa. 38.2. *Nachath*
A.V. stick fast   II. 1. 690

Psa. 38.3. *Mippenei*
A.V. because of
    II. 2. 532–534. ". . . there is a *Multiplication,* a plurality too, for it is indeed, *Mippenei, à faciebus,* the faces, the divers manifestations of Gods anger; . . ."

Psa. 38.4, and *Prov.* 14.31. *Chabad*
A.V. burden
    II. 4. 370–371. "In the Originall language, the same word, that is here, *a burden, Chabad,* signifies *honour,* and *wealth,* as well as a *burden."*

Psa. 38.4. *Jikkebedu* (Jikebbedu)
A.V. are too heavy
    II. 5. 426–429. ". . . our word, in the originall, . . . is *Jikkebedu,* which is not altogether, as we read them, *graves sunt,* but *graves fieri;* not that they *are,* but that *they were as a burden, too heavy for me; . . ."*

Psa. 38.9. *Adonai*
A.V. Lord   II. 6. 583–585, 605; III. 5. 137; III. 14. 153

Psa. 51.7. *Ezob*
A.V. hyssop
  V. 15. 480–491. ". . . the word in Hebrew is *Ezob*, . . . And the Hebrew Rabbins think this word of our text, *Ezob*, to signifie any of three or foure plants, rather then our Hyssop."

Psa. 55.19, also *Job* 14.14. *Kalaph*
A.V. change
  I. 4. 309–310. "The very same word, which is here [*Psa.* 55.19], *kalaph*, is in *Job* also: . . ."

Psa. 66.3. *Norah*
A.V. terrible
  VIII. 4. 132, 511–512. "this word . . . *Norah*, which is rather *Reverendus*, then *Terribilis*, . . ."

Psa. 66.3. *Cacash*
A.V. submit themselves (mg. *yield feigned obedience, Heb. lie*)
  VIII. 4. 672–673. "The word is *Cacash*, and *Cacash* is but *Mendacem fieri*, to be brought to lie, to dissemble, . . ."

Psa. 66.5, 16. *Lechu*
A.V. Come
  VIII. 4. 445–446. ". . . in both places it is not, *Venite*, but *Ite*, It is *Lechu*, not *Come*, but *Goe*, . . ."

Psa. 89.48. *Gheber*
A.V. man   II. 2. 257; II. 9. 114, 140; IX. 1. 557, 588

Psa. 103. 2. *Gamal* [should be *Gemul*]
A.V. benefits   VII. 17. 138

Psa. 140.1, 4. *Meish . . . Meadam*
A.V. from the man . . . from the man   IX. 16. 521, 525
  Meadam is in verse 1, *Meish* in verse 4.

Psa. 144.15. *Asherei*
A.V. happy   III. 2. 195, 198

Prov. 14.31. *Ebion*
A.V. poor   VIII. 12. 291 . . . 323

Prov. 14.31. *Gnashak*
A.V. oppresseth   VIII. 12. 213, 260

Prov. 14.31. *Gnoshehu* ('Osehu)
A.V. his Maker   VIII. 12. 498

Prov. 14.31. *Dalal* [should be *Dal*]
A.V. poor   VIII. 12. 323, 625

Prov. 14.31, also 1 *Kings* 8.33, *Job* 19.21, *Psa.* 6.2. *Chanan,* also *Canan* [less correct]
A.V. hath mercy
 VIII. 12. 651–654. "... the same word, which the holy Ghost uses in this text, and in *Exodus,* for mercy, which is *Canan,* he uses in other places, particularly in the dedication of the *Temple,* for *prayer.*" [mg. 1 Reg. 8]. On *Job* 19.21: X. 5. 155–157. "the same Translators use this word for *Chanan,* which is to oblige and binde a man by benefits, or to have *compassion upon him;* ..." On *Psa.* 6.2: V. 17. 62. "For this word *Chanan* used in this place ... is onely *Deo mihi gratiam,* Lord shed some drops of grace upon me, ... For this word is used, where *Noah* is said *to have found grace in the eyes of the Lord* [mg. Gen. 6.8]; ... And this word is used, not onely of God towards men, but also of men towards God [mg. Psal. 102.14] ..."

Prov. 22.6. *Chanach*
A.V. train up (mg. *catechise*)   IV. 7. 882

Prov. 22.11. *Ragnah* [misprinted in the Folio as *Nagnah* in lines 1084, 1086, 1090 and as *Dagnah* in line 1099]
A.V. his friend   I. 3. 1084, 1086, 1090, 1099
 See our note in Vol. I, p. 326, on line 1084. The initial consonants "N" and "D" in *F* must be misprints. Our conjecture is that the Hebrew word intended is as given above. We may note that in VIII. 8. 309 mg., *F* misprints "Nab." for "Rab." (i.e., Rabbi).

Prov. 24.12. *Tochen*
A.V. pondereth   II. 15. 241

Prov. 25.21. *Lachem,* and *Maiim*
A.V. bread ... water
 III. 18. 281. The usual vocalization of *Lachem* is *Lechem.* It is vocalized *Lachem* in this text, which Donne is quoting, because it comes at the end of a clause, and its position causes a lengthening of the first vowel from "e" to "a."

Eccles. 1.1. *Coheleth*
A.V. the Preacher
 IX. 12. 191. Donne's comment that the word means 'a Shee-preacher' is wrong. He probably derived it from the commentary of Johannes Lorinus, to whom his marginal note refers. See our note in Vol. IX, p. 440.

Eccles. 12.1. *Bechurotheica*
A.V. in the days of thy youth
 II. 11. 26, 321. In line 26, *F* reads *Bechucocheica,* but in line 321 *Bechurotheica.* The MSS *D* and *L* read *Bechurotheica* in both places. The Ashmole MS reads *Becharathica.* The Hebrew should be transliterated as *Bechurotheca.*

Isa. 1.9. (*et passim*) *Tzebaoth*
A.V. of hosts
   I. 6. 354–355; VIII. 4. 654. This is the rendering of A.V. throughout
the Old Testament, but where this text is quoted in *Rom.* 9.29 A.V. trans-
lates "of Sabaoth," and again in *James* 5.4, following in both places the
Greek σαβαὼθ and Vulg. Sabaoth. I. 6. 354–355: "The name of the true
God is *Dominus tzebaoth,* the Lord of Hosts; ..."

Isa. 13.21. *Ziim ... Ochim*
A.V. wild beasts ... doleful creatures [mg. *Heb. Ziim ... Heb. Ochim*]
   IV. 1. 174–176. "... Indeed God knowes what, *Ochim,* and *Ziim,* words
which truly we cannot translate." Donne usually transliterates sadhe
(tsaddi) as "tz," but here he followed the margin of A.V. in writing "Z."

Isa. 32.8. *Iagnatz*
A.V. deviseth   VIII. 10. 136

Isa. 32.8. *Nadib*
A.V. liberal   Vulg. princeps
   VIII. 10. 214–221. "... the vulgat Edition ... reads this very Text thus,
Princeps verò ea quæ principe digna sunt, cogitabit, ... A Translation
herein excusable enough; for the very Originall word, which we translate,
Liberall, is a Royall word, *Nadib,* and very often in the Scriptures hath so
high, a Royall signification."

Isa. 47.11. *Shakrah*
A.V. from whence it rises [mg. *Heb. the morning thereof*]
   I. 5. 443–444. *"Evill shall come upon thee, and thou shalt not know,
Shakrah,* the morning, the beginning of it; ..."

Isa. 52.3. *Machar*
A.V. Ye have sold   I. 1. 44

Isa. 52.3. *Kinnan* [should be *Kinnam*]
A.V. for nought   I. 1. 61

Isa. 52.3. *Casaph* [should be *Ceseph*]
A.V. money   I. 1. 113

Jer. 17.9. *Gnacob* ('Aqob)
A.V. deceitful   IX. 7. 263

Jer. 25.38. *Ionah*
A.V. oppressor   Vulg. columbæ
   II. 2. 492–496. "... wee read it the *fiercenesse of an oppressour,* but
Saint *Hierome* reads it, *The anger of a Dove.* And truly there is no other
word then that, in that tongue, (the word is *Ionah,*) that signifies a *Dove,*

and that word does signifie a *Dove,* in many other places of Scripture; . . ."
Donne has been misled by the Vulgate. Besides the ordinary noun meaning 'dove,' there is also a verbal form (the active participle *Iona[h],*
singular absolute of the simple conjugation of the verb *Iana[h],* which
means 'oppress' or 'suppress') and so A.V. rightly translates the words as
"oppressor," and the passage of Donne's sermon quoting the views of "the
Fathers of the Latine Church," interpreting the word as *Dove,* could only
have confused and misled his hearers.

Jer. 50.25. *Otzar*
A.V. armory　　Vulg. thesaurus　　IX. 7. 414
(See note on Donne's treatment of this word on p. 311 of the present
volume.)

Lamentations [title]. *Sepher Kinoth*
A.V. Lamentations　　IV. 9. 857
The title in A.V. is derived from the Septuagint. In the Hebrew Bible
the title is *Echah,* from its first word, but in the Talmud the title is *Kinoth,*
Lamentations.

Lam. 3.1. *Gnabar* עָ בַ ר
A.V. wrath
X. 9. 709. Here the Hebrew characters are printed in the margin of *F*
without vowel points. Cp. the note on *Job* 13.15, where the vowel points
are printed. The word in *Lam.* 3.1 is the noun, while *Gnabar* is the root.

Lam. 4.7. *Mippeninim*
A.V. rubies
X. 7. 306–309. ". . . redder then pearle: *Mippeninim* is the originall
word, which the *Rabbins* translate pearle; And the Vulgate Edition hath
it, *Rubicundiores ebore antiquo,* redder then the oldest yvory . . ." In his
verse translation of *Lamentations,* "*for the most* part according to *Tremellius,*" Donne renders the words "they were more ruddy in body than
rubies" (A.V.) as "As carbuncles did their pure bodies shine."

Lam. 4.20, also *Gen.* 1.2. *Ruach*
A.V. breath　　IV. 9. 517, 542, 546

Ezek. 34.19. *Mirpas*
A.V. fouled
X. 6. 466–467. "The word is *Mirpas;* and it denotes not onely *Conturba-
tionem,* a troubling, a mudding, but *Obturationem* too, . . ."

Dan. 11.38. *Mauzzim*
A.V. of forces (mg. *Or, munitions. Heb. Mauzzin*)
I. 6. 353; III. 5. 693; VII. 13. 840–841

Hos. 2. 19. *Erash*
A.V. betroth
 III. 11. 2–6. "...and *Erash* signifies not onely a betrothing, as our later Translation hath it, but a mariage; ...and so our former Translation [i.e., the Geneva version] had it, and so we accept it, ...*I will mary thee unto me for ever.*"

Hos. 3.4, also *Exod.* 2.14 and *Isa.* 9.6. *Sar*
A.V. prince VII. 17. 475, 477, 484, 486

No specific reference given:
Caphar
 VII. 17. 183–186. "...for...*Ingratitude,* the holy language, the *Hebrew,* lacks a word. The nearest root that they can draw Ingratitude into, is *Caphar,* and *Caphar* is but *Tegere,* to hide, to conceal a benefit; ..." This is not quite correct. The word means 'to hide or conceal,' without mention of a benefit.

Nata
 IX. 11. 348. "...*Nata,* which is to Decline, to step aside, or to be withdrawne, ..."

Kut (Chut)
 IX. 11. 349. "...*Kut,* which is *filum,* a thread, or a line ..."

Sepher Chinnuch
 IV. 7. 886–889. "And *Sepher Chinnuch,* which is *Liber Institutionum,* that is, of *Catechisme,* is a Book well knowne amongst the *Iewes,* every where, where they are now: ..."

Elah [should be *'Alah*]
 II. 15. 281–283. "...that great name of God, ...*Elohim,* is not inconveniently deriv'd from *Elah,* which is *Iurare* to swear, ..."

Pharas (Paras)
 IX. 6. 468–471. "...the Pharisee hath his name from *Pharas,* which is Division, Separation; But *Calvin* derives the name (not inconveniently) from *Pharash,* which is Exposition, Explication."

Hiphil
 V. 7. 148–151. "...as the *Grammarians* call it, it is in *Hiphil,* and it signified *Induere fecit eos;* God caused them to be cloathed, or God caused them to cloath themselves; ..." Also in II. 1. 688–691 the parallel form "in *Niphal*" is correctly used by Donne, "...that word...is here, (as the Grammarians in that language call it) in *Niphal, figere factæ,* they were made to stick; ..."

Hebrew usage. (1) Tense in Hebrew:

IX. 15. 45–59. "... as God himselfe is eternall and cannot bee considered in the distinction of times, so hath that language in which God hath spoken in his written word, the Hebrew, the least consideration of Time of any other language. Evermore in expressing the mercies of God to man, it is an indifferent thing to the holy Ghost whether he speak in the present, or in the future, or in the time that is past ... [On *Psa.* 32.7:] The present word, *Thou art,* is but inserted by our Translators; In the Originall it is onely, *Tu refugium, Thou my hiding place,* There is no *fuisti,* nor *es,* nor *eris,* That he was, or is, or will be so, ..." Donne's comment is correct. Hebrew verbs do not distinguish actions as past, present, or future, but indicate them simply as completed (perfect) or not yet completed (imperfect). In this Hebrew resembles other Semitic languages in contrast to the Indo-European group.

(2) No superlative:

Donne is correct in stating that Hebrew has no superlative for adjectives. It has to employ circumlocutions such as "a sleep of Jehovah" for "a very deep sleep" (see I. 3. 1003–05 and X. 9. 344–345), or it doubles the adjective or adverb as in 1 *Sam.* 2.3, "talk no more proudly, proudly," A.V., "talk no more so exceeding proudly."

Chapter II

Donne's Sources (Continued)

THE EARLY FATHERS, ESPECIALLY ST. AUGUSTINE

IN THIS chapter we are dealing with secondary sources. The Bible, as we have shown in chapter i, was Donne's great and primary source. Without a knowledge of the Fathers and of later commentators Donne would almost certainly have been still a great preacher, but he would have been a preacher of a different kind. His acquaintance with the works of the Fathers gives a particular flavour to his work, pleasant to some tastes, unpleasant to others. Augustine and Jerome, Basil and Chrysostom were men of towering intellect and wide human sympathies. Through them and the other Fathers the Middle Ages were linked with the civilizations of Greece and Rome. The whole Christian Church is deeply indebted to them.

Donne quotes or refers to the following Fathers, Doctors of the Church, or ecclesiastical historians who lived in the first eight centuries of our era: St. *Ambrose* (*ca.* 340–397), St. *Athanasius* (*ca.* 296–373), *Athenagoras,* a Christian apologist who lived in the second century under Marcus Aurelius, St. *Augustine* (354–430), St. *Basil* (330–379), *Chrysologus* (400–450), St. John *Chrysostom* (347–407), *Clement* of Alexandria (born about 150, died about 215), *Clement* of Rome, bishop of Rome at the end of the first century, St. *Cyprian* (martyred in 258), St. *Cyril* of Alexandria (died 444), St. *Cyril* of Jerusalem (died 386), St. John *Damascen* (died in the middle of the eighth century), the pseudo-*Dionysius* the Areopagite, variously named by Donne as *Areopagitica, Dionyse, Denys,* and *Dyonisius* [*sic*], whose writings probably belong to the sixth century, *Epiphanius* (died 402), *Eusebius* (*ca.* 260–340), *Fulgentius* (468–533), St. *Gregory* the Great (540–600), St. *Gregory Nazianzen* (*ca.* 329–390), St. *Gregory Nyssen* (*ca.* 331–394), St. *Gregory Thaumaturgus,* or *Neocæsariensis* (died *ca.* 270), *Hilarius,* bishop of Poitiers (died 368),

St. *Ignatius* of Antioch (martyred *ca.* 107), *Isidore,* bishop of Seville (560–636), St. *Jerome* or *Hieronymus,* generally cited by Donne as St. *Hierome* (*ca.* 342–420), *Justin Martyr* (martyred *ca.* 165), *Maximus* the Confessor (580–662), *Melito,* bishop of Sardes (flourished in the second century), *Origen* (*ca.* 185–253), *Tertullian* (*ca.* 160–*ca.* 220), *Theodoret* (*ca.* 393–*ca.* 457). It is convenient to include here two Greek authors who flourished later than the other Fathers but who cannot well be classified with the medieval authors of the Roman Church. These are Œcumenius (believed to have flourished in the tenth century), who left a number of commentaries on parts of the New Testament, in which he collected many passages from the earlier Greek Fathers, and Theophylact, archbishop of Bulgaria (flourished in the late eleventh and early twelfth centuries), who wrote commentaries on the Gospels, Acts, St. Paul's Epistles, and also on the Minor Prophets. It should be noted here that Donne quotes all the Greek Fathers in Latin versions.

St. Augustine is above all others the Father to whom Donne turned most constantly. This is proved by the lists which Mrs. Holtby has drawn up for me of references to the Fathers in Volumes III, VI, and IX. In Volume III we find 55 references to Augustine against 29 to Tertullian, his nearest rival in this volume, and 24 to Jerome. In Volume VI there are 84 references to Augustine against 21 to Chrysostom, 20 to Basil, and only 10 to Tertullian. In Volume IX there are 87 references to Augustine, 37 to Jerome, 17 to Chrysostom, 11 to Tertullian, and 9 to Basil.[1] From our knowledge of the remaining volumes Mrs. Holtby and I estimate that Augustine is quoted or referred to about 700 times in the whole edition. These citations are not, however, distributed at all evenly among the individual sermons.

---

[1] The three lists are printed in full in the accompanying table. It will be found that in addition to the Fathers mentioned above there are a fair number of references to Ambrose, Gregory the Great, Origen, Gregory Nazianzen, Cyprian, and Cyril of Alexandria. The figures for these Fathers fluctuate considerably from volume to volume. It should be noted that where Donne quotes a number of Latin sentences from a single passage, he often intersperses his own very free translations, and sometimes comments of his own; we then number the series of quotations as one single reference. Throughout this discussion we omit the prefix "St." partly because space is wanting and partly because certain Fathers, such as Tertullian and Origen, were never canonized.

REFERENCES TO THE FATHERS

Vol. III		Vol. VI		Vol. IX	
Augustine	55	Augustine	84	Augustine	87
Tertullian	29	Chrysostom	21	Jerome	37
Jerome	24	Basil	20	Ambrose	18
Chrysostom	20	Jerome	15	Chrysostom	17
Ambrose	10	Gregory the Great	12	Gregory the Great	12
Gregory the Great	9	Tertullian	10	Tertullian	11
Basil	8	Ambrose	9	Basil	9
Gregory Nazianzen	7	Cyprian	7	Origen	6
Cyprian ⎫ Origen ⎭	6	Clement of Alexandria ⎫ Cyril of Alexandria ⎬ Irenæus ⎭	6	Damascen ⎫ Lactantius ⎭	5
Lactantius ⎫ Cyril of Alexandria ⎬ Hilary ⎭	4	Athanasius	5	Athanasius ⎫ Cyril of Alexandria ⎬ Theodoret ⎭	4
Justin Martyr	3	Justin Martyr ⎫ Origen ⎭	4	Justin Martyr	
Athanasius ⎫ Gregory Nyssen ⎪ Dionysius the Areopagite ⎬ Clement of Alexandria ⎪ Irenæus ⎪ Damascen ⎭	2	Epiphanius ⎫ Theodoret ⎭	3	Gregory Nazianzen ⎫ Gregory Nyssen ⎬ Chrysologus ⎭	3
		Gregory Nazianzen ⎫ Gregory Nyssen ⎪ Lactantius ⎬ Leo the Great ⎪ Gregory of Valentia ⎭	2	Epiphanius ⎫ Cyprian ⎪ Hilary ⎬ Theophylact ⎪ Leo the Great ⎭	2
Athenagoras ⎫ Clement of Rome ⎬ Epiphanius ⎪ Gregory of Valentia ⎭	1	Hilary	1	Clement of Alexandria ⎫ Œcumenius ⎪ Cyril of Jerusalem ⎬ Gregory of Valentia ⎪ Dionysius the Areopagite ⎭	1

There are 5 sermons in which Augustine is not mentioned at all.[2] On the other hand, while the average number of references per sermon is 3 or 4, there are much higher figures for a number of sermons.[3]

[2] These are Vol. II. (No.) 4, Vol. III. 6, Vol. IV. 6, Vol. VIII. 4, Vol. IX. 13. It is possible that there may be some unidentified allusion to Augustine in one or another of these.

[3] For example, Vol. II. 3 (10 references), Vol. IV. 3 (11), Vol. V. 10 (13), Vol. VII. 8 (12), Vol. IX. 3 (11, of which 2 are very long passages full of quotations from the *Confessions,* and there are 9 other quotations from at least two others of Augustine's works).

Donne had a particular regard for Augustine for several reasons. He recognized the greatness of the Saint intellectually, morally, and spiritually. He saw in Augustine the supreme thinker of the Early Church. But also he recognized Augustine's warm humanity, and displayed an interest in his life and personality which he does not show for any other Father. He saw a parallel between the sins and failures of his own youth and those of Augustine as narrated by the Saint himself in his *Confessions*. Augustine, the son of a pagan father and a Christian mother, hesitated for many years before he was converted and baptized. His youth was dissolute,[4] and in his early manhood he studied and taught the art of rhetoric, aiming at worldly success. He joined the heretical Manichæans,[5] and for nine years strove to induce others to join them. Even when at last he abandoned the Manichees, and became a catechumen in the Christian Church, he was troubled by many doubts and difficulties, and delayed baptism for some time. All this struck an answering chord in Donne's mind, and when he considered the amazing change from sinner to saint in Augustine, he took courage for himself. He expressed his love for Augustine's memory by calling him "that blessed and sober Father," that "tender blessed Father," that "blessed Father of tender bowels."[6]

The *Confessions* seems to have been the work which Donne knew best. Again and again he picked out from it some wonderful scene or some unforgettable phrase. Thus he recalled the passage in Book IX which describes how Augustine and his mother talked together at Ostia of the glories of the heavenly life shortly before her death:

The day now approaching whereon she was to depart this life, (which day Thou well knowest, we knew it not,) it came to pass, Thyself, as I

---

[4] Both Augustine and Donne show what some have considered an excessive sense of guilt for sexual errors. The Rev. Dr. J. N. D. Kelly, in his *Early Christian Doctrines*, London, 1958, p. 365, describes Augustine as "obsessed with the ravages which unbridled sexuality produces in human beings."

[5] Manichæism is more properly called a separate religion than a heresy, for it was compounded of Zoroastrian, Gnostic Christian, and pagan elements, and believed in a dualism in which the evil principle (the Devil) was co-eternal with the good (God). It was widely accepted from the third to the fifth century A.D.

[6] See Vol. VII, p. 343; II, p. 107; IV, p. 78; also IX, p. 94.

believe, by Thy secret ways so ordering it, that she and I stood alone, leaning in a certain window, which looked into the garden of the house where we now lay, at Ostia;... We were discoursing then together, alone, very sweetly; and *forgetting those things which are behind, and reaching forth unto those things which are before,* we were enquiring between ourselves in the presence of the Truth, which Thou art, of what sort the eternal life of the saints was to be, *which eye hath not seen, nor ear heard, nor hath it entered into the heart of man....* And when our discourse was brought to that point, that the very highest delight of the earthly senses, in the very purest material light, was, in respect of the sweetness of that life, not only not worthy of comparison, but not even of mention; we raising up ourselves with a more glowing affection towards the Self-same [i.e., God], did by degrees pass through all things bodily, even the very heaven, whence sun and moon, and stars shine upon the earth; yea, we were soaring higher yet, by inward musing, and discourse, and admiring of Thy works; and we came to our own minds, and went beyond them, that we might arrive at that region of never-failing plenty, where *Thou feedest Israel* for ever with the food of truth, and where life is the *Wisdom by whom all* these *things are made.*[7]

Donne summarizes this very briefly, and his Latin quotations are evidently taken from memory, in the following passage in his Easter sermon of 1628:

S. *Augustine* speaking of discourses that passed between his mother, and him, not long before her death, sayes, *Perambulavimus cuncta mortalia, & ipsum cœlum,* We talked our selves above this earth, and above all the heavens; *Venimus in mentes nostras, & transcendimus eas,* We came to the consideration of our owne mindes, and our owne soules, and we got above our own soules; that is, to the consideration of that place where our soules should be for ever; and we could consider God then, but then wee could not see God in his Essence.[8]

A good example of the way in which Donne takes up a phrase of Augustine's and makes it part of his own prose can be found in the opening of the prayer which closes the sermon on *Proverbs* 8.17: "Therefore shall every one that is godlie make his Prayer unto thee O God, in a time when thou may'st be found: we acknowledg this to be that time, and we come to thee now early, with the confession of thy servant *Augustine, sero te amavi pulchritudo tam antiqua, tam*

---

[7] *Confessions,* IX. chap. 10 (old numbering), trans. E. B. Pusey, Everyman's Library, 1942.
[8] Vol. VIII of our edition, p. 232.

nova; O glorious beauty, infinitely reverend, infinitely fresh and young, we come late to thy love, if we consider the past daies of our lives, but early if thou beest pleased to reckon with us from this houre of the shining of thy grace upon us; . . ."[9]

The words in this passage, ". . . we come late to thy love, if we consider the past daies of our lives," point the resemblance which Donne himself perceived between the excesses of his own youth and those of Augustine, and the delay in both, due partly to doubt and to intellectual pride, and partly to a desire for worldly success. Elsewhere Donne quotes Augustine's own description of his sensual love from the *Confessions,* II. 2, and dwells on the misery which flowed from it: ". . . but what got I by all that, *Ut cæderer virgis ardentibus ferreis, zeli suspicionis et rixarum;* nothing but to be scourg'd with burning iron rods, rods of jealousie, of suspition, and of quarrels; . . ."[10]

In the last three books of the *Confessions* Augustine broke off his autobiography in order to meditate on the Scriptures, and especially on *Genesis* 1.1: "In the beginning God created the heaven and the earth." This was a subject which often occupied Donne's mind, and he quoted freely from Augustine in a number of places. Even before his ordination he wrote in the *Essays in Divinity:*

> Let me in thy beloved Servant *Augustine's* own words, when with an humble boldnesse he begg'd the understanding of this passage, say, *Moses writ this, but is gon from me to thee; if he were here, I would hold him, and beseech him for thy sake, to tell me what he meant. If he spake Hebrew, he would frustrate my hope; but if Latine, I should comprehend him. But from whence should I know that he said true? Or when I knew it, came that knowledge from him? No, for within me, within me there is a truth, not Hebrew, nor Greek, nor Latin, nor barbarous; which without organs, without noyse of Syllables, tels me true, and would enable me to say confidently to Moses, Thou say'st true.*[11]

This reappears in a sermon preached in January, 1624/5, in this form:

> S. *Augustine* puts himselfe earnestly upon the contemplation of the Creation, as *Moses* hath delivered it; he findes it hard to conceive, and he

---

[9] Vol. I, p. 250. The quotation is from Aug. *Confessions,* X. 27.

[10] Vol. I, p. 238.

[11] *Essays,* ed. Simpson, pp. 15–16. The passage in Augustine is from *Conf.* XI. 5 (3 in the older arrangement).

sayes, *Si esset ante me Moses* [in margin, *Confes.* L. xi. c. 3], If *Moses* who writ this were here, *Tenerem eum, & per te obsecrarem,* I would hold him fast, and beg of him, for thy sake, O my God, that he would declare this worke of the Creation more plainly unto me. But then, sayes that blessed Father, *Si Hebræa voce loqueretur,* If *Moses* should speake Hebrew to mee, mine eares might heare the sound, but my minde would not heare the voyce; I might heare him, but I should not heare what he said.[12]

The sermon in which he made the fullest use of these three books of the *Confessions* was that which he preached on Whitsunday, 1629. There in a passage which occupies eight pages of our edition, he ranges backward and forward from the second chapter of the eleventh book to the eighteenth chapter of the twelfth book, then to the thirtieth chapter, next to the tenth chapter of the thirteenth book, and so on:

First then, undertaking the consideration of the literall sense, and after, of the spirituall, we joyne with S. *Augustine, Sint castæ deliciæ meæ Scripturæ tuæ;...Nec fallar in eis, nec fallam ex eis;...Non frustra scribuntur,* says he; Lord, thou hast writ nothing to no purpose; thou wouldst be understood in all: ... *Confiteor tibi quicquid invenero in libris tuis;* ... Thus that blessed Father meditates upon the word of God; he speakes of this beginning of the Book of *Genesis;* and he speaks lamenting, *Scripsit Moses & abiit,* a little *Moses* hath said, and alas he is gone; ... But says he, since I cannot speake with *Moses, Te, quo plenus vera dixit, Veritas, rogo,* I begge of thee who art Truth it selfe, as thou enabledst him to utter it, enable me to understand what he hath said. So difficult a thing seemed it to that intelligent Father, to understand this history, this mystery of the Creation. But yet though he found, that divers senses offered themselves, he did not doubt of finding the Truth: For, *Deus meus lumen oculorum meorum in occulto,* says he, O my God, the light of mine eyes, in this dark inquisition, since divers senses, arise out of these words, and all true, *Quid mihi obest, si aliud ego sensero, quam sensit alius, eum sensisse, qui scripsit?* What hurt followes, though I follow another sense, then some other man takes to be *Moses* sense? for his may be a true sense, and so may mine, and neither be *Moses* his. Hee passes from prayer, and protestation, to counsell, and direction; *In diversitate sententiarum verarum, concordiam pariat ipsa veritas,* Where divers senses arise, and all true, (that is, that none of them oppose the truth) let truth agree them. But what is Truth? God; And what is God? Charity; Therefore let Charity reconcile such differences. *Legitimè lege utamur,* says he, let us

---

[12] Vol. VI, p. 218.

use the Law lawfully; Let us use our liberty of reading Scriptures according to the Law of liberty; that is, charitably to leave others to their liberty, if they but differ from us, and not differ from Fundamentall Truths.[13]

Another of St. Augustine's works which influenced Donne profoundly was the *De Civitate Dei*. Some years before his ordination he had shown in *Biathanatos* by numerous references that he was familiar with this work. He had there made an interesting comparison of Augustine with Calvin as an expositor of Scripture:

> To speake a little of Saint *Augustine* in generall, because from him are derived almost all the reasons of others [i.e., against suicide], he writing purposely thereof, from the 17 to the 27 Chapter of his first book *De Civitate Dei*, I say, ... though Saint *Augustine* for sharpe insight, and conclusive judgement, in exposition of places of Scripture, which he alwaies makes so liquid, and pervious, that he hath scarce been equalled therein, by any of all the Writers in the Church of God, except *Calvin* may have that honour, whom (where it concernes not points in Controversie,) I see the *Jesuits* themselves often follow, though they dare not name him, have a high degree and reverence due to him, yet in practique learning, and morall Divinity, he [Augustine] was of so nice, and refin'd, and rigorous a conscience, (perchance to redeeme his former licenciousnesse, as it fals out often in such Convertits, to be extreamely zealous) that for our direction in actions of this life, Saint *Hierome,* and some others, may bee thought sometimes fitter to adhere unto, then St. *Augustine* ...[14]

We can only enumerate a few of the leading ideas of the *De Civitate Dei* which Donne inherited and set forth in his *Sermons*. God, being perfectly good, creates everything good. Evil is a negative condition, like darkness, cold, or vacancy. "For evil has no positive nature, but the loss of good has received the name *evil*" (*De Civ. Dei,* XI. 9). That which we call *bad* is a perversion of what was originally good

---

[13] Vol. IX, pp. 94–95. On p. 97 Donne turns aside from Augustine for a moment to consider the opinions of Basil, Ambrose, and Jerome, but he speedily returns to Augustine, and continues to quote the Saint till on p. 101 he quotes again from the eleventh book, and observes, "I am loath to part from this father, and he is loath to be parted from, for he says this in more then one place; ..."

[14] *Biathanatos,* p. 98. Donne continues his examination of Augustine's opinion throughout pp. 99–101. He returns to the *De Civitate Dei* in marginal references on pp. 91, 146, 148, 200, 211. *Biathanatos* was probably written in 1607 or 1608, though it was not published till after Donne's death.

(XIV. 11).[15] Such a perversion arises when a conscious creature becomes more interested in itself than in God, and wishes to exist by itself independently of God, "esse in semet ipso" (XIV. 13). This is the sin of pride, and it was first committed by Satan, "the proud angel who turned from God to himself, not wishing to be a subject, but to rejoice like a tyrant in having subjects of his own" (XIV. 11). Though God has made all things good, He foreknows that some will become evil, and He foreknows the good use which He will then make of their evil. "Sicut naturam bonarum optimus creator, ita voluntatum malarum iustissimus ordinator" (XI. 17).

Through the writings of St. Augustine, Donne got some idea of the Platonic and Neoplatonic view of the world. Donne mentions the Platonic doctrine of Ideas on several occasions:

God had conceived in himselfe, from all eternity, certaine Idea's, certaine patterns of all things, which he would create.[16]

Of God himselfe, it is safely resolved in the Schoole, that he never did any thing in any part of time, of which he had not an eternall pre-conception, an eternall Idea, in himselfe before. Of which Ideaes, that is, pre-conceptions, pre-determinations in God, S. *Augustine* pronounces, *Tanta vis in Ideis constituitur,* There is so much Truth, and so much power in these Ideaes, as that without acknowledging them, no man can acknowledge God, for he does not allow God Counsaile, and Wisdome, and deliberation in his Actions, but sets God on worke, before he have thought what he will doe. And therefore he, and others of the Fathers read that

---

[15] With this we should compare Donne's treatment of the text, "Why callest thou me good? There is none good but one; that is, God" (*Mat.* 19.17): "First then, there is nothing good but God: neither can I conceive any thing in God, that concerns me so much as his goodnesse; for, by that I know him, and for that I love him. . . . But, *ineffabili dulcedine teneor cum audio, Bonus Dominus;* [August. in mg.] I am . . . replenished with all sweetnesse, established with all soundnesse, when I hear of my God in that name, my good God. . . . He is so good, goodnesse so, as that he is *Causa bonorum, & quæ in nos, & quæ in nobis,* the cause of all good either received by us, or conceived in us; . . . In a word, he is *Bonum cætera bona colorans, & amabilia reddens* [Idem in mg.], it is his goodnesse, that gilds and enamels all the good persons, or good actions in this world." Donne continues with the corollary, "That there is nothing ill; that this goodnesse of God is so spread over all, (all actions, all persons) as that there is nothing ill." (Vol. VI, pp. 232, 236.) He continues with quotations from Augustine.

[16] Vol. VIII, p. 120.

place, (which we read otherwise) *Quod factum est, in ipso vita erat* [*John* 1.3, 4]; that is, in all their Expositions, whatsoever is made, in time, was alive in God, before it was made, that is, in that eternall Idea, and patterne which was in him. So also doe divers of those Fathers read those words to the Hebrews, (which we read, *The things that are seene, are not made of things that doe appeare*) *Ex invisibilibus visibilia facta sunt, Things formerly invisible, were made visible;* that is, we see them not till now, till they are made, but they had an invisible being, in that Idea, in that pre-notion, in that purpose of God before, for ever before.[17]

God had no external pattern in the Creation, for there was nothing extant; but God had from all Eternity an internal pattern, an *Idæa*, a preconception, a form in himself, according to which he produc'd every Creature.[18]

Donne's quotations cover almost the whole field of Augustine's thought. They are drawn for the most part (as far as we have been able to identify them) from the *Confessions, De Civitate Dei,* the *Sermons, Enarrationes* on the Psalms, *De Doctrina Christiana,* and the *Epistles,* with occasional references to *De Gen. con. Man., De Moribus Ecclesiæ, De Trinitate, De Vera Religione, Enchiridion, Quæst. in Heptateuchum, Retractationes,* etc. They deal with such immense subjects as the Nature of God, the Creation of the Universe, the relation between soul and body, the fall of Adam and its consequences, original sin, the saving work of Christ in all its aspects, death and immortality, the nature of the Church and its Sacraments, and the authority of Scripture. For the most part Donne accepts Augustine's views[19] on these subjects, and it was natural that he should do

---

[17] Vol. VII, pp. 60–61. In his *Essays in Divinity* (ed. Simpson, 1952), p. 29, Donne had written: "The greatest Dignity which we can give this world, is, that the *Idæa* of it is eternall, and was ever in God: And that he knew this world, not only *Scientiâ Intellectus,*...but also *Scientiâ Visionis,* by which he knows only infallible things; and therefore these *Idæas* and eternall impressions in God, may boldly be said to be *God;* for nothing understands God of it self, but God; and it is said, *Intellectæ Jynges à patre, intelligunt et ipsæ* [marg. note, *Zoroast. Oracul.* 4]: And with *Zoroaster* (if I misconceive not) *Jynx* is the same as *Idæa* with *Plato.*" See M. P. Ramsay, *Les Doctrines médiévales chez Donne,* pp. 155–158, for a discussion of these passages.

[18] Vol. IV, p. 98.

[19] For a comparison of Augustine's views on most of these topics with those of other Early Fathers, and the differences between them, see the Index to Kelly, *op. cit.,* pp. 491–501.

so, for Augustine had a very large part in shaping the theology of the Western Church; but as a commentator he often rejects Augustine's interpretation of particular texts, and in a few doctrinal matters he shows himself ready to follow the more liberal lead of some of the Greek Fathers.[20] This may be seen in his wish to follow Clement of Alexandria, Chrysostom, and others in believing that the righteous heathen, such as Socrates and Plato, were saved by God. In one of the Easter sermons he writes:

And as those blessed Fathers of tender bowels, enlarged themselves in this distribution, and apportioning the mercy of God, ... so did they inlarge this mercy farther, and carry it even to the Gentiles, to the Pagans that had no knowledge of Christ in any established Church. You shall not finde a *Trismegistus*, a *Numa Pompilius*, a *Plato*, a *Socrates,* for whose salvation you shall not finde some Father, or some Ancient and Reverend Author, an Advocate. ... To me, to whom God hath revealed his Son, in a Gospel, by a Church, there can be no way of salvation, but by applying that Son of God, by that Gospel, in that Church. Nor is there any other foundation for any, nor other name by which any can be saved, but the name of Jesus. But how this foundation is presented, and how this name of Jesus is notified to them, amongst whom there is no Gospel preached, no Church established, I am not curious in inquiring. I know God can be

---

[20] In particular Donne did not agree with Augustine in thinking that unbaptized infants "must pass to eternal fire with the Devil, although their sufferings will be relatively mild as compared with those of adults who have added sins of their own to their inherited guilt" (Kelly, *op. cit.,* p. 366, quoting Augustine, *Serm.* 294. 2–4; *De pecc. mer. et remiss.* 1.55). He asserted strongly that God saves such innocent children, and that their place is in heaven. Thus he writes: "If I had no other errand to heaven, but the *communion of Saints,* the fellowship of the faithfull, to see that flock of *Lambs,* Innocent, unbaptized *children,* recompensed with the twice-baptized *Martyrs,* ... this fellowship of the faithfull, is worth all the paynes, that that sight costs us in this world." (Vol. IV, pp. 176–177.) Again, when he has made it clear that Baptism is God's usual seal of admission to the Church, he blames parents who allow a child to die unbaptized, "though God preserve that child out of his abundant, and miraculous mercy, from spirituall destruction." (Vol. V, p. 162.) A little later he says, "I speake not this, as though the state of *children* that died without baptisme were desperate; God forbid, for who shall shorten the Arme of the Lord? God is able to raine downe *Manna* and *Quailes* into the soules of these children, though negligent parents turne them out into the wildernesse, and put God to that extraordinary work." (*Ibid.,* p. 163.)

as mercifull as those tender Fathers present him to be; and I would be as charitable as they are. And therefore humbly imbracing that manifestation of his Son, which he hath afforded me, I leave God, to his unsearchable waies of working upon others, without further inquisition.[21]

This passage does not stand alone, but is supported by several others. Donne would not limit salvation to any particular branch of the Christian Church, nay, not even to the Christian Church itself.[22] "There are an infinite number of *Stars* more then we can distinguish, and so, by Gods grace, there may be an infinite number of souls saved, more then those, of whose salvation, we discerne the *ways,* and the *meanes.*"[23]

Donne differs from Augustine over the question whether God's grace is resistible, which is connected with Augustine's strong emphasis on predestination and election. In the latter part of his life

[21] Vol. IV, pp. 78–79. It might be objected that in Vol. VI, pp. 118–119, Donne seems to be arguing against Justin Martyr, and in later times Andradius and Tostatus, who held that "rectified reason did the same office in the Gentiles, as faith did in the Christians," and that "originall sin is absolutely remitted to them, *In prima bona operatione in charitate,* In their first good morall work that they do." But his purpose in this later passage was not to argue that Socrates and Plato and their like had not been saved, but to dispute that any could have been saved by reason, philosophy, or morality. He prefers in such matters to trust to the infinite mercy of God, and not to magnify the power of human reason.

[22] Vol. X, pp. 169–170: "For though God have revealed no other way of salvation *to us,* but by breeding us in his Church, yet we must be so far, from straitning salvation, to any *particular Christian Church,* of any subdivided name, *Papist* or *Protestant,* as that we may not straiten it to the *whole Christian Church,* as though God *could* not, in the largenesse of his power, or *did* not, in the largenesse of his mercy, afford salvation to some, whom he never gathered into the Christian Church."

[23] Vol. VI, p. 161. In this passage Donne agrees with Augustine that in the promise to Abraham that his seed should be as the stars and as the sands, the stars may represent the saved among the Jews, and the sands those who will be lost, but his conclusion from this is much more charitable than Augustine's. The latter thought (in the state of astronomy in his day) that the stars were comparatively few in number, and therefore few Jews would be saved. But the invention of the telescope by Galileo had shown Donne that there were infinitely more stars than had been previously distinguished, and therefore his view of the salvation of the Jews is more hopeful.

Augustine held that there were a fixed number of God's elect, who were to fill up the places of the fallen angels.[24] These elect are moved by an irresistible impulse of God's grace. Augustine found himself obliged by these views to twist the text "God wills all men to be saved" (1 *Tim.* 2.4), making it mean that he wills the salvation of all the elect, among whom men of every race and type are represented.[25]

Though the Council of Carthage (418), as confirmed by Pope Zosimus, had supported Augustine by outlawing Pelagianism and confirming his doctrine of original sin, it did not uphold his belief in the irresistibility of grace. There was no noticeable impact on the East, and in the West many supporters of the Council found some of Augustine's ideas distasteful, especially his view that the will, though supposed to be free, is incapable in its fallen state of choosing the good.

Augustine on predestination was a precursor of Calvin and Calvinism. Donne's practical experience of the misery caused by this doctrine of predestination led him to combat this side of Calvinism with vigour. He has many passages in which he maintains that man's will is free, that the promises of the Gospel are not illusory, and that salvation is offered to all who will repent and believe.[26]

Donne certainly owed much of value to Augustine. But we may perhaps wonder whether Augustine's influence on him was altogether healthy. A modern reader cannot help feeling that an undue number of Donne's sermons are devoted to four of the Penitential Psalms (21 out of 34 sermons on texts from the whole Book of

---

[24] Kelly, *op. cit.*, pp. 368–369. He quotes *De Civ. Dei*, 22. 1, 2, *De Corrept. et Grat.* 12–16, *Enchir.* 98 f.

[25] Kelly, pp. 368–369, quoting *De Corrept. et Grat.* 44, *Enchir.* 29.

[26] See Vol. V, pp. 53–54: "They are too good husbands, and too thrifty of Gods grace, . . . that restraine Gods generall propositions, *Venite omnes,* Let all come, and *Vult omnes salvos,* God would have all men saved, so particularly, as to say, that when God sayes *All,* he meanes some of all sorts, some Men, some Women, some Jews, some Gentiles, some rich, some poore, but he does not meane, as he seemes to say, simply All. Yes; God does meane, simply All, so as that no man can say to another, God meanes not thee, no man can say to himselfe, God meanes not me. . . . *Perditio nostra ex nobis,* Our destruction is from our owne sin, and the Devill that infuses it; not from God, or any ill purpose in him that enforces us. The blood of Christ was shed for all that will apply it, . . ."

Psalms) and that in many other sermons there is too much emphasis on sin and its punishment. Donne himself draws attention to Augustine's reverence for these particular Psalms,[27] but the sermons which he based on them are for the most part tedious, and we could well have dispensed with at least half of them. However beautiful the *Psalms* may be as a manual of devotion, they do not and could not anticipate the whole Gospel. Christ came to bring salvation to men, to give them light and life and forgiveness. Therefore the Christian should have a repentance deeper than any of the Jewish psalmists could feel, but he should also have a joy and assurance which they knew only in part.[28] To meditate too long on human guilt and frailty, as Donne is apt to do, is to distort the Christian message, and in this distortion Augustine, with his emphasis on original sin and his description of humanity as a *massa damnata*[29] (a phrase which Donne quotes several times), must have had a share.

As an example of one of the Greek Fathers whom Donne quotes constantly in Latin, we may take St. Basil. In the sermon on *John* 1.8 preached at St. Paul's on Christmas Day, 1621, Donne asserts in his first paragraph that the doctrine of the whole of St. John's Gospel is summed up in the first chapter. In the first verse of this chapter he finds the assertion of Christ's Divinity, and also the distinction of Persons in the Godhead, and on this latter point Donne invokes the aid of Basil. "And then, as his *Eternitie,* so his *distinction of Persons,* is also specified in this 1. verse, when the *Word,* (that is, *Christ*) is

---

[27] Vol. VI of our edition, p. 293: "So also hath there beene a particular dignity ascribed to those seven Psalmes, which we have ever called the *Penitentiall Psalmes;* Of which S. *Augustine* had so much respect, as that he commanded them to be written in a great Letter, and hung about the curtaines of his Death-bed within, that hee might give up the ghost in contemplation, and meditation of those seven Psalmes." Fortunately Donne did not imitate Augustine's example in this. His own last words were taken from the Lord's Prayer, "Thy Kingdom come, Thy will be done."

[28] There is one great penitential Psalm, the fifty-first, which anticipates the Christian experience in a remarkable way, and Donne's sermon on this psalm (Vol. V, No. 15) is a fine one.

[29] Augustine, *Enchiridion,* c. 27. See the present edition of Donne's *Sermons,* Vol. I, p. 273; Vol. III, p. 109; Vol. IV, p. 148, "man was sowr'd in the lumpe, . . . in the loins of *Adam";* Vol. V, p. 186.

said to have been *apud Deum, with God.* For, therefore, (saith Saint *Basil*) did the *Holy Ghost* rather choose to say *apud Deum,* then *in Deo, with God,* then *in God, ne auferendæ Hypostaseos occasionem daret,* lest he should give any occasion of denying the same *Nature,* in divers *Persons;* for it doth more clearly notifie a distinction of Persons, to say, he was *with him,* then to say, he was *in him;* for the severall Attributes of God, (*Mercy* and *Justice,* and the rest) are *in God,* and yet they are not distinct Persons."[30] For this quotation see the sixteenth Homily of St. Basil (Migne, *Pat. Græc.,* 31, col. 479).

In the *Sermon of Valediction,* preached on April 18, 1619, we find (Vol. II, pp. 239–249) a rather free adaptation of a number of sentences from Sermo viii, *De Pœnitentia,* of Basil (Migne, *Pat. Græc.,* 32, cols. 1218–38): "*Viximus mundo; vivamus reliquum nobis ipsis* [*Basil,* in mg.]; Thus long we have served the world; let us serve our selves the rest of our time, that is, the best part of our selves, our souls. *Expectas ut febris te vocet ad pœnitentiam?* [*Idem,* in mg.]. Hadst thou rather a sickness should bring thee to God, than a sermon? hadst thou rather be beholden to a Physitian for thy salvation, than to a Preacher?" After an interval of a few pages, Donne returns again to this source: "*Labore fracta instrumenta, ad Deum ducis, quorum nullus usus?* [*Basil,* in mg.] wouldest thou consecrate a Chalice to God that is broken? no man would present a lame horse, a disordered clock, a torn book to the King.... *Temperantia non est temperantia in senectute, sed impotentia incontinentiæ,* chastity is not chastity in an old man, but a disability to be unchast; and therefore thou dost not give God that which thou pretendest to give, for thou hast no chastity to give him." And after another interval Donne quotes again: "Remember then the Creator, and *remember thy Creator,* for, *Quis magis fidelis Deo?* [*Basil,* in mg.] who is so faithful a Counsailor as God? *Quis prudentior Sapiente?* who can be wiser than wisdome? *Quis utilior bono?* or better than goodness? *Quis conjunctior Creatore?* or neerer then our Maker? and therefore remember him."

In his Christmas Day sermon of 1624 Donne draws twice on Basil. He says: "And therefore much more, when we come to these super-

---

[30] Vol. III, p. 349.

naturall points, such as this birth of Christ, we embrace S. *Basils* modesty, and abstinence, *Nativitas ista silentio honoretur,* This mysterie is not so well celebrated, with our words, and discourse, as with a holy silence, and meditation: *Immo potius ne cogitationibus permittatur,* Nay, (saies that Father) there may be danger in giving our selves leave, to thinke or study too much of it. *Ne dixeris quando,* saies he, *præteri hanc interrogationem:* Aske not thy selfe overcuriously, when this mystery was accomplished; . . . *Præteri hanc interrogationem,* pass over this question, in good time, and with convenient satisfaction, *Quando,* when Christ was borne: But *noli inquirere Quomodo,* (saies S. *Basil* still) never come to that question, how it was done, *cum ad hoc nihil sit quod responderi possit,* for God hath given us no faculties to comprehend it, no way to answer it."[81]

In Volume V we have noted as many as twenty references to St. Basil. These will be found on pp. 42, 104, 108, 110, 143, 162, 171, 203, 284, 289, 293, 299, 342, 348, 350, 352–353, 355, 364, 374, 378.

For St. Cyril of Alexandria we can draw on Donne's Christmas Day sermon of 1621. In that sermon (Vol. III, p. 350) Donne discusses the call of St. Andrew and another disciple in *John* 1.38, and writes: "In his [Andrew's] first question, *Master, where dwellest thou?* there is not onely, (as *Cyrill* observes) a reverent ascribing to him *a power of instructing* in that compellation, *Master,* but a desire to have more time afforded to his instructions, *Where dwellest thou, that I may dwell with thee?*" This is a reference to Cyril's *In Joannis Evangelium,* lib. II, c. 1: "Primum enim magistrum ipsum vocant, clare significantes velle aliquid discere. Tum rogant uti domum suam indicet, tanquam ibi opportune dicturi quod sit operæ pretium." (Migne, *Pat Græc.,* 73, cols. 215–218.)

A little later (p. 352) he appears to be using a different chapter of Cyril's commentary on St. John with reference to *John* 1.4–8. "Though most expositors, as well ancient, as modern agree with one generall, and unanime consent, that *light* in this *verse* [verse 8] is intended and

---

[81] Vol. VI, p. 179. This is from the *Homilia in sanctam Christi generationem* (Migne, *Pat. Græc.,* 31, cols. 1458–76, the Appendix). Dr. J. N. D. Kelly tells us that though J. P. Migne's editor doubted the authenticity of this sermon (*Pat. Græc.,* 31, cols. 30–35), more modern criticism, starting with Usener, has accepted it as a genuine work of St. Basil's.

meant of *Christ,* Christ is this light, yet in some precedent and subsequent passages in this Chapter, I see other senses have been admitted of this word, *light,* ... particularly in the *fourth verse (In it was life, and that life was the light of men)* there they understand *life,* to be nothing but this *naturall life,* which we breath, and *light* to be onely that *naturall light, naturall reason,* which distinguishes us *men,* from other creatures. Now, it is true that they may have a pretence for some ground of his interpretation in antiquity it selfe, for, so says Saint *Cyrill, Filius Dei Creativè illuminat,* Christ doth enlighten us, in creating us." Here the late Dr. F. E. Hutchinson gave us this note: "See *In Joannis Evangelium,* lib. i, c. vii. The exact phrase, as here quoted, does not occur in this chapter, but Donne was probably quoting from memory, and intended merely to give the general sense of the passage."

Donne made considerable use of the threefold method of interpreting Scripture, which he inherited from medieval theologians, and which goes back ultimately to such early Fathers as Origen and Clement of Alexandria. They derived it from the Hellenized Jew, Philo of Alexandria, who was active in the first half of the first century A.D. He was a practicing Jew, who was eager to show that whatever the letter of the Old Testament might say, it had an inward or spiritual meaning which was in harmony with Platonism. "For Origen, as for Philo, the whole of Scripture, not merely certain passages, has a deeper meaning to be explained by the commentator. Clement of Alexandria, who may have been Origen's teacher, had anticipated him here. ... Scripture for him [Origen] was a mirror, which reflected the divinity now darkly, now brightly; it had body, soul, and spirit, a literal, moral, and allegorical sense, the first two for 'simple believers' who were 'unable to understand profounder meanings,' the third for the initiates, the Christian gnostics, who were able to investigate *the wisdom in a mystery, the hidden wisdom of God."*[32]

The Latin Fathers took over the allegorical method from the Alexandrian school. Thus St. Ambrose made the work of Philo Judæus the basis of his commentary on Genesis, though he explained that Philo as a Jew could understand only the moral, not the mystical

[32] Beryl Smalley, *The Study of the Bible in the Middle Ages,* Oxford, 1952, pp. 6–9.

sense, and a Christian expositor must supplement him by finding types of Christ and the Church.[33] St. Jerome's commentaries contain many examples of a scholarly literal interpretation and of an allegorical. St. Augustine put the spiritual sense of Scripture above the literal, but he liked to give both a literal and a spiritual interpretation to the same text, and he very seldom sacrificed the literal sense to a subjective spiritual interpretation.[34] St. Gregory the Great was regarded by later ages as the master of spiritual (i.e., allegorical) interpretation. He reduced the literal exposition to a bare minimum, and exercised much ingenuity in finding in the Old Testament types of Christ and the Church,[35] and of the Last Things.

Donne distinguishes clearly the three senses—literal, moral, and mystical—and makes them the basis of his plan of exposition for a series of six sermons preached at Lincoln's Inn. Thus he writes of his text [*Psa.* 38.3], "Which words we shall first consider, as they are our present object, as they are historically, and literally to be understood of *David;* And secondly, in their *retrospect,* as they look back upon the first *Adam,* and so concern *Mankind collectively,* and so *you,* and *I,* and all have our portion in these calamities; And thirdly, we shall consider them in their *prospect,* in their future relation to the *second Adam,* in *Christ Jesus,...*"[36] And in the next sermon he puts it more briefly: "First then, all these things are *literally* spoken of *David:* By *application,* of us; and by *figure,* of Christ. *Historically, David; morally,* we; *Typically,* Christ is the subject of this text."[37]

Though Donne frequently makes use of the moral and anagogical senses of Scripture, he is quite definite in asserting the supremacy of the literal sense.[38] This is particularly evident in the sermon which

[33] *De Cain et Abel,* i. 4–5.

[34] Smalley, *op. cit.,* pp. 23–24.

[35] For example, he explains the text *Job* 28.19, "the topaz of Ethiopia shall not be equal to it [i.e., wisdom]," as meaning that the virtues of the Gentiles shall not be equal to the holiness of the Son of God (*Moralia* XVIII, lii, Migne, *Pat. Lat.,* 76, col. 88).

[36] Vol. II of our edition, p. 75.

[37] *Ibid.,* p. 97.

[38] This point is admirably made by Helen Gardner in her book, *The Business of Criticism,* Oxford, 1959, pp. 136–137: "Compared with other preachers of his Church and age, and certainly with those of the age pre-

he preached before the King on *Job.* 16.17–19. Here he rejects the exposition which Gregory the Great had given of the words of the text: "Difference of Expositions makes us stop here, upon this inquisition, in what affection *Iob* spake this.... S. *Gregory,* according to his manner, through all this book, which is, to apply all *Iobs* sufferings to Christ, and to make *Iob* some kinde of type of Christ, makes no more of this, but that it is an adjuration of the earth, in the person and behalf of Christ, not to suck in, or smoother his blood, but that it might be notified, and communicated to all the world. And truly, this is a good use, but it cannot be said to be a good sense of the place, because it cannot consist with the rest of the words."[39]

And in his Christmas sermon of 1621 at St. Paul's he says: "And therefore though it be ever lawfull, and often times very usefull, for the raising and exaltation of our devotion,... to induce the *diverse senses* that the Scriptures doe admit, yet this may not be admitted, if there may be danger thereby, to neglect or weaken the *literall sense* it selfe. For there is no necessity of that *spirituall wantonnesse* of finding more then necessary senses; for, the more *lights* there are, the more *shadows* are also cast by those many lights. And, as it is true in

---

ceding, Donne makes a great deal of reference to the mystical senses. It would be possible to amass a formidable number of quotations, and on their evidence argue, in all good faith, that Donne held the view which Professor Willey puts forward as the view of the age, and valued the mystical sense as the sweet kernel hidden in the husk of the literal. Such a view, however impressively supported by quotation, would, I believe, be false. Donne's prime concern is always to establish the literal sense of his text, which he defines more than once as 'the principal intention of the Holy Ghost in that place.' He has profited by the long struggles of the exegetes of the Middle Ages to distinguish the problem presented to the interpreter of Scripture by its figurative nature, from the problem of whether it has different senses. Like St. Thomas, he includes in the literal sense the figurative, metaphorical, and parabolic..."

[39] Vol. IX, p. 221. Elsewhere in the same sermon he remarks, "S. *Gregory* hath, (to good use) given us many Morals, (as he cals them) upon this Booke, but, truly, not many Literals,... *Origen,* who (except S. *Gregory*) hath written most of this Booke, and yet gone but a little way into the booke neither, doth never pretend much literalnesse in his expositions, so that we are not to looke for that at *Origens* hands. We must not therefore refuse the assistance of later men, in the exposition of this Text,..." (*ibid.,* p. 214).

religious duties, so is it in interpretation of matters of Religion, *Neces-sarium & Satis convertuntur;* when you have done that you ought to doe in your calling, you have done enough; ... so when you have the *necessary sense,* that is the meaning of the holy Ghost in that place, you have senses enow, and not till then, though you have never so many, and never so delightfull."[40]

MEDIEVAL AND RENAISSANCE COMMENTATORS
AND CONTROVERSIALISTS

DONNE's indebtedness to medieval writers and especially to Aquinas, Scotus, and other Schoolmen, is very considerable. To examine it fully would require a whole volume, and such a book was devoted to it several years ago by Miss M. P. Ramsay, whose *Les Doctrines médiévales chez Donne,* Oxford, 1917, gained her a doctorate at Paris.[41] It would be useless for us to try to summarize her results in the small space at our disposal. It must suffice for us to say that we ap-preciate the great influence which Aquinas exercised on Donne's thought, and which is more apparent in the earlier prose works than in the *Sermons.* Our Index at the end of this volume gives a large number of references under the heading "Aquinas" and "the School."

Out of the mass of Catholic commentators whom Donne consulted there are three who deserve special notice.[42] They are Nicholas of Lyra, representing the early fourteenth century, Benedictus Pererius, who lived in the late sixteenth century, and Cornelius à Lapide, a contemporary who outlived Donne, and whose commentaries were published in the early seventeenth century.

Nicholas of Lyra (1270–1340) represented the culmination of a medieval movement for the study of Hebrew and rabbinical lore. It

---

[40] Vol. III, p. 353.

[41] Miss Ramsay's book, though useful, is one-sided, as it represents Donne throughout as a medievalist, omitting the renaissance element in his thought.

[42] These are not necessarily the ones quoted most often by name in the *Sermons.* For example, Donne mentions Calvin's expositions of the Scrip-tures much more often in the *Sermons* than he mentions those of the three with whom we deal in detail. He knew that the name of Calvin would awaken a readier response from his hearers than would that of Lyra, a medieval commentator whose work was nearly three hundred years old.

is only recently that scholars have recognized how much work on this subject was done by the school of the Abbey of St. Victor, of whom the Masters Hugh, Richard, and Andrew were the outstanding exponents of Biblical scholarship. As early as the twelfth century, Jewish sources such as the commentaries of Rashi (called "Rabbi Solomon" by Donne) and the Hebrew lexicon known as "Mahbereth" were being used by Christian scholars.[43] Lyra used this knowledge and added to it in his famous *Postillæ* or Postils (probably derived from "post illa verba"), that is, they formed a comment written out as a continuous gloss interposed after certain words in the text of Scripture. The Bible with Lyra's postils which Donne presented to the Benchers of Lincoln's Inn when he resigned the Readership there, was a copy printed at Douai in 1617 in six volumes folio.[44]

Until Donne himself became a Hebrew scholar he seems to have drawn his knowledge of the Jewish Rabbis chiefly from Lyra, and in *Biathanatos* he has a number of quotations from the postils.[45] Thus on p. 203 he writes, "And therefore saith *Lyra*, [*all Iews and some Christians agree, that least by his reproach dishonour might redound upon God, a good and zealous man may kill himself, as* Samson *did, and the Virgins.*]" The square brackets here are Donne's, and are used, as sometimes in the *Sermons,* as a mark of quotation. In another early work, the *Essays in Divinity,* he quotes Lyra even more frequently.[46]

In the *Sermons,* however, when Donne mentions Lyra by name, it

---

[43] See Smalley, *op. cit.,* pp. 353, 367, and Spicq, *Esquisse d'une histoire de l'exégèse latine au moyen âge,* Bibliothèque Thomiste, XXVI (Paris, 1944).

[44] See our account of this gift in Vol. II of our edition, pp. 2–3.

[45] *Biathanatos,* pp. 158, 198, 203, 212. This book has been assigned by Gosse (I, 258) and others (Keynes, p. 86) to 1608, but we are inclined to think that it may have been written somewhat earlier.

[46] Ed. Simpson, pp. 5, 26, 33, 42, 48, 58–59. On p. 33 Donne writes, "For with, and since *Lyra,* (of whom his Apologist *Dornike* sayes, *Delirat qui cum Lyra non sentit*) they [the Expositors] agree much, that Heaven and Earth in this place, is the same which it is now." Donne evidently relished Dornike's atrocious Latin pun. On p. 48 he writes, "*Lyra,* who is not so refined [i.e. subtle], yet very Judaick too, thinks, that as with the Latin, *Cholaus, Choletus, Cholinus,* and *Nicolaus* is one Name; so it is in the variation of names in the Scriptures."

is generally to disagree with him. Thus when he expounds *Psa.* 6.10 he remarks that the words may be taken either as a curse or as a prediction. "And because *Lyra* takes them to be so, a curse, he referres the words *Ad Dæmones,* To the Devill: That herein *David* seconds Gods malediction upon the Serpent, and curses the Devill, as the occasioner and first mover of all these calamities; ..."[47] Donne, however, prefers to consider the words as a prediction, and gives them a different interpretation. Again, in his Christmas sermon of 1627 he writes that the words of this text (*Exod.* 4.13) are to be taken as a prayer by Moses that God would send Christ as a deliverer: "And that, not as *Lyra* takes them; *Lyra* takes them to be a petition, and not a reluctation; but a petition of *Moses,* that hee would send *Aaron;* That, if he would send any, he should send a man of better parts, and abilities, then himselfe; ..."[48]

Though Donne mentions Lyra by name only a few times in the *Sermons,* there are passages which show that Lyra's commentary was still consulted by him, though he does not supply the name. Thus in Vol. VIII, p. 200, when Donne is discussing 1 *Sam.* 7.6, he writes: "And so when at *Samuels* motions, and increpation, the people would testifie their repentance, *They drew water,* sayes the story, *and poured it out before the Lord, and fasted, and said, We have sinned against the Lord.* They poured water, *Vt esset symbolum lacrymarum,* That that might be a type, and figure, in what proportion of teares, they desired to expresses their repentance." He supplies in the margin against *"Vt esset symbolum lacrymarum"* the name "Rab. Oziel," unfortunately misprinted in the Folio which we followed as "Nab. Oziel."[49] Donne's use of the form "Oziel" for Rabbi Jonathan ben Uzziel, to whom the Targums on the books of *Samuel* and *Kings* are ascribed, betrays that he had been using Lyra's commentary, which contains this passage (with the Vulgate numbering I. Reg. vii. 6): "...hoc fecerunt in signum humiliationis....Ionathan filius Oziel maximæ reputationis apud Hebræos, hoc exponit de conversione cordium ad Deum, et sic per istas aquas intelliguntur lacrymæ contri-

---

[47] Vol. VI, p. 53.

[48] Vol. VIII, p. 152.

[49] This mistake is corrected in the list of Corrigenda on p. 445 of the present volume.

tionis exeuntes a corde ..."[50] Also when Donne mentions "Rabbi Solomon" as he does in Vol. III, p. 315, and Vol. VIII, p. 152, he is referring to the great Jewish scholar Rashi (1040–1105), whom Lyra quotes by that name.[51]

Two renaissance commentators on whom Donne drew more heavily than would appear from his marginal references in the *Sermons* are Benedictus Pererius (Bento Pereyra), a Jesuit who taught theology and philosophy at Rome, and Cornelius à Lapide (van den Steen), a Jesuit hebraist and theologian who taught at Louvain and Rome. Pererius was the elder by thirty years, and his masterpiece was his commentary on *Genesis,* which appeared in four volumes from 1589 to 1598 at Rome. These were published together as a unit at Cologne in 1601, and six more editions followed in the seventeenth century. This great commentary was deservedly popular with Protestants as well as Catholics. Raleigh in his *History of the World,* Donne in his *Essays in Divinity* and *Sermons,* and Sir Thomas Browne in *Religio Medici* and *Vulgar Errors,* all made liberal use of Pererius on *Genesis.*[52] Also Protestant commentators like Paræus and Rivetus cite Pererius on *Genesis* more often than they quote Luther and Calvin.[53]

In *Essays in Divinity*[54] Donne quoted Pererius by name at least

[50] We owe this reference and further explanation about the Targum to Rabbi Lehmann of Oxford, who kindly gave us the Aramaic for the passage.

[51] It used to be thought that Lyra was the first Latin scholar to use this name, but the recent discovery of a manuscript by Herbert of Bosham, who wrote in the late twelfth or early thirteenth century, shows that Herbert quotes a "litterator hebreus" who is generally Rashi. "A marginal note in the same hand as the text has, against two passages where Rashi is quoted: Salomon." Smalley, *op. cit.,* p. 190.

[52] See A. Williams, *The Common Expositor,* pp. 35–37. Williams shows that Raleigh, who occasionally cited Pererius, used him also in other passages without acknowledgment. We know from the sale of Browne's library and that of his son in 1710–11 that he owned the commentaries on *Genesis* of Pererius and Mersenne (Williams, p. 32), and yet "he never cites or quotes either Pererius or Mersenne. Instead he seems trying to give the impression that he is using original sources."

[53] Williams, *op. cit.,* p. 33.

[54] Ed. Simpson, pp. 10, 11, 15, 19, 27, 52, 74. On pp. 17, 18, 32, 60, 72, 83, 89, Pererius, though not mentioned by name, was evidently Donne's authority.

seven times, and in many other places he drew on the commentary without acknowledgement. In the *Sermons* Donne made less use of Pererius than he had done in the *Essays*. This is natural, for the *Essays* were based exclusively on texts taken from the first chapters of *Genesis* and *Exodus,* whereas in the *Sermons* Donne took the whole range of Scripture for his province. Also his method as a preacher was different from that used in the *Essays*. However, he cites Pererius by name in five places, and in our Appendix to Volume VIII of the *Sermons* we have shown that in the Christmas Sermon of 1627 he made considerable use of the commentary on *Exodus* by Pererius. In the Easter sermon of 1629[55] he appears to be drawing on Pererius in the passage where he discusses the creation of the Angels. Pererius (*Gen*. I, pp. 194–199) has a long dissertation "Cur Moses hoc loco, creationem Angelorum non exposuerit." He dismisses the theory that Moses had included the angels under the name of "heaven" or "light." He then discusses whether they were created before the world, as nearly all the Greek Fathers and St. Jerome and others had thought, or at the same time as the world, as St. Augustine and most of those who followed him had believed. He writes: "Verum ea de re magna lis est inter Patres. Etenim fere Græci scriptores, et de Latinis quicunque fuere ante Augustinum, censuerunt, multis ante hunc mundum sæculis, Angelos esse a Deo conditos, hoc tradit Origenes . . . Basilius, Nazianzus . . . Damascenus . . . Ambrosius . . . Hieronymus." He goes on to state that Augustine, Theodoret, and the Schoolmen held that they were created at the same time as the world, but Augustine did not make this an article of faith.

In the Easter sermon Donne does not follow Pererius slavishly, but he summarizes the chief points in a lengthy discussion, which has occupied many pages. He writes: "That *Moses* did speak nothing of the fall, or of the confirmation of Angels, may justly seem a convenient reason to think, that he meant to speak nothing of the creation of Angels neither. . . . And therefore, that the Angels are wrapped up in that word of *Moses, The Heavens,* and that they were made when the heavens were made, or that they are wrapped up in that word of *Moses, The Light,* and that they were made, when Light was made, is all but conjecturall, and cloudy: . . . That they were created long before this world, all the Greek Fathers of the Eastern Church did constantly think; And in the Westerne Church, amongst the Latine Fathers, S. *Ierome* himself was so cleare in it, as to say, *Sex millia, nostri orbis, nondum implentur anni, ... Et quantas æternitates, quantas sæculorum origines, ... Theodoret* that thinkes not so, thinks it not against any article of Faith, to think that it was so. *Aquinas,* that thinkes not so, will not call it an errour, to think so, out of a reverence to *Athanasius,* and *Nazianzen,* who did think so; ..." He then deals with St. Augustine's views at some length.

Without the help of Pererius, Donne would hardly have been able to state that "all the Greek Fathers" held that the angels were created long before the world was made, for this would have involved extensive research on his part. However, he must have taken down his volumes of Jerome and Augustine to complete the passage, for Pererius does not quote the sentences from these two which Donne inserts. He uses the commentary to supply his own deficiencies, and then enlarges the passage by quoting from two of his favourite Fathers.[56]

In the *Sermons* Donne made still more extensive use of the commentaries of Cornelius à Lapide (Cornelius van den Steen), a Flemish Jesuit, all of whose works belong to the seventeenth century. His earliest commentary, that on the Epistles of St. Paul (among which he included the Epistle to the *Hebrews*), was published at Antwerp in 1614, and it was followed by a commentary on the Pentateuch in 1616, by one on *Jeremiah, Lamentations,* and *Baruch* in 1621, and by a larger work, which included the last-named, on the four Major Prophets in 1622. These were followed by commentaries on the Minor Prophets in 1625, and on *Acts* and *Revelation* (*Apocalypse*) in 1627. He wrote commentaries on other parts of the Bible, which were published too late for Donne to have seen them, and according to the Jesuit Directory his commentary on the Gospels was not published till 1639, two years after Lapide's death and eight years after Donne's. It is therefore evident that it is only with Lapide's earlier commentaries that we need concern ourselves, and that Donne should have made use of these is proof of his desire to keep abreast of Continental

---

[56] We have quoted this as a single example of the type of passage in which careful students can trace Donne's use of the commentaries, and of Pererius in particular.

learning. Lapide's enormous digest of patristic and medieval comments on the Scriptures was immensely popular in the seventeenth,
eighteenth, and nineteenth centuries. His numerous separate commentaries were collected together, with supplements, into a huge
series of twenty-four volumes, *Commentaria in Scripturas Sanctas*
(Paris, 1857–1863), and this in the edition of 1865, which is well
known in most libraries, is the one from which my quotations are
drawn, though I have also consulted the original separate editions.
Protestants as well as Catholics made much use of it,[57] and it was translated into English in an abbreviated form in 1876 by T. W. Mossman,
and again in 1896–97 by W. F. Cobb.

Donne's indebtedness to Cornelius à Lapide has already been dem-
onstrated in Volume VIII of our edition, Appendix, pp. 393–396, with
regard to the Christmas Sermon of 1627, which was printed in that
volume. Donne himself supplied the names of Cornelius and Pererius
in the margin of one passage, and quoted some of their words ver-
batim. Moreover, the influence of these two commentators was evident throughout a large part of the sermon. There, however, the
subject was complicated by the fact that Lapide had himself made
use of Pererius. There are a number of other sermons in which Donne
makes use of Lapide alone. One of these is the Christmas sermon of
1624[58] on *Isaiah* 7.14, and Donne begins it with these words: "Saint
Bernard spent his consideration upon three remarkable conjunctions,
this Day. First, a Conjunction of God, and Man in one person, Christ
Jesus; Then a conjunction of the incompatible Titles, Maid and
Mother, in one blessed woman, the blessed Virgin *Mary:* And thirdly
a conjunction of Faith, and the Reason of man, that so beleeves, and
comprehends those two conjunctions." This is from *Sermon* iii *in
Vigilia Nativitatis,* and it is possible that Donne may have taken it
straight from the works of St. Bernard which he was fond of quoting.
We may note, however, that Cornelius à Lapide places it at the be-

---

[57] It was still used by Anglicans in the nineteenth century. Dr. Percy
Simpson says that in his schoolboy days at Denstone College, Staffordshire,
in the years 1879 to 1884, Canon Edward Lowe frequently based his sermons in college chapel on interpretations supplied by Lapide. His boyish
hearers were much amused by some of these allegorical and far-fetched
explanations.

[58] Vol. VI, No. 8, pp. 168–185.

ginning of his exposition of *Isa.* 7.14: "Tria opera tres mixturas fecit omnipotens illa majestas in assumptione nostræ carnis.... Conjuncta quippe sunt ad invicem Deus et homo, mater et virgo, fides et cor humanum."[59]

The earlier part of the sermon is very fine, and in it Donne draws entirely on his own inspiration, but there is a tedious discussion of virginity in lines 428–475 which is largely borrowed from Lapide. Donne writes: "That which *Gellius,* and *Plinie* say, that a Virgin had a child, almost 200. yeares before Christ, that which *Genebrard* saies, that the like fell out in France, in his time, are not within our faith, and they are without our reason;..." This is very close to the words of Lapide: "Nam quod scribunt Gellius, lib. ix. c. iv, et Plinius lib. vii. iv, virginem peperisse, pro ficto, non pro facto habendum est, uti et illud quod ævo nostro sub Henrico II Franciæ rege scribit Genebrardus Ambianis in Francia factum, ut virgo pareret."

A little later Donne quotes Cyprian: *"Virgo non tantum esse, sed & intelligi esse debet, & credi:...Ita, ut nemo, cum virginem viderit, dubitet an sit virgo,* saies that Father,... The word in the Text, is derived *à latendo,* from retiring, from privatenesse: And *Tertullian,* who makes the note, notes withall, that *Ipsa concupiscentia non latendi, non est pudica,...Studium placendi, publicatione sui, periclitatur,* saies the same Author:... It is usefully added by him, *Dum percutitur oculis alienis, frons duratur, & pudor teritur,...*"

These two passages from Cyprian and Tertullian, which Donne quotes in a slightly shortened form, are found in full in Lapide, who gives the references to Cyprian, *De Habitu et Disciplina Virginum,* and Tertullian, *De Velandis Virginibus,* c. xiv. Their close collocation with the passage about Gellius, Pliny, and Genebrardus suggests strongly that Donne was drawing his quotations here from Lapide, and not directly from the Fathers.

There are some other minor resemblances in this latter part of the sermon, but it is clear that Donne consulted other sources besides Lapide. For example, Donne and Lapide both mention the views of Calvin, but Lapide does not mention Cramerus, whose name Donne puts in the margin against the words, "And yet there have beene some so impious, as to charge *Calvin,* with that impiety, with denying her

[59] *Commentaria in Isaiam.*

[the Blessed Virgin] to be a Virgin then." Also Lapide violently attacks Calvin, while Donne defends him, though briefly.

A sermon in which Donne seems to have made use of Lapide for a single paragraph in which he refers to the Fathers is that on 1 *Corinthians* 16.22: "If any man love not the Lord Jesus Christ, let him be Anathema, Maranatha" (Vol. III of our edition, No. 14). In the last paragraph but one Donne gives an explanation of the Aramaic word *Maranatha:*

"The word seemes to be a Proverbiall word amongst the Jews after their returne, and vulgarly spoken by them, and so the Apostle takes it, out of common use of speech: *Maran*, is *Dominus, The Lord,* and *Athan* is *Venit, He comes:* Not so truly, in the very exactnesse of Hebrew rules, and terminations, but so amongst them then, when their language was much depraved: but, in ancienter times, we have the word *Mara* for *Dominus,* and the word *Atha* for *Venit;* ... S. *Hierom* seems to understand this, *Dominus venit,* That the Lord is come; come already, come in the flesh; *Superfluum,* sayes he, *odiis pertinacibus contendere adversus eum, qui jam venit;* It is superabundant perversnesse, to resist Christ now; Now that he hath appeared already, ... And so S. *Chrysostome* seemes to take it too; Christ is come already, sayes he, *Et jam nulla potest excusatio non diligentibus eum;* ... But that is not all, that is intended by the Apostle, in this place."

This is fairly close to the words of Lapide, who, however, gives a slightly different Hebrew rendering, though his quotations from Jerome and Chrysostom are almost exactly the same: "Rursum patet linguarum peritis, *Maran atha* esse vocem Hebræo-syriacum ... *Maran,* hoc est Dominus noster, ... *etha,* hoc est venit ... quod pure hebraice diceritur ... *morenu atha* ... insinuet, ait S. Hieronymus, quod superfluum sit odiis pertinacibus adversus eum velle contendere, quem venisse jam constat ... ait Chrysostomus: Ratio cur anathema denuntiam eis ... est quod ipse jam venit ... ut nulla possit esse eum non diligentibus excusatio."

In his sermon on 2 *Corinthians* 5.20, preached at St. Paul's, undated, Donne introduces an earlier verse (verse 13 from the same chapter) and writes: "S. *Paul* was under the imputation of *madnesse.* Nay, our blessed Saviour himself [*Mar.* 3.21 in mg.] did some such act of vehement zeal, as that his very friends thought him *mad. S. Paul,* because his madnesse was imputed to a false cause, to a pride in his much *learning,* disavowed his madnesse, *I am not mad, O noble Festus* [*Acts,* 26.25]. But when the *cause* was justifiable, he thought his *madnesse* justifiable too; *If we be besides our selves, it is for God* [2 *Cor.* 5.13 in mg.]; and so long well enough. *Insaniebat amatoriam insaniam Paulus* [*Theophil.* in mg.], S. *Paul* was mad for love; S. *Paul* did, and we doe take into our contemplation, the beauty of a Christian soul; ..."[60]

All this material, though differently arranged, can be found in Lapide (in 2 *Cor.* 5.13), who comments on the words *Sive enim mente excedimus,* If we be beside ourselves, "Imò Syrus, Chrysostom, Theophilus ... vertent *sive insanimus.* ... Sic de Christo dicunt consanguinei Marci 3. v. 21, *quoniam in furorem versus est.* ... Sic enim habet Theophilus. ... *Insaniebat itaque Paulus amatoria quadam insania Deus amans ...*" Lapide, like Donne, contrasts this text with St. Paul's words in *Acts* 26.25 where the Apostle says, "I am not mad, most noble Festus, but speak forth the words of truth and soberness." When we find that Donne has joined together different books of the New Testament plus a quotation from Theophilus,[61] an author whom he hardly ever quotes, and that all these are found together in Lapide, the conclusion is plain that he had Lapide's commentary at his elbow while he was planning this sermon.

A passage in which Donne himself gives us the name of Lapide as his authority is in the Fourth Prebend Sermon, preached on January 28, 1626/7, where he writes, "In the name of *Iesus,* S. *Paul* abounded, but in the Name of *Christ* more; for, (as a Jesuit [*Corn. Lap.* in mg.] gives us the account) he repeats the name of *Iesus* almost three hundred times, but the name of *Christ* more then foure hundred, in his

---

[60] Pp. 124–125 of our present volume.

[61] Theophilus, bishop of Antioch, lived in the latter part of the second century, and wrote an apology for the Christian faith. St. Jerome mentions that he wrote a commentary on the Gospels, of which Jerome himself made use. There are four books of commentaries on the Gospels, in Latin only, which bear the name of Theophilus, but critics have decided that these are much later than his time. We have not found any other reference to this Theophilus in Donne's work, so it appears that he was drawing on Lapide.

Epistles."[62] This is in Lapide's *Commentaria in Epistolas Pauli Sancti,*
Antwerp, 1614, on *Ephesians* 1.10.

Because of Donne's considerable indebtedness to Lapide in a few
sermons, the reader might perhaps form the opinion that Donne knew
much less of the Fathers than has been supposed, and that his learning
has been exaggerated. This would be a mistake, as we have examined
a large number of passages, and have decided that most of them show
that Donne referred to the original authorities, or that at any rate
Lapide was not his chief source.[63]

We may conclude by saying that Donne showed his openness of
mind and his determination to make use of the best and most up-to-
date Biblical commentaries in securing the volumes of Lapide almost
as soon as they were published. In two or three sermons he followed
Lapide rather slavishly, and overloaded his work with an excessive
number of quotations. But on the whole he seems to have used Lapide
intelligently, as a pointer to relevant passages in the Fathers and the
Schoolmen.

[62] Vol. VII, pp. 309–310.

[63] Two examples may be briefly summarized. In Donne's sermon on a
difficult text, 1 *Corinthians* 15.29 (Vol. VII, No. 7, pp. 190–214), he first
devotes several pages to refuting the opinion of Cardinal Bellarmine.
Then he considers the opinions of the Italian Jesuit Justinian, and of
Cardinal Cajetan. After this he examines the opinions of Tertullian,
Theodoret, Chrysostom, and Theophylact among the Fathers, and then
turns to Aquinas. Among those whom Donne calls "the later men" he
considers the Jesuit Maldonatus, then Luther, Melanchthon, and Piscator
[Fischer]. Lapide's examination is much shorter, and he begins with the
interpretation of Aquinas. He mentions Tertullian, Theodoret, and
Chrysostom, but not Theophylact, and he omits altogether Luther,
Melanchthon, Piscator, and Maldonatus. His mention of Bellarmine is so
much shorter than Donne's that it is evident that Donne consulted Bellarmine's own works and was not content with Lapide's brief summary, if
he used him at all for this sermon. His chief object was to show that Bellarmine was wrong in using the text as an argument for the existence of
Purgatory.

In another sermon upon the same text, Donne turns aside to interpret a
passage from 1 *Corinthians* 10.13, and cites the opinions of Chrysostom,
Jerome, and Gregory the Great (Vol. VII of our edition, p. 187). Lapide
in his commentary on this passage quotes Augustine, Ephrem, Theophylact, Œcumenius, Ambrose, and Anselm—a quite different range of
authors.

Of the Protestant commentators Calvin is the one most frequently quoted by Donne. In *Biathanatos* (p. 98) Donne had linked Calvin with St. Augustine "for sharpe insight, and conclusive judgement, in exposition of places of Scripture," and in *Essays in Divinity* (pp. 26, 59, 93, 95) there are several references to Calvin. In the *Sermons* Donne quotes Calvin both as an expositor of Scripture (Vol. III, p. 101, where Calvin is described as "one, to whom we all owe much, for the interpretation of the Scriptures," and p. 177, where he is called "a later Divine, worthy to be compared to the *Ancients,* for the exposition of Scriptures"),[64] and as a theologian, with whose doctrines Donne did not always concur.

Donne also has frequent references to Luther as an expositor. For example, on the text *Gen.* 18.25, when he is discussing the visit of three men (angels) to Abraham, he writes: "*Luther* sayes well upon this text, If there were no other proofe of the Trinity but this, I should not believe the Trinity; but yet sayes he, This is *Singulare testimonium de articulo Trinitatis,* Though it be not a concluding argument, yet it is a great testimony of the Trinity....I confesse, in the literall sense, there is nothing but a recommendation of hospitality, and therefore, to the Jews, I would urge no more out of this place:..."[65] Other passages where Donne quotes Luther as an expositor can be found in III, p. 315; V, pp. 139, 303, 321; VII, pp. 206–208, 308; VIII, pp. 233, 236, 319.

Other Protestant commentators quoted by Donne are Beza, Chemnicius, Drusius, Peter Martyr, Melanchthon, Musculus, Pellicanus, Piscator, Polanus, Rupertus, etc. Particulars about them will be found in Appendix B to this chapter.

---

[64] For other references to Calvin see our Index. They are particularly frequent in Vols. VII, VIII, and IX.

[65] Vol. III, pp. 143–144.

APPENDIX A

LIST OF IDENTIFIED PASSAGES FROM ST. AUGUSTINE'S WORKS QUOTED OR REFERRED TO BY DONNE IN THE SERMONS

Vol. I. 1. 414–417. Of which will of God, whosoever seeks a reason, *Aliquid majus Deo quærit,* says S. *Augustin,* he that seeks what perswaded or inclind the will of God, seeks for somthing wiser, and greater than God himself.
Also Vol. II. 6. 298–299, VI. 9. 98–101.
See also *Essays in Divinity* (ed. Simpson), p. 48, lines 21–22.
　　Aug. *De Gen. con. Man.* I, c. 2.

Vol. I. 3. 549–561. St. *Augustine* considers that question of *David, Quis ascendet,* and *quis stabit . . .?* And he applies the answer, *Innocens manibus, & mundo corde; . . .* [on *Psa.* 24. 3, Vulg. 23.3]
Also Vol. II. 5. 151–154.
　　Aug. *De Perf. Justitiæ hominis,* c. 15, sec. 36.

Vol. I. 3. 794–795. *Amor est pondus animæ; sicut gravitas, Corporis*
Also V. 10. 37, IX. 11. 299.
　　Aug. *Ad Inquis. Januarii,* L. II (*Epist.* 55), c. 10, sec. 18.

Vol. I. 4. 308–309. *Mortalitas Mutabilitas,* says St. *Augustine: . . .*
　　NOTE: This is probably an adaptation of *De Trinitate,* II, c. 9, Mutabilitas non inconvenienter mortalitas dicitur.

Vol. I. 5. 60–61. *Quid erat quod me delectabat nisi amare et amari?*
　　Aug. *Confessiones,* II, c. 2.

Vol. I. 5. 65–68. *Amatus sum, et perveni occulte ad fruendum, . . .* but what got I by all that, *Ut cæderer virgis ardentibus ferreis, zeli suspicionis et rixarum; . . .*
　　Aug. *Confes.* III, c. 1.

Vol. I. 5. 536–537. *. . . sero te amavi pulchritudo tam antiqua, tam nova*
　　Aug. *Confes.* X, c. 27.

Vol. I. 6. 232. *Rusticani insultant*
　　Aug. *Ser.* 130 *De Tempore.* [Migne, App., Serm. 155]

Vol. I. 6. 284–286. *. . .* as S. *Augustine* sayes, *Latro Laudabilis & mirabilis* [F. *miraculis*] *. . . imitabilis*
　　Aug. *Ser.* 120 *De Tempore.* [Migne, App., Serm. 154]

Vol. I. 6. 312–315. Saint *Augustine* some times eases himself upon so long Texts, as needed no great preparation, no great study; for a meer paraphrase upon this Text, was enough for all his hour, when he took both Epistle and Gospel, and Psalm of the day for his Text.
Also IV. 7. 907–909, V. 1. 270.
    Aug. *De Verbis Apostoli,* Serm. 10 [Migne, Serm. 176].

Vol. I. 6. 488–490. S. *Augustine* (if that Sermon which is the 130. *de Tempore,* be his, for it is in the copies of *Chrysostome* too) reads those words thus: *Nonne times Deum tuum?* [mg. *Tom.* 10 *in Append. Ser.* 49]
    NOTE: Donne's doubts were justified. This is a homily of Chrysostom's in an abbreviated and adapted version beginning *Hodierna die.* For Chrysostom's text see Migne, *Pat. Græc.* 49, cols. 399 ff. The Maurine editors, and Migne following them, print the sermon *Hodierna die* (to which Donne alludes) in their Appendix: see *Pat. Lat.* 39, cols. 2047 ff.

Vol. I. 7. 204–205. . . . he lay smothered up in *massa damnata,* in that leavened lump of *Adam,* where he was wrapped up in damnation.
Also III. 3. 663; IV. 5. 122; V. 9. 95.
    Aug. *Enchiridion,* c. 27.

Vol. I. 7. 284. *Perdidimus possibilitatem boni*
Also II. 1. 242–243, VII. 3. 534.
    Aug. Ser. 12 *De Verb. Apost.* [Migne, 30 *De Script.*], c. 2, sec. 3: "Per malum velle perdidit bonum posse."

Vol. I. 7. 481–483. It is S. *Augustins* observation, that that land, which is so often called the land of promise, was their land from the beginning, . . .
Also IV. 7. 180–182, V. 9. 386.
    Aug. *Ser.* 105 *De Temp.* [Migne, App., Serm. 34], c. 7, sec. 9.

Vol. II. 1. 725–730. There is a *probatum est* in S. *Augustine, Sagittaveras cor meum . . . à nundinis loquacitatis . . .* in his Church.
    Aug. *Confes.* IX, c. 2.

Vol. II. 3. 461 ff. S. *Augustine* . . . confesses of himself, *Ne vituperarer, vitiosior fiebam, . . . Et ubi non suberat, quo admisso, æquarer perditis, . . . Fingebam me fecisse quod non feceram, ne viderer abjectior, quo innocentior, . . . Audiebam eos exaltantes flagitia,* sayes that tender blessed Father, . . . *Et libebat facere, non libidine facti, sed libidine laudis, . . .*
Also Vol. II. 14. 310–313, IX. 17. 345–346.
    Aug. *Confes.* II, c. 3, sec. 7.

Vol. II. 3. 763 ff. It is true, that most of the *Eastern Fathers*, and it is true that S. *Augustine* himselfe was of that opinion, that S. *Paul* said of himselfe, *that he was sold under sin*, respecting himself before his re generation. . . . S. *Augustine* ingenuously retracts that opinion, which (as he says) he had held, when he was a *young Priest* at *Carthage*, . . .
Aug. *Retract.* I, c. 23.

Vol. II. 5. 39 ff. It is one of Saint *Augustines* definitions of sinne, *Conversio ad creaturam* . . . *Est quoddam bonum, quod si diligat anima rationalis peccat.* . . . *Quia infra illum ordinantur,* . . .
Aug. *De Ver. Relig.* c. 38 [20 in *F*].

Vol. II. 8. 138–142. Saint *Augustine* saith . . . that this place [1 *Cor.* 3.11] . . . is one of these places of which Saint *Peter* saith *Quædam difficilia* There are some things in Saint *Paul* hard to be understood: . . .
Aug. *De octo Dulcitii Quæstionibus,* I, 3.

Vol. II. 10. 596–599. As Saint *Augustine* said, when hee came out of curi osity to hear Saint *Ambrose* preach at *Milan,* . . . *Appropinquavi, & nesciebam,* I came neer God, but knew it not; . . .
Also IV. 9. 862–864, V. 17. 219, IX. 10. 231–233.
Aug. *Confes.* V, c. 13.

Vol. II. 13. 170–173. *Nec quæsivit per Oratorem piscatorem,* He sent not out Orators, Rhetoricians, strong or faire-spoken men to work upon these fisher-men, *Sed de piscatore lucratus est Imperatorem,* . . .
Aug. *En. in Ps. XXXVI,* II, sec. 14.

Vol. II. 18.349–351. *Navem quæro,* says he, *sed & patriam,* When I goe to the Haven to hire a Ship, it is for the love I have to my Country; . . .
Aug. ? *De Doct. Christiana,* I, c. 4.

Vol. III. 1 (i). 78 ff. Saint *Augustin* apprehended somewhat more in it, but upon a mistaking; for accustoming himself to a Latin copy of the Scriptures, and so lighting upon copies, that had been miswritten, he reads that, *vanitas vanitantum:* . . . though, as he saies, in his Retracta tions, his Copies misled him, . . .
Aug. *Retract.* I, c. 7, sec. 3.

Vol. III. 1 (ii). 1–3. That Riches were hurtful even to the owners, St. *Augustin* hath well and fully expressed, *Eris præda hominum, qui jam es diaboli;* . . .
Aug. *En. in Ps. CXXXI,* sec. 25.

Vol. III. 2. 149. *Caro conjux,* sayes the same Father in another place, . . .
Also V. 10. 364, IX. 14. 153.
Aug. *En. in Ps. CXL,* sec. 16, and *CXLIII,* sec. 6.

Vol. III. 7. 416–417. Saint *Augustine* contracts that prayer, and fixes it, *Liberet te Deus à temet, noli tibi esse malus;* ...
Also IX. 4. 159.
> Aug. *Ser.* 297 *De Sanctis* [Migne], "In Natali apostolorum," c. 6, sec. 9.

Vol. III. 10. 192 ff. S. *Augustine* hath brought it nearer, *Qui alienum negat, si posset, tolleret,* ... S. *Augustine* puts a case to the point: ... a poore Usher of a Grammar Schoole found a bag of money, ...
> Aug. *De Verb. Apost.* Serm. 19 [Migne, Serm. 178], c. 8.

Vol. III. 14. 461 ff. It was *Licentius,* to whom S. *Augustine* writes his 39. Epistle. He had sent to S. *Augustine* a handsome Elegie ...
> Aug. *Epist.* 39 [26].

Vol. IV. 2. 541–543. And of this errour [i.e., Chiliasm] ... S. *Augustine* himself had a touch, and a tincture, at beginning.
Also IV. 10. 181–183.
> Aug. *De Civ. Dei,* Lib. XX, c. 7.

Vol. IV. 2. 747–748. Those Vapours and *Clouds* which *David* speaks of, S. *Augustin* interprets of the Ministers of the Church; ...
> Aug. *En. in Ps. CXXXIV,* sec. 17.

Vol. IV. 4. 412–414. If you will enquire whether any of the Fathers of the Primitive Church did at any time pray for any of the dead, you shall be told (and truly) that *Augustine* did, ...
Also IV. 13. 300, VII. 6. 556, IX. 8. 395.
> Aug. *Confes.* IX, c. 13.

Vol. IV. 8. 874. *Perfectiorum est nihil in peccatore odiisse præter peccata*
Also III. 18. 234 ff., VI. 16. 318.
> Aug. *En. in Ps. CXXXVIII,* sec. 28.

Vol. IV. 13. 715–717. ... *Monicaes* Confessor said still unto her, in the behalfe of her Son S. *Augustine, filius istarum lachrymarum,* the son of these teares cannot perish; ...
Also V. 11. 295 ff., X. 2. 262.
> Aug. *Confes.* III, c. 12.

Vol. V. 1. 458–460. They [the Arians] made, sayes S. *Augustine, Filium creaturam,* The Son, they accounted to be but a creature; but they made the Holy Ghost *Creaturam Creaturæ,* ...
> Aug. *De Hæres.* xlix.

Vol. V. 2. 573–575. In that state, when he had a disposition to Baptisme, he sayes of himselfe, *Inferbui exultando, sed inhorrui timendo;* ...
> Aug. *Confes.* IX, c. 4, sec. 9.

Ibid. 578 ff. *Insinuati sunt mihi in profundo nutus tui, ... Et gaudens in fide, laudavi nomen tuum, ... Sed ea fides securum me non esse sinebat*
Ibid. sec 12.

Vol. V. 5. 456–457. *Cum tota dicat ecclesia, quamdiu hîc est, Dimitte debita nostra, non utique hîc est sine macula et ruga*
Aug. *Retract.* I, c. 7, sec. 5.

Vol. V. 10. 338 ff. Saint *Augustine* preaching upon those words, *Qui posuit fines tuos pacem, ...* observed ... such an alteration in his auditory, as that he tooke knowledge of it in his Sermon; *Nihil dixeram, nihil exposueram, verbum pronunciavi & exclamastis, ...*
Aug. *En. in Ps. CXLVII,* sec. 15.

Ibid. 364. See III. 2. 149.

Vol. V. 15. 182–183. *Berseba* was far off; *Mulier longè, libido prope,* but *Davids* disposition was in his owne bosome.
Aug. *En. in Ps. L,* sec. 3.

Ibid. 309–314. *Audiunt male viventes, & quærunt sibi patrocinia peccandi;* Wee heare of *Davids* sin, and wee justifie our sins by him; *Si David, cur non & ego? ... Qui facit, quia David fecit, id facit, quod David non fecit, ... Quia nullum exemplum proposuit, ...*
Ibid.

Ibid. 315–319. So that he that sins as *David* did, yet sins worse then *David* did; and hee that continues as unsensible of his sin, as *David* was, is more unsensible then *David* was; *Quia ad te mittitur ipse David,* For God sends *Nathan* to thee, with *David* in his hand; ...
Ibid. sec. 5.

Vol. V. 16. 505 ff. S. *Augustine* thinks, that these two words, to *Rebuke,* and to *Chasten,* doe not differ at all; or if they doe, that the latter is the lesser. ... Disputing, Impleading, Correcting, in S. *Augustines* interpretation, amount but to an Instruction, and an Amendment, yet saies he of *David, In ira emendari non vult, erudiri non vult, ...*
Aug. *En. in Ps. VI,* sec. 3.

Vol. V. 17. 219. See II. 10. 598.

Vol. VI. 1. 606–608. S. *Augustine* himselfe, undervalued and despised the Scriptures, because of the poore and beggerly phrase, that they seemed to be written in, ...
Aug. *Confes.* III, c. 5.

Vol. VI. 3. 295–298. Aswell Saint *Gregory,* as Saint *Augustine* before, interpret this [*Deut.* 25.5] of our elder, our eldest brother *Christ Iesus.* That *hee* being dead, we mary his wife, the Church, and become husbands to her.
Aug. *En. in Ps. XLIV,* sec. 23.

Vol. VI. 4. 268–270. St. *Augustine,* and not he alone, interprets this whole Psalme of Christ, that it is a *thankesgiving of Christ* to his *Father,* ...
Aug. *En. in Ps. XXXIII.*

Vol. VI. 8. 303–306. ... though St. *Augustine,* and some with him, ascribe this refusall of *Achaz,* to a religious modesty, yet St. *Hierome,* and with him, the greatest party, justly impute this, for a fault to *Achaz:* ...
Aug. *Quæst. in Heptateuchum,* I, 63.

Ibid. 397–398. *In talibus rebus, tota ratio facti, est potentia facientis*
Aug. *Epist.* 137, c. 2, sec. 8.

Vol. VI. 11. 263–264. *Nihil est falsitas, nisi cum esse putatur, quod non est*
Aug. *Confes.* VII, c. 15.

Ibid. 330–331. But, *ineffabili dulcedine teneor cum audio, Bonus Dominus;* ...
Aug. *En. in Ps. CXXXIV,* sec. 4.

Ibid. 350–352. ... and *quale bonum ille,* sayes that Father, what kinde of goodnesse God is, this doth sufficiently declare, *Quòd nulli ab eo recedenti bene sit,* ...
Aug. *De Gen. ad Litteram,* XI, c. 5.

Ibid. 411–413. Fortune her self, is but such an Idol, as that S. *Augustine* was ashamed ever to have named her in his works, and therefore repents it in his Retractations; ...
Aug. *Retract.* I, c. 1, sec. 2.

Ibid. 524 ff. And therefore when the *Manichees* pressed S. *Augustine* with that, *Vnde malum?* ... S. *Augustine* saies, *Vnde malum? Quid malum?* From whence comes evill? ...
Aug. *De Duabus Animabus con. Man.* c. 8.

Vol. VI. 12. 403–404. *Nihil in Ecclesia catholica salubrius fit, quam ut Rationem præcedat Autoritas*
Aug. *De Mor. Eccles.* c. 25

Vol. VI. 13. 90–92. ... though S. *Augustine* say, That to convert a man from sin, is as great a miracle, as Creation, yet S. *Augustine* speaks that of a mans first conversion, ...
Aug. *En. in Ps. LXXXVIII,* Serm. 1, sec. 6.

Ibid. 155 ff. S. *Augustine* moves a question ... whether torture be to be admitted at all, or no. ... For, many times, sayes S. *Augustine* againe, *Innocens luit pro incerto scelere certissimas pœnas;* ... *Ignorantia Iudicis est calamitas plerumque innocentis,* ...
Aug. *De Civ. Dei,* Lib. XIX, c. 6.

Ibid. 291–293. ... mariage with a contract against children, or a practice against children, is not (sayes S. *Augustine*) a mariage, but a solemne, an avowed, a dayly Adultery.

Aug. *De Bono Conjugali*, c. 5, sec. 5.

Vol. VII. 1. 342 ff. Of which Ideaes, ... S. *Augustine* pronounces, *Tanta vis in Ideis constituitur,* There is so much truth, and so much power in these Ideaes, as that without acknowledging them, no man can acknowledge God, ...

Aug. *De diversis Quæstionibus LXXXIII*, 46.

NOTE. Actually Augustine writes, "... siquidem tanta in eis vis constituitur ut nisi his intellectis sapiens esse nemo possit."

Vol. VII. 5. 533–534. *Quid peto, ut venias in me, qui non essem si non esses in me?*

Aug. *Confes.* I, c. 2.

Vol. VII. 6. 557 ff. *Pro peccatis Matris meæ deprecor te, ... Credo quòd jam feceris, quæ rogo ... Voluntaria oris mei accipe Domine*

Aug. *Confes.* IX, c. 13.

Vol. VII. 7. 681 ff. ... for S. *Augustine* remembers it ... in an extreame sicknesse, *Flagitavi baptismum à Matre ... Sonat undique ... Sine eum, faciat quid vult, nondum baptizatus est* ... But ... would they say to a man that lay wounded ... *Sine eum, vulneretur ampliùs, nondum enim sanatus est* ... ?

Aug. *Confes.* I, c. 11.

Vol. VII. 8. 580 ff. *Ordo est, per quem omnia aguntur, quæ Deus constituit* ... But (as the same Father sayes in the same book) it is *Ordo, quem si tenueris in vita, perducet ad Deum, ... Nihil ordini contrarium, ... O si possem dicere quod vellem! ... Rogo, ubi ubi estis verba, succurrite; ...*

Aug. *De Ordine*, I, c. x, 28; c. ix, 27; c. vi, 15, 16.

Vol. VII. 12. 457 ff. *Invocat te fides mea,* sayes he to God; ... *Dedisti mihi per ministerium Prædicatoris* ...

Aug. Confes. I. c. 1.

Vol. VII. 13. 638–641. S. *Augustine* had written against a Bishop who was of the sect of the Anthropomorphits, ... *Istius corporis oculos non videre Deum, nec visuros,* ...

Aug. *Epist.* 148, to Fortunatianus, c. 1, sec. 1.

Ibid. 693–694. *Facies Dei ea est, qua Deus innotescit nobis*
Also VIII. 6. 564, 11. 482; IX. 4. 757, 16. 633; X. 4. 167.

Aug. *En. in Ps. X*, sec. 11.

Vol. VII. 15. 176–179. When we heare S. *Augustine* in his Confessions, lament so passionately the death of his Son, and insist so affectionately, upon the Pregnancie, and Forwardnesse of that Son; . . .
    Aug. *Confes.* IX, c. 6.

Ibid. 665 ff. *Sunt qui patienter moriuntur . . . Sunt qui patienter vivunt, & delectabiliter moriuntur*
    Aug. *In Epist. Johan.* 4. Trac. ix, sec. 2.

Vol. VII. 17. 348–354. . . . that hatred which *David* calls *Odium perfectum,* . . . Saint *Augustine* calls it *Odium Charitativum,* . . .
    Aug. *En. in Ps. CXXXVIII,* sec. 28.

Vol. VIII. 3. 393–395. *Esse firmissimè credo, quænam sint nescio;* that there are distinct orders of *Angels,* assuredly I beleeve; . . .
    Aug. *Ad Orosium, con. Priscill.* c. 11.

Ibid. 395–396. *Dicant qui possunt; si tamen probare possunt quod dicunt*
    Aug. *Enchiridion,* c. 58.

Ibid. 473. . . . *fatendum est Angelos natura mutabiles*
    Aug. *De Ver. Relig.* c. 13, sec. 26.

Vol. VIII. 6. 424 ff. And therefore does S. *Augustine* say in his behalfe, whatsoever can be threatned him, *Si potest vivere, tolerabile est,* . . . *Si non potest vivere,* . . . *Opus cum fine, merces sine fine;* . . .
    Aug. *Serm.* 279 *De Script.* [Migne], "De Paulo apostolo," c. 1, sec. 4.

Vol. VIII. 7. 487–488. *Si Stephanus non orasset,* . . . the Church had had no *Paul:* . . .
    Aug. *Serm.* 4 *De Sanctis* [Migne, 382], "De sancto Stephano," c. 4.

Vol. VIII. 8. 473–476. S. *Augustine* . . . puts himselfe to that question, If *Davids* constitution be shaken, . . . *Præ indignatione,* . . . from whom proceeds this Indignation, and this Anger? . . .
    Aug. *En. in Ps. XXXVI,* Serm. 2, sec. 9.

Ibid. 709–711. . . . in Martyrdome, as S. *Augustine* sayes, *Injuriam facit Martyri,* He wrongs a Martyr that praies for a Martyr, as though he were not already in Heaven; . . .
    Aug. *Serm.* 15 *De Verb. Apost.* [Migne, 159] c. 1.

Ibid. 747–754. S. *Augustine* observes out of the words of this Text [*Ps.* 6.6, 7], that because some of *Davids* afflictions are expressed in the Preter tense, . . . and some in the Future, . . . therefore *David* hath a speciall regard to his future state, . . .
    Aug. *En. in Ps. VI,* sec. 7.

Vol. VIII. 9. 627–628. *Imo solus se diligere novit, qui Deum diligit*
Aug. *De Trinitate*, XIV, c. 14, sec. 18.

Vol. VIII. 11. 96–98. . . . S. *Augustine* professes, *Plura se nescire quam scire*, That there are more places of Scripture, that he does not, then that he does understand.
Aug. *Ad Inquis. Januarii*, L. II (*Epist.* 55), c. 21, sec. 38.

Vol. IX. 2. 307–312. Saint *Augustine* excuses *Tertullian* from heresie: because (says he) *Tertullian* might meane, . . . that God was so far from being nothing, as that he had rather a body. Because it was possible to give a good interpretation of *Tertullian*, that charitable Father Saint *Augustine*, would excuse him of heresie.
Aug. *Epist.* 190, c. 4, sec. 14.

Vol. IX. 3. 65 ff. . . . we joyne with S. *Augustine, Sint castæ deliciæ meæ Scripturæ tuæ;* . . . *Nec fallar in eis, nec fallam ex eis;* . . . *Non frustra scribuntur,* . . . *Confiteor tibi quicquid invenero in libris tuis;* . . .
Aug. *Confes.* XI, c. 2, sec. 3.

Ibid. 77 ff. . . . he speakes of this beginning of the Book of *Genesis;* and he speaks lamenting, *Scripsit Moses & abiit,* . . . *Si hic esset, tenerem eum, & per te rogarem* . . . But sayes he, since I cannot speake with *Moses, Te, quo plenus vera dixit, Veritas, rogo,* . . .
Also IV. 8. 184–187.
Aug. *Confes.* XI, c. 3.

Ibid. 89–92. For, *Deus meus lumen oculorum meorum in occulto*, sayes he, . . . *Quid mihi obest, si aliud ego sensero, quam sensit alius, eum sensisse, qui scripsit?*
Aug. *Confes.* XII, c. 18.

Ibid. 95 ff. Hee passes from prayer, and protestation, to counsell, and direction; *In diversitate sententiarum verarum, concordiam pariat ipsa veritas,* . . . *Legitimè lege utamur*, sayes he, . . . *Si quis quærat ex me, quid horum Moses senserit,* . . . *Non sunt sermones isti confessiones,* . . .
Aug. *Confes.* XII, c. 30.

Ibid. 114–117. *Ego illuminem ullum hominem, venientem in mundum?* saies he; Is that said of me, that I am the light, that enlightned every man, any man, that comes into this world?
Aug. *Confes.* XIII, c. 10.

Ibid. 118–119. *Quod luce veritatis, quod fruge utilitatis excellit*
Aug. *Confes.* XII, c. 30.

Ibid. 271–277. S. *Augustine* observing aright, That at this time, of which this Text [*Gen.* 1.2] is spoken, The waters enwrapped all the whole substance . . . of which all things were to be created, . . . And so the holy

Ghost moving, and resting upon the face of the waters, moved, and rested, did his office upon the whole Masse of the world, and so produced all that was produced; ...

Aug. *De Gen. ad Litteram*, III, c. 14 and 15.

Vol. IX. 3. 308–313. *Mira profunditas eloquiorum tuorum; ... Ecce, ante nos superficies blandiens pueris, ... Sed mira profunditas, Deus meus, mira profunditas*

Aug. *Confes.* XII, c. 14.

Ibid. 317–329. *Rara anima, quæ cum de illa loquitur, sciat quid loquatur, ... Contendunt & dimicant, & nemo sine pace videt istam visionem*

Aug. *Confes.* XIII, c. 11.

Ibid. 334 ff. *Da quod amo; amo enim, nam & hoc tu dedisti; ...* he sayes this in more then one place; ...

Aug. *Confes.* XI, c. 2 and c. 22.

Vol. IX. 4. 639–641. *Fecisti nos Domine ad te, & inquietum est Cor nostrum, donec quiescat in te*

Aug. *Confes.* I, c. 1.

Vol. IX. 11. 130–135. S. *Augustine* confesses, that the reading of *Cicero's Hortensius, Mutavit affectum meum,* began in him a Conversion from the world, *Et ad teipsum, Domine, mutavit preces meas,* That booke, sayes he, converted me to more fervent prayers to thee, my God; *Et surgere jam cœperam ut ad te redirem,* By that help I rose, and came towards thee.

Aug. *Confes.* III, c. 4.

Vol. X. 1. 689–694. *Puto Prædicatores & nubes & ventos,* sayes S. *Augustine, ... Nubes propter carnem, ventos propter spiritum, ... Nubes cernuntur, venti sentiuntur; ...*

See IV. 2. 747.

Vol. X. 3. 332–336. ... S. *Augustine* reports, (if that Epistle be S. *Augustines*) that when himselfe was writing to S. *Hierome, ...* suddenly in his Chamber there appeared *ineffabile lumen, ... nostris invisum temporibus, ...*

Epist. 205 *ad Cyrill:* Jerosolym [mg. of F].

NOTE: The letter beginning *Gloriosissimi christianæ fidei athletæ,* which Donne numbers 205, has long been recognized to be apocryphal. Apart from other points, St. Cyril of Jerusalem, to whom it pretends to be addressed, died in 386, long before St. Jerome. The Maurine editors, and following them J. P. Migne, placed it, along with the corresponding letter supposed to be from St. Cyril, in the Appendix to the genuine letters of St. Augustine. See *Pat. Lat.* 33, cols. 1120 ff.

Vol. X. 7. 612–615. Saint *Augustine* saith excellently, . . . to a holy Virgin, who was ready to leave the Church, for the ill life of Church-men, *Christus nobis imperavit Congregationem, sibi servavit separationem;* . . .
Aug. *Epist.* 209 [208]. Feliciæ virgini.

Vol. X. 10. 244–249. *Debuit dicere fructum, non laborem,* saith *Augustine,* . . . *Sed ipsi labores non sunt sine gaudio,* . . . *Si labor potest manducari & jucundari, manducatus fructus laboris qualis erit?*
Aug. *En. in Ps. CXXVII*, sec. 10.

Ibid. 480–483. *Ne miremur illos lætari continuò subiecit, Dominus in illis,* . . . to take away all wonder, it is added, the Lord is in the midst of them, and then, be what they will, they must rejoyce; . . .
Aug. *En. in Ps. LXVII*, sec. 24.

Ibid. 530. *Quis sic delectat quam ille, qui fecit omnia quæ delectant?*
Aug. *En. in Ps. XXXII*, Serm. I, sec. 6.

Ibid. 533–549. *Si in nomine suo, non tota die* . . . *Nullo modo beatus, nisi scias unde gaudeas*
Aug. *En. in Ps. LXXXVIII*, sec. 17 and 16.

Vol. X. 11. 454–463. *Quia Domini Domini sunt exitus mortis* (as Saint *Augustine* interpreting this *text* answeres that question) . . . *Quid apertius diceretur?* sayes hee there . . . *Nec oportuit eum de hac vita alios exitus habere quam mortis.*
Aug. *De Civ. Dei, XVII*, c. 18, sec. 2.

APPENDIX B

List of Medieval and Renaissance Commentators and Controversialists Quoted by Donne in the Sermons and Other Main Prose Works

Aben Ezra (1092–1167). Spanish rabbi. Commentary on Sacred Books (exc. *Paralipomenon*). This is according to the literal sense, but elsewhere he follows cabbalistic views. *Book of the Name*, etc.
III. 9. 603–604, 18. 398; IX. 9. 302.

Abulensis. *See* Tostatus.

Acosta (José, 1539?–1600). Spanish Jesuit who took part in the evangelization of South America.
IV. 10. 504. X. 7. 509. *Essays in Divinity*, p. 84. *Pseudo-Martyr*, p. 126.

Agrippa (Heinrich Cornelius, of Nettesheim, 1486–1535). Taught in Cologne, Paris, Spain, England—alchemy, medicine, Hebrew, theology. Influenced by cabbalism of Reuchlin and Lully. *De incertitudine et vanitate scientiarum* (1527); *De occulta philosophia* (1531).
IV. 8. 354.

Alcazar (Luis d', 1554–1613). Spanish Jesuit, teacher of theology. *Investigatio arcani sensus in Apocalypsi.*
VI. 2. 60.

Alensis (Alexander of Ha[y]les, *ca.* 1170–1245). Taught scholastic philosophy at Paris, where Bonaventura and Thomas Aquinas were his disciples. Known as "Doctor irrefragibilis." Donne quotes *Postillæ in universa Biblia, summa universæ theologiæ* (Bale, 1502).
III. 12. 317; IX. 15. 167.

Alvarez (Alphonso Alvarez Guerrero, d. 1577). Doctor of canon and civil law. Bishop of Naples. *Speculum utri digni.*
IV. 5. 434. *Pseudo-M.*, pp. 35, 38, 147, etc.

Andradius (Diego Andrada de Payva, 1528–1575). Portuguese. Professor of theology at Coimbra. At Council of Trent. Important in sixteenth-century theology. *Decem libri orthodoxarum explicationum, Defensio Tridentiæ fidei catholicæ* (1578) (unfinished)—both against Chemnitz. Three volumes of sermons.
VI. 5. 180; VIII. 10. 382.

Aquinas (St. Thomas, *ca.* 1225–1274). Dominican philosopher and theologian. Leader of the Schoolmen and author of the great *Summa Theologica* (printed 1485).

I. 9. 113, 552; II. 2. 273, 16, 259; III. 1 (i). 31, 3. 725, 4. 178; IV. 3. 886, 5. 243, 6. 195–206, 7. 466, 577, 630, 707, 8. 287, 10. 497; V. 3. 192, 4. 442, 7. 260. (For references in the remaining volumes see Index under "Aquinas" and the "School.") *Biathanatos,* pp. 32, 38, 48, 71, etc. *E. in D.,* pp. 16, 24, 28, 33, etc. *Pseudo-M.,* pp. 179, 194, 195, 204, etc.

Ardoinus (Santes de, *fl. ca.* 1430). Doctor in Padua. Supposed author of various medical works. *Opus de venenis*...(Venice, 1492, after his death).

> III. 6. 304. *Biathanatos,* p. 135.

Arriba (Franciscus de, early 17th cent.). Franciscan Bishop of Ciudad Rodrigo. Confessor to Anne of Austria. *De gratia et libero arbitrio* (1622).

> VII. 4. 286.

Aureolus (Petrus Aureoli, 1280–1322). Franciscan philosopher and theologian who taught at Toulouse and Paris. Commentary on *Sentences.* Also *Quodlibeta, Breviarum Bibliorum.* Criticized doctrines of St. Thomas and defended Scotus.

> IX. 4. 702.

Ayguanus (Michele Angriani, d. 1401 or 1416). *Super Sententiarum libros IV. Commentaria in Psalmos* (1603), *Opus de conceptione S. Mariæ,* etc.

> V. 16. 510.

Azorius (Juan Azor, 1533–1603). Spanish Jesuit. *Institutiones morales.*

> IV. 5. 435; IX. 6. 213. *Biathanatos,* pp. 42, 62, etc. *E. in D.,* p. 70. *Pseudo-M.,* pp. 35, 114, 122, etc.

Baldus (de Bartholinis, 1327–1400). Professor of law at Perugia and Bologna. Left incomplete works, printed at Venice, 1496, later editions 1508, 1515, etc.

> VI. 11. 402; VII. 16. 482. *Biathanatos,* p. 105. *E. in D.,* p. 35. *Pseudo-M.,* p. 42.

Bannez (Domingo Bañez [Benius], 1528–1604). Spanish Dominican theologian. Leading exponent of Thomism. Confessor of St. Theresa of Avila. Concerned with dispute on free-will between Dominicans and Jesuits. Commentaries on Aquinas, Aristotle; treatise on free-will.

> VII. 4. 176 (as "Benius"); X. 7. 524; 10. 52. *Pseudo-M.,* pp. 95, 100 (as "Benius").

Baronius (Ven. Cesare, 1538–1607). After Eusebius, "Father of ecclesiastical history." *Annales ecclesiastici* finished (up to 1198) in year of death.

Martyrology (revision commissioned to deal with confusions resulting from calendar reform) (1586, 2d. ed. 1589).
II. 18. 455; III. 9. 618; IV. 5. 432, 10. 494; IX. 6. 158, 337. *Biathanatos*, pp. 60, 69–70, 147, etc. *Pseudo-M.*, pp. 10, 37, 91, etc.

Bede, the Venerable (*ca.* 673–735). Historian. Northumbrian monk. Scientific treatises, verse, expositions of Scripture. Most important work *Historia ecclesiastica gentis Anglorum* (completed 731).
V. 14. 768; VIII. 7. 231. *E. in D.*, pp. 15, 28. *Pseudo-M.*, pp. 106, 271.

Bellarmine (St. Robert, 1542–1621). Italian Jesuit. Professor of theology at Louvain and Rome. Cardinal 1599, Archbishop of Capua 1602–1605. Great anti-Protestant writer. *Disputationes de controversiis Christianæ fidei adversus hujus temporis hæreticos* (1586–1593).
I. 1. 426; III. 9. 611, 11. 88, 15. 74, 16. 22; VI. 3. 318; VIII. 2. 386; IX. 12. 516, etc. *Biathanatos*, p. 176. *E. in D.*, p. 18. *Pseudo-M.*, pp. 42, 43, 80, etc.

Benius. *See* Bannez.

Bernard of Clairvaux, St. (1090–1153). Founded Cistercian monastery at Clairvaux. One of most influential religious forces in Europe. Mystic, saintly character. *De diligendo Deo, De gratia et libero arbitrio*, etc.
III. 1 *passim*, 4. 529, 5. 395, 12. 550, 569, 606, 13. 401, 15. 192 ff.; VI. pp. 127, 129, 7. 328, 8. 1, 579, 9. 213, 411, 571, 13. 570, 16. 230, 278, 17. 214, etc. See Index.

Beza (Theodorus, 1519–1605). Friend and disciple of Calvin. Translated and commented on the New Testament. Donne owned two of his works (Keynes, p. 210).
IV. 7. 1020; VII. 4. 16, 7. 629, 15. 537–538. *Biathanatos*, pp. 17, 157. *E. in D.*, p. 79.

Biel (Gabriel, d. 1495). Philosopher and theologian, professor at Tübingen. *Epitome seu collectorium circa Lombardi sentiarum libros*, etc.
III. 12. 383. *Pseudo-M.*, p. 251.

Binnius (Severin, 1573–1641). Historian and critic. Taught ecclesiastical history at Cologne. *Concilia generalia et provincialia*—new survey of Councils, 1606.
X. 5. 664. *Biathanatos*, pp. 87, 92, etc. *Pseudo-M.*, pp. 20, 24, 269, etc.

Bodin (Jean, 1530–1596). Political writer and demonologist. *La République* (1576), *La Démonomanie des sorciers* (1580).
IX. 8. 119. *Biathanatos*, pp. 35, 91, 172. *Pseudo-M.*, p. 11.

Bolduc (Jacques, d. 1646). Capuchin, professed 1581. Superior of several monasteries. Commentary on *Job* and *Jude* (compared with 2 *Peter*), *De ecclesia ante legem, De ecclesia post legem, De orgio christiano ... eucharistiæ typica mysteria.*
VIII. 16. 68; IX. 9. 337, 422.

Bonaventura, St. (Giovanni di Fidanza, 1221–1274). Franciscan theologian, called "Doctor seraphicus." Studied and taught at Paris. Became Minister General of his order and doctor 1257. Created Cardinal Bishop of Albano 1273. Took prominent part in Council of Lyons (1274) and died while it was still sitting. Theologian in tradition of SS. Augustine and Anselm.
VII. 12. 312; IX. 4. 710. *Biathanatos*, p. 127.

Boverius (Zacharias, 1568–1638). Italian Capuchin. *Demonstrationes symbolorum,* etc.
IV. 6. 192.

Bradwardine (Thomas, *ca.* 1290–1349). Archbishop of Canterbury. Famous mathematician. *De geometria speculativa, De quadratura circuli* (1495). Principal theological work *De causa Dei contra Pelagium, et de virtute causarum libri III.* Honoured by Chaucer and Dante in their poems.
VI. 11. 574.

Cajetan (Tommaso de Vio Gaetani, 1469–1534). Dominican, who made a close study of humanism. General of Dominicans 1508, Cardinal 1517. Chosen to plead with Luther. One of foremost defenders and exponents of Thomism. Translated much of Bible, using versions of Jerome and Erasmus. Modern attitude to *Genesis,* authorship of Epistles, etc., for which he was attacked by Catharinus. Commentaries on many books of the Bible.
I. 3. 765; II. 9. 302; III. 4. 111; VII. 7. 210, 460; VIII. 7. 329; IX. 6. 199, 9. 301, 13. 294. *Biathanatos,* pp. 36–37, 126. *E. in D.,* p. 26. *Pseudo-M.,* B1ᵛ, 245.

Calvin (John, 1509–1564). Famous French reformer and theologian.
II. 3. 598, 9. 307, 310, 353, 12. 157, 15, 390; III. 3. 393, 7. 212, 15. 90, etc. Quoted constantly in all volumes except I and IV. *Biathanatos,* pp. 29, 44, 98, 104, etc. *E. in D.,* pp. 26, 59.

Canisius (St. Peter, 1520–1597). Dutch Jesuit. Took part in the Council of Trent. *Summa doctrinæ Christianæ* (1585), *Institutiones Christianæ Pietatis,* etc.
IV. 7. 924, 1029.

Cantiprat (Thomas Cantipratani, d. ? 1263). Dutch Dominican. *Bonum universale, De natura rerum,* etc.
    X. 3. 324; 6. 177.

Canus (Melchior Cano). Spanish Dominican. Professor of theology at Salamanca 1546–1552. At Council of Trent 1551. Somewhat anti-Jesuit. *De locis theologis* (1563) marks new epoch in history of theology. Treatise on theological method. Restoration of best patristic learning advocated. *De sacramentis, De pœnitentia.*
    IV. 8. 272, p. 408 (n.); VII. 4. 186; VIII. 5. 191. *Pseudo-M.,* p. 106.

Carbo (Ludovicus Carboni à Costaciano, d. 1597). Thomist theologian and casuist. Commentaries on St. Thomas. *Introductio in universam philosophiam, Summa summarum casuum conscientiæ.*
    VII. 4. 266. *Biathanatos,* pp. 38, 60, 121. *Pseudo-M.,* pp. 229–230, 237.

Carthus (Ludolphus of Saxony [Carthusiensis], d. 1378). Wrote a *Life of Christ,* which was very popular; many editions and translations. *Expositio in Psalterium* (1491). Strong influence of his writings shown in *Imitatio Christi,* which is sometimes attributed to him.
    IV. 3. 472.

Castro (Leon, d. 1589). Of Valladolid. Greek and Hebrew scholar. Commentaries on *Isaiah* and *Hosea.*
    IV. 9. 11; VIII. 4. 16.

Catharinus (Ambrosius, *ca.* 1484–1553). Dominican theologian. Controversialist against Lutheran doctrines. Defended Immaculate Conception and other doctrines opposed to Dominican tradition. Prominent part in Council of Trent. Bishop of Minori 1546. Treatises on sin and grace, etc.; commentaries on *Genesis,* Pauline Epistles.
    II. 3. 158, 9. 303; IV. 11. 250; V. 2. 521; VIII. 16. 329. *E. in D.,* p. 26.

Chemnicius (Martin Chemnitz, 1522–1586). German Lutheran theologian. Attacked Council of Trent, defended Lutheran doctrines. *Loci theologici,* etc.
    VII. 6. 633, 11. 257. *E. in D.,* p. 15.

Chiffletius (Jo. Jac., 1588–1660). Studied medicine at Paris, Montpellier, Padua; doctor to Archduchess Isabella of the Netherlands, then to Philip IV of Spain. Wrote on historical and archæological subjects as well as natural science. *De linteis sepulchralibus Christi servatoris.*
    IX. 8. 314.

Choppinus (René Choppin, d. 1601) (Cheppinus). French jurist. *Monasticon, seu de Jure cœnobitarum* (1601), *De privilegiis prædiorum* (1590), etc.
    V. 13. 384. *Pseudo-M.,* pp. 36, 134.

Coccius (Jodœus, 1581–1622). German Jesuit. *Parallelon biblicum visionum Johannis, Historia Sanctorum Alsatiæ, Disputatio de arcanu S. Scripturæ sensu,* etc.
X. 6. 217.

Collius (Francesco Collio, ?–1640). Italian theologian. *Conclusiones in sacra theologia, De sanguine Christi, De animabus paganorum* (1622).
IV. 2. 645.

Coquæus (Leonardus, ? – ?). Augustinian. *Examen præfationis monitoriæ Jac. I. M. Brittaniæ regis, præmissæ apologiæ suæ pro juramento fidelitatis* (1610), *Apologia pro summis Ecclesiæ Romanæ pontificibus* (1619).
IV. 9. 783.

Coster (Francis, 1532–1619). Jesuit. Professor at Cologne. Works on ascetical subjects, meditations on B.V.M., and sermons on the Gospel for each Sunday of the year. *Annotatione in N. T. et in præcipua loca, quæ rapi possent in controversiam.*
II. 3. 183.

Cramerus (Daniel, 1568–1637). Professor of logic at Wittenberg. Became archdeacon and professor at Stettin. *Pommersche Kirchenchronik* (1602).
VI. 8. 514.

Drusius (Jan van der Driesche, 1550–1616). Dutch Protestant refugee, professor of Oriental languages at Oxford. Commentaries on Scriptures; Hebrew, Chaldaic, and Arabic grammars. Donne owned copies of *Miscellanea* (1586), *Ad Minerval Seraria* (1606), *Tetragrammaton* (1604).
VIII. 3. 450. *E. in D.,* pp. 11, 25.

Duns Scotus (Johannes, *ca.* 1264–1308). Franciscan. Philosopher and theologian. Studied at Oxford, taught at Paris and Cologne. First great theologian to defend the Immaculate Conception. Wrote commentaries on Aristotle and Peter Lombard.
I. 9. 320; IV. 6. 195–208. *Biathanatos,* p. 92. *E. in D.,* pp. 27, 29.

Durandus (Gulielmus, 1230–1296). Bishop of Mende from 1285. Well-known writer on canon law. *Speculum judiciale; Rationale Divinorum Officiorum,* of which Donne possessed a copy (Lyons, 1605).
VIII. 7. 328.

Durantius (Jean-Étienne Duranti, d. 1589). Liturgiologist. President of Parliament of Toulouse. Killed in Huguenot rising. *De Ritibus Ecclesiæ Catholicæ* (Rome, 1591) dealt with all the liturgical rites according to the method of Durand's *Rationale.*
I. 3. 140.

Erasmus (Desiderius, *ca.* 1466–1536). Dutch humanist. Editor and translator of N.T., editor of Fathers. Attacked monastic corruptions; did not join Protestants in spite of paving the way for the Reformation.
VII. 11. 280. *Pseudo-M.*, B1ᵛ, D4ʳ.

Escalante (Ferdinand, ? – ?). Spaniard, of the Order of the Holy Trinity. Professor of theology at Seville about 1612. *Clypius concionatorum verbi Dei.*
IV. 8. 356.

Estius (Wilhelm Est, 1541–1613). Chancellor of University of Douai. Commentaries on Epistles of Paul, *Apocalypse; Annotationes in præcipua ac difficiliora Scripturæ loca.*
VII. 7. 157, 747.

Eugubinus (Augustinus Steuchius, of Gubbio, 1496–1549). Bishop of Kisamos in Crete, director of Vatican library, legate to Council of Trent. *Recognitio veteris testamenti ad Hebraicam veritatem* (1529), *Cosmopœia* (1535).
VIII. 5. 789. *Biathanatos,* p. 22. *Pseudo-M.*, p. 18.

Ferus (Jo. Wild, d. 1554). Wrote much, including *Enarrationes* or *Annotationes* on different books of the Bible.
VIII. 5. 822. *Pseudo-M.*, pp. 104–105.

Feuardentius (François Feuardent, 1539–1610). Minorite friar. Preached against Henri III and IV, and attacked reformers. Published several theological treatises. Edition of Irenæus (1576).
VII. 7. 245. *Biathanatos,* p. 60. *Pseudo-M.*, pp. 12, 215.

Galatinus (Petrus, d. 1539). Franciscan—converted Jew. *De Arcanis Catholicæ Veritatis* (1518).
V. 16. 249–250; VII. 11. 186. *E. in D.*, pp. 9, 25, 26, etc. *Pseudo-M.*, pp. 92, 146.

Gavantus (Bartolommeo, 1569–1638). Italian Barnabite, famous for liturgical studies. General of his Order. Chief work (dedicated to Pope Urban VIII) *Thesaurus sacrorum rituum seu commentaria in rubricas Missalis et Breviarii Romani* (1628).
VIII. 14. 692.

Genebrard (Gilbert, d. 1597). French Dominican. Wrote on Hebrew and Chaldean languages, history of the Jews, theological treatises. *De sacrarum electionem jure ad ecclesiæ gallicanæ redintegrationem.*
VI. 8. 430. *E. in D.*, p. 25.

Gerard (Johann, 1582–1637). Lutheran theologian. Wrote many theological works and Biblical commentaries.
VII. 4. 405.

Gerson (Jean le Charlier de, 1363–1429). Chancellor of Paris. Worked for reform of Church from within. Took important part in the four Articles of Constance. Extreme Nominalist. Mystical teaching. Augustinian. *De consolatione theologiæ, De unitate ecclesiæ,* etc. Commentaries on *Magnificat* and *Song of Solomon.*
VII. 3. 95; IX. 8. 763. *E. in D.,* p. 41.

Gherson (Levi ben, 1288–1344 [Gersonides]). Doctor and philosopher. Writings on mathematics, logic, philosophy, and *Les guerres du Seigneur.*
III. 18. 399.

Gregory de Valentia (1551–1603). Spanish Jesuit. Taught philosophy at Rome, Dillingen, and Ingolstadt. Wrote principally against the doctrines of Luther and Calvin.
III. 16. 19; VI. 16. 398. *Pseudo-M.,* p. 123.

Gretzer (Jacob, 1562–1625). German Jesuit. Taught philosophy and dogmatic and moral theology at Ingolstadt. Corresponded with Bellarmine. Edited patristic and medieval works. Donne owned copies of *De Modo Agendi Jesuitarum,* 1600; *Summula Casurum Conscientiæ,* 1611; *Mysta Salmuriensis,* 1614; *De Benedictionibus,* 1615. (Keynes, p. 215.)
V. 11. 242; VIII. 4. 238. *Pseudo-M.,* pp. 86–87, 120, 130, etc.

Heshusius (Tilemann, 1527–1588). Lutheran theologian. Author of numerous theological works and a commentary on *Isaiah.*
VIII. 10. 63.

Holkot (Robert, d. 1349). English Dominican. Doctor of theology in Oxford. Expositions of Bible. Commentaries published posthumously. *Quæstiones* on the *Sentences* of Peter Lombard, and *De Sapientia.*
II. 5. 104; III. 15. 645.

Hosius (Stanislaus, 1504–1579). Born of German parents in Cracow. Cardinal and Prince-Bishop of Ermland. Studied at Padua and Bologna. Converted Prince Maximilian of Bohemia. Great defender of Roman Catholicism against Protestant incursions.
X. 6. 325–326.

Hugo de S. Victor (*ca.* 1096–1141). Theologian and mystic, influenced by Augustine and Dionysius. *De Sacramentis Christianæ Fidei.*
IV. 13. 287.

Ivo, St. (*ca.* 1040–1116). Bishop of Chartres. Works on canon law, letters, sermons. *Decretum, Panormia* (with important Prologus).
VI. 12. 478.

Lapide, Cornelius à (Cornelius van den Steen, 1565 or 67–1637). Jesuit Hebraist and theologian. Taught at Louvain and Rome. Commentaries on Pentateuch, four Major Prophets, Minor Prophets, *Acts,* Epistles, *Apocalypse.*
    III. 16. 24; VI. 8. 596; VII. 5. 295, 12. 350; VIII. 5. 793.

Lerinensis or Lyrinensis (Vincentius, "Peregrinus," d. *ca.* 450). Monk on island of Lérins, opposed Augustinianism. In *Commonitorium duplex adversus hæreticos* laid down threefold test of Catholicity "quod ubique, quod semper, quod ab omnibus creditum est."
    II. 13. 398; VIII. 4. 272, 5. 566.

Lombard (Peter, *ca.* 1100–1160). "Master of the Sentences." Taught at Cathedral School in Paris. In 1148 opposed Gilbert de la Porrée at Council of Rheims; 1159, made Bishop of Paris. Commentaries and *Sententiarum Libri Quattuor.*
    III. 4. 181; IV. 13. 291; V. 2. 200–201; VIII. 16. 305. *Biathanatos,* pp. 32, 182. *E. in D.,* pp. 26, 36, 64.

Lorinus (Johannes, 1559–1634). French Jesuit. Commentaries on Pentateuch, *Psalms, Wisdom; Epistolæ Catholicæ, Com. in Aristotelis Logicam.*
    VI. 6. 219; VII. 12. 330; VIII. 3. 256, 4. 18; IX. 12. 191.

Luther (Martin, 1483–1546). Founder of the German Reformation.
    I. 4. 282; II. 9. 310–315; III. 5. 355–357, 15. 86, 158; VI. 6. 184, 9. 42. *E. in D.,* pp. 8, 26. *Pseudo-M.,* p. 100.

Lyra (Nicholas of, 1270–1340). French Franciscan, professor at the Sorbonne. *Postillæ perpetuæ in universam S. Scripturam,* first Biblical commentary printed, favourite manual of exegesis, emphasizes importance of literal interpretation of the Bible. Numerous theological works.
    VI. 1. 503; VIII. 5. 806. *Biathanatos,* pp. 158, 198, etc.; *E. in D.,* pp. 5, 26, 33, etc. *Pseudo-M.,* pp. 38, 45, 252.

Maldonatus (Juan Maldonato, 1533–1583). Spanish Jesuit, popular theological lecturer. Commentaries on the Gospels, *Jeremiah, Baruch, Ezekiel, Daniel.*
    I. 3. 750; III. 7. 189; VI. 16. 403; VII. 4. 147, 5. 629 and 705, 7. 556; IX. 6. 138; X. 6. 214. *Biathanatos,* p. 124.

Martyr, Peter (Pietro Martiro Vermigli, 1500–1562). Augustinian friar converted to Protestantism. Professor of theology at Strasburg, and at Oxford 1548 to 1553.
    II. 9. 296; IV. 7. 93, 337; V. 19. 107. *Biathanatos,* pp. 102–104, 151.

Maximus (St., "Confessor," *ca.* 580–662). Greek theologian, determined opponent of Monothelitism. Refused adherence to "Typus" of Constantius II; died in exile. Prolific writer on doctrinal, ascetical, exegetical, and liturgical subjects.
VIII. 8. 44; IX. 5. 65.

Maynardus (Johannes Philippus). Author of the treatise *De privilegiis ecclesiasticis pro defensione censurarum Pauli V adversus Venetos* (Ancona, 1607).
IV. 5. 436. *Pseudo-M.*, pp. 32, 44, 91, etc.

Medina (Miguel, 1489–1578). Spanish Franciscan. Composed a Chain of Holy Scripture, *De sacrorum hominum continentia,* etc.
IV. 4. 341.

Melanc(h)thon (Philip Schwarzerd, 1497–1560). One of the leaders of the Reformation. Donne calls him "a man of more learning and temperance then perchance have met in any one, in our perverse and froward times" (VII. 7. 607). *Loci communes rerum theologicarum* (1521).
III. 4. 147; IV. 12. 435; VII. 4. 492, 7. 607. *E. in D.*, p. 9.

Mendoza (Franciscus, 1572–1626). Portuguese Jesuit. Commentary on *Kings; Discursus morales in libros Samuelis.*
IV. 13. 682, 704.

Mesues (Johannes Damascenus, b. 777 or 780). Director of hospital in Baghdad. Translations of Greek medical works and many other medical writings.
II. 2. 708.

Moses, Rabbi (Maimonides, 1135–1204). Greatest Jewish philosopher of the Middle Ages. Strong Neoplatonic tendencies. Called by Donne "the saddest and soundest of the Hebrew Rabbins."
IV. 3. 475; IX. 5. 119 and 309, 15. 525. *E in D.*, p. 11.

Musculus (Wolfgang Mosel, 1497–1563). Benedictine converted to Protestantism by reading Luther. Commentaries on St. Paul's Epistles, other books of the Bible, and the Fathers; sermons; and a treatise *De abominabili usura.*
III. 4. 154. *Biathanatos,* pp. 103, 188. *E. in D.*, p. 49.

Mussus (Cornelius Musso, 1511–1574). Born at Piacenza. Belonged to order of preaching brothers, and was famous as a preacher. Professor of metaphysics at Pavia. At Council of Trent. *De visitatione et modo visitandi, Historia divina Synodus,* etc.
IX. 6. 143.

Oleaster (Hieronymus, d. 1563). Portuguese Dominican.
III. 13. 565; VI. 7. 458; IX. 2. 372.

Osiander (Andreas, 1498–1552). Lutheran Hebrew scholar. Professor at Königsberg, where he published *De justificatione* (1550). Writings include a revised edition of the Vulgate and a harmony of the Gospels.
III. 3. 387; VII. 15. 597; IX. 10. 262.

Oziel, Rabbi (Jonathan ben Uzziel, ? – ?)
VIII. 8. 309 mg. (Unfortunately printed as "Nab. Oziel" in *LXXX Sermons,* and in our edition.)

Pamelius (Jacques de Pamèle, 1536–1587). Doctor of theology, Bishop of St. Omer. *Rituale SS Patrum latinorum,* etc.
V. 1. 604.

Panigorola (Francesco, 1548–1594). Franciscan. Famous preacher. Bishop of Asti. *Sermons,* works on *Canticles, Lamentations,* and *Psalms,* etc.
IV. 15. 405; VI. 11. 191.

Pellicanus (Conrad Kursner, 1478–1556). Swiss reformer, professor of theology at Basle and Zurich. Compiled a Hebrew primer, and wrote a commentary on the Bible.
III. 3. 389, 15. 92; VII. 15. 598. *E. in D.,* p. 42.

Peltanus (Theodor Anton, d. 1584). German Jesuit, professor of Greek and Hebrew and then of theology, at Ingolstadt. *De peccato originale, De satisfact. Christi, De majestate Corporis Christi,* etc.
III. 18. 89.

Pererius (Benedictus Pereyra, 1535–1610). Jesuit who taught theology and philosophy at Rome. Commentaries on *Genesis, Exodus,* and other books of the Bible.
V. 2. 555; VII. 4. 177; VIII. 5. 785, 792, 795. *Biathanatos,* pp. 28, 199. *E. in D.,* pp. 10, 11, 15, etc.

Picus (Pico della Mirandola, 1463–1494). Brilliant Italian scholar and Platonist, friend and pupil of Ficino; studied Oriental languages and the Jewish Cabbala.
V. 19. 103. *Biathanatos,* pp. 49, 174. *E. in D.,* pp. 10, 13, 30, etc.

Piscator (Johannes Fischer, 1546–1626). German Protestant theologian. Author of many theological, exegetical, and controversial works (against Baronius, Bellarmine, etc.), Hebrew grammar, translation of the Bible.
III. 3. 389; VII. 4. 17, 7. 620; VIII. 5. 519, 779.

Polanus (Amandus, 1561–1610). German Protestant theologian. *Symphonia catholica* (1607), treatise on predestination, Biblical commentaries, etc.
III. 3. 389; VIII. 2. 682; X. 5. 612. *Pseudo-M.,* p. 16.

Porrecta (Serafino Capponi a, b. 1536). Dominican theologian. Taught philosophy at various Italian universities. Lived for twenty-three years in Venice. Prolific preacher and writer.
III. 9. 609; VIII. 7. 431.

Possevino (Antonio, 1533/4–1611). Jesuit, born at Mantua. Missions for Pope Gregory XIII in Germany, Hungary, Sweden, Poland, and Russia. Treatise on the Mass translated into English with a life of the author 1570.
X. 6. 565.

Prateolus (Gabriel Dupréau, 1511–1588). Controversialist who wrote much against Protestants.
X. 7. 138. *Biathanatos,* p. 68. *E. in D.,* p. 79. *Pseudo-M.,* pp. 9, 134.

Remigius (d. 874). Archbishop of Lyon. *Liber de tribus episcoporum epistolis, Absolutio cujusdam quæstionis de generali per Adamum damnatione et speciale per Christum ex eadem ereptione electorum,* etc.
IV. 11. 206; V. 2. 594.

Reuchlin (Johannes, 1455–1552). First of great German humanists. Hebrew scholar and follower of Mirandola. Interested in the Cabbala. *Penitential Psalms.*
VIII. 8. 458. *Biathanatos,* p. 118. *E. in D.,* pp. 24, 91.

Rhegius (Vincentius, 1544–1614). Jesuit of Palermo. *De Sanctissimo Trinitate, Enchiridion evangelicorum,* etc.
III. 7. 193.

Ribadineyra (Pedro de, 1527–1611). Spaniard who worked with St. Ignatius Loyola in establishing the Society of Jesus in other countries, especially Belgium.
IV. 4. 363. *Pseudo-M.,* pp. 121, 122, 252, etc.

Ribera (Franciscus, 1537–1591). Spanish Jesuit. Professor of theology in Salamanca. Commentaries on Minor Prophets and New Testament; *De templo Hierosolymitano et iis, qui ad templum pertinent; Meditationes de præcipuis mysteriis vitæ J. Christi.*
III. 4. 567; VI. 2. 68.

Rupertus (Tuitensis, 1591–1635). German Dominican who left his order to join the Lutheran church. Commentaries, treatises on various doctrines, *Commentariorum de S. Trinitate et ejus operibus in utrumque testamentum libri XLII.*
VIII. 5. 884; IX. 1. 414; X. 10. 134.

Salmeron (Alfonso, 1516–1585). Spanish Jesuit. One of the original members of the society.
IX. 6. 134.

Sanctius (Gaspar Sanchez, 1554–1628). Spanish Jesuit. Wrote commentaries on many books of the Bible.

III. 15. 188; IV. 1. 576.

Sandæus (Maximilian van der Sanden, 1578–1656). Jesuit, professor of theology and philosophy at Mayence and Cologne. Wrote various theological works, and others defending the Society of Jesus.

VII. 12. 549–551; IX. 6. 542.

Saunders (Nicholas, ?1530–1581). Regius professor of theology at Louvain. Wrote various treatises on the Church in opposition to Bishop Jewel's *Apology*. Worked for dethronement of Elizabeth in favour of a Catholic sovereign. Papal agent in Ireland 1579. *De visibili Monarchia Ecclesiæ* (1571), etc.

IV. 4. 341. *Pseudo-M.*, pp. 252, 261.

Schonfeldius (Gregorius, 1559–*ca.* 1620). Calvinist. *Centuria IV thesium theologiæ*, etc.

VII. 4. 404.

Scribanius or Scribonius, also known under pseudonym Clarius Bonarscius (Carolus, 1561–1629). Jesuit writer.

II. 18. 445. *Biathanatos*, p. 72 (as "Clarus Bonarsicus"). *Pseudo-M.*, p. 150 (where name and pseudonym are both given).

Serarius (Nicholaus, b. 1555). Jesuit, born at Metz. Learned in Latin, Greek, Hebrew, Syriac. Friend of Baronius. In controversy with Luther. Author of commentaries on various books of the Old Testament. *Prolegomena biblica.* Donne owned three of his books.

III. 15. 222; IV. 7. 94, 338. *Biathanatos*, pp. 19, 146, 183. *Pseudo-M.*, pp. 42, 46, 87, etc.

Sextus Senensis (1520–1569). A Jew converted to Christianity, who became a celebrated Dominican preacher. Wrote *Bibliotheca Sacra* (1586).

VII. 6. 664. *Biathanatos*, p. 162. *E. in D.*, pp. 18–19. *Pseudo-M.*, pp. 105, 119–120.

Solomon, Rabbi (Rashi, 1040–1105). Jewish biblical scholar, born in Troyes, where he became a rabbi after studying at Mainz and Worms. One of the most highly reputed exegetes of Hebrew Scriptures and Talmud. Aimed to interpret according to literal sense (against trend of his time).

III. 15. 69; VIII. 5. 811. *E. in D.*, p. 53.

Spondanus (Henri de Sponde, 1568–1643). Lawyer; renounced Protestantism, took Roman orders, became Bishop of Pamiers. *De cœmeteriis sacris;* also an epitome of Baronius' *Annales* up to 1640.

III. 9. 621.

Stevartius (Peter Stevart, d. 1621). Doctor of theology. Commentaries on the New Testament, *Apologia pro S. Jesu, Oratio de colloquio ratisbonensi.*
IX. 15. 347.

Stunnica (Zunniga, "Didacus," 16th cent.). Hermit of Augustinian order, doctor of theology of Toledo. Commentaries on *Job* and *Zechariah; Philosophia prima pars; In omnes sui temporis hæreticos sive de vera religione lib. III.*
IX. 9. 419.

Tannerus (Adam, 1571–1632). German Jesuit and neo-Thomist. *Theses theologicæ. . . . divi Thomæ, De summo pontifice et conciliis,* etc. Various controversial works. Donne owned a copy of his *Defensio Ecclesiæ Libertatis* (Keynes, p. 221).
IX. 15. 340. *Pseudo-M.,* pp. 168, 183, 184.

Tapperus (Ruard Tapper, 1487–1559). Belgian anti-Protestant preacher and writer. Dean of faculty of theology at Louvain. *De clamatio articulorum . . . adversus nostri temporis hæreses* (1554), *Orationes theologicæ* (1557), etc. Complete works printed 1582.
X. 6. 653–654.

Tostatus (Alonso Tostado, "Abulensis," *ca.* 1400–1455). Bishop of Avila 1449. Known as "the wonder of the world" for learning. Assisted at Council of Basel. His views were derogatory to Papal authority, but he protested orthodoxy in his *Defensorium* (1443) written against Torquemada and others. Also wrote commentary on Eusebius and on historical books of the Old Testament, and *Matthew.* Editions of works published in Venice 1507, 1547, and (more nearly complete) 1615.
III. 6. 366; IV. 11. 428; VI. 5. 182, 7. 456; VIII. 10. 384. *E in D.,* p. 26.

Tremellius (John Immanuel, 1510–1580). Son of Ferrarese Jew, converted to Christianity 1540 through influence of Reginald Pole, to Protestantism by Peter Martyr. Became King's Reader of Hebrew at Cambridge 1549; professor of Hebrew studies at Heidelberg 1561, expelled 1577 for Calvinistic opinions; finally teacher of Hebrew at Sedan. Translation of the Bible into Latin: N.T. 1569, O.T. 1575–1579; Hebrew and Greek Catechism 1551; Chaldean and Syriac grammar 1569.
III. 3. 388, 529, 574; VII. 4. 9, 12. 516; IX. 9. 332, 485, 11. 20.

Turrecremata (Juan Torquemada, 1388–1468). Dominican, later cardinal. Numerous works on canon law, theology, dogma, etc.; most important, *Commentarium in Decretum Gratiani* (1519) and *Summa de Ecclesia* (1489).
IX. 15. 168.

Vegas (Manuel de Vega, d. 1640). Portuguese Jesuit. *De Missa, De Eucharistia, De cultu . . . sanctorum,* etc.

V. 2. 553.

Vives (Juan Luis, 1492–1540). Spanish philosopher and theologian. Left Spain for fear of the Inquisition, studied in Paris, visited England in 1523 and became professor of theology at Oxford. *De institutione fœminæ, De initiis, sectis et laudibus Philosophiæ, De Disciplinis,* etc.

X. 7. 457.

Vossius (Gerhard Jan Voss, 1577–1649). Dutch humanist theologian. Most important works *Historia pelagiana* (1618), *Dissertationes Tres de tribus symbolis* (1642), in which he decisively disproved the traditional authorship of the Athanasian Creed, and *Libri IV de theologia gentili* (1642).

VII. 4. 173.

Zambran (Melchior Zambrano, "Xereciencis," Aloares Didacus). Archbishop of Trani. Commentary on *Isaiah; Decisio casuum in articulo mortis occurentium circa sacramenta* (1604).

I. 3. 759. *Biathanatos,* p. 30. *Pseudo-M.,* p. 129 mg.

NOTE: The references given in this list are not complete. Many more might be found in *Biathanatos* and *Pseudo-Martyr.*

Chapter III

The Folios

COMPOSITION AND ARRANGEMENT

THE GREAT majority of Donne's sermons are contained in the three Folios of 1640, 1649, and 1661, which were all published by the authority of Donne's elder son. In our Vol. I, pp. 1–12, we gave a bibliographical account with full collations of these three volumes, but we left over to the present volume the plan and arrangement of their contents.

The *LXXX Sermons* of 1640 has a definite plan which is based on two principles. The first 49 sermons are grouped according to the main events of the Church's year. We have 7 sermons for Christmas, 5 for Candlemas Day, 5 for Lent (all of them preached at Whitehall), 10 for Easter, 10 for Whitsunday, 7 for Trinity Sunday, 1 for All Saints' Day, 5 for the Conversion of St. Paul. After this we leave the Church's calendar, and are given what is apparently a collection of sermons preached at St. Paul's: 15 sermons on the Penitential Psalms, and 5 Prebend sermons on the psalms allotted to Donne as a Prebendary. After this we have a collection of 11 sermons on several occasions. In this last group are included two sermons (71 and 72) which represent Donne's revision and enlargement of a single sermon which he preached at The Hague on December 19, 1619. We have also 4 sermons preached at Whitehall (70, 73, 74, 75), and 4 preached at St. Paul's (77–80), plus a single one (76) "preached to the Earle of Carlile, and his Company, at Sion" [the London house of the Earl of Northumberland, Carlisle's father-in-law].

Closer examination will show that most of the sermons in the earlier part of the volume were preached at St. Paul's, although Sermon 42 was preached at Lincoln's Inn on Trinity Sunday, 1620, and Sermon 43 at St. Dunstan's on Trinity Sunday, 1624. We have stated our reasons in Volume III, pp. 26–28, for thinking that Sermons 38–41 were preached at Lincoln's Inn in the Trinity Term, and not on Trinity Sunday itself. We are also told in the heading of Sermon 27 that it was *"preached to the Lords upon Easter-day, at the Communion, The King being then dangerously sick at New-Market."*

The arrangement of the *Fifty Sermons* of 1649 is less satisfactory. It opens with 3 sermons preached at marriages, 4 sermons at baptisms, and 3 sermons at churchings. Then come 13 sermons preached at Lincoln's Inn, followed by 6 at Whitehall, 6 "preached to the Nobility," 9 preached at St. Paul's, 6 at St. Dunstan's (so described, but the last was more probably preached at St. Paul's).[1] It is difficult to find any guiding principle in this arrangement after the first 10 sermons beyond a mere grouping according to place. "Sermons preached to the Nobility" is an absurdly vague title, especially as one of the sermons (34) has no title to connect it with any specific nobleman.

It seems possible that Donne himself may have devised the arrangement of the 1640 Folio. In his last illness at Aldborough Hatch, where the heading of Sermon 71 tells us that he made a revision of some sermons at least, he may have fastened together several bundles of sermons for the festivals of the Church's year without arranging them all according to their dates. The Christmas sermons are placed chronologically, but there is some disorder in most of the other groups. It is evident that this big volume was intended to include what Donne considered to be his most significant work—the sermons he had preached at St. Paul's for the great festivals, and his Prebend sermons, and sermons on the Penitential Psalms, together with some occasional sermons.

The *Fifty Sermons* was entered in the Stationers' Register in 1639/40 along with the *LXXX Sermons*,[2] but John Donne junior realized that a volume of 80 sermons would be sufficient for the

---

[1] See pp. 29–31 of the present volume.

[2] See the entries from the Stationers' Register for January 3, 1639/40, and February 19, 1639/40, in my *Study of the Prose Works of John Donne* (1948), pp. 276–277, especially the third entry "eodem die [i.e., February 19, 1639/40] Master fflesher Master Marriott and Richard: Roiston Entred for their Copie under the hands of A: ffrewen, vice-chancellor of the university of Oxford and master Bourne warden a booke called *ffifty Sermons* penned and preached by the reverend John Dunne doctor: [of] D[ivinity]: and late deane of Saint Pauls vjᵈ. . ."

public for some time. Over the printing of *Fifty Sermons* he had a quarrel with Francis Bowman the printer, which resulted in a lawsuit the outcome of which is not clear.[3] In the course of litigation the

[3] See "Bowman v. Donne," by J. Milton French, *Times Literary Supplement*, December 12, 1936.

While this volume was passing through the press, additional information on the licensing and printing of the *Fifty Sermons* has been supplied by Mr. Robert Kreuger, who has kindly told me of his recent discovery in Magdalen College Library of two documents. The first is a piece of paper which has been folded into two leaves and pasted into a modern binding, among the papers of Accepted Frewen, Vice-Chancellor of the University of Oxford. It is a statement by John Donne junior, dated September 26, 1638, that when he had been asked by Dr. Frewen whether the 42 sermons listed below had been offered to the Chaplains of the Archbishop of Canterbury and the Bishop of London [i.e., for licensing] his answer was that the sermons had not been offered to them nor seen by them. The second is Frewen's license to print the sermons, written throughout in the hand of William Strode, followed by a list of 22 sermons.

The interesting points about these documents are the date of Donne's answer to Dr. Frewen and the fact that the list contains only 42 sermons. The sermons in *Fifty Sermons* which are missing from the list are Nos. 3, 16, 19, 20, 26, 34, 47, 50 (*Hos.* 2.19, *Col.* 1.24, *Psa.* 38.2, *Psa.* 38.3, *Isa.* 65.20, *Luk.* 23.34, *Gen.* 3.24, 1 *Thes.* 5.16). Two in the list (those on *Prov.* 22.11 and 2 *Cor.* 4.6) were postponed from the *Fifty* to the *XXVI Sermons*.

Mr. Kreuger also gives some additional information taken from the Public Record Office documents (C8/118/14) mentioned by J. M. French about the suit brought by Bowman against the younger Donne on November 14, 1648. Bowman stated that about September in the 15th year of King Charles's reign Donne offered him 50 sermons by his father, which had been licensed, claiming that these were "the only presente-remaining peeces of the said Deanes labours in that kind & all perfetted and completed." Bowman said that 42 sermons were immediately delivered, and that he agreed to print within 5 years, to pay £50 for them, and to put up a bond of £100 in case he should not perform the agreement. Donne promised to deliver the remaining 8 sermons within the month, and that they would also be properly licensed. Bowman agreed with Royston and Flesher and with Lichfield of Oxford for the printing of the sermons, but before they could be printed Donne appeared with 80 sermons which he offered to Bowman, saying that if he would not take them also, he [Donne] would deal with others for the printing of the said 80, and that he would procure a narrative of his father's life to be added to them,

younger Donne stated that the sermons had been transcribed by "two ancient servants" of his father's, Thomas Roper and Robert Christmas.[4]

Our experience in completing our edition has shown that our statement in Vol. I, p. 7, that the *Fifty Sermons* was not printed as carefully as the *LXXX Sermons* was something of an understatement. The *Fifty* has more gross misprints than the *LXXX*, but its chief failing is its inability to use italics properly. Donne's custom was to italicize all Scriptural quotations, as is done in the six sermons which were printed within his lifetime, but the *Fifty Sermons* constantly breaks into roman in the middle of an italicized quotation.[5] Also on some pages (e.g., p. 247) we find a number of Scriptural passages

---

"which noe doubt would spoile the sale of the said 50. Sermons or much invalidate the same." Donne then sold the 80 to Flesher and Marryott for a large sum of money, and so dealt with them that the 80 "should be printed & come forth before it was possible that the 50. Sermons could be made readie. . . ."

On December 15, 1648, the younger Donne replied, stating that he did not give anyone other than Bowman permission to print the *Fifty Sermons*. He accused Bowman of having taken 3 additional sermons, and claimed that Bowman admitted that he had these. He denied having offered the 80 sermons to Bowman, and said that he did not deal with Marryott and Flesher until Bowman showed that he was not going to print the 50, but out of "commemoration" to his father he printed the 80, to force the printing of the 50 by Bowman. He claimed that Bowman sold the sermons for £30 more than he paid for them. Finally, he admitted having sued Bowman for £100 in common law, and he ended by professing his grief that his father's 50 sermons had not yet been printed.

Mr. Kreuger hopes to publish an article containing the full text of the Magdalen College documents, and also the inferences which he draws from the statements of Bowman and of John Donne junior.

[4] In his will Donne left to these two servants five pounds each "to make them seal rings engraved with that figure which I usually seal withal of which sort they know I have given many to my particular friends."

[5] For example, on p. 29 (Vol. V of our edition, p. 109) the *Fifty* has "Be *Baptized every one of you*" though "Be" is part of the text, and a few lines later "*Can any Man forbid water,* that *those should not be baptized, which* have *received the holy Ghost,*" where "that" and "which" are part of the quotation. We commented on this irritating practice, which has necessitated a large number of trivial alterations in the text, on pp. 403–404 of Vol. III of our edition.

printed in roman: "...that which we translate What is man, that thou art mindefull of him," and "Man liveth not by bread onely, says Christ." Some pages are overcrowded with unnecessary italics, others are printed almost entirely in roman. The punctuation is also much less satisfactory than that of the *LXXX Sermons*.

For the contents of *Fifty Sermons,* Donne had selected a number of sermons preached at Lincoln's Inn and a smaller number preached at St. Dunstan's, and had kept a small collection of baptismal, churching, and marriage sermons. If we consider that Donne was Reader at Lincoln's Inn from October 24, 1616, to February, 1622, and that he preached twice on every Sunday in term, and once on the Sundays immediately before and after term, we can see that the total (excluding the period when he was on the Continent with Doncaster from late April, 1619, to January, 1620) must have been nearly 200. Yet we have only 18 sermons described as preached at Lincoln's Inn, and two of them were preached when he visited the Inn after he had ceased to be a Reader. If we include the five sermons which we have tentatively assigned to Lincoln's Inn,[6] the number 23 is still so small that we can see that Donne must have rejected most of his Lincoln's Inn sermons as unworthy of publication. It may be that he had lost or destroyed the notes of most of the early ones. At any rate the earliest sermons described as "preached at Lincoln's Inn" do not appear to be earlier than the spring or summer of 1618,[7] and the earliest which is dated in the Folio is the *Sermon of Valediction* preached on April 18, 1619, which was printed in *XXVI Sermons*.

It is a puzzle why the three sermons on *John* 1.8 which were all preached at St. Paul's should not have been included in the *LXXX Sermons* instead of this later volume. The first of the three is the splendid Christmas sermon of 1621, which should chronologically have headed the series of Christmas sermons in the *LXXX*. It was apparently excluded in order that it might be printed together with the two other sermons, which were preached on Midsummer Day, 1622, and October 9, 1622, respectively. But the *LXXX* contains another triplet of sermons, this time on 1 *Cor.* 15.29, of which the first was in an Easter series as No. 21 of the *LXXX* (Vol. VII, No. 3,

---

[6] These are Nos. 12–15 in Vol. III and No. I in Vol. V.

[7] Vol. II of our edition, Nos. 1–6, and 10.

in our edition) while its two fellows were printed much later, as Nos. 77 and 78 (Vol. VII, Nos. 6 and 7, in our edition). We can only suppose that it was by accident that the much finer triplet on *John* 1.8 were banished to the limbo of the latter part of the *Fifty Sermons*.

By the time that *Fifty Sermons* appeared, in 1649, the political situation had changed greatly since the title was entered on the Stationers' Register in 1639/40. Charles the First had been deposed and executed, and the Parliament was supreme. John Donne junior therefore prefaced this volume by a dedicatory epistle to Basil Earl of Denbigh, a parliamentarian peer whose chaplain he was, and by a short address to the three Lords Commissioners of the Great Seal. We do not know how much he may have changed the contents of the volume from that originally planned. It seems clear that he deleted names from some of the titles,[8] and he may have deliberately excluded such a sermon as that on *Psa.* 38.9,[9] which recommended auricular confession, and may have substituted another in its place, but he does not seem to have tampered with the text itself in any way. It is quite possible that the collection of sermons preached at Whitehall before the King which were finally published in *XXVI Sermons* were originally intended for this second volume but were omitted by John Donne junior because they would have given the book a predominantly royalist flavour. He did in fact include six Whitehall sermons, which he placed in the middle of the book, but he may well have been unwilling to include an additional fifteen. He may have replaced them by the miscellaneous sermons "preached to the Nobility," and the baptismal and churching sermons. He certainly did not omit them on literary grounds, for a number of them—particularly the two on 1 *Timothy* 1.15 (Vol. I, Nos. 8 and 9), that on 1 *Timothy* 3.16 (Vol. III, No. 9), that on *Acts* 7.60 (Vol. VIII, No. 7), and that on *Matthew* 6.21 (Vol. IX, No. 7) are notable examples of Donne's skill. These all found their place later in the *XXVI Sermons,* when this final volume was hurriedly published in 1661 with a fulsome dedication to "His most Sacred Majesty Charles II." It seems certain that Donne him-

---

[8] See Vol. III, pp. 20–21, and Vol. V, pp. 7–9.

[9] Printed from MSS alone as No. 6 of our Vol. II. See our brief discussion in Vol. I, pp. 71–72, of its exclusion from the Folios.

self must have wished to preserve and publish these sermons, which were quite as carefully polished as those preached at St. Paul's.

We have already pointed out that the title *XXVI Sermons* for the 1661 Folio is a misnomer, as it contains only 24 sermons,[10] 2 of which are printed twice over. It is predominantly a Whitehall volume, for 14 of the sermons were preached there, and one was preached before Queen Anne at Denmark House. These are collected together in the first part of the volume, except that Donne's last sermon before the King is placed at the end. The rest of the volume contains 1 sermon preached at Greenwich, 2 sermons at Lincoln's Inn, 1 at St. Dunstan's, 1 (described in the title as 2) before the Prince and Princess Palatine at Heidelberg, 1 at the Temple, 1 at Paul's Cross, 1 at the Spital.

The printing of this volume differs in excellence according to its different parts. Apparently it was printed on two separate presses at once,[11] and the two sets of workmen had before them two (possibly three) manuscript volumes, written by different scribes. Thus the sermon on *James* 2.12 (Vol. VIII, No. 15, in our edition), which appears in *XXVI Sermons* both as No. 3 and No. 17, is printed more accurately in its first than in its second appearance.[12] But on the whole the printing of the volume was hasty and careless, and many corrections were made while the sheets were passing through the press.

A recent article, "The Text of John Tillotson's Sermons," by David D. Brown,[13] throws some light on the methods of seventeenth-century preachers, though Tillotson, who was born in 1630 and died in 1694, belonged to a generation later than Donne's. In 1663 he became Divinity Reader at Lincoln's Inn, and continued to hold the office till he became Archbishop of Canterbury in 1691, although he had meanwhile a number of other appointments, the chief one being that of Dean of Canterbury. The Bodleian Library contains a manuscript (MS Rawlinson E. 125), in Tillotson's own hand, of a number of his

---

[10] Or 23, if the two sermons on *Eccles.* 5.12, 13, are regarded as being really one sermon. See our Vol. III, pp. 391–392.

[11] See our discussion of this point in Vol. I, pp. 10–11.

[12] A list of the substantive variants between these two texts will be found in Vol. VIII, pp. 385–389. Occasionally the reading of No. 17 has been preferred, but for the most part our text of the sermon is based on No. 3 (called "A" in our textual notes).

[13] *The Library,* 5th Series, Vol. XIII, No. 1, 1958, pp. 18–36.

sermons. "The notes against the head of each sermon provide new information of a kind which can seldom be obtained from *Barker* [Barker's edition of *Two Hundred Sermons* by Tillotson], and show clearly that Tillotson—like most preachers in the ordinary course of their ministry—would often preach a sermon more than once, to different congregations, and sometimes in the same place after an interval of some years." Brown shows that many of Tillotson's sermons at Lincoln's Inn on Sundays were preached again two days later at the fashionable church of St. Lawrence Jewry, where he was Tuesday lecturer. One sermon which was first preached at St. Andrew Undershaft in 1680 was repeated at Whitehall before the Royal Family in 1681, and was delivered six times in all. Yet he was careful "to prepare or adapt a sermon to a particular auditory," and in this he reminds us of Donne. Tillotson had his own views on what "the Style of Popular Sermons ought to be." Brown states that the tradition that he "used to preach after a much more popular Manner to the City Congregations" was known to Swift more than a generation later.

Tillotson's avowed repreaching of old sermons makes us wonder whether Donne employed the same method at his different churches. We have already suggested that the sermon on *Luke* 23.34, which lacks a title altogether, may have been preached at both Sevenoaks and Blunham.[14] It is possible that some of the other undated sermons in the Folios which have no place of preaching mentioned in their titles may have been used first at St. Paul's and then at other churches.

---

[14] Vol. V, pp. 19–20.

APPENDIX A

List of Variants in Copies of
XXVI Sermons

(Universities of Chicago, Cincinnati, Harvard, Yale, Bodleian Library Oxford, British Museur University Library Cambridge, Lincoln's Inn, Carlisle Cathedral Library, St. Paul's Cathedr Library, Fellowes, Simpson, Sparrow.)

Page	Line	*1st state* (*uncorrected*)		*2d state* (*corrected*)	
L3ʳ (p. 77)	34	anothers wife	*Yale*	another wife	*The rest*
O4ᵛ (p. 104)	25	you memory	*Cinn ULC*	your memory	*The rest*
U2ʳ (p. 147)	14	fill'd	⎫	fil'd	⎫
	14	of in	*BM Chic Cinn*	off in	
	24	histᵒry	*ULC Sp*	history	*The rest*
	25	Silvᵉr	*Fell*	Silver	
	40	*insi*	⎭	*nisi*	⎭
Y2ʳ (p. 163)	21	becaus	⎫ *Chic*	because	⎫ *The rest*
	21	bee nprodigall	⎭	been prodigal	⎭
Y3ᵛ (p. 166)	21	glasses	⎫ *Chic*	glases	⎫ *The rest*
	21	vanitys	⎭	vanities	⎭
Aa1ʳ (p. 177)ᵃ	5–6	particular	⎫	particular,	⎫
	11–12	enconrage		encourage	
	13	show		shew	
	15	showed		shewed	
	22	*strengths*		*strength*	
	23	sort,	*Chic*	sort:	
	25	thee, why	*Yale*	thee. Why	
	28	God;	*Har*	God,	
	29	stewards	*ULC*	stewards,	*The rest*
	30	showed	*BLO*	shewed	
	35	here	*Linc*	there	
	38	Gods,		Gods	
	45	*compedite*		*compedite,*	
	45	*confitere duo,*		*confitere, Domino*	
	45	*& vertentus*		*& vertentur*	
	46	fortune;		fortune,	
		thee,	⎭	thee;	⎭

ᵃ While this volume was passing through the press, it was found that *Sim*, a large-paper copy, has this page in partly corrected state, intermediate between the two states given.

Page	Line	1st state (uncorrected)		2d state (corrected)	
Aa1ᵛ (p. 178)	1	colars		collars	
	1	garthers		garters	
	9 *mg.*	Quid		*Quia*	
	15	*bands,* for		*bands.* For	
	21	so ever	*Chic*	soever	
	23	phylosophers	*ULC*	philosophers	*The rest*
	27	actions,	*Linc*	actions;	
	28	no,		no;	
	34	theirs,		theirs;	
	37	reservation,		reservation	
	39	worse,		worse;	
	44	a recusant		aRecusant	
Aa4ʳ (p. 183)	1	onely *Ephod*		onely *Ephod,*	
	4	was, returned,		was returned,	
	5	*C*ommandements;		Commandement;	
	6	Testified		testified	
	6	Angels;		Angels,	
	7	manifested,		manifested;	
	9	Heres		Here's	
	9	far h is		far his	
	10	*hread*		*bread*	
	12	*safty*		*safety*	
	15	wifes	*Chic*	wives	
	16	him;	*ULC*	him,	
	19	hnndred	*Linc*	hundred	
	21	spiritualll		spirituall:	*The rest*
	23	*mundum*		*mundum;*	
	23	*rediit*		*rediit:*	
	24	Crose, musters		Cross, muster'd	
	25	Gentils, we		Gentiles. We	
	26	literally;		literally,	
	26	devided		divided	
	36	staes		states	
	36	*Orientis*		*Orientis,*	
	41	Thirdly,		Thirdly;	
	42	retnrns		returns	
Cc2ʳ (p. 187)	28	niether	*Sp*	neither	
Cc2ᵛ (p. 188)	3	true,	*Sp*	true;	
Cc3ʳ (p. 189)	7	*forence*	*Sp*	*forense*	
Cc3ʳ (p. 189)	23 *mg.*	(blank)ᵇ	*Chic Cinn Har* *Linc Car Sp*	Rom. 1.12	Yale BLO BM ULC Fell Sim

ᵇ It should be noted that the margins and marginal notes were printed separately from the body of the text. This explains why the division of the MSS over this marginal reading is different from that in 1.7, where Mr. Sparrow's copy stands alone.

Page	Line	1st state (uncorrected)		2d state (corrected)	
Cc3ᵛ (p. 190)		*mg.*ᵉ April 2. 1621	*Yale BLO* *BM ULC* *Fell Sim*	(heading) April 19. 1618	Chic Har Cinn Linc Sp Car (also in Dr. Williams's Library)
	7	we rereserved		were reserved	
	21	*Sio*		*Silo*	
	29	And then	*Sp*	and then	*The rest*
	30	this world,		this world;	
	30	she world		the world	
Dd1ʳ (p. 193)	20–21	that / that in	*BLO*	that / in	*The rest*

Dd4ᵛ (p. 200)   4   *1st state:* run, *BLO   2d state:* run; *BM ULC   3d state;* run;   *The rest*

13–14 *1st state:* their understanding, and he rectified their will saies God their; *BLO* (line 13)

2d state: their understanding, and he rectified their will; but still their understanding, and their will I draw them saies God their;   *BM ULC*

3d state: their understanding, and he rectified their will; but still their understanding, and their will. I drew them saies God there;   *The rest*

29–30 *1st state: ille de ipso san- / guie medciamenta facit*   *BLO*
2d state: ille de ipso sanguine medicamenta facit   *BM ULC*
3d state: ille de ipso sanguine medicamenta facit   *The rest*

37   *1st state:* drawing,   *BLO*
2d state: drawing;   *BM ULC*
3d state: drawing;   *The rest*

40   *1st state:* assurance,   *BLO*
2d state: assurance   *BM ULC*
3d state: assurance   *The rest*

41   *1st state:* He . . . save / sinners   *BLO*
2d state: he . . . savesinners   *BM ULC*
3d state: he . . . savesinners   *The rest*

Page	Line	1st state (uncorrected)		2d state (corrected)	
Ff3ʳ (p. 213)	1	Shephaerd of Shephears		Shepheard of Shepheards	
	10	*Diaconas*	*ULC*	*Diaconos*	*The rest*
	24	Church,		Church,)	
	44	vehementst		vehementest	
Gg4ʳ (p. 223)	26	pouering	{ *ULC*	pouring	*The rest*
	43	in, me	*Yale* }	in me,	

ᵉ Here the sermon heading is placed above and beyond the lines which separate the margins from the body of the sermon. In Vol. I, pp. 142–143, we gave our reasons for thinking that the date "April 19, 1618" is the correct one, and that "April 2. 1621" is a blunder. We have therefore treated this latter date as occurring in the uncorrected state of the margin, and the earlier date as belonging to the corrected state, found in seven copies including that belonging to Mr. Sparrow. In the body of the sermon, however, this particular copy has a number of blunders on this page which are lacking in all other copies known to us.

Page	Line	*1st state* (uncorrected)		*2d state* (corrected)	
Gg4ᵛ (p. 224)	21	inconsidaration	⎱ *Yale*	inconsideration	⎱ *The rest*
	38	concluded, etermine	⎰	conclude, determine	⎰
Ii1ᵛ (p. 242)	15	Rome,	⎱ *Yale BM*	Rome,	⎱ *The rest*
	42	and	⎰ *BLO Fell*	and	⎰
Nn1ᵛ (p. 274)	10	*mnndi*	⎫	*mundi*	⎫
	20	Ghospel	⎪ *Har*	Gospel	⎪
	25	*Ecubescere*	⎬ *Cinn*	*Erubescere*	⎬ *The rest*
	34	things	⎪ *Linc*	things;	⎪
	34	brighter;	⎭	brighter	⎭
Nn2ᵛ (p. 276)	35	in thee; the	⎫	in thee the	⎫
	39	in Christ,	⎬ *Sp*	in Christ	⎬ *The rest*
	43 *mg.*	*Sumentatis*	⎭	*Juventutis*	⎭
Oo2ᵛ (p. 288)	41	ovious	⎱ *Chic Har*	obvious	⎱ *The rest*
	41–42	pass- / over	⎰ *Linc*	pas- / over	⎰
Pp1ʳ (p. 285)	Sign.	Ppp	*Yale Cinn* *BLO BM Fell*	Pp	*The rest*
Pp2ʳ (p. 287)	Sign.	Aaa2	*Har Sp*	Pp2	*The rest*
Rr3ʳ (p. 305)	14 *mg.*	Jos. ult. 85	*Cinn Har Yale*	Jos. ult. 15	`"`
Ss4ᵛ (p. 316)	27–28	Reli- / gion	*Chic Fell*	Reli- / gion,	`"`
Yy4ᵛ (p. 348)	19	Kings	*Chic*	King!	`"`
Aaa4 & 4ᵛ (pp. 361ᵈ–364)		evil / *Egypt*	*Cinn Har Yale* *BLO Fell*	evil / evil	`"`
Bbb2ᵛ (p. 368)	10	stuff;	*Cinn Chic Har* *Yale BLO Fell Sp*	stuff	`"`
Bbb3ʳ (p. 369)	39	shine;	*Chic Sp Yale* *Cinn BM Linc* *Will Fell*	shines;	`"`
Bbb3ᵛ (p. 370)	32	Son from	*Chic Sp*	Sun from	`"`
Ggg1ᵛ (p. 406)	2	exampls;	*Har*	examples;	`"`
	5	thetefore		therefore	`"`

ᵈ Should be 363.

NOTE: A few insignificant variants have been found in sheets Nn, Oo, Pp, and Qq of the *Fifty Sermons.* These have been recorded in our Textual Notes. See also Vol. I, p. 7, and footnote.

APPENDIX B

LIST OF SERMONS IN THE FOLIOS, THE PRESENT EDITION, AND ALFORD'S EDITION

Folio		Text	Potter & Simpson	Alford	
LXXX.	1	Col. 1.19, 20	IV. 11; p. 283	I.	1
	2	Isa. 7.14	VI. 8; p. 168	I.	2
	3	Gal. 4.4, 5	VI. 17; p. 331	I.	3
	4	Luke 2.29, 30	VII. 11; p. 279	I.	4
	5	Exod. 4.13	VIII. 5; p. 130	I.	5
	6	Isa. 53.1	VIII. 13; p. 292	I.	6
	7	John 10.10	IX. 5; p. 131	I.	7
	8	Mat. 5.16	X. 3; p. 84	I.	8
	9	Rom. 13.7	IV. 12; p. 303	I.	9
	10	Rom. 12.20	III. 18; p. 376	III.	63
	11	Mat. 9.2	X. 2; p. 65	III.	64
	12	Mat. 5.2 [5.8]	VII. 13; p. 325	I.	10
	13	Job 16.17, 18, 19	IX. 9; p. 213	I.	11
	14	Amos 5.18	II. 18; p. 348	I.	15
	15	1 Cor. 15.26	IV. 1; p. 45	I.	12
	16	John 11.35	IV. 13; p. 324	I.	13
	17	Mat. 19.17	VI. 11; p. 223	I.	14
	18	Acts 2.36	IV. 14; p. 345	I.	16
	19	Apoc. 20.6	VI. 2; p. 62	I.	17
	20	John 5.28, 29	VI. 13; p. 262	I.	18
	21	1 Cor. 15.29	VII. 3; p. 94	I.	19
	22	Heb. 11.35	VII. 15; p. 370	I.	20
	23	1 Cor. 13.12	VIII. 9; p. 219	I.	21
	24	Job 4.18	VIII. 16; p. 355	I.	22
	25	Mat. 28.6	IX. 8; p. 189	I.	23
	26	1 Thes. 4.17	IV. 2; p. 63	I.	24
	27	Psal. 89.47 [89.48]	II. 9; p. 197	I.	25
	28	John 14.26	VII. 18; p. 434	I.	26
	29	John 14.26	VIII. 11; p. 253	I.	27
	30	John 14.20	IX. 10; p. 232	I.	28
	31	Gen. 1.2	IX. 3; p. 92	I.	29
	32	1 Cor. 12.3	VI. 5; p. 114	II.	30
	33	Acts 10.44	V. 1; p. 35	II.	31
	34	Rom. 8.16	V. 2; p. 58	II.	32
	35	Mat. 12.31	V. 3; p. 77	II.	33
	36	John 16.8, 9, 10, 11	VI. 16; p. 311	II.	34
	37	John 16.8, 9, 10, 11	VII. 8; p. 215	II.	35
	38	2 Cor. 1.3	III. 12; p. 256	II.	36
	39	1 Pet. 1.17	III. 13; p. 274	II.	37
	40	1 Cor. 16.22	III. 14; p. 292	II.	38
	41	Psal. 2.12	III. 15; p. 313	II.	39

414

Folio		Text	Potter & Simpson	Alford
Fifty	9	Micah 2.10	V. 9; p. 184	IV. 89
	10	Micah 2.10	V. 10; p. 198	IV. 90
	11	Gen. 28.16, 17	II. 10; p. 213	IV. 92
	12	John 5.22	II. 15; p. 311	IV. 93
	13	John 8.15	II. 16; p. 325	IV. 94
	14	Job 19.26	III. 3; p. 91	IV. 95
	15	1 Cor. 15.50	III. 4; p. 114	IV. 96
	16	Col. 1.24	III. 16; p. 332	IV. 97
	17	Mat. 18.7	III. 6; p. 156	IV. 98
	18	Mat. 18.7	III. 7; p. 171	IV. 99
	19	Psal. 38.2	II. 1; p. 49	IV. 100
	20	Psal. 38.3	II. 2; p. 72	IV. 101
	21	Psal. 38.4	II. 3; p. 95	IV. 102
	22	Psal. 38.4	II. 4; p. 119	IV. 103
	23	Psal. 38.4	II. 5; p. 131	IV. 104
	24	Ezek. 34.19	X. 6; p. 140	IV. 105
	25	Ezek. 34.19	X. 7; p. 159	IV. 106
	26	Isa. 65.20	VII. 14; p. 349	IV. 107
	27	Mark 4.24	VII. 16; p. 393	IV. 108
	28	Gen. 1.26	IX. 1; p. 47	IV. 109
	29	Gen. 1.26	IX. 2; p. 68	IV. 110
	30	Job 13.15	III. 8; p. 187	IV. 111
	31	Job 36.25	IV. 6; p. 163	IV. 112
	32	Apoc. 7.9	VI. 7; p. 150	IV. 113
	33	Cant. 3.11	VI. 14; p. 280	V. 114
	34	Luke 33.24 [23.34]	V. 12; p. 231	V. 115
	35	Mat. 21.44	II. 8; p. 179	V. 116
	36	John 1.8	III. 17; p. 348	V. 117
	37	John 1.8	IV. 5; p. 145	V. 118
	38	John 1.8	IV. 8; p. 210	V. 119
	39	Phil. 3.2	X. 4; p. 103	V. 120
	40	2 Cor. 5.20	X. 5; p. 119	V. 121
	41	Hosea 3.4	VII. 17; p. 415	V. 122
	42	Prov. 14.31	VIII. 12; p. 270	V. 123
	43	Lam. 4.20	IV. 9; p. 235	V. 124
	44	Mat. 11.6	IX. 4; p. 109	V. 125
	45	Deut. 25.5	VI. 3; p. 81	V. 126
	46	Psal. 34.11	VI. 4; p. 95	V. 127
	47	Gen. 3.24 [3.14]	X. 8; p. 178	V. 128
	48	Lam. 3.1	X. 9; p. 192	V. 129
	49	Gen. 17.24	VI. 9; p. 186	V. 130
	50	1 Thes. 5.16	X. 10; p. 213	V. 131
XXVI.	1	Luke 23.40	I. 6; p. 252	V. 132
	2	Ezek. 33.32	II. 7; p. 164	V. 133
	3 } 17 }	Jas. 2.12	VIII. 15; p. 335	V. 134
	4	1 Tim. 3.16	III. 9; p. 206	V. 135

SERMONS ISSUED SEPARATELY

APPENDIX C

Index of Scriptural Texts of the Sermons

TEXT		POTTER & SIMPSON	FOLIO	ALFORD
Gen.	1.2	IX. 3	LXXX. 31	I. p. 570
	1.26	IX. 1	Fifty. 28	IV. p. 490
	1.26	IX. 2	Fifty. 29	IV. p. 512
	2.18	II. 17	Fifty. 2	IV. p. 17
	3.14	X. 8	Fifty. 47	V. p. 289
	17.24	VI. 9	Fifty. 49	V. p. 325
	18.25	III. 5	LXXX. 42	II. p. 206
	28.16, 17	II. 10	Fifty. 11	IV. p. 168
	32.10	I. 7	XXVI. 12	V. p. 551
Exod.	4.13	VIII. 5	LXXX. 5	I. p. 79
	12.30	VI. 18	XXVI. 21	VI. p. 53
Deut.	12.30	IV. 4	XXVI. 23	VI. p. 85
	25.5	VI. 3	Fifty. 45	V. p. 255
Judges	5.20	IV. 7	Issued separately	VI. p. 191
Est.	4.16	V. 11	XXVI. 22	VI. p. 70
Job	4.18	VIII. 16	LXXX. 24	I. p. 428
	13.15	III. 8	Fifty. 30	IV. p. 537
	16.17–19	IX. 9	LXXX. 13	I. p. 214
	19.26	III. 3	Fifty. 14	IV. p. 216
	36.25	IV. 6	Fifty. 31	IV. p. 556
Psal.	2.12	III. 15	LXXX. 41	II. p. 186
	6.1	V. 16	LXXX. 50	II. p. 375
	6.2, 3	V. 17	LXXX. 51	II. p. 396
	6.4, 5	V. 18	LXXX. 52	II. p. 423
	6.4, 5	V. 19	LXXX. 53	II. p. 439
	6.6, 7	VIII. 8	LXXX. 54	II. p. 449
	6.8–10	VI. 1	LXXX. 55	II. p. 478
	11.3	VI. 12	Issued separately	*Omitted*
	32.1, 2	IX. 11	LXXX. 56	II. p. 502
	32.3, 4	IX. 12	LXXX. 57	II. p. 526
	32.5	IX. 13	LXXX. 58	II. p. 549
	32.6	IX. 14	LXXX. 59	II. p. 570
	32.7	IX. 15	LXXX. 60	III. p. 1
	32.8	IX. 16	LXXX. 61	III. p. 17
	32.9	IX. 17	LXXX. 62	III. p. 39
	32.10, 11	IX. 18	LXXX. 63	III. p. 60
	34.11	VI. 4	Fifty. 46	V. p. 270
	38.2	II. 1	Fifty. 19	IV. p. 308
	38.3	II. 2	Fifty. 20	IV. p. 333
	38.4	II. 3	Fifty. 21	IV. p. 357
	38.4	II. 4	Fifty. 22	IV. p. 382
	38.4	II. 5	Fifty. 23	IV. p. 394
	38.9	II. 6	MSS	*Omitted*

TEXT		POTTER & SIMPSON	FOLIO	ALFORD
Mat.	18.7	III. 6	Fifty. 17	IV. p. 277
	18.7	III. 7	Fifty. 18	IV. p. 292
	19.17	VI. 11	LXXX. 17	I. p. 273
	21.44	II. 8	Fifty. 35	V. p. 28
	22.30	VIII. 3	Fifty. 1	IV. p. 1
	28.6	IX. 8	LXXX. 25	I. p. 447
Mark	4.24	VII. 16	Fifty. 27	IV. p. 468
	16.16	V. 13	LXXX. 76	III. p. 364
Luke	2.29, 30	VII. 11	LXXX. 4	I. p. 57
	23.40	I. 6	XXVI. 1	V. p. 361
	23.34	V. 12	Fifty. 34	V. p. 14
John	1.8	III. 17	Fifty. 36	V. p. 46
	1.8	IV. 5	Fifty. 37	V. p. 75
	1.8	IV. 8	Fifty. 38	V. p. 94
	5.22	II. 15	Fifty. 12	IV. p. 191
	5.28, 29	VI. 13	LXXX. 20	I. p. 343
	8.15	II. 16	Fifty. 13	IV. p. 206
	10.10	IX. 5	LXXX. 7	I. p. 126
	10.22	IV. 15	Issued separately	*Omitted*
	11.21	VII. 10	LXXX. 80	III. p. 469
	11.35	IV. 13	LXXX. 16	I. p. 251
	14.2	VII. 4	LXXX. 73	III. p. 304
	14.20	IX. 10	LXXX. 30	I. p. 552
	14.26	VII. 18	LXXX. 28	I. p. 515
	14.26	VIII. 11	LXXX. 29	I. p. 534
	16.8–11	VI. 16	LXXX. 36	II. p. 82
	16.8–11	VII. 8	LXXX. 37	II. p. 104
Acts	1.8	IV. 10	Issued separately	VI. p. 225
	2.36	IV. 14	LXXX. 18	I. p. 307
	7.60	VIII. 7	XXVI. 15	V. p. 604
	9.4	VI. 10	LXXX. 46	II. p. 297
	10.44	V. 1	LXXX. 33	II. p. 19
	20.25	VIII. 6	LXXX. 47	II. p. 316
	23.6, 7	IX. 6	LXXX. 49	II. p. 356
	28.6	VIII. 14	LXXX. 48	II. p. 333
Rom.	8.16	V. 2	LXXX. 34	II. p. 42
	12.20	III. 18	LXXX. 10	III. p. 103
	13.7	IV. 12	LXXX. 9	I. p. 169
	13.11	II. 12	XXVI. 20	VI. p. 33
1 Cor.	12.3	VI. 5	LXXX. 32	II. p. 1
	13.12	VIII. 9	LXXX. 23	I. p. 410
	15.26	IV. 1	LXXX. 15	I. p. 233
	15.29	VII. 3	LXXX. 21	I. p. 362
	15.29	VII. 6	LXXX. 77	III. p. 388
	15.29	VII. 7	LXXX. 78	III. p. 414
	15.50	III. 4	Fifty. 15	IV. p. 240
	16.22	III. 14	LXXX. 40	II. p. 164

TEXT		POTTER & SIMPSON	FOLIO	ALFORD
2 Cor.	1.3	III. 12	LXXX. 38	II. p. 127
	4.6	IV. 3	XXVI. 25	VI. p. 143
	5.20	X. 5	Fifty. 40	V. p. 137
Gal.	3.27	V. 7	Fifty. 7	IV. p. 102
	4.4, 5	VI. 17	LXXX. 3	I. p. 39
Ephes.	5.25–27	V. 5	Fifty. 5	IV. p. 63
Phil.	3.2	X. 4	Fifty. 39	V. p. 120
Colos.	1.19, 20	IV. 11	LXXX. 1	I. p. 1
	1.24	III. 16	Fifty. 16	IV. p. 261
1 Thes.	4.17	IV. 2	LXXX. 26	I. p. 472
	5.16	X. 10	Fifty. 50	V. p. 344
1 Tim.	1.15	I. 8	XXVI. 13	V. p. 569
	1.15	I. 9	XXVI. 14	V. p. 585
	3.16	III. 9	XXVI. 4	V. p. 415
Heb.	11.35	VII. 15	LXXX. 22	I. p. 387
James	2.12	VIII. 15	XXVI. 3 and 17	V. p. 393
1 Pet.	1.17	III. 13	LXXX. 39	II. p. 145
2 Pet.	3.13	VIII. 2	Issued separately	VI. p. 244
1 John	5.7, 8	V. 6	Fifty. 6	IV. p. 80
Rev.	4.8	VIII. 1	LXXX. 44	II. p. 247
	7.2, 3	X. 1	LXXX. 45	II. p. 271
	7.9	VI. 7	Fifty. 32	IV. p. 572
	7.17	V. 4	Fifty. 4	IV. p. 45
	20.6	VI. 2	LXXX. 19	I. p. 324

Addenda and Corrigenda
for Volumes I-IX

Addenda: Volume I

INTRODUCTION I: ON THE BIBLIOGRAPHY

1) Note to pages 1–32:

The following copies of various early editions have come to our attention since the publication of Volume I, and should be added to our lists: The Library of Lincoln's Inn possesses a copy of *XXVI Sermons*, and one of *Fiue Sermons upon Speciall Occasions*. The Princeton University Library possesses a copy of the Sermon to the Virginia Company (edition of 1622), with the name "F. Bridgewater" on the flyleaf. The Princeton Theological Seminary Library possesses a copy of the 1633 edition of *Deaths Duell*, and one of *Six Sermons* (1634). John Sparrow, Warden of All Souls College, Oxford, possesses a copy of *XXVI Sermons* with the first cancel title page. Carlisle Cathedral Library has a copy of *XXVI Sermons* with the second cancel title page.

2) Add to item concerning Wilford's *Memorials and Characters*, 1741, on page 31:

The surviving editor (E. M. Simpson) has acquired an earlier volume, *Memorials of Worthy Persons: Two Decads*. By Cl. Barksdale.... London, Printed by I.R. 1661, which contains the source of "The Character of Sir Willm Cokayne" in Wilford. It was Clement Barksdale who first excised this "character" from Donne's sermon at the funeral of Sir William Cokayne (Vol. VII, pp. 257–278). Wilford corrected the date of this sermon, which had been given erroneously by Barksdale as preached on December 23, 1626, instead of December 12 (the date given in *LXXX Sermons*), but otherwise his text follows Barksdale's in its alterations and omissions, and he introduces an occasional minor variant of his own.

INTRODUCTION II: ON THE MANUSCRIPTS

3) Note to pages 33–38:

Early in 1960 Dr. Esmond de Beer presented to the Bodleian Library three valuable Donne MSS which he had bought from the library of the late Wilfred Merton. Two of these are the Dowden (*D*) and the Wilfred Merton (*M*) MSS described in Volume I, pages 33–38, of our edition. I have now had the opportunity of reëxamining these with the help of Dr. R. W. Hunt, Keeper of the Western MSS, and Miss M. C. Crum, his assistant. In our account of *D* we mentioned (p. 37) the inscription on fol. 1 "Ex dono M^ri Gregg: de Ilkeston park: May 29th 1683." There is a monogram before this inscription which can be read as "JW," and Miss

The Text
Remember nowe thy Creator in the dayes of thy youthe. 12:1: Ecclesiastes.

Wee may consider Two greate

Vertues, One for the Sonetye of the Esse, Thankfullnes, And another for attayning the next Esse. Repentaunce, As the precious met-
talles, Silver and gould, of the Silver, of the vertue of Thankfullnes,
there are whole mynes in the earth. Bookes written by Morrall men,
by Philosophers. A man maye growe ritch in that mettall, in that vertue
by digging in that Myne, in the workes of Morall men. But of this
goald, the vertue Repentaunce, there is noe Myne in the earth, in the
Bookes of Philosophers, noe doctrine of Repentaunce; This gould is for
the most part, in the washes: This Repentaunce for the most p[ar]te in
the waters of Tribulacion: But God directs thee to it in the Texte,
before thou comest to these waters: Remember nowe thy Creator, &
before these evill dayes come, and thou wilt repent, &c. If thou didst not
remember him till nowe, there then the holy Ghost takes the neerest
waye to bring man to god, by awaking his memorye, for y[e] vnderstanding
required long instruction, and severe demonstracion; And the will &
required an instructed vnderstanding before, and is oft deceaved, by
Cendors, and the boundlesse ffacultye; and if the memorye doe faste[n]
vpon any of those thinges w[hi]ch god hath done for vs, that is neerest
waye to him.

Remember therefore, and Remember nowe, youe y[t] memo[r]ye
so placed in the Endowments p[ar]te of the soule, Doe serve not y[ou]
Remembringe to the Endowments p[ar]te of thy Esse, But Doo it Now,
Nunc maye, while you have lifte, And Nunc in diebus, as it is in y[e]
Texte, Nowe, while God gives thee many, Enioye, many meanes to come
to him! And in Diebus Iuuentutis, in the dayes of thy youth, of thy
Strength, while thou art able to doo that, w[hi]ch thou purposest to
doo.

FIRST PAGE OF "A SERMON OF VALEDICTION"

From the Merton manuscript, in the Bodleian; by kind permission
of the Curators

Crum tells me that the incumbent at Ilkeston in 1683 was John Wylson. It may have been to him that William Gregg gave the manuscript. After the eight sermons by Donne there is a ninth, obviously an author's draft, in the same hand that wrote the inscription. This sermon may have been Wylson's own—it is certainly not by Donne. Certain passages in the Donne sermons have been marked by hand. This manuscript was bound for Mr. Merton by Katherine Adams, who laid the original vellum binding inside the covers. These are small details, but they seem worth adding to our original account. The three MSS are described by Helen Gardner in an article which gives special attention to the Dowden MS of the *Poems,* "Donne MSS. for the Bodleian," *Times Literary Supplement,* March 11, 1960.

The Wilfred Merton MS (*M*) was formerly identified by Keynes and others with a manuscript mentioned by John Payne Collier in his *History of Dramatic Poetry,* II, 432–433, and *Bibliographical and Critical Account of the Rarest Books,* I, p. i. In Volume I of our edition we disputed this identification partly on the ground that Collier stated in his *Bibliographical Account,* p. i, that he had "lent the MS. to a clergyman, and in some way, during the transit, Alabaster's sonnets accidentally escaped . . . they were accompanied by some other rare unprinted poems of the time." Mr. Merton urged on us the view that no pages could have been abstracted from his manuscript, which appeared to be absolutely complete. The Bodleian librarians have shown, however, that the volume contains a large number of gatherings each of which contains either one or, occasionally, two sermons. The scribe took great pains to enlarge or contract his writing in such a way that the end of each gathering should coincide with the end of a sermon or a pair of sermons. This means that the Alabaster poems must have occupied one or more separate gatherings, and if the manuscript was at one time in a state of bad repair it would have been quite easy to extract such gatherings without disturbing the appearance of the manuscript as a whole.

Inside the front cover there is a pencil notation, "Mr. Collyer 3 Bouverie St. Fleet St." The handwriting is not Collier's, and, as far as we know, Collier never spelt his name as "Collyer." However, the pencil note may have been made by the bookseller or his assistant who sold the volume to Collier. A strong reason for connecting the volume with Collier lies in Archdeacon Hannah's account of Collier's manuscript as containing "several of Donne's MS. sermons, along with other valuable relics, and amongst them a sermon preached 'By Doctor King Biŝ: of London before yᵉ Kinges Maiestye' on Ps. ii. 10, 11, 12" (Hannah, *Poems and Psalms of*

Henry King, 1843, p. xci). This corresponds exactly with the inscription before John King's sermon in the Merton MS.

I feel therefore obliged to state that our doubts about the identification of the MS can hardly be justified, and that the Merton MS is probably the same as the one described by Collier and Hannah.

4) Note to pages 42–45:

[This note is added on the basis of material collected by the late George R. Potter and his assistants.]

A considerable amount of work has been done on the history of the Dobell MS (*Dob*)[1] since Volume I went to press. Although the results are not conclusive, some progress has been made and a good deal of useful matter collected.

The major part of this inquiry is concerned with the origin of *Dob*. In seeking to determine where and for whom the manuscript was made, a large number of Donne's contemporaries have been considered and a few of his close friends and patrons singled out for special study, particularly those who were known to have connections with Cambridgeshire, where *Dob* eventually appeared. The investigation has yielded a wealth of information, some of which is significant; but no positive proof of original ownership can be claimed.

One difficulty has been the lack of sufficient evidence to affix a definite date to *Dob*. The manuscript cannot have been completed before Donne's illness in 1623/4, since it includes *To Christ* (in some editions entitled *A Hymne to God the Father*), which was written at that time, and there is reason to believe that it may have been compiled several years later. Helen Gardner, Reader in English Literature in the University of Oxford, and Evelyn M. Simpson, the surviving editor of this edition, have noted similarities in the text of the poems between *Dob* and other manuscripts written after Donne's death in 1631. W. A. Jackson, Director of the Houghton Library, Harvard University, and H. M. Nixon, Deputy Keeper in charge of book bindings in the British Museum, have each given the opinion that the original binding of the manuscript was probably made as late as 1630.

It has already been established that *Dob* became the property of William Balam (1652–1726) in the latter part of the seventeenth century and was used by him as a commonplace book for a number of years. The scribblings which cover the margins of the manuscript give us an insight into the character and personality of Dr. Balam as well as providing us with an interesting picture of the Isle of Ely in its legal, political, and religious

---

[1] Harvard Library, fMS Eng 966.4 (formerly Nor 4506).

till, by seuall wayes, we haue mett in ye gates of brass, yet wthin yt gate
of heauen I may meett wth you all and yere say to my satio and your
satio, that wch ye sayd to his ffather and our ffather, Of those whome
thou gauest me, haue I not lost one. Remember me thus, you that stay
in this kingdome of peace, where not sword is drawne but ye sword of
Iustice, as I shall remember you in those kingdomes, where ambition on
one side, and a neceffary defence against iminent perfecution on ye
other side, are drawne many swords already; and Christ Iesus remember vs all in his kingdome: to wch, though we must sayle through
a sea, yet it is ye sea of his blood, in wch neuer soule suffered ship-
wrackt: though we must be blowne with strong winds wth vehement sighes and groanes for our sinnes, yet it is ye spirit of god
that bloweth all that wind in vs, and shall blowe away all contrary winds
of diffidence in his mercy. It is that kingdome, where we shall all
be souldiers, but of one army, the lord of hosts, and all children of one
Quire, ye god of harmony did consent: where all clyents shall retaine
but one aduocate, ye aduocate of vs all, Christ Iesus, and yet euery
clyent receiue a sentence on his side, not only in a verdit of not
guilty, a non misputacon of his sinnes, but a venite benedicti a reall
participacon of an immortall crowne of glory. where there shalbe noe
difference in affection, nor in voyce, but we shall all agree as fully and
as perfectly in our Hallelujah, and our Gloria in excelsis, as god ye father and god ye sonne and god ye holy ghost agreed in fiat faciamus
hominem; we shall prayse ye whole Trinity as vnanimely, as ye Trinity concurrd in making vs. To end, it is ye kingdome where we
shall end, and yet beginne but then; where we shall haue continuall rest, o
yet neuer growe lazy; where we shall haue more strength and noe enemies; where we shall liue and neuer dy; where we shall meete and neuer
part. But heere we must.

preach'd at Lincolnes Inne before his
departure with my L. of Doncaster Ev. 1619

aspects. They also claim some historical value in reference to several celebrated and colorful figures of that period. Of more importance is the discovery that William Balam was a student of literature and an admirer of Donne's poetry. His treatment of the poems, including corrections, additions, underscoring of lines, and critical comments—in one instance comparing an idea of Donne's with one of Dryden's, in another paraphrasing fifty lines of one of Donne's Satires,—indicates that he read them with interest and understanding. That he admired Donne's poetry is evidenced by the fact that he owned at least one other manuscript copy of Donne's poems which he also used as a commonplace book (CUL Add. MS 5778).

The immediate fate of the manuscript after 1726 seems to be clearly defined. Under the terms of William Balam's will, "Tenn of the best Bookes in my whole Library" were left to his friend Charles Fleetwood,[2] the official records to his clerk Samuel Newby (Mrs. Newby received a large quarto Bible), and the rest of his property to his nephew William Towers.[3] It is unlikely that Charles Fleetwood chose *Dob* as one of the ten, for the Rossall Sale Catalogue for 1844,[4] which includes an inventory of the Rossall-Fleetwood library,[5] fails to show any item of this description. Certainly it could not be described as an official record. Thus it can be assumed that William Towers fell heir to the manuscript. He died in 1745 and his estate[6] passed to his wife Anne, who died May 5, 1785. No data have been found for the period between that time and 1914, when the manuscript appeared at Sotheby's and was purchased by Percy Dobell.

The material relating to the Dobell MS contains a report on the extent of this study, and includes notes on the manuscript, bibliographies, and memoranda on Donne's contemporaries, William Balam, and Cambridgeshire. All of it is now the property of Harvard University and has been placed in the Houghton Library.

INTRODUCTION III: ON THE TEXT

5) Addition to footnote 12, on page 49:

The clause from the sermon on *Ecclesiastes* 5.12 and 13 (the text should be emended to 5.13 and 14) should not have been quoted as a corrupt passage. See notes to this sermon, in Volume III.

---

[2] Son of William Fleetwood, Bishop of Ely, 1714–1723.

[3] Master of Christ's College, Cambridge, 1734–1745.

[4] Harris Library, Preston, Lancashire.

[5] For this information we are indebted to Major Roger Hesketh-Fleetwood, Meols Hall, North Meols, Lancs.

[6] Two friends, the Rev. Josias Cockshutt, Rector of Kegworth, Leicestershire, and the Rev. Thomas Cartwright, Fellow of Christ's College, Cambridge, each received "one ffolio Book out of my Library."

6) Note to page 71, lines 8-9:
The source manuscript for *D* and *L* did, as indicated here, evidently omit "of," change "though" to "through," and change "write" to "waite"; but this last change was a mere misreading, not a deliberate change, for *M* misread the word as "wayte," also. "Were" for "was" is not a change by *D* and *L*, but a preservation of the correct word, in which these two manuscripts agree with *M*. For corrected details see the notes to the sermon on *Psalms* 38.9, in Volume II.

INTRODUCTION TO THE SERMONS

7) Addition to footnote 57, on page 143:
Since Volume I was published, a third state of the forme containing this page has come to light, in a copy of *XXVI Sermons* owned by John Sparrow, which contains several errors that are corrected in all other copies, and which gives the date as April 19, 1618. This discovery creates a puzzling situation, since it indicates that the state containing the date April 2, 1621, is the *corrected* state of the forme. We still, however, are convinced that 1618 is the right date for both the sermons on 1 *Timothy* 1.15; they were clearly not preached several years apart, and if 1621 had been the correct year it is hard to see why the date of the *first* sermon was not also changed and why the date 1618 was originally assigned to *both* sermons, not simply the second one. Possibly John Donne junior acquired a second copy of the second sermon, with the date 1621, and without thought changed the date to correspond with that on his new copy. Certainly there is no reason for supposing the date 1621 to be any *more* reliable than 1618.

Addenda: Volume III

INTRODUCTION

8) Note to page 41:
In Sermon 17, when Donne speaks (line 985) of "your *twelve Companies,*" he is addressing the representatives of the twelve great livery companies of London, who accompanied the Lord Mayor and the Sheriffs to St. Paul's for divine service on Christmas Day and six other feast days in the year (see Stow, *Survey of London,* ed. Kingsford, II, 190). These companies were the Mercers, the Grocers, the Drapers, the Fishmongers, the Goldsmiths, the Skinners, the Merchant Tailors, the Haber-

dashers, the Salters, the Ironmongers, the Vintners, and the Clothworkers. See W. Herbert, *The History of the Twelve Great Livery Companies of London*, London, 1837, I, 1–224, and P. H. Ditchfield, *The Story of the City Companies*, London, 1926.

Addenda: Volume IV

INTRODUCTION

9) Note to page 34:

On page 2 we pointed out that in Elizabethan and Jacobean times the Holy Communion was celebrated in Cathedrals once a month and on the great festivals. In St. Paul's the second Sunday of the month was chosen as Communion Sunday, and in 1622 this fell in October on the 13th. This explains Donne's appeal to his hearers in Sermon 8 (see page 233 of this volume): *"Ecce agnus Dei, Behold the lambe of God, Here, here* in this his ordinance he supplicates you, when the Minister, how meane soever, prays you, *in his stead, be yee reconciled to God.* Here he proclaims, and cries to you, *Venite omnes, come all that are weary and heavy laden.* Here he bleeds in the *Sacrament,* here he takes away the sinnes of the world, ..." This page (233) contains a number of references to parts of the office of Holy Communion in the Prayer Book of the Church of England. Similar references can be found in certain of Donne's sermons on Christmas and Easter Day, but this appears to be the only sermon for the monthly Communion Sunday at St. Paul's which has been preserved.

Addenda: Volume VIII

INTRODUCTION

10) Additional note to pages 15–19:

Sermon 7, lines 472 ff.: "We have a story in the Ecclesiastical story of *Nicephorus* and *Sapricius,* formerly great friends, and after as great Enemies: ..." Cp. *Biathanatos,* p. 186: "... these words will justifie the fact of the Martyr *Nicephorus,* ... Whose case was, That having had some enmitie with *Sapritius,* who was brought to the place where he was to receive the bloudy crowne of Martyredome, he fell downe to *Sapritius,* and begged from him then, a pardon of all former bitternesses. But *Sapritius* elated with the glory of Martyredome, refused him; but was presently punished; for his faith coold, and he recanted, and lived. And *Nicephorus* standing by, stepped into his roome, and cryed, I am also a Christian, and so provoked the Magistrate to execute him; . . ." The marginal note is *"Metaph. in Niceph. Martyr."*

This is a striking example of the way in which Donne in the *Sermons* repeats the general sense of passages in *Biathanatos* or *Essays in Divinity* without repeating the exact words. It appears that he had a stock of abbreviated notes from authors whom he had read, and that he expanded such notes in different words each time that he repeated them.

Corrigenda: Volume I

INTRODUCTIONS

PAGE	SERM. NO.	LINE	For:	Read:
44		17	March 17, 1727	April 3, 1727
101		29	another version	another vision
111 n. 4		9	tenerrimus	tenerrimis
127		20	cricitisms	criticisms
135		9	thirst hath	thirst hast
145		23	*iste*	*ista*

SERMONS

PAGE	SERM. NO.	LINE	For:	Read:
215	3	1197	*Amici*	*Amice*
257	6	208	*compositorem*	*composito rem*
307	9	229	hell (*F*)	help

Also, the following emendations of the Latin in the Folios should be made:

PAGE	SERM. NO.	LINE	For:	Read:
224	4	51	*vocatia*	*vocantia*
240	5	170	*Dominis*	*Domini*
244	5	295	*affectum*	*effectus*
260	6	284–285	*miraculis*	*mirabilis*
261	6	321	*Loquemar*	*Loquemur*
282	7	520	*defectu*	*[de] defectu*
299	8	539	*Immolatam*	*Immolatum*
303	9	95	*humanus*	*humanum*
304	9	123	*iste*	*ista*
309	9	300	*Adetur venia*	A *detur venia*
312	9	411	*medici*	*mederi*
312	9	421	*adhibitur*	*adhibetur*
312	9	421	*exitatur*	*excitatur*
312	9	428	*habet*	*habent*

TEXTUAL NOTES

PAGE	SERM. NO.	LINE	
324	3	140 mg.	Add to TN the following:

NOTE: The reference is to *Joannis Stephani Duranti Secretioris Regii Consistorii Consiliarii, Amplissimiq. Senatus Tolosani Primi Præsidis, De Ritibus Ecclesiæ Catholicæ Libri Tres* (Rome, 1591), Lib. I, cap. xix ("De Baptisterio et sacro fonte"), § 30.

PAGE	SERM.	LINE	
327– 334	5		Lines 4, 10, 21, 23, 36, 63, 65–66, 82, 93, 94, 110, 113, 113–114, 191, 272–273, 279–280, 300, 343, 372 *mg.*, 441, 493, 514, 526, *M* reads as *E* (apart from minor variants in spelling and capitalization).
328	5	35	Add TN: upon God, but also securely employed] *om. M*.
328	5	67	Add: *suspicionem M*
328	5	72 mg.	Add: Divisio *M*
329– 334	5		Lines 133, 141 *mg.*, 210 (second TN on this line), 233, 447, *M* reads as *F*
330	5	197	Add: that he that hath *M*
330	5	233	Add TN: love; if] love, and if *M*
331	5	279	Add TN: to] *om. M*
331	5	279– 280	Read: to any . . . rather then] *om. E*
332	5	362	Read: and seek him, and seek him with a heavy heart] and seek him with heavy hearts *M, E*
333	5	449	Read: *vigilaverint*] vigelauerint *M*
333	5	470	Read: besieged] be seet *M* (followed by space) : be-sett *E*
334	6	554	In NOTE, for: Publius read: Publilius
343	9	421	For: *adhibitur* read: *adhibetur*

Corrigenda: Volume II

INTRODUCTION

PAGE	SERM. NO.	LINE	For:	Read:
17		10	volcme	volume

SERMONS

PAGE	SERM. NO.	LINE	For:	Read:
69	1	741	are	art (F)
138	5	265–266	For: Christ would not. / They were *sins*, that lay upon him, †part with† *our sins* read: Christ would not part with *our sins*. / They were *sins*, that lay upon him, *our sins Edd.*	

			For:	Read:
142	5	409	*fieri (F)*	*fuere*
153	6	336	*dissolui (Dob)*	*dissolvi*
155	6	420	*pecatorem (Dob)*	*peccatorem (M)*
158	6	528	howe when (Dob)	howe and when (Dob)
159	6	559	them to (D, L)	then to (Dob, M)
163	6	699	conclude, (Dob)	conclude
192	8	450	unite (F)	reunite (M, Dob, D, L)
204	9	260	denied (F)	defined
220	10	243	Chrysotome	Chrysostome (F)
228	10	570	are	art (F)
243	11	305	plac'd in (F)	plac'd thee in (Ash, D, Dob, E, L, M)
251	12	19	*saluta (F)*	*soluta*
258	12	277	*operator (F)*	*operato*
258	12	296–297	the word ... they (F)	the words ... they
259	12	321	man	mans (F)
299	14	447 mg.	*in vitæ*	*in vita (F)*
321	15	387	*has*	*hast (F)*
349	18	31	*wo? (F)*	*wo,*
352	18	153	whatsover	whatsoever (F)
354	18	239	*quod (F)*	*quid*
358	18	378	*intramittendo (F)*	*intromittendo*
362	18	540	satified	satisfied (F)

TEXTUAL NOTES

PAGE	SERM. NO.	LINE	
398	5	265–266	Add TN: Christ would not part with *our sins.* /They were *sins,* that lay upon him, *our sins Edd.* : Christ would not. / They were *sins,* that lay upon him, part with *our sins F*
398	5	266	Delete TN Retain NOTE
399	6	13	Read: *omne desiderium* : omne desiderium *M, D, L* : omnia desideria *Dob*
402	6	143	Delete *"mg."* in numbering, and for ὀκύριος read ὁ κύριος
402	6	149 mg.	Read: 2 Cor. 7.5 *M, D, L* : *om. Dob*
402	6	156	Read: and so *D, L* : and *Dob* : and to *M*
402	6	156	Add TN: ther's] theis *M* : there's *D, L*
404	6	226–227	Read: not to be *M, D, L* : not be *Dob*
404	6	273	For: never [?] read: ever ["n" crossed out]
405	6	277	For: mola *M* read: *mala M*
405	6	323	Delete TN
405	6	329	Read: God *M, D, L* : good *Dob*
406	6	347	For: word] now *M* read: word] noū [noun] *M*
406	6	347	Read: *Jetzer* : Jetzer *Dob, M* : *Jeezer D, L* NOTE: Neither the "Jetzer" of *Dob* and *M* nor the *"Jeezer"* of *D* and *L* [etc.]
406	6	350	Read: tentacōns *M*
406	6	353	For: *denominàntur a* read: *denominantur à*
407	6	375	For: [not italicized in *M, D, L*] read: [not italicized in *D, L*]
408	6	399	Read: allwayes have *M, D, L* : have *Dob* Delete NOTE
408	6	420	Add TN: *peccatorem M* : *pecatorem Dob*
408	6	427	For: Cains *Dob* : Davids *M* read: Cains *Dob, M*

PAGE	SERM. NO.	LINE	
409	6	450	For: like *D, L* : life *Dob, M* read: like *M, D, L* : life *Dob* Delete NOTE
410	6	485	Read: *desiderium M, D, L* : desiderius *Dob*
410	6	502 mg.	For: Ps. 102.18 *Dob* read: Ps. 102.18 *Dob, M*
410	6	528	Delete TN
410	6	534	Read: things *M, D, L* : thinge *Dob*
411	6	550	For: this *M* read: his *M*
412	6	559	For: them to *D, L* : thou to *Dob* read: then to] them to *D, L*
412	6	576	Read: groanings *M, D, L* : groanes *Dob* Delete NOTE
413	6	622	Read: gronings *M, D, L* : groanes *Dob* Delete the bracketed direction
414	6	670–671	Delete second sentence of NOTE
414	6	678	For: in In Manus *M* read: in *In Manus M*
421	8	135	For: and so *M* read: and he *M*
424	8	264 mg.	For: 1 Sam. 14.15 *F, L* read: 1 Sam. 14.15 *F, M, D, L*
429	8	450	For: unite] revet *Q* : reunite *M, Dob, D, L* read: reunite *M, Dob, D, L* : unite *F* : revet *Q*
430	8	459	For: stopping *M* read: stepping *M*
432	8	550 mg.	For: Dan. 11.18 *F* read: Dan. 11.18 *F, M*
433	8	593	Read: Innocency] an Innocence *M, D*
434	9	260	Add TN: defined *Edd. conj.* : denied *F*
436	11	305	Add TN: plac'd thee in *Ash, D, Dob, E, L, M* : plac'd in *F*
437	12	296–297	Add TN: the words...they : the word ...they *F*
438	12	479	Add to NOTE: A friend has suggested the emendation "alimented."
441	15	29	Delete TN
445	15	246	For: father] read: farther]

PAGE	SERM. NO.	LINE	
445	15	250 *mg.* }	For: Psal. 42.80 *M* : Psal. 42.8 *E* read: Psal. 42.8 *M, E*
448	15	432	For: memory *M* read: memories *M*
455	17	H'd'g	For: Donne read: Donn and for: Nethersole's read: Nethersoles
458	18	31	Add TN: *wo,* : *wo? F*
462	18	528 *mg.* }	For: Psal. 119.17 *F* read: Psal. 119.17 *F, M*

Corrigenda: Volume III

PREFATORY NOTE

ix		14	For: Hereford read: Herford

INTRODUCTION

23		14–15	For: meet in such a read: meet without (*F*)

SERMONS

			For:	Read:
69	1	320	*Domini* (*F*)	*Donum*
78	2	207	blessednesse (*F, M*)	blessings (*D, L, P*)
93	3	81	say they (*F*)	say they,
125	4	424	is is	it is (*F*)
144	5	367	Luther	*Luther* (*F*)
191	8	153	*Devestation*	*Devastation* (*F*)
194	8	281 *mg.* }	[The Hebrew characters should have the vowel points, as they have in the Folio.]	
246	11	179	*in them* (*F*)	*of them*
259	12	112	Colledge, (*F*)	Colledge)
264	12	317 *mg.* }	Aleus. (*F*)	Alens. [I.e., Alensis]

TEXTUAL NOTES

PAGE	SERM. NO.	LINE	
396	1	320	Add TN: *Donum* : *Domini F*
400	2	206	Delete TN
400	2	207	Add TN: blessings *D, L, P* : blessednesse *F, M*
402	2	480 mg.	For: *F, L* read: *F, D, L, M*
403	2	541	For: gangred *M* read: gangrēd [gangrend] *M*
404	3	81	Add TN: say they, *Edd.* : say they *F*
410	9	87	Read: so, as a *M* : so, a *F* : soe that *P* : as a *D, L*
411	9	204 mg.	For: *F, D, L* read: *F, D, L, M*
413	9	354	Read: Shepherds *P* : Shepherd *F, D, L, M* [final "d" exaggerated]
417	9		In NOTE at end, read: "... Donn's ... Whithall ... 1620" [no question mark]
420	11	179	Add TN: *of them* : *in them F*
423	12	112	Add TN: Colledge) : Colledge, *F*
425	16	61	Delete TN
427	16	170	Delete second TN on this line
428	16	209	Delete first TN on this line
428	16	246	For: for *D,L,E* : soe *M* read: for *D,L,M,E*
429	16	268	For: ranne *M, E* read: ranne *E*
429	16	278	For: yee *E* read: yee *M, E*
431	16	453	Delete first TN on this line
432	16	494	For: myne by disteaming it, mine by disavowing by *M* read: myne by disclameing it, myne by disavowing by *M*
432	16	504 mg.	For 2 Cor. 12.15 *L* : 1 Cor. 12.15 *F, M, E* read: 2 Cor 12.15 *L, M* : 1 Cor. 12.15 *F, E*

Corrigenda: Volume IV

PAGE	SERM. NO.	LINE	For:	Read:
viii		12	[March 28]	[April 13]

SERMONS

61	1	609	*neutiquam* (*F*)	*ne utiquam*
123	3	1259	come (*F*)	come not (*M*)
135	4	101 mg.	[This reference belongs to line 112 *mg.*]	
152	5	264	forebeare	forbeare (*F*)
265	10	6	part (*Q*)	parts
365	15	34	then were (*F*)	they were
368	15	146	thanks giving (*F*)	thanksgiving

TEXTUAL NOTES

384	1	90–91	Delete [*M* reads "and" for "one"]
384	1	147–148	Delete [*M* omits "thou hast"]
389	3	142	Delete TN
393	3	757	Read last sentence of NOTE as follows: *M* does italicize in places, but here it reads "oportune ... importune" though in lines 757–758 it has "*oportune ... importune nolentibus.*" In line 766 it does not italicize.
393	3	773	For: *P, Al* read: *M, P, Al*
393	3	791	For: *F* read: *F, M*
397	3	1259	Read: come not *M* : come *F* NOTE: Cp. "come not" in lines 1257 and 1261.
413	10	6	Add TN: parts ... are *Edd.* : part ... are *Q*

Corrigenda: Volume V

SERMONS

221	11	171	For: *Domem* (*F*) read: *domem*
231	12	Text	For: Luke 23.24 read: Luke 23.34

TEXTUAL NOTES

PAGE	SERM. NO.	LINE	
404	12	150	For: thus *M* read: this *M*
404	12	173–174	For: ruinous *M* read: ruinent *M*
406	12	435	For: *considereth*] considers *M* read: 434–435 *considereth ... considereth*] considers . . . considers *M*
407	12	460–484	Add TN: *M* uses italics for this prayer.
408	13	63	Add TN: that] *om. M*
408	13	65	Add TN: it] *om. M*
408	13	69	Add TN: worship of that God] worship and a certayne tyme supposed for that outward worshipp of that God *M*
408	13	71	Add TN: that all things] all things *M*
408	13	75	Add TN: those] these *M*
408	13	75–76	For: exemplifie *F* read: exemplifie *F, M*
408	13	76–77	Add TN: may seeme most] may seeme to be most *M*
408	13	77	Delete TN
408	13	98	Add TN: are but] are all but *M*
409	13	192–194	For: with . . . stand . . . *M* read: which . . . have . . . *M*
409	13	200	Delete TN
410	13	215	For: that a thing *M* read: thats a thing *M*
411	13	354	Add TN: *those*] *om. M*
411	13	381	Delete second TN on this line
411	13	410	For: we] *om. M* read: we finde] *om. M*
412	13	500	For: *Edd.* read: *M*
413	13	683	Add TN: preaches] preaches but *M*

Corrigenda: Volume VI

SERMONS

PAGE	SERM. NO.	LINE	For:	Read:
39	I	3	one (*F*)	ones
45	I	226, 229	retained (*F*)	retaine
55	I	609	wee (*F*)	Wee
56 57	I	646 *mg.*, 647	*Erubescent* (*F*)	*Erubescant* (Vulg.)
90	3	321	says (*F*)	say
94	3	490	*Pastor*	Pastor (*F*)
119	5	179	them (*F*)	him
187	9	61	it	it. (*F* has: it,)
192	9	215	*sentiva* (*F*)	*sentina*
192	9	232	*Dedit* (*F*)	*Deditum*
200	9	535	*Excedere* (*F*)	*Excidere*
233	11	373	*par* (*F*)	*paris*
236	11	496	*nostram* (*F*)	*nostrum*
270	13	291	children (*F*)	mariage
289	14	322	hath (*F*)	both

TEXTUAL NOTES

367	I	3	Add TN: ones : one *F*
367	I	226, 229	Add TN: retaine : retained *F*
367	I	609	Add TN: Wee : wee *F*

NOTE: The capital is required in order to show that this was the answer of the Christians.

367	3	321	Add TN: the *Jesuites* ... say : the *Jesuites* ... says *F*
369	5	179	Add TN: him : them *F*
370	9	42, 45, 57	*Depuerascendum* (*F*)

[J. B. Leishman suggests that we should read *Repuerascendum*. The verb *depuerascere* is unknown to the *Thesaurus Linguæ Latinæ*, and to Ducange and Forcellini.]

PAGE	SERM. NO.	LINE		
370	9	61	Add TN: it. : it, *F*	
372	13	291	Add TN: mariage : children *F*	

NOTE: The printer of *F* was misled by the occurrence of "children" a few words before, and again afterward, but the sense demands "marriage" (spelt as "mariage" throughout the sermon).

372	14	322	Add TN: both : hath *F*

NOTE: The reading of *F,* which was followed by *Al* and ourselves, is just possible, but "both" (suggested by J. C. Maxwell) makes better sense.

Corrigenda: Volume VII

INTRODUCTION

			For:	Read:
9		32	With him	Wish him

SERMONS

			For:	Read:
78	2	165	*pace* (*F*)	*space*
93	2	733	unrepeated	unrepented (*F*)
129	4	404	*Schoufeldius* (*F*)	*Schonfeldius*
132	4	523	very similitude (*F*)	verisimilitude
209	7	691	*eum*	*eum,* (*F*)
213	7	870	in (*F*)	*in*
220	8	199	gooodnesse	goodnesse (*F*)
225	8	364	that that they (*F*)	that they
302	12	57	*are*	*art* (*F*)
304	12	133	*wtih*	*with* (*F*)
334	13	339	man (*F originally*)	man may (*F corr. in errata*)
366	14	616	yes (*F*)	yet
378	15	287	[Add marginal reference:] Mat. 19.12 *F*	

PAGE	SERM. NO.	LINE		
442	18	290	[Add marginal reference:] [Psa. 115.1]	
442	18	306	*Holy Ghost, (F)* *Holy Ghost*	

TEXTUAL NOTES

455	2	165	Add TN: *space* : *pace F*	
456	4	523	Add TN: verisimilitude : very similitude *F*	
457	7	738	NOTE: For loti read: lati	
458	7	870	Add TN: *in Baptismate* : *in Baptismate F*	
458	8	364	Add TN: that they : that that they *F*	
460	13	339	Add TN: man may *F corr. in errata* : man *F originally*	
461	14	616	Add TN: yet [as in line 614] : yes *F*	
463	18	306	Add TN: *Holy Ghost* : *Holy Ghost, F*	

Corrigenda: Volume VIII

SERMONS

			For:	Read:
44	1	248	*fluttereth*	*fluttereth (F)*
200	8	309 mg.	Nab. Oziel *(F)*	Rab. Oziel

TEXTUAL NOTES

379	6	583	For: see the read: see thy	
379	7	142	For: arcis *F* read: *arcis F*	

Corrigenda: Volume IX

SERMONS

			For:	Read:
51	1	147	Philosphers	Philosophers *(F)*
161	6	225	λατρέια *(F)*	λατρεία
223	9	360–361	Admiration *(F)*	Adjuration

PAGE	SERM.NO.	LINE	For:	Read:
299	13	122	sin	sin. (*F*)
343	15	346–347 *mg.* }	Stenartius (*F*)	Stevartius

TEXTUAL NOTES

416	1	155	For: Philosphers *Q* read: Philosophers *Q*
439	9	360–361 }	Add TN: Adjuration : Admiration *F*

NOTE: See line 338, "adjuration, or imprecation."

General Index to
All the Volumes of the
Present Edition

Acknowledgments will be found in the Prefaces to Volumes I–IV and X. Occurrences of the same names on later pages are included in this Index. Sources of illustrations are given therewith.

Index

Abbot, or Abbott, George, Archbp. of Canterbury, I. 112, 113, 125; III. 36; IV. 15, 26 n., 33 n., 39, 201; VII. 38–39; IX. 27 n.

Aben Ezra, III. 222, 387 mg.; IX. 221; X. 387

Abulensis. *See* Tostatus

Acosta, IV. 279; X. 173, 267, 387

Adams sermon, at St. Dunstan's, X. 24 n., 25, 28, 178–191

Adiaphorists, VII. 174

Adrian II, Pope, III. 223

Aelfric's *Exodus*. *See* Bible

Aerius, VII. 171–172

Agbarus, or Abgarus, IV. 125, 397

Agrippa, Cornelius, IV. 220 mg.; X. 387

Alabaster, William, *Divine Meditations,* I. 33, 34; X. 427

Alcazar, VI. 63 mg.; X. 387

Alciate, V. 242

Aldborough Hatch, I. 47; II. 38, 269; III. 391 n.; IX. 12, 31; X. 31, 32, 403

Alensis, III. 264 mg.; IX. 338; X. 387

Alford, Henry, ed., *The Works of John Donne,* I. 17, 18, 28, 29, 105, 327; II. 397, 398, 415, 434, 438; III. 396, 397, 407; IV. 387, 400, 405, 411, 412, 416, 418; V. 399, 415, 417, 419, 421; VI. 23, 371; VII. 458, 463; IX. 432, 440, 441; X. 12 n., 33 n., 264, 273, 318, 414–421

Allen, D. C.
—— "Dean Donne Sets His Text," X. 307 n., 308, 310 n., 314 n., 324
—— *The Harmonious Vision,* III. 30 n.

Alleyn, Edward, IV. 6 n., 13; VII. 12, 13 n.; X. 31

Alogiani, the, III. 348

Alsop, B., I. 23

Alvarez, IV. 157; VII. 320 mg.; X. 387

Ambrose, St.
—— I. 138, 159, 163, 214, 222, 244 mg., 259 mg., 272, 285, 298
—— II. 59 mg., 60, 67, 88 mg., 152, 154, 161 mg., 218 mg., 227, 229, 240 mg., 262, 320, 330, 345, 380
—— III. 47, 98 mg., 149, 242, 244 mg., 286 mg., 290 mg., 320, 327
—— IV. 80, 108 mg., 111, 115, 116, 123, 143, 153 mg., 196, 208, 210 mg., 215 mg., 261, 306, 309, 332, 336, 341, 373

—— V. 37, 42, 87, 100, 121 mg., 141, 146, 154, 162, 164, 170, 206, 210, 212, 215, 241, 308, 344
—— VI. 162, 181, 182, 233, 251, 277, 287, 339
—— VII. 79, 85, 92, 144, 178–179, 209, 246, 297, 343–344
—— VIII. 41, 75 mg., 96, 153, 162, 179 mg., 214, 267, 298, 341 mg., 342 mg., 362
—— IX. 5, 18, 21, 84, 85, 97, 119 mg., 139, 190, 200, 238, 253, 284, 304 mg., 325 mg., 339, 342 mg., 366 mg., 373
—— X. 64, 71, 72, 73, 82, 122 mg., 175 mg., 196 mg., 201, 216, 224 mg., 345, 346 n., 352 n., 361, 368, 374 n.

Anabaptists, II. 10, 112–113; III. 213; IV. 142, 202, 207, 208, 313; V. 83, 101, 109; VI. 136, 182, 338; VIII. 349

Ancrum. *See* Ker

Anderdon, J. H., X. 307 n.

Andradius, VI. 119; VIII. 247; X. 356 n., 387

Andrewes, Lancelot, Bp. of Winchester, later Bp. of Ely, I. 40, 113; IV. 6, 21, 25; VII. 45 n.; VIII. 23; X. 14, 19 n., 34, 308
—— *XCVI Sermons,* I. 40

Anne of Denmark, Queen of England (consort of James I), I. 115–117, 129, 134, 236; II. 26; III. 15; VI. 27; X. 408

Anomæi, the, VIII. 228

Anselm, VI. 238; X. 374 n., 390

Antwerp, IV. 7; X. 369

Antwerp Polyglot. *See* Bible

Apostles' Creed, VI. 249; VII. 200, 402; VIII. 263

Aquinas, St. Thomas, I. 304, 316; II. 79 mg., 332 mg., 453; III. 48 mg., 110 mg., 119 mg.; IV. 113, 151 mg., 168, 169, 192, 195, 196, 198 mg., 218 mg., 278, 330; V. 82 mg., 108 mg., 158 mg., 374; VI. 19, 20, 180; VII. 102, 200, 201, 230, 376, 378, 384; VIII. 96, 155, 205, 206, 231, 360; IX. 98, 105 mg., 127; X. 83, 214 mg., 223, 259, 364, 369, 374 n., 387, 391
—— Thomism, X. 388, 390, 391
—— Thomists, I. 310; IV. 168; IX. 139. *See also* Schoolmen

Arabic. *See* Bible

449